International Bonds and Certificates of Deposit

International Bonds and Certificates of Deposit

Terence Prime

Solicitor, Lecturer, University of Liverpool

Butterworths
London, Boston, Dublin, Edinburgh, Kuala Lumpur,
Singapore, Sydney, Toronto, Wellington
1990

United Kingdom	Butterworth & Co (Publishers) Ltd, 88 Kingsway, LONDON WC2B 6AB and 4 Hill Street, EDINBURGH EH2 3JZ
Australia	Butterworths Pty Ltd, SYDNEY, MELBOURNE, BRISBANE, ADELAIDE, PERTH, CANBERRA and HOBART
Canada	Butterworths Canada Ltd, TORONTO and VANCOUVER
Ireland	Butterworth (Ireland) Ltd, DUBLIN
Malaysia	Malayan Law Journal Sdn Bhd, KUALA LUMPUR
New Zealand	Butterworths of New Zealand Ltd, WELLINGTON and AUCKLAND
Puerto Rico	Equity de Puerto Rico, Inc, HATO REY
Singapore	Malayan Law Journal Pte Ltd, SINGAPORE
USA	Butterworth Legal Publishers, AUSTIN, Texas; BOSTON, Massachusetts; CLEARWATER, Florida (D & S Publishers); ORFORD, New Hampshire (Equity Publishing); ST PAUL, Minnesota; and SEATTLE, Washington

A CIP Catalogue record for this book is available from the British Library.

ISBN 0 406 11460 9

Typeset by Kerrypress Ltd, Luton, Beds.
Printed by Mackays of Chatham Ltd, Chatham.

Preface

There can be no doubt that the development of the free currency markets has been one of the most important post-war innovations limiting or even extinguishing national economic sovereignty, and thereby subtly diminishing political sovereignty. On the one hand it has made possible the rapid expansion of multinational corporate activity; on the other it has brought the economic order to the edge of a massive debt crisis with the potential to produce recession of 1930s proportions. Within free currency techniques the international bond and CD are of undoubted significance, and, from a legal point of view, constitute perhaps the most interesting sector.

Whilst the economic significance of the subject area has been appreciated and benefited from a large volume of study and publication, the legal issues have not been subjected to much scrutiny. Indeed except for Philip Wood's excellent 'Law and Practice of International Finance' and Peter Gabriel's 'Legal Aspects of Syndicated Loans' little has been attempted. Yet international bond markets exist worldwide with the associated dealers and issuers and lawyers seeking to advise them. It is hoped that this work will be of some assistance to them in the important and demanding practical tasks which constitute their daily work.

Inevitably in the production of a work of this nature the author's indebtedness ranges widely. Sadly the theft of a brief case containing correspondence with various financial and legal professionals part way through the project prevents my acknowledging all but a few of the many who have listened patiently to usually obvious questions and pointed out the frequently less than obvious answer. It has proved to me beyond all argument that the practitioners in the City are generous of their time, with all genuinely interested in their work; they are as fascinated by the interest of what they do as they are motivated by the financial rewards which it generates. To all many thanks. Particular thanks are due to Richard Youard and Rupert Beaumont at Slaughter and May, Philip Wood at Allen and Overy and Jonathan Lass at Lass and Company who have borne the brunt. Finally without the enthusiasm and expert advice of Professor Roy Goode OBE, Professor of English Law, Oxford University, and latterly Professor Ross Cranston, of the Centre for Commercial Law Studies, Queen Mary College, the work would have certainly not proceeded at all. In addition I should acknowledge the help of Professor A H Hudson of Liverpool University who has read several chapters and made helpful comments, and my son Jeremy who has helped greatly with the proof reading.

A final and special acknowledgment is due to the International Primary Markets Association who have permitted me to quote freely from their recommendations. The address of the Association is 1–3 College Hill, London EC4R 2RA.

It is unlikely that this work is so comprehensive as to deal with all aspects of a massive subject. I am interested to know what may have been missed. I am also interested in other arguments and conclusions to those which have impressed me. I hope that users of this book will at least be sufficiently interested in the subject to wish to comment where comment is necessary.

The Faculty of Law
Liverpool University
PO Box 147
Liverpool L69 3BX

TP
October '89

Contents

Table of statutes

References in this Table to *Statutes* are to Halsbury's Statutes of England (Fourth Edition) showing the volume and page at which the annotated text of an Act may be found.

Table of cases

E

F

N

PAGE

W

Z

1 Definition and economic background

A bond may be said to be a marketable instrument, usually unsecured, issued by a legal person (known as the issuer), being one of a number of similar documents issued at the same time, which are intended to be capable of transfer by the persons to whom they are issued and which are usually intended to be fully negotiable. These characteristics are important as the intention of the issuer is to sell its debt among as wide a range of lenders as possible within the market to which the bonds are addressed. Further, it is usually intended that subsequently a secondary market in the bonds will be established after issue, wherein the instruments can be traded, and any holder will be able to obtain the current market value for his bond without waiting for the repayment of the bond by the issuer on maturity.

Bonds can be categorised depending upon the market to which they are addressed as each market gives rise to its own demands requiring different financial and legal solutions.

There are three such markets of which only two have an international aspect. The non-international bond market is the domain of the domestic bond, which is a bond issued on the market of a particular country by a resident of that country. It naturally follows, both from the residence of the issuer and the choice of the domestic market as the place of issue, that such a bond will comply with the legal and other requirements of the domestic venue for issue and that legal issues, so far as they are not covered by the terms of the bond itself, will be resolved by domestic legal institutions in accordance with domestic law.

Of the two types of bond with international aspects one has strong similarities with the domestic bond. This is known as the foreign bond which is a bond sold by an issuer on the market of a single country, in which it is not resident, and which is denominated in the currency of that country. Such a bond will be underwritten by, and sold to, underwriters who are national to the country in which the bond is issued. As an example a British company may issue a bond on the New York market, underwritten by New York underwriters and denominated in dollars. If the English company had issued those bonds on the English market they would have been domestic bonds.

The third type of bond has the most international aspects of all. This is the true international bond. This has been defined as ‘an international bond underwritten by an international syndicate and sold in countries other than the country of the currency in which the issue is denominated'[1] An example of an international bond transaction would be the issue by a Japanese company of dollar denominated bonds through a consortium of European banks and overseas branches of U.S. investment banks on markets throughout the world, excluding U.S. markets. An attempt at a statutory definition of an international bond issue, recognising the features of a bond issue and the marketing practices thereof, was made in the Companies Act 1980, s 71(2), as amended by the Companies Act 1981, s 112.[2] Unfortunately, the statutory definition was created for the particular purpose of modifying the general restrictions on insider dealing contained in Part V of the 1980 Act in so far as they might otherwise bear upon international bond issues and dealers therein, and is limited to that function. Thus it does not apply, for instance, to issues by sovereign issuers, although these are in fact undoubtedly issues of international bonds bearing similar characteristics to issues by corporate issuers. The statutory definition thus cannot be considered one of general guidance or effect.

Subsequent attempts at statutory definition have been no more effective in producing a good general definition of an international bond. The Finance Act 1982, s. 57 in providing international bond dealers with exemption from bond washing provisions, defined an international bond as meaning a security

(a) which is neither preference stock nor preference share capital; and
(b) which is in bearer form; and
(c) which carries a right to interest either at a fixed rate or at a rate bearing a fixed relationship to a standard published base rate: and
(d) which does not carry a right to any other form of benefit whether in the nature of interest, participation in profits or otherwise; and

1 Morgan Guaranty Trust 'World Financial Markets' last page of each issue quoted Rita M. Rodriguez and E. Eugene Carter 'International Financial Management' Prentice-Hall, Englewood Cliffs (N.J.) (1976) p. 567.

2 By this definition an international bond issue means an issue of debentures of a company (the 'issuing company') which satisfies two conditions. Firstly, all the debentures must either be or to be offered by an off-market dealer to persons (whether principals or agents) whose ordinary business includes the buying or selling of debentures. Secondly, where debentures are denominated in sterling, not less than 50 per cent in nominal value of the debentures must be or to be offered to persons who are neither citizens of the U.K. and Colonies nor companies incorporated or otherwise formed under the law of any part of the U.K.

International bonds have been referred to in only three modern English cases and then without discussion of their character. The cases of *R v Guildhall Justices, ex p DPP* (1983) 78 Cr App Rep 269 and *R v Guildhall Justices and DPP ex parte Carsons Selignman, Knight and Pimm* (1983) 148 JP 385 concerned criminal procedural aspects arising from alleged counterfeiting and fraud involving international bonds. *Trustees of the British Museum v A-G* [1984] 1 WLR 418 concerned the powers of the court to extend trustees' powers of investment in the light of changed conditions including new forms of investment such as unit trusts and international bonds.

(e) the interest on which is payable without any deduction in respect of income tax or of any tax of a similar character imposed by the laws of a territory outside the U.K.;

but the definition specifically provides that a security is not prevented from being a Eurobond by reason only that it carries a right to convert into a security of another description or to subscribe for further securities. The Finance Act 1984, s 35, which exempted quoted international bonds from deduction of income tax on interest payments also contained a definition which has been referred to subsequently in the Finance Act 1986, ss 46 and 47. Under this definition an international bond is a security carrying a right to interest, in bearer form, issued by a company and quoted on a recognised stock exchange. The latter definition excludes bonds issued by sovereign issuers and both ignore the international aspect of the international bond; any foreign bond which satisfied the conditions would be defined as an international bond under the statute because each definition was drafted for specific and limited purposes.

As has been seen the foreign bond is far less complex and international in its implications than the international bond. While there is a foreign connection arising from the foreign nationality of the issuer it can, and will, be formalised for issue in the single market in the same way as a domestic bond. Because of this the bond will incorporate the law applicable to the domestic market and give jurisdiction to the courts of that country. By contrast the international bond is of necessity geared to a wide range of markets.

Certificates of deposit can also be domestic or international in character. A certificate of deposit has been described as 'a negotiable, interest-bearing instrument evidencing a time deposit with a commercial bank'.[1] A legal definition of a certificate of deposit is given by the U.S. Uniform Commercial Code, Article 3 s 3–104, which defines it as 'an acknowledgement by a bank of a receipt of money with an engagement to repay it'. The only English statutory attempt at definition appears to be that contained in the Finance Act 1968, s 55(3) and therefore made for tax purposes. This reads:

> 'certificate of deposit' means a document relating to money, in any currency, which has been deposited with the issuer or some other person, being a document which recognises an obligation to pay a stated amount to bearer or to order, with or without interest, and being a document by the delivery of which, with or without endorsement, the right to receive that stated amount, with or without interest, is transferable.

There is a secondary market in certificates of deposit in the same way as for international bonds. If, therefore, the holder of the certificate of deposit wishes to realise his investment before maturity of the deposit he may sell his certificate on the secondary market in the same way as he could sell an international bond on the bond market. The first certificates of deposit were issued as domestic negotiable securities in 1961 by First

[1] F.G. Fisher *Eurobonds* Euromoney Publications 2nd edn, London (1988), p. 216

National City Bank in the United States of America. It was the same bank which in 1966 issued dollar denominated certificates of deposit in London to tap the international market. Whereas with a bond the issuer can be any legal person and will only rarely be a bank, certificates of deposit, from their very nature as evidence of a time deposit, can only be issued by a bank.[1] The documentation for the issue of a certificate of deposit is considerably simpler than that of an international bond. However, the very fact that the international certificate of deposit can be sold across a number of jurisdictions in the same way as the international bond means that many of the legal issues to which international bonds give rise are also applicable to the international certificate of deposit.

EURODOLLARS AND OTHER EUROCURRENCIES

To understand the function and purpose of both the international bond and the international certificate of deposit a knowledge of the eurocurrency market is essential, for the eurocurrency market and the market for international bonds and certificates of deposit together constitute the free currency market in which funds can be borrowed in large amounts, substantially free from domestic governmental regulation.

To explain eurocurrency it is easiest to move from the specific of the eurodollar to the generality of eurocurrency.[2] A eurodollar has been summed up as representing 'a debt denominated in U.S. currency owed by a bank institution located outside the U.S. as a result of a dollar on deposit in that institution'.[3] However, while the eurodollar deposits exist and are traded outside the U.S., every eurodollar deposit originates from and depends upon a deposit in a bank within the U.S.

These apparently conflicting statements can only be understood against the complex background of modern transfers of funds as currently practised by the international banking system. Today the vast sums of money involved in capital investment or as the proceeds of international trade are not moved in location from A to B as so many dollar bills but merely by some book-keeping transactions on the accounts of the parties affected. The book-keeping transactions are prompted by means of 'a bank transfer' which is simply a transfer directed by telex or some other speedy means of communication between one bank and another.

The transfers creating the eurodollar can arise either as a result of an investment decision or as the consequence of international trade.

Each movement of the deposit within the banking system is therefore

1 In fact, it seems that any authorised deposit-taking institution under Part I of the Banking Act 1987 could legally issue certificates of deposit but, in practice, they are only issued by authorised institutions entitled to call themselves banks under Part III of that Act.

2 Apart from other general works cited see Effros 'The Whys and Wherefores of Eurodollars' (1968) 23 Business Lawyer 629.

3 Stuart W. Robinson *Multinational Banking* A.W. Sijthoff (1972) p. 162.

not a movement of money but a movement of a claim against a bank.[1] The consequences of movement are of potentially far-reaching significance; 'as this claim is transferred from hand to hand . . . new debtor-creditor relationships are established which may differ substantially from each other, according to the laws which regulate them.'[2]

It can be clearly seen that eurodollars arise directly from the modern methods employed within the international banking system to move large sums of money from one international financial centre to another.[3]

Because of the very way in which eurodollars are created they are always linked by what has been described as 'an umbilical cord'[4] tied to a dollar deposit in an American bank. It should also be noted carefully that the word eurodollar is misleading. It suggests they are dollars traded within Europe. In fact the concept and term are applicable to all similar trading of dollar deposits outside the U.S. (although to make confusion worse confounded comparable trading in Asia is usually referred to as trading on the Asian dollar market).

In this explanation attention has been focussed upon the eurodollar. This has been because it is usually easier to explain the general concept in terms of the specific. The dollar was chosen because it is easily the most common currency within the eurocurrency market.[5] Nevertheless, it must clearly be understood that what is being considered is a true eurocurrency market, since many currencies other than the dollar are traded in a similar way outside the country of the currency involved. There is thus a eurocurrency market in euro-German marks, Swiss francs, pounds sterling, Dutch guilders, French francs, Japanese yen and other currencies. In each case the eurocurrency involved is tied to a deposit of that currency in the country of origin as eurodollar deposits are always tied to a dollar deposit in a bank in the U.S. (e.g. euro-guilders are tied to guilder deposits in the Netherlands and euro-French francs to bank deposits of francs in France).

THE CENTRAL BANK AND CORRESPONDENT BANKS

The analysis undertaken so far has concentrated on the transactions outside the country of the currency involved. In fact the situation within the U.S.

1 Joseph Dach 'Legal Nature of the Eurodollar' (1964) 13 AJCL 32. Thus, for instance, the proper law applicable to each particular deposit as it is traded will be the law of the jurisdiction where the deposit is made, with the result that what appears to be different links in one piece of trading will in fact be a number of individual legal relationships each possibly covered by a different system of law—see *Libyan Arab Foreign Bank v Bankers Trust Co* 26 ILM 1600 at p. 1615.

2 Dach *op. cit.* p. 34.

3 The economic and institutional mechanism has been widely discussed in financial literature—see, for example, Robinson *op. cit.*

4 Rodriguez and Carter *op. cit.* p. 431.

5 Eurodollars comprise approximately 75 per cent of the eurocurrency market. David K. Eiteman and Arthur Stonehill *Multinational Business Finance* 3rd edn Addison-Wesley, Reading (Mass.) (1983) p. 400; Rodriguez and Carter *op. cit.* p. 522.

will be rather more complex. As has been seen, a eurodollar deposit is always based and dependent upon a dollar deposit in a U.S. bank, that deposit being the original from which the eurodollar deposits were created. As such it will be shown both on the books of the particular U.S. bank, say Bank of America, and in the books of the Federal Reserve Board as the U.S. central bank. If the European bank entitled to the deposit transfers the deposit to another European bank and both use Bank of America as correspondent bank, the U.S. part of the transaction will be shown by entries in the books of Bank of America alone. Where, however, the two European banks have different correspondent banks the position becomes more complex. Let us suppose that Lloyds bank wishes to transfer eurodollar deposits to Credit Lyonnais and that the U.S. correspondent bank of Lloyds is Citibank and that of Credit Lyonnais is the Bank of Chicago. When the original deposit was created Bank of America would, on the instructions of Lloyds Bank, credit the account of Citibank, who would show the receipt of the deposit from Bank of America and a debit in favour of Lloyds Bank. Settlement would take place through Chips, the automated U.S. clearing house, and the accounts of the two U.S. banks at the Federal Reserve Board would be adjusted by showing the transfer so that Bank of America would drop out of the picture. When the deposit was transferred on to Credit Lyonnais similar entries would be made to effect the transfer between Citibank and Bank of Chicago with Bank of Chicago crediting the deposit in favour of Credit Lyonnais.

Thus while all eurodollar deposits must be settled via the U.S., the use of different correspondent banks involves the full use of New York clearing procedures through Chips.

THE EUROCURRENCY EXPANSION POTENTIAL

Given that the essential source of eurodollars is 'the book-keeper's pen', it would seem that there is potential for a vast increase of eurodollar deposits by a series of transactions within the banking system from one initial deposit.[1] While the theoretical model is regarded as valid by economists (and indeed may be the actual fate of some initial deposits, subject to each bank in turn in fact making a prudent deduction for reserves), it does not represent the majority of transactions.[2] When deductions for reserves of 10 per cent are taken, the initial deposit will indeed increase the supply of the eurodollar deposits by tenfold, but only if the funds are retained within the banking system for ten transactions. It is not likely that this will occur. Instead, at some stage they will probably disappear from the system. The phenomenon is known as leakage. Leakage occurs on a vast scale for complex reasons which it is not necessary to consider further here. Suffice it to say that

1 See the classic illustration and argument of Milton Friedman in 'The Eurodollar Market: Some First Principles' in the *Morgan Guaranty Survey* October 1969 at pp. 7–9.

2 When lending to customers other than depositing with another bank, a bank lender will consider it prudent to take a proportion for reserves.

most commentators who have considered the phenomenon have concluded that the multiplier effect in practice of the euro-dollar phenomenon is close to one.[1]

FREE-CURRENCY MARKET TECHNIQUES

The techniques of the free-currency markets have been developed to solve two fundamental problems. The first is that borrowers require a reasonable length of loan to finance capital investments, whereas the funds underpinning the markets have been essentially short-term funds. The classic formation of a unit of eurocurrency has been the creation of a time deposit held by a bank abroad from a demand deposit in the country of the currency of denomination of the deposits. However, time-deposits themselves tend to be of short duration such as a week or a month.[2] A prospective depositor may be persuaded to contract to deposit his money for longer against a higher rate of interest, but even this technique is not likely to produce deposits committed for more than three or six months. In general, the additional rates of interest are not likely to be sufficiently attractive to persuade a businessperson, who does not immediately need the money, to lose the availability of liquid capital for long periods of time in the uncertain world in which we live. The essential problem is how to create a long-term lending medium out of funds which will not be committed long term.

The second problem is the size of loan. The demand for money in the free-market has been in the form of the huge borrowing requirements of the very largest organisations, namely multinational companies and sovereign borrowers. No single bank would be likely to be able to finance a loan of the size required by such organisations without breaking the basic banking principle of spreading risk. The only way in which loans of such a size could be met is through multiplicity of lenders.

The classic and most widely used means of solving these twin problems is the syndicated loan. The syndicated loan is a loan by a syndicate of banks each of which takes an agreed portion of the loan by which the funds are put together for the particular borrower. The syndication of the loan solves the problem of the sheer size of the loan demanded. The financial problems of turning money held on essentially short-term commitment into a loan of five or ten years, or even more, are tackled by means of important provisions within the agreement which connect the syndicated banks to one another and to the ultimate borrower. Being dependent upon short-term funds the banks making the loan will have to face varying interest rates during the lifetime of the loan. In theory at least in order to be able to obtain the currency underpinning the loan the banks will have to go out into the market place at regular intervals to borrow that currency short term. The syndicated loan agreement therefore requires the borrower to

1 Friedman *op. cit.* at p. 10. Rodriguez and Carter *op. cit.* p. 526; Brian Kettle *The Finance of International Business* Graham and Trotman Ltd London (1979) p. 232 *et seq.*

2 There is even a flourishing overnight deposit market.

pay a fluctuating amount of interest which is fixed at three or six monthly intervals, at a percentage above a specified rate of interest related to the cost of raising short-term deposits on the London inter-bank market, usually the London Inter-Bank Offer Rate.[1] There are further provisions which require early repayment of the loan in the event that it becomes impossible for a banking syndicate to obtain the necessary supporting funds in the short-term market, or it becomes illegal for a syndicate bank to continue its lending operations to the borrower.[2] The net effect is that legally the borrower takes the risk that the short-term funds underpinning his long-term loan remain available.[3]

A second solution to the twin underlying problems is to use a form of borrowing in the short-term market, which combines a longer-term commitment with a short-term possibility of realisation if the lender so requires. The means of achieving this is to devise an instrument of borrowing with a more substantial commitment in terms of time but with the instrument capable of being traded upon a market after issue. This then enables a prospective lender who is unsure whether he will have need of his capital in the short term to undertake a long-term commitment knowing that, if the need arises, he can simply sell his debt instrument upon the market and recover his fund at the then market price. Such instruments are used in the free-market, and are in the form of negotiable certificates of deposit and negotiable international bonds.[4]

A negotiable certificate of deposit is an acknowledgment in writing by a bank that a certain sum of money has been deposited with it and that that sum will be repaid at the due date to the holder of the instrument. In the meantime the instrument bears interest at six or twelve monthly intervals, entitlement to which is proved by coupons attached to the certificate itself. On the date of an interest payment the holder of the certificate simply detaches the appropriate coupon from the certificate and, on production of this, is paid the interest. The certificates are issued by a single issuer bank in a number of countries at once and large sums of money may be obtained by the bank in this way. The bank, of course, will anticipate that it will be able to lend on the money raised at a higher rate of interest than it is paying on the coupons, thereby making a profit from its operations. The device has been very useful to banks in raising

1 The rate of interest offered by commercial banks within the eurocurrency market on deposits taken by them. This therefore represents the cost to the syndicated banks of raising the money required.

2 Logan and Rowntree 'Term Loan Arrangements' in Rendell ed. *International Financial Law*, Euromoney Publications, 2nd edn (1983).

3 Although, in practice, getting actual repayment of the loan part-way through its term from a borrower who has committed his borrowed funds may well be practically impossible despite the legal position. The ultimate practical consideration for the banks participating is probably that it is always possible to borrow funds at a price.

4 So important has this aspect become that flexibility has been brought to the syndicated loan with techniques allowing the sale of loan assets now having been developed.

money in the free-currency market and has been particularly favoured by American banks raising dollar loans outside the U.S.

The international bond market is similarly constituted but with one essential difference. In the international bond market the ultimate borrower of the money is brought into direct contact with the initial lender with the bank operating as a financial intermediary. The ultimate borrower issues negotiable documents of indebtedness upon the international market, the whole issue being organised by an international consortium of banks and underwriters. As with certificates of deposit the bonds are normally interest-bearing, and carry coupons against the production of which the interest due will be paid on the various payments dates to the bearer.[1] The bonds themselves are payable to bearer and a secondary market is established on which they can be traded.

There is, however, an important structural difference between the international bond part of the free currency market and the rest. As has been mentioned, in the international bond market the position of the banks is merely organisational. If a bond issue is not repaid by the borrower it is the ultimate investors who suffer the loss. For the rest of the free-currency market the money is lent to the participating bank or banks who then lend on to the ultimate borrower. Should that borrower not repay, the loss is that of the banks who are therefore in the exposed position.

It should be noted further that the international bond market is a substitute for the eurocurrency market. The eurodollar market has been described as 'a network of *bank* liabilities and *bank* claims denominated in dollars'[2] which description is remarkably accurate. The effect of a successful international bond issue is either to take money out of the eurocurrency system by causing it to be used to purchase bonds thereby going out of the banking system or, alternatively, to cause some funds which otherwise would have gone into the eurocurrency system to be used to purchase the bonds instead.

Whilst there is an element of substitution between the two systems the two markets also display elements of linkage. An international bond issuer may deposit the proceeds in an overseas bank at least for a period of time, leading to some growth in the eurocurrency market. More significantly it seems probable that underwriters and market markers depend upon the euro-currency market to fund and establish their positions, particularly with regard to the initial establishment of the secondary market essential to a successful international bond issue.[3]

Nevertheless, it cannot be pretended that the two markets are other than basically substitutory. Little is known about the ultimate investors in the two markets, but there is good reason to suppose that significant differences in yields will cause funds to shift between them. However, whilst no doubt many investors straddle the two markets, it is probable that there are others

1 Some bonds are coupon (i.e.) interest-free and are issued at a discount, the return to the lender being the ultimate capital appreciation on redemption day.

2 Morris Mendelson 'The Eurobond and Capital Market Integration' Journal of Finance, March 1972, at p. 113.

3 Mendelson *op. cit.* pp. 113–115.

who find attraction in one only. For all the element of competition between the two they are perhaps best viewed as ultimately complementary, and a means by which the international banking community has managed to meet the large financial requirements of the modern state and industry with considerable effectiveness and sophistication.

HISTORY OF THE MARKET[1]

The period 1945 to 1973

The Eurobond market was conceived within, and ultimately born into, an existing international free-currency market serving the needs of large scale borrowers. The eurodollar market already existed and its early history is also the history of the Eurobond market. It arose as a consequence of the cold war immediately after the Second World War. Holders of dollars in eastern Europe, including the various state trading banks of the Soviet Union, were reluctant to hold their dollar deposits in the U.S., fearing that such accounts might be blocked for political purposes.[2] They were also concerned that such deposits might be attached in the U.S. by U.S. residents with claims against the Communist governments of eastern Europe.[3] To avoid these risks the eastern European holders chose to place their deposits with banks in western Europe, choosing in particular the Moscow and Narody Bank, London and the Banque Commerciale pour l'Europe du Nord, Paris. Once deposited within the banking system the funds flowed through the inter-bank system of the western banks, much of it finding its way to London.[4]

However, such a limited cause would not have produced a consequence as great as a massive new international source of funding. The important point was that within the new market better terms could be obtained by depositors in London than were available in the U.S. Western central banks and commercial institutions were soon prepared to use the same means to earn a better return on their deposits. The funds handled on the new

1 See generally, I.M. Kerr *History of the Eurobond Market* Euromoney Publications London (1984) an interesting anecdotal history bringing out the contributions of the individuals within the market whose initiative, energy, vision and skill enabled the advantages of the economic circumstances to be fully utilised to establish the procedures and instruments of the market. See also F.G. Fisher III *Eurobonds*, Euromoney Publications, London (1988), Chapter 1.

2 This has occurred in the case of dollar deposits held in the U.S. by Iran as a result of political differences arising as an aftermath of the Iranian Revolution and the taking of U.S. hostages and, subsequently, in respect of dollar deposits held in the U.S. by Libya, as a result of the political differences leading to the U.S. bombing of Libya. In the years immediately after the Second World War, Russians would no doubt remember distinctly that during that war their dollar holdings in the U.S. had been impounded by the Alien Property Custodian, Milton Friedman *op. cit.* p. 5.

3 The two factors were closely linked in the action taken by the U.S. against Iran.

4 P. Einzig *The Eurobond Market* Macmillan, London (1969); Eiteman and Stonehill *op. cit.* p. 316; Robinson *op. cit.* p. 164.

market were in huge amounts with the overheads in setting up the loan spread over a vast sum. No domestic regulations required specified proportions of deposit to be allocated to reserve thus preventing them from being lent on. Consequently, the banks were able to give a more generous return on their deposits and still earn good profits.

Two of the three external factors which occasioned and characterised the development of the international bond market and its techniques were present from the very beginning. These three factors are comparative freedom from national intervention, freedom from domestic regulation, and the use of techniques and approaches developed by the U.S. in its own domestic market.

As if the external and economic advantages were not sufficient U.S. economic policy, never, since the end of the Second World War, the most far-sighted aspect of U.S. policy in its international ramifications, threw highly volatile fuel into the flames. By the end of the 1950s the U.S. balance of payment account had moved from surplus to deficit, and an increasing haemorrhage of dollars made their way to Europe. This process was intensified by domestic regulations to control some of the effects of the U.S. economic policies, which increased the returns which Americans could obtain in Europe. In particular, as an anti-inflationary measure U.S. banks were limited as to the amount of interest they could pay on domestic deposits by regulations[1] or overseas branches of U.S. banks. The flight of capital from the U.S. consequently continued and intensified.

Parallel to these developments changes were at work in Europe. London had for many years held the position of being the world's major financial centre.[2] This has been built up through the availability of sterling through the U.K. domestic market to finance development world-wide coupled with a highly developed expertise in marshalling both domestic and overseas capital for both domestic and foreign needs. However, industrial decline hastened by the cost of financing two world wars had left it so weakened that the provision of sterling from the domestic market for world finance was no longer a practicable proposition. In 1957 an economic crisis necessitated the political recognition of this situation with strict governmental restrictions being imposed on the lending of sterling to non-residents. However, London was saved from the ignominy of surrendering its premier position by return to external currency convertibility among the European nation signatories of the European Monetary Agreement. At the end of 1958 the French franc, sterling, and Dutch guilder all became externally convertible and the Swiss and Belgian francs and the German mark fully convertible. Thus all these currencies held by a *foreign* resident could be freely converted. With the guidance and encouragement of the Bank of England, U.K. banks turned their attention and their expertise

1 United States, Board of Governors of the Federal Reserve System Regulation Q 12 CER para. 217 3(a) introduced 1 January 1936. No interest at all is payable on demand deposits—para. 217 2(a). Deposits with maturities of less than 30 days are classed as demand deposits.

2 McLea and Cairncross *Capital City* Eyre Methuen, London (1974).

to dollar lending from non-domestic sources to retain their position as the world international financial centre.

The European developments were assisted by contemporary developments in the U.S. The ever increasing flow of dollars from the U.S. and the associated developing balance of payments deficit caused that country to take further steps to protect its own economy. President Kennedy and his Treasury Secretary of State, Douglas Dillon, adopted a policy of seeking to encourage Europeans to raise capital in their own markets. In 1962 Treasury Secretary Dillon made speeches in Europe advertising this option which were noted and discussed by European banks in general and the British banks in particular.

In fact the Americans were preaching to the already converted. During the 1950s and early 1960s a booming U.S. economy had produced a situtation in which the dollar was the primary sources of funds for international borrowing. Because of the dollar connection the U.S. domestic market monopolised the market through its foreign bond sector. As a consequence issues were structured around a U.S. lead manager with an underwriting syndicate receiving a commission of at least 1 per cent. If the foreign bonds had been placed among U.S. investors this would have been unexceptional, but U.S. investors were much more interested in U.S. investments and the bonds were largely placed with foreign investors provided by European and other international institutions from among their overseas clients. For this the European and international institution who actually placed and sold the bonds received a commission of 0.5 per cent. In reality the U.S. participation was an unnecessary, and, in the light of the commission structure, an expensive irrelevance.[1]

If President Kennedy and Treasury Secretary Dillon were anxious to remove pressure from the U.S. domestic capital market by encouraging Europeans to raise their capital outside the U.S., they were equally concerned to achieve the same result by the parallel expedient of encouraging U.S. citizens to invest their capital in the U.S., by financial sanction if necessary. On 18 July 1963 President Kennedy made a speech to Congress concerning the balance of payments issue and other economic problems, in which he mooted *inter alia* the imposition of an Interest Equalisation Tax, which was subsequently approved by Congress to apply retrospectively from the date of the President's speech. The tax was designed to stem the outflow of U.S. capital in so far as it was ascribable to foreign borrowers tapping the domestic market.[2] The tax was a deliberate disincentive to investors and existed as a flat rate of 15 per cent on the purchase value of shares bought by U.S. residents. In respect of bonds the tax was graded from 2.75 per cent for bonds with a maturity of less than 3½ years to the full 15 per cent for bonds with long maturities. Thus, U.S.-resident investors, who had previously been prepared to invest in foreign bonds, were deterred from choosing this form of future investment.

Even before President Kennedy's proposal of the new tax the warnings

1 Kerr *op.cit.* p. 17

2 Interest Equalisation Tax Act Pub Law 88–563, 2 September 1964, 78 Stat 809; 26 U.S.C. para 4911-31.

of Treasury Secretary Dillon had struck home. It was already clear that the U.S. domestic market would shortly be closed to outside issuers. The subscription agreement for the first international bond issue was signed on 1 January 1963. The issue was for a $15,000,000 amount by Autostrade, the builder and operator of Toll Motorways in Italy for a term of 15 years. The issue was guaranteed by IRI, the financial holding corporation of the Italian State.[1] The modern international bond market was born.

President Kennedy's Interest Equalisation Tax proved to be merely the first move by the U.S. government to segregate its domestic capital market from the rest of the world. Accumulating balance of payment difficulties, arising from U.S. efforts to simultaneously build a new society with vast increases in social expenditure and to fight the ever more expensive war in Vietnam, caused President Johnson to announce a Voluntary Restraint Programme in February 1965 intended to limit, or even stop, the outflow of dollars from the U.S. Under the guidelines of the Programme, corporations were to limit direct investment outflows unless they could show counter-balancing balance of payment savings. Such savings could take the form of increased exports from the U.S., increased repatriation of dividends from overseas subsidiaries, and increased foreign earnings from fees and licences. At the same time U.S. banks were discouraged from making medium and long term loans to international borrowers, including the overseas subsidiaries of U.S. corporations. These subsidiaries were encouraged to raise capital in overseas capital markets where they were carrying on business or from international funds as a new source of capital. The Voluntary Programme proved to be unsuccessful. Confronted also with the additional pressure on the dollar arising from the devalution of sterling in 1967, the voluntary nature of the policy was abandoned and mandatory restrictions were imposed on direct overseas investment. U.S. corporations were each given quotas. These were based on two factors. First, the actual record of the individual corporation with regard to investment was taken into account. Secondly, countries were categorised into one of three categories with the highest priority given to developing countries. Foreign earnings of overseas U.S. subsidiaries and liquid cash balances held abroad were to be repatriated to the U.S. in terms equal to, or exceeding, previous recent patterns. To oversee the working of the mandatory pattern an Office of Foreign Direct Investments responsible to the U.S. Treasury Secretary was created.

The effect of U.S. policies embraced by President Kennedy and President Johnson were twofold, both working to the advantage of the free currency market. First, since the problem of the balance of payments deficit was left unsolved, there were plenty of dollars available outside the U.S. to

[1] The dollars raised were immediatley converted into lira and re-lent to Finsider, the Italian government-owned steel producer. The effect of this was that Italian withholding tax on interest payments was avoided—Fisher *op.cit.* p. 15. There are other contenders for the title of 'First Eurobond Issue'—see Kerr *op.cit.* p. 16. The importance of the Autostrade issue, at the very least, is that it changed market perception and established the concept—as such it was decisive and this history treats it as such.

be borrowed. Secondly, both overseas borrower and the overseas branch, subsidiary, and associate, of U.S. corporations were frozen out of the U.S. domestic capital market, which was the largest domestic capital market in the world. This last factor was particularly important because it occurred when changing patterns of world trade and organisation were prompting a need for the general availability of money for these very types of borrower. As the mandatory restrictions had already acknowledged (but inadequately provided for), developing countries needed capital to finance the development of their resources at a time when, in most cases, the state was taking a much more active role in development through state agencies and corporations set up to this end. Further, the restrictions were themselves largely necessary because, for both political and economic reasons, world trade norms were changing from successful companies exporting to countries overseas to that of establishing subsidiaries within their foreign markets to satisfy the demand there.[1] New and dominant units in the world trading pattern had been thus established in the forms of the large state owned enterprise and the multinational corporation. Yet for these very organisations the domestic sterling capital market could not provide the necessary finance and the domestic dollar capital market would not.

Many of the new multi-national corporations were U.S. by origin and in many cases the proposed destination for their subsidiaries was Europe because of its political stability coupled with its economic resurgence, to which a useful stimulus was provided by the establishment of the European Economic Community pursuant to the Treaty of Rome.[2] Even those countries outside the European Community were considered to be good places for investment, with the U.K. being particularly popular, partly because of the close political and defence ties arising from a war which was then still viewed as recent, and partly because of the common ties of culture, history, and language. All these developments helped foster London's leadership in the develpoment of the free eurocurrency and eurobond markets.

Inevitably, as U.S. corporations established European subsidiaries, American banks proved anxious to follow them to keep as much of the banking busines arising from their operations as possible. To achieve this, major branches of U.S. banks were set up in Europe, with once again London proving to be a popular location. With the U.S. influence came the third factor causing and directing development of the free currency markets, namely U.S. experience and techniques of financing which could be adapted to the new international bond market.

The effect of these various changes on the new concept of an international bond market after 1963 is interesting in the close parrallel between cause and effect, the most significant being the mandatory requirements initiated by President Johnson in 1968. The 1963 Autostrade issue excited interest and showed the means but, in the following two years, the flow of new

1 The phenomenon and its causes are excellently discussed in D. Wood and J. Byrne *International Business Finance* Macmillan, London (1981) ch 1.

2 Signed 25 March 1957 Council of Europe, IV European Yearbook (1958 413-537).

issues has been characterised as 'steady rather than spectacular'.[1] The pace quickened in 1966 and 1967 with the impact of the Voluntary Restraint Programme so that in the latter year the total for new issues reached a level of nearly U.S. $1.5 billion. It was, however, 1968 which proved the decisive year, for the effect of the abandonment of the Voluntary Programme in favour of mandatory restriction was to turn the attention of U.S. borrowers to the new international bond market, in which they had, hitherto, shown only moderate interest. In 1968 the total had doubled to over U.S. $3 billion, of which nearly U.S. $2 billion was raised by U.S. corporate issuers.[2] The new international bond market could then be seen as truly fully established.

The period 1973 to 1982

By 1968 the international bond market was an established and vital component of the free capital market. It was, however, a minor if very significant part of the whole and it was the euro-dollar market, particularly through the syndicated loan, which was the much larger and more important area of the free market. Developments in the period 1973 to 1983 simply reinforced this overall situation.[3]

In the final months of 1973 the Yom Kippur war was fought and, as part of the conflict, the oil embargo was imposed by the Arab suppliers who then proceeded to organise a cartel of all suppliers and, when oil came to be supplied again, it was on the basis of vast increases in price and therefore of profits to the supplying countries. Many of the Arab suppliers with large supplies of oil available also have small populations and, thus, large credit balances were generated by those countries, which they were anxious to invest internationally. Whilst some of this wealth was, no doubt, invested in Eurobonds via Swiss bank accounts, vastly greater amounts were invested by being put on deposit with banks in international centres, from which it found its way into the eurocurrency market.

At the same time that oil suppliers, as the new winners in the game of international trade and finance, had vast sums to invest, the new losers, those countries with no oil reserves but a great need for oil to enable their industries and economies to function, had a need to borrow to purchase the necessary oil supplies. This was particularly true of poorly developed countries, for the fully industrial countries could at least seek to trade their way through the problems generated by the great increase in the cost of this important commodity. However, the functioning of the economies of the poorer and less developed countries was also of concern to the developed economies of the west, who saw the developing countries as important markets for the industrial products of the west. With the encouragement of western governments, particularly that of the U.S., western banks saw that there was a huge opportunity to generate business and profits by recycling, through the syndicated loan mechanism, the oil profits

1 Kerr *op.cit.* p. 22.
2 Source Kerr *op.cit.* pp. 30–31.
3 See the excellent account of H. Lever and C. Huhne in *Debt and Danger, The World Financial Crisis*, Penguin (1985).

being deposited with them to the countries needing to borrow. As a result western banks made vast loans to apparently credit-worthy developing countries in the period now under consideration with a consequent huge increase in Eurocurrency lending.

The borrowers of these funds were all apparently credit-worthy developing countries but with very differing backgrounds. Some were simply the very poorest countries of the world including the poorest African and Asian countries who borrowed to the limits of their limited credit-worthiness simply to be able to survive. Some were countries in potentially better circumstances that borrowed to develop only to find that much of the proceeds disappeared in a welter of internal corruption. Some were countries such as Argentina and Brazil and some countries of eastern Europe who were generating a fast rate of ecomonic growth which they wished to sustain, but whose borrowing only generated a short-term consumer boom. Finally, there were well populated oil exporting countries such as Mexico, Venezuela and Nigeria, which wished to use their wealth to generate industrial development for their peoples, but were at risk that by doing so the money borrowed would be misapplied and the means of repayment disappear if the artificially achieved oil price fell substantially. By the end of the period under review western banks had lent huge sums to borrowers such as these. It was not expected that the loans would be repaid, for it was anticipated that as loans fell due for repayment new ones would be granted of at least equal amount so that the borrower's obligation was merely to pay interest at the going rate. In the jargon of the time 'debt does not get paid; debt just gets rolled'.[1] Underlying all this was the assumption of the banking system, in flat denial of their own historical experience, that states cannot go broke and always pay, at least, in the medium term.

The period of securitisation—1982 to date

States cannot be bankrupt in the same way that an individual can face bankruptcy or a corporation can be wound up. In fact when faced with a situation where repayment is too uncomfortable the time-honoured way out for a state is simply to stop paying on its debt. The debt might be rolled at maturity but the whole process demanded that the sovereign borrowers should repay the interest. The great increases in oil prices achieved in the previous decade eventually came to have economic consequences which made the position achieved by sovereign lenders untenable. First, world economic activity declined. As a consequence commodity prices fell and it was on those prices that so many borrowers were dependent to be able to pay the interest on their debts. The high oil prices resulted in more efficient use and this together with reduced world economic activity reduced demand for oil and made inevitable a fall in price. The oil revenues on which Mexico, Venezuela and Nigeria were relying to be able to service their euro-debt were soon much reduced. Finally, an increasingly unsettled world economy produced great volatility with regard to currency relationships and overall high interest rates. The high interest rates came

1 Delfim Neto, Brazilian Government Minister quoted in Lever and Huhne.

quickly to be reflected in the eurocurrency loans due to the very nature of the mechanisms employed, and developing countries could not generate the necessary income from the reduced commodity prices obtainable to pay the vastly increased interest bills. With the cross-default clauses usually included in each syndicate loan, by mid-1982 the whole system was verging on the edge of default. In August of that year Mexico indicated that it could no longer sustain the financial burdens upon it.

Mexico's problems were huge, but only the tip of the iceberg as full investigation by the world's financial community revealed. There were many other countries in similarly desperate positions with borrowings well beyond their capacity to repay. Frightened by what they had discovered the bank's initial reaction was to refuse new loans. Roll-over became roll-up.

In fact such was the scale of the problem that neither borrower nor lender would allow the whole situation simply to blow up. Governments and international financial institutions such as the IMF also became involved, and complex loan renegotiations took place so that loans were not called in and, indeed, often further sums were advanced to cover unpaid interest. The process is ongoing so that, while the loans have not been called into default, they equally remain unpaid and, indeed, grow as interest is capitalised into new loans.

While the banks have found themselves thus support of their existing loans, they have not felt any great desire to extend this form of financial activity into new sectors because of the risks which they now perceive as existing for themselves. Instead, they have calculated that profits can be generated as financial intermediaries, organising and distributing new issues of securities. As a result there has been a great upsurge in the amount of activity on the international bond market with new issues of traditional bonds and similar securities. The process has been called that of securitisation. In addition, experiment and innovation have brought in new shorter- and medium-term instruments and mechanisms in euronotes and eurocommercial paper. The common denominator in the process is that the bank is merely intermediary with the investor (lender) buying the issuer's (borrower's) security, which is in a negotiable form capable of being traded to a willing purchaser. If the new euronote and eurocommercial paper sectors are classed as part of the international bond sector because of these common characteristics, it is the international bond market which is now comfortably the largest sector of the free capital market.

If, in the period 1973 to 1982, it was Arab money which fuelled the eurocurrency market and supported the international bond market, more recently it has been Japanese investment which has fulfilled the same purpose as the economic importance of the Arab countries has diminished while that of Japan has gone from strength to strength. Much of this investment has been placed via Swiss banks. In recognition of the increasing interest of the Japanese investor and his importance to the market, his needs have been influential in the marketing strategies of the last five to ten years.

Marketing and innovation

From 1968 the history of the market can be seen as that of an established market thriving in good times and, perhaps more important, surviving bad times. The present size and structure of the market is considered in Chapter 2. From a historical point of view many interesting developments have arisen in the bad times, when high interest rates and volatile currency markets have made new issues difficult to market. To overcome investor resistance at such times the professional advisers within the market have been the most innovative with their ideas on the basis that new ideas often have a degree of interest to investors which well tried and established means lack. Where those innovations have actually addressed the problems of the market they have been accepted into the mechanics of the market and have earned a sector for themselves. Where, however, the difficulties of the market have not been addressed the innovation has only achieved, at best, a temporary following as 'flavour of the month' and then disappeared into neglect. Only those innovations which have shown successful staying power will be considered here.

The traditional bond has been an unsecured debt security of medium- to long-term duration at a fixed rate of interest. The length of term obtainable and the rate of interest necessary to make an issue marketable have depended on the economic stability prevailing at the time of issue and also, to an extent, on the perceived credit-worthiness of the issuer. Economic stability favours longer terms and general low interest rates in line with those prevailing world wide at such times. Perhaps the most successful innovation within the market has been the Floating Rate Note introduced in 1970.[1] By 1970 the economic stability of the previous years had given way to a period of monetary instability. In August 1970 the U.S. Treasury authorities suspended the official convertability of the U.S. dollar into gold, thus heralding the era of floating exchange rates. Inflation was on the increase throughout the world, to be taken even higher by the increased price of oil imposed by OPEC in 1973–4 and again in 1979. The concept underpinning the Floating Rate Note is that the security is issued not at a fixed rate of interest but at a rate which is recalculated at six monthly intervals at a percentage above the short term borrowing rates on the inter bank market so that, if interest rates generally go up, so does the rate paid to the investor on the note. Thus, provided that the note is not defaulted, the investor does not lose out if interest rates generally go up, for the risk of this is placed on the issuer/borrower. Equally, of course, if interest rates go down, the rate of return to the investor declines and where decreases in interest rates are anticipated, use of the role by an issuer is advantageous to it, for the investor would be better off in a fixed term bond of an equal initial interest rate. The first use of the concept was in May 1969 in the U.S. $14.7 million issue of debentures by Dreyfuss Offshore Trust NV due 1974,[2] but the form was not really to receive general market recognition until May 1970 with the issue of U.S. $50 million FRNS for Ente Nazionale per l'Ernergia Electtrica (ENEL), the Italian national electricity agency. The particular issue paid interest at 0.75 above six month Libor, and would

[1] See Kerr *op. cit.* pp. 34–40. Georges Ugeux *Floating Rate Notes* Euromoney Publications (2nd edn London 1985) ch 2.

[2] Kerr *op.cit.* p. 36.

be redeemed by the issuer if interest rates exceeded 13 per cent. The time was considered right for the concept, for the issue was followed by six further FRN issues in the same year, and a fast evolution of the form to a very significant proportion of the total bond market.[1]

A later period of market nervousness produced the antithesis of the FRN in the Zero Coupon bond.[2] In the first half of 1981 the market was listless and resistant to new issues. To obtain market interest Pepsico Overseas reverted to an idea first tried in June 1966, when BP Tanker-Erksberg issued non-interest bearing promissory notes at a discount of 71.87 per cent. The 1966 move had not excited the accolade of limitation until taken up by Pepsico in 1981 with an issue of U.S. $75 million three year zero coupon notes at an issue price of 67.25 per cent. The form has proved an immediate success on its reintroduction particularly because of Japanese demand and is now an established form within the international bond market.[3]

A very early concept in the market was that of the convertible bond, which is one issued by a company convertible into shares of the issuer at a future date at the option of the investor. An early example was the U.S. $25 million issue of 5¾ per cent 15 year bonds, which carried warrants to purchase shares in the Italian Steel Company, Societa Finanziaria Siderurgica (FINSIDER), made in June 1964.[4] In fact, convertibility can be conferred by either of two separate forms. The entitlement to convert can be contained in the bond terms themselves, in which case the right to convert passes with the bond itself as it is sold from investor to investor. Alternatively, as in the case of this early issue, the right to convert can be contained in a warrant, which can be traded separately. The warrants to purchase shares in Finsider eventually became very valuable. The equity-convertible sector has proved to be a constantly significant sector of the market.[5]

A different form of warrant is the debt warrrant, a U.S. innovation subsequently applied to the international bond market. The first public issue was a Yankee bond issue in December 1980, when a U.S. $200 million issue by the Kingdom of Sweden was made on the U.S. market. The five year notes carried coupons of 13.65 per cent, and each note had attached to it a warrant entitling the holder to buy one new four year note from the issuer at par, exercisable within six months. Clearly, the attraction of such a warrant depends on whether or not it is anticipated that interest rates will decline. The particular issue was a tremendous success, and the U.S. example was soon being repeated on the international bond markets.[6]

Another U.S. innovation transplanted to the international bond market is the certificate of deposit. The first deposit was the domestic dollar C.D.

[1] For the present position see Chapter 2, pp. 24 et seq. For an account of the terms of the Floating Rate Note see Chapter 6, pp. 177 et seq.

[2] Kerr *op.cit.* pp. 69-71.

[3] The zero coupon bond is considered *post* Chapter 6 p. 179.

[4] Kerr *op.cit.* p. 22

[5] See Chapter 2, p. 24. Convertibles are discussed *post* Chapter 7 p. 194.

[6] See Kerr *op.cit.* p. 67.

issued in 1961 in the U.S. by the First National Bank. The experiment was successful, and in 1966 the London Branch of the same bank made the first issue on the international bond market.[1] The issue was to be the first of many and certificates of deposit are now an important part of this capital market. Inevitably, the basic form was not immune from market developments and, in April 1977, the first eurodollar *floating rate* certificate of deposit issue was made by the the Dai-ichi Kangyo Bank Ltd in an issue of U.S. $10 million. Significantly, the issuer was a Japanese bank which, like all Japanese banks, was denied access to the straight Floating Rate Note market by the Japanese Ministry of Finance.[2]

1 Fisher *op.cit.* p. 67.
2 Kerr *op.cit.* p. 48.

2 Issuing in the market

If the eurocurrency and international bond markets fulfil an important strategic function within the world economy, it is clear that borrowers will continue in the future to seek there the funds they need as they have done in the past. It is also likely that individual governments will tolerate these transnational phenomena as long as they are perceived to fulfil these, or other, vital functions which are not fulfilled elsewhere.[1]

It cannot be emphasised too strongly that the euro-currency and international bond markets are markets, and subject to the ordinary laws of the market place. If there is more money available to be borrowed than borrowers require, the latter are able to secure more favourable terms than is otherwise the case. Where, however, there is a shortage of money available to be borrowed the lender is in the strong position, and able to negotiate loan terms closely adapted to his own requirements.

The most significant factor at work within the euro-currency and international bond market affecting the supply and demand for money within it is economic certainty and uncertainty. At times when it appears that the economies of the developed nations are functioning stably and predictably, and there is a feeling of certainty among investors, money for loans becomes readily available in the market. Where the position is otherwise and the economies of developed nations appear disrupted, usually with high levels of inflation in at least some of them and associated problems of currency fluctuation, investors become uncertain and retreat from the market. Equally such conditions very often generate a greater need for borrowers to borrow, particularly in the public sector, where countries throughout the world find a need to borrow money to cover an adverse

1 It has been written that 'however much . . . governments may wish to regulate the euro-dollar market (out of existence) neither they nor their influential banker and industrial constituents will be willing or able to do so. For the Euro-dollar market exists precisely because the dollar not only facilitates but is necessary to current levels of business profit in today's international economy'. Hopkins, 'Money, Monopoly and the Contemporary World Order' 2 (1972) Journal of International Law and Policy 63. While Professor Hopkins is wrong in putting his total emphasis on the dollar and the euro-dollar in world trade and finance his remarks are precisely apposite to the position of the free currency market *as a whole*.

balance of trade position, which they hope will be a temporary phenomenon.

The most obvious factor directly affected by uncertainty in the world economy is length of term available on the international bond market. Bonds are essentially long-term investments and usually have a fixed interest rate throughout their term. When investors perceive certainty in the world economy they are prepared to lend long term at fixed interest rates. Conversely, where uncertainty prevails they are not prepared to make such long-term commitments, and the length of term of bond issue possible to a borrower is much more restricted.

Further, uncertainty also affects the interest rate or, as it is expressed in the market, the coupon value. At times of uncertainty not only does the length of term that the market will accept reduce, but, as interest rates rise generally in all money markets, so the coupon value in the international bond market increases as the market struggles to remain competitive with other conflicting claims on investment money.

A further factor strongly influenced by the certainty or otherwise of the world economy is issue size. In times of uncertainty the market has available less funds for borrowers, and, accordingly, the size of issue is of necessity reduced.[1]

CURRENCY FLUCTUATIONS

A further factor of considerable interest to both borrowers and lenders in the market is currency fluctuation. The market for both international bonds and certificates of deposit is international. Further, they can be denominated in any currency that the issuer chooses. At its most obvious this reflects itself in differing rates of interest within the market for issues of different currencies of denomination. For instance, the Swiss franc is generally perceived to be a strong currency by issuers and investors alike. On the other hand, the Italian lira is often perceived as a weak currency. Accordingly, it is often possible to launch an issue denominated in Swiss francs with a coupon value considerably less than that which a similar issue denominated in Italian lira would require for the bonds or certificates of deposit to be taken up.

For the issuer, however, a much more sophisticated problem is associated with this point. The issuer wishes to raise his borrowing requirement as cheaply as possible. What concerns him is the total amount that he will have to pay to service his borrowing over the whole life of the loan represented by the bond or certificate of deposit issued. Whether he is sensible to issue in a strong or a weak currency will, in the end, depend upon the amount of currency fluctuation which goes on during the life of the issue. Let us suppose that the issuer wishes to borrow 100,000,000 Italian lira on the international bond market. He can do a straight issue denominated in Italian lira. Alternatively, he could do an issue in Swiss francs for the equivalent value, and convert the Swiss francs raised into

[1] These points are more fully discussed by F.G. Fisher *Eurobonds* (1988) Chapter 2.

Italian lira for the purposes of the expenditure which he has in mind. Let us suppose that an issue in Italian lira could accomplished with a coupon of 9 per cent, and one in Swiss francs at a coupon value of 6 per cent. The length of term of the issue is a straight 10 year.

It would seem at first sight that the issuer would be well advised to issue in Swiss francs, and convert into Italian lira, thereby saving himself 3 per cent per annum in interest on the coupon. However, subsequent events might well make nonsense of this approach. If the Swiss franc were to appreciate by 4 per cent per annum against the dollar, and the Italian lira depreciate by 3 per cent per annum against the dollar, the relative values of the Swiss franc and the Italian lira would be moving apart at a rate of 7 per cent per annum. On a Swiss franc denominated issue, the issuer will eventually have to repay the bond in Swiss francs. Clearly, the rate of currency drift between the denominated Swiss franc and the U.S. dollar (which was the currency of use by the issuer after the conversion) at 7 per cent per annum is considerably more than the 3 per cent per annum interest difference. The result would be that in our hypothetical situation an issuer who had chosen to denominate his issue in Swiss francs would be borrowing the amount of the issue very expensively.[1]

These factors are of course relevant to all borrowings in the free-currency market, the growth of which have made possible much greater arbitrage by borrowers in seeking to take intelligent positions with regard to currency movements as a sensible commercial defence to this phenomenon. However, the very availability and use of the facility tends to emphasise the extent of currency movement, and the markets are, of course, capable of being used for outright speculation. One writer has been prompted to declare:

> Over the years the international money markets have facilitated movements of funds out of weak currencies and into strong currencies, but the scale and immediacy of these movements has grown immeasurably alongside the expansion of the euro-currency markets . . . The die was cast after 1967, but it took another four years or so before governments realised that their defences against currency movements were totally insufficient to maintain a system of fixed parities and, once asset holders realised that they could force governments to exchange rates against their will, the day of floating exchange rates had arrived.[2]

1 There are nevertheless considerable possibilities for arbitrage in both the euro-currency and international bond markets — see Dach 'Legal Nature of the euro-dollar' (1964) 13 A.J.C.L. p. 33 Fisher *op. cit.* p. 151. The overall effect has been well summed up; 'Side by side with an elaborate, and well functioning market for (Euro) currency deposits — resulting in interest arbitrage — there is an equally dynamic market for foreign exchange rates. These two 'markets' are interwoven, are manned usually by the same persons, and bring the funds from surplus centres to areas of relative shortage, thus equalising the cost of money.' Dach *op. cit.*

2 Geoffrey Bell 'The Euro-dollar Market and the International Financial System' Macmillan London, 1973 p. 2.

WHO ARE THE ISSUERS AND WHO ARE THE INVESTORS?

In the case of certificates of deposit, quite clearly, the issuers and banks as certificates of deposit are merely a means for a bank to give a tradeable security based upon a deposit paid to it. In the case of international bonds the position is much more complex. Here there is a clear division between private sector and public sector borrowing. The relative size of the shares of these two sectors has, over the years, varied from time to time in relation to one another, but in the years 1974–78[1] the private sector represented 47 per cent of the total market and the public sector 53 per cent. The private sector could be further sub-divided by type. Straight debt issues represented 31.7 per cent of the total international bond market, floating rate notes[2] represented 8.3 per cent of the total, warrant bonds[3] represented 0.4 per cent, and convertible bonds[4] 6.6 per cent. The private sector borrowers as a whole represented the largest companies in the world, each with a major share of the international market for its particular product.

The public sector could be further sub-divided. Government borrowing was 14.6 per cent of the total of the international bond market, public organisations such as state trading organisations and nationalised industries represented 21.6 per cent, municipalities 5 per cent, and supranational borrowers such as the World Bank 11.8 per cent.

With regard to country of issuer the vast majority of issues were by borrowers from the developed countries. North America, Australia, New Zealand, Western Europe and South East Asia between them accounted for approximately 80 per cent of the total borrowing. This had the result that only approximately 20 per cent of the total market was available to developing countries, and, in obtaining a share of that percentage, those countries whose economies were judged to have the greatest potential for development at the time of issue did best overall.

In 1983, a total of 46,376,500,000 U.S. dollars' worth of bonds were issued on the market which represented a slight decline on the 1982 total of 47,266,100,000 U.S. dollars.[5] The currencies of denomination were as follows:

Australian dollars	218,540,000 U.S. dollars
Canadian dollars	1,121,910,000 U.S. dollars
Deutsche marks	4,516,470,000 U.S. dollars
Dutch guilders	709,420,000 U.S. dollars

1 Source Fisher *The Eurodollar Bond Market* (1979) Euromoney Publications Chapter 3.

2 Floating Rate Notes are international bonds issued with a variable rate of interest by way of return on the coupon. They are discussed in Chapter 6.

3 Warrant bonds are bonds issued by companies with warrants entitling the holder to purchase equity shares in the issuing company. The warrants themselves have a market value and are separately tradeable. They are discussed in Chapter 7.

4 Convertible bonds are international bonds convertible in certain circumstances into equity shares in the issuing company. The bond itself contains the conversion element which in the case of a warrant bond is separately contained in the warrant. See the discussion in Chapter 7.

5 Source *The Euromoney International Bond Annual 1984*.

European currency units 1,709,420,000 U.S. dollars
Japanese yen 276,650,000 U.S. dollars
New Zealand dollars 15,300,000 U.S. dollars
Norwegian kroners 13,720,000 U.S. dollars
U.K. sterling 1,955,410,000 U.S. dollars[1]
U.S. dollars 34,847,200,000 U.S. dollars

The vast majority of issues were by governments of, or corporations within, developed and stable countries with a high credit rating. Indeed, the proportion of the market taken up by issues from developing countries had declined dramatically as a result of the international debt crisis. The proportions of issue were 16.5 per cent by supranational organisations, 38 per cent by other public sector issuers, and 45 per cent by private sector issuers. The form of issue was 64.1 per cent by way of straight debt, 31.5 per cent by way of floating rate note, and 4.4 per cent by way of convertible bonds.

By 1986 year fixed rate bonds had a new issue volume of $126 billion, and the turnover of the secondary market averaged $40 billion per week. New issues of F.R.N.s totalled $46,564,000, and convertible bonds and warrants $21,747 million. The newly established London based Eurocommercial paper market (including euronotes) had, by the end of 1986, an estimated debt outstanding of $30 to $35 billion.[2] By the period 1984–87 the private sector accounted for 62.1 per cent of the international bond market and the public sector 37.9 per cent. The public sector could be subdivided into governmental issues which held 13.6 per cent of the market, public organisations which held 14.8 per cent, municipalities holding 1.9 per cent, and supranationals holding 7.6 per cent. The private sector contributed straight debt issues of 33.9 per cent, FRNs 19.1 per cent, warrant bonds 5.2 per cent, and convertible bonds 3.9 per cent. A breakdown by country or borrower for the same years reveals European countries and their corporations were responsible for 43.6 per cent, North America 28 per cent, Asia 14.8 per cent, Australia and New Zealand 5.1 per cent, Africa 0.4 per cent, the Middle East and Eastern Europe 0.2 per cent each, and Central and South America 0.1 per cent, leaving the supranationals with their 7.6 per cent.[3]

While considerable information is available as to the identity of the issuers far less is known about the identity of the lenders. Both certificates of deposit and international bonds are issued as bearer instruments so that they can be freely negotiated. Once issued, therefore, the instrument can, and is, negotiated freely and without record of the identity of the holder. They are negotiable securities which are internationally tradeable and, therefore, 'can change hands almost like currency'.[4]

Given the nature of the form of the investment, combining ease of

1 Proportionally a very substantial increase over the preceding year.
2 Simon Perry ed. *International Finance Yearbook*, 1987 Edn, Euromoney Publications.
3 Fisher *Eurobonds* pp. 62–65.
4 Fisher *The Eurodollar Bond Market* p. 43.

marketability with anonymity, it is reasonable to suppose that these instruments will appeal to investors seeking these particular characteristics in their investments. Some will be held by institutions such as pension funds, insurance companies, investment trusts, and central and commercial banks. It has been estimated that institutional investors represent approximately 25 per cent of the total investors in terms of volume held.[1] However, it seems probable that many international bonds and certificates of deposit are held by private individuals, having been purchased by banks for their account. It has been estimated that between 40 per cent and 60 per cent of all international bonds find their way into portfolios managed by Swiss banks.[2] However, more recently a trend of rising participation in the markets by institutions for their own accounts has been noted.[3]

At this point one may reflect that a picture emerges with increasing clarity. The centre is an international capital market on which money is raised in vast amounts, which can only be achieved by issues of international size. Investors within the market appear to be sophisticated, either because they are institutional, or wealthy and knowledgeable individuals, or wealthy individuals represented by sophisticated institutions. Issuers show greater variety from a large multi-national company, with a battery of dynamic accountants seeking to borrow money as cheaply as possible, to developing countries, where financial expertise will vary from good to weak.

SYNDICATION AND THE BOUGHT DEAL

Inevitably linking issuer and investor on an international basis is a complex task of considerable proportions. Traditionally, it has only been achieved by a syndication of effort. However, more recently increased competition between institutions, with greater emphasis on purchasing and placing power, has led to an involvement of a smaller number of institutions, and an erosion of traditional syndicate structures under the bought deal. This will be considered separately. Since the bought deal is much easier to understand against the background of traditional syndicate structures, it is the traditional syndicate which will be considered first.

THE TRADITIONAL SYNDICATE

The syndicate consists of an assembly of financial institutions whose obligations to one another are controlled by a network of lengthy agreements defining their legal responsibilities *inter se*. Of prime importance are the *managers* or *management group*, to whom the responsibility of taking action on behalf of the issue and its underwriters is devolved. These are selected as being the most important of the *underwriters* to be involved in the issue,

1 Union Bank of Switzerland *The Euromarket: Financial Centres Across National Borders* quoted Fisher *op. cit.* p. 43.

2 Union Bank of Switzerland, *op. cit.* Here the bonds will be held for private clients such as the wealthy Arab or European investor (in the mythology of the market typically the prosperous Belgian dentist) or, of increasing recent importance, the rich Japanese investor.

3 *International Finance Yearbook* 1987 Edn, *supra*.

and given management status; responsibility is devolved on this inner group primarily because of the difficulty of obtaining quick and effective management decisions from a large group. The obligations of the managers *inter se* are governed by an agreement among managers. Their relationship to the issuer is defined by the subscription agreement which they enter into direct with the issuer. The prince among the managers is the lead bank or lead manager whose pivotal position is considered separately.[1]

The underwriters as a whole are bound to each other by the terms of the underwriting agreement, to which the managers (who are themselves underwriters) will be party. The underwriting agreement, in an English issue, will also connect the underwriters directly to the issuer, for the management group enter into this agreement with the underwriters as agent for the issuer. The function of the underwriting of the issue is that the issuer is assured of receiving the full proceeds of the new issue at the issue price, for the banks undertaking the underwriting agree to purchase the shares at that price, in the event that the issue is not fully subscribed by investors. Ideally underwriters are chosen for their financial strength to be able to take on this substantial residual commitment, their institutional reputation within the market, and, since underwriters often participate in the active selling of the securities, their capacity to place the sale of large numbers of securities from the issue within the market.

The differentiation of the underwriters and the management group within the team has been noted, and is reflected in the positioning of names on the prospectus, with the more prestigious positions going to the managers.[2] This is legitimate as it represents a difference of both function and legal responsibilities. However, sometimes other groups of underwriters are given specially prominent positions on the prospectus by means of special bracketing of their names in a prominent position.[3] Those selected are usually the more prestigious of the underwriters after the management group. The purpose of special bracketing is purely that of prestige and advertisement, and has no bearing on the functions or legal obligations undertaken.

The final participants in the syndicate are the selling group who are securities dealers, banks, and other financial institutions, who each assume responsibility for selling a certain proportion or number of the securities issued. Each enters into an agreement (the selling group agreement) which defines its obligations. In an English issue the agreement will be made by the managers with the dealers as agent of the issuer. In principle, participants to the selling group are selected on the basis of their ability to sell large numbers of securities, their reputation within the market and their general prestige.

Each participant within the syndicate is rewarded by the allowance of a commission calculated on the size of the responsibilities he undertakes.

1 See *post* p.28.
2 Self-advertisement is an important motivating factor for institutions participating in the market.
3 Fisher *The Eurodollar Bond Market* p. 82.

Where a particular institution undertakes dual responsibilities, e.g. underwriting and sale it becomes entitled to the commission on each.

The lead bank or lead manager

In making the organisational and distributive effort essential for a successful issue there is one pivotal figure of particular importance, namely the lead bank or lead manager, who manages the operation on behalf of the issuer. It is the lead bank who will be given the instructions by the issuer to prepare the issue for the market. It is the lead bank who will investigate with the issuer the state of its affairs, to ensure that the issue will be acceptable to the market and be presented in its best and most attractive light. It is the lead bank who will assemble the syndicate of co-managing banks, underwriters, and selling banks and institutions to enable the whole international marketing operation to proceed, and the issue to be fully sold at the best price realiseable.

At first sight it might seem that the lead manager is a mere cipher or agent only of the issuer, acting merely as a sort of advertising agent to present the issuer's case to the market as attractively as possible, so that the bonds can be sold for the best possible price. The reality is far more complex, with the lead bank occupying a more complex and potentially confusing position. On the one hand it certainly wishes to do the best that it can for its client, the issuer. On the other hand it is also aware that the co-managing banks, underwriters, and selling institutions with whom it works, will be relying heavily upon it to have carried out as thorough investigation of the background of the issuer (including the issuer's financial situation) as possible. This is to prevent a commitment to sell being undertaken by them which cannot, in fact, be fulfilled, because the investors to whom, at the end of the chain, the bonds must be sold will not purchase the issue. For the members of the underwriting team failure to sell the bonds at the proper market price as agreed can be disastrous, for each member of the group undertakes to sell an agreed portion at an agreed price thus underwriting a share of the issue. Failure to sell the issue because the issuer lacks the standing to convince the market that its bonds represent fair, or indeed any, value for money will leave the underwriters buying in, out of their own pocket, an issue which is only saleable, if at all, at a considerable loss.

Further the lead bank, by agreeing to lead the issue to market at all, is putting its own reputation behind the issue to the ultimate investor. In a market which is as highly institution influenced as the international bond market a reputable name as a lead manager undoubtedly will influence institutions to buy bonds, either for their own investment or for the portfolio of their clients. If it subsequently appears that the conditions of the issue, or the financial situation of the issuer, were such at the time of the issue that the issue should not have been made, the lead manager will find his reputation badly affected in subsequent similar transactions. Nor is the concern to obtain accurate financial information limited to a desire to avoid marketing bond issues which will run into difficulty before redemption.

The bonds are marketed by issuing a prospectus containing detailed financial information with regard to the purposes of the issue and the status and background of the issuer. It is against this that investors will make their decision to invest in the bonds. As will be seen any misstatement in the prospectus may lead to complex issues of liability in tort, both for the issuer itself and for those who have been instrumental in its preparation, and also for those who have, as part of the selling group, sold the securities to the investors.[1]

Further, some at least of this investigation by the leading bank is related to an important legal topic, which will have direct relevance to the legal validity of the issue. Someone must investigate whether the proposed borrowing by the issuer is within its constitutional power, as there is a clear legal consequence that borrowings either without, or in excess of, the constitutional powers of the issuer will be invalid and unenforceable against it. Clearly, it is not practicable for all of the members of the managing banks, underwriters, and selling group to make individual investigations of these important points. Nor is it practicable for so much to be left to the investors themselves. The duty of a careful investigation is undertaken by the lead bank, and the process of carrying out this research into the borrower's fitness to undertake the issue is called due diligence.[2]

It is clear that the accuracy of prospectus carrying this vital investment information is essential for the well-being of all concerned. From the issuer's point of view it enables an accurate case to be presented in the best possible light, and prevents potential tort liabilities which would otherwise occur. From the point of view of the managing banks, underwriters and members of the selling group it prevents being caught with issues which are not effectively saleable or which, if sold, could give rise to problems of liability in tort to the investor and, in any event, loss of market reputation. From the investors point of view full and accurate information in the prospectus enables him to make an informed choice of investment; inaccurate information in the prospectus would leave him at best with only problematical rights to compensation in law rather than the good investment security which he thought he was buying.

The network of relationships

The marketing of a multimillion dollar issue of bonds or certificates of deposit, by international co-operation across many countries through a syndication effort of a large number of institutions, calls for a complicated network of relationships tied together by a corresponding network of interlocking agreements. Before the practicalities of bringing an issue to market can be considered, this network of relationships forming the structure of the syndicate requires further consideration. The network itself is slightly

1 These are considered in Chapter 5.

2 A comprehensive consideration of matters to be investigated by the lead manager by way of due diligence for both corporate and sovereign issuers is contained in Fisher *Eurobonds* pp. 96–98.

differently structured depending upon whether the issue is led by an American or British lead manager.

In an American issue the lead manager concentrates on getting together his underwriting team. The underwriting team itself will select and appoint a group of co-managers, which will act as an inner group working closely with the lead manager. These managers will add to the underwriters, if further underwriting commitment is needed. They will also get together the selling group.

The structure of a typical United States style issue is shown in figure 1 below.

Figure 1

United States Style Issue Structure

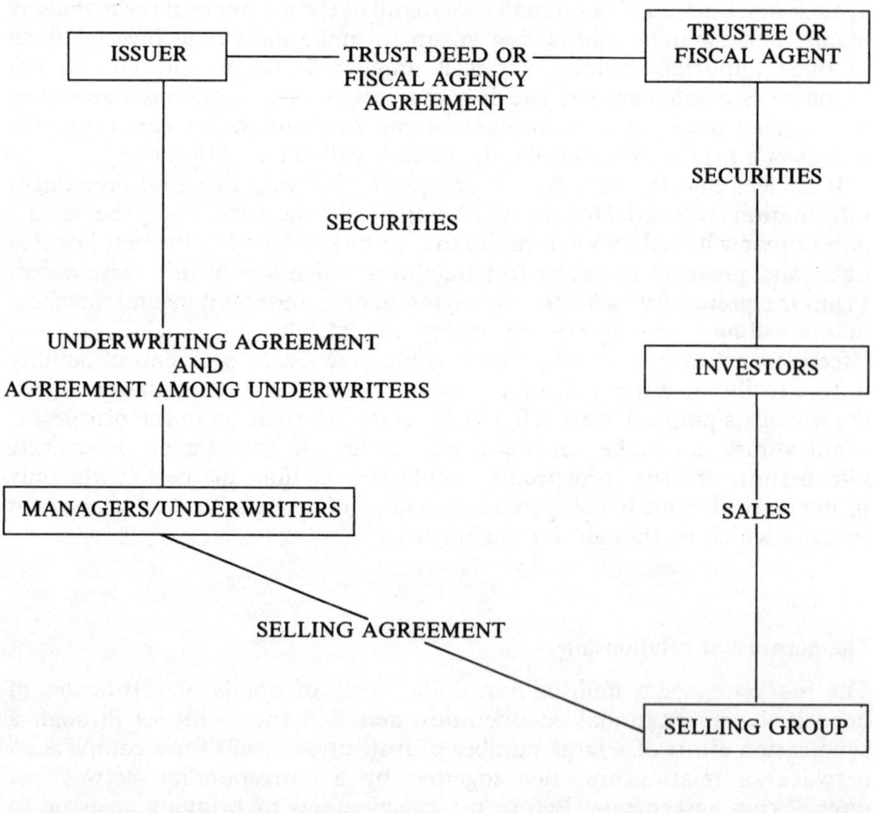

In a U.S. style issue, therefore, the managers have twin roles, namely to manage the issue, and for each to take his share of the underwriting commitment. The managers are connected to the issuer by means of the underwriting agreement, which they sign on behalf of the underwriters. Under this agreement each underwriter's obligation is several and not joint, so that he is responsible to the issuer for taking up his agreed share of the total issue. The issuer also undertakes responsibilities under this agreement, including obligations to disclose any deterioration in its financial position, and an agreement to indemnify the underwriters against any liabilities arising from materially inaccurate information in the prospectus. Further, there is an escape clause for the management group which enables them to abort the issue before it is closed, if there is such a significant change in either the issuer's credit-worthiness or the general economic circumstances surrounding the issue that the issue cannot be completed successfully.

All the managers and the underwriters have their relations regulated by an agreement among underwriters. It is by this document that the management team are appointed, and which gives them the power to act as representatives of the underwriters as a whole. Further, even among the management team, considerable discretions are given to the lead manager with regard to decisions necessary to market the securities and stabilise the secondary market when this opens. This recognises the need for instantaneous action on the international financial market where events move extremely rapidly. Whatever division of responsibilities is achieved under the agreement among underwriters, it affects only the relations of the underwriters *inter se*, and has no effect whatsoever on their obligations to the issuer embodied in the underwriting agreement itself.

The management group enter into an agreement with the selling group. This contains restrictions on the investors to whom the bonds can be sold, the terms on which they can be marketed, and the general obligations of the participants in the selling group. It also sets out the commissions to which they are entitled on sales. Each selling group member enters into the agreement on a several basis.

In fact most, if not all, of the underwriters and managers will also be engaged in selling the issue. To the extent they do so they bind themselves to the terms of the selling group agreement. The selling group members sell on to the end investors. When all the bonds or certificates have been sold then clearly the issue is complete.

This, however, does not bring to an end the necessary relationships. In accordance with the terms of the issue it will be necessary for interest to be paid from time to time. Further it is necessary for the bonds to be redeemed on the redemption date. To cope with these administrative matters, which will go on throughout the life of the bond and to form the link between the issuer and the bondholders, there are two alternative possibilities.

The first is the appointment by the issuer of a fiscal agent. His functions and responsibilities are set out in the fiscal agency agreement, but it should be noted that the function of a fiscal agent is limited. As its very name implies it is an agent of the issuer, appointed for the purpose of carrying out the functions given to it by its principal. Those functions extend to receiving the money necessary for payment from the issuer, and dispersing it via the various paying agents in the different jurisdictions where the bonds have been sold.

The alternative form is the appointment of a trustee by trust deed to act on behalf of the bondholders. In this case the relationship between the trustee and the bondholder/investor is fiduciary, and his obligation is to represent their interests. In addition the trustee will be responsible to carry out the administrative responsibilities normally given to the fiscal agent where a trustee is not used.

The critical difference between these two forms becomes most apparent in a situation of default on the bonds where, if there is a trust deed, the responsibility and power to take action on behalf of the bondholders is conferred by the trust deed upon the trustee. Where there is no trust deed and only a fiscal agency agreement each bondholder is left to fend for himself.

Finally, it should be noted that there will be but one trustee or fiscal agent. In fact, the bonds will have been issued in numerous jurisdictions, and it is necessary for payment to be made on interest dates and at redemption at various places in the world. Accordingly, a number of paying agents at various centres are appointed by the issuer, and their powers and responsibilities are contained in the paying agency agreements. These are purely administrative in character.

Much of this basic network is retained in the U.K. framework although these do differ from the U.S. in certain important respects.

Before the introduction of Value Added Tax (V.A.T.) in the U.K. an issue was made under the following framework. The lead manager assembled his management group, and these entered into a subscription agreement with the issuer roughly equivalent to the main underwriting agreement in the U.S. type issue.

FIGURE 2

U.K. PRIOR TO V.A.T.

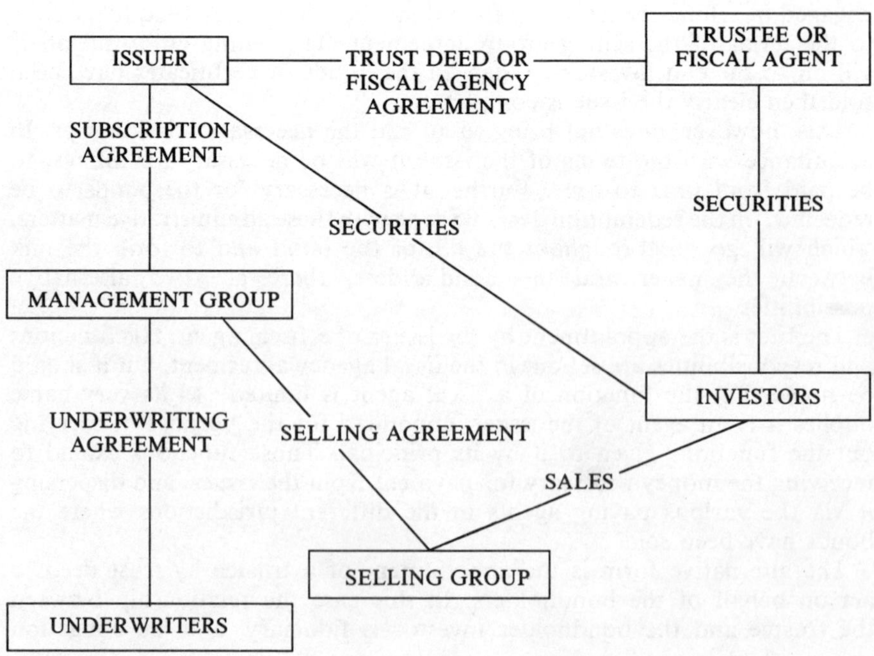

There were however important differences. By the subscription agreement the managers contracted as principals to assume the obligations of the issue, and they did so on a joint and several basis. It therefore follows that, as against the issuer, each member of the management group was liable to take up the whole of the issue if these were to prove necessary. Between the members of the management group there may be a subsidiary agreement (called the agreement between managers), by which they divided their obligations *inter se*, but this did not remove their underlying obligation to the issuer.

The management group is connected with the underwriters by means of the underwriting agreement, whereby the underwriters agreed the amount of commitment which each was prepared to take of the total issue. This agreement corresponded to the agreement among underwriters in the U.S. issue. The management group entered into the selling agreement with the selling group. The other relations of investor, trustee or fiscal agent, and issuer, remained constant.

With the advent of V.A.T. in Britain it became desirable to change the structure somewhat so that the issuer was in direct contractual relationship with the managers, underwriters and the selling group, rather than with the managers only as before. V.A.T. is a tax on goods and services supplied as a percentage of the value thereof.[1] However, when the goods or services are provided for an overseas consumer the V.A.T. rate is zero.[2] Issuers through the London market are overseas countries or companies. Hence the structure was changed, so that the issuer was placed in direct legal relationship with each of the institutions that were providing services for him.

The mechanics of this are that the managers enter into the underwriting agreement with the underwriters as agents for the issuer, thereby creating a direct legal relationship between the issuer and the underwriters. Thus, under the new style agreement, the underwriters contract directly with the issuer to underwrite their agreed portion of the total issue. In addition they contract on a several basis with the issuer to assume responsibility for the share of any defaulting underwriter, subject to their own total responsibility not being increased by more than an additional 10 per cent of their basic commitment. Thus, if a particular underwriter underwrote £1,000,000 worth of an issue which proved to be disastrous, and one or more of his fellow underwriters failed to fulfil his share of the obligation, he could be called upon to take up his basic commitment of one million pounds plus a further 10 per cent making a total of £1,100,000 in total. Any residual underwriting risk beyond this limit would fall upon the managers.

1 Currently 15 per cent.

2 F.A. 1972 Sched. 4 Group 9 item No. 6. There is, however, an exception in the case of Certificates of Deposit issued by a person who belongs in a country other than the Isle of Man which is not a member of the European Economic Community Item 6(a)(ii). However, these are *exempted* by F.A. Group 5 Item 4.

The remainder of the relationships and documentation are as in a U.S. style issue. This is hardly surprising since the form of syndication used has its origin in the U.S., and has simply been adapted to the particular needs of the international bond market. In the past there has, however, been criticism that the model has not travelled well.[1] The U.S. domestic market and the international bond market are distinct, and the participating institutions differ substantially. In particular, whereas U.S. syndications to their domestic market are composed exclusively around houses and institutions whose main business is dealing in securities, in international bond issues the syndicate was often composed around a wider array of houses many of whom were only incidentally engaged in the marketing of securities. The point with regard to international bonds has been well put:

> 'The diversity is not only geographical, which would be manageable, but is also functional. Whereas a uniformity of function exists in the U.S. syndicate, in Europe the syndicates include banks of every description, nationalized and private, commercial and investment, international and national, not to speak of stock exchange firms, secondary market dealers, foreign exchange specialists — in fact almost every conceivable financial institution.'[2]

The diversity arose because of the desire of so many large financial institutions to participate in the glamorous international market for reasons both of profit and of national and international prestige. It is a mark of that prestige — and also a useful advertisement — for an institution to have its name as a member of the syndicate in a prominent position in the prospectus of the issue (or, as it is known on the market, the tombstone). In forming a syndicate an institution were often asked to participate on the basis of its past prestige or long standing reciprocal commercial relationship with an existing member. Its inclusion frequently added little to the real needs of the syndicate, which are organisational facility and the power to place the sale of large amounts of the issued securities. Inevitably the inclusion of dead wood in a syndicate reduced its overall efficiency to the detriment of both issuer and the ultimate investor. However, in recent years increasing competition within the market has driven participants to put greater weight upon selection by placing power within the market, thereby leading to greater syndicate efficiency. This increased pressure has its ultimate expression in the bought deal.

COMING TO MARKET

If these are the contractual relationships eventually produced, and the documentary means which are used, they in fact represent the legal definition of a complex process evolved through the means of the market itself.

This process starts with the lead manager who, having considered the background and the needs of the issuer, concluded that an issue is possible, and calculated its size, announces in the press the news of the forthcoming

1 Yoon S. Park *The Eurobond Market; Function and Structure* Praeger Publishing Co, New York and London, 1974 pp. 37–49; Rischer *The Role of Underwriters in the Euro-capital Market Euromoney* April 1973.

2 Park *op. cit.* p. 45.

issue. This date, referred to as announcement date, is a critical point as once the announcement has been made, and news of the projected issue become public, it is not likely that the issue can be abandoned without loss of face to both issuer and lead manager, and, probably, the credit–worthiness of the issuer being detrimentally affected.

Also on announcement date, the lead manager starts to try to assemble his syndicate by telexing his proposed underwriters and selling group members inviting them to participate. This is known as the *invitation telex*. Ideally, preliminary prospectuses are sent to the proposed participants, a draft subscription agreement to the manager, a draft underwriting agreement to the proposed underwriters, and draft selling agreements to the selling group. A draft trust deed or fiscal agency agreement is also available for inspection.

The invitation telex is a critical document in the formation of legal obligations between the syndicate members. It is usually preceded by a telephone call or an invitation to participate conveyed via a trading screen. The telephone or screen offer may be accepted by the invitee but he will nevertheless receive an invitation telex to which he is expected to react to confirm more formally the agreement he had given. Eventually, all these preliminary agreements will culminate in the signed syndicate agreements. The significance of this increasingly formal documentation is clearly set out in the rules of the International Primary Markets Association, the self-regulatory body formed by market participants to help the market develop in an orderly and predictable manner.[1]

These rules specify that the invitation telex should be considered as the basis of the syndicate participant's commitment subject to the signed syndicate agreements which are thus recognised as the overriding legal documents. The head managers should however advise all invited parties by screen or telephone at the earliest possible moment of the basic terms of the issue, both commercial and non-commercial.

Apart from the commercial terms of an issue, the screen or telephone invitation and/or the invitation telex should, under the rules, as a minimum address the following subjects, namely,

(1) guarantees;
(2) ratings;
(3) ranking;
(4) negative pledges;
(5) market rated call provisions;
(6) taxation, tax redemption, and protection against identification or certification;
(7) sales restrictions, lock-up provisions and private placement arrangements;
(8) expense caps, payment of commission, deductibility of expenses, and stabilisation accounts;

[1] Post p. 42.

(9) force majeure; and
(10) cross default.[1]

Further, under the rules, an early positive response to a screen or telephone invitation may be reversed upon receipt of the invitation telex only if there are changes in or additions to the basic commercial or non-commercial terms of the issue. If there are subsequent material changes in or additions to the invitation telex (whether in the agreements or otherwise), commitments may be withdrawn but for these reasons only.

As yet the pricing of the issue will not have been finalised, although unofficial indication will be given. The various proposed participants are invited to agree to participate in the venture.

Over the succeeding days the lead manager works hard to stabilise his syndicate, making sure that all necessary participation is forthcoming. The lead manager is also concerned to try to work out the degree of demand for the particular issue. This is no easy task. The quality of feedback from the participants is not uniformly good. Some institutions will indicate precisely the amount of interest they are receiving with regard to sales, whereas others will inflate the degree of demand, so as to try to increase their standing with the managing banks in an effort to ensure their inclusion in subsequent syndicates.

The problem for the manager, which arises from overestimation by participating institutions of their ability to sell the issue, is the risk that the excess bonds taken up by the offenders will simply be dumped on the secondary market when this opens leading to erratic price fluctuation, a depressed market, and the issue and all the participating institutions getting a bad name as a result. Institutions exaggerating the demand and their placing power may not be limited to the selling group. It may extend to some of the underwriters or even co-managers.[2]

The desire of the lead manager is to establish a stable and realistic secondary market. This is in the interests of the reputation of the issuer and also the long-term reputation of the participating institutions. To achieve this the issue must be accurately priced in relation to the demand. Hence the need to gauge real demand precisely and effectively.

Before the announcement of the issue a pricing date will have been fixed when the price of the issue will be finalized. The date chosen is usually approximately 13 days after the announcement date. On pricing day the lead manager will consider carefully the feedback of information it has managed to obtain with regard to the demand for the issue. This will then be discussed with the co-managers and pricing finalised. If it is felt that demand is thinner than had been hoped, investor interest can be stimulated by either, or both, of two courses of action. The first is to price the issue at below par; the second is to increase the size of the interest on the coupon. The effect of either course of action is to increase the yield to the investor. Alternatively, if the demand is far greater than had been anticipated, the lead manager may conclude that to release the issue at par would be to

1 Post Chapter 12 p. 288.
2 Fisher *Eurobonds* p. 78.

underprice it and may in these circumstances decide to issue at above par, thereby increasing the return to the issuer as well as stabilising the market. The range of adjustment is between 1 per cent below par to 1 per cent above par.[1]

The manager's decision is communicated to the issuer, who may or may not adopt it. It is likely that the recommendation will be adopted, as the issuer relies heavily on the expertise of the lead manager to make the issue a success. If accepted the terms of the issue can be finalised, and communicated to the participating institutions. This also enables the documentation to be finalised, and the network of legally binding agreements is then created. The day following pricing day is called offering day, when all the underwriters are informed of the amount of allotment to them by telex. Similarly, those selling group members to whom bonds have been allotted are also notified of their allotment by the same means.

It should be noted that it may well be that, under the terms of the underwriting and selling group agreements into which the participants have entered, the amount of their allotment is not fixed but left to the discretion of the lead manager. In such a situation the only right of the participants is to be consulted with regard to the pricing terms, the amount of allotment falling to them being determined by the lead manager, although a prospective syndicate member can always refuse all participation in the light of the bond price decided upon.

From the offering to the closing of the issue, the primary concern of the lead manager, on behalf of the syndicate, is the stabilisation of the market price of the issue on the secondary market.[2] The secondary market is maintained by a network of bond dealers, who trade in issued bonds on behalf of themselves and their investors. By and large they are the same institutions who will undertake issues on behalf of borrowers if approached. Once the price of the issue has been fixed the means available to the lead manager to stabilise the market are limited. No longer can he alter the terms of issue to try to make them more or less attractive to investors. What he and the syndicate members can do is to alter the amount of supply and demand within the market at any particular point of time. This is done in two ways. On a particular day syndicate members can themselves buy in the secondary market, if it is felt desirable that this be done to stabilise the price. Where there is excessive purchase demand bonds can then be released back into the market to satisfy this. Throughout the lead manager is concerned to make sure that the price of the securities moves through only a narrow range.

After pricing the most important decision that the manager makes with regard to issue stabilisation is his decision to go long, or short, on the issue. If he decides to go long he arranges an allotment of bonds available to buyers to an amount less than the full principal amount of the issue. The remainder are held by him on behalf of the syndicate as a whole,

1 The effect of premium and discount pricing on yield is discussed by Fisher *Eurobonds* at pp. 78 and 79.

2 The legal implications of price and market stabilisation are considered in Chapter 3, p.67.

and sold into the secondary market when there appears to be any excess of investor demand forcing the price of the issue up. If the lead manager, instead of going long goes short, it means that a greater value of bonds is allotted to underwriters and selling group members than the full amount of the issue. As and when necessary to meet the obligations on the short the lead manager buys in the second market to meet its commitments. It is likely that a short position is one which can only be maintained at some cost, and this forms part of the expenses which are charged to the underwriters, as the effect of the operation is to secure the ultimate placing of the issue at a proper price thereby preventing them from being called upon to fulfil their underwriting obligations.

There is thus, during this period of price stabilisation, a market created by the lead manager which is referred to as the 'syndicate bid'. However, syndicate members themselves, who cannot fulfil their commitments by selling to investors, will avoid using this market to unload their securities, as this would publicise their difficulties to the lead manager. Instead, a second secondary market develops away from that established by the lead manager.

The process of price stabilisation does not come to an end with the closing of the issue. On the announcement day not only will the subsequent pricing day have been fixed, but also the day for the actual closure. This is usually approximately 15 days after pricing day. By this date it is anticipated that the whole of the issue will have been sold. In any event the syndicate members will be charged for and sold the bonds which they have committed themselves to take. On this date the bonds due to each institution are allocated to it, and paid for by that institution.

The process of allocation is interesting. International bonds are usually held by institutions in one or other of two depositary networks, Euroclear and Cedel. The workings of these two systems are discussed when the secondary market is considered.[1] Suffice it to say here that the workings of these two systems are sufficiently sophisticated that a temporary global bond for the full amount of the issue can be deposited in one or other of them, with details of the individual holdings of the syndicate members. The definitive bonds are printed subsequently and deposited at a later day, when, of course, individual investors, to whom the participating institutions have made sales, can obtain physical possession of their bonds if they so desire. Most do not, and almost all bonds never leave the depositary to which they are allocated from issue to redemption.

When making payment for the bonds allocated to it each syndicate member is entitled to deduct the amount of the agreed commission for the particular function which it has fulfilled, with the exception of the underwriting commission where the commitment can only be calculated later. These vary with the length of maturity of the issue, but on a ten-year maturity will total 2 per cent consisting of 0.5 per cent for manager's fee, 0.5 per cent underwriting commission, and 1.5 per cent selling group commission. A special account is set up to receive these net sums, which is then passed on to the issuer who has thereby fulfilled his borrowing requirement.

[1] See Chapter 9.

The whole technique for mounting an issue has given rise to criticism. Members of the syndicate are not supposed to sell the securities on the secondary market or to each other (they are after all included in the syndicate to strengthen the syndicate by their operations), and the agreements often impose penalties if they are caught behaving in this way. Even more important than the financial penalties flowing from the agreement is the fact that any offending institution, which can be detected, will probably be excluded from future syndicates. However, detection is unlikely and real policing of the syndicate practically impossible.[1] Further, the syndicate member should place his securities at the offering price, but it is quite usual for sales to be discounted by the member using part of his underwriting or selling group commissions to create the discount. Such means are likely to be used in respect of an issue which is going poorly. Indeed, cases have even been noted of underwriters passing on their entire selling commission and part of their underwriting commission.[2] This is done, of course, to avoid having to undertake their underwriting commitment, but the very fact that commissions have a sufficiency of spread to enable an underwriter to escape his responsibilities by these means without any loss, coupled with the other techniques to stabilise the market in the hands of the managers, has led to the suggestion that in the international bond market there is no true underwriting because the so-called underwriters shoulder no real risk.[3] It has been argued that the commission structure is too generous for the tasks actually performed[4] rather than those nominally alloted. Any inefficiency in the system is not to the issuers detriment alone. Where a particular syndicate member uses his commissions to discount an issue investors will pay different prices on the issue, depending upon the source of their purchase.

The grey market[5]

The lack of control which the lead manager has, in practice, over the sale of bonds has become institutionalized within the market by the development of a grey market, which is the name given to market dealings in bond issues before even a formal offering has been made. The formal offering cannot be made until the offering documents have been executed. Two factors seem to give rise to the market. The first is the continued participation in syndicates of institutions with inadequate placing power, who cover their position in advance by dealings at discount in the grey market, eating into their commission to ensure that they are not left with unplaced stock on their books, thereby tying up large amounts of capital. This factor, however,

1 Rischer *op. cit.* Fisher *Eurobonds* p. 80.
2 Park *op. cit.* p. 47.
3 W.J. Hopper *Some Practical Aspects of Raising International Finance* Moorgate and Wall Street. Autumn 1971.
4 In fact, the structure is no more expensive than that for issue of foreign bonds on the domestic market of any particular European country — Park *op. cit.* p. 40–41.
5 See, generally, Fisher *Eurobonds* pp. 92–94.

is emphasised by the second consideration, which is the aggressive attitude of some lead managers in overpricing a new issue beyond investors' willingness to pay, in order to secure the mandate from the issuer in the first place. The issuer is, of course, cost conscious, and wishes to raise its funds as cheaply as possible by floating a non-discounted issue with the lowest possible coupon price. If, as frequently happens, the result appears to be likely to be unattractive to investors, the pressure upon syndicate participants, to cover their position by operations in the grey market, becomes extreme. As a result the grey market has grown up, and is now a tolerated phenomenon within the new issue mechanism of the international bond market. To eliminate this market would probably require both a combination of greater discipline of pricing and a reduction in the commissions earned. The traditional high commissions earned within the market reflects the original design of retailing to individual investors, which is expensive, rather than wholesaling to institutional investors. Greater participation in the market by institutional investors, and increased competition has led to some tightening of commission structures.

Purchasers of bonds on the grey market will be institutions (including sometimes syndicate members) who have clients, often large institutional investors, who are prepared to buy at the right price. If the issue is overpriced they are, therefore, prepared to commit their funds if the bonds are sufficiently discounted. Equally, if an issue is underpriced, investors may be prepared to buy on the grey market at a premium in order to ensure a sufficient holding of an attractive investment. To the extent that the effect of the grey market is to ensure that, in practice, bonds are sold at their proper value, it can be argued that the grey market fulfils a useful function. However, its existence undoubtedly makes life more difficult for a lead manager in securing an orderly issue, and the establishment of a firm secondary market, which reflects the price at which the issue was officially marketed. Indeed, the final pricing may even be influenced by the grey market trading already established. The unfortunate effect of the grey market, and the dumping of bonds on a secondary market away from the lead manager's operations, is often that different investors end up paying different prices for the same investment.

THE BOUGHT DEAL[1]

The concept behind the bought deal is the marketing of an issue which is priced as soon as instructions to issue are given by the issuer, and in which the management group agree to buy the issue at the fixed price. The concept was first used in early 1979. It is a response to three factors characteristic of the last decade. First, greater efficiency within the market place, with market institutions with placing power using that power to great effect and leaving less room for less effective institutions. Secondly, it is a reflection of increasing volatility of interest rates and market reaction, when opportunities to bring issues to market relatively cheaply appear and disappear quickly. Finally, it reflects the increasing tying of bond issues

[1] See generally, Fisher *Eurobonds* pp. 89–91.

to interest and currency swaps, where speed and precision are of paramount importance. Because these factors have remained characteristic of the market, the bought deal has moved, from being the exception, to the principal method by which straight fixed rate bond issues are marketed. Full syndication tends to be used for more complex issues such as convertibles.

Because of the needs which the bought deal serves, the precise obligation of which is undertaken by the management group, syndicates are small, and consist of a tightly knit group of institutions confident of their ability to place the whole issue. Indeed, a small issue might be bought by a single institution. Underwriters may or may not be included by the management group to underwrite the risk they have assumed. The result is that fewer institutions will earn greater fees, for there are less to share the commissions. Also greater competition for the mandate may result in commission spreads being reduced. A typical bought deal syndicate, where underwriters are included, is shown below, from which it will be seen that a bought deal is, indeed, a simplified version of a traditional U.K. syndicate.

In it the managers, on a joint and several basis, commit themselves to the purchase of the entire issue, if the selling effort does not dispose of the entire issue. This agreement is contained in the underlying or subscription agreement between the issuer and managers. If underwriters are included, it is thus the managers' responsibilities which are underwritten in part by the sub-underwriting group. The agreement between managers and issuer is not conditional on the arrangement of a sub-underwriting group, even if it is intended to use one. Pricing and offering date are the same day since the deal is thus unconditional, and the price is part of the agreed deal between issuer and manager.

FIGURE 3

BOUGHT DEAL SYNDICATE

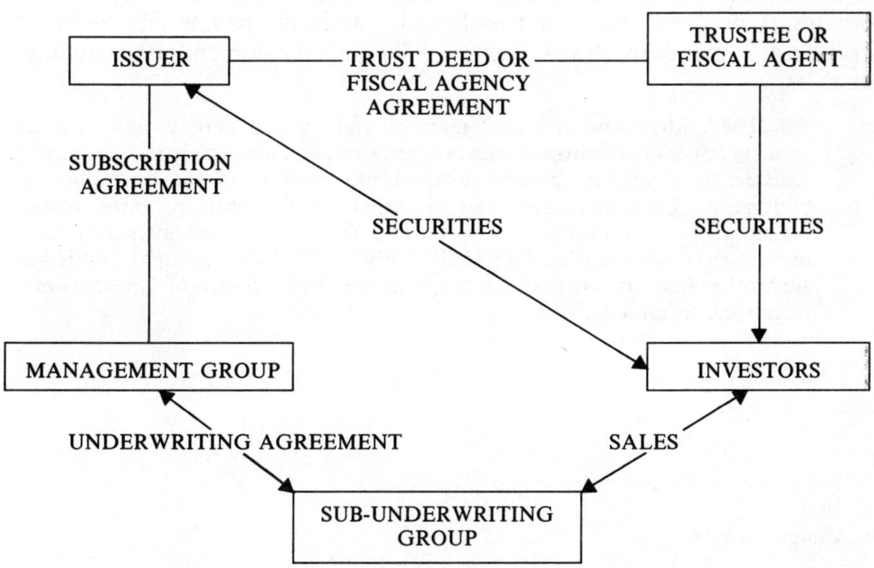

In addition there is an agreement amongst managers to bind the group together, which typically gives control of the offering and marketing of the securities to the lead manager. Under the agreement amongst managers each manager is in a direct contractual relationship with every other manager. The rest of the structure, terms, and relationships are on the same pattern as a traditional syndicate.

THE INTERNATIONAL PRIMARY MARKET ASSOCIATION[1]

The International Primary Market Association (IPMA) is an association of some seventy bond houses, and is concerned to standardise new issue procedures and documentation, and to maintain standards with regard to new issue arrangements. It was incorporated under English law in 1984 and is based in London. While it is not in any way a regulatory body it works closely with the Association of International Bond Dealers (AIBD). Its concern is to try to standardise new issue procedures and to maintain standards, so that communication and decision making with regard to new issues is facilitated. Thus it makes recommendations as to the form and content of new issue documentation. While these are not obligatory, it does require of its members that, if these standard procedures are to be departed from with regard to a new issue, full disclosure should be made. Market participants can be assured of the required levels of disclosure and information, and make speedier decisions, thus speeding up syndication and investment decisions. It focusses entirely on new issue procedures. While it has no regulatory authority, it carries such considerable influence that it is now estimated that at least 90 per cent of new issues conform to its guidelines.[2]

The closeness of the relationship between the IPMA and AIBD has been noted. The AIBD is primarily concerned with the activities of dealers on the market and it is therefore considered later when the securities regulation is discussed.[3] There is considerable duplication of personnel in the two organisations and the relationship is actively promoted by both organisations. Indeed IPMA has the following recommendation amongst its rules.

> All IPMA Members who lead manage and co-lead manage international security issues or offerings should register, or ensure that an associate company register, as reporting dealers under AIBD rules from the day following allotments. Lead managers should under normal circumstances remain registered for a minimum of twelve months and co-lead managers for a minimum of six months. This shall apply to US dollar straight bonds and such other instruments and currencies as the IPMA Board of Directors may from time to time decide.

[1] See generally, Fisher *Eurobonds* p. 212.
[2] Ibid.
[3] Chapter 4 p.90

ISSUES OF PARTLY PAID BONDS

Some issues of partly paid bonds have been made. The terms of such an issue are that the subscribed price is payable by more than one instalment, the first being made on first issue and the other or others subsequently. The issuer is obviously adequately covered in respect of the first instalment by the fact that this will be required as a condition to subscription. The problem is to cover the issuer's position if subsequent instalments are not paid at the agreed dates. Most bonds include express terms to cover this situation. It is commonly provided that the clearing agent will not clear transactions in respect of partly paid notes, thus leaving the purchaser from the issuer the holder of the security in the case of registered bonds until the complete purchase price is paid. Secondly, the terms will provide that definitive bonds will only be issued to fully paid bondholders. Thirdly, it is normal for the bond terms to provide that, while the issuer may accept late payments with interest, it has the right to forfeit a partly paid bond, keeping the instalments already paid and resell the forfeited bonds as fully paid at any price.

The power of forfeiture usually reserved is clearly a most effective weapon in the hands of an issuer. Under English law it has to be reserved expressly for it does not arise by implication of law.[1] If a prescribed procedure is set out for forfeiture it must be complied with strictly, for any irregularity will be fatal to the validity of the forfeiture, which is viewed as being in the nature of a penal procedure.[2] It appears that under English law, where a forfeiture has been carried out duly and bona fide, equity will not intervene to grant relief.[3] However, if application is made to a court of equity before the securities being forfeited the court has power to grant relief against forfeiture if it is just so to do under its ancient jurisdiction to relieve against the forfeiture of property. It is a settled head of jurisdiction that, 'where it is possible to state that the object of the transaction and of the insertion of the right to forfeit is essentially to secure the payment of money, equity has been willing to relieve on terms that the payment is made with interest, if appropriate, and also costs.'[4] The effect of forfeiture is that the former owner of the securities is discharged from his obligations under them, unless the terms of issue expressly keep open his liabilities for any short fall on the issue price which the resale still leaves.[5] As the bonds can only be resold as fully paid, no question of any continuing obligation of the subsequent purchaser can arise.

SECURITIES REGULATION ISSUES

The purpose of the gathering together of the large and complicated syndicate of participants is the marketing of a large issue of the issuer's securities

1 *Clarke v Hart* (1858) 6 HL Cas 633.
2 *Johnson v Lyttle's Iron Agency* (1877) 5 CH.D. 687.
3 *Sparks v Liverpool Waterworks Co* (1807) 13 Ves. 428.
4 *Shiloh Spinners Ltd v Harding* [1973] AC 691 per Lord Wilberforce at p.722.
5 *Re Blakely Ordnance Co, Stockens Case* (1868) 3. Ch. App. 412; *Re Bolton* [1930] 2 Ch 48 at 59.

on an international basis. The syndicate is deliberately composed so as to maximise the selling power of the syndicate in a considerable number of countries and, therefore, legal jurisdictions. Each jurisdiction will have its own individual system of securities regulation, adapted to the requirements of its own particular market. These regulations will vary in nature, therefore, from jurisdiction to jurisdiction, and range from the very permissive to the highly regulatory. It is therefore necessary to devolve the responsibility for satisfying the requirements of each specific jurisdiction to the syndicate participant who is to sell securities in that particular jurisdiction. This is done by provisions in the selling group agreement.[1]

ISSUES OF CONFLICT OF LAW AND JURISDICTION

The international nature of the syndication, and of the issue of securities, gives rise to complex issues as to the law applicable to the documentation, and the courts of which legal system is to have jurisdiction over them. It is plainly in the interest of all the syndicate participants, and of the issuer and investor, that certainty, predictability and uniformity should prevail. However, the potential complexities are considerable.

With regard to the syndicate documentation itself, for instance, it is perfectly possible for there to be a selling agreement between the London-based branch of an American Bank, which acts as lead manager on behalf of a Japanese issuer and a German selling agent. In the event of any dispute leading to litigation the potential problem is, therefore, which system of law is to apply, and the courts of which legal system are to have jurisdiction. In the example given the law of Japan, England, the U.S., and Germany could each be argued to be involved, as could the courts of each of the four legal systems be seen as potentially having jurisdiction.

Equally, the bonds, the subject of such an issue, have some connection with the law and legal systems of each of the four jurisdictions. Further, after issue, they may be sold by the German member of the selling group to an Austrian investor who, in due course, might sell them on in Switzerland to an Italian purchaser, who in due course sells to a Spanish purchaser.

In order to resolve some of these issues use is frequently made in the syndicate documentation of choice of law and jurisdiction clauses, which are also included in the ultimate bond or certificate of deposit, the subject of the issue. The international effectiveness of this solution is considered subsequently.[2]

CERTIFICATES OF DEPOSIT

Certificates of deposit fall into two basic categories. The simplest form are tap certificates, which are offered, on a time to time basis, in amount, and at rates of interest, which the market will stand at each moment of offer. Securities vary between one month and five years. Issue size will depend on the state of the market. Typically, they are issued with fixed interest rates, which remain unvaried throughout the life of the security,

1 Securities Regulation in the various jurisdictions give rise to complex issues which are examined in Chapter 4.

2 See Chapter 13.

interest being paid annually in arrears, except where the security has less than one year's life, when the interest is payable at redemption calculated on a daily basis fixed to a 360-day year for ease of calculation.

Typically tap issues are made without the complex documentation essential for an international bond issue, arrangements being made simply over the telephone direct with the issuing bank.

The second form of certificate of deposit is a more sophisticated instrument, both as to its nature and as to its form of issue. This is the floating rate certificate of deposit.[1] As its name implies it pays interest, which varies with the general level of interest rates applicable to the eurocurrency markets. This is calculated by a fraction of a per cent (usually one-quarter) over LIBOR, as in the case of syndicated loans. The applicable rate of interest is similarly fixed at six-monthly-intervals. Maturities vary, but average two to three years. Denominations and size of issue also vary immensely. The shorter average term makes floating rate certificates of deposit popular with investors when the market is uncertain, and they are looking for a shorter-term investment than the maturities usual in the international bond market.

Issues of floating rate certificates of deposit are made by procedures similar to those employed in the international bond market, although on a somewhat simplified basis. There is a syndicate to manage and sell the issue, but the documentation between the members of the syndicate is simpler. The issuing bank will usually act as lead manager, consequently issues of due diligence will not arise although full and accurate disclosure will be expected.[2] The issue will not usually be underwritten.[3]

TAXATION ON ISSUE

The nature of withholding taxes

The incidence of withholding taxes or, as they are more familiar to English eyes, taxes levied at source on the payer of interest, have a very significant impact upon the structure of international bond financing. The idea behind a withholding tax is quite simple, and dictates that the payer of interest should deduct from the interest payment the tax at the appropriate rate attributable to the payment, and forward this to the relevant revenue authorities. Such taxes are well accepted revenue devices facilitating the collection of tax, and, indeed, are commonly used even where borrower and lender are resident in the same jurisdiction. They become of even more crucial importance in international transactions, since, once the interest has departed from the jurisdiction of the borrower, the revenue authorities of that jurisdiction would be left with no effective means of collection in the absence of the use of the device.[4] It is a feature of the Eurobond market

1 There is a comparable creature of the international bond market — the floating rate note. See *post* Chapter 6.

2 On certificates of deposit generally see Fisher *Eurobonds* pp. 125–127.

3 Specific issues may be underwritten for particular reasons but this is not the norm.

4 Foreign courts will not usually enforce the tax laws of other jurisdictions.

that interest on the coupon should be paid free of tax, so that the set interest rate is actually received by the bondholder. Given this expectation of the bondholder, an issue will not be generally acceptable to the market unless the bondholder's position is secured in this respect.

Bond terms

The bonds themselves usually make explicit provision in their terms to cover the difficulties of the tax situation. The terms provide that payment of principal and interest will be made without deduction on account of any present, or future, taxes or duties, levied by the jurisdiction of the issuer. If, however, the matter was simply left there the issuer would be left in an unsatisfactory position, because he would be left to pay the commercial rate of interest and the tax upon it at a grossed up amount. His borrowing would, therefore, be crippling to him.[1]

Arrangements on issue

Accordingly, as a matter of practice, international bonds are not issued by issuers subject to a withholding tax in their own jurisdiction at the time the issue is made. The sophistication of the techniques used in the international financial market is such that this problem can be overcome by companies incorporated in a jurisdiction which imposes a withholding tax. The means employed is the use of one of the many countries in the world, operating a tax system which looks kindly upon the tax implications of commercial transactions (and often the acquisition of wealth by individuals as well), commonly referred to as 'tax havens'. In particular, what is needed is a country which allows payment of interest to be made free of withholding tax, such as the Netherlands Antilles and the Cayman Islands.

The means employed is for the corporation wishing to undertake the loan to form a subsidiary in the tax haven, and for the issue to be made by the foreign subsidiary, which then receives the results of the issue, and lends them on to the parent company. The loan made by the subsidiary to the parent company is interest bearing, and the interest is at a rate which allows the subsidiary to finance the interest on the coupons of the bonds. In this way the parent corporation receives the required funds, and is able to undertake the issue on normal commercial terms.

Choice of tax haven

The choice of a satisfactory tax haven depends upon two separate sets of considerations. The first of these relate to the tax haven itself. To be satisfactory as a tax haven for the location of the subsidiary in an international bond issue, the laws of the jurisdiction must be such as to allow the subsidiary to make payments of interest to the bondholders without

1 He would pay in all the notional interest which would, less the tax at the appropriate rate, give the actual interest agreed — a significantly higher figure than the appropriate rate of tax on the net agreed figure.

the deduction from the agreed sum of any withholding tax. Secondly, the tax haven must either charge no local stamp or documentary taxes, or, if any are levied, they must be at such an insignificant level as not to give rise to any major cost to the issuer. Thirdly, the jurisdiction chosen must not seek to impose any capital, or inheritance, taxes upon bondholders merely because the issue was made within that jurisdiction. Fourthly, the chosen jurisdiction must be free of any local exchange control regulations, which would either prohibit or make difficult the payment of interest to bondholders, or the ultimate repayment of their capital to them, or the repatriation of the proceeds of the issue to the jurisdiction of the parent company. Fifthly, since the subsidiary is incorporated merely to raise the loan, there must be no requirements of the local corporate law that a significant porportion of share capital be subscribed in relation to the borrowing being undertaken, for the parent would find this an unacceptable burden since its interest in the subsidiary is purely for the raising of capital and not for trading purposes. Sixthly, the cost of incorporation and administration of the subsidiary under local corporate law must be inexpensive. Finally, the political complexion of the local jurisdiction must be considered, for it is important that the benign fiscal and commercial environment should continue and not be brought to an abrupt end by political developments, causing a new administration with radically opposed policies to come into power.

The second set of considerations arise from the jurisdiction of the parent company, and the relations between that jurisdiction and the tax haven itself. In particular, not only is it important that the subsidiary be able to make payments of interest without deduction of tax, but the parent must be entitled to make payments free of tax to the subsidiary without the imposition of a withholding tax, and also, in due course, be able to repatriate the funds to the subsidiary to redeem the bonds without falling foul of tax or exchange control regulations. Secondly, the subsidiary having no significant assets of its own, the issue will be made palatable to the market by the parent company guaranteeing its subsidiary's issue, thereby substituting its own credit-worthiness for that of the subsidiary.[1] If, therefore, the parent is called upon to make payment under the guarantee, it is important that these too can be made free of any tax or exchange control regulations. Finally, since in the hands of the parent the interest paid on its bonds is an operational expense for its trading purposes, it is vital that the interest should be deductible in the computation of the parent's tax liability for its trading operations in its own jurisdiction.

In evaluating the position of the parent company with regard to both the allowance of interest in the calculation of its tax liability and the impact of exchange control regulations, the law of its own jurisdiction must be considered at the time that the issue is made. If the laws of that jurisdiction prove to have insurmountable obstacles, it will not be possible to undertake an issue by the parent corporation beneficially. With regard to the impact of withholding taxes, the matter to be investigated is whether the country

1 See *post* pp 290–291.

in which the subsidiary is to be incorporated has a sufficiently favourable double taxation treaty with the jurisdiction of the parent.

Stamp duties and other documentary taxes levied in many jurisdictions are another area of taxation which may give rise to difficulty to an issuer by increasing the cost of the issue. In international finance they can take the form of taxes imposed upon the securities which are issued, and which may be calculated by reference to a small percentage of their face value. Equally, some jurisdictions levy a straight issue tax on the value of bonds issued, or, in the case of convertible bonds, on the share capital into which the bonds may be converted. It is necessary to investigate the tax position in the jurisdiction of the issuer with regard to these matters, which can significantly increase the cost of the issue to the issuer.

A further area of difficulty in the field of taxation, which can significantly affect the attractiveness of a bond issue to the bondholders, arises from the possible extra jurisdictional impact of the capital taxation of some countries. Capital taxes comprise taxes on capital gains made by taxpayers on realisation of their investments, inheritance taxes payable on the death of a property holder, and gift taxes which are often supportive of inheritance taxes and which tax gifts made by one person to another. A particular jurisdiction may seek to levy one or all of these forms of capital taxation. So far as they affect only residents within that jurisdiction no difficulties arise, but some jurisdictions may seek to levy them on a different basis which can have the result that a bondholder, having no connection with the country of the issuer, may find himself liable to pay the tax simply because of his holding bonds issued by an issuer resident in the jurisdiction concerned.[1]

Of course, in any event, the mere fact that the issuer's jurisdiction passes a withholding, capital, or inheritance tax does not necessarily mean that this will necessarily be enforced except by the courts of that jurisdiction. An English court will not enforce a foreign tax where the agreement affected is governed by English law.[2] This is probably also true of the attitude of the English courts in dealing with an agreement governed by the law of some other country,[3] unless presumably the chosen law would give effect to the tax.

However in dealing with foreign stamp duties a further distinction must be drawn. Where the effect of the foreign law is to make the unstamped contract unenforceable and inadmissible, the English courts take the view that the failure to stamp is merely a procedural matter, and will ignore it.[4] On the other hand, where under the foreign stamp law the agreement

1 Philip Wood *Law and Practice of International Finance* Sweet and Maxwell 1980 p. 286.

2 *Indian and General Investment Trust Ltd v Borax Consolidated Ltd.* [1920] 1 KB 539.

3 *Re Visser* [1928] Ch 877; *Keiner v Keiner* [1952] 1 All ER 643; *Rossano v Manufacturer's Life Insurance Co.* [1963] 2 QB 352.

4 *Bristow v Sequeville* (1850) 5 Exch 275.

is void due to defective stamping, the English courts will recognise this and give effect to it.[1]

UNITED KINGDOM COMPANIES IN THE EUROBOND MARKET

The U.K. is one of the many jurisdictions which operates a withholding tax on interest payments.[2] The exact impact of this on issues of international bonds by U.K. companies was not entirely clear. In practice, before 1979 the Inland Revenue were prepared to accept that international bonds issued by a U.K. resident company could constitute a foreign source of interest payable gross, without deduction of income tax, under Case V of Schedule D, rather than being chargeable under Case III and therefore subject to the U.K. withholding tax. The reasoning behind the Revenue's approach was quite simply that, under the U.K. exchange control regulations which were in force until 1979, U.K. investors would need to use premium investment funds to make the purchase, which made it unlikely that they would invest in international bonds. The suspension of U.K. exchange control regulations in 1979 brought about a change of attitude by the Revenue. After this it became clear that the Inland Revenue would strive for the widest possible impact of the tax upon international bond issues by U.K. companies. The Revenue was fearful that the abolition of exchange control would lead to a massive increase in investment in such issues by U.K. taxpayers who, because the bonds enjoy the anonymity of bearer instruments, would not declare the interest which they earned on their tax returns. Equally, however, U.K. companies are anxious to raise capital on the international bond market because of its inherent efficiency, and, indeed, looking at the matter from the point of view of corporate investment, the U.K. government is by no means opposed to their wish to do so.

In any event U.K. companies have a traditional vehicle available to them to raise money in the international bond market. The technique employed is merely a specific form of the general use of the foreign subsidiary incorporated in a country with a benign tax system already discussed. In addition there are advantages from the point of view of securities regulation with regard to distribution to U.K. purchasers.[3] In the case of U.K. companies, a subsidiary is located in the Netherlands which satisfies the general requirements previously discussed. In particular, there is no withholding tax on interest under the Dutch tax law, and, in relation to the payment of interest by the U.K. company through its Dutch subsidiary, no withholding tax is applicable under the U.K. and Dutch double taxation treaty. The Dutch revenue authorities were content that the issue proceeds realised by the Dutch finance subsidiary should be lent on to the U.K. company at only $\frac{1}{8}$ more than the rate of interest of the issue itself, and on this small fraction of a percentage they levy Dutch tax at 48 per cent

1 *Alves v Hodgson* (1797) 7 Term Rep. 241 See the statutory exception created for bills of exchange by the Bill of Exchange Act 1882 s. 72(1) to ensure maximum negotiability of foreign bills.

2 Finance Act 1972 s. 1 now Value Added Tax Act 1983 ss. 1 and 2.

3 *Post* Chapter 4 p.85 et seq.

— a small enough price to pay for all of the tax advantages which had accrued.[1]

More recently, however, the Dutch authorities have sought to impose a large 'turn' of ¼ per cent rather than the ⅛ per cent traditionally imposed.[2] Further, the need for a financial intermediary added complication, clumsiness, and the expenses and delays of formation. The U.K. government set about analysing its objectives more fully and precisely than it had in the past. It became clear that it had no wish to drive U.K. issuers to the expense and complication of forming a foreign financial intermediary, and so far from having any objection to U.K. companies raising finance on the international bond market, it was prepared to promote this result. What it did not want to assist, rather it wished to discourage, was the interest being paid to U.K. residents on such issues being without deduction of tax.

This analysis led to legislation in the Finance Act 1984, s 35, the object of which was to remove from the requirement of deduction at source of income tax on the coupon, payments payable to persons outside the U.K. in respect of issues by U.K. companies. Unfortunately, the legislation is less than successful. It provides that s. 54 of the Income and Corporation Taxes Act 1970 (which requires deduction of tax at source on payment of interest) shall not apply to interest paid on any quoted Eurobond, where either the person by or through whom the payment is made is not in the U.K., or the payment is made by or through a person who is in the U.K., but either of two conditions are satisfied. The first condition is that it is proved, on a claim in that behalf made to the Board, that the person who is the beneficial owner of the quoted Eurobond and who is entitled to the interest is not resident in the U.K. The second condition is that the quoted Eurobond is held in a recognised clearing system. A quoted Eurobond is defined as meaning a security which is (1) issued by a company, (2) is quoted on a recognised stock exchange (within the meaning of s 535 of the Income and Corporation Taxes Act 1970), (3) is a bearer form, and (4) carried a right to interest. A 'recognised clearing system' is defined as meaning any system for clearing quoted Eurobonds designated by the Board of Inland Revenue as a recognised clearing system.

The defects of the legislation appear to be twofold. To give rise to the exemption from the effect of the withholding tax it is necessary that the international bond be quoted on a recognised stock exchange and whilst quotation is usual it is not a universal practice. Further, the Luxembourg Stock Exchange has not been recognised for this purpose. Secondly, bondholders require that interest be paid gross, that there should be no

1 It is for this reason that the risk of currency fluctuation on the funds if converted to sterling from some other currency is left on the shoulder of the U.K. parent company rather than the Dutch subsidiary despite the fact that under Dutch law any such losses are of an income nature allowing them to be set against profits realised in any year unlike the more complex and less benign taxation of foreign currency fluctuations. See generally Jill C. Pagan *Taxation Aspects of Currency Fluctuations*, Butterworths 1983, particularly at p. 81 *et seq*.

2 See Henbrey 'Company Finance' 1984 B.T.R. 7.

uncertainty that they are entitled to gross interest and that, to preserve their anonymity, they should not have to take positive steps to show their entitlement to gross interest under the first condition, if the bonds are not held in a recognised clearing system. Under the terms of the legislation these requirements can only be satisfied where the issue is made by an overseas subsidiary. In practice, new issuers in the market have relied on the legislation in view of the costs involved in establishing an overseas subsidiary. Issuers who have issued before and who have a Dutch subsidiary have continued, in general, to use the subsidiary. The Dutch subsidiary seems set for a longer life yet.

U.S. CORPORATIONS IN THE EUROBOND MARKET

The U.S. also operates a withholding tax. This was introduced in 1936[1] at a rate of 10 per cent. Slight modifications were made in the following two years, and the modified version of the tax became part of the Internal Revenue Code of 1939 at general rates of 10 per cent for individuals and 15 per cent for corporations.[2] Subsequently, by degrees, the rates were raised to 30 per cent where they remain to this day.[3]

Inevitably therefore, when the international bond market developed and U.S. corporations wished to participate, this tax represented a problem to be overcome. The finance subsidiary was pressed into use, but the form depended on whether or not the parent corporation's activities were almost exclusively foreign or largely domestic. If the U.S. parent corporation's activities were almost exclusively foreign, and the money raised was to be invested in foreign affiliates, the parent corporation could use a domestic international finance subsidiary (IFS). The intermediary is usually referred to as an 'eight-twenty company'. The domestic IFS would be wholly owned by the U.S. parent, issuing securities guaranteed by the parent, and lent the proceeds to the foreign affiliates. The affiliates would necessarily pay interest on the money borrowed to the affiliate and this would represent the whole, or virtually the whole, of the income of the domestic I.F.S. Since the operations of the foreign affiliates were largely, or even exclusively, overseas, the interest payments paid to the I.F.S. would be largely non–U.S. source income in its hands. Under the terms of the Internal Revenue Code a U.S. company (which includes a domestic I.F.S.), which derives less than 20 per cent of its gross income from U.S. sources, is not required to withhold tax on interest paid to foreigners.[4]

This was an effective means of dealing with the problem of withholding tax where the parent company's interests were largely overseas, and the bond issue was made to capitalise this. Where however this was not the case, or if it was likely that its operations would not continue to be so

1 Revenue Act of 1936, Pub. L. No. 74–740, ss 143(b), 144.211(a), 231(a), 49 Stat 1648, 1701–02, 1714, 1717.

2 Internal Revenue Code of 1939, Pub. L. No. 76–1 ss 143(b)(144) 211, 231, 53, Stat. 1, 61–62, 75, 78.

3 I.R.C. ss 871 (a)(1), 881 (a), 1441(a), 1442(a).

4 I.R.C. s 861(a)(1)(B).

heavily based overseas, other means had to be considered. In such circumstances the natural solution was the overseas I.F.S. Naturally, such an I.F.S. would need to be situated within a jurisdiction offering the advantages already considered, and, while a number of satisfactory locations were available, it was the Netherlands Antilles which came to be the most used.

The use of the Netherlands Antilles for this purpose depended on the terms of the tax treaty between itself and the U.S.,[1] and the local law of the Netherlands Antilles. Under local law non-residents are free of withholding tax on their income receipts, and also free of any other taxes which would adversely affect the position. Under Article VIII of the treaty, interest receipt of the Netherlands Antilles subsidiary from the U.S. are in general not subject to U.S. withholding tax. Effectively, the only real cost in respect of the borrowing were comparatively minor administrative and legal costs.

However, since 1980 the U.S. has applied deeper thought to the position of the U.S. corporation in relation to the Eurobond market. On the one hand, to have a tax system which drives its own corporations to the necessity of complex overseas arrangements to raise the capital they need to develop and expand their overseas activities, was hardly beneficial to U.S. economic (and probably political) interests. On the other hand, there was a concern that holders of bearer securities could draw income entirely anonymously from their investments, and not declare it as part of their income on their tax returns. This latter consideration was of far wider implication than the Eurobond market, since so many different forms of investment can be held in bearer form with the consequent anonymity which this brings. Having thus analysed the real issues with which it wished to deal, the U.S. passed legislation accordingly. The effect of the legislation is that U.S. issuers may now issue direct into the market without the use of an I.F.S., and will not suffer fiscally as a result, provided strict conditions are met.

In order to issue bearer securities that will be free of withholding taxes U.S. issuers must now comply with three separate, but interrelated, sets of tax rules. These are contained in or based on three separate statutes, the Tax Equity and Fiscal Responsibility Act of 1982 (TEFRA), the Tax

1 Convention on Income Taxes, 29 April 1948, U.S.-Netherlands 62 Stat. 1757, T.I.A.S. No. 1855, Protocol Facilitating Extension of Convention to the Netherlands Antilles, June 15th, 1955, 6 U.S.T. 3696, T.I.A.S. No. 3366. The resultant regime is discussed by Alan S. Lederman in 'The offshore finance subsidiary: An analysis of the current benefits and problems' (1979) 51 *Journal of Taxation* 86, who pointed out the potential of vulnerability of the arrangement to Revenue attack if friendly toleration turned to hostility. See also the excellent and lengthy analysis of A.J. Alex Gelinas in 'Tax Considerations for U.S. Corporations using Finance Subsidiaries to Borrow Funds Abroad' (1980) *The Journal of Corporation Taxation* 230, who voiced the same concerns.

Reform Act 1984 (the TRA), and the Interest and Dividend Tax Compliance Act of 1983 (I.D.T.C.A.).[1]

The fundamental purpose of TEFRA was to move issuers away from the use of bearer securities to those requiring registration by means of fiscal disincentives. It achieves this with the aid of temporary regulations introduced in August 1984 by worsening the tax position of parties on the issue of bearer securities, with a view to ensuring that they would not be sold to U.S. investors in the initial distribution of the securities. The particular fiscal disincentive applied is the imposition of an excise tax equal to 1 per cent of the face value of the securities issued multiplied by the number of years to maturity.[2] However, since the U.S. authorities were primarily concerned with their foreign and domestic markets and not with the Eurobond market, in which they wished their corporations to be able to issue freely as desire and necessity arise, they were content to include an express 'Eurobond exception' applicable if three criteria are satisfied. First, interest must be payable on the bearer securities only outside the U.S. Secondly, the face of each security and detachable coupon must bear a legend setting out that any U.S. person holding such security or coupon will be subject to various limitations under the revenue laws of the U.S. Finally, the securities must be sold under 'arrangements reasonably designed' to ensure that the securities will not be sold or distributed to any U.S. person (other than qualified U.S. financial institutions such as banks, brokers and insurance companies).[3]

IDTCA was introduced to build on the basis established by TEFRA. IDTCA imposed stronger information and reporting requirements than TEFRA to improve compliance with U.S. tax laws, particularly the taxation of interest and dividends. Issuers, paying agents, and brokers are all required to obtain and report the tax identification numbers of investors receiving payments of interest or dividends on, or the proceeds of sale of, securities. If this is not done a 20 per cent withholding tax must be withheld from the payments of interest, dividends, or sales proceeds.

The choice imposed by the form of the legislation is plainly unacceptable to the international bond market, which has always demanded payment of interest free of taxes, and also respect for and preservation of the traditional anonymity of the market. As a result of pressure from those who are involved in, or wish to use, the Euromarkets, temporary regulations have now been introduced to protect the needs of the market. Issues made in compliance with the TEFRA Eurobond exception are free of the information and reporting requirements if all payments of interest and principal are made outside the U.S., and neither the issuer nor the paying

1 The legislation is discussed by Alan B, Beller and Gail S. Berney in 'Eurobonds' in (1986) 19 *Review of See and Commodities Reg.* 39 and James P. Holden 'Repeal of the Withholding Tax on Portfolio Debt Interest to Foreigners . . . in the context of Eurobond Financing' (1985) 5 *Virginia Tax Review* 375.

2 In addition certain allowances and reliefs are removed which would otherwise be available.

3 This last requirement is exactly parallel to the security regulation requirements discussed *post* p 102 et seq.

agent has actual knowledge that the holder is a U.S. person. Further, information and reporting requirements do not apply to sales proceeds paid to investors by non-U.S. custodians and brokers that are not controlled by a U.S. person and derive most of their income from outside the U.S. Where, however, the custodian or broker is controlled by a U.S. person, or derives most of its income from the U.S., information must be reported, unless the institution has on its files evidence of the holder's non-U.S. status.

If the thrust of these reforms were to insist on less anonymity for investors and therefore greater fiscal rectitude, at some risk to the traditions of the international bond market until specific exemptions were made for it, the thrust of the Tax Reform Act was to try to assist the market by eliminating the need for a foreign I.F.S. This it achieved by repealing the 30 per cent withholding tax on 'portfolio interest' in the case of a debt-securities issued by non-resident alien individuals and foreign corporations after 18 July 1984. Three types of debt-securities produce income qualifying as portfolio interest, two of the exceptions relating to registered debt securities in particular circumstances and the third being 'obligations in bearer form issued in compliance with the TEFRA Eurobond exception.'[1] Coupled with the creation of this means for U.S. issuers to issue international bonds without the use of an IFS, the Inland Revenue Service took steps to clamp down on the use of the Netherlands Antilles finance subsidiary structure.[2]

The overall effect of these provisions is, therefore, now to create a means whereby U.S. issuers can freely make use of the international bond market without the impositions of financial penalties. Indeed U.S. issues are now made direct without the use of an I.F.S.[3]

1 IRC sections 871(h) (2) (A), 881 (c), (2) (A).

2 In October 1984 the I.R.S. ruled that Netherland Antilles finance subsidiary structures would not be recognised for U.S. federal tax purposes in the future. Instead, the U.S. affiliate to which the proceeds were on lent would be treated as the issuer. Rev. Rule. 84-152 1984-2CB. 381 and Rev. Ruling 84-153 1984 2 CB. 383. It may be that the I.R.S. ruling would not, in fact, stand up to judicial scrutiny see Holden *op. cit.* p. 399 *et seq.*

3 Holden *op. cit.* at p. 406.

3 The issue documentation and issues arising

This chapter falls naturally into two parts. First, the issue documentation and its typical provisions will be considered, and, secondly, two general issues arising from them, namely the provisions for time of performance and the legality of the various indemnity provisions which are included.

THE ISSUE DOCUMENTATION[1]

Of the documentation already mentioned a division can be made between that documentation which is related solely to the issue of the securities, and which (if the issue is competently and successfully launched) will cease to be of significance, and that documentation which is permanent in the sense that it remains effective throughout the life of the securities and is created for this purpose. Into the first category may be placed the documentation relevant to the actual issue of the securities, namely the prospectus, subscription agreement, underwriting agreement and selling group agreement. The permanent documentation consists of the bonds[2] themselves, and the related trust or deed or fiscal agency agreement.[3] It is to a detailed examination of the first group that the following chapter is devoted.

THE PROSPECTUS

The prospectus comprises three major parts. It sets out details of the securities being offered including their form, denomination, and terms. In particular, it specifies the existence of the trust deed or the fiscal agency agreement, and provides that the bondholders and coupon holders are entitled to the benefit of, and are bound by, the provisions of any trust deed which governs the issue of which they are deemed to have notice. It also summarises

1 While there is considerable standardisation of the issue documentation the standardisation is not total. Further, of course, standardisation does not mean uniformity of treatment by the courts of the various jurisdictions in which they are issued — se Professor N. Horn 'A Uniform Approach to Eurobond Agreements' 9 Law and Policy in International Business 753 (1977).

2 The various forms of security and their terms are discussed *post* Chapter 5 6 and 7.

3 The trust deed and the position of the trustee is discussed *post* Chapter 12, p 317.

the relevant terms of the underwriting and selling arrangements. It then goes on to describe the issuer. In the case of a corporate issuer details of the business carried out by the corporation, its management, and something of its history, will be set out. The purpose for which the funds are being raised by the issue will be explained and also the company's future intentions. The company's financial structure will be analysed and financial statements covering the most recent five years prepared by independent auditors will be included.

In the case of a sovereign borrower a description of its government is included to take the place of the description of the management in the case of a corporate borrower. Its history is similarly reviewed. By way of financial information details of past government budgets are set out, the country's economy analysed sector by sector, and projected development plans are described. Financial information with regard to its balance of trade and payments are included, together with details of its external public debt, and gold and foreign exchange reserves.

The prospectus is presented in such a way that, while giving the serious information needed by investors and their advisors to decide whether they wish to invest or not, the document also constitutes a considerable publicity outlet for the issuer and the financial institutions within the syndicate.

As has been noted, ideally a draft prospectus should be circulated in plenty of time for proposed syndicate members to be able to consider their position before signature of the subscription agreement, and the commitment of the various members. However, acceleration of bond issue timings has caused a drastic movement away from this ideal position. Often a prospectus is only sent after the issue has been finalised and on occasion, in the case of very well-known issuers, no prospectus may be sent at all (though there may be the issue of an Extel card). The position became so worrying that IPMA has now recommended that a draft prospectus be sent to co-managers at least one business day before signature of the formal subscription agreement, although in exceptional circumstances a copy may be made available for inspection at the London ofice of the lead manager.. Even this, of course, leaves little time for a full and proper review of the borrower's financial position prior to commitments being undertaken, and there is a danger that a guideline intended to establish a minimum position will, in practice, succeed only in establishing a norm.

THE SUBSCRIPTION AGREEMENT

(1) Recitals

Typically the subscription agreement entered into between the issuer and the managers recites the legal authority, if any is needed, obtained by the issuer to make the issue, the size of issue and the terms thereof, the existence of the trust deed or the fiscal agency agreement, the underwriting agreement, and the selling group agreement.

In the case of an English issue made since the introduction of V.A.T. it further recites that the managers have agreed to act as agents to the issuer in relation to the issue and, in any event, their willingness to subscribe to the issue.

The substantive provisions vary from issue to issue but will usually include the following:

(2) Issue commitment

First, that the managers jointly and severally agree, on behalf of the issuer, to offer the securities for subscription to members of the selling group. Secondly, it provides that the managers will subscribe, or obtain subscriptions for, the whole of the issue at 100 per cent of the principal amount, from which the selling group concession will be allowed, to the extent that the securities are not wholly subscribed by members of the selling group, or are not wholly underwritten pursuant to the underwriting agreement. The percentages of the selling group concession is fixed by the terms of the agreement.

(3) Interest and stock exchange listing

The issuer and the managers agree the rate of interest and the terms of payment of the coupons. The issuer confirms that it authorises the lead manager to make, and the lead manager agrees that it will make, an application on the issuer's behalf and at the issuer's expense for listing of the securities on whatever national stock exchange (or stock exchanges if more than one are to be used) as are agreed. The issuer further agrees that in connection with such application it will furnish all documentation and information as may, in the reasonable opinion of the lead manager, be necessary or advisable both to obtain, and subsequently maintain, such listing.[1] The issuer further warrants that it will use its best endeavours to obtain and maintain listing of the securities on the agreed stock exchange and, in the event that the obtaining or maintenance of the listing proves impossible, that it will then use its best endeavours to obtain, and maintain, a listing of the securities on such other stock exchange or exchanges as the issuer and the lead manager may agree to substitute.

(4) Publication

The issuer agrees that it authorises the lead manager to arrange for such publication of the terms of the securities and their issue as the issuer and the lead manager may agree.

(5) Issuer's undertaking

The issuer undertakes with the managers that the securities will be validly issued, and in the form set out in either the trust or the fiscal agency agreement, depending upon which is being used.

[1] While dealings in the securities will take place through the network of international dealers specialising in the trading of bonds, listing on a stock exchange does create investor confidence and is, therefore, usual. The matter is considered in connection with the secondary market *post* p.230. From a practical point of view the matter is of considerable importance.

(6) Managers commissions

The agreement sets out the management commission to which the managers are entitled for managing the issue, and the underwriting commission for the underwriting commitment which is to be allowed to the underwriters, to the extent to which they underwrite the issue. The managers are specifically empowered to deduct both commissions from the subscription money for the issue prior to that being paid to the issuer. The managers are further authorised to offer the securities to the selling group on terms which define the selling group commission.

(7) Closing of issue

The agreement agrees the closing date of the issue or contains the machinery by which the closing date will be fixed. On that date it is agreed that the amount of the subscription, less the agreed commission and expenses payable by the issuer, shall be paid into the issuer's bank account. The payment is agreed to be made against the delivery of the temporary global security for the aggregate principal amount of the issue in the form set out in either the fiscal agency agreement or trust deed, depending upon which is being used for the issue.[1]

Where the agreement contains not a fixed closing date, but a machinery provision whereby one will subsequently be fixed or agreed, the closing date may be much later than originally contemplated with the risk that the issuer is kept out of the borrowing requirement for the excess period. Accordingly, in this situation, it is usual to provide some form of compensation to the issuer should that date be unduly lengthened. This is usually done by a provision to the effect that, should the closing date be later than specified, a further sum should be payable to the issuer by way of adjustment for interest. However, the agreement will fix a rate of interest, which is only payable if the members of the selling group and underwriters are informed of the amount due from them before the close of business on the business day before the date of payment by them. Where this is not possible the responsibility of the individual participants in the syndicate will be to pay the actual interest earned on the money they received from the date agreed up to, but excluding, the closing date. The agreement will provide further that none of the participants in the syndicate are to be under any further or other obligation to the issuer in respect of such delay.

(8) Delivery of securities

The agreement will provide that the bonds will be delivered to the lead manager by a specified date, and then will be held by the lead manager to the order of the issuer until the temporary global security is surrendered. Thereafter they will be held to the order of the persons entitled thereto and lodged with the appropriate bond depositary.

1 As already indicated the temporary global bond will be lodged with either Euroclear or Cedel, the constituted bond depositories. Issues arising from the clearing systems are discussed in Chapter 9 p.233 et seq.

(9) Issuer's warranties

Within the subscription agreement, as a condition of the managers reciprocal agreements, the issuer enters into a series of warranties with each of the managers for the benefit of the managers and the underwriters. First, the issuer warrants that the prospectus contains all the material information with regard to the issuer, and that such information is true and accurate in all material respects, and is not misleading. The issuer further warrants that any opinion and intentions expressed therein with regard to the issuer are honestly held, that there are no other facts the omission of which would make the information or expressions of opinions or intentions misleading, and that the issuer has made all reasonable enquiries to ascertain the material facts. However, this warranty and agreement is expressly made not to extend to statements and omissions pertaining to the subscription, underwriting, and selling of the securities, which remain the responsibility of the managers.

Secondly, the issuer warrants that the issue, its terms, the issue documentation including the securities, and the fiscal agency agreement or trust deed and the issuer's obligation thereunder, comply with the laws of the issuer's jurisdiction and that they will not infringe the terms of, or constitute a default under, any other trust deed, agreement, or obligation by which the issuer is bound. The issuer also warrants that the issue documentation, and its obligations thereunder, have been duly authorised by it according to any legal requirements necessary, and that the securities will, when the issue is completed, constitute valid and legally binding obligations of the issuer in accordance with the terms of the documents and issue.

Thirdly, the issuer warrants that no event has occurred which, had the securities already been issued, would, or potentially could, constitute an event of default under the terms of the securities.

Fourthly, the issuer warrants that it is not involved in, and has no knowledge of, any threat of any litigation or other proceedings material to the issue of the securities.

Fifthly, the issuer warrants that any consents, approvals, authorisations, and other orders necessary for the issue of the securities, and the legal validity of the issue documentation, from any regulatory authority constituted by the laws of the issuers jurisdiction have been obtained and are in full force and effect. Thus, if any consents or approvals for the issue are necessary under the laws of the issuer's jurisdiction, the issuer contracts that they have been obtained. It further warrants that it has complied with all legal and other requirements necessary to ensure that upon due signature, issue and delivery, the securities will represent valid and legally binding obligations of the issuer payable in accordance with their respective terms, and that due payment of all amounts payable in respect of the securities and compliance with both their terms and of the issue documentation will not infringe any existing laws of the issuer's jurisdiction or the terms of any consent, approval, or authorisation, obtained from any such regulatory authorities.

Sixthly, the issuer warrants that, between the date of the issuer's entry into the subscription agreement and the closing date, the issuer will not, without prior authorization, issue any public announcement which could materially affect the issue of securities.

It should be noted carefully that the issuer's warranties are given only to the managers. It follows from this that breach of them is not an event of default in the bond issue which can only be determined from the terms themselves. Further breach of the warranties does not, *per se*, confer any remedy on the bondholders whose rights will be limited to the common law remedies for misrepresentation in the prospectus.[1]

(10) Stamp duties and issue taxes

Under the terms of the subscription agreement responsibility for the payment of any stamp or document duty payable in the issuer's jurisdiction, or the jurisdiction of the lead manager, in connection with the issue of securities, the fiscal agreement or trust deed, and the syndicate documentation will be the responsibility of the issuer.

(11) Indemnities

The manager's responsibility to subscribe for the securities, or to procure subscribers for them, is made on the basis of the issuer's warranties and agreements. It is intended that these warranties will remain true and accurate up to, and including, the closing date. The issuer therefore gives certain undertakings to each of the managers for their own benefit and as agents for the underwriters. First, it undertakes that it will hold the managers and the subscribers of the securities indemnified against all losses, costs, and liabilities which they may incur, or to which they may be subjected, as a result of any misrepresentation, or alleged misrepresentation, in breach, or alleged breach, of the issuer's warranties and agreements. The issuer similarly undertakes to hold the managers and subscribers of the securities indemnified from any such liability arising from the issuer's omission, or alleged omission, to perform its warranties and agreements.

(12) Issuer's obligations to inform of changing circumstances

The issuer undertakes that, if at any time prior to the subscription money being paid to it on the closing date, any material change affecting the warranties or agreement occurs, it will forthwith notify the lead manager of the change. In this event the lead manager is empowered to take all reasonable steps to remedy the difficulty, or alternatively the lead manager may require the issuer to take such steps. In the event of the lead manager and co-managers taking steps themselves, the issuer undertakes to reimburse them in respect of the cost of such action.

(13) Machinery for defending claims against the issuer

Plainly the issuer's warranties and indemnities have the potential to cause considerable difficulties if a claim is indicated to the managers in respect of which indemnity may subsequently be sought against the issuer. If an

[1] As to which see *post* Chapter 5.

investor alleges that he has purchased a security on the basis of matters in the prospectus which constitute a misrepresentation, and that he has an action for damages, it may be that the claim is a good one which ought to be met, or a spurious one which ought to be contested. There is a potential conflict of interest between the manager, who would be disposed to compromise even weak claims from investors, knowing that they could obtain indemnity from the issuer, and the issuer, who would want to contest such cases on the basis that there was no liability to be discharged. Machinery is needed to determine how such third party claims should be dealt with. Traditionally, the subscription agreement provides that a manager, receiving notice of any claim which may lead it to rely upon the issuer's indemnity, shall promptly notify the issuer of the claim in writing, and that such legal advisers shall be employed to deal with the claim as may be agreed between the manager and the issuer. If agreement cannot be reached the managers are usually given the power of selection of legal advisers. Finally, it is usually provided that the issuer shall not be liable for any settlement of any such action effected without his consent, thus preventing the compromise of spurious claims out of the issuer's pocket.

(14) Managers' right to abort issue for issuer's failure to perform agreement or material change

However important the provisions for indemnity might be, the subscription agreement will confer upon the managers even greater rights pertaining to the issuer's warranties and agreements. It will provide that upon any material breach of the warranties, or the issuer's material failure to perform any of the agreements, or any other change affecting any of the warranties or agreements, coming to the notice of the managers before payment being made to the issuer on the closing date, the lead manager, on behalf of the managers and the underwriters and the selling group, shall be entitled by notice to the issuer to elect to treat the breach, failure, or change, as discharging all the participants from their respective obligations under the agreement. It should be noted that this is permissive. The lead managers are empowered to treat the agreement as at an end, but are not bound to do so. This enables the lead manager to consider whether the breach or change is so material in extent as to prevent the issue being brought to a successful conclusion, or whether it is still practicable to proceed. The agreement will further provide that the failure of the lead manager to make an election in respect of a particular breach or change does not affect its right to treat any breach or change subsequently coming to its notice as releasing the participants from their obligations.

Clearly, this confers a power upon the lead manager of devastating proportions with the wildest possible discretion. However, the power is but rarely exercised. Both the issuer and the syndicate participants are eager to make a successful issue. Even if the issuer is in breach of a warranty the participants in the syndicate will still be keen to complete the issue, provided that it is practicable to do so honestly. As a practical matter, therefore, the vital consideration will be whether the breach or change when disclosed so significantly affects the marketability of the securities that a successful issue is not longer possible.

The subscription agreement will expressly provide that the issuers warranties and agreements continue in full force and effect notwithstanding the successful completion of the subscription and issue of the securities to investors.

(15) Conditions precedent

The power of the managers to withdraw from the issue is reinforced by terms within the subscription agreement which make it clear that the agreement is conditional upon certain events. The first of these is that as at the closing date there has been no adverse change in the condition of the issuer from that disclosed in the prospectus, nor that any event has occurred having the effect of rendering untrue or incorrect any of the warranties given by the issuer. The further conditions are, secondly, that any legal opinions required by the managers have been obtained, thirdly, that the securities have been admitted for listing to the chosen stock exchange, and, fourthly, that the fiscal agency agreement or trust deed has been executed and is effective. Again, if any of these conditions are not satisfied the lead manager on behalf of the managers is entitled, but not bound, to terminate the agreement on behalf of the managers and other participants. The effect of termination is to terminate all parties' rights with regard to the agreement, except the responsibility of the issuer to reimburse the managers for expenses incurred in connection with the issue.

The provisions with regard to conditions precedent and also the managers' right to abort the issue for material change create a number of events referred to as force majeure. Under I.P.M.A guidelines these must be clearly defined and the impact which they might have on an issue must be clearly set out if the management group is released from its underwriting obligations on the occurrence of the events. The provisions must be clear as to who determines and has authority to invoke the release of obligations, and how expenses and other responsibilities are to be dealt with after release. I.P.M.A. further recommends that such releases should not be made dependent on third party contracts, such as swaps. If they are so dependent this should be very clearly disclosed.

(16) Expenses

A successful international bond issue involves considerable expense. The various syndicate agreements have to be prepared, the securities have to be printed, inspected, and delivered, the listing of the securities on the chosen stock exchange has to be obtained, fees and expenses are payable to the fiscal agent or trustee, and the paying agents, and finally considerable expense is incurred with regard to publicity. By the terms of the selling agreement the issuer will assume responsibility for all of these. In addition it will traditionally agree that it will reimburse a global sum towards the travelling, telephone, and postage expenses, incurred by the managers, as well as the legal fees and expenses of the managers' legal advisers.

(17) Sales by managers

Under the subscription agreement the managers will agree that any securities offered by them for sale, or subscribed to for their own benefit, will be offered or subscribed on the terms set forth in the selling group agreement. This is intended to prevent the managers effecting sales at a price less than that to which the selling group is bound, thereby prejudicing the efforts of that group to place its commitment. It also binds the managers to the obligations with regard to securities regulation undertaken by the members of the selling group.[1]

(18) Market stabilisation

The steps which the managers take with regard to the stabilisation of the price have already been noted. By the subscription agreement a wide power to stabilise is conferred upon the managers including the power to over-allot, but it is made clear that in the exercise of such powers the managers act as agents of the underwriters, and not of the issuer. On the other hand, the issuer undertakes with the managers that it itself will not, before the expiration of a specified period after the closing date, enter into any transactions which would affect the market price of the securities, thereby preventing the issuer achieving an artificial value for the issue independently of the managers. The legal power, therefore, to stabilise the secondary market is vested exclusively with the managers on behalf of the syndicate.[2]

(19) Market disruption or force majeure clause

One of the most controversial provisions of the subscription agreement is the market disruption clause. This empowers the lead manager, on behalf of the managers, by notice given at any time before closing date to determine the agreement, if, in the opinion of the lead manager, market conditions have changed to such an extent that a successful issue cannot be mounted. The clause is widely worded and traditionally covers changes in the national or international financial, political, or economic conditions, or currency exchange rates, or exchange controls, likely to prejudice materially the success of the offering and distribution of the securities. Upon notice being given pursuant to the provision all the participants are released from their respective obligations, save that the issuer remains responsible for the payment of the fees costs and expenses that it has agreed to bear.

The exact form of the clause when used can vary. It can, and often is, drawn as here so that the judgment of whether or not there is market disorder is that of the lead manager. The test thus hardly objective, and confers a very wide discretion on the lead manager. In practice, where possible, the lead manager would be likely to consult with his fellow managers and the issuer where consultation is possible, but some times this will not be possible where the market is developing quickly. Often a position will have to be adopted on the basis of incomplete information and the

1 As to which see *post* p.71.
2 Stabilization is discussed *post* p.67.

justification for a discretion which effectively removes legal liability from the lead manager, if he aborts the issue in circumstances where it is subsequently clear that it could have been made successfully, is quite simply that it would be unreasonable to hold otherwise, and, where a market is already volatile, it would be impossible to find managers on any other terms.

In fact, it is all too easy to become over-excited by the clause since it has only been used very rarely. Both managers and issuer have a common interest in an issue being mounted if, and only if, it can be brought to successful fruition. Where this is impossible it is in the interests of both that the issue should not be made. This common interest has prevented the clause being used except in the most exceptional situation.[1]

IPMA has a number of provisions dealing with such clauses. It recognises that

> 'the managers and underwriters are normally discharged from their underwriting obligations if certain events occur between the signing and before the payment date (or occasionally earlier). The force majeure or termination clause usually has the following elements:
>
> *(a)* *a description of the types of event that qualify;*
> *(b)* *a description of their required effect in order to effectuate a release (normally a material prejudice to the issue, sale or distribution of the bonds or notes);*
> *(c)* *specification of in whose opinion such changes have occurred and in whose authority the right to invoke the provisions is vested;*
> *(d)* *treatment of expenses and certain other surviving obligations in the event of a release.*
>
> Whilst various styles of these clauses exist, with variations in the degree of generality of the qualifying events, the co—managers and under writers should be able to assume that the lead manager will negotiate a clause which is sufficiently broad to afford a reasonable protection against unforseen developments.
>
> Conclusion of third party agreements, such as swaps, have sometimes been made conditions precedent to the closing of a euro-issue. This is to be discouraged.

There are also provisions with regard to the screen, telephone invitation and invitation telex:

> 1. The absence of a force majeure clause or the inclusion of a force majeure clause which does not afford reasonable protection prior to payment against unforeseen developments should be disclosed.
>
> 2. If the closing is made dependent on the conclusion of third party contracts like swaps, the existence of such conditions should be noted.

1 It was precisely this lack of community interest in the recent national sale of BP shares *by the government* which gave rise to the underwriting difficulties which arose consequent on the October 1987 stock-market 'crash'. If BP had been issuing the shares it might well have been best advised to abort the issue.

(20) Conflict of laws and time of the essence

Finally, by the terms of the agreement, the issuer will submit for all purposes in connection with the issue to the jurisdiction of the courts of the legal system designated to have jurisdiction, agree that the agreement is governed by, and is to be construed in accordance with, the chosen law, and, where that law is English law, agrees that time shall be the essence of the agreement thereby giving legal reinforcement to the speed of occurrences on the market and the need for prompt reaction thereto.

(21) Circulation of the subscription agreement

Sadly, similar problems have arisen with regard to the circulation of a draft subscription agreement as have arisen with regard to the draft prospectus with the consequent result that it is then impossible for a proper review of their contents prior to commitment.[1] Again I.P.M.A. now recommends that such documents should be delivered by the lead manager one full business day prior to signing the subscription agreement.

THE UNDERWRITING AGREEMENT

The underwriting agreement makes provision for the underwriting of the issue. The concept of underwriting within the international bond market is consistent with its strict conventional commercial sense. Whilst the Companies Act 1985 uses the term underwriter, it contains no definition of the term, which is not defined elsewhere in the companies legislation. However, it appears that the courts will restrict the meaning of the term to its normal commercial use. This is hardly surprising as in the past the courts have been prepared to receive evidence as to the meaning of the term in commerce. Thus in 1889 Cotton LJ stated precisely the normal commercial use of the term;

> From the evidence which has been given as to the meaning of the expression 'underwriting' as applied to shares, it appears that an 'underwriting' agreement means an agreement entered into before the shares are brought before the public that in the event of the public not taking up the whole of them, or the number mentioned in the agreement, the underwriter will, for an agreed commission, take an allotment of such part of the shares as the public has not applied for. This is what is meant when it is said that a person has agreed to underwrite a certain number of shares in a company.[2]

The same remarks will apply, *mutatis mutandis*, to the underwriting of an international bond issue.

At the point of time that the underwriting agreement will be entered into the subscription agreement will not be signed in its final form, and, inevitably, the form of underwriting agreement reflects this.

1 *Ante* p.56.

2 *Re Licensed Victuallers' Mutual Trading Association, ex p Audain* (1889) 42 Ch D 1 at 5 and 6. Within a decade the term had acquired a legal definition in these terms without the need for evidence see *Re London-Paris Financial Mining Corpn.* (1897) 13 TLR 569 at 570-571 *per* Lindley LJ.

The underwriters on the announcement date will have been informed by telex of the terms of the issue in its proposed form. The underwriting agreement refers to this telex, the terms of the securities, and the terms of the prospectus, a copy of which is sent with the draft underwriting agreement. Typically the underwriting agreement will be in a form containing terms similar to those set out below.

(1) Recitals

By the proposed agreement the underwriters are invited to accept an underwriting participation of a specified proportion of the total issue. The offer is expressed to be made upon the terms and conditions of the prospectus, and is subject to the subsequent signing of the subscription agreement between the issuer and the management group. The underwriting agreement confirms that on a specified date the managers anticipate entering into the subscription agreement with the issuer, and that on the same date the securities will be offered on behalf of the issuer to the selling group, which will include the managers and other underwriters.

(2) Commission

The agreement specifies the amount of underwriting commission as a percentage of the principal amount of the securities underwritten, and confers on the managers the right to deduct from the commission the individual underwriter's pro rata proportion of the expenses incurred in connection with the issue of the securities, so far as not reimbursed by the issuer, and any sums which become due to the managers under the stabilisation and over-allotment provisions contained within the underwriting agreement.

(3) Managers' agent of issuer

The terms further establish that the managers are acting as agents of the issuer, except in relation to the provisions regarding stabilisation and over-allotment.

(4) Impact of subscription agreement

Similar provisions with regard to the closing date as are contained in the subscription agreement are contained in the underwriting agreement. The fact is recited that the subscription agreement contains provisions whereby, in certain circumstances, on the lead manager giving notice to the issuer before payment being made to the issuer for the issue, the participants are released and discharged from their obligations. The underwriting agreement specifies that if the responsibilities of the managers are determined in this way all underwriting commitments previously made cease to be of effect, and, except as otherwise provided within the underwriting agreement, no party shall have further rights or liabilities thereunder.

(5) Underwriting commitment

The essence of the underwriting agreement is the obligation of the underwriter to underwrite his agreed proportion of the issue. Accordingly, the agreement binds the underwriter, in the event that the aggregate principal amount of the securities subscribed and paid for by members of the selling group falls short of the total principal amount of the securities, to take up his underwritten proportion at the issue price, less the amount of the selling group concession, on the terms of the selling group agreement if called upon by the managers so to do.

This central obligation of the underwriter is usually modified when the underwriter is also a member of the selling group so as to enable the underwriter to sell his way out of the commitment. The modifying provision provides that an underwriter who is also a member of the selling group will only be called upon to subscribe any securities if the aggregate principal amount of the securities subscribed and paid for by it as a member of the selling group falls short of its underwriting commitment, and then only up to the amount of the shortfall. If therefore an issue is going badly an underwriter, who is also a member of a selling group, can, by increased sales effort, limit its residual commitment. For instance if the underwriter's commitment is to subscribe $1,000,000 and only one half of the issue is sold but the particular underwriter has managed to effect sales of $800,000 worth of securities, its underwriting obligation is reduced to the $200,000 difference between its actual sales and its underwriting commitment. If there was no such modification of the agreement its obligation would remain at one half of its underwriting commitment, namely $500,000.

This general approach of the underwriting agreement can be varied by different provisions with the agreement. Sometimes the managers are given the right to arrange the subscription of the securities elsewhere, without prejudice to the issuer's rights against the defaulting underwriter. Where it is not possible for the managers to arrange for the subscription of the securities each of the underwriters not in default is liable to subscribe and pay for the securities in the proportion that its underwriting participation bears to the aggregate principal amount of the securities. Customarily, however, this latter obligation is limited by a provision that no underwriter shall be called upon to subscribe securities the aggregate principal amount whereof exceeds a fixed percentage (usually 10 per cent) of its underwriting participation.

(6) Market stabilisation

The underwriting agreement contains covering provisions with regard to market stabilisation. The underwriters authorize the managers as their agents to make purchases and sales of the securities at the manager's discretion for the underwriters' account in the open market or otherwise, for long or short account, on such terms as the managers deem advisable, and, in allocating the securities, to over-allot. The managers are further authorised to cover any short position, or sell any long position, incurred pursuant to the stabilisation and over-allotment powers on such terms as the managers deem advisable, and the managers are empowered to close any transaction so entered into at any time at their discretion. It is agreed that all such purchases, sales and over-allotments shall be made for the account of the underwriters as nearly as practicable in proportion to their respective underwriting participations. Accordingly, the underwriters agree to indemnify the managers against any net loss and the managers in turn agree to credit the underwriters with any net profit arising from such transactions in the proportion that the underwriters' participation bears to the aggregate principal amount of the securities. Traditionally, the potential liability of the underwriters is limited by a provision that the underwriters' net liability shall not exceed their underwriting commission. Their liability is, however, expressed to continue under these provisions whether or not the proposed issue of the securities is consummated.

However, the clause is usually restricted in its operations by two express provisions. First, there is a time limit on these operations, if they are to fall within the clause, of 30 days following the closing date, or 60 days following the execution of the subscription agreement, whichever occurs the sooner. This is important not merely in limiting the amount of time that authorised stabilisation can continue, thus putting the underwriters at risk if losses are made, but also enables an early pay out of the underwriting commission to be made. Secondly, the powers given to the managers are to be used with a 'view to stabilising or maintaining the market price of the bonds' and consequently operations carried out with different objectives could not be charged to the general syndicate account. Further, while a wide discretion is conferred on the lead manager as to the operations which might be undertaken' his powers are merely to trade on the account. Thus, he cannot distribute a long position directly among the underwriters nor can he call on the underwriters to supply securities to meet a short position adopted on behalf of the syndicate.

The justification for stabilisation is that it is necessary for an orderly distribution to the market for otherwise wide fluctuations might occur as a result of undesirable speculative transactions entered into by the unscrupulous, which have the potential for particularly violent disturbance on what is often a market used only by large financial institutions. However, the whole concept of stabilisation is, of course, contrary to rules commonly adopted by most developed institutions against insider-trading.[1] Accordingly, when English company law adopted a formal statutory prohibition against insider-trading by the Company Securities (Insider Dealing) Act 1985 international bonds were excluded from its operation.[2] However, when the operation of the insider-trading prohibition was extended

1 In fact stabilisation was probably contrary to public policy at common law prior to statutory intervention so that contractual provisions forming the framework for stabilisation would be unenforceable — see *Scott v Brown, Doering McNab & Co* [1892] 2 QB 724; *North v Marra Developments Ltd* (1981) 56 LJR 106. In the former case the Court of Appeal were also of the opinion that where a market was manipulated pursuant to an agreement among a number of people there may be a criminal conspiracy to defraud.

2 Companies Securities (Insider Dealing) Act 1985, s 6. For the definition of, international bond see *ante* Chapter 1 p 2.

by the recently enacted Financial Services Act 1986 the operation of the prohibition in relation to market and price stabilisation was modified. No longer is there a specific exemption for international bonds for there has been substituted an exemption applicable to both international bonds and domestic securities. The detail is to be supplied through detailed rules to be introduced by the Securities Investment Board which will apply to shares and stock, debentures, government and public securities, instruments containing entitlement to shares and securities and to certificates representing securities.[1] SIB issued a consultation paper 'Stabilisation — The New Approach' and, having considered reactions to this, has made rules with regard to stabilisation, as has also the TSA.[2]

IPMA also has clear provisions governing price stabilisation as practised by its members. It is clear that price stabilisation by a lead manager should assist in the orderly distribution of the issue, thus promoting an orderly secondary market and ultimate liquidity. Lead managers should therefore only enter into stabilisation activity on behalf of the syndicate in order to encourage the orderly distribution of securities. Stabilisation actions with objections other than orderly distributions are inappropriate.

IPMA rules provide further that a syndicate participant should not be liable for any stabilisation losses or unreimbursed expenses which together exceed the actual underwriting commission or if management and underwriting fees are combined, the 60 per cent of the combined fee which is deemed to be underwriting commission. Lead managers should not be obliged to credit the stabilization account for stabilsation profits in excess of one additional actual or deemed underwriting fee. Stabilisation losses or unreimbursed expenses in excess of these amounts should not be deducted from the management fee and should be borne in their entirety by the lead manager.

Under the IPMA regime stabilisation provisions in underwriting agreements may permit the lead manager to 'hedge' the stabilisation account in instruments considered by him to be appropriate and the rules provide that the economic results of that hedging will be charged or credited to the stabilisation account. However, the lead manager should not have the right to distribute a syndicate long position to the underwriters nor should the lead manager have the right to require underwriters to supply securities to meet a syndicate short position. Under IPMA rules stabilisation activity for the account of the syndicate should cease as soon as practicable after the closing date and the syndicate account should be closed out and all positions covered within 30 days following the signing date. In this regard, it is accepted that the lead manager may purchase or sell to or from his own account to settle a position which exists in the stabilisation account.

(7) Relationship to the selling group agreement

Acceptance of the participation as an underwriter under the terms of the

1 Financial Services Act 1986, ss 48(2)(1), 175.

2 The respective positions of the SIB and TSA within the regulatory framework created by the Financial Services Act discussed in Chapter 4.

agreement also, by the terms of that agreement, acts as acceptance of the terms and conditions set forth in the selling group agreement, a copy of which is sent with the draft underwriting agreement, and securities subscribed or purchased by underwriters as members of the selling group, or pursuant to the provisions of the underwriting agreement, are deemed to have been subscribed on the terms of the selling group agreement.

(8) Conflict of law and time of the essence

The underwriting agreement provides that it shall be governed and construed in accordance with the chosen system of law and that, where the law chosen is English law, time shall be the essence of the agreement.

(9) Variations

Under the underwriting agreement the managers are empowered to vary both the total amount of the issue (by increasing or decreasing it) and to vary the individual underwriting agreements. The timetable of the issue and the term of the bonds can also be varied.

(10) Commissions

Underwriting commissions cannot be deducted from the proceeds of the sale of the securities prior to these being passed by the underwriter to the issuer for usually the state of account cannot be finally determined. There may be unsold securities giving rise to underwriting liabilities or the stabilisation efforts may be running at a loss causing potential but unquantified underwriting liabilities. I.P.M.A. stipulates that normal underwriting fees may be paid up to 90 days after closing after making appropriate deductions for stabilisation and any expenses which the issuer is not responsible to reimburse. If payment is delayed beyond four months underwriters are to be paid 100 per cent of their fee without deductions and after five months interest at 1 per cent should be paid on all sums outstanding. If these standards are not met by appropriate provisions in the documentation this should be fully disclosed.

(11) Acceptance

It is expressly provided that on notification of the final bond terms after the price has been fixed the underwriters can decline to participate but if they do not do so will be taken to have accepted their allocation. The provision reverses the general rule of offer and acceptance that mere silence is not an acceptance.

THE SELLING GROUP AGREEMENT

The main purposes of the selling group agreement are first to throw the burden of compliance with the securities regulations of the various jurisdictions, and any other national laws affecting sales within those jurisdictions, upon the individual members operating in each jurisdiction and, secondly, to place on their shoulders any liabilities which may arise from any unauthorised representation made by them. Much of the form of the agreement is dictated by the complex selling restrictions necessitated by the former purpose.

Like the underwriting agreement the selling group agreement will be entered into by the managers prior to the conclusion of the subscription agreement. It might at first appear that the managers could be at risk in creating liabilities to the selling group without having any assurance that the subscription agreement will be entered into and the issue take place. In fact, this is carefully controlled by the terms of the selling agreement itself.

Typical terms are as follows.

Recitals

The selling agreement recites the proposed terms of the subscription agreement but makes it clear that no such agreement has been entered into. It specifies a date on which it is anticipated that the agreement will be concluded. The managers indicate that, on the same day, they expect on behalf of the issuer to offer the securities to a selling group of banks, brokers, and dealers, including the managers and other underwriters, on the basis of the prospectus and on the terms of the selling group agreement. The agreement further provides that the managers have not made to the selling group member any offer of any securities at all. On the contrary that offer will be made only on the day the subscription agreement is entered into. The terms of the selling group agreement will apply to the offer which is made at that time. In the meantime, while bound by the terms of the selling group agreement, the individual dealer has no assurance that any securities will be allocated to him at all.

The agreement refers to the telex or cable sent to the selling group members, informing them of the terms of the proposed issue on the announcement date. A copy of the prospectus is also sent.

The agreement gives the details with regard to the closing date contained in the draft subscription agreement.

By the terms of the selling group agreement the dealer agrees the following conditions:

(1) *Dealer is principal*

The securities are subscribed by the dealer as principal and not as agent for another legal person.

(2) *Issuer's jurisdiction*

The dealer agrees that he will not directly or indirectly offer, sell, or deliver any securities in the jurisdiction of the issuer, nor to any resident of the issuer's jurisdiction, nor to others for sale within that jurisdiction or to residents thereof, except in compliance with the applicable laws governing such transaction (eg the securities regulations of theat jurisdiction). The dealer further undertakes that any securities dealers to whom he in turn sells the securities will agree that he purchases them as principal and that he in turn will not directly or indirectly re-offer or re-sell them within that jurisdiction or to any resident thereof except pursuant to an exemption available under the issuer's law.

(3) *U.S. selling restrictions*

Where an issue is to be marketed widely, restrictions on selling within the U.S. are included to avoid the effect of U.S. securities regulation. Traditionally these have been verbose as on the following lines.

(a) Securities not to be registered

The dealer understands that the securities have not been and will not be registered under the Securities Act of 1933 of the U.S.A., and may not be offered or sold, directly or indirectly, in the U.S. or to U.S. persons, as part of the distribution of the issue. Re-offers and re-sales of the securities in the U.S. or to U.S. persons, after completion of the distribution of the issue, must be made in compliance with the registration requirements of the Securities Act of 1933, or pursuant to an exemption therefrom: the availability of any such exemption would depend upon the facts and circumstances existing at the time of such re-offers and re-sales.

(b) No U.S. sales

Further the dealer represents and agrees that any securities subscribed by it will be subscribed as principal for distribution in conformity with the provisions of the agreement, and, in particular, the dealer agrees that it will not offer or sell directly or indirectly, any securities acquired by it pursuant to the agreement in the United States, or to any U.S. person other than an underwriter or member of the selling group, prior to 90 days from the closing date.

(c) Purchaser confirmations

The dealer agrees that the circumstances that the issue is not registered under U.S. Securities Act 1933, and the consequences thereof, will be brought to the attention of any purchaser from the dealer by notice in writing, and that such purchaser will enter into agreements similar to those of the dealer with regard to sales or offers within the United States, or to U.S. residents, or any sub-sale.

(d) Definition

For these purposes the U.S. is defined by the agreement as the United States of America, the possessions, territories, and all areas subject to its jurisdiction. A U.S. person means any person who is a national, or resident of or normally resident in, the U.S. (including the estate of any such person), and any corporation, partnership, or other entity, formed or organised in the U.S.

(e) U.S. fiduciaries

The restictions on dealings with a U.S. connection are modified by the agreement in two respects. Offers or sales of the securities may be made to persons outside the U.S. who are not U.S. persons through U.S. agents or fiduciaries provided that such agents or fiduciaries confirm in writing that they are acting pursuant to specific instructions from the principal or beneficiary, and not on any discretionary authority conferred upon them. Also any member of the selling group may act on behalf of purchasers who are not U.S. persons, who have made payment for, and taken delivery of, securities outside the U.S., whether personally or by an agent, in transmitting such securities to a custodian or fiduciary in the U.S. for safekeeping at the request to the purchaser.

However I.P.M.A. now specifies a standard form of U.S. sale restrictions:

Each underwriter agrees:

(i) not to offer, sell or deliver at any time directly or indirectly in the U.S. or to a U.S. person (or company or other entity organised in the U.S.) any bonds or notes acquired in connection with the contemplated distribution, except for offers or sales to U.S. underwriters or through a private placement (which are not considered sales to the public),

(ii) not to offer, sell or deliver directly or indirectly in the U.S. or to a U.S. person any bonds or notes acquired in any other matter within (usually) 90 days from the completion of the distribution as (usually) determined by the lead manager,

(iii) to give notice to any person who buys any bonds or notes from the underwriter during the distribution process to the effect that the securities have not been registered under the U.S. Securities Act 1933 and to require the agreement of any dealer to similar restrictions and to giving notice to any purchaser and require similar undertakings from succeeding dealers.

In the case of an issuer with U.S. connections the impact of U.S. securities regulation is of particular concern, and the above provisions will be supported by a lock-up provision. I.P.M.A. recommends the following wording:

> A temporary global note in bearer form without coupons will be deposited on the closing date with a bank depositary common to Euroclear and Cedel S.A., and will be exchangeable for definitive notes not earlier than 90 days after completion of the distribution of notes as determined by [the lead manager] upon presentation of certificates as to beneficial ownership.

Sometimes an issue is made, intended and structured to make use of the U.S. private placement provision to allow some sales to take place in the U.S. without the need for registration under, and other difficulties with, their system of securities regulation. I.P.M.A. guidelines require disclosure, in such a situation, of the private placement option, to which managers it is available, and for sales to what categories of clients, the form of the securities (whether bearer or registered), and the minimum denominations specified.

(4) *General Restriction*

The dealer will comply with all applicable laws and regulations in each jurisdiction in which it may offer, or sell, or distribute, the securities, and will not publish any prospectus, application form, offering circular, or other offering material in any country, except in circumstances that will result in compliance with any applicable laws and regulations. All offers, sales, and deliveries of securities by the dealer will be on similar terms.

If the securities legislation of any jurisdiction in which the dealer operates requires any consent, approval, or permission for the subscription, offer, or sale, that the dealer will obtain such consent or approval, and neither the issuer nor the managers have any responsibility in respect thereof.

(5) *U.K. Restrictions*

Restrictions on sales within the U.K. are also necessary in respect of issues not listed on the U.K. stock exchange, if the issue is to be controlled so as to avoid conflict with U.K. securities regulation. The following is the wording specified by I.P.M.A.

Each underwriter agreed:

(i) not to offer, sell or deliver any bonds or notes in the U.K. (except under circumstances which do not constitute an offer to the public under the U.K. Companies Act) other than to persons whose ordinary business it is to buy or sell securities,

(ii) not to distribute in or from the U.K. any offering material except if the underwriter is authorised to do so under the security laws of the U.K. (largely members of the Stock Exchange or of the recognized associations of dealers) or if the distribution of this material is to persons whose ordinary business it is to buy or sell securities.

Where securities are listed on the U.K. stock exchange sales can be effected without breach of U.K. securities regulation if made under the document containing the listing particulars. In such a situation, therefore, the above restriction can be included in the documentation modified by the recital of the exemption for sales made under the listing particulars.

Disclosure of selling restrictions

With regard to both U.S. and U.K. selling restrictions I.P.M.A. allows deviation from its prescribed wording. However, since it wishes to create a situation in which the market may normally assume that the standard wording has been used, it requires that any deviation must be disclosed. I.P.M.A. also requires that disclosure should be made of any other applicable national selling restrictions, or if the issuer's mandate requires that the securities should not be offered for sale in particular countries. The same applies if the lead manager has reserved the sales rights in specific countries to itself.

(6) *Unauthorised representations*

The dealer is not authorised to give any information, or make any representation, in connection with the offering, issue, subscription, or sale of the securities, other than those contained in the prospectus in its final form. The dealer agrees that it will indemnify the issuer and the managers against any losses, liabilities, claims, charges, expenses, actions and demands, which the issuer, or any manager, may incur as a result of the dealer's failure to observe any of the conditions to which it has agreed, and, in particular, those arising from any unauthorised representation, or the giving of any information not contained in the prospectus in its final form.

(7) *Termination of subscription agreement*

The selling group agreement refers to the provisions in the subscription agreement containing the issuer's warranties and indemnities in favour of the managers and other subscribers. the dealer authorises the managers, at their absolute discretion, to waive and take any other action in respect of breach of such warranties as the managers shall deem fit. The dealer agrees that the managers shall incur no liability by the use of their discretion, and it undertakes that it will not take any action against the issuer in respect of such warranties and indemnities without the prior consent of the managers, coupled with the terms of the subscription agreement itself, the effect of this is to confer all powers to deal with an issuer's breach of its warranties on the managers, who can either waive an unimportant breach, or cause the issuer to face all the claims for compensation to which the breach may give rise under the indemnity provision.

The fact that the subscription agreement itself may be determined by the managers in certain circumstances, or come to an end otherwise under its own terms in other circumstances, is recorded in the selling group agreement. In such event it is agreed that any contract for subscription of the securities is automatically rescinded, and no party shall have any rights or liabilities thereunder.

(8) *Payment procedures*

The requirements for payment of the subscription are detailed as are the arrangements for distribution of the securities. If the dealer is late in making payment for his subscription the managers reserve the right to advance funds to the issuer to cover his delay, and to charge the dealer interest thereon at current rates.

(9) *Conflict of laws and time of the essence*

The chosen law governing the agreement and its construction is specified. Where that law is English law it is provided that time shall be of the essence of the agreement.

(10) *Procedure for acceptance*

Similar arrangements for the dealer's acceptance of the terms of the agreement are made as in the case of underwriters' acceptance of the underwriting agreement.

TIME OF THE ESSENCE[1]

To understand the effect of this provision it is necessary to analyse the possibilities under English law with regard to provisions in relation to time in commercial contracts.

The issue of time in a commercial contract raises two separate questions. The first issue is the time at which the parties agreed, or must be taken to have agreed, that the particular obligation which is the subject of consideration was to be carried out. The second, and separate, question is the issue of what consequences the parties must be taken to have intended if the obligation being considered was not performed by the party obligated to carry it out on the agreed date. Is the contractual responsibility of the party owing the duty an obligation which is to be construed as a breach of warranty sounding in damages only, or is the obligation to perform on the due date a condition of the contract entitling the other party to terminate the contract and to refuse to carry out its obligations thereunder?

Time for performance

Normally, a commercial contract will specify when the various obligations thereunder are to be performed. If it does not do so the normal inference will be that obligations are to be performed within a reasonable time. What

1 See generally, R.M. Goode, *Payment Obligations in Commercial and Financial Transactions* Sweet and Maxwell (1983) pp. 71-78; M.P. Furmston in Cheshire, Fifoot and Furmston's *Law of Contract* 11th edn, Butterworths (1986) pp. 538-542; G.H. Treitel *Law of Contract* 7th edn, Sweet and Maxwell (1987) pp. 631-635

is reasonable is a matter of inference from all the facts of the particular case.[1] In such a situation the party obligated is not in breach of his obligation until a reasonable time for performance has gone by.

The consequences of breach

Once the time for the carrying out of the obligation has passed consideration must be given to the consequences of the breach. At common law the time for the stipulated performance would be likely to be construed as a condition of the contract, and, therefore, breach would entitle the innocent party to terminate the contract. On the other hand, equity did not consider that stipulations as to time were necessarily of crucial importance, and would only allow the innocent party to treat the contract as at an end where it was clear from the major terms of the contract that the parties intended the stipulation to be an essential condition. In these circumstances time was said to be of the essence of the contract. This in turn came to have an effect upon the common law, and statute now expressly provides that contractual stipulations as to time are to be construed to have the same effect in law as in accordance with the rules of equity.[2] Where such a contractual stipulation is not of the essence it can be made so, by giving notice to the other party requiring him to complete his performance within a reasonable time, once that party is in breach of his contractual obligations. What is reasonable notice depends on the facts of the case, but it appears that where the innocent party prior to the breach has consistently pressed for performance on time, a shorter period of notice will be reasonable than if no pressure has been exerted.[3]

The construction of the original contract to ascertain whether time is or is not of the essence relies heavily, in the absence of express provisions in the contract, on the effect of the breach on the innocent party which should have been within the anticipation of the parties at the time that the contract was made. Thus, traditionally, under a contract for the sale of goods a stipulation as to the time when the seller is to deliver the goods is treated as of the essence,[4] whereas a stipulation as to the time at which the buyer is to pay for the goods will not normally impose such an obligation.[5]

Given the general importance to the participants to the syndicate agreements that their terms be duly performed on time to enable the complex arrangements and obligations to be perfected within the precise time sequence necessary for a successful issue, it is likely that the obligations

1 The true explanation of *Green v Sevin* (1879) 13 Ch D 589.

2 The Law of Property Act 1925, s 41 re-enacting Supreme Court of Judicature Act 1873, s 25(7).

3 *Stickney v Keeble* [1915] A.C. 386

4 *Hartley v Hymans* [1920] 3 KB 475 at 484. Even early delivery may justify repudiation *Bowes v Shand* (1877) 2 App Cas 455; Sale of Goods Act 1979: s 10(1).

5 Sale of Goods Act 1979 s10(1); *Martindale v Smith* (1841) 1 QB 389. The position appears to be similar where payment is not made on the agreed date under a distributorship agreement: *Decro-Wall International SA v Practitioners in Marketing Ltd.* [1971] 1 WLR 361.

of performance on time by the respective parties would in any event be held to be conditions, the breach of which would entitle the other parties to withdraw from the agreement. However, the inclusion of the actual term that time should be 'of the essence' of the agreements puts the issue beyond doubt for under English law the parties may make any, or every, term pertaining to performance of the contract a fundamental condition by express provision, and the courts will give effect thereto.[1]

It should perhaps be noted that, where a stipulation as to performance is not an essential condition of the contract, the party obligated is not left free to breach his responsibility with impunity. While failure to perform on time does not entitle the other party to refuse to perform his part of the contract, the party in breach will be liable in damages under normal contractual principles.[2]

THE INDEMNITY PROVISIONS

The most important contractual terms arising from this related network of documents are the various indemnity provisions, the object of which is to apportion the final legal risk between the parties in respect of the liabilities covered. As has been seen these are twofold. First, those of the issuer to the syndicate participants covering the responsibility for inaccuracies in the prospectus, and, secondly, those given by members of the selling group to the issuer and the managers in respect of responsibility for either factual inaccuracies given by a selling group member in information not included in the prospectus, or responsibility for sales in breach of the laws of the jurisdiction in which a selling group member sells, or attempts to sell, the securities which it has agreed to subscribe.

A misrepresentation may occur in a prospectus either through inadvertence, or through a deliberate act on the part of the person supplying the information who puts it forward knowing full well that it is untrue. Where the untruth is put forward deliberately the tort of deceit is committed. A contract to indemnify a person in respect of liability for deceit is illegal.[3]

1 *Steedman v Drinkle* [1916] 1 AC 275; *Hudson v Temple* (1860) 29 Beav, 536; *Harold Wood Brick Co Ltd v Ferris* [1935] 2 KB 198.

2 *Raineri v Miles* [1981] AC 1050 noted by Alec Samuels (1981) 44 MLR 100.

3 *Brown Jenkinson & Co Ltd v Percy Dalton (London) Ltd* [1957] 2 QB 621. Lord Evershed MR dissented on the basis that no dishonesty was involved — a matter immaterial to the tort of deceit. See the discussion of illegal indemnities in Treitel *op. cit.* at p. 330. Similarly, a contract to defraud prospective shareholders will also be void for illegality *Begbie v Phosphate Sewage Co. Ltd* 1875 LR 10 QB 491 or to rig the market by contracting to buy shares at a fictitious premium *Scott v Brown, Doering McNab and Co* [1892] 2 QB 724. It seems that this is so even though the fraud may not be criminal *Chitty on Contracts* 25th edn Sweet and Maxwell (1983), General Principles p. 556 citing *Cockshott v Bennett* (1788) 2 Term Rep 763; *Mallalieu v Hodgson* (1851) 16 QB 689; *Miller v Karlinski* (1945) 62 TLR. 85; *Napier v National Business Agency Ltd* [1951] 2 All ER 264 and see especially the remarks or Pearce LJ in *Brown Jenkinson & Co. Ltd v Percy Dalton (London) Ltd.* [1957] 2 QB 621 at 638 and Morris LJ at 634, 635.

Clearly, as a matter of fact, either the issuer or the managers may promote the deceit by deliberately causing the inaccurate information to be included in the prospectus, or, alternatively, both issuer and managers may act in concert in deliberately promulgating the untrue prospectus, thereby jointly issuing the deceit.

Where the promotion of the deceit is a joint venture neither the managers nor issuer can rely on the agreement in the courts as it is totally void for illegality, being clearly contrary to public policy. However, where it is the issuer who promoted the deceit and the managers acted innocently in issuing the prospectus on its behalf, the managers will be able to rely on the provisions for indemnity,[1] unless they had continued to promote the issue by the use of the prospectus after learning of the true state of the affairs and therefore of the issuer's illegal purpose.[2] Clearly, if the prospectus has been issued and securities sold upon the basis of it, the giving of a remedy to the innocent managers in respect of sales made prior to the true state of affairs becoming known to them, so far from promoting the unlawful purpose of the guilty, is likely to have a deterrent effect upon the issuer in leaving it with the prospect of having to bear the whole financial burden of the results of its own unlawful acts.[3] The only policy consideration for the alternative result of leaving the burden upon the syndicate participants would appear to be that it is an incentive for greater care to be taken by them in the preparation of the prospectus. However, the enquiries made are extensive and the syndicate, through its lead manager, is largely dependent on the factual information gained from the issuer to its detailed questions. So exhaustive are the enquiries that it is difficult to see how, in the practical world of commerce, greater care could be taken than traditionally occurs. It is therefore submitted that where the syndicate acts innocently both on authority, and by reason of policy, its participants are entitled to rely on the indemnity.[4] If, however, the managers have deliberately refrained from making the usual enquiries of, and to, the issuer, it is probable that they will be taken to have participated in the deceit by not caring

1 *Mason v Clarke* [1955] AC 778; *Bank fur Gemeinwirtshaft Akt v City of London Garages Ltd.* [1971] 1 WLR 149; *Archbolds (Freightage) Ltd v S Spanglett Ltd.* [1961] 1 QB 374.

2 *Cowan v Milbourn* (1867) LR 2 Exch. 230; *Clay v Yates* (1856) 1 H & N 73 *Alexander v Rayson* [1936] 1 KB 169 at 182; *Ashmore Benson Pease Co. Ltd v AV Dawson Ltd.* [1973] 1 WLR 828.

3 See Treitel *op. cit.* p. 374 *et seq,* Treitel does not follow the traditional classification of illegality in performance adopted by Chitty *op. cit.* p. 549 *et seq.* and Furmston *op. cit.* 11th edn p. 357 *et seq.* which distinguishes between a contract illegal at formation and one illegal in performance, the latter being enforceable at the hand of an innocent party who did not know of or participate in the illegal performance.

4 Even if this were not so deliberate deceit by the issuer within the prospectus would be a fraud on both the ultimate investors and the syndicate participants. In these circumstances the syndicate participants may well be able to claim damages for misrepresentation *Burrows v Rhodes* [1899] 1 QB 816; *Shelley v Paddock* [1980] QB 348 (Brandon LJ *dubitante*).

whether the contents of the prospectus were correct,[1] and be unable, therefore, to rely on the indemnity.

On the other hand, where the inaccuracy occurs in the prospectus only by reason of inadvertence, there is no illegality in the indemnity and it will be enforced by the courts. Illegality only effects contracts to indemnify a person against the consequences of a civil liability deliberately committed. Where the civil liability against which the indemnity is sought is one incurred negligently or innocently there can be no objection to the indemnity.[2] Since the act is not deliberate no illegal purpose is being promoted by the giving of indemnity.

Where, however, is the line to be drawn between the managers issuing the prospectus recklessly, not caring whether the contents are true or false, where reliance on the indemnity will not be allowed, and mere negligence where it will? The answer under English law is probably that managers will be reckless and participate in the deceit where either they make no enquiries of and about the issuer, or where their enquiries are so perfunctory that they were clearly unconcerned as to the truth of the information given to them.[3]

A similar analysis covers the enforceability by the managers and issuer of a selling group members indemnity where a dealer has performed its sales by giving inaccurate information to investors which was not contained in the prospectus. Where the information is given inadvertently no question of illegality arises. Where the giving of the information is deliberate, and therefore constitutes deceit, the issuer and managers can rely on the indemnity provided that they did not participate in the deceit. However, as no fraud has been practised on them, there can be no question of an independent action for fraud by them against the offending selling group members.

In the case of the dealer's indemnity in respect of sales in breach of the law of the jurisdiction where he sells the securities, or offers them for sale, different considerations apply. Here the mode of performance conflicts with statutory requirements enacted for the safeguarding of investors and therefore their benefit. Breach of the statutory requirements will lead to the offending dealer and the issuer incurring criminal liability. The issuer may also be involved in civil responsibilities to the investors as a result of the breach.

It appears that where a contract requires that performance be carried

1 The tort of deceit from the leading case of *Derry v Peek* discussed *post* p 126

2 *Betts and Drewe v Gibbins* (1834) 2 Ad El. 57; *Adamson v Jarvis* (1827) 4 Bing 66; *Lister v Romford Ice and Cold Storage Co Ltd* [1957] AC 555; *Bradstreets British Ltd v Mitchell and Carapanayoti & Co. Ltd* [1933] Ch 190; *Daily Mirror Newspapers Ltd. v Exclusive News Agency* (1937) 81 Sol Jo 924. The latter two cases involved consideration of the contractual liability between the parties on the innocent publication of a defamation by one of them, see now Defamation Act 1852, s 11.

3 Contrast this with the U.S. cases *Henzfeld v Laventhol, Krekstein, Horwath and Horworth* F.2d 2734–35 (2nd Cir. 1976); *McLean v Alexander* 420 F. Supp. 1078 (D. Del 1976) discussed *post* Chapter 5 at p.154.

out in a lawful manner and confers a right of indemnity on one party in the event that the other performs his obligations unlawfully, there is no objection under English law to the innocent party relying on the indemnity. By allowing the indemnity the party to perform is more likely to ensure that the performance is lawful, as liability for failure to perform lawfully will ultimately be placed on his shoulders by reason of the indemnity.[1] Different considerations apply if the issuer encouraged the unlawful acts. By so doing he would be party to a conspiracy to break the law. For the courts to allow reliance on the indemnity would deter issuers from behaving unlawfully.[2] Further, where the issuer encourages the unlawful performance without realising its illegality the indemnity will be illegal, for ignorance of the law is irrelevant and the issuer will not be able to rely thereon.[3] If, however, the dealer induces the issuer to believe that the legal requirements have been satisfied, as by the consent of a foreign stock exchange being given on the dealer's application for the distribution where no such application has been made, it appears that an issuer may be able successfully to sue the dealer on a separate collateral warranty[4] or in deceit.[5]

Similarly contracts made with the intention of defrauding a third party are illegal under U.S. law, and it appears that this is so whether the fraudulent activity constitutes a crime or only a tort. [6] Thus, as in England, agreements which have the effect of rigging a stock market are illegal.[7] Where there is a contract between the promoters of a company and a subscriber for shares that the subscriber will not have to pay for the shares allotted, or will only have to pay out of dividends, the contract is void as an illegal fraud on the other subscribers, if it is intended to keep the bargain secret and to use the subscriber's name to induce subscriptions.[8] It follows from this that a contract to indemnify from the consequences of a tortious or criminal act which is intended to be committed is illegal. One to indemnify in the case of inadvertence and negligence will be upheld.[9]

As in English law also, where the illegality arises only because of one party's intention to perform the contract in an illegal manner, the other

1 Treitel *op.cit.* pp. 326–322.
2 *Bostel Bros Ltd v Hurlock* [1949] 1 KB 74; *Bigos v Bousted* [1951] 1 All ER 92.
3 *Belvoir Finance Co Ltd v Stapleton* [1971] 1 Q.B. 210; *Nash v Stevenson Transport Ltd* [1935] 2 KB 341; *J.M. Allan (Merchandising) Ltd v Cloke* [1963] 2 QB 340.
4 *Strongman (1945) Ltd v Sincock* [1955] 2 QB 525.
5 *Shelley v Paddock* [1980] QB 348.
6 *Corbin on Contracts* West Publishing 6 (1963) Vol. 6A p. 525 *et seq.*; *Williston on Contracts* 3rd Ed (1957) Baker Voorkis and Co. Inc., New York. Vol.15 p. 126 *et seq.*
7 *Harper v Crenshaw* 82F 2nd 845; 102 ALA 362 (1936); *Goess v Lucinda Shops* 93 F. 2nd 449, 115 ALR 264 (1937).
8 *Clifton v Tomb* 21 F. 2nd 893 (1927); *Reiff v Nebraska-Cal Colony Co.* 277 F. 417 (1921).
9 *Hanover Fire Insurance Co. v Merchants Trans. Co.* 15 F. 2d 946 cert den. 273 U.S. 758; *Hiroshima v Bank of Italy* 78 Cal. App. 362.
Restatement Contracts 2nd edn para. 192 and explanatory notes.

party may enforce the contract against the guilty if he had no knowledge of that party's illegal purpose.[1] If, however, the innocent party becomes aware of the illegal purpose, he must take no steps to carry out his side of the bargain, if this would assist the accomplishment of that purpose, because by so doing, he would participate therein and be unable to rely upon the contract.[2]

1 *Corbin on Contracts* Vol. 6A p. 746 and authorities therein referred to.
2 *Corbin on Contracts* Vol. 6A p. 747.

4 The regulation of issues of securities

An issue of international bonds will cause the bonds to be sold in many different legal jurisdictions. Each system will have its own laws governing the responsibilities involved in the sale of securities on issue. In any particular jurisdiction it is probable that there will be two areas of law potentially applicable to a securities issue. The first is a specific system of securities regulation actually designed to control the issue of a dealing in securities with the object of protecting the investor. Such a system may be highly developed as in the U.S. where the degree of regulation is considerable or one which is little developed and, as such, offers liberal scope to an issuer and its advisers to market the issue as it pleases with relatively little control over the manner in which this is done. Secondly, each country will have within its system of general criminal law the offences which are potentially applicable to issuers of securities, particularly where fraud or dishonesty is involved.

GENERAL CRIMINAL LIABILITY

In addition to the specific structure erected by way of securities regulation in any individual jurisdiction there will be general criminal restrictions on deceptive and fraudulent operations. It therefore follows that these must be borne in mind as well as the offences created by the system of securities regulation itself.

In England and Wales, the most relevant offences are obtaining property by deception, under section 15 of the Theft Act 1968, false accounting under section 17 of the same Act, and the use of false statements under section 19.[1]

INVESTOR PROTECTION AND DEPOSITS OF MONEY

Not all investments have been considered traditionally to be securities. The classic investment in the private sector generally considered as a safe

[1] In fact, under English law there are complex jurisdictional limitations on crimes under the Theft Act when carried out internationally, on conspiracies and attempts to commit them, and on international conspiracies to defraud. The Law Commission has recently recommended their reform: The Law Commission: 'Jurisdiction over Offences of Fraud and Dishonesty with a Foreign Element', (Law Com No 180, 1989).

investment is the deposit of a sum of money with a bank. In general, invitations for such deposits do not fall to be protected by the disclosure provisions governing risk type investments such as company shares. The protection given to investors is contained in the Banking Act 1987, which erects a considerable supervisory position for the Bank of England, and gives a system of insurance in respect of deposits.[1]

Under the 1987 Act the responsibilities for the supervision of the banking sector, and hence protection of the depositor, is placed on the shoulders of the Bank of England, and in carrying out this responsibility that Bank has a duty to keep under review the operation of the statutory scheme of protection, and developments in the field of banking relevant to the exercise of its powers and the discharge of its duties.[2] To assist it in the discharge of these burdens there it is to be a Board of Banking Supervision, consisting of three ex-officio members, being the Governor of the Bank of England (Chairman), the deputy Governor, and the executive officer of the Bank for the time being responsible for the supervision of the system. In addition there will be six independent members, jointly appointed by the Chancellor of the Exchequer and the Governor of the Bank of England.

The system of regulation revolves around s 3 of the Act, which provides that no person can lawfully accept a deposit in the course of carrying on a deposit-taking business unless authorised by the Bank of England.[3] A business is a deposit-taking business if in 'the course of business money received by way of deposit is lent to others', or if 'any other activity of the business is financed wholly, or to any material extent, out of the capital of or the interest on money received by way of deposit.'[4] A deposit for the purposes of the Act is 'a sum of money paid on terms under which it will be repaid, with or without interest or a premium, either on demand, or at a time or in circumstances agreed by or on behalf of the person making the payment and person receiving it.'[5]

The Bank of England has considerable powers to regulate advertisements for deposits by authorised institutions.[6] Further, the Bank is given considerable powers to monitor and police the regulatory framework. In another effort to protect the investor, only businesses with £5 million in capital behind them will be able to describe themselves as banks, which word implies to the man in the street a business of some real substance.

However, the most obvious protection to investors built into the new Act is the deposit protection scheme, which is thus continued.[7] The scheme

1 On the 1987 Act see Arora 'The Banking Act 1987' 9 Co Law pp. 9 and 39.

2 Banking Act 1987, s 1.

3 This abolishes the distinction between recognised banks and deposit-taking institutions introduced by the Banking Act 1979. There are, however, certain exemptions from the effect of s 3 set out in s 4.

4 This recognises the basis of banking business as traditionally conceived—see *Re The Bottomgate Industrial Cooperative Society* (1891) 65 L.T. 712. Occasional acceptances of deposit not in the course of business are excluded (s. 6(2)).

5 S. 5. The section does contain modifications of this basic provision.

6 S. 32.

7 The 1979 Act provided for such a scheme.

is built around a Deposit Protection Fund raised by contribution levied on authorised institutions by the Deposit Protection Board created by the legislation, and charged with administering the scheme. If an authorised institution becomes insolvent the Board must, as soon as practicable, pay to each depositor an amount equal to three-quarters of his deposit to a maximum of £20,000.[1]

It is worth noting that a separate elimination of risk system to protect investors with regard to their deposits applies also to the U.S. under the famous Glass Steagall Act,[2] and a regulatory scheme which constitutes an entirely separate system applies to their risk type investments under the Securities Act of 1933 and the Securities Exchange Act of 1934.

The situation of issues of certificates of deposit under these provisions is discussed at the end of this chapter.[3]

SALE OF SECURITIES IN ENGLAND

Traditionally the securities regulation operative in this country has been by means of the control of the prospectus governing a new issue by means of the Stock Exchange, the Companies Acts, the control of securities dealers and investment advisers under the Prevention of Fraud (Investments) Act 1958, and the criminalisation of fraudulent marketing under the latter Act. However, this system, whilst of interest as forming a historical context for developments, under the Financial Services Act 1986, has been superseded, and both regimes will be examined. The traditional system will be examined first.

THE TRADITIONAL CONTROLS: THE PROSPECTUS

With regard to investments which are considered to be of a higher risk nature, English law has taken to control of the prospectuses advertising the offered securities as the keystone of its policy of seeking to get before the prospective investor all information necessary for an informed investment decision to be made. Indeed, the very use of the term prospectus is likely to send an English lawyer's mind racing over the complex body of the law which has been erected around this critical document. Regulations cover when a prospectus must be used, what must be in it, and confer both civil remedies and criminal sanctions for prospectuses which fail to comply with the requirements or which are inaccurate or misleading. Important though this is, it does tend to disguise a simple point. A prospectus is essentially a convenient selling tool. When shares or debentures are marketed the simplicity of the basic security sold disguises the complex bundle of legal rights and responsibilities and economic assets and liabilities which

1 S. 58 *et seq.*
2 Banking (Glass-Steagall) Act 1933. For a discussion of the inter-connecting system of investor protection constituted by the Glass-Steagall Act and the system of securities regulation see Mitchell S. Berkey 'Bank Certificates of Deposit—Notes not in tune with Securities Regulation' (1982) 10 Fordham Urban Law Journal 469.
3 P. 115.

they represent. A share in a company is as valuable as the price which the market will pay for it, but that very value will be largely determined by the legal and economic factors which it represents. Many of these factors will themselves depend upon a wide network of factual considerations. To be understood it is necessary that the facts and the seller's conclusions thereon should be expressed in a digestible form to the prospective purchaser, whether that purchaser be a single individual with a long pocket or a wide section of the general public. Comprehension is eased if the information is contained in a permanent form, which can be pursued, studied, and digested over a period of time. The prospectus evolved essentially because it was the natural form to satisfy the need.

Because of the complexity of the legal rights and obligations embodied in a bond, and the economic considerations which affect them, it is natural therefore that a prospectus should be used. While this is so and the use of a prospectus is, in consequence, general, sight should not be lost of the fact that use of a prospectus may not be merely convenient but compulsory.

THE ISSUE OF DEBENTURES

The legislation compelling the issue of a prospectus to support the sale of securities in this country was traditionally that affecting companies. In so far as the market for international bonds is used to a significant extent by a sovereign borrower there was no compulsion requiring the use of a prospectus. However, corporate borrowers also comprise a significant portion of market users and here different considerations applied.

In English law the prospectus requirements as in the Companies Act 1985 applied to the issue of shares and debentures. The question therefore which arose, when securities denoting a loan to a company were issued, was whether this did or did not constitute an issue of debentures within the meaning used by English company law. Undoubtedly, the issue of bonds by a company did constitute the issue of a debenture given the wide construction given to the word debenture in the case law[1] and specific definition conferred by the statute itself.[2]

An international bond issue, if made by a corporation, will normally be made by a foreign company. Issues by foreign companies were not caught by the general prospectus provisions of the Companies Act,[3] because the provisions only applied to domestic issues.[4] However, foreign companies

1 See, eg *British India Steam Navigation Co v IRC* (1881) 7 QBD. 165; *Edmunds v Blaina Furnaces Co.* (1887) 36 Ch D 215; *Levy v Abercorris Slate and Slab Co* (1887) 37 Ch D 260; *Lemon v Austin Friars Investment Trust Ltd* [1926] Ch 1; *Knightsbridge Estates Trust Ltd v Byrne* [1940] AC 613. See in particular, the extensive review of the evolution of the Companies Act definition coherently set out by Lord Romer in the latter case.

2 Companies Act 1985 s 744, which makes use of a statutory definition first used in the Companies Act, 1929 s 380 and patently taken from the common law.

3 Contained in s 56

4 See the definition of company in s 744 of the Act.

were caught by the other specific provisions dealing with issues of foreign companies.[1]

In respect of such companies it was not lawful for any person to issue, circulate, or distribute in Great Britain a prospectus offering for subscription shares in, or debentures of, a foreign company unless it complied with s 72 of the Act. Further it was unlawful to issue to any person in Great Britain a form of application for shares in, or debentures of, such a company unless the form was issued with a lawfully constituted prospectus; but this did not apply if it was shown that the form was issued in connection with a bona fide invitation to a person to enter into an underwriting agreement with respect to shares or debentures. Apart from requiring contents similar to those required of an English company to be included in the prospectus, the Act further required additional information. There had also been included the instrument constituting or defining the constitution of the company, the enactments (or provisions having force as an enactment) under which the incorporation of the company was effected, and an address in Great Britain where the documents could be inspected. Where they were in a foreign language a certified translation had to be provided. The additional information was not required in the case of a prospectus issued more than two years after the date at which the company was entitled to commence business. The constitution of the company replaced the articles in the applicability of the English legislation to them. The prospectus had further to disclose the date on which, and the country in which, the company was incorporated, and whether the company had established a place of business in Great Britain (if it had such an established place of business the address of its principal office in Great Britain had to be given). Any condition requiring or binding an applicant for shares or debentures to waive compliance with these provisions, or purporting to affect him with notice of any contract document or matter not specifically referred to in the prospectus, was rendered void.[2]

If these various provisions controlled when a prospectus had to be used and, their contents, what then was a prospectus? It was expressly provided that the terms 'prospectus', 'shares', and 'debentures' had the same meanings in respect of foreign companies as when used in respect of a company incorporated under the Act.[3] This brought in the general definition of terms contained in s 744 of the Act where prospectus was defined as 'any prospectus, notice, circular, advertisement, or other invitation offering to the public for subscription or purchase any shares or debentures of a company.'[4] Clearly, the words 'invitation' and 'offer' were not used in the

1 Companies Act 1985, s 71 *et seq.*
2 The legislation had particular provisions covering the use of opinions and reports by experts in ss 74 and 75.
3 S. 79.
4 It was held in *Government Stock and other Securities Investment Co v Christopher,* [1956] 1 All ER 490 [1956] 1 WLR 237 that, at least for the purposes of s. 37 of the Act the term prospectus should be given no wider meaning than that contained in s 455.

technical meaning given to them in the law of contract.[1] Equally, however, the context seems to demand that there should be the use of some form of document. However, the main difficulty of the definition was to resolve when the document constituted an offer to the public and where an offer was made without the public being involved.

The professionals-only exemption

It is because of this structure that a much exploited exemption existed. An offer of shares or debentures for subsrciption or sale to any person whose ordinary business is to buy or sell shares or debentures, whether as principal or agent, was deemed not to be an offer to the public.[2] The effect of this was to place the professional dealer in a position different to that of the general public by making the provision compelling the issue of a prospectus, and controlling its contents, inapplicable to an offer to him. The professional was presumed to be able to look after himself.

Unfortunately, there was no statutory guidance to clarify who was a person whose ordinary business is to buy or sell debentures whether as principal or agent. It would clearly cover any dealer previously licensed, recognised or exempted under the recently repealed Prevention of Fraud (Investments) Act 1958, whether buying or selling on his own or a client's account. The client was presumed to be sufficiently protected by the advice given to him by his professional adviser ie the licensed dealer. Beyond this there was a twilight world which was not clarified by litigation and resultant judicial decisions. It seems that practitioners operating in the field took the view that it probably covered:

> bankers, insurance companies, discount houses, stockbrokers, institutional investors e.g. pension funds and investment managers. It should also cover insurance brokers, solicitors and accountants where, in actual practice, their business involves acquiring and disposing of securities, for example in connection with the administration of trusts and of estates.[3]

The provision was unfortunate in being so imprecise, for what was needed was a precise designation of the exempted persons to whom the offer was made. Only this could have achieved a resolution of the twin policy considerations involved. The investor did not need to be protected because he was a professional or had the benefit of professional advice, but the issuer needed to be able to identify the sale as an exempt one at a glance, without enquiry as to whether in reality the investor was properly protected by the professional intermediary. The effect of the exemption required

1 Schmitthof, *Palmer's Company Law* 23rd edn Stevens, London (1982) p. 224.

2 Companies Act 1985, s 58.

3 PD Daniels *Tolley's Company Law* (1983) ed. A.L. Chapman and R.M. Ballard p. 604. The fact that the professionals covered were wider in scope than dealers recognised, licensed, or exempted under the Prevention of Fraud (Investments) Act 1958 is clearly indicated by s 2 of that Act which exempted from the restrictions on dealing the acquisition, subscription, or underwriting, or the effecting of transactions as principal with a person whose business involved the acquisition and disposal or holding of securities whether as principal or agent.

limitation to those advisers who were clearly professionally skilled at investment advice, and therefore fully capable of protecting those of whom they are agents. It is by no means clear that this was or is true of the average solicitor, insurance broker and accountant.

Private placement

English law also had a traditional private placement exemption, but in general this was too narrow to constitute an adequate mechanism through which a bond issue can flow. It was contained in the Companies Act 1985, ss 59 and 60. Its effect has been summed up in the following words: 'Consequently where an issuing house places the whole or part of a new issue privately with a few institutional investors, eg pension funds, *which have agreed to hold the securities as long-term investments*, the investment should appear to be made to the public'.[1] The consequence of this was that since there was no issue to the public the prospectus requirements did not apply. U.S. private placement rules are much more generous, and since sometimes an international bond issue is marketed in part in that jurisdiction, using the private placement facility to preclude the necessity for registration, the U.S. position is dealt with in an appendix to this thesis.

PREVENTION OF FRAUD (INVESTMENTS) ACT 1958

The licensing requirements

Plainly, therefore, where an international bond issue could be placed through a chain of dealings limited to professionals, the prospectus requirements of the Companies Act could be avoided, and the result would not constitute a public issue. Wide use was made of the exemption.[2] Traditionally the position was unsatisfactory, because of the complexity of the licensing requirements of the dealers, and the lack of overall control excercisable, under the now repealed Prevention of Fraud (Investments) Act 1958.[3]

The Prevention of Fraud (Investments) Act 1958 was not concerned only, however, with erecting a system of licensing control over dealers in securities. Its most effective provisions were contained in ss 13 and 14, which constituted a separate portion of the Act bearing the heading General Provisions for the Prevention of Fraud. It is noteworthy that the range of transactions covered by these provisions was considerably wider than that covered by the licensing provisions. This was because the scheme of the licensing system applied only to securities as precisely defined in the Act, whereas those concerning fraud also affected 'arrangements with respect to property other than securities' thereby having effect over all types of international bonds. It may, therefore, be claimed with some truth that it was these two sections which formed the cornerstone of the statutory

1 *Palmers Company Law* p. 324—italics author's.

2 Gower discussion document 'Review of Investor Protection' H.M.S.O. January 1982 para 3.04. (hereafter referred to as Gower 'Review')

3 The statutory structure and its limitations as a means of regulation were extensively discussed in the Gower discussion Review.

basis of securities regulation of issues under the English system. The Financial Services Act has substantially re-enacted these provisions, and their effect will be considered in the discussion of the effect of that Act since its regime represents the future, and, by the time these words are read in all probability also the present.[1]

The detail of the system of English statutory regulation thus created ample provision under which foreign securities could be traded largely free of the system of securities regulation.

Even where the use of the exemption was required for a British company means were available with a little ingenuity. In such a situation the British company would be advised to form a foreign subsidiary[2] with the subsidiary making the issue and using the exemption, and the parent British company giving strength to the issue by guaranteeing the resultant bonds.

THE FINANCIAL SERVICES ACT

The traditional scheme of securities regulation of international bonds on the London market has been superseded by the implementation of the Financial Services Act. Different regimes under the Act exist for securities listed on the London Stock Exchange and those not so listed, (for instance) because they are listed on the Luxembourg exchange. The regime applicable to securities listed on the London market is more fully developed and implemented than that applicable to bonds not so listed.

BONDS LISTED IN LONDON

The purposes of the Financial Services Act 1986 is to control and regulate the manner in which investment securities are sold. This is done by two separate but integrated approaches. First, securities are to be sold only via 'authorised' persons under the Act. Secondly, the manner in which such securities are sold is controlled, partly by regulations emanating from the appropriate authorities and partly by the provisions of the Act itself.

Institutional regulation

The institutional regulation emanating from the appropriate authorities is effected through a complex system of self-regulation through five Self Regulating Organisations (SROs) responsible ultimately to the Securities and Investment Board. Members of the Stock Exchange are controlled by The Securities Association which is the appropriate SRO. Consequently, the TSA rulebook must be followed. Since many of the dealings in the market for these international securities would not take place between Stock Exchange members there was a need for some other more general institution

1 Post p. 97.

2 Usually in Holland both because of physical proximity and the fact that there is a double taxation convention between Holland and the U.K. In addition the resultant interest payments will not be paid after deduction of tax under the Income and Corporation Taxes Act 1970, s 54 for they are paid by a person not in the U.K. and are therefor exempt under the Finance Act 1984 s 35, provided that the bonds are quoted on a *recognised* stock exchange.

to be brought within the system. The institution on which this mantle has fallen is the Association of International Bond Dealers.

THE ASSOCIATION OF INTERNATIONAL BOND DEALERS

The international bond market early in its history felt the need for a system of self-regulation to try to control the activities of the institutions participating in the market and to facilitate the development of the market in an orderly manner. The Association of International Bond Dealers (AIBD) was formed in 1969 and had as its objectives:

(1) To promote good relations amongst its members and to provide a basis for joint examination and discussion of questions relating to the international securities markets and to issue rules and to make recommendations governing their operations.

(2) To provide services and assistance to participants in the international securities markets.

The enactment of the Financial Services Act created the need for a SRO within the framework to cover the international securities market and those who deal within it. The AIBD was appointed a designated investment exchange, a special category of supervisor devised by the Department of Trade and Industry to meet the particular needs of the international bond market. Designated exchanges are subject to a much smaller degree of restriction than recognised investment exchanges with regard to the reporting requirements and capital adequacy required of their members. Of course a particular institution can always be a member of an alternative SRO, such as the TSA (the Securities Association) and subject themselves to the stricter regime which such membership entails.

The AIBD is organised under Swiss law and has two offices with its centre and secretariat in Switzerland and an administrative centre in London. This reflects the weight of its membership and the importance of London as a financial centre within the international bond market. Of the just over 860 members, nearly half are located in the U.S. alone. The AIBD runs educational courses and also represents its membership in its dealings with government bodies and other institutions capable of affecting the development of the international bond market.

However, within the scheme created by the Financial Services Act it is undoubtedly the AIBD's rule-making capability and arbitration process which are its most important aspects. Its effect was general prior to the implementation of the Financial Services Act for its membership already included virtually all the major institutions active in either the primary or secondary markets. Its rulebook enabled members to deal with each other on agreed terms and conditions and this will continue. The rules themselves are concerned with the everyday workings of the market covering dealing practices, settlement procedures (including the role of the clearing houses and depositaries) and the printing and format of the bonds themselves. In addition there is an arbitration process to resolve disputes between members where the parties in dispute consent to submit the issue to the procedure. If the rules of the AIBD are not complied with the ultimate sanction it can impose is expulsion which, in view of the statutory requirement of membership on participating institutions under the Financial Services Act to be able to operate within the U.K., is now a very real power over institutional operation. On the other hand, since its function is to ensure that the market operates in an orderly way and to protect the well-being of its memberships within the market, its rule-making function will be used to promote the international bond market in a practical manner rather than to promote a fully developed system of securities regulation appropriate to the protection of the average investor, who is unlikely to use this market.

Listing requirements

Where an issue is to be listed on the U.K. market the Stock Exchange requirements for listing must be fully complied with. Part IV of the Financial Services Act which deals with official listing of securities has been implemented. It applies to debentures, bonds and certificates of deposit issued by corporations, and similar instruments issued by governments, local authorities or other public authorities outside the EEC, or by any international organisation involving at least one EEC Member State.[1] However, it is constructed so as to work through the Stock Exchange regulations by empowering the Exchange to introduce listing rules to comply with the three EEC Directives on official listing.[2] In particular, the Stock Exchange can require specified disclosures to be made in a document called 'the listing particulars' before the securities are admitted to listing, which, in practice, will be achieved by requiring that they be made as part of any offering. The prospectus provisions of the Companies Act do not apply if the securities are listed, or subject to an application for listing, but do apply if they are not. Thus the new listing system is very similar to the one it replaced, once it is realised that the new system cannot be fully appreciated by simply reading the Act, for the new structure is designed to position the Stock Exchange and its rulebook at the centre of the stage.

The Stock Exchange rules

The Stock Exchange rules pertaining to the issue of international bonds are set out its 'Admission of Securities to Listing' generally referred to as the Yellow Book, the relevant Part being Section 7. Section 7 is a list of rules mostly modifying the provisions of earlier rules and hardly makes exciting reading. The Exchange has issued a most useful paraphrase of the rules in a booklet 'Eurocurrency Debt Securities—Guide to Listing', which is considerably easier to follow, and also contains something of the interpretation and emphasis which the Exchange places on the various rules. While the rules themselves represent the authoritative document the Guide

1 Financial Services Act 1986, s 142(3) and Sch 1 para 2 and 3.

2 These are Directives 79/279/EEC, 80/390/EEC and 82/121/EEC. The first dealt with co-ordination of the conditions for the admissions of securities to stock exchange listing, the second with the co-ordination of the requirements for the contents and distribution of the listing particulars and the third with the publication of regular information with regard to listed securities.

represents orthodoxy, and since the Exchange has the responsibility of enforcing and interpreting its own rules, it is unlikely that issuers and their advisers will do other than play by the book and accept the guidance of the Exchange. Indeed the Exchange openly invites those wih difficulties and queries with regard to listing of these forms of securities to contact their quotations department who will, no doubt, give appropriate official guidance.

Certain basic conditions are required to be fulfilled by an issuer as set out in Chapter 2 of Section 1, although paras 15 and 16 will not generally apply.[1] In particular, except in the case of states and their regional or local authorities and other specified special types of issuer, the issuer must both (i) be incorporated or otherwise established in conformity with applicable laws, and (2) have published accounts in accordance with those applicable laws for the five preceeding years. However, in the case of guaranteed bonds the requirement for five years' published accounts may be waived in respect of the issuer where satisfied by the guarantor. The securities themselves must, where applicable, be issued in conformity with the laws of the place where the issuer is incorporated, and with the issuer's memorandum and articles of association or equivalent document, have an anticipated market value in excess of a minimum required by the rules, and be freely transferable. Convertible bonds are normally permitted only to be listed where the securities into which they are convertible are themselves listed, which may be either in the Stock Exchange itself or on another regulated, regularly operating, recognised open market.

The listing application must relate to all the securities of the class proposed to be issued, and a participation must be offered to two houses who normally make markets in the relevant type of security: these need not be independent of the management or selling group.

The information required to be included in the listing particulars depends on the circumstances of the issue and the issuer, but in general the requirements are less demanding than for a domestic or foreign issue. There are four separate regimes contained in the rules:

(1) *General* (applicable where (2),(3) and (4) do not apply). For these issues the listing particulars should include information set out in para 6.4(i). In fact para 6.4(i) contains two separate regimes, depending on whether the issue is by an issuer who is already listed or a new applicant. The requirements made of new applicants are the greater. Where the securities are guaranteed by another company, the listing particulars should contain the information required by the schedule in respect of both guarantor and issuer. In each case the precise information to be furnished will depend on whether the legal person is, or is not, already listed.

Where the issuer or, where relevant, the guarantor is not a listed company but is an international company listed on another major stock exchange, it may by treated by the Exchange as a listed issuer and, if so dealt with by the Exchange, it is relieved of the responsibility to include the additional information required of new applicants.

1 S 7, para 2

(2) *Issues by states and their regional and local authorities* The requirements for the contents of the particulars of such issues (known technically as an equivalent offering document) are set out in para 6.4(iv). There are the fewest requirements for such issues.

(3) *Issues of state guaranteed debt securities* The requirements pertaining to the issuer are contained in para 6.4(ii) if both principal and interest are guaranteed. Information relating to the guarantor need only comply with Sch 4 in so far as it is appropriate. Paragraph 6.4(ii) requirements also apply to certain special types of issuer, state trading enterprise, and international economic institutions such as the EEC, IMF and the African and Caribbean Development Banks.

(4) *Convertible bond securities* The requirements for these are set out in para 6.4(3) and are the most extensive of all. In addition, the particulars should include information concerning the nature of the shares offered by way of conversion, exchange or for subscription, and the rights attaching thereto, and the conditions of and procedures for conversion, exchange or subscription, and details of the situations in which they may be amended.[1]

(5) *Overriding considerations* The rules also contain general overriding provisions. The rules expressly remind issuers of the general duty of disclosure contained in s 146[2] and go on expressly to give effect to the general standards evolved by the market. 'The listing particulars (together with the details required to be circulated in the statistical services) will be expected to comply with the content generally recognised and accepted in the international eurocurrency securities market where the securities concerned are to be issued by way of a eurocurrency selective marketing.'[3]

(6) *Publication of information* The Stock Exchange has sought to recognise the way in which international bonds are, in fact, marketed, labelling the process eurocurrency selective marketing, which it defines as a selective marketing of eurocurrency securities with a syndicate of dealers with a view to their reselling such securities as principals off market.

Realising the need to give information freely to be able to assemble such a syndicate in the first place the Exchange recognized that this gave rise to considerable difficulties with the general requirement of the rules that particulars or equivalent offering documents might not be circulated or made available publicly unless they had first been formally published. It did not seek to place unnecessary burdens on issuers or their advisers in making arrangements for syndication, underwriting, and selective marketing of these forms of security, and therefore circulation is permitted of *draft* listing particulars or equivalent offering documents clearly marked as such, for the purpose of arranging such syndication, underwriting, and selective marketing. Further circulation is also permitted of other documents of a marketing nature such as the invitation or offering telex (or its equivalent in another medium) and press release, and documents which consist of,

1 S 7 para 6(4).
2 Discussed *post* p. 94
3 S 7, para 6(2)(b).

or are drafts of, or relate to, agreements to be entered into in connection with the issue of the securities, provided that any such obligations thereunder to issue, subscribe, purchase, or underwrite securities are conditional on listing being granted.[1]

(7) *Continuing obligations* Continuing obligations to give information to the Exchange throughout the lifetime of the securities are contained in para 8. In particular, issuers and their guarantors should submit copies of their annual accounts to the Company Annoucements Office, and should notify any material information affecting a company's ability to meet commitments on listed debt securities.

The general disclosure information

In addition to the information specified by the listing rules of the Stock Exchange s 146 requires that the listing particulars should contain 'all such information as investors and their professional advisers would reasonably require and reasonably expect to find there for the purpose of making an informed assessment of the assets and liabilities, financial position, profits and losses, and prospects of the issuer of the securities and the rights attaching to those securities'. In determining what information is to be included in listing particulars to meet these requirements regard is to be had to (1) the nature of the securities and of the issuer of the securities, (2) the nature of the person likely to consider their acquisition, (3) the fact that certain matters may reasonably be expected to be within the knowledge of professional advisers of any kind which those persons may reasonably be expected to consult, and (4) to any information available to investors or their professional advisers disclosed pursuant to other requirements to the Act.[2] The information to be included is such of the specified information as is within the knowledge of any person responsible for the listing particulars or which it would be reasonable for him to obtain by making enquiries. In the case of international bonds the persons responsible for listing particulars are (1) the issuer of the securities to which the particulars relate, and (2) any person who accepts and is stated in the particulars as accepting responsibility for, or who has authorised the contents of, the particulars of any part thereof.[3] However nothing in the section is to construed as making a person responsible for any particulars by reason of giving advice as to their contents in a professional capacity.[4]

The general requirement to disclose is thus considerable, but there are a number of exemptions from disclosure, one of which is likely to be of particular importance to Eurobond issues. The Stock Exchange may without prejudice to any of its powers under the listing rules exempt from disclosure specific information where such disclosure is unnecessary bearing in mind the potential buyers and dealers in such securities.[5] Such an exemption

1 Yellow Book, s 7 para 5.4
2 Financial Services Act 1986, s 146(3).
3 S 152(1) and (5).
4 S 152(8).
5 S 148(1)(c).

is clearly particularly relevant to securities traded in by experts such as Eurobonds.[1]

Cold calling

A further provision of importance to the international bond market affecting the sale of listed securities is the prohibition of the practice of cold calling contained in s 56. By its provisions no person shall, in the course of, or in consequence of, an unsolicited call by way of business, enter into an investment agreement with the person on whom the call is made, or procure or endeavour to procure that person to enter into such an agreement.[2] Unsolicited call means a personal visit or oral communication made without express invitation. The prohibition exists whether the unsolicited call is made on a person in the U.K. or made *from* the U.K. on a person elsewhere.[3] The prohibition is thus not limited to those carrying on business within the U.K. and extends also to those carrying on investment business but not authorised under the Act. However the object of the provision is not to protect privacy, and it therefore only applies if the unsolicited call is linked to the person on whom the call is made entering into an investment agreement or an attempt being made to procure that person to enter into an investment agreement.

Since an investment agreement is defined by s 44(9) of the Act as meaning any agreement the making or performance of which by either party constitutes an activity forming an investment business and this includes 'buying, selling and subscribing for or underwriting investments', telephoning an institution to invite it to enter into a subscription or underwriting agreement for an international bond issue could constitute an unsolicited call under the Act. Further where a financial institution purchased bonds and subsequently telephoned one of its long standing customers, recommending the bond as a good investment well suited to the particular needs of that investor, the telephone call could again constitute an unsolicited call.

The section does permit the Secretary of State to make regulations allowing unsolicited calls and the power to make such regulations can be transferred to a designated agency and can thus be exercised through an SRO.

In fact both the SIB and TSA have made regulations covering unsolicited calls. These permit calls which would have otherwise be unlawful in a variety of different situations. As examples both permit calls to be made on professional investors, who are, essentially, dealers in investments, and existing clients of the caller covered by a written investment agreement signed by the investor permitting unsolicited calls for whom the caller has

1 It is at least open to the Stock Exchange to exempt information under this head from disclosure which is essential to an investor to make an informed assessment for this is expressly prohibited in relation to another ground of exemption conferred, namely where disclosure would be seriously detrimental to the issuer (Financial Services Act 1986, s. 148(1)(b)).

2 S 56(1).

3 S 56(8).

done business in the previous twelve months[1]. Thus in international bond sales calls can be made by dealers to their peers to arrange the syndicate and by dealers to their established customers to sell bonds to them as investors.

Restriction on advertising

Cold calling is only one manner in which would-be investors can be approached to make an investment in an investment security. An alternative is by means of advertising so that the investor responds by contacting the marketer of the security. Advertising is controlled by s 57, which prohibits any person, other than an authorised person, from issuing or causing to be issued an investment advertisement in the U.K. unless its contents have been approved by an authorised person.[2] An investment advertisement is any advertisement inviting persons to enter or offer to enter into an investment agreement, or exercise any rights conferred by an investment to acquire, dispose of, underwrite, or convert an investment, or containing information calculated to lead directly or indirectly to persons doing so.[3]

It should be noted that an investment advertisement issued outside the U.K. is to be treated as issued in the U.K. if it is directed to persons in the U.K. or is made available to them otherwise than in a newspaper, journal, magazine, or other periodical publication published and circulating principally outside the U.K., or in a sound or television broadcast transmitted principally for reception outside the U.K., or in a sound or television broadcast transmitted principally for reception outside the U.K.[4]

The word 'advertising' is given a very wide definition to include 'every form of advertising, whether in a publication, by the display of notices, signs, labels or showcards, by means of circulars, catalogues, price lists or other documents, by an exhibition of pictures or photographic or cinematographic films, by way of sound broadcasting or television, by the distribution of recordings, or in any other manner.'[5] Given the width of the definitions given to 'advertising' and 'investment advertising', it would seem probable that the display of an investment name together with a price guide on a trading screen constitutes an investment advertisement since its very purpose is to publicise the availability of the investment and invite a response.

It is not envisaged that the applicability of the restrictions on advertisements will have a great deal of impact on the international bond market, for any advertisement will normally be issued by the lead manager

1 SIB Unsolicited Calls Regulation 4(1)(f) and TSA Unsolicited Calls Rules, rule 2(c). The text is a brief summary and the precise terms of each rule should be studied.

2 In fact, a non-authorised person can lawfully issue an advertisement, or cause one to be issued, if the issue is made to persons whom he reasonably believes to be authorised or exempted persons within the Act—Financial Services Act 1986 (Investment Advertisements) (Exemptions) Order 1986 Article 9.

3 Financial Services Act 1986, s 57(2).

4 S 207(2).

5 S 207(3)

who will almost invariably be authorized within the Act, and who will be content to issue for he will have carried out the extensive process of due diligence to satisfy himself as to the issuer's well being, and will therefore feel able to issue the advertisement with a deep knowledge of the issuer.

Misleading statements and practices

The old anti-fraud provisions of the Prevention of Fraud (Investments) Act 1958 have been substantially re-enacted in the Financial Services Act s 47. This provides that any person who makes a statement, promise or forecast, which he knows to be misleading, false or deceptive, or which he makes recklessly, or any person who dishonestly conceals any material facts, will be guilty of a criminal offence provided either (1) he makes the statement or concealment for the purpose of inducing, or is reckless as to whether it may induce, another person to enter or to offer to enter into (or refrain from doing so) an investment as to whether it may induce another person, to exercise (or refrain from exercising) any rights conferred by the investment.[1]

It should be noted that an offence can be committed under the section even if the person being induced by the statement or concealment is not the person at whom it was directed. Further, since the offence can be committed by recklessness actual conscious dishonesty does not have to be established. Over-zealous statements lacking any reasonable basis in fact, and which a reasonably diligent person would have recognised as likely to have one of the specified effects on the investment decision of another, are likely to be caught by the provision.[2]

To support its prohibition of fraud the Act creates a second offence in relation to acts or practices likely to defraud, deceive or mislead. By s 47(2) it is an offence for any person to do any act, or engage in any course of conduct, which creates a false or misleading impression as to the market in, or the price or value of, any investments, if he does so with the purpose of creating that impression, and of thereby inducing another person either (1) to acquire, dispose of, subscribe for, or underwrite those investments or to refrain from doing so, or (2) to exercise or refrain from exercising any rights conferred by those investments. However, it is a defence for a person to show on the balance of probabilities that he reasonably believed that his act or conduct would not create a false or misleading impression as to the matters specified. The overall effect of this provision is therefore to make unlawful the deliberate undertaking of an act or course of conduct giving a false or misleading impression which deceives investors as to the price or value of any investments. Actions taken to stabilise the price of bonds as the issue is made and immediately thereafter could clearly

1 The Law Commission in its report 'Jurisdiction over Offences of Fraud and Dishonesty with a Foreign Element' (Law Com No 180, 1989) made no recommendations for reform of the jurisdictional ambit of provisions in the Financial Services Act 1986 for those provisions prescribe their own territorial ambit and do not rely on the general criminal law.

2 *R v Seymour* [1983] 2 AC 493, [1983] 2 All ER 1058, HL.

breach this prohibition unless stabilisation is undertaken pursuant to lawful authority.[1]

BONDS NOT LISTED IN LONDON

As we have seen international bonds may be listed in London or in Luxembourg or, indeed, not listed anywhere. When bonds are not to be listed in London a different regime applies to that which has been considered and this regime is as yet only part implemented so that the position which will be established in the future must be considered separately from the position which obtains at the present time.

THE PRESENT POSITION

It is intended that the position of bonds not listed on the London market should ultimately be covered by Part V of the Financial Services Act 1986. However, this as yet has not been implemented although the 1986 Act has repealed the Prevention of Fraud (Investments) Act 1958. The position which is left is that the conduct of business provisions of the Financial Services Act 1986, already discussed in relation to London issues, relating to cold calling, advertising and misleading statements and practices must be met.

THE FUTURE

The structure of Part V is to control offers of non-listed securities by restricting advertisements for the offer unless a prospectus, or its equivalent, has been registered with the registrar of companies. An advertisement offers securities if it invites a person to enter into an agreement for, or with a view to subscribing for, or otherwise acquiring or underwriting any securities, or if it contains information calculated to lead directly to a person entering into such an agreement. Such an advertisement falls within Part V if it is issued in the U.K. although this apparent territorial restriction is considerably widened by statutory definition.[2]

Part V applies to debentures bonds and certificates of deposit issued by corporations, but not to securities issued by or on behalf of governments, local authorities and other public authorities.[3] In this respect, the applicability of Part V is more restricted than Part IV.

In general terms, therefore, bonds issued by corporations will be subject to the requirements of a prospectus unless they are to be sold without any form of advertisement within the wide definition of the Act. Where a prospectus is necessary there are requirements as to the contents contained in the Act,[4] and a general requirement that such a prospectus should contain all the information which investors and their professional advisers would reasonably require, and reasonably expect to find there, for the purpose

[1] Stabilisation is discussed *ante*, ch 3.
[2] By s 207(3) discussed *ante*, p 96.
[3] S 158(1), Sch. 1, para 2 and 3.
[4] S 162.

of making an informed assessment of both the financial position including prospects of the issuer and the rights attaching to the securities.[1]

To this general requirement there are three exemptions of potential applicability to an issue of international bonds, one or more of which is likely to be exploited by the international bond market given the institutional and sophisticated bias of its investors. First, the Act provides that the requirements do not apply if other securities issued by the same person (whether or not securities of the same class as those to which the offer relates) are already dealt in on an approved exchange, and the exchange certifies that persons likely to consider acquiring the securities to which the offer relates will have sufficient information to enable them to decide whether to do so, having regard to the steps that have been taken to comply in respect of those other securities to the requirements, to the nature of the securities to which the offer relates, to the circumstances of their issue, and to the information about the issuer which is available to investors by virtue of any enactment.[2] Unfortunately, this exemption depends on a certificate from the approved exchange (in the case of a corporation whose *shares* are listed in this country, the Stock Exchange), and since approved exchanges have no immunity from suit at the hands of disgruntled investors, it is not likely that certificates will be granted with any liberality.

Fortunately, however, two further relevant exemptions exist under the Act. Section 160(6)(a) creates a private placement exemption by allowing the Secretary of State to exempt by order advertisements appearing to him to have a private character, whether by reason of a connection between the person issuing them and those to whom they are addressed or otherwise. Further, s 160(6)(c) creates a potentially wide professional-only exemption by allowing the Secretary of State to exempt by order advertisements issued to persons appearing to him to be sufficiently expert to understand any risks involved. Unfortunately, as yet the Secretary of State has issued no regulations pursuant to his powers and it is plainly impossible to consider the width of these exemptions without the detailed rules continued in the regulations. However, given the way in which the market has used the professionals only exemption in the past, and the probability that a government devoted to assisting the effectiveness of British trade and commercial institutions will reflect the needs of the London bond market, it is unlikely that the smooth flow of the London issuing vase will be interrupted.

INTERNATIONAL DISTRIBUTION

International bonds and certificates of deposit are issued as an international security aimed at an international market. The explanation given shows how they are successfully marketed in this country without being subject to the full protection given to purchasers of securities by the English statutory provisions of securities regulation, but does not explain how the same result is achieved in other jurisdictions. The explanation is simple. Most systems

1 Financial Services Act 1986, s 163.
2 S 161(3).

of law have an exemption for essentially private placements parallel to, but often more generous than, the English exemption eg France,[1] Holland,[2] Mexico,[3] Japan,[4] The Phillipines[5] Canada,[6] and Australia.[7] Use is made of the exemption in each jurisdiction in which the securities are marketed. The precise nature of the exemption varies from jurisdiction to jurisdiction, and is more restricted in some than others. However there is something of a general tendency to use them as liberally as possible, which could have repercussions if any particular borderline transaction were ever litigated in the courts.

INTERNATIONAL BOND ISSUES AND U.S. SECURITIES REGULATION

The U.S. enjoys probably the most comprehensive system of securities regulation in the world. Erected by a system of statutes in the 1930's in the light of the Wall Street Crash and the events which led up to that traumatic experience, which brought so much misery not merely to that country but throughout the industrialized world, it was designed to restore investor confidence in the national capital markets, and made a major contribution to the effectiveness of the Roosevelt policies of the New Deal. The statutory provisions have been much developed by the interpretation of the courts, which have been keen to ensure that the policies behind the statutes be given full effect, and by the Securities and Exchange Commission, which is the Federal Agency created to enforce and monitor the regulatory scheme. The Commission has proved to be a dynamic (some would argue an over-dynamic) agency, and its rulings and adjudications have added greatly to the law and practice of the scheme. Its releases are as much studied by American practitioners as are the Acts themselves and the rulings of the courts.

The basic structure

The cornerstone of the comprehensive system of the U.S. lies in the reporting and registration provisions contained in the Securities Act of 1933 and the Securities Exchange Act of 1934 which together produce a unified disclosure system erected in the following manner. First, public offerings of securities have to be registered by the issuer under the Securities Act of 1933. A prospectus must be used to effect their sale. Secondly, where

1 International Securities Project (1975) 30 'The Business Lawyer' at p. 586.
2 ibid. at p. 624.
3 ibid. at p. 617.
4 ibid. at p. 603.
5 International Bar Association *Comparative Survey of Securities Laws* (1980) p. 148.
6 ibid. at p. 43.
7 There has been greater judicial consideration and analysis of the concept of non-public offering in other Commonwealth jurisdictions than there has been in this country—see, eg *Corporate Affairs Commission (South Australia) v Australia Central Credit Union* (1985) 59 ALJR 785.

a company offers securities under the 1933 Act, it becomes liable in principle to file regular information with regard to its affairs under the continuous reporting requirements of the Securities Exchange Act 1934.[1] Securities listed on one of the national exchanges of the U.S. have to be registered under the Securities Exchange Act 1934[2] and thereby become liable to the continuous reporting requirement of that Act.[3]

In view of the strictness of the U.S. regulation, and the expense required to obtain all the information necessary to satisfy the detailed prospectus and reporting requirements, an international bond issuer will be advised to avoid being caught by the registration and disclosure requirements. The advice will be reinforced by reflections of the dynamic enforcement policy of the S.E.C., and the severe penalties which breach any of the detailed provisions of the regulatory scheme entails.

Overseas issues

At first sight it may seem that the answer is simply for an issuer not to issue within the U.S. or list the securities on any of the national exchanges. However, matters are not so simple. Clearly, as a matter of fact, merely issuing the securities abroad does not prevent U.S. nationals or residents from purchasing the issue. The possibility that purchases by U.S. nationals will occur is increased when the issue is by a U.S. company, which may well be a particularly attractive investment to a U.S. national, and the possibility becomes even stronger where the issue includes a jurisdiction adjacent to the U.S. such as Canada. Indeed, an issuer of a foreign issue of securities in for instance Canada may actually seek to find purchasers within the U.S.

The jurisdictional hook

The U.S. system of securities regulation makes provision to catch issues made outside the U.S. national markets by certain key provisions around a specific jurisdictional hook. The jurisdictional hook is aimed at those who use the U.S. mails and instrumentalities of inter-state commerce as the means of effecting their purposes. There are certain key statutory provisions built around these means. The 1933 Act makes it unlawful to use these means to sell or deliver unregistered securities, whether the use be direct or indirect.[4] Further, it is unlawful to sell or deliver registered securities by these means if the security is not accompanied by a prospectus complying with the Act.[5] The same Act confers a civil remedy on the purchaser where the means are unlawfully used.[6] Further any use of the specified means to effect transactions in unlisted securities is *per se* unlawful

1 Securities Exchange Act 1934, s 156(d).
2 Securities Exchange Act 1934, s 12(b); 15 USC s 781(b).
3 Securities Exchange Act 1934, s 13(a); 15 USC s 78m(a).
4 15 USC, s 77e(a) (1970).
5 15 USC, s 77e(b) (1970).
6 15 USC, s 77(1) (1970).

unless undertaken by a broker dealer registered under the 1934 Act.[1] These provisions related to the jurisdictional bite of the registration and disclosure provisions. The anti-fraud provisions are given even greater compass and are considered separately.

The use of the U.S. mails and use of interstate commerce are concepts which have been given a wide meaning. The Securities Act itself defines 'interstate commerce' to include 'trade or commerce in securities . . . between any foreign country and any State, Territory or the District or Columbia'.[2] The Exchange Act contains a definition similarly as wide.[3] The use of the means need not be directly related to the sale. Thus the mailing of annual reports after the sale has been effected has been held to establish the jurisdictional base, at least where post-purchase mailings are designed to lull the victim into a false sense of security, postpone inquiries or complaints, or make the transaction less suspect.[4] Nor need the mailings to be directed at the purchaser. If part of the distribution, a communication mailed by the issuer to an associate will establish jurisdiction.[5]

Nor can the jurisdictional hook be avoided by non-user of the mail. Interstate commerce will have occurred if the security is brought into the U.S. by motor car for delivery[6] or if a representative of the defendant travels into the U.S. to contact or discuss the securities with a prospective investor.[7] Further, if a U.S. investor buys the securities and gives a cheque in payment the use of the mails to clear the cheque may afford the jurisdictional base.[8] Overall, therefore, it is clear that the jurisdictional potential of the legislative scheme is enormous.

Limitation of jurisdictional claims

The S.E.C., however, has not concerned itself with taking the jurisdiction to its greatest theoretical limits. It has been more concerned about issues by U.S. corporations outside the jurisdiction than with similar foreign issues, because of the special attractions of the former to U.S. investors, and the way in which U.S. corporations could evade the regulatory scheme with ease if their ability to issue to U.S. investors by means of foreign issues were not curtailed. Even with regard to U.S. issuers the Commission has announced that it would refrain from taking action in respect of a failure to register under the 1933 Act with respect to offerings made exclusively to foreign nationals by U.S. issuers, provided that 'the distribution is effected in a manner which would result in the securities coming to rest outside

1 15 USC, s 77o(a) (1970).
2 15 USC, s 77b(7) (1970).
3 15 USC, s 78c(a) (17) (1970).
4 *United States v Ashdown* 509 F2d 793 (5th Cir 1975).
5 *United States v Monjas* 147 F2d 916 (3rd Cir 1944); *Hill York Corp. v American International Franchises Inc* 448 F2d 680 (5th Cir 1971); *Belhumer v Dawson* 229 F Supp 78 (D Mont 1964).
6 *Moses v Michael* 292 F.2d 614 (5th Cir 1961).
7 *Hill York Corpn v American Franchises Inc., ante.*
8 *Kann v United States* 323 U.S. 88 (1944); *Little v United States* 331 F2d 287 (8th Cir 1964).

the U.S.'[1] This is so even though the offer originates from the U.S. and involves U.S. broker-dealers in the underwriting. The foreign nationals must not acquire the securities with a view to redistribution in the U.S. and in the case of sales within Canada it is considered probable that securities are acquired with a view to such redistribution.[2] It is for the U.S. issuer to ensure that the distribution is in such a manner as to prevent the securities flowing back into the U.S.

This, of course, passes the burden back to a U.S. issuer of international bonds to ensure that the bonds sold outside the U.S. are not immediately resold to U.S. residents. The technique which has been evolved to meet this is in the form of the so-called 'lock-up' arrangement. The arrangement has evolved specifically in connection with the offering of an international bond outside the U.S. by a U.S. issuer in a currency other than the U.S. dollar. The Commission are prepared to bless an issue subject to an appropriate lock-up by giving a no-action letter, which indicates that, on the basis of the information put before the commission by the issuer as to the circumstances of the issue the commission does not feel that action on its part in respect of the issuer is necessitated.[3] However, the use of the lock-up has become common practice on the international bond market even when undertaken by a non-U.S. issuer, and as a precautionary step no-action letters are often sought from the S.E.C. in respect of them.[4]

Perhaps the two no-action letters which best illustrate the specific restrictions placed on overseas distributions to ensure that such securities would come to rest abroad are those in respect of the Pacific Lighting Corporation[5] and the Singer Company[6] both issued in 1974. The eight central procedures proposed and accepted by the S.E.C. have been summarised as follows:

(1) Each member of the underwriting or dealer syndicate of the offering signs an agreement contractually obligating it not to offer and sell securities it is acquiring as part of the distribution in the U.S. or to citizens, nationals or residents. Generally, the contractual restrictions further preclude such offers of any of the securities being distributed, however they may be acquired (including through ordinary secondary market trading), during the ninety-day lock-up period;

(2) Once each member of the underwriting or dealer syndicate has sold its allotment, it is required to send the lead manager an 'all-sold' telex advising that its allotment has been fully sold outside the U.S. and to non-U.S. persons;

(3) Each member of the underwriting or dealer syndicate agrees in writing

1 Sec Act Rel No. 33-4708 (9 July 1964).

2 ibid.

3 See, for instance, *Sanchez-O'Brien Oil and Gas Corpn S.E.C. Div Corpn Fin* No Action Letter (21 May) Fed Sec L. Rep (CCH) 76, 734. *Fairchild Camera and Instrument, Int. Finance NV* (15 December 1976).

4 eg *Vizcaya Int NV* S.E.C. Div Corpn Fin No Action Letter (5 April 1973).

5 S.E.C. No-Action Letter (14 May 1974) (Lexis, Fed Sec Library, No act file).

6 S.E.C. No-Action Letter [1974-75 Transfer Binder] Fed Sec L Rep (CCH) 79,979 (2 Aug 1974).

to send to each purchaser to which it sells securities a confirmation in connection with such a sale. If the purchaser is not a dealer, the confirmation will in effect state that, by purchasing the securities, the purchaser represents that it is not a U.S. person, that it is not purchasing for the account of any U.S. person prior to the completion of the 90-day lock-up period. If the purchaser is a dealer, the confirmation is somewhat more elaborate and will state that, by purchasing the securities, the dealer represents (i) that it is not purchasing for the account or, or for resale to, any U.S. person, (ii) that it will not sell the securities so acquired prior to the completion of the 90-day lock-up period, (iii) that it will not sell any other such security, however acquired (including again, through normal secondary market transactions), prior to the completion of the 90-day lock-up period, and (iv) that it will send to each purchaser to which it sells any of the securities the confirmation described in this sentence or the previous sentence, as appropriate.

(4) All marketing documents for the issue, particularly the offering circular or prospectus and the initial invitation telex to potential syndicate and selling group members, must refer to the restrictions on offers and sales in the U.S. and to U.S. persons;

(5) Generally, to ensure further that the ban on sales to U.S. persons is observed and that the securities have come to rest abroad, no definitive securities are issued initially. A single temporary global certificate representing the entire issue is delivered to a depository for Euro-clear and (CEDEL), S.A. (CEDEL), the two European clearing systems for Eurobonds. Interests in the certificate are recorded on Euro-clear's and CEDEL'S books in favour of their account holders and all trades in the securities prior to the end of 90-day lock-up period are carried out through CEDEL and Euro-clear. Certification of non-beneficial U.S. ownership is given by the record owners of interests in the temporary global certificate as shown in the records of Euro-clear and CEDEL.[1]

The lock-up procedure

The object of the lock-up procedure is to try to ensure that the securities are not resold to U.S. nationals until the expiration of a minimum period from the completion of the distribution of the issue outside the U.S. The minimum period which has become hallowed by custom is ninety days.[2] To add belt to braces when distribution is completed the individual bonds capable of negotiation are not issued to the individual purchasers. Instead, a temporary global bond equal to the totality of the issued bonds is lodged with an authorised depositary. Thus no investor has a bond to be able to negotiate. At the end of the 90 day lock-up period it is the authorised

1 Virginia K. Troia 'An Overview of the Eurobond Market' (1987) 12 North Carolina Journal of International Law and Commercial Regulation at p. 340.

2 See the relevant provisions in the management underwriting and selling agreements ante pp. 72–3.

depositary which issues the individual bonds to each particular purchaser in substitution for the global bond.[1]

The logical conceptual basis for sheltering a jurisdiction from sales of securities for a long time is that distribution may be a continuing process but it does not go on for ever. There must come a point of time when distribution of an issue must be taken to have been completed, even a two-stage distribution, and subsequent sales thereafter are genuine sales on the secondary market rather than the second stage of a two-stage distribution. The choice of 90 days is entirely arbitrary,[2] but it seems to have been chosen so as to allow sufficient certainty within a comparatively short period so that U.S. issuers are not denied access to foreign security markets.

In one particular area the effectiveness of these procedures as protection from S.E.C. interference has been questioned. This is on the issue of an international security with detachable warrants for another debt security of the same issuer. This is because traditionally the distribution of the securities underlying the warrants is deemed, for obvious reasons, to continue until the exercise or expiration of the last warrant, which will probably be after the expiration of the 90-day lock-up period. As a result both the warrants and underlying securities remain locked up for the entire term of the warrants, unless they are all exercised before expiration. Further, prior to the exercise of the warrants it must be certified that neither they nor the underlying securities will be beneficially owned by U.S. persons.[3] However, even with these the S.E.C. has now issued a no-action letter allowing the adoption of procedures to ensure that the original securities and warrants would be distributed and come to rest abroad and that there is little chance that the warrants or new securities obtained through them

1 As a matter of practice most of the individual investors will probably decline to take physical delivery of the bonds and be content to leave them in the safe keeping of the depositary.

2 See Harold S. Bloomenthal *Securities and Federal Corporate Law* (Clark Boardman Ltd New York 1984 rev.) Vol. 3c para. 15, 11[2]. In fact the S.E.C. have conceded only the minimum point. While if the 90-day lock-up is observed the *S.E.C. will not pursue the issuers or underwriters* if the securities are sold in the U.S. after the three month lock up period, the S.E.C. have never conceded that such securities may be sold once the 90 days are up. This leaves U.S. dealers at risk that if bonds are sold which have never come into the hands of the public the *dealers* may be seen as participating in a two stage issue, and therefore breaching U.S. requirements even though the 90 days have elapsed. In practice, therefore, U.S. dealers apply their own internal seasoning rules and do not trade in international securities issued in this way until 9 months or 1 year from issue. The nine month period is borrowed by analogy from the seasoning period fixed by Rule 147 in relation to a restricted exemption from security regulation namely inter-state offerings. See Natham 'Trading in Multiple Markets' (1982) 4 Comparative Corporate Law and Securities Regulation p. 244 . No doubt a dealer could, in fact, sell the securities within the jurisdiction immediately the 90 days have expired pursuant to an exemption, e.g. the private placement exemption.

3 Beller and Berney, 'Eurobonds' 19 Sec and Commodities Reg 39,40 (19 Feb 1986).

would come into the hands of U.S. residents. To satisfy S.E.C. requirements the initial distribution must comply with the requirement identified from the Pacific Lighting and Singer no-action letters and further procedures were also to be carried out. These have been summarised as follows:[1]

(a) The warrants were to be issued in definitive form only to holders confirming non-beneficial U.S. ownership under procedures identical to those set forth for the original securities (ie delivery at the closing date of temporary forms of bearer securities and warrants, exchangeable for definitive securities only (a) at least 90 days after the date the lead manager advised the fiscal agent that the distribution has been completed, and (b) by presentation of certification of non-U.S. beneficial ownership).

(b) The warrants were to bear a legend stating that they were not registered under the Securities Act of 1933, were not to be offered to U.S. persons and were not to be 'exercised by any such U.S. national or resident.' Further, the warrants were to provide that they could be exercised only upon presentation of a warrant exercise letter (see (c) below) through the office of Euro-clear in Brussels or at the warrant agent's office in London.

(c) The Warrant Exercise Letter was to provide:
   (i) that none of the Warrants . . . exercised hereby is beneficially owned by a U.S. person;
   (ii) that the exerciser, if a dealer, agreed, if not a dealer, not to offer, sell or deliver in the U.S. or to U.S. person prior to 90 days after distribution of the original securities; and
   (iii) that the exerciser, if a dealer, agreed and represented that it had not and would not offer, sell or deliver in the U.S. or to U.S. persons prior to 90 days and after distribution of the original securities, and agreed to deliver to purchasers upon exercize of the warrants a written confirmation stating that the new securities had not been registered under the 1933 Act and that accordingly dealers and non-dealers agreed to comply with their respective duties as set forth in this paragraph.

(d) The new securities were to be credited to holders' accounts or issued in definitive form only upon receipt of signed Warrant Exercise Letters.

EXTRA-TERRITORIAL REACH OF THE ANTI-FRAUD PROVISIONS

It might well be that a nation will wish to give a greater ambit to the anti-fraud provisions of its securities law than to its registration and disclosure requirements. Fraud is a serious matter and will in general be more strongly proscribed than breaches of registration and disclosure requirements which can be seen as basically regulatory in character. Further, one might think, what objection can be taken to a nation framing the territorial application of its anti-fraud provisions in the widest possible terms? If the English anti-fraud provisions have such wide impact that the English courts have jurisdiction, under English statutes, over the fraudulent distribution by a Japanese issuer on the North American markets, with the result that a German national seeks redress here for a sale effected

[1] Troia *op cit* p. 343 footnote 77.

to him by a French dealer when both were in Switzerland, why should anyone object? Is not fraud dishonest wherever committed? Do not all civilised and developed countries oppose fraud?

In fact, as will be seen, considerable objections may be taken by other countries. What, however, cannot be ignored is that there is a real problem. Securities regulation remains an essentially national concern. Many securities are sold internationally. The possibilities that arise therefore for the unscrupulous and dishonest are considerable. In the absence of a system of international securities regulation of a width commensurate with the actual international distribution of securities it may well be that, if it were not for national legislation capable of being applied to fraudulent practices undertaken outside the territorial confines of the enacting state, such practices would be both more frequent, and extensive and the likelihood of an offender being punished would be even less. Certainly in the case of the anti-fraud provisions of the U.S.A., which have been given the widest territorial effect, the main stimulus for this has been examples of international fraud of a massive and obvious nature.

It will be recollected that the anti-fraud provisions of the English system were contained in s 13 and 14 of the Prevention of Fraud (Investments) Act 1958.[1] The jurisdiction of the English courts under these provisions, when dealing with an internationally fraudulent sale of securities, fell to be considered by the House of Lords in the important case of *R v Markus*[2] In that case the defendant had 'played a leading part' in the fraud. The investment was known as 'Agri-fund', and was held out as a Panamanian fund established to invest in food producing industries. The sales organisation was an English company, Agri-International (U.K.) Ltd., operating from London offices managed by the defendant, who was a director. The securities were in the form of units, and were marketed in Western Europe by teams of salesmen in the target markets, who sought offers from members of the public. The public's offers and cheques were remitted to London, where they were dealt with so as eventually to credit the London company's account in a Swiss bank. The London company sent to the investors their security certificates, which eventually proved to be worthless.

The old s 13(1)(b) dealt with two differentiated offences. The first was that of inducing a person to take part in any prohibited arrangements; the other of inducing a person 'to offer to take part in such an arrangement'. The House of Lords held that these were two seperate offences but that they were not mutually exclusive, in that the mere fact that one of them had been committed did not mean that the other could not be committed as the transaction proceeded. On the actual facts the victims had offered to take part in the arrangement in Western Europe when they had offered to buy the units. Western Europe was outside the jurisdiction of the English courts. However, the victims had been induced to take part in the arrangement in England, where their offers and cheques were dealt with, and accordingly the English courts had jurisdiction under the second limb.

1 *ante* pp. 88 and 89.
2 [1976] AC 35.

Any act of the victim in England carried out to enable him to receive profits or income constituted taking part in the arrangements, and such acts could be carried out through persons acting on his behalf (in this case the English company which was, in fact, defrauding him).

It is interesting to note the care exercised by the House of Lords in basing the jurisdiction under the section on acts actually occuring within England. In the event little objection can be taken to a finding of jurisdiction by the English courts over the fraudulent activities emanating from London and carried out through an English company. This approach is continued in the Financial Services Act 1986. This imposes territorial restrictions on the applicability of both offences created by s 47. For there to be an offence of making a misleading statement or forecast contrary to s 47(1) one or more of the following conditions must be satisfied:

(a) The statement must be made, or the facts concealed, in or from the U.K.; or
(b) The person affected must be in the U.K.; or
(c) The agreement is, or would be, entered into, or the rights are, or would be, exercised in the U.K.

Thus, if a prospectus which is issued in the U.K. solely for distribution abroad contains a misleading statement the territorial connection will be established under (a). Equally, if a prospectus is issued abroad for distribution in the U.K. the territorial connection will be established under (b). Further, if a prospectus is issued abroad for distribution abroad but with applications for bonds to be accepted in London the territorial connection would be established under (c).

With regard to the offence of creating a false impression contrary to s 47(2) the territorial requirements are different. Here there is no offence unless either the act is done, or the course of conduct engaged in, in the U.K., or the false or misleading impression is created there. Thus, if a misleading impression is created in the U.K. in a prospectus for distribution abroad, the necessary territorial connection will be established, as it will if a misleading prospectus is issued abroad for distribution in the U.K. If, however, a misleading prospectus is issued abroad for distribution abroad, there is no offence even though the application for bonds is to be made to this country.

The principal anti-fraud provisions of the U.S. securities legislation to be the subject of consideration in the light of possible extra-territorial effect is s 10(b) of the 1934 Securities Exchange Act and rule 10(b)(5) promulgated by the S.E.C. thereunder. Rule 10(b)(5) provides:

> It shall be unlawful for any person, directly or indirectly, by the use of any means, or instrumentality of inter-state commerce, or the mails, or of any facility of any national securities exchange,
> (1) to employ any device, scheme or artifice to defraud,
> (2) to make any untrue statement of a material fact, or to omit to state a material fact necessary in order to make the statements made, in the light of the circumstances under which they were made, not misleading, or
> (3) to engage in any act, practice, or course of business which operates or would operate as a fraud or deceit upon any person, in connection with the purchase or sale of any security.

It is at this point that the objections to a state giving extra-territorial effect to the anti-fraud provisions of its system of securities regulation become clearer. The jurisdictional hook supporting the U.S. provisions are exactly the same as the jurisdictional hook of the general regulatory provisions, including those governing disclosure and registration, namely the use of inter-state commerce or the U.S. mails for the prohibited act. Potentially at least the wider the extra-territorial effect given to the one the wider the effect of the other.

Secondly, different jurisdictions may have differing concepts of fraud. Some may be far more general than others. Further, different emphases may arise from the interpretation of the courts. No doubt all jurisdictions could unite around a concept of fraud limited to telling deliberate lies in order to take investors money in exchange for worthless pieces of paper. However, different considerations apply where the untruth is peripheral to the value of the investment and may appear to many to be immaterial. Similarly, the omission of facts with the result that an aspect of the prospectus becomes misleading, involves subjective decisions as to whether or not the omitted facts were material. It will be seen that with regard to both these issues that rule 10(b) demands the finding that the wrongly stated or omitted fact be material for liability to attach, but concepts of materiality may well differ significantly from jurisdiction to jurisdiction thereby imposing on an issuer and its advisers a burden ranging from the insignificant to the overwhelming.

Further the means employed by differing jurisdictions to deal with securities regulation may vary considerably. One country, such as the U.S., may rely on a strict statutory scheme with a vigorous agency to ensure that the investor protection is fully observed, whereas another may well prefer to base its control far more upon a system based upon self-regulation by its investments institutions such as the stock market as in the U.K. This will in part reflect different histories and experiences of abuses perpetrated on investors.[1] In part, it will reflect different policies. One country may feel that a system involving a large element of self-regulation actually confers more protection than a fully statutory scheme. Finally, a country may feel that by limiting its regulation it encourages the growth and vigour of its capital markets; another may feel that its markets are best encouraged by a comprehensive system of regulation thereby increasing investor confidence. A country promoting its capital markets by a conscious decision of little regulation may well feel aggrieved when its policies appear to be restricted by another country giving a vigorous extra-territorial application to its regulatory provisions, and even its anti-fraud provisions, when acts are designated as fraudulent in the second state which would not be viewed as such in the first.

What then determines the territorial effect of the U.S. system? Initially

1 In the last 150 years the U.K. has not suffered from the degree of abuses of the scale which led to the trauma of the Wall Street Crash of 1929.

the starting point in the U.S. (as in this country) is to read the relevant statute.[1] Usually the statute is silent and the matter must be resolved by a literal application of its provisions[2] or by a determination of the legislative intent. Given that the definition of inter-state commerce includes 'trade commerce transportation or communication between any foreign country and any state', there can be little doubt that the legislative scheme was intended by Congress to have some effect upon foreign issuers. The exact degree of effect is, however, more difficult to determine, although the broad definition of inter-state commerce to include 'trade commerce transportation and communication', and the width given to the relationship between the use of the means and distribution process,[3] would allow a simple literal construction influenced by the clear Congressional purpose to cover almost any use of the jurisdictional means within any part of the distribution, preparation, or the handling of the immediate consequences of distribution such as the clearing of cheques.

There is an apparently limiting provision of the Exchange Act 1934. Section 30(b) provides:

> The provisions of this title or any rule or regulation thereunder should not apply to any person insofar as he transacts a business in securities without the jurisdiction of the U.S., unless he transacts such business in contravention of such rules and regulations as the commission may prescribe as necessary or appropriate to prevent evasion of this title

This would appear to put outside the ambit of the Act any person transacting a business in securities outside the U.S. unless he falls foul of any regulations made by the S.E.C. under the power conferred by the section—a power which they have not as yet exercised. However, both the S.E.C. and the courts have taken he position that this provision is very limited in effect. Its protection so far as it extends, is to the professional involved in the distribution, and not to a particular issue and issuer, and even then relieves them from the reporting and registration requirements applicable specifically to broker-dealer registration requirements under the Act.[4] Thus, obligations to register an issue and the anti-fraud provisions do not fall within the provision. As such s 306(b) cannot be said to have any general limiting effect.

A more general possible limitation arising from U.S. principles of statutory interpretation is the general requirement that Acts of Congress be constructed, so far as possible, so as to avoid the violation of accepted principles of international law.[5] Clearly under international law a state has jurisdiction over actions which take place within its territory.[6] Therefore,

1 A statute might be perfectly clear. Prohibition of a non-complying but regulated prospectus under the Companies Act 1985 by overseas companies applies only to distribution of the prospectus in Great Britain. Companies Act 1985, s 72(1).
2 As in *R v Markus, ante* p. 107.
3 *ante* pp. 102–102.
4 Brief of S.E.C. as Amicus Curiae *Schoenbaum v Firstbrook* 405 F2d 215 (1967).
5 *Murray v Schooner Charming Betsy* 6 US (2 Cranch) 64 (1964); *McCullock v Sociedad Nat'l* 373 UD 10 (1962); *Lauritzen v Larsen* 345 US 571 (1953).
6 *The Lotus* (1927) PCIJ Series A No 10.

if a U.S. resident deliberately circulates a non-complying prospectus within that jurisdiction, there can be no doubt that the U.S. courts and their law have jurisdiction. Nor can there be any doubt that an alien deliberately undertaking the same act falls within the province of the U.S. courts and their law. Similarly, an issuer whether U.S. or foreign must be taken to intend the normal consequences of his acts, and it can be no answer by him that he did not intend the consequences of his act when those consequences were the probable result of his actions. It is to avoid the possible consequences within the U.S. of distributions undertaken abroad that the lock-up procedure was introduced with the blessing of the S.E.C.[1]

There remain, however, other possibilities of jurisdiction based on concepts of international law operated within the U.S. These are set out in the Restatement (Second) of the Foreign Relations Law of the United States (1965), to which extensive reference has been made by courts considering the territorial effect of its securities law. These include the so-called conduct test of jurisdiction, whereby a state has the right of international law to impose sanctions on conduct carried out in its territory even though its effects are felt exclusively elsewhere. The Restatement recognises such a power in s 17 which provides, expressly that:

> A state has jurisdiction to prescribe a rule of law
> (a) attaching legal consequences to conduct that occurs within its territory, whether or not such consequences are determined by the effects of the conduct outside the territory.[2]

Further the U.S. recognises the right of a state to prescribe a rule of law imposing legal consequences on an act undertaken outside the territory which cause an effect within its territory—the so-called effects basis of jurisdiction. The Restatement, s 18 provides:

> A state has jurisdiction to prescribe a rule of law attaching legal consequences to conduct that occurs outside its territory and causes an effect within its territory if either
> (a) the conduct and its effects are generally recognized as constituent elements of a crime or tort under the law of states which have reasonably developed legal systems, or
> (b)(i) the conduct and its effects are constituent elements of activity to which the rule applies; (ii) the effect within the territory is substantial; (iii) it occurs as a direct and foreseeable result of the conduct outside the territory; and (iv) the rule is not inconsistent with the principles of justice generally recognized by states that have reasonably developed legal systems.

Finally the Restatement recognises the right of state to prescribe rules attaching legal consequences to its nationals even though not resident within

[1] *ante* p. 85 et seq.

[2] *R. v Markus* is based on an interpretation of the statutory provisions which keeps it exactly within the conduct basic approach although of course this formed no part of the reasoning of the English courts.

its territory. The nationality principle has been little used in discussion relating to securities regulation.[1]

Under both the conduct based and effects based jurisdiction, the courts of two different jurisdictions and their respective law may have an interest in the acts giving rise to the effect complained of. These are the jurisdiction in which the acts took place and the jurisdiction in which the effects are felt. The classic and most used example of the principles in action is that of a defendant who fires a gun over the boundary of State A into State B, hitting and injuring a national of B. State A might claim to deal with the defendant under its own laws of attempted murder because the shooting occurred in its territory (the conduct base); State B might claim to deal with the defendant on the basis that the effects of the shooting were felt in its territory (the effect base).

The shooting example is, however, a comparatively straightforward example. If before proceeding to jurisdiction A the defendant had put the bullets in the gun in jurisdiction C, would jurisdiction C have any claim over the defendant, or would this purely preparatory act be insufficient to found jurisdiction? And how about jurisdiction D where the defendant purchased the gun, and jurisdiction E where he purchased the bullets? Is it only the pulling of the trigger which has its consequences determined by its effects outside the jurisdiction?

Further, in the situation of securities fraud is not the position even more complex because of the very complexity of the distribution process? Is it only the making of a misrepresentation which constitues the use of the jurisdictional means to defraud, or may any step in the distribution and associated process constitute the conduct giving rise to the fraudulent effect? These issues have given rise to significant difficulties for the U.S. courts.

In the case of *Leasco Data Processing Equipment Corpn v Maxwell*[2] the total transaction was only brought to fruition by conduct both in the U.S. and outside. The case involved an allegation of fraud under rule 10b-5. The allegation was the Leasco, through a subsidiary, had been induced to purchase stock on the London Stock Exchange at an over valuation on the basis of fraudulent mispresentations made to them. Since the Stock was purchased overseas the question was whether the preliminary U.S. conduct was completed by the effects elsewhere. The actual conduct consisted of the defendant's communication with the American company in America by international means of communication, and meetings with Leasco's representatives in New York to make his misrepresentations, and the signing of the agreement in New York to sell the stock.

These actions in the U.S. were held to give rise to conduct based jurisdiction on the basis that they were significant and not merely preparatory, and

1 Restatement, s 30(1) provides 'A state has jurisdiction to prescribe a rule of law
(a) attaching legal consequences to conduct of a national of the state wherever that conduct occurs, or
(b) as to the status of a national, or as to an interest of a national, wherever the thing or other subject matter to which the interest relates is located.'

2 468 F2d 1326 (2nd Cir 1972).

their consequences were to be determined by the effects in England. However, by demanding that the conduct undertaken within the U.S. be significant, the court did place some limitation on the transnational implications of U.S. conduct based jurisdiction. Similar distinctions were drawn in the subsequent case of *ITT v Vencap,*[1] a case arising from the collapse of I.O.S., as have a number of other cases involving the extra territorial reach of the U.S. securities laws. Provided that the conduct undertaken in the U.S. is not merely preparatory, the U.S. courts would impose jurisdiction and U.S. law even though the only sufferers from the U.S. conduct were foreigners. The court said quite expressly: 'We do not think Congress intended to allow the U.S. to be used as a base for manufacturing fraudulent security devices for export, even when these are peddled only to foreigners. This country would surely look askance if one of our neighbours stood by silently and permitted misrepresented securities to be poured into the U.S.[2]

From this background a complex approach, distinguishing between the position of U.S. nationals and foreigners, was laid down in the central case of *Bersch v Drexel Firestone Inc.*[3] This case was a class action on behalf of a group of investors brought by the plaintiff Howard Bersch. The plaintiff was an American resident in New York, but the class represented by him included many foreigners. Also within the class were Americans resident within the U.S. and Americans resident abroad. The common complaint was that they had been induced to purchase worthless securities in I.O.S., a Canadian investment corporation, on the basis of misrepresentations both within the prospectus and made by the underwriters. The plaintiff also alleged that the underwriters had failed to use due diligence with regard to the preparation and presentation of the prospectus, and that an accounting firm who had prepared accounts published to support the issue had failed to abide by generally accepted accounting principles.

Representatives of I.O.S. had had meetings in New York with their lawyers and accountants and major underwriters to arrange the offering, had drafted a portion of the prospectus in New York, and had opened accounts in New York to receive the proceeds of the issue. The bulk of the prospectus was, however, prepared overseas and the whole, when completed, was published exclusively overseas where the issue was marketed. The securities were to be offered to Americans including Bersch.

The issue therefore arose as to whether American courts had jurisdiction arising from the conduct within the U.S. to give a remedy to the class represented by the plaintiff under, *inter alia*, rule 10b-5. The Second Circuit recognised that Congress, preparing a statute, might well not wish to go to the full extent of jurisdiction permitted by international law as set out in the Restatement. Judge Friendly recognised that in circumstances where 'a court is confronted with transactions that in any view are predominantly foreign, it must seek to determine whether Congress would have wished

1 519 F2d 1001 (2nd Cir 1975). See also *SEC v Kasser* 548 F2d 109 (3d Cir 1977).
2 ibid. at 1017-1018.
3 519 F2d 974 (2d Cir 1975).

the precious resources of U.S. courts and law enforcement agencies to be devoted to them rather than to leave the problem to foreign countries'.

From these premises the court went on to consider the jurisdictional position from the point of view of both the conduct and the effects basis. This involved considering both the resident status of the various individuals within the class represented by the plaintiff, and also the significance of the conduct within the U.S. The court took the view that the conduct occurring within the U.S. was 'merely preparatory' and 'relatively small in comparison with those abroad'. Essentially, the conduct was nothing more than conduct preparatory to the fraud itself, and therefore insufficient to support conduct based jurisdiction in respect of the foreigners purchasing outside the U.S. Graphically, the court stated:

> The fraud if there was one, was committed by placing the allegedly false and misleading prospectus in the purchaser's hands . . . Not only do we not have the case where all the misrepresentations were communicated in the nation whose law is sought to be applied . . . or the case where a substantial part of them were (as in the Leasco case) but we do not even have the oft cited case of the shooting of a bullet across a state line where the state of the shooting as well as the state of the hitting may have an interest in imposing its law. At most the U.S. helped to make the gun whence the bullet was fired from places abroad.

If foreigners purchasing abroad were not protected under the conduct basis they were no more successful under the effects basis. The U.S. had no direct interest in the effect of sales of securities outside the jurisdiction to foreigners, and a direct interest was necessary to found jurisdiction. General arguments that actions such as those alleged against the defendant must have an adverse effect on the American economy, or the confidence of American investors in their financial institutions, were insufficient.

With regard to U.S. investors resident with the U.S. the court found jurisdiction based on the effects test, because the plaintiffs in this category had relied upon the prospectus, which they had managed to obtain from abroad. The court was prepared to assume jurisdiction over predominantly foreign conduct causing such a direct effect within the U.S.[1]

This left the issue of the U.S. citizens who were resident abroad. In this case the court combined the conduct and effects basis of jurisdiction. It appears that if there is some significant preparatory conduct within the U.S., and there is an effect on U.S. residents abroad this will be sufficient for U.S. courts to claim jurisdiction. While merely preparatory activities in the U.S. are not enough to trigger application of the securities law for injury to foreigners located abroad, they are sufficient when the injury is to Americans so resident.[2] From this it follows that the U.S. courts see a direct effect upon their nationals resident abroad when the predjudice to their nationals is contributed to by significant preparatory conduct arising within its jurisdiction. The court in Bersch found that there was such

1 See also *Travis v Anthes Imperial Ltd* 473 F2d 515 (8th Cir 1973).
2 ibid. at p. 992.

significant preparatory conduct within the U.S. on the facts alleged before it.

AVOIDANCE OF EXTRA-TERRITORIAL EFFECT OF U.S. ANTI-FRAUD PROVISIONS

Given the fact that part of the jurisdictional reach of the U.S. anti-fraud provisions is conduct related, it is clear that the most elementary way to avoid this part of the potential jurisdictional hook is to ensure that no conduct in preparing or making the issue occurs in the U.S. It is, however, unfortunately clear that merely structuring an issue so as to avoid the registration requirements, as is commonly done in international bond issues, does not itself avoid the anti-fraud provision.[1] There is, however, an argument that such structuring, if fully carried out, may avoid the effects based claim to jurisdiction. It will be remembered that use of the lock-up and other devices is specifically aimed at preventing the securities being issued into U.S. hands and they are of considerable sophistication. If carefully used by an issuer and its non-U.S. resident advisers it may be that they could argue that any impact, which may occur in spite of their endeavours upon any U.S. interest, was not a foreseeable effect or consequence within s 18 of the Restatement.[2] The possibility of being able to deploy the argument is a strong reason for making full use of these devices by a non-U.S. issuer, who might otherwise feel that he would escape the U.S. registration and disclosure requirements in any event.

CERTIFICATES OF DEPOSIT

The English position pre-Financial Services Act 1986

In general it appears that certificates of deposit escaped the regulatory provisions of both the Companies Act 1985 and the Prevention of Fraud (Investments) Act 1958.[3] In relation to the former Act the word securities, when used in the definition of debenture in s 455, would be construed *ejusdem generis* with debenture stock and bonds, which words precede it.[4] Conceptually, a certificate of deposit it not an emblem of loan but evidence of a deposit on terms. Further, the protective regulatory scheme of the Banking Act 1979 would cover such an investment, and there should be no need of the alternative informative scheme of securities regulation.[5] Thus,

1 A point made by Bersch at p. 986
2 The point is made by Chaikin in 'Fraud Securities Laws and Extra-territoriality in United States' Chapter 11 of *Regulation of British Securities Industry* ed. Barry Rider, Oyez Publishing Ltd, London (1979).
3 Gower *Principles of Company Law* 4th edn Stevens, London (1979) p. 353; Goode *Commercial Law* Penguin books/Allen Lane (1982) p. 525.
4 ante p. 85 et. seq.
5 Further it has been pointed out that a certificate-holder contributes funds to a bank . . . in exchange for a simple pledge to pay fixed interest payments and repayment of capital. The entrepreneurial or managerial efforts of the promisor have little bearing on the promisee's return on his investment. Berkeley *op.cit.* p. 487.

reliance on private placement and professionals-only exemptions was unnecessary.

With regard to the 1958 Act, which also used the word securities as the main concept with regard to its regulatory scheme, specific provision was made in the definition of the term to include deposits with industrial and provident societies and building societies.[1] It followed logically therefore, on the principle *expressio unius est exclusio alterius*, that deposits with other institutions were outside the definition and therefore the regulatory scheme. The very fact that specific provision was necessary in this later Act for certain deposits supports the contentions of the previous paragraph that all deposits were outside the scheme of the Companies Act 1948, and therefore of the 1985 legislation which re-enacted its provisions.

On the other hand, the anti-fraud provisions of the 1958 Act undoubtedly applied to certificates of deposit, as both s 13 and 14 were drawn to apply to property other than securities.

The English position under the Financial Services Act 1986

There can be no doubt that certificates of deposit now fall fairly and squarely within the regulatory scheme introduced by the Financial Services Act 1986. By virtue of Sch 1, para 2 debentures are investments under the Act, and debentures are defined to include *inter alia* certificates of deposits excluding instruments covered by para 3 dealing with government and public securities. This is widened in its application to the compulsory listing obligations under Part 4 of the Act, for s 142(3)(b) provides that for the purposes of Part IV the word debenture shall include any instrument issued by governments or public authorities within para 3 except Member States of the EEC and their local authorities.

The U.S. position

In the U.S. the courts have held that certificates of deposit fall outside the regulatory scheme of the 1933 and 1934 Acts. The S.E.C. had consistently argued the contrary view, pointing out that 'solicitation of investors' funds is not significantly different from any other corporate enterprise seeking debt financing'. In *Marine Bank v Weaver*[2] the Supreme Court rejected this contention, and accepted the arguments advanced, *inter alia,* from the American Bankers Association Brief as Amicus Curiae, that 'Congress intended to protect bank depositors by means of the banking laws'[3] and that application of the 1933 and 1934 Acts would amount to regulatory overkill.[4] The Court expressly held that certificates of deposit lay outside the statutory definition of security, since 'the holders of the bank certificates of deposit are abundantly protected under the federal banking laws'.[5] The court did add the qualification that it 'does not follow that a certificate of deposit between transacting parties invariably falls outside the definition

1 S 26.
2 102 s Cl 1220 (1982), 50 USLW 4285.
3 *Weaver v Marine Bank* 637 F2d (3rd Cert. 1980) argued 50 USLW 3569 (January, 1982) at p. 21.
4 at p. 22.
5 at 4287.

of a security . . . Each transaction must be analysed and evaluated on the basis of the content of the instrument in question, the purposes intended to be served, and the factual setting as a whole'[1] Neverthless it would appear that the status of the typical certificate has now been settled.[2]

The latter point is reinforced by the fact that the approach of the Supreme Court in *Marine Bank v Weaver* has been followed subsequently. In *Wolf v Banco Nacional de Mexico* F 2d (9 Cir 1984) the U.S. Court of Appeals for the Ninth Circuit was confronted with the question of whether a certificate of deposit issued by a U.S. bank was security. The particular certificate of deposit under scrutiny was one issued by a Mexican bank. The Court of Appeals referred to *Marine Bank v Weaver*, and noted that the rationale of the earlier case was that a certificate of deposit issued by a U.S. bank was not a security because of the protection from loss arising from the protection of the federal banking laws. From this is deduced that the issue which it was called on to consider was whether Mexican regulation of Mexican banks was equivalent to federal regulation of U.S. banks. The test to be applied was whether a foreign bank is sufficiently well regulated that the risk that the certificates of deposit will not be repaid in full at maturity is virtually eliminated. In the particular case it came to the conclusion that Mexican regulation produced such a result, and held that the certificate of deposit was, therefore, not a security within the U.S. system of securities regulation.

It follows from the test selected that had the Mexican system left any substantial risk of loss the case would have had a different conclusion. In *Gary Plastic Packing Corpn v Merrill Lynch, Pierce Fenner and Smith* (2nd Cir 1985) the Court of Appeals for the Second Circuit was again presented with a certificate of deposit, which was unconventional in form, and again used as the basis for its deliberation the Supreme Court decision in *Marine Bank v Weaver*. The certificates of deposit in the later case were created by unusual means pursuant to a system. Under the Merrill Lynch system for the issue of the certificates Merrill Lynch arranged for a number of banks to issue specially created certificates of deposit to customers of Merrill Lynch, bearing rates of interest lower than that paid by issuing banks to their own customers. Merrill Lynch placed the certificates with its own customers receiving the differential between the two rates of interest as commission. In return for the lower rates of interest accepted by its customers it undertook to create and maintain a secondary market for their benefit, and to provide continuing monitoring of the issuing banks.

The Court of Appeals for the Second Circuit referred to *Marine Bank v Weaver*, and noted that the Supreme Court had held that a conventional certificate of deposit was not a security because investors were adequately protected by federal and state banking laws. The court concluded, however, that the certificates of deposit issued through Merrill Lynch were securities, for investors in them were buying something more than an individual certificate of deposit, as they were buying an opportunity to participate

1 at 4288.

2 The American Law Institute specifically excludes certificates of deposit from its proposed Federal Securities Code.

in the overall programme and the secondary market, and the investor's decision to invest was plainly made in reliance upon the efforts, knowledge, and skill of Merrill Lynch. These were significant matters setting the case apart from the position in *Marine Bank v Weaver*. In this case the decision of the Court of Appeals appears to have been based upon the form of the investment rather than the risk which the investor was left to carry, for repayment of the certificates purchased by investors under the Merrill Lynch programme was insured by the Federal Deposit Insurance Corp and the Federal Savings and Loans Insurance Corp in the same manner as they would have been if issued by the banks directly to their own customers, or to the market in general. In these circumstances it is at least likely that the case is wrongly decided in the light of the decision in *Marine Bank v Weaver* as it is that it successfully adds tests related to the form of the investment to that of the risk born by the investor put forward in the earlier case.

CONCLUSION

The implications of national systems of securities regulation impose a considerable burden on issuers of international bonds and their advisers. It is necessary to avoid conflict with the securities regulation of any jurisdiction in which the securities are issued. Fortunately, the private placement provision generally available in most systems of regulation provides a means of avoidance, of which full advantage is taken by professionals within the market in structuring an issue. Consequently most issues are marketed so as to avoid the regulation of any national system.

However, the apparent strength of the position of the international issuer is less secure than it appears. The very lack of clear definition of the private placement and professionals-only exemptions in most jurisdictions could lead to surprising results if their terms were ever litigated in terms of a particular issue to the discomfort of the issuer and his advisers. This lack of definition of these exemptions tends to encourage exploitation to the widest conceivable extent to which they may extend thus potentially compounding the problem.

Finally, there is the issue of extra-territorial effect of national systems which has the potential to upset the most careful planning. This may lead an issuer to face penalties in a jurisdiction to which it was not even planned that the issue should extend. The penalties may be financial or even extend to imprisonment and, as if that were not enough, may give a civil remedy to purchasers of securities from the issuer and those involved in the distribution, for in both the *Bersch* and *ITT* cases it was made clear that breach of Rule 10(b)-5 could enable a purchaser to pursue a civil claim in U.S. courts where those courts had jurisdiction under the principles discussed.[1]

1 See *post*, ch 5 for a fuller discussion.

5 Civil liability for the prospectus

For prospectuses issued by companies falling within the technical definition of prospectus within the Companies Act, the Act itself, principally by s 67, conferred vital remedies upon investors injured by misrepresentations, or from whom information prescribed by the Act to be publicised is withheld.[1] However, as an issue of international bonds is carefully constructed so as to avoid, so far as possible, the application of each jurisdiction's domestic securities regulations and any civil remedies conferred thereby, the remedies of the 1985 Act did not apply to most, if not all, international bond issues. Instead, traditionally, an investor was be thrown back under English law upon the general principles and rules of the law of contract and of tort to determine whether or not he had any remedy in respect of any sale of bonds to him upon the basis of an inaccurate prospectus. Apart from his remedies at common law new statutory remedies now arise under the Financial Services Act 1986.[2]

Before looking at the remedies available to him, it is worthwhile considering just what result the investor will be anxious to achieve in these circumstances. It is most likely that he will simply want to get rid of the securities that he has acquired, and recover the purchase price that he paid for them, thereby getting back to the position he would have occupied had he never embarked upon his investment. Occasionally, a particular investor may wish to achieve more than this. It may well transpire that an investor entered into a transaction upon the basis of the misrepresentation, anticipating that the securities being offered were worth, not merely their issue price in the form that they were represented, but more than this. In such a case the investor would clearly be anticipating that he would make a speedy profit from the resale of the securities at the enhanced value. No doubt represented the securities would be worth more than the

1 The remedies applicable to prospectuses published in connection with conventional issues of shares and debentures by domestic companies are discussed by Professor Gower, *Modern Company Law* (4th edn) Stevens, London (1979) Chapter 16 and Professor Penningtons *Company Law* 5th edn Butterworths Chapter 8 pp. 302–323. Under the 1948 Act the governing section was s 43.

2 On the whole topic of misrepresentation at common law see David K. Allen's reliable *Misrepresentation* (1988) in Sweet and Maxwell's Modern Legal Studies series.

issue price, but the question nevertheless remains as to whether, if these facts can be established, the investor is entitled to damages for loss of profit as well as recovering, by one means or another, the full amount of the purchase price of the securities.

RESCISSION OF THE CONTRACT

Under English law a contract, which is entered into as a result of a misrepresentation by one party, is voidable at the instance of the other, who was misled. This is part of the general English law of contract, and is not limited in its effect to contracts for the sale and purchase of securities.

For a statement to amount to a misrepresentation certain matters must be proved by the plaintiff. These are as follows:

False statement

Plainly for there to be a misrepresentation there must be a representation which is false.[1] The representation complained of must be one of fact. Misrepresentations of the law, or inaccurate statements of opinion, do not constitute representations the falsity of which will give rise to a remedy under English law.

These bald statements have, however, to be modified in the light of the actual practice of the courts. These have been quite liberal in their construction of what is a question of fact. In the case of an English company it has been held that a misrepresentation as to the contents of the company's memorandum of association is a misrepresentation of fact, and not of law, and, therefore, gives rise to a remedy.[2] It would follow from this that a misrepresentation as to the borrowing powers of the issuer under its own constitution would also be treated as factual, and, of course, under English law foreign law is both proved and categorised as a matter of fact. On the other hand, a statement of opinion is clearly not factual. In *Bentley & Co Ltd v Black*[3] the directors of the company had calculated an estimate of future profits based upon an accountant's certificate which was misleading. It was held by the Court of Appeal that the director's estimate was a mere statement of opinion and not one of fact.

Of course, it might be the case in such a situation as this that the company itself asserts the truth of the matters recited in the accountant's report. There is no reason, in principle, why the mere publication of such a report or certificate should not be held to be an assertion of the truth of the

1 A mere omission to provide information will, in principle, only give rise to liability in negligence for pure financial loss where there has been a voluntary assumption of responsibility on the part of the party who has omitted to disclose the information. No such liability arises from a failure to provide information within the context of negotiations for an ordinary commercial contract even though it be a contract *uberrimae fidei*; *La Banque Financière de la Cité SA v Skandia (UK) Insurance Co Ltd* (1988) Times, 24 August.

2 *Oakes v Turquand and Harding* (1867) LR 2 HL 325.

3 (1893) 9 TLR 580.

facts contained therein, and in such a case, should the facts be erroneous, the company will have made a misrepresentation through the prospectus. On the particular facts of *Bentley and Co Ltd v Black* the Court of Appeal held that this was not the situation. Lord Esher, M.R. said, referring to the accountant's certificate:

> that certificate asserted the existence of certain facts. It was necessary for the defendant to show that the directors in the prospectus asserted the existence of those facts . . . The true meaning of what they said in the prospectus was, we have employed a Chartered Accountant to go through the books and report to us the result of his examination, and he has made a certain report[1]

The severity of the principle that the statement of an inaccurate opinion is not a misrepresentation of fact is modified, to an extent, by the attitude of the courts that the expression of an opinion by a person with regard to the performance of securities does at least imply that he honestly possesses that particular opinion, and if the opinion is not, in fact, held there is a misrepresentation of fact.[2] Similar considerations apply with regard to statements of intention, which again are not treated as representations of fact beyond being an assertion that the person making the statement honestly has that intention at the time of stating it. Statements of both opinion and intention in fact refer to the state of a person's mind which can be seen as being 'just as much a fact as the state of his digestion'.[3]

Clearly, for there to be a liability with regard to misrepresentation there must be a positive representation which is false.[4] *Prima facie* therefore, there is no liability for omissions from a prospectus or other document inducing the purchase of securities, even though the omission is a material omission from the document in that it would have been a determining factor in the investment decision of a prudent investor.

While the common law principle remains valid in the case of a prospectus not covered by the terms of the Companies Act, the common law itself

1 While the principle of liability by adoption of another's misrepresentation is clear its application to the facts of the particular case is more doubtful. Were the facts to recur it is submitted that the outcome would be likely to be different.

2 *Aarons Reefs Ltd v Twiss* [1896] AC 273 at 284 *per* Lord Halsbury LC

3 *per* Bowen LJ in *Edgington v Fizmaurice* (1885) 29 Ch D 459 at 483.

4 If an accurate representation of fact is made and subsequent changing circumstances render this inaccurate prior to a contract being entered into the new material facts must be disclosed so that the representee is not misled: *With v O'Flanagan* [1936] Ch 575. It may be that there is no such duty of further disclosure where a person makes a representation as to his present intention but changes his mind before the conclusion of the contract: *Wales v Wadham* [1977] 1 W.L.R. 199, but see *contra Traill v Baring* (1864) 4 De GJ & Sm 318 and the comments of Professor Treitell in *The Law of Contract* (1987) (7th edn) Sweet and Maxwell at p. 304. Further it appears that in English law one party may be under a duty, *after contract*, to inform the plaintiff when a change of circumstances makes it dangerous to rely on information which was correct when given: *Cherry v Allied Insurance Brokers* [1978] 1 Lloyd's Rep 274; *contra Argy Trading Development Co Ltd v Lapid Developments Ltd*[1977] 1 WLR 444.

has modified the operation of its first simple premise. The prospectus or other documentation must be read as a whole, and, if the omission of material information has the effect that the information left within the prospectus becomes misleading, there is in law a positive misrepresentation. The mere fact that the retained statements themselves are literally true is irrelevant in the light of the totally misleading nature of the prospectus itself.[1]

Since promoters and users of the prospectus will wish to emphasize the positive advantages to investors of purchasing the securities with which the prospectus deals, it is inevitable that most prospectuses will contain positive inducements supporting the purchase of the investments. This readily opens the way for a court to take the view that the suppression of material facts gives rise to a suggestion of falsehood, taking the prospectus as a whole, and it appears that this the courts are readily prepared to do, at least where the remedy sought is merely rescission of the contract, the finding of which involves no allegation of fraud or negligence against the user of the misrepresentation. Thus, a contract for the sale of securities upon the basis of a prospectus has been said to be one of modified *uberrima fides*.[2]

The false representation must induce the contract

It is not sufficient that a false representation should have been made by one party to the contract with the intention that the other should rely upon it. In addition, as a matter of fact, the innocent party must have relied upon the misrepresentation for it to be actionable, for it is only in these circumstances that the misrepresentation will have induced the contract the rescission of which is being sought.[3] If, therefore the plaintiff never read the prospectus there will be no reliance upon it and the contract would not have been induced by the misrepresentation. Similarly, if the plaintiff had read the prospectus but had placed no weight on the matter misrepresented as he considered that it was immaterial or, alternatively, if he ignored the mis-statement preferring to rely upon his own investigation and inspection of the issuer's property and means of production, the contract

1 See, eg *R v Lord Kylsant* [1932] 1 KB 442: and *Aarons Reefs Ltd v Twiss (ante)*. The authority of the former case is strengthened by the fact that it was a criminal prosecution under the Larceny Act 1864 (now repealed) where the operation of the section should in case of uncertainty, be limited in favour of the accused. In the latter case the words of Lord Halsbury LC at p. 281 are particularly in point.
See also *inter alia Peek v Gurney* (1873) LR 6 HL 377, *Central Rly Co of Venezuela v Kisch* (1867) LR 2 HL 99; *Greenwood v Leather Shod Wheels Co* [1900] 1 Ch 421; *Clark v Urquhart* [1930] AC 28.

2 Gower *op. cit* p. 379 quoting Kindersley V–C in *New Brunswick and Canada Rly and Land Co v Muggeridge*
(1860) 1 Drew & Sm 363 at 381 described by Page Wood V–C as a 'golden legacy' in *Henderson v Lacon* (1867) LR 5 Eq 249 at 262.

3 *Smith v Chadwick* (1884) 9 App Cas 187; *Cackett v Keswick* [1902] 2 Ch 456, 464; *Jennings v Broughton* (1853) 5 De GM & G 126.

will not have been induced by the misrepresentation on which the plaintiff will not have relied.

However, the mere fact that the plaintiff has inspected the issuer's premises and means of production does not *per se* mean that he has not relied upon the statements in the prospectus. It might, for instance, be the position that a prospectus contains estimates of the volume of production of which the company's factories are capable. A particular plaintiff, with no knowledge of the particular industry, may well be unable to form any firm view as to the accuracy or otherwise of the estimates from a visit to the issuer's factory. In this situation, he will clearly be relying upon the estimates in the prospectus rather than his own inspection, and if the estimates in the prospectus were a material consideration to him in deciding upon making the investment he will have relied upon the misrepresentations. The matter is essentially factual. The fact of an inspection prior to investment is merely evidential although it might have the effect of altering the burden of proof.

The factual nature of the plaintiff's reliance upon the misrepresentation is reinforced by the principle that it is not necessary that the misrepresentation should be the sole inducement causing him to purchase the securities. The misrepresentation may be merely one of several factors inducing the purchase and, it appears, need not even be the main one.[1]

The plaintiff will not lose his remedy simply because the defendant, having made representations which were false in the prospectus, gave the plaintiff the opportunity of verifying the accuracy of the facts for himself.[2] This is hardly surprising since the whole purpose of the inclusion of the positive assertions within the prospectus is to induce people to accept those statements without putting themselves to the trouble of verification. Clearly in such a situation where a plaintiff does not seek to verify the inaccurate facts he will be relying upon the misrepresentations in the prospectus, which will, therefore, induce the contract if they are a cause of his purchase of the securities. Because of this it seems that a plaintiff will be able to rescind even though he fails to make enquiries which a reasonable man in his position would be expected to make.[3]

The representation must be made by a party to the contract

To give rise to a remedy the misrepresentation must have been made by one party to the contract to the other. It will be remembered that, in the normal international bond issue, the dealers under the selling group agreement agreed to take a certain number of securities from the issuer, for whom the managers, as managers, acted as agent. The issuer's contract is therefore with the selling group dealers, who act on their own behalf in the arrangements which they make subsequently to distribute the securities, either direct to the ultimate investor or on to the institutions

1 *Re Royal British Bank, Nicol's Case* (1859) 3 De G & J 387; *Edgington v Fitzmaurice* (1885) 29 Ch D. 459.
2 See the remarks of Sir George Jessel MR in *Redgrave v Hurd* (1881) 20 Ch D 1 at p. 14.
3 *New Brunswick and Canada Railway and Land Co v Muggeridge ante.*

and dealers, who in turn will, possibly via a network of contacts, distribute to the ultimate investor. This therefore means that the issuer has no direct contract with the investor, and therefore any mis-statement in the prospectus will not, *per se*, allow the investor who has been misled to rescind the purchase of the securities and reclaim his money.

It is worth noting that with regard to sales of company shares and debentures within the Companies Act 1985 the problem was resolved by s 58 of the Act.[1] It will be recollected that this provided that, where a document is used to promote a public offer, it should be deemed for all purposes to be a prospectus, and, if allotment took place, the prospectus was deemed for all purposes to have been issued by the company, and the purchasers equally were deemed to be subscribers thereby creating the contractual nexus.

However in our international bond issue the prospectus provisions could not be relied on, and both traditionally and at the present time a remedy will therefore only be available to an investor if the dealer from whom he purchased the security made use of the prospectus to induce the investor to purchase. It is only in these circumstances that, by adopting the prospectus, the dealer will have made the misrepresentation contained within it to the investor. If the investor independently has seen the prospectus, and the dealer makes no reference to it in the course of making the sale, it is difficult to see how the dealer can have made a misrepresentation with regard to the contact between itself and the investor.

Where, however, the dealer does make the sale upon the basis of the prospectus, thereby adopting the prospectus and its representation for the purposes of its dealings with the investor, and the prospectus contains a report which contains a mis-statement, the report is adopted with the prospectus unless the prospectus makes it clear that the issuer accepts no responsibility for its accuracy.[2]

The effect of misrepresentation

The effect of misrepresentation is that the purchaser is entitled to rescind the contract as against the vendor of the securities.

Before 1967 it was believed on the authority of *Seddon v North Eastern Salt Co*[3] that a contract for the sale of securities could not be rescinded once the sale had been completed by their transfer. However, by the Misrepresentation Act 1967, s. 1 it is now clear that the completion of the contract does not bar the relief. For the purpose of rescission for misrepresentation it matters not that the party making the false representation was neither fraudulent nor negligent; a purely innocent

1 Formerly Companies Act 1948, s 45. This has now been repealed by the Financial Services Act 1986.

2 *Re Pacaya Rubber and Produce Co Ltd, Burns Application* [1914] 1 Ch 542; *Mair v Rio Grande Rubber Estates Ltd* [1913] AC 853 distinguishing *Bentley and Co v Black* to its individual facts.

3 [1905] 1 Ch 326.

misrepresentation made in good faith and after the exercise of all due care will still give rise to the remedy.

The result of misrepresentation may therefore be seen to be somewhat complex. If an inaccurate prospectus is used by an issuer the dealer will be entitled under English law to rescind as against the issuer; whether the investor purchasing from the dealer will be entitled to rescind a contract with the dealer will depend upon whether the sale was effected by the dealer putting before the purchaser the inaccurate prospectus or the inaccurate information contained therein and the purchaser relied thereon.

Loss of the right to rescind

The use of a misrepresentation to induce a contract makes the contract voidable but not void *ab initio*. Consequently the contract remains in existence unless and until a positive act is taken by a plaintiff to bring the contract to an end. The right may be lost if the plaintiff waives it.

Waiver may occur by reason of a positive act on the part of the plaintiff, or by implication by unreasonable delay in making use of the remedy. Unreasonable delay is the allowance of the expiration of an unreasonable time after the falsity of the statements which induced the contract have come to light. The reasonableness of the length of time left to the plaintiff during which positive action must be taken to determine the contract is a question of fact, and depends upon all the circumstances of the case. If a plaintiff merely has grounds to suspect the untruth of the statements, but does not positively know of their untruth, he is allowed a reasonable period in which to investigate the facts and ascertain the truty. If he rescinds before the expiration of this period the rescission will be effective. The amount of time available to him will depend upon the complication and difficulty of the enquiries necessary to ascertain the truth.[1] In the case of an international bond issue it may often be a complicated and time consuming matter to discover the truth. However, if the purchaser knows positively that the offending statements in the prospectus are untrue he must act promptly, and in a case where a company informed an investor of the falsity of the statements in the prospectus it was held that a delay of 15 days by the investor constituted waive of his right to rescind.[2]

Waiver of the right to rescind by positive act may take the form of any act which indicates an election to affirm the contract. If therefore a bondholder were to accept interest payments on the bond,[3] or exercise any of the rights conferred by the bonds,[4] or attempts to sell his bonds, he will be taken to have waived his right.[5]

Further the whole purpose of rescission is to rescind the contract and put both parties in the position which they occupied before the contract was entered into. In order, therefore, for the investor to reclaim his purchase

1 *Central Rly Co of Venezuela v Kisch* (1867) LR 2 HL 99.
2 *Re Scottish Petroleum Co* (1883) 23 Ch D 413.
3 *Scholey v Central Railway of Venezuela* (1869) LR 9 Eq. 266n.
4 *Sharpley v Louth and East Coast Rly* (1876) 2 Ch D 663.
5 *Re Royal British Bank, Nicol's Case* (1859) De G & J 387.

price he must be able to return the securities to his vendor. If he is no longer able to do this rescission is impossible. Plainly, therefore, the remedy ceases to be available if the investor has sold or transferred his securities. It further appears that the remedy ceases to be available to the investor if he has sold some of the securities, because the contract for sale must be rescinded as a whole and this can only be done if all the securities within the contract can be returned to the dealer.[1] If, however, securities have been purchased under several contracts by an investor, and he has sold part or all of the securities purchased in one contract only, it appears that rescission remains possible with regard to the other contracts.[2] These artificial distinctions have however not been uniformly applied, and in some cases a proportional rescission of a contract where some of the securities have been sold has been allowed.[3] The validity of the distinction is doubted by both of the foremost modern commentators.[4]

CLAIMS FOR DAMAGES

If an investor wishes to pursue a claim for damages for false representations in a prospectus, a number of possibilities are available to him. The most common way to achieve this end is to bring an action in tort for deceit. This will be considered first.

Action in deceit

The essential difference between the requirements which a plaintiff must satisfy to bring an action for damages in deceit, and the action for rescission for misrepresentation, is the state of mind of the person making the misrepresentation. All the other requirements remain constant, and thus there must be a statement of fact which is false, and which induces the other party to enter into the contract to purchase the securities, in exactly the same manner as if the action were one of rescission for misrepresentation.

As laid down by the House of Lords in the leading case of *Derry v Peek*,[5] the action of deceit is essentially one based upon the allegation of fraud and for the action to be established the maker of the misrepresentation must make it either with knowledge of its falsity or recklessly, not caring whether it is true or false. The principles applicable, and the implications that follow from them, were admirably set out by Lord Herschell in that case:

> First, in order to sustain an action of deceit, there must be proof of fraud, and nothing short of that will suffice. Secondly, fraud is proved when it is shown that a false representation has been made (1) knowingly, or (2) without belief in its truth, or (3) recklessly, careless whether it be true or

1 *R Mount Morgan (West) Gold Mines Ltd* (1887) 3 TLR 556.

2 *Re Metropolitan Coal Consumers Association Ltd, Grieb's Case* (1890) 6 TLR 416.

3 *Re Mount Morgan (West) Gold Mines Ltd* (1887) TLR 556.; *Maturin v Tredinnick* (1864) 10 LT 331.

4 Pennington *op. cit.* pp. 309–310; Gower *op. cit.* p. 382.

5 (1889) 14 App Cas 337.

> false. Although I have treated the second and third as distinct cases, I think the third is but an instance of the second, for one who makes a statement under such circumstances can have no real belief in the truth of what he says. To prevent a false statement being fraudulent there must . . . always be an honest belief in its truth. And this probably covers the whole ground, for one who knowingly alleges that which is false, has obviously no such honest belief. Thirdly, if fraud be proved, the motive of the person guilty of the offence is immaterial. It matters not that there was no intention to cheat or injure the person to whom the statement was made.[1]

The burden therefore upon a plaintiff is severe, modified only by further observations of Lord Herschell in the same case:

> . . . when a false statement has been made the questions whether there were reasonable grounds for believing it, and what were the means of knowledge in the possession of the person making it, are most weighty matters for consideration. The ground upon which an alleged belief was founded is a most important test of its reality. I can conceive many cases where the fact that an alleged belief was destitute of all reasonable foundation would suffice *of itself* to convince the court that it was not really entertained, and that the representation was a fraudulent one.[2]

It follows from this that a plaintiff can seek to discharge the heavy burden of proof by establishing that the maker of the representation knew of facts from which it was reasonable to deduce that the representation was false. The effect of this would seem to be to switch the burden of proof on to the maker of the representation to establish to the satisfaction of the tribunal that he had not been fraudulent, or to run the risk that the tribunal will find deceit proved.

However, in the final analysis it does appear that fraud involves a strong element of dishonesty. The courts have steadfastly refused to impose objective responsibility on a defendant, and have been careful to view matters through the defendant's own eyes. Thus, if a representation is made which can be reasonably understood in more than one way, the court will consider the position not from the point of view of any objective meaning which the court infers itself as to the words used, nor as to how they are understood by the person to whom the representation was made, but only as to the meaning which the person making the representation intended them to have. If in that latter meaning he honestly believed the representation to be true then there is no fraud and no deceit.[3] Further, an appellate court will not intervene to impose an adjudication of fraud, where the judge at first instance has found that there was no deceit, unless the appellate court is totally convinced that the judge who saw and heard the defendant in the original trial was wrong in his adjudication.[4]

1 at p. 374.
2 at pp. 375 and 376.
3 *Akerheilm v De Mare* [1959] 3 All ER 485 PC.
4 *Gross v Lewis Hillman* [1970] Ch 445.

Action for damages for negligence

As a result of the principles enunciated by the House of Lords in *Derry v Peek* it was regarded as established law that, whereas rescission of a contract for misrepresentation was available for any misrepresentation of fact inducing a contract, whether fraudulent, negligent, or entirely innocent, an action for damages could be maintained only where fraud could be established. In recent years, however, developments both by statute and at common law have undermined these simple principles, and have given rise to remedies in certain situations which depend not upon fraud but rather upon negligence.

Unfortunately both developments are in their infancy and it is difficult to be dogmatic as to the exact scope of the possible remedies.

The first development to be considered is that which has arisen at common law as a result of the landmark decision of the House of Lords in *Hedley Byrne & Co Ltd v Heller Partners Ltd.*[1] In that case advice had been sought from professional men who, *prima facie*, appeared to have been less than careful in the advice they gave.[2] There was no contract between the person giving the advice and those seeking it. In the circumstances the House of Lords held that a duty of care could arise where advice or information was sought from a person in circumstances where the person seeking the advice would clearly be relying upon the skill and judgment of he from whom the advice or information was sought, and further, that the giver of the information knew, or should have been aware, that reliance was being placed upon him. In such circumstances the duty would be broken if due care was not taken to see that the information or advice given was sound and accurate.

The principle is capable of the widest possible application and its exact limits remain to be defined. It seems probable that, like the great principle of negligence outlined by Lord Atkin in *Donoghue v Stevenson*,[3] the principle will prove to be capable of endless development which may prevent its outer limits ever being defined with finality. Indeed, within *Hedley Byrne v Heller* two of their Lordships who heard it seemed to accept that the duty of care does not arise in the case of directors or others who seek a public subscription of shares or debentures by means of a prospectus.[4] At first sight, it is difficult to see why the principle should be restricted in such an arbitrary fashion and one may be forgiven for dismissing their Lordships' reservations as merely typical judicial caveats often used on the pronunciation of a broad principle and which are subsequently abandoned as the principle is evolved.

Subsequently, the Privy Council by majority has restated the provision in *Mutual Life and Citizens Assurance Co. Ltd. v Evatt*[5] that a duty of care arises where the defendant 'lets it be known to the recipient of the advice

1 [1964] AC 465 [1963] 2 All ER 575.
2 No liability was imposed because they had disclaimed responsibility.
3 [1932] AC 562.
4 Lords Morris and Devlin [1964] AC at 500 & 501 and 518–519.
5 [1971] AC 793.

that he claims to possess that degree of skill and competence and is willing to exercise that degree of diligence which is generally possessed and exercised by persons who carry on the business or profession of giving advice of the kind sought'. Such a definition of the duty involved is plainly of easy application in the case of claims for negligent advice, but not for the supply of false information, which will be the more usual source of difficulty on a distribution of securities. Issuers and syndicate members are more concerned with supplying information via the prospectus to induce investors to purchase than giving positive advice so to do.

The purpose of the carefully restrictive formulation of the majority in *Mutual Life v Evatt* seems to have been to ensure that no liability could arise in the case of advice given casually. However, the problems arising in applying the test to cases where information is given are obvious, and in this connection the better test appears to be to ask whether the information was given in a business context — the test applied by Cairns J in *WB Anderson and Sons Ltd v Rhodes (Liverpool) Ltd.*[1] This was the test preferred by the dissenting minority in *Mutual Life v Evatt*[2] which comprised Lords Reid and Morris, who had been part of the House of Lords who had originally decided *Hedley Byrne v Heller*. Further, this approach has also been endorsed by the Court of Appeal in *Esso Petroleum v Mardon*,[3] in which Lord Denning expressly said that the *Hedley Byrne* principle:

> covers this particular proposition: if a man, who has or professes to have special knowledge or skill, makes a representation by virtue thereof to another — be it advice information or opinion — with the intention of inducing him to enter into a contract with him, he is under a duty to use reasonable care to see that the representation is correct, and that the advice, information or opinion is reliable. If he negligently gives unsound advice or misleading information, or expresses an erroneous opinion, and thereby induces the other side to enter into a contract with him, he is liable in damages.[4]

Nor can it make any logical difference that the information is given as in *Anderson v Rhodes* to induce the recipient to enter into a contract with a third party, at least where the information is supplied in a business context and the supplier has his own commercial reasons for inducing the contract.

Unless an exemption is specifically made for the issuers of prospectuses, it would therefore seem that they will be subject to the duty unless responsibility is disclaimed for the prospectus as a whole or for the portion

1 [1967] 2 All ER 850. The duty has been stated even more widely than this by Lord Denning as Master of the Rolls. In *Ministry of Housing v Sharp* [1970] 2 QB 223 at 268 he said . . . 'the duty to use due care in a statement arises, not from any voluntary assumption of responsibility, but from the fact that the person making it knows, or ought to know, that others, being his neighbours in this regard, would act on the faith of the statement being accurate.' However, in the particular case the defendant was under a statutory duty to supply the information which was inaccurate.

2 at p. 811.

3 [1976] QB 801.

4 at p. 820.

in which the alleged misrepresentation occurs.[1] Logically, too, an expert, including an auditor, who consents to his report being included in the prospectus will similarly be subject to the duty.[2]

The only reasons against imposing liability under the *Hedley Byrne* principle for misstatements in the prospectus on the sale of securities are the policy considerations arising from the large number and size of possible claims to which the application of the principle may give rise — in short the famous floodgates argument. While this principle has been apparently rejected by the House of Lords in recent years in refusing to restrict the natural growth of the concepts of negligence arising from *Donoghue v Stevenson* via *Hedley Byrne v Heller* in *Junior Books Ltd v Veitchi Ltd*[3] the brave words have not been supported by weight of decision. In the *Junior Books* case both Lord Fraser and Lord Russell said that the particular decision was based on the special facts of the case. The invitation has been heeded,[4] and, indeed their lordships even taken literally at their word.[5] This, of course, is but an illustration of the essential gradualism of the development of English law and this very phenomenon makes it questionable whether the *Hedley Byrne* principle would be applied to a careless misstatement in a prospectus.[6]

In the case of an issuer of international bonds it would seem that any duty of care will be broken where the issuer failed to exercise reasonable care in verifying the contents of the prospectus from the knowledge of its servants and the information in its records. In the case of the lead manager who causes the issuer to issue the prospectus to the dealers and, if so used by the dealers, to members of the public, it seems quite probable that such responsibility could arise if the lead manager had failed to ask reasonably probing questions of the issuer in exercising his responsibilities of due diligence. Certainly there can be little doubt that the rest of the syndicate rely heavily upon the lead manager for this purpose, and that a lead manager cannot be other than aware of this. With regard to others

1 Such an exclusion will be subject to the test of reasonableness *Smith v Eric S. Bush (a firm)*, *Harris v Wyre Forest District Council* [1989] 2 WLR 790, [1989] 2 All ER 514.

2 In general an auditor uses his duty to shareholders and not to potential investors *Caparo Industries plc v Dickmen* [1989] 2 WLR 514 but the position is otherwise when he knows that the company is in financial difficulties and seeking financial support from third parties to whom the accounts will probably be shown : *JEB Fastners Ltd v Marks Bloom & Co* [1981] 3 All ER 289.

3 [1983] AC 520.

4 It was likely to be. Apart from Lord Fraser's and Lord Russell's invitation Lord Brandon dissented.

5 See the criticism of the Court of Appeal in *Muirhead* v *Industrial Tank Specialities* [1985] 3 All ER 705, of the Privy Council in *Candlewood Navigation v Mitsui OSK Lines* [1985] 2 All ER 935 and of the House of Lords itself in *Leigh and Sillavan Ltd v Aliakman Shipping Co Ltd* [1985] 2 All ER 145.

6 It cannot be said that the English courts have been other than reluctant to provide a remedy for the disappointed investors — see, eg *Stafford and another v Conti Commodity Services Ltd* [1981] 1 All ER 691; *Royal Bank Trust Co (Trinidad) Ltd v Pampellonne* [1987] I Lloyd's Rep 218.

in the syndicate in their dealings, it is submitted that responsibility would be only likely to arise in circumstances where information within their possession gave rise to suspicion that the contents of the prospectus might be incorrect, thereby placing them on enquiry before they made use of the prospectus in connection with their own advice. Certain it is, however, that the principle of the case where applicable extends beyond the limits of contractual relationship, and clearly is not limited as is the law of misrepresentation to mis-statements of fact, but extends to careless opinions and inaccurate forecasts for which there is no reasonable basis.

The second significant alteration in English law, which has given rise to the possibility of maintaining an action in respect of negligent misrepresentation, is the enactment of s 2(1) of the Misrepresentation Act 1967. This provides that where a person has entered into a contract after a misrepresentation has been made to him by another party thereto, and as a result thereof he has suffered loss, then, if the person making the misrepresentation would be liable in damages in respect thereof had the misrepresentation been made fraudulently, that person should be so liable notwithstanding that the misrepresentation was not made fraudulently, unless he proves that he had reasonable grounds to believe, and did believe up to the time that the contract was made, that the facts represented were true.[1] The effect of the provision is to 'impose an absolute obligation not to state facts which the representor cannot prove he had reasonable grounds to believe'.[2] Once the plaintiff has established that he has entered into a contract as a result of a misrepresentation made to him and has therefore suffered loss, the burden passes to the defendant to show that he had reasonable ground to believe, and did believe up to the time the contract was made, that the representation he had made was in fact true. If this burden is not discharged by the defendant he is liable in damages.

There is no definition of misrepresentation in the statute, and it would seem that the legislature intended that the definition evolved by the common law should be applied.

Damages under English law without negligence or fraud

Finally, two situations arise under which it is possible that damages may be recoverable under English law without proof of either negligence or fraud. The first of these arises by operation of statute for s 2(2) of the Misrepresentation Act 1967 which gives a power to a court to award damages in circumstances where a contract is capable of rescission by reason of

1 The provision is based on the Companies Act 1948, s 43. This, of course, would not usually apply to an international bond issue because there is no prospectus within the meaning of the 1948 Act. Potentially therefore the provisions of the Misrepresentation Act 1967 are of particular importance in the case of international bond issues.

2 *per* Bridge LJ in *Howard Marine and Dredging Co Ltd v A Ogden & Sons (Excavations) Ltd* [1978] QB 574. See the discussion in Allen *op. cit.* p. 46 et seq.

misrepresentation. The statutory provision provides that in circumstances where a contract is rescindable for misrepresentation then, if the victim of the misrepresentation claims the rescission of the contract in any proceedings arising out of the contract, the tribunal considering the matter may declare the contract subsisting, and award damages in lieu of rescission, if it is of the opinion that it would be equitable to do so, having regard to the nature of the misrepresentation, and the loss that would be caused by it if the contract were upheld, as well as the loss that rescission would cause to the other party. Damages in these circumstances may be granted under s 2(2) in circumstances where there is a negligent statement entitling a person to damages under s 2(1), and it is expressly provided that any award given in lieu of rescission will be taken into account in assessing the misrepresentor's liability for negligent misrepresentation under s 2(1).[1]

For damages to be claimable under these provisions all the requirements with regard to misrepresentation which could give rise to the right to rescind must be satisfied. Further the plaintiff must still be entitled to rescind by reason of the misrepresentation, and, if the right to rescind has been lost by express or implied waiver, the court's power to grant damages must also be terminated. Finally, the provisions restricting the effectiveness of exclusion clauses applicable on a claim for negligent misrepresentation under s 2(1) apply equally in respect of the court's powers to grant damages under s 2(2).

A second possibility which might allow a remedy for a misrepresentation that the legislature intended the common law definition evolved in connection with the giving of the right to rescind and the imposition of liability for fraud to be the applicable meaning. The representation concerned must therefore be one of fact, unlike that which arises under the principles announced in *Hedley Byrne v Heller*. On the other hand under both the *Hedley Byrne* principle and the Misrepresentation Act a provision purporting to exclude responsibility for the misrepresentation within the resultant contract will not be effective against a person suing on the misrepresentation unless the disclaimer satisfies the requirements of reasonableness set out in s 11(1) of the Unfair Contract Terms Act 1977.[2] This provides that the requirement of reasonableness is satisfied if the term is a fair and reasonable one to have included in the contract having regard to the circumstances which were, or ought reasonably to have been, known to or in the contemplation of the parties when the contract was made. Where the effect of the contractual term being considered is not to exclude liability totally, but to seek to limit it to a specified sum of money, in determining whether the provision is fair and reasonable on the above basis regard is to be

1 S 2(2) and s 2(3).

2 See now *Smith v Eric S Bush (a Firm), Harris v Wyre Forest, District Council* [1989] 2 WLR 790, [1989] 2 All ER 514. There used to be some doubt as to whether a disclaimer of all liability was subject to the reasonableness test when the Hedley Byrne principle was relied on — see the discussions by Michael A. Jones 'Excluding Liability for Negligent Statements' 7 *Litigation* 222 (1988) and Allen *op. cit* p. 87 et seq.

had to (1) the resources which the misrepresentor could expect to be available to him for the purposes of meeting the liability should it arise, and (2) how far it was open to him to cover himself by insurance. The burden of proof lies upon he who seeks to rely upon the exemption provision to show that the requirement of reasonableness is satisfied.[1]

It is not likely that on an international bond issue or, for that matter, a domestic issue of shares and debentures, that an issuer will seek to limit its liability by a restriction of such liability to a specified sum. The question therefore of reasonableness in this connection is likely to arise only with regard to the total exclusion of liability. In favour of a finding of reasonableness of such a provision would be the great complexity of the creation of a prospectus and the extraction of the information to be placed within it, the fact that the amount involved in an issue on the international bond market is likely to be beyond the capital resources of any institution within the syndicate to discharge, and that this made without fraud or negligence is if that representation becomes a term of the contract. In principle, a representation may exist merely as a representation inducing a contract or may be incorporated as a term within a contract. Whether a term becomes incorporated within a contract depends upon the intention of the parties as to whether they intended the representation to have contractual effect or not.[2] If the representation does become a term of the contract, and it subsequently appears that the representation is incorrect, this will represent a breach of the term, and the purchaser will have a claim for breach of contract against the vendor, whether the vendor was at fault or not. This would have the particular advantage that an action for damages for a false representation could be maintained where the representation was in the form of a promise rather than a representation of an existing fact. However, as Professor Gower points out, this possible advantage is unlikely to arise with any frequency in practice as prospectuses rarely contain definite promises.[3]

If a representation does become a term of the contract, it is clear that these principles are applicable in relation to any contract made between a dealer and an investor, in which the prospectus has been used by the dealer to induce the contract. A greater problem, however, arises in the case of the contract between the issuer and the dealer. The question which arises is whether the securities are issued as a total replacement of the terms of the agreement to sell based upon the prospectus. Are they a complete novation between the parties of the previous agreement? In *Re Chicago and North West Granaries Ltd.*[4] in seeking to resolve the question of the terms of the contract between a debenture holder and the company from whom he had bought the debentures, North J expressed the opinion that the debenture was the whole contract between the company and the debenture holder, and consequently the prospectus could not be looked

1 S 11(1)(4) and s 11(1)(5).

2 Cheshire and Fifoot *The Law of Contract* (1986) (11th edn), Butterworths p. 120 et seq. The intention of the parties in this connection is looked at objectively.

3 Gower *op. cit.* at p. 382.

4 [1898] 1 Ch 263. See also *British Equitable Assurance Co v Bailey* [1906] AC 35

at for the purpose of defining the terms of the contract.[1] In the subsequent case of *Re Tewkesbury Gas Co*[2] Parker J adopted North J's view only adding that, if the terms of the debenture did not fully comply with the terms of the agreement between the debenture holder and the company for the purchase of the debenture because this incorporated terms from the prospectus, there was a possible claim in equity to have the debenture rectified to conform with the contractual terms.[3] However, these views were distinguished in the case of *Jacobs* v *Batavia and General Plantation Trust Ltd*,[4] where the application for the securities expressly made their acquisition subject to the terms of the prospectus.[5] Some of the rights expressed to be attached to the security in the prospectus were not set out in the securities. In these circumstances the Court of Appeal held that the plaintiff was entitled to rely on all the rights conferred by the prospectus on either of two grounds. First, that the entire contract was contained in the two written instruments, namely the deposit notes and the prospectus, which the court reconciled by incorporating the additional rights into the contract between the security holder and issuer as though they were inserted in the security itself. Alternatively, the court was prepared to hold that the promise was a binding collateral contract in consideration of a separate contract on the part of the plaintiff to take up the notes.[6] Only Sir Ernest Pollock MR referred to the earlier cases of *Re Chicago and North West Granaries Co and British Equitable Assurance Co v Baily*, and then only to distinguish them on the basis that in the case before him the application form expressly incorporated into the contract for sale the terms of the prospectus, thereby indicating a common intention of the parties that the securities when issued should not be an entire novation of a contract for sale. The majority of the court (Warrington and Sargant LJJ) preferred to base itself upon the collateral contract, and from this line of reasoning could evade completely the novation point because the novation would apply only to the original contract of sale. Warrington LJ said:

> The contract may be stated in this way: the terms of the deposit note have already been settled. An applicant for a deposit note in those terms which have already been settled, if the deposit note is allotted to him, shall be entitled to the benefits which have been stipulated for by the prospectus; that is, it is an independent contract, it *does not vary the terms of the deposit note*; it is an independent obligation, to the benefit of which the holders of every deposit note in that particular form shall be entitled, an additional benefit given to each holder of the deposit note.[7]

The reconciling of the conflicting authority is difficult. Does the Court of Appeal decision turn upon its own narrow factual distinction from the

1 at p. 266.
2 [1911] 2 Ch 279.
3 at p. 283.
4 [1924] 2 Ch 329.
5 The form of the securities was that of interest-bearing deposit notes.
6 This latter is the line of reasoning of the majority (Warrington and Sargant LJJ).
7 at p. 335. Italics mine.

earlier cases? If it does, modification of the terms of the security from representations in the prospectus will only be possible where some part of the contractual documentation expressly incorporates the terms of the prospectus. If not it would appear that a representation in a prospectus, which is intended to be a contractual term, will normally constitute a term of a collateral contract between the issuer and the purchaser, which will not merge into the terms of the security itself, unless that security expressly states that it, and it alone, set out all contractual terms arising between the issuer and the security holder. This latter is an attractive solution since it enables a representation, which was intended to have contractual force, to retain that status in accordance with the common intention of the parties.

Who can sue and be sued?

The related questions of who can sue and who can be sued in an action for misrepresentation in respect of the prospectus gives rise to answers which differ, depending upon the form in which the action is brought, and the circumstances which led to the misrepresentation.

Plainly in cases of an action for rescission of a contract for misrepresentation damages under the Misrepresentation Act 1967 (whether associated with a claim for rescission or sought independently), and actions alleging breach of contract, where it is claimed the misrepresentation became a term of the contract, it is clear that the action is limited to the parties of the contract. Further the party to whom the representation was made will only have a remedy if the other party himself made the misrepresentation, or, alternatively, the misrepresentation was made by an agent on his behalf acting within the scope of his authority. If therefore an expert has produced an inaccurate opinion which has been placed within a prospectus and the prospectus used by a dealer to sell securities, the expert cannot be liable in respect of the remedies at present under discussion. Whether the dealer using the prospectus will be liable will depend upon whether or not he has made an active representation of the inaccurate facts, by inducing the sale upon the basis of the prospectus without indicating that the portion emanating from the expert was included without responsibility for its accuracy being vouched for.

When the responsibility under the common law rule of *Hedley Byrne* is examined the position is more complex. Plainly the only persons liable will be those who owed and broke the duty of care, and they will be liable only in respect of those to whom the duty of care was owed. This has far greater potential than the boundaries of contract, and could put legal responsibility upon an issuer who has put a prospectus into circulation, even though a particular sale to a particular investor was by a dealer who was acting independently and not as agent for the issuer. Similarly, the inclusion of an expert's opinion within the prospectus with the consent of the expert (for instance an auditor's opinion) could give rise to the expert being responsible to the ultimate investors if the opinion is inaccurate and the expert has been negligent. The only obvious limitation on liability under the *Hedley Byrne* principle is that the statement must have been intended by its maker to be relied upon by the recipient. If therefore the maker of the statement had no such intention and, particularly, if he disclaimed legal responsibility for the statement, the condition would not be met and a remedy would not be available.[1]

In case of an action in deceit anyone who caused the statement to be included in the prospectus, participated in the issue of the prospectus, or promoted sales of the securities upon the basis of the prospectus with the necessary fraudulent state of mind will be liable to an action in deceit on the part of those who have suffered loss from his action. In the case of a corporate issuer this would appear to cover both the company and its directors, and would also cover any expert whose opinion was included in the prospectus with his consent and who knew of the inaccurate information within his opinion.

An important limiting factor, however, with regard to liability for deceit, under the common law principle of negligence, and for misrepresentation under the Misrepresentation Act 1967, arises from the fact that in order to succeed in an action the plaintiff must show that he was one of a class of persons intended to act upon it. This arises from the very definition of the duty of care in the common law principle. In an action for deceit the principle was held to apply in the leading case of *Peek v Gurney*.[2] Any restrictions on an action for deceit must also apply to an action under s 2(1) of the Misrepresentation Act 1967, for that subsection expressly provides that it applies if the person making the misrepresentation would be liable to damages had the misrepresentation been made fraudulently. As set out in *Peek v Gurney* the implications of the principle are considerable.

In that case a prospectus had been issued full of misrepresentations and deceit. The plaintiff had read the prospectus. He did not, however, apply for any of the securities on the issue. Instead, some three to five months later the plaintiff purchased securities on the secondary market. Fairly shortly thereafter the fraudulent nature of the venture became obvious and the securities worthless. In these circumstances the plaintiff sought damages in deceit.

The House of Lords held that the action could not be maintained. The misrepresentations within the prospectus were not addressed to persons who, like the plaintiff, had bought upon the secondary market, but to those who were to subscribe to the issue thereby guaranteeing its success. Once the issue was closed the prospectus was spent as it had served its purpose, and there was nothing further for it to do. If the effect of the issue of a prospectus were not limited in this way it would be difficult to draw any line limiting the responsibility of those who issued it.

Plainly this is a great limitation upon those seeking to obtain relief for misrepresentation. The difficulties are particularly strong in the international bond market, where, as has been seen, it is extremely difficult to decide when an issue has been completed and the secondary market opened. Further

1 A disclaimer of responsibility in a situation falling under the principle of *Hedley Byrne v Heller* will need to satisfy the test of reasonableness within the Unfair Contract Terms Act 1977, s 2(2). *Smith v Eric S Bush (a firm), Harris v Wyre Forest District Council* [1989] 2 WLR 790, [1989] 2 All ER 514.

2 (1873) LR 6 HL 377.

the mode of the sale is via a succession of dealers to the ultimate purchaser rather than direct from the issuer on the subscription of the investor. Therefore the problems of being clear that the issue is complete, and that particular sales were in fact genuine purchases on a secondary market, are compounded.

One general exception to the principle of *Peek v Gurney* was established by the Court of Appeal in *Andrews v Mockford.*[1] In that case the fraud had been perpetrated not merely by the use of the prospectus, but by other documentation used subsequently. From this the court was prepared to infer that the prospectus had been issued not merely to induce application for the allotment of shares, but also to induce members of the public to purchase shares on the secondary market. In such circumstances the Court of Appeal held that the prospectus's function was not exhausted when the allotment was completed but continued to induce subsequent purchases by members of the public on the secondary market as had been intended.

The precise effect of *Peek v Gurney* today is obscure. As has been well expressed its principle 'fails to recognise the result of modern issuing techniques'.[2] Where a prospectus is issued as part of the requirement to obtain a listing on the London Stock Exchange it is plain that it is intended to influence purchasers on that market.[3] In some international bond issues the prospectus will be issued for this very purpose.[4] As has been well put today 'those who publicly advertise a prospectus know that it will be relied on indiscriminately by investors who apply on allotment and those who buy on the market'.[5]

These arguments apply equally, however, where a prospectus is not issued with a view to obtaining a quotation on the London market. On an international bond issue the prospectus is issued to induce purchases throughout the dealer network and will be so used. As such it will be relied upon to place the whole of the issue and to influence both the issue, and the subsequent establishment of the secondary market. It is inevitable that the very fact that it is used in this way will mean that it will continue to have an effect upon investors, and their decision to invest on the secondary market for some time thereafter.

However, in these circumstances it is at least possible that if these issues were again to come before a court *Peek v Gurney* would be seen as establishing the principle that a person is only responsible in damages for misrepresentation in a prospectus to those who were intended to act upon it. The issue of when a prospectus has been exhausted would therefore be seen simply as one of fact, and *Peek v Gurney* as a product of its time. The line between the primary and the secondary market is no longer as clear cut as it was particularly in respect of international bonds, and one has no need to look further than the complexities which arise on stabilisation and the establishment of the secondary market after issue to have clear

1 [1896] 1 QB 372 CA.
2 Gower *op. cit.* at p. 374.
3 Gower *op. cit.* at p. 374.
4 Listing on the Luxembourg exchange is more usual.
5 Gower *op. cit.* at p. 375.

evidence of this. The prospectus is clearly intended to influence investors and will do so on both markets. In these circumstances, it seems difficult to deny that investors will be widely influenced, and this must be taken as the natural consequence of the machinery of publication. An investor so influenced is acting in the way contemplated by the issuer and its advisers, whether the purchase is at first, second, or even third hand. Nevertheless, it must be accepted that the older a prospectus becomes before the particular purchase is made the more difficult will it be for the purchaser to claim that he relied upon it, that the matters complained of were false at the time that they were made, and that they actually gave rise to the loss alleged rather than circumstances subsequently developing. This should not, however, prevent a remedy where a plaintiff can overcome the difficulties of proof. The injustice of the consequence of the ruling in *Peek v Gurney* were made clear in the arguments for the plaintiff a century ago: 'The mischief done was like that occasioned by a person throwing a lighted squib into a crowd, not one particular person but any or all might suffer from it . . ..'[1]

THE DAMAGES ISSUE

Further significant differences in the remedies available to an investor for misrepresentation arise in the field of measure of damages. Clearly any remedy available to a plaintiff previously discussed will enable the plaintiff to recover the price that he has paid for the securities. However, the various remedies are not equally useful in enabling him to recover damages for anticipated profits from the purchase of the securities. It may well be that a plaintiff purchased the securities on the basis that as represented they were worth more than the price at which they were being marketed, and therefore envisaged being able to make a speedy profit from the transaction. In this case his true loss is not what he paid for the securities but the value of the securities, in the condition that they were represented to be, and which, therefore, he reasonably expected to be able to realise. If therefore a plaintiff paid £10,000 for a security which, had the representations been true, would have been worth £12,000 then, if the security turns out to be worthless, his actual perceived loss is not £10,000 but £12,000. Where the plaintiff can sue in contract, because the misrepresentation became a term of the contract, there is little doubt that he is entitled to his full claim for failure of his expectations. The general principles, however, governing tortious liability traditionally do not take cognisance of damages for expectancy loss, and in general, the plaintiff would not be able to succeed. Whilst there was some movement in English law to allow damages for loss of bargain in a case brought under the Misrepresentation Act, s 2(1)[2]

1 at p. 380.

2 *Watts v Spence* [1976] Ch 165. In that case there was a contractual relationship between plaintiff and vendor but the plaintiff was prevented from seeking damages for breach of contract by reason of the rule in *Bain v Fothergill* (1874) LR 7 HL 158. See also *Kitcher v Fordham* [1955] 2 Lloyd's Rep 705; *Jarvis v Swan Tours* 1973 QB 233; *Davis & Co (Wines) Ltd v Afa-Minerva (EMI) Ltd* [1974] 2 Lloyd's Rep 27.

this has been sustained and the proper basis is tortious.[1] This is inevitable since the possible explosion of the distinction between tort and contract in assessing damages represented by the decision of the House of Lords in *Junior Books Ltd v Veitchi Co Ltd.*[2] has never been completed given the subsequent retreat from principle in later cases.[3]

REMEDIES FOR BREACH OF THE STATUTORY REGULATORY FRAMEWORK

(1) The traditional situation

It might be thought that in general, since the statutory framework controlling securities regulation is to protect investors, a breach of the statutory framework would give rise to a civil cause of action in the hands of the injured investor. In general in respect of international bonds this has not been the position.

The machinery of regulation contained in the Companies Act making compulsory the use of a regulated prospectus does not apply to international bond issues. In any event the Companies Act in its various provisions are usually clear as to whether the consequence of breach of a provision is civil or criminal. Because of the particularity of the statute the courts have not been willing to confer a civil right of action when the statute does not expressly confer such a right.[4]

This left the position under ss 13 and 14 of the Prevention of Fraud (Investments) Act 1958 and the provisions of the Banking Act itself. Historically, the English courts have been reluctant to deduce civil remedies from regulatory provision and all major commentators took the view that civil remedies do not arise from breaches of the regulator's provisions of these Acts.[5] However, English law will not permit a contract to be enforced in breach of the regulatory framework of any Act of Parliament to the detriment of those for whose protection that framework was erected. Consequently, while no civil remedy flowed from breach of these provisions to an injured investor when the contract had been executed, if the investor had not yet paid the price of the securities, he could rely upon breach of the provisions as justifying him in refusing to pay and in the knowledge

1 The measure seems to be that available in tort where deceit is shown *F and H Entertainments Ltd v Leisure Enterprises Ltd* (1976) 120 Sol Jo 331; *Andre & Cie SA v Ets Michel Blanc & Fils* [1977] 2 Lloyd's Rep 166. See the discussion by Allen *op. cit.* p. 49 *et seq.*

2 [1983] 1 AC 520 See Holyoak 'Tort and Contract after Junior Books' (1983) 99 LQR 591.

3 ante p. 130.

4 The exception was Companies Act 1948, s 38 re-enacted as ss 56 and 66 of the Companies Act 1985 discussed by Gower pp. 387–391. This has been repealed by the Financial Services Act 1986.

5 Gower *op. cit* at p. 391. Pennington makes no suggestion of the existence of a remedy.

that the court would not enforce the contract against him because of the illegality of the actions of the issuer and the issuer's advisers.[1]

(2) Under the Financial Services Act

The nature of the control of issues under the Financial Services Act depends on whether or not they are to be listed on the London Stock Exchange.[2] In addition there are separate controls on cold calling, advertising, and misleading statements.[3] The civil position under each will be discussed in turn.

Listed bonds Bonds listed on the London Stock Exchange are subject to compulsory disclosure of specified information in the listing particulars. The amount of disclosure necessary depends on the nature of the issue and the form of the securities. However, in general the amount of disclosure required is less than that generally demanded in a domestic issue. In addition, under s. 148 of the Act the Exchange is empowered to exempt the omission from listing particulars of otherwise necessary information in certain circumstances.[4] Nevertheless, there thus remains, in modified form, a general duty to make material disclosures,[5] and for breach of this residual duty civil remedies are attached. This civil liability is attached by virtue of ss 150, 151 and 152.

Section 150 creates a general liability to pay compensation for false and misleading particulars by the person or persons responsible for them to any person, who has acquired any of the securities in question, and suffered loss in respect of them as a result of any untrue or misleading statement in the particulars, or any omission from them of any material required to be included. If material required to be included is omitted the particulars are to be treated as a statement that there is no such matter. This remedy is additional to any other liability which the person or persons responsible may have created by their acts. It is an acquisition of securities if a person contracts to acquire them or an interest in them.

To this general liability to compensate there are five specific defences created by s 15.

(1) If the defendant can show that, having made reasonable enquiries, he reasonably believed, at the time when the particulars were submitted, either that the statement was true or not misleading or that any omission was properly omitted then in certain circumstances he has a valid defence.[6]

(2) This applies where the offending statement purports to be made by

1 For a general discussion of the effect of illegality on contractual provisions see *ante* ch 3. As it is normal for the price of securities to be paid on issue this situation is unlikely to occur.

2 *ante* p. 89 *et seq.*

3 *ante* p. 95 *et seq.*

4 Discussed *ante* p. 94

5 In a most limited form in respect of sovereign issuers see *ante* p. 93

6 S 150(1) reproducing in modified form the defence in s 68(2)(a) of the Companies Act 1985.

or on the authority of an expert and is, and is stated to be, made with the expert's consent. If this is the position, and the defendant can show that he believed on reasonable grounds that the expert was competent to make or authorise the statement and consented to its inclusion in the form and context in which it was included, then, in certain circumstances, he has a defence.[1]

(3) If the defendant can show either that a correction, or the fact that an expert was not in fact competent or had not consented to publication, was published in a manner calculated to bring the fact to the notice of potential investors, or that he took reasonable steps to secure such publication before the time when the securities were acquired, he will have a defence.[2]

(4) A defendant is not responsible for any loss resulting from the accurate and fair reproduction of a statement by an official person or contained in a public official document.[3]

(5) The defendant has a defence if he can establish that the person suffering the loss acquired the securities 'with knowledge' that the statement was false or misleading, or of the omitted matter, or of the changed or new matter, as appropriate;[4]

The general liability thus created attaches, subject to the defences, to the person or persons responsible, who are defined in s 152 of the Financial Services Act as:

(a) the issuer of the securities to which the particulars relate;
(b) in the case of a company all directors at the time the particulars are submitted;
(c) in the case of a company each person who has authorised himself to be named in the particulars as a director, or as having agreed to become a director, of that body either immediately or at a future time;
(d) each person who accepts, and is stated in the particulars as accepting responsibility for, or for any part of, the particulars;
(e) each person not falling within (a) to (d) above who has authorized the contents of, or any part of, the particulars.

However in respect of international bond issues the responsibilities of directors and those who have agreed to become directors is modified by

1 S 150(2). The defence is based on the defence in s 68(2)(b) of the Companies Act 1985. An expert includes any engineer, valuer, accountant, or other person whose profession, qualifications, or experience gives authority to a statement made by him (s 151(7)).

2 S 150(3) based on s 68(1)(c) of the Companies Act 1985. This defence depends not on proof of reasonable belief but on prompt and effective action.

3 S 150(4) based on s 68(2)(d) of the Companies Act 1985. The Act contains a definition of 'official person' or 'official document'.

4 S 150(5). But does the investor have to show that he suffered the loss as a result of the inaccuracy of omission and, if so, is not this defence an irrelevance? There was no equivalent in s 68 of the Companies Act 1985 and it has all the hallmarks of a bodge arising from legislative compromise.

a special provision relating to 'international securities'.[1] Here the director or director designate cannot be liable as director designate under (b) and (c) above but may be liable under (d) and (e) for accepting or authorising the contents of the particulars.

Unlisted bonds Securities not to be listed on the London Stock Exchange are covered by Part V of the Financial Services Act which will function when brought into force similarly to the old companies legislation provisions by requiring a compulsory prospectus to be delivered to the registrar of companies unless the sale of the securities is to be of a private character only (private placement) or to persons appearing to him to be sufficiently expert to understand any risks involved (professionals only).[2] Documents circulated under a private placement or professionals-only arrangement are not a prospectus for the purpose of the Act but only an advertisement (even if entitled prospectus on their front cover). Consequently, the provisions of s 166, 167 and 168 giving statutory entitlement to compensation for false and misleading prospectuses do not apply.

Misleading statements and advertising (s 47) This section, like ss 13 and 14 of the Prevention of Fraud (Investments) Act 1958 creates criminal liability only.

Cold calling (s 56) By contrast with the position under s 47 civil consequences do flow from breach of s 56. Any investment agreement entered into as a result of the call is unenforceable against the person on whom the call was made and that person is entitled to recover any money or property paid or transferred under the agreement together with the compensation for any loss sustained by him as a result of parting with it.[3] However, in certain very limited situations the court may allow such an agreement to be enforced.[4] The person on whom the call was made is responsible for returning what he has received in exchange for what he has parted with — normally the security for the return of the purchase price.[5] However, the investor may well have parted with the investment by selling it on to a third party in which case he must return its value at the date of the cold call.[6]

Restrictions on advertising (s 57) Where the restrictions on advertising are breached a criminal offence is committed with a penalty on conviction on indictment of imprisonment for a term not exceeding two years or a

1 S 151(5). International securities are defined as a debenture 'which is of a kind likely to be dealt in by bodies incorporated in or persons resident in a country or territory outside the United Kingdom, is denominated in a currency other than sterling, or is otherwise connected with such a country or territory.'
2 S 160.
3 S 56.
4 S 56(2).
5 S 56(4).
6 S 56(6).

fine or both. In addition the investor has civil remedies parallel to those for cold calling.

COMPLICATIONS OF CORPORATE LIABILITY

Complications can arise with regard to the liability of corporations because corporations are necessarily abstract and can only act through their employees.

The essential liability of an employer in tort rests firmly on principles of agency. Nor does it make the slightest difference that the employer is a corporation. The position was well summarised by Lord Diplock in *Tesco Supermarket v Nattrass*.[1]

> A corporation is an abstraction. It is incapable itself of doing any physical act or being in any state of mind. Yet in law it is a person capable of exercising legal rights and of being subject to legal liabilities which may involve ascribing to it not only physical acts done by a natural person on its behalf but also the mental state in which that person did them. In civil law, apart from certain statutory duties, this presents no conceptual difficulties. Under the law of agency the physical acts and state of mind of the agent are in law ascribed to the principal, and if the agent is a natural person it matters not whether the principal is also a natural person or a mere legal abstraction. *Qui facit per alium facit per se: qui cogitat per alium cogitat per se.*[2]

The majority of civil cases can thus be disposed of by the established conceptions of agency which allows the knowledge of the agent to be imputed to the principal. Different considerations apply, however, where the responsibility of the employer is to be determined by processes which demand a reprehensible state of mind in the principal itself. This was also recognised by Lord Diplock in *Tesco Supermarkets v Nattrass* for his Lordship went on to say:

> But there are some civil liabilities imposed by statute which, exceptionally, exclude the concept of vicarious liability of a principal for the physical acts and state of mind of his agent; and the concept has no general application in the field of criminal law.[3]

The position of a company in such a situation was ably summed up by Denning LJ thirty years ago when he said:

> Some of the people in the company are mere servants and agents who are nothing more than the hands to do the work and cannot be said to represent the mind or will. Others are directors and managers who represent the directing mind and will of the company, and control what it does. The state of mind of these managers is the state of mind of the company and is treated by the law as such. So you will find that in cases where the law requires personal

1 [1972] AC 153.
2 at pp. 198–199.
3 at p. 199.

> fault as a condition of liability in tort, the fault of the manager will be the personal fault of the company.[1]

In the *Tesco* case Lord Reid went on to explain:

> Normally the board of directors, the managing directors and perhaps other superior officers of a company carry out the functions of management and speak and act as the company. Their subordinates do not. They carry out orders from above and it can make no difference that they are given some measure of discretion. But the board of directors may delegate some part of their functions of management giving to their delegate full discretion to act independently of instructions from them. I see no difficulty in holding that they have thereby put such a delegate in their place so that within the scope of the delegation he can act as the company. It may not always be easy to draw the line but there are cases in which the line must be drawn.[2]

In short, by being given actual authority to carry out the particular task the agent becomes the alter ego of the company by a process of delegation.

The question, however, then arises as to whether these limitations on the knowledge of the agent giving rise to liability are restricted to the criminal sphere or extend to civil liability. It will be recollected that Lord Diplock was of the opinion that it did for he said, after stating the straightforward agency principle, 'there are some civil liabilities imposed by statute which exclude the concept of the vicarious liability of the principle for the . . . state of mind of his agent'. This must necessarily be so given the supremacy of Parliament; whether a statute has such an effect will be a matter of construction of the particular statute involved with all its attendant difficulties and potential inconsistencies.

An important illustration of such restriction of liability by reason of statute applicable to the issue of international bonds and certificates of deposit arises from The Statute of Frauds Amendment Act 1828, s 6 of which provides:

> No Action shall be brought whereby to charge any Person upon or by reason of any Representation or Assurance made or given concerning or relating to the Character, Conduct, Credit, Ability, Trade or Dealings of any other Person, to the intent or Purpose that such other Person may obtain Credit, Money or Goods upon, unless such Representations or Assurance be made in Writing, signed by the Party to be changed therewith.

In *UBAF Ltd v European American Banking Corpn*[3] the defendant U.S. bank invited the plaintiff British bank to participate in two loans to be made to two associated corporate clients of the U.S. bank. Information was given

1 *H L Bolton (Engineering) Co Ltd v T J Graham & Sons Ltd* [1957] 1 QB 159 at p. 172. See also Viscount Haldane in *Lennard's Carrying Co Ltd v Asiatic Petroleum Co Ltd* [1915] AC 705 at 713.

2 *Tesco Ltd v Nattrass* [1972] AC 153 at 171. Lord Diplock pointed out that the correct starting point to ascertain those who represent the directing mind of the company was from a construction of the articles of association (p.199). The delegation principle was accepted by the House but none of their Lordships found that there was a delegation on the facts.

3 [1984] 2 All ER 226.

by the U.S. bank relating to the loans, the securities for the loans, and the affairs of the two client companies. The loans were made but the two companies ran into increasing difficulties and it became clear that large sums would never be repaid. The plaintiff alleged *inter alia* that the information given to it, which had induced it to participate in the loan, was inaccurate at the time it was supplied and known to be so by the defendant. The information had been supplied with a covering letter signed by one Francios Macheras as assistant secretary of the defendant—a position which to English ears is without any clear definition. The defendant argued that the signature did not constitute the signature of a party to be charged (the defendant company) within the meaning of the section.

In the nineteenth century the purpose of the section had been clearly stated by Bramwell B in *Swift v Jewsbury*[1] when he said: 'In my opinion the effect of the statute is this, that a man should not be liable for a fraudulent representation as to another person's means unless he puts it down in writing and acknowledges his responsibility for it by his own signature.' The requirement of the maker's own signature had led the argument to be advanced that the section could not apply to corporations since they can only sign through human means but this argument had been rejected in the early part of the century.[2]

What then would constitute the signature of a company? In *UBAF Ltd v European American Banking Corpn* counsel for the defendant sought to restrict the term to those who, in the words of Lord Reid, speak and act for the company conceding only that the alter ego principle would extend to make acceptable a signature where the signer had been specifically authorized by the board to sign the documents in question. These, of course, are the most obvious examples of actual authority. Often, however, an agent's authority will be implied from the status conferred upon him by his actual employment within the company, because it is generally understood that those holding a particular function have particular powers, and these will be viewed as part of the agent's contract unless the contrary is agreed. The fact that the powers are implied makes them no less actual. The Court of Appeal was prepared to take the signature requirement as being satisfied by such an implied authority, saying 'the signature on behalf of a company of its duly authorised agent acting within the scope of his authority is, for the purpose of s 6 of the 1828 Act, the signature of the company'.

The overall effect of the approach of the Court of Appeal to the statute was therefore less restrictive than that argued for by counsel for the defendant. The essential restriction which appears to derive from the judgment is that, in evaluating whether or not the signature is that of the company, the court will not use the concept of constructive authority, limiting its approach to actual authority although allowing the actual authority to arise by implication. Such an approach is consistent with the

1 (1874) LR 9 QB 301.

2 *Hirst v West Riding Union Banking Co Ltd* [1901] 2 KB 560; *Banbury v Bank of Montreal* [1918] AC 626 affirming [1917] 1 KB 409 CA.

concepts used by the House of Lords in *Tesco v Nattrass* demanding only that the alter ego be actually appointed.

One general area in which there has been careful control of the general agency approach at common law has been the field of fraudulent misrepresentation. Even a civil allegation of fraud in English law has always been treated as a serious matter necessarily involving a reprehensible state of mind on the part of the defendant. English common law has refused to hold a master liable for his employee's misrepresentation on the basis of fraudulent misrepresentation where the servant making the misrepresentation honestly believed it to be true, but another servant or the master himself knew the statement to be false but did not know that it was being made.[1] To do so from the moral point of view is to take two innocent states of mind and by adding them together to produce the fraudulent one, a position no doubt of little difficulty to justify from the point of view of the theoretical moralist, but perhaps more remarkable from the point of view of simple legal analysis of civil liability. Nevertheless, the law has been left on its simple moral basis.

This is not a true exception to the principal of employer liability for the acts of its agents. It is simply a refusal to allow the addition of fragmented knowledge, innocent in its fragmented state, to produce a guilty whole. Thus if a servant makes a statement, known by him to be untrue, to his master or a fellow servant, in the expectation that the untruth will be passed on to the person to be deceived the master will be liable, for here all elements of deceit are drawn together in the prime actor, the deceitful servant, and the master or fellow servant are merely his agent for the distribution of the information.[2] The position can be reversed, so that if a servant makes an inaccurate statement innocently but a fellow servant or the master knows that the statement, whilst inaccurate, will be made but does not inform the innocent servant of the inaccuracy, the master will be liable, for the necessary guilty state of mind exists in the master or servant with the necessary knowledge and the innocent servant becomes merely the agent of the guilty.[3] The distinctions, whilst logically justifiable, seem somewhat narrow as a basis for imposing or refusing legal liability. Fortunately, the importance of this somewhat arcane area has, in general, decreased with the imposition of liability for negligent misrepresentation.

1 *Cornfoot v Fowke* (1840) 6 M & W 358; *Armstrong v Strain* [1952] 1 KB 232, CA.

2 *London County Freehold and Leasehold Properties Ltd v Berkeley Property and Investment Co Ltd* [1936] 2 All ER 1039 CA as explained in *Armstrong v Strain.*

3 *Ludgate v Lowe* (1881) 44 LT 694 CA. But what of the position where the master or servant while knowing the information to be false has no intention of misleading the third party? Is not a vital element of deceit missing?—Wright (1937) 15 Can Bar Rev 716. It is difficult to see an English court allowing a defendant to escape on this argument—it would almost certainly find against him on the facts.

CIVIL REMEDIES IN THE UNITED STATES

While in England and Wales and most other jurisdictions international bonds are marketed pursuant to the private placement or professionals-only exemption, in the case of the U.S., as has been discussed,[1] every effort is made to prevent the securities being distributed in that jurisdiction. What, however, are the civil liabilities which occur when the arrangements made are inadequate to satisfy the requirements of that jurisdiction, and bonds are issued to U.S. residents? In fact considerable remedies are conferred by the laws of that jurisdiction on purchasers of securities the subject of an unregistered issue, which stand in marked contrast to the position at common law in England and Wales.[2]

In the U.S. there are general common law remedies roughly parallel to those available at English law. Since these are so unremarkably similar no further reference will be made to them. Of more crucial interest are the statutory remedies arising from breaches of the system of U.S. securities regulation, the severity of which do constitute a significant consideration in structuring a bond issue so that no part of the initial distribution is made to the U.S., and which, through the reach of rule 10(b)(5), have had the potential to give a remedy to a purchaser even when the issue is not made to the U.S. To understand the plethora of remedies it is necessary to look at both of the major sections of the 1933 Act, ss 11 and 12, as well as rule 10(b)(5). Rule 10(b)(5) will be examined as it has had, on previous judicial interpretation, the capacity to impinge on an international bond issue structured so as not to include the U.S. within the area of initial sales. Section 11 will be examined because, although it does not apply to an international bond issue unless the issuer chooses to register it pursuant to the 1933 Act, the width of the remedy created by the courts pursuant to the section illustrates clearly the radical imposition of liability which would arise if rule 10(b)(5) were ever to be applied by the U.S. courts to an international bond issue. Section 12 will be examined because it is precisely the section applicable where an unregistered issue is made where no exemption is applicable to justify the lack of registration, as could arise if an issue were not structured in such a way as to satisfy the requirements of the S.E.C.'s no action letters or the demands of the Commission itself. The position under s 12 will be examined first.

Section 12—the unregistered issue

Where an unregistered issue is made, and no exemption is applicable to justify the lack of registration, s 12(1) specifically allows the purchaser to recover the consideration paid for the securities purchased by him together with interest by tendering the security. He must, however, give credit for any income received from the security during the time that he has held it. Where he has sold the security he is entitled to sue for damages for any loss suffered, if he has obtained a price for the security less than that

1 *ante* ch 4.

2 In the case of a distribution *registered* under the 1933 Act, extensive protection is given to investors by s 11.

which he paid for it. Any action in reliance on this provision must be brought by the purchaser within one year from the sale of the security in violation of the registration requirements.[1] Responsibility under this provision arises even though the seller of the securities acting in good faith and reasonably, but erroneously, believed that the distribution was in accordance with an applicable exemption from the registration requirements.[2] Potentially, this is a provision of wide application when it is remembered that, where an exemption from registration is claimed in respect of an issue, it is for the seller to establish that such an exemption is applicable.

This provision is buttressed by s 12(2) of the same Act, which makes actionable any statement of a material fact which is false or misleading because of the omission of a material fact in the sale of a security to a purchaser, unless the purchaser was aware of the falsity or misleading nature of the statement. In these circumstances there is a liability upon the defendant, unless the defendant can prove 'that he did not know, and in the exercise of reasonable care could not have known, of such untruths or omission'. This provision is applicable not merely to an unregistered issue which should have been registered, but also to an unregistered issue which can fairly rely on one of the exemptions from the registration requirements. Again a sale in breach of these requirements entitles the purchaser to recover the price he paid plus interest, less any income received from the investment on returning the securities to the seller. If the purchaser has ceased to own the securities he may sue for damages.

The basic effect of s 12 is therefore to give a remedy to a purchaser but that remedy is bounded by the basic requirement of privity of contract; the investor can only sue the person who sold to him. This is an important restriction on the liability of underwriters for, where an issuer sells the securities to the underwriters, and the underwriters resell to the investors, the investors have no privity with the issuer and there is no direct liability of the issuer to them.[3] The exact extent, however, by which the operation of the remedies is restricted by the privity concept is not entirely clear. Purchasers have been allowed by the courts to sue successfully persons other than the actual seller to them where those other persons' participation 'is a substantial factor in causing the transaction to take place'. On the other hand their 'mere participation in the events leading up to the transaction is not enough'.[4]

The position of the S.E.C. is that s 12 imposes liability not merely on the seller but anyone who aids and abets him in the actual sale of the securities.[5] The courts do seem to have been prepared to adopt the S.E.C. view by a process of statutory interpretation which has led to the introduction

1 Securities Act 1933, s 13.
2 *Woodward v Wright* 266 F 2d 108, 115 (10th Cir 1959).
3 *Collins v Signetics* 605 F 2d 110 (3rd Cir 1979).
4 *Pharo v Smith* 621, F 2d 656 (5th Cir 1980).
5 Brief for the S.E.C. as *amicus curiae* 71–76 *Blackwell v Bentsen*, 203 F 2d 690 (5th Cir 1953); *Petit v American Stock Exch* 217. F Supp 21 (S.D.N.Y. 1963).

of 'an extremely liberal standard of privity . . .'[1] The cases are confused and not easy to reconcile[2] but perhaps one illustration can be given. In *Katz v Amos Treat & Co*[3] the investor was a dentist and an experienced and knowledgeable investor. The shares were purchased from the issuer. The transaction was a preliminary to the actual issue which was to be underwritten by the defendant underwriters. An employee of those underwriters, one Nardone, had interested the plaintiff in the purchase of the securities, had recommended them to him, and had introduced him to the President of the issuing company. The underwriters received no commission, however, in respect of the transaction between the plaintiff and issuer. Also involved in the plaintiff's deliberations as to whether to purchase the stock was one Wofsey, a lawyer in charge of preparing the registration statement for the subsequent public issue, who had recommended the issue as a good one. The court held that it would be permissible for a jury to find that the underwriters were participating in the sale as brokers for all that there was no underwriting commission, and could therefore be liable on that ground. Further, that a jury could find, on the evidence available, that the underwriters actively solicited the plaintiff's offer to buy and were liable on that basis. Presumably Nardone would equally be responsible on this latter basis. Further, the courts were of the opinion that Wofsey's actions were sufficient for a jury to be able to find that he had been a party to the solicitation, and had therefore participated in the sale.

Clearly, the way is open for liability to be imposed on issuers, underwriters, dealers, and professional advisers who actually promote the sales of securities in breach of s 12 whether privity exists or not.[4]

Apart from the liberal interpretation given to the privity requirement there seems to be a general move in the U.S. to allow s 12 to have a wide effect upon those involved in the distribution of an issue of securities. A decisive case is the case of *Sanders v John Nuveen & Co Inc*[5] where the distribution of securities by a finance company had been effected with 42 purchasers pursuant to exempt transactions. The defendant had acted as underwriter. Some of the purchasers had received written reports relating to the company from the defendant, and the defendant had made oral representations to some of the others. However, the defendant had neither sent the report nor made any oral representations to many of the purchasers. The issuer of the securities had completely and fraudulently misrepresented his financial position and in this the issuer's auditors had knowingly assisted.

1 *In re Caesars Palace Securities Litigation* 360 F Supp 366 (E.D. pa 1973).
2 The case law is discussed Bloomenthal *Securities Regulation* Vol 3a 8.20 et seq.
3 411 F 2d 1046 (2nd Cir 1969).
4 It should also be noted that anyone controlling the seller can be separately liable for breach of s 12 by virtue of the provisions of s 15.
5 619 F 2d 1222 (7th Cir 1980) cert. denied 450 U.S. 1005 (1981). (Justices Powell and Rehquist dissented both on the meaning put on reasonable care and the denial of the right of the underwriter to rely on the auditors' report without investigation.)

The defendant, however, was not aware of the fraud. Nevertheless he was found liable.

The court held that the fact that many of the purchasers had been the recipients neither of a report nor any oral representations was irrelevant. The plaintiffs in an action based on s 12(2) do not have to establish reliance on the inaccurate material.[1] It would appear that it is merely sufficient that the material is used as part of the general promotion of the sales effort. The court pointed out that s 12(2) requires merely that the defendant should sell a security by 'means of a prospectus or oral communication which includes an untrue statement'. The court held that once a prospectus (in the particular case the reports) containing a misleading statement was distributed to some of the purchasers the requirement of the section was satisfied.

Secondly, the court held that there was no responsibility on the plaintiff to exercise reasonable care, and that therefore in giving a remedy against the defendant no distinction should be made between sophisticated and unsophisticated investors.

Finally, the court held that for an underwriter (but no other type of defendant) to establish the defence that he had exercised 'reasonable care', it was necessary for him to prove that he had made a reasonable investigation before accepting and using the inaccurate information which had been placed before him. In the case of defendants other than underwriters there may or may not arise a responsibility to make investigation to discharge the burden of exercising reasonable care. In respect of these defendants their responsibilities will be decided upon their particular role in the distribution process and the circumstances of the distribution.

In so doing the effect of the court's decision is to put the burden on the defendant in establishing 'reasonable care' within s 12(2) on the same basis as the burden upon a defendant to establish the due diligence defence under s 11 which expressly requires the proof of reasonable investigation. Indeed, in one respect, it appears that the burden that arises under s 12(2) is wider than that which arises under s 11 for in general under s 11 there is no duty to investigate that portion of the material given to the underwriters which was prepared by experts. This is because it is clearly impracticable to expect that a non-expert will be able to investigate and pass judgment upon an expert's report. However, the expert par excellence has generally been considered to be the auditor. The effect of the *Sanders* case therefore appears to be that where under s 12(2) the duty to investigate arises it extends to both the expertised and the non-expertised portions of the issuer's material.

Clearly, the remedies available to a U.S. investor in respect of misleading statements in promotional material including the prospectus are considerably wider than those available to their English counterpart at common law. Under s 12(2) the investor is helped by a considerably widened and liberal use of the privity concept, and further assistance comes from the fact that it is not necessary that he should have relied on the promotional material

[1] See also on this point *John Hopkins Univ v Hutton* 422 F 2d 1124 (4th Cir 1970).

in making his investment decision. In part this arises because of the U.S. willingness to use the civil remedies made available to purchasers as part of the policing mechanism of the system of securities regulation. Those involved in issuing and distributing securities are likely to regard the possibility of being sued by disgruntled investors for considerable sums of money as a considerable penalty if care is not used. Plainly, this will not deter the desperate and the fraudulent, who will envisage being either insolvent or absent from the jurisdiction when the law-suits flow in. However, with regard to the respectable institutions within the distribution process, the threat of a multiplicity of law-suits is likely to ensure that they take the greatest possible care, and apply the highest possible standards to the issues in which they become involved.

The anti-fraud provision—Rule 10b-5

The evolution of a wide use of s 12 would seem unlikely to be motivated entirely by the public good aspect of the policing function. As with England. the principal common law remedy against the misleading prospectus has been the action of deceit with all the difficulties of proof which this entails. It is almost certainly legal impatience with the traditional common law remedies which has caused the courts to seek to evolve s 2 to its fullest extent. The same process has had a dramatic effect elsewhere in the evolution of remedies for investors. In contrast to the English reluctance to give civil remedies for breach of the regulations governing securities distribution, except where statutes specifically provide for one, the U.S. courts have taken a much more creative role and to this end have made use of rule 10b–5. However, it must be acknowledged that recent decisions of the Supreme Court indicate a clear movement toward restricting the use of this rule to give civil remedies.

The terms and potential scope of this broad anti-fraud device has already been examined.[1] The very width of the provision makes it an important weapon in the armoury of the investor if a breach of its terms confers a civil remedy upon the person affected. The rule applies to any purchase or sale by any person of any security whatsoever. It therefore applies to securities which are registered and those which are not, either because they are sold pursuant to some exemption such as a private offering, or which should have been registered pursuant to the terms of the legislation but were not. It therefore follows that a particular set of facts may disclose both a breach of s 11 or s 12 and also a breach of rule 10b–5. Given the frequent overlap it might be thought that there is little reason for a court to imply a civil remedy under the rule when express civil remedies are conferred by s 11 and s 12. However if a civil remedy is implied for a breach of a rule this will have the effect that an investor will have a remedy in circumstances where no remedy is available elsewhere,[2] or there is a remedy but the investor is in difficulties with procedural matters governing

1 *ante* p. 108.

2 As in *Fischman v Raytheon Mfg Co* 188 F 2d 783 (2nd Cir 1951) where the securities had been purchased on the open market and not from the issuer.

the remedy, for instance the short one-year time limit for commencing an action under s 12.

The effect of rule 10b–5 is simply to prohibit certain functions. By virtue of the prohibition the actions become unlawful. However, the courts have been prepared to confer a remedy upon a purchaser by implying a private right of action in favour of a person injured as a result of a violation of the rule, who was within the class of persons that the prohibition was intended to protect.[1] The mere fact that a private right of action is conferred does not, of course, indicate its boundaries. Much depends upon the policy which the courts perceive as underlying the legislation. This can clearly be seen by the changing view which the courts have expressed with regard to the issue of defining who can bring an action. In the 1960s and early 1970s the courts were prepared to give as wide reading as possible to imply private rights of action for anyone who could show some loss however remotely connected with the alleged violation. This was done by the broad meaning put upon the words 'purchase or sale' and 'connection' that related them.[2] However, in 1975 in the important case of *Blue Chip Stamps v Manor Drugstores*,[3] the Supreme Court indicated a clear and dramatic change in their perception of the requirements of the underlying policy. The court indicated clearly that it was concerned that 'vexatious' litigation should be limited, and that priority should be given to this end. The court took the view that actions based upon federal security law were particularly liable to give rise to vexatious litigation. It further was concerned about broadening the class of potential plaintiffs so as to create 'a liability in an indeterminate amount for an indeterminate time to an indeterminate class'. Finally, the court was concerned at the clear potential conflict between the procedural restrictions placed upon the express remedies conferred by the Act and the lack of such requirements in the implied remedy under rule 10b–5[4]. In the circumstances the court was prepared to allow a remedy only to 'a purchaser' or 'seller', and these terms should be strictly construed.

If the delineation of the class of persons on whom a civil right of action is conferred has proceeded from a broad liberal approach to the imposition of a conservative and restrictive approach since 1975, a similar history can be detected in the evolution of the mental elements required to lead to a defendant having liability imposed upon him. It should not be forgotten that the provisions of rule 10b are anti-fraud. The issue that has arisen is whether a defendant will be found to have breached the rule only if a defendant's actions were deliberate, or whether liability would be imposed also where he was reckless, or even when he was merely negligent as by

1 The earliest authority is now nearly 40 years old. *Kandon v National Gypsum Co* 69 F Supp 512 (E.D. Pa 1946). In doing so the courts were merely applying traditional tort principles. The same approach has been applied to other prohibitions within the securities legislation eg SEA s 10(b), 15(c)(1), SA s 17(1).

2 *S.E.C. v National Securities* 393 US 453 (1969); *Sup't of Insurance v Bankers Life and Casualty Co* 404 US 6 (1971).

3 421 US 723 (1975). See also *Piper v Chris – Craft Industries* 430 US 1 (1977).

4 pp. 938–9.

failing to prevent wrongdoing by others for whose actions he had some responsibility. The extent of a defendant's responsibility for the acts of others is, of course, of the greatest importance in respect of civil liability for misrepresentations involved in an issue. If the issuer is corporate and a prospectus is issued on the authority of the directors, half of whom know of its inaccuracy and the other half of whom do not because they rely upon the bona fides of their more active colleagues, those who are ignorant will not be liable in damages unless responsibility arises in negligence. Further, those who advise an issuer, whether corporate or otherwise, such as underwriters, lawyers, and accountants, may be responsible for failing to exercise due care where they rely upon information given to them by the issuer, but would escape responsibility when they innocently assist in the distribution of securities.

In the expansionist period of the 1960s and early 1970s the Supreme Court was prepared to give wide effect to the anti-fraud provisions. A wide meaning was placed upon the concept of fraud so that liability could be imposed upon people who had been involved in the distribution without deliberately participating in the fraud.[1]

In 1976 the Supreme Court in *Ernst & Ernst v Hochfelder*[2] reversed the previous liberal approach, and adopted a restrictive approach based upon a literal reading of the rule and the statute under which it was made. The court noted that s 10(b) under which the rule was made proscribed 'any manipulative or deceptive device or contrivance'. In the view of the court 'manipulative' had a precise meaning: 'it connotes intentional or wilful conduct designed to deceive or defraud investors by controlling or artificially affecting the price of securities'. This coupled with the use of the terms 'device' and 'contrivance' clearly indicated that the intention of Congress was to proscribe conduct quite different from negligence and 'clearly connotes intentional misconduct . . .'[3] The court buttressed its view by looking at the legislative history of the legislation,[4] and pointed out that those provisions of the Act which impose liability for negligent conduct do so explicitly, and 'subject to significant procedural restrictions not applicable under s.10(b)'.[5]

The effect of the Supreme Court's decision is that a civil remedy will only be conferred for breach of rule 10b–5 where knowledge, or to use the word prominent in the American writing 'scienter', can be shown.[6]

1 *S.E.C. v Capital Gains Research Bureau* 375 US 180 (1963); *Affiliated Ute Citizens of Utah v US* 406 U.S. 128 (1972).

2 96 S Ct 1375 (1976). See also *Santa Fe Industries v Green*, 430 US 462 (1977). *Aaron v S.E.C.* 446 US 680 (1980). The latter case is interesting for the Supreme Court demanded scienter for an implied remedy under s 10(b) but not for a comparable remedy under Securities Act 1933, s 17(a). In fact, it appears that rule 10b–5 was adapted from the language of s 17a.

3 at p. 1384.

4 at p. 1385.

5 at p. 1388.

6 The court did not consider whether scienter was necessary for the S.E.C. to be able to obtain an injunction to prevent breaches of Rule 10b–5. It is probable that it is not.

Nor did they consider the question whether in some circumstances reckless behaviour is sufficient for civil liability to arise. The court defined scienter for the purposes of its decision simply as an intention to deceive. It seems probable that the scienter requirement will be satisfied by proof of the defendant's recklessness and that recklessness will be applied at least as widely as the formula in *Derry v Peek*.[1] Whether any more liberal interpretation will be placed upon recklessness to widen the scope of the remedy for potential plaintiffs is not clear, but the present composition and attitude of the Supreme Court would seem to suggest that a liberal approach along these lines would not be likely to receive support if the issue reaches the highest U.S. court.

However, not all cases do reach the highest court and some federal district courts continue to hold the scienter satisfied in circumstances where it is sometimes difficult to see conduct which could be categorised as reckless on the *Derry v Peek* formulation.[2] The courts have been particularly severe on accountants. In one case the accountants were held liable in drawing accounts which showed a receipt in respect of a transaction which had not at that time been effected, and in respect of which the monies shown had not in fact been received. The court emphasised the positive responsibility of the accountants to ensure that the accounts were properly drawn in accordance with generally accepted accounting principles, and that their obligations extended beyond the mere checking of the arithmetic of the company's book-keepers.[3] In another case accountants were held liable where they failed to disclose material facts known to them although they did not appreciate their significance.[4] A further firm of accountants has been held responsible when, in the view of the court, they failed to observe generally accepted auditing procedures.[5] It may well be that as yet the full implications of the change of policy evidenced by the Supreme Court have not established themselves at district level; at best the cases reveal a considerable potential for difference between one judge and another in applying the recklessness formula. In any event there remains a considerable element of uncertainty.

One area in which the remedies available under rule 10b–5 have been, and remain, liberal is on the issue of whether or not a plaintiff must have relied upon the false information put forward by the defendant. The courts have recognised that it may be that someone, who has not read the false information, may nevertheless suffer as a result of it. Accordingly, there are decisions which have allowed actions to proceed even where some at least of the plaintiffs purchase their securities without having read the

1 Bloomenthal *Securities and Federal Corporate Law*, Clark Boardman Ltd, New York (1987 Rev.) Vol. 3A 9–135. See eg *Sanders v John Nuveen* 554 F 2d 790 (7th Cir 1977).

2 The point is discussed Bloomenthal *op. cit.* 9–136 *et seq.*

3 *Henzfeld v Laventhol, Krekstein, Horwath and Horwath 540* F 2d 27 34–35 (2nd Cir 1976).

4 *McLean v Alexander*, 420 F Supp. 1078 (D. Del 1976).

5 *Adams v Standard Knitting Mills* ['76–'77 Transfer Binder) Fed Sec L Rep (CCH) 96, 683 (E.D. Tenn. 1976).

allegedly false information put forward. To meet the problem a general rather than a specific reliance test has been put forward. To be able to recover a plaintiff who has not read the misleading information must prove that the effect of the false information had been to inflate the market price of the security because the general public had relied upon it, and that he, the plaintiff, had purchased at the inflated price without realising the artificiality of the market price.[1] This seems to be a considerable improvement upon the simple requirement of specific reliance, which was represented by the traditional U.S. approach and is still the governing principle behind English law. The simple approach does not recognise the sophisticated workings of the financial market, and the ways in which investors can be injured as a result of the deceitful conduct of others. Of course, in dealing with the imposition of liability for mere negligence there would be strong policy arguments for limiting the defendants' liability to those who have directly acted on the misleading information supplied to them.

A further mitigation of the reliance principle introduced by some courts would appear to be no longer reliable in the light of the restrictive policy now adopted by the Supreme Court. In its earlier more liberal days, however, the Supreme Court in a rule 10b–5 action had held that if there was a duty to disclose, and the information not disclosed was material, the plaintiff could recover without the need to establish reliance.[2] It would appear from that case itself that the court was not merely dealing with the failure to disclose material information required to be included because of the scheme of securities regulation, but also failure to disclose material information the absence of which would have affected the judgment of a prudent investor.

Liability under section 11

The effect of increasing restrictions, which the Supreme Court has placed upon the use of rule 10b–5 as a means of giving investors civil remedies, contrasts starkly with the liberality of the statutory remedies conferred on investors for misleading information by the Securities Act 1933, s 11. While s 11 will rarely, if ever, apply to an international bond issue because of the means employed to keep the issue out of the U.S. and prevent registration being necessary, s 11, and some of the cases decided under it, are of considerable interest as the previously liberal approach of the courts in conferring a wide civil remedy for investors under the anti-fraud provisions had the effect of increasingly assimilating those remedies to the wide base of those available under s 11. Given the extra-territorial effect which the

1 *Siegal v Realty Equities Corp.* 54 FRD 420 (S.D.N.Y. 1972); *Accord Blackie v Barrack*, 524 F 2d 891 (9th Cir 1975); *Pearson v Ecological Science Corp*, CCH Fed Sec L Rep 94, 030 (S.D.N.Y. 1973). See also the important 5th Cir decision *Shores v Sklar* 647 F 2d 462 (5th Cir 1981) and *Panzirer v Wolf* 663 F 2d 365 (2nd Cir 1981) cert. granted 6–28–82 (Dkt. 81–1998).

2 *Affiliated Ute Citizens of Utah v United States*, 406 US 128 (1972). See also *Korn v Franchard Corp* 456 F 2d 1206 (2nd Cir 1972); *Victorian Investors v Responsive Environments Corp.*, CCH Fed Sec L Rep ('72–'73 Transfer Binder) 93, 661 (S.D.N.Y. 1972).

U.S. courts have given to the anti-fraud provisions, it can readily be seen that a change of policy by the Supreme Court from its present restrictive and conservative stance could lead the issuers of international bonds and their advisers to have great interest in the potential lengths to which the U.S. courts will go in giving wide ranging remedies to investors against all those involved in the distribution process. In such a situation the clearest indications of the policy of the U.S. courts, and the concepts with which they most customarily work, will be found in s 11 and its accumulated case law.

The purpose of Congress in enacting s 11 was to provide a wide remedy to investors purchasing securities on the faith of misleading information in which the obstacles to recovery inherent in the technicalities of the action for deceit, and, to a lesser extent, the right to rescind a contract would play no part. It seems probable that inherent in the policies underpinning s 11 is the belief that one of the most effective ways of policing the operation of the system of securities regulation is to give to the disgruntled investor the widest possible remedies, thus both protecting the injured investor, and deterring issuers and their advisers from acting other than with the highest possible probity and care.

Accordingly, s 11 provides that if a registration statement, when it became effective to cover an issue, 'contained an untrue statement of a material fact or omitted to state a material fact required to be stated therein or necessary to make the statements therein not misleading', an investor acquiring any security covered by the registration document can maintain an action.

It should be noted that there is no restriction limiting the remedy conferred to purchases upon the initial issue of the securities. In this connection all that an investor has to prove is that he acquired the security and that it was covered by the registration document.

The purchaser's right is to sue those responsible for the difference between the price which the purchaser paid for the security (not being greater than the public offering price), and the price for which he eventually sold the security, or, where he still owns it, its value at the time of the action.

As with s 12(2) there is no requirement that the investor should have relied upon the misleading information given to him.[1] There is, however, an exception to this as s 11(a) provides that a plaintiff cannot recover if it is proved that at the time of his acquisition of the security he knew of the untruth of the misleading statement.

While the investor need not show that he relied upon the misleading information he must show that it was 'material'. This is defined in Securities Act, rule 405 as 'matters to which an average prudent investor ought reasonably to be informed before purchasing the security registered'. In

1 There is, however, an exception where the investor bought the securities after the issuer had made generally available an earnings statement covering a period of at least twelve months from the effective date of the registration statement. In such circumstances an investor must show reliance: s 11(a). Will general reliance be sufficient?

the leading case of *Escott v Bar Cris Corpn*[1] the court accepted the view of the S.E.C. that a material fact is 'a fact which if it had been correctly stated or disclosed would have deterred or tended to deter the average prudent investor from purchasing the security in question'.[2] The court pointed out that the average prudent investor would not concern himself with minor inaccuracies, but would be concerned with 'facts which have an important bearing upon the nature or condition of the issuing corporation or its business'.[3]

Given that under s 11 an investor can sue for the difference between what he paid for the security and its value at the time of the action, it might be thought, at first sight, that the investor is given an insurance policy against bad investments regardless of whether the loss arises from the false information. In fact this is not so. Section 11(e) allows a defendant to defeat or reduce a claim to the extent that he can show that the decline in value of the security resulted from causes other than the mis-statement in, or omission from, the registration statement. The effect of this is of course to reverse the burden of proof and place it upon the defendant, but if the defendant can discharge that burden, he can eliminate or reduce the investor's claim.[4] In this s 11 differs from s. 12(2) which has no comparable provision. In the leading case of *Feit v Leasco Data Processing Equipment*[5] the court took judicial notice of the fact that there had been a considerable general decline in stock market prices which would have affected the investment in any event. Accordingly, they reduced the plaintiff's damages by an appropriate percentage to reflect this extraneous and inevitable loss. Nevertheless, given the difficulties of proving the precise cause of the decline in value of an investment the effect of reversing the burden of proof is to improve dramatically a plaintiff's chance of recovery from that which obtains under the traditional principle of recovery at common law, which, in both the U.S. and England, leaves the burden upon the plaintiff of showing that his loss was directly caused by the misleading prospectus.

To English eyes perhaps the most remarkable thing about s 11 is the range of persons who are liable to an action brought by the investor. The investor is entitled to sue every person who signed the registration statement, ie the issuer itself, the issuer's principle executive, financial and accounting officers, and the majority of the board of directors.[6] In addition, every director of the issuer and every person who has consented to being named as a director or as a prospective director of the issuer are made liable as is every accountant, engineer or other expert who has consented to being named, or certified a part of the registration statement, and finally, but by no means least, every underwriter. The liability is joint and several and the purchaser is entitled to sue any one of them to recover his entire loss.

1 283 F Supp 643 (S.D.N.Y. 1968).
2 at 681.
3 ibid.
4 *Beecher v Able* 435 F Supp 397 (S.D.N.Y. 1977).
5 332 F Supp. 544 (E.D.N.Y. 1971).
6 S 6.

The only exceptions are that an expert is liable only in respect of mis-statements or omissions in the portions of the registration statement which he prepared or certified, and an underwriter who underwrote only a portion of the issue on a several basis is responsible only to the aggregate public offering price of the securities which it underwrote.

The considerable burden placed upon the various personnel involved in the distribution is modified only by the provision of the 'due diligence' defence of s 11(b). While the issuer itself remains absolutely liable for the mis-statement or omission, any of the other potential defendants can escape liability if he proves that he exercised due diligence with respect to the information in the registration statement. In deciding the standard of diligence required the registration statement is divided into two portions, the expertised and non-expertised. The expertised portions are those prepared by the expert as expert and specifically referred to in his certificate or opinion included in the registration statement. The mere fact that people with an expertise have been instrumental in preparing other parts of the registration statement does not expertise those portions where the expert's job has merely been a general collator of information.[1]

With regard to the expertised portions the due diligence requirement of any defendant other than the expert himself is limited. A defendant satisfies it if 'he had no reasonable ground to believe and did not believe' that there was any material mis-statement or omission. However, with regard to the unexpertised portions the burden for all defendants is greater. The standard required is that 'he had, after reasonable investigation, reasonable ground to believe and did believe' that there was no material mis-statement or omission. This latter is also the burden placed upon the expert with regard to the expertised portion which the expert has prepared.

The greater burden imposed by the latter test is considerable for s 11(c) demands that in determining the reasonableness of the investigation and ground for belief 'the standard of reasonableness shall be that required of a prudent man in the management of his own property'. Depending upon the particular facts of the issue, the position of the defendant, his knowledge of the matters within the registration document and of the company's affairs, and his own particular expertise, the burden placed upon him may be a positive one to make investigation of facts put forward.[2] The only circumstances in which the prospective defendant can be taken to be safe in simply relying upon portions of the registration document which were put before him without investigation, is therefore with regard to expertised portions which he did not prepare, and in respesct of which he had 'no reasonable ground to believe and did not believe contained any material mis-statement or omission'.

When enacted s. 11 was considered to be so severe in the responsibilities that it imposed that some commentators saw it as the end of the underwriting and stockbroking business of the U.S. In fact, it took 35 years from enactment for the first case upon the section to be fully litigated in the U.S. courts. During those 35 years not only had Wall Street continued in business,

1 *Escott v Bar Chris Construction Corp* at 683 & 4.
2 ibid at p. 697.

but it had maintained its position as one of the leading capital markets of the world with some 27,000 registration statements having become effective involving public offerings of more than $384 billion.[1] There would seem, therefore, to be little reason to suppose that the imposition of the firm liability upon those involved in the distribution process is necessarily an impediment to the well-being of a nation's capital markets.

The leading case is *Escott v Bar Cris Construction Corpn* and it is well worth examining to see how s 11 can be used to give an investor a remedy against a wide range of personnel involved in the distribution process who have failed to maintain proper standards. While the decision is that of one district court judge alone, the case has been generally accepted as authoritative because of the cogency of the reasoning of the court,[2] and has been much discussed by writers on American securities regulation because of the wide range of issues raised by the litigation.

The action was a class action on behalf of the purchasers of debentures in the company. The debentures were sold pursuant to a registration statement which had become effective on 16 May. The issue was closed on 24 May 1961.

The issuer was a company engaged in the construction of bowling alleys and the sale of them and the supply and sale of equipment to them. From very early on after the issue of the securities the company was encountering financial problems and by 29 October 1962 it had filed a petition for arrangement under Chapter 11 of the Bankruptcy Act. Three days later it defaulted in the payment of the interest due on the debentures.

The complaints made by the plaintiffs were extensive. In essence they were that the overall picture painted by the prospectus was that of a healthy company competing strongly in a healthy industry, where the true position was that the industry was in difficulties and the company on the verge of disaster.

The court seized its opportunity to demonstrate just how far-reaching are the implications of the U.S. system of regulation. All of the many defendants were held liable but the basis of the liability and the nature of the duty they owed varied in relation to the position they held in the company or the function they had discharged in the preparation of the prospectus. All the executive internal directors of the company were held liable on the basis that they had signed a prospectus which they knew, or should have realised, was essentially false or misleading. Even those of limited education were unable to defend successfully on the basis of reliance on the expertised portions of the registration statement.[3] By contrast non-executive internal directors and company officers who had signed the document were dealt with on the basis of the knowledge which they had from the particular areas in which they dealt. A financial assistant who had signed the prospectus was held liable because he knew sufficient to know that the prospectus was misleading. The young lawyer who had collated

1 Ratner *Securities Regulation* (1980) (2nd edn) 2nd edn West Publishing Co. St Paul, Minn. p. 157.
2 The case was dealt with by Judge McLean.
3 at 685.

the information for the registration document internally was held liable because he had made no investigation of the matters referred to in the prospectus. External non-executive directors who had only joined the company shortly before the registration statement became effective were held liable on the same basis. Total inactivity and reliance on others is not sufficient. Similarly, the firms of accountants, lawyers and underwriters who had been involved in the issue were held liable on the same basis.

The framework of s 11 is of considerable interest to the international bond market for all that its offerings are rarely registered pursuant to that section. The evolution by the U.S. courts of the civil remedy available for breach of rule 10b–5, prior to the abrupt action of the Supreme Court in 1975 and subsequently, appeared increasingly to be leading to a width of remedy comparable to that achieved under rule 10b–5. The liabilities imposed in the *Bar Cris* case can therefore be seen as indicative of the sorts of liabilities which might well have been imposed under rule 10b–5 had that evolution continued. The potential extra-territorial effect of the anti-fraud provisions in those circumstances could easily have led to the application of the similar remedies to international bond issues. A change of political direction in the U.S. could, of course, still lead to a more liberal Supreme Court, and a reinstatement of the position which had evolved prior to 1975.

The class action

It is certainly clear that the system of securities regulation in the U.S. leads to considerably more litigation. It is only in part that this can be ascribed to the more effective remedies given to investors under the U.S. scheme. Equally important is a vital procedural difference. In England an investor who has lost money as a result of a misrepresentation and has a cause of action is left to pursue his action alone. It may therefore be that a considerable number of investors each suffer small losses individually, which they do not feel worth pursuing as individual matters, although the composite loss to the public is considerable. By contrast in the U.S. full use is made of the 'class action' permitted by the federal rules of civil procedure. This enables one or more of the affected persons to bring an action on behalf of the entire class.[1] The U.S. clearly recognises the practicalities of litigation, the expense of which is not conducive to small and complicated claims being litigated. While in one direction the class action may be said to encourage litigation by enabling a number of claims to proceed as one action, none of which would have been litigated as separate matters, it can also be said to be an efficient use of litigation, since it leads to the resolution of an amalgam of claims by the decision of one case. This coupled

1 The class action is not limited to securities litigation but is part of the U.S. general rules of procedure.

no doubt with the contingency fee, has enabled much freer litigation of investor protection issues than has been customary in this country.[1]

The bringing of a class action is governed by the Federal Rules of Civil Procedure, Rule 21, which provides that such an action may be brought where: (1) the class is so numerous that joinder of all members is impracticable, (2) there are questions of law or fact common to the class, (3) the claims of the representative parties are typical of the claims of the class, and (4) the representative parties will fairly and adequately protect the interest of the class. Over and above this a plaintiff must show one of three alternatives. First, he may establish that separate actions involve a risk of inconsistent adjudication. Secondly, he may establish that separate actions create no risk of impairment of the rights of any of the parties to the action. Finally, he may establish that the issues involving members of the class in common predominate over issues involving only individual members and the class action is the best method for adjudicating the issues.

Clearly, where a misrepresentation has been made in issued documents which have been widely circulated joinder of all parties usually will be impracticable.[2] It is not usually difficult to find someone within the class with a typically representative claim and no conflicting interests to represent the class adequately. If necessary where mis-statements have been made in a number of documents possibly relating to several issues the court may divide the class into sub-classes.[3]

Thus, in general, under s. 11 the class action is admirably suited to the task of underpinning the litigation. It was, in fact, used in both the *Bar Cris* and *Leasco* cases to which reference has already been made.

The limitations on the action, however, become more apparent when consideration is turned to the more complex issue as to whether the issues common to the class predominate over the issues individual to particular investors. Where the misrepresentation is in written form there will be no individual difficulties in showing that it was made. On the other hand where oral representations are shown to have been made, the means of proof in respect of each investor may well be substantially different in each case and accordingly in such a situation a court is reluctant to permit a class action.[4] This principle may cause some difficulties on the use of the class action for litigation involving the seeking of civil remedies under rule 10b–5. The essential point under rule 10b–5 giving rise to difficulty is the requirement that the plaintiff should show a reliance upon the document. This, of course,

1 The granting of effective practical remedies to injured investors is not merely desirable for the protection of those investors but is also one of the most effective and cheapest means of deterring breach of the highest standards in issuing procedures. Lord Denning, at least, has been prepared to contemplate the use of the contingency fee in England on the case of derivative actions but not more generally because of the lack of availability of legal aid for such actions—see his remarks in *Wallersteiner v Moir (No 2)* [1975] 1 QB 373 at p.393 et seq.

2 See, eg *Cannon v Texas Gulf Sulpher 6*, 47 FRD 60 (S.D.N.Y. 1969).

3 The power is conferred by F.R.C.P. Rule 23(c)(4)(B). See, eg *Green v Wolf Corp.* 406 F 2d 291 (2nd Cir 1968); *Blackie v Barrack* 524, F 2d 891 (9th Cir 1975).

4 *Moscarelli v Stamm* 288 F Supp 453 (E.D.N.Y. 1968).

is not a general requirement in the action under s. 11. Since each plaintiff in an action under Rule 10b–5 must show reliance, and it is a matter on which any defendant is likely to take sharp issue, it may well be that the issues involving individual members will predominate over those common to the class. This would have the effect of stunting the application of the class action to the rule 10b–5 situation. It may, however, be that the means round the problem lie in the various methods already discussed of circumventing the problem of reliance generally in rule 10b–5 actions.[1]

The burden placed upon professional advisers such as accountants, lawyers, and underwriters in cases under s 11 is considerable as shown by the *Bar Cris* case itself. Each, within the areas for which they are responsible, is converted from a mere adviser of the issuing company to a policeman on behalf of the prospective investors to which the issue will be made, and a policeman with a responsibility to make individual enquiry into the matters for which it assumes responsibility and behind which, therefore, they put their reputation. Even if the evolution of case law under rule 10(b)–5 has now been brought to an end for the foreseeable future, it may well be that the professional advisers involved will find that an equivalent responsibility is placed upon them by reason of the evolution of the principles of professional responsibility, both with regard to the class of people to whom the duty is owed and also by a consistent raising of the standards of professional care involved.

1 *Karn v Franchand Corpn* 456 F.2d 1206 (2nd Cir. 1972).

6 Bond terms[1]

The purpose of the arrangement made by the syndicate is to effect an issue of securities, whether of international bonds or international certificates of deposit, payable in accordance with their terms, and lawfully issued in accordance with the requirements of the various legal jurisdictions whose laws might have some application to them. When this has been done the securities are issued, exist in the hands of investors, and, as soon as the secondary market is established, are capable of being traded.

The securities themselves, however, come in a number of different forms, and it is worth while examining the particular provisions of the various types of security. Despite a considerable similarity between the terms of the various securities, differences do arise in relation to the variation in function between them. Convertible issues raise special complications and these will be considered in the next chapter.

THE INTERNATIONAL BOND

An instrument bond is an instrument denominated in a particular amount of specified currency (eg $5,000) and bears an individual number. The bond face recites the issue of which it is part and certifies that the issuer will pay to the bearer of the bond the principle sum of .....thousand United States dollars on .... of .... upon presentation and surrender of the bond and will further pay interest at ... per cent per annum from ... day in each year with the first payment to be made on the ... day upon presentation and surrender of the interest coupons as they become due.

The bond also refers to the trust deed where applicable and recites that the bond is subject to and carries the benefit of the provisions of the trust deed.

Interest

The coupons which carry the payment of the interest portion of the bond

[1] While there is considerable standardisation of terms in a bond issue standardisation is not complete and in any event would not guarantee standardised treatment by the courts of the various jurisdictions—see Professor N Horne 'A Uniform Approach to Eurobond Agreements' (1977) 9 *Law and Policy in International Business* 753.

are annexed to the bond itself. When one becomes payable it is simply detached from the bond and presented for payment. The coupon recites that it is payable to bearer on, and subject to, the terms and conditions endorsed on the bond to which the coupon appertains.

It therefore follows that both the bond and the coupon are issued subject to specified terms and conditions, and these can be found endorsed upon the bond itself (one is, however, bound to complain that not infrequently the conditions are set out in such small print that they are difficult to read even with the aid of a magnifying glass!). They begin by reciting much of the material which is contained on the face, but specifically provide that the holders of the bonds and the coupons are deemed to have notice of all provisions contained in the trust deed where applicable, and specify its whereabouts for consultation.

The specific individual terms may be summarised as follows:

1. *Negotiability* The securities are usually specified as being in bearer form and title thereto shall pass by delivery.[1]

2. *Interest provisions* The rate of interest is set out and the dates of payment thereof. It is normal for the bonds to contain an express provision to the effect that bonds will cease to bear interest from their due date for redemption unless, upon due presentation, payment of the principal or premium (if any) is improperly withheld or refused. The reason for this express provision is that under English law if interest is not expressed to cease on the due date then, unless the issuer makes legal tender of payment, interest will continue to run in favour of a bondholder no matter how he delays presentation, subject only to the outer limits of the period of prescription fixed by the bonds or applicable statutory limitation periods.[2] A further point of practice needs to be noted in respect of interest. It is the practice of the Eurobond market to calculate interest on the basis of 12 months of 30 days each and, where there is an incomplete month, the number of days actually elapsed where interest payable in respect of part of a year must be calculated.[3]

3. *The status of the bonds* This will be specified. It is most unusual for an international bond to be secured, and the terms will recite that the bonds constitute unsecured obligations of the issuer, and will at all times rank *pari passu* and without preference among themselves. Further, the bonds will rank *pari passu* with all other unsecured obligations of the issuer (other than subordinated obligations), subject to any mandatory exceptions applicable under the laws of the issuer's country.

4. *Negative pledge* Because the bonds are not secured obligations of the issuer, it is important that the issuer will not create further indebtedness by subsequent borrowing which creates a security ranking in preference to the particular issue of international bonds. The terms and conditions

1 Negotiability is dealt with in ch 8.
2 *Fowler v Midland Electricity Corp* [1917] 1 Ch 527.
3 This contrasts with the practice on the Eurocurrency markets while the 360-day year is utilised, the calculation is on the basis of the exact number of days which have elapsed.

will include a negative pledge clause in an effort to cover this situation.

5. *Payment* The bonds have detailed provisions with regard to payment of the sums due under the notes and coupons. The details of these and the legal responsibility to pay are examined subsequently.[1]

6. *Taxation* Complications may arise by reason of the effect of the application of withholding and other taxes to the issuer's obligation to pay. The terms will contain a provision to deal with this possibility and its effect is discussed subsequently.[2]

7. *Limitation and prescription* The obligation to pay is an obligation which could go on indefinitely if an investor does not present his bonds and coupons for payment. Plainly, an issuer will be anxious to know that his obligations will come to an end at some clear and specified time in the future. The obligation to pay, being a legal obligation, will be brought to an end by the expiration of any limitation period applicable to it, under the laws of any jurisdiction in which the obligation is litigated. Nevertheless, to leave the matter there is unsatisfactory. Different jurisdictions apply very different approaches to matters of limitation and an issuer requires finality at some stage. Further, two investors litigating similar securities, both of which were payable on the same day, and who commence their actions also on the same day, may find that the results obtained are very different. Under one jurisdiction it may be that the period of limitation has run and the investor has lost his remedy. In the other, where a longer limitation period is applied, the other investor may proceed to a successful remedy. In an attempt to deal with this and other problems, the terms and conditions specify common period of prescription applicable to the securities and coupons. Choice of period may vary, but a ten-year period in respect of bonds, and five years in respect of coupons, are common periods applied.

While an issuer and its advisers may hope that the inclusion of such provisions will effect a common period of limitation to all bonds wherever held and litigated, the actual result is far more questionable due to the different characterisation of limitation periods in different legal systems. In civil law systems statutes of limitation of actions are classified as substantive rules. This is true of the U.S.S.R., Poland, Czechoslovakia, both East and West Germany, France, Italy, the Benelux countries, Scandinavia and Portugal.[3] Consequently, the topic is governed by the proper law of the contract, and the courts of these countries will apply that law regardless of their own statutes of limitation and the periods applicable thereunder. Where a contract includes a choice of law clause recognised by the courts of such countries, *prima facie* therefore the limitation periods of the chosen proper law will be those applied. Where, as in the typical international bond terms, particular periods of limitation are specified, then,

1 *post* Chapter 10.

2 *post* Chapter 11.

3 O. Lando *International Encyclopedia of Comparative Law* Vol. 3 Private International Law J.C.B Mohr (Paul Siebeck) Tübingen (1976) pp. 123 and 124; G. Delaume *Transational Contracts* Oceana Publications, New York (1983 rev) p. 44 et seq.

if they are the same periods as the selected proper law, the outcome is straightforward and the designated periods will be applied in these jurisdictions. Where on the other hand the designated periods are not the same as the limitation periods arising under the statutes of limitation of the proper law, the validity of the modification must be determined by the proper law. Unfortunately, the substantive rules of different legal systems with regard to the effect of modification vary considerably, and in this situation therefore the outcome is difficult to predict.[1]

Fortunately, in civil law jurisdictions the position does not appear to be further complicated by the courts of those jurisdictions refusing to apply as *lex fori* the limitation period of, or recognised by, the proper law on the grounds of public policy, where there is a substantial difference between the two. Thus, in civil law jurisdictions foreign statutes have been given full effect even though they allowed much longer time limits than the *lex fori*[2] although in one case the German Supreme Court did refuse to apply a Swiss statute to a claim under which the claim could never be barred.[3]

The position in civil law systems contrasts dramatically with the position in common law jurisdictions, where periods of limitation are characterised as a matter of procedure. As a procedural matter the period of the statutes of the *lex fori* are viewed as the applicable time limit, and the limitation periods of the proper law are ignored. Thus an action brought within the limitation period prescribed by the proper law, but within the period allowed by the *lex fori*, will be allowed. This result inevitably encourages forum shopping amnong common law jurisdictions. On the other hand common law jurisdictions recognise express contractual periods of limitation as matters of substance and the validity of such provisions and its effect will fall to be decided by the proper law of the obligation.[4]

The procedural approach of the common law was true of England,[5] and is true of the Commonwealth.[6] It is also true of the U.S., where s 142 of the Second Restatement of the Conflict of Laws provides that an action will not be allowed if it is barred by the statute of limitation of the forum.[7]

1 Delaume *op. cit.*p. 45; *Uncitral Yearbook 1972* Vol. 3 supplement p. 125 *et seq.*

2 Lando p. 124.

3 RG 19 Dec 1922, RG2 106, 82, 85. Interestingly, the German court did not apply German limitation rules but directed that the case should be decided in accordance with the Swiss limitation rules which would apply in the absence of the particular offending statute.

4 *Allan J Panozza & Co Pty Ltd v Allied Interstate (Qld) Pty Ltd* [1976] 2 NSWLR 192.

5 *Williams v Jones* (1811) 13 East 439; *Ruckmaboye v Mottichund* (1853) 8 Moo PCC4; *Huber v Steiner* (1835) 2 Bing. NC 202; *Harris v Quine* (1869) LR4 QB 653; *Re Low* [1894] 1Ch 147: *Black-Clawson International Ltd v Papierweke Waldhof-Aschaffenburg AG* [1975] AC 591.

6 Lando *op. cit.* p. 123

7 This is subject to the U.S. 'borrowing statute' formulae—see generally Wurfel 'Statutes of Limitations in the Conflict of Laws' (1974); 54 North Carolina Law Review 489 Developments in the Law—Statutes of Limitations' (1950); 63 Harv L Rev 1177 and J. W. Ester 'Borrowing Statutes of Limitation and Conflict of Laws' (1962) 15 University of Florida Law Review 33.

The validity of a provision in the bond terms specifying a particular period of limitation is thus even more questionable in common law jurisdictions than in civil law jurisdictions. There is, however, one possible line of argument. Common law countries, in refusing to apply the limitation periods of other legal systems, have been prepared to draw a distinction between provisions which bar a remedy and those which extinguish a right. Recognition has been accorded to the latter, at least when shorter than the limitation period of the forum.[1]

In England the legislature has come to the rescue. In 1980 the Law Commission published a working paper[2] reviewing the classification within the English conflicts of laws of statutes of limitation in which it provisionally recommended that all periods of limitation, whether English or foreign should, for the purposes of English private international law, be classified as substantive. The working paper was subsequently confirmed by the report 'Classification of Limitation in Private International Law'[3] containing a draft bill and the substance of the draft bill became the Foreign Limitation Periods Act 1984.[4]

The general effect of the Act is to provide that the proper law of the obligation is to be applied by the English courts to determine matters of limitation and prescription rather than English law.[5] To this a gloss is added that in any case in which the application of the new principle would conflict with public policy the new principle should not apply to the extent that its application would so conflict.[6] If the purpose of this provision with regard to public policy were restricted to situations in which the proper law provided either an inordinate period of limitation or no period at all, no substantial objection might be raised apart from difficulties inherent in deciding what is 'inordinate' or 'excessive'. However, public policy is clothed much more brightly than this, for statute provides there is a conflict with public policy to the extent that the application of the new principle would 'cause undue hardship to a person who is, or might be made, a party to the action or proceedings.'[7] Thus attention is centred not on the particular rule of the proper law itself, but on its impact upon the particular circumstances of the case and the situations of the parties thereto. This inevitably makes more difficult the situation of those involved in pre-planning conflict avoidance by the selection of proper law and jurisdiction,

1 *Goodman v LNW Ry* (1877) 14 Sc LR 449; *McElroy v McAllister,* 1949 SC 110; *The Harrisburg* 119 US 199 (1886); *Davis v Mills* 194 US 451 (1904); Restatement Second s 143.
2 Working Paper No 75, 'Classification of Limitation in Private International Law'.
3 Law Com No 114 1982.
4 On the Act generally see PB Carter *The Foreign Limitation Periods Act 1984'* (1985) 101 LQR 68.
5 S 1.
6 S 21(1).
7 S 2(2).

as well as advisers seeking to predict the probable results of any litigation raising issues of limitation, should disputes arise.[1]

On the other hand the distinction betwen prescription as a bar to a remedy and as a bar to a right is abrogated for practical purposes, for the English courts are required to treat any adjudication on a matter of limitation by a foreign court as an adjudication on the merits of the matter,[2] thus preventing a subsequent action in the English courts where adjudication on limitation was considered to be a bar to the remedy only.

English law is, however, preserved to assist in the calculation of the limitation period. Plainly as the *lex fori* the English courts are well equipped to determine when proceedings are commenced before them for this is essentially a matter for their own procedure. In accordance with common sense the Act provides that whether proceedings have been commenced and, if so, at the time at which they were begun, shall be determined by English law.[3]

Many systems of law provide for the suspension of the running of the limitation period in certain circumstances; some confer a discretion on the court to allow proceedings to be brought out of time in certain circumstances. Under the Act the English courts must apply any suspensive provisions of the foreign law,[4] except such suspensive provisions as apply because of the absence of a party from any specified jurisdiction or country.[5] On the other hand, the English court is not merely left to apply the provisions of the applicable foreign law allowing the exercise of a discretion but are

1 See the trenchant criticism by Carter *op. cit.* at p. 72. However, the insulation of issues of limitation from English law is promoted in other respects. If the rules of private international law of the proper law refers issues of limitation back to the English courts as the *lex fori* (renvoi) the reference is to be ignored, for the Act provides that references to the law of any country excludes their body of private international law (s 1(5) and 4 (2). There was no equivalent to s 1 (5) in the Law Commission's draft bill). The insulation of the operation of limitation and prescription from English law is however, not in all respects complete. The Act provides that, with regard to matters in the determination of which both the law of England and Wales and the law of some other country fall to be taken into account, the law remains unchanged (s 1 (2)). The applicable rules of tort in English private international law are determined by such a double reference under the principles of *Boyes v Chaplin* ([1971] AC 36) and the applicable limitation principles in this area remain unchanged from those established at common law.

2 S 3.

3 S 1(3).

4 S 4(1).

5 S 2(3). This exception to the general applicability of the provisions allowing for the suspension of the running of the limitation period of the applicable foreign law was justified by the Law Commission as 'bearing in mind the practical difficulties which would be created by attempting to apply foreign suspensive provisions and the fact that such provisions are generally falling into disfavour'. *Classification of Limitation in Private International Law* (Law Com No 114, Cmnd 8570, 1982) p. 24.

positively enjoined to excerise the 'discretion in the manner in which it is excercised in comparable cases by the courts of that other country.'[1]

It is difficult to summarise the impact of the various rules of the private international law of the jurisdictions in which proceedings may be brought on a bond. Where the proceedings are brought in a common law jurisdiction other than England and Wales, where limitation periods are classified as procedural, that effectiveness of a bond term restricting the period in which proceedings can be brought will fall to be determined by the private international rules of the *lex fori*. Where proceedings are brought in a civil war jurisdiction the effectiveness of such a bond term will fall to be determined by the proper law of the obligation. The same is true if proceedings are brought in the English courts. Where English law is the proper law, or the English courts apply a proper law which would itself recognise such bond term, much will depend on the development by the English courts of concepts of public policy.

8. *Default* It is necessary to make precise provision for what is to happen if the user does not comply with the terms and conditions pursuant to which the bonds are issued. In addition, investors may need to be able to take action to preserve their investment if, despite the issuer carrying out all of his current obligations under the bonds themselves, circumstances indicate that it will not be possible for his satisfactory position to be maintained. This is traditionally dealt with by specifying certain events of default which entitle an investor or (where there is a trust deed) the trustee to accelerate matters by declaring the securities due and payable forthwith. The issues that arise with regard to default and acceleration, and the position with regard to the trustee, are complicated matters which are considered separately.[2]

9. *Terms of the trust deed* The terms and conditions will include a summary of the contents of the trust deed.

10 *Replacement of notes and coupons* It may be that a bond or coupon is lost or accidentally destroyed. The terms and conditions customarily provide that where any bond or coupon is defaced, mutilated, stolen, lost or destroyed, it may be renewed at one of the offices of the various paying agents on such terms as to evidence and indemnity as the issuer may require. The investor is made responsible for any cost incurred in connection therewith. He will be expected also to enter into an indemnity with the issuer under which he agrees to reimburse to the issuer any loss which may fall upon the issuer. A defaced or mutilated bond must be surrendered prior to a new bond or coupon being issued.

11. *Notices* The bondholders are a disparate collection of individuals and institutions, situated in a number of countries of the world. The bonds customarily move from hand to hand on the secondary market without the necessity of registration to perfect the transfer. Accordingly, it is not

[1] S 1(4). It is not envisaged that the English courts will be able to achieve a precisely similar result to that which would have been achieved by the foreign court had that court dealt with the matter but a broadly similar approach should be possible—Law Com No 114 *op. cit.* p. 21.

[2] *post* ch 12.

possible to ascertain, at any specific moment, full details of the names and addresses of all bondholders'. From time to time the trustees or fiscal agent, or even the issuer itself, may need to give notice to bondholders with regard to their investment. This is of particular importance with regard to the arrangement of bondholders meetings, should the necessity for one arise. Accordingly, the terms and conditions provide that all notices to the bondholders regarding the bonds will be published in one leading daily newspaper in the financial centre around which the bond issue has been constructed, or if that is impossible, then a daily newspaper (approved by the trustee where there is a trust deed), having general circulation within the continent in which the greater part of the issue is being placed. If a notice is published more than once, the terms and conditions provide that it is to be deemed to be given on the day on which it was first published.

12. *Governing law* The bonds and coupons and the trust deed are, under the conditions, to be governed by, and constructed in accordance with the chosen system of law. The issuer irrevocably submits to the non-exclusive jurisdiction of the courts of the chosen legal system for all matters arising out of the trust deed and the securities. (Where there is a trust deed, this provision is usually repeated within it).

13. *Authentication* The conditions provide that the bond is not to be valid, and authentic for any purpose, until a certificate of authentication endorsed upon it shall have been signed by, or on behalf of, the principal paying agent. The certificate is printed as part of the bond.

Endorsed on the bond are details of the name and office of the principal paying agent, and the names and offices of the various paying agents within the group. Identical details are endorsed upon each coupon.

SPECIAL CONDITIONS

Conditions affecting maturity

Unless special provision is made, bonds will not run to their full maturity prior to redemption,[1] except for the one provision which we have seen is normally provided for, namely where the imposition of additional taxes upon the payment obligations under the bonds increases the cost to the issuer.[2]

Flip-flops It is, of course, possible to issue bonds with no final maturity—a perpetual bond. These are known on the English domestic debenture market. However, the more usual variation encountered on the international bond market is the flip-flop issue. This is an issue under which the bonds have no final maturity, but which give the bondholder the right within a specified period to convert into a fixed term bond. He may also be given subsequent rights of reconversion back to a perpetual bond and out to a fixed bond again.

Retractables and extendibles Equally, it may be that, with regard to a particular issue, an issuer wishes to make other arrangements for flexibility. An issuer may feel that he can increase the attractiveness of the investment

[1] *Hooper v Western Counties and South Wales Telephone Co.Ltd.* (1982) 68 L.T.78.
[2] *post* Ch 11.

to the investor in the circumstances of the market at the time of the particular issue by giving the investor the opportunity of prolonging the length of the investment if the investor so chooses. In these circumstances, the investor is effectively given a choice of bringing the investment to an end at either an earlier or a later point of time. This can be achieved by either of two mechanisms. One is the extendible maturity, where the security is issued for a limited and comparitively short period of time, such as five years.[1] At the end of the five years the investor is given the right, by notice, to continue the investment for an additional period (possibly a further five years). If the investor exercises this option the terms of the security remain the same as on original issue, except that the redemption date is put back to the extended period. Much the same effect can be achieved by an alternative variation, the retractable security. This is the opposite of the extendible security in that it is issued for the longer period with the investor having the right to give notice requiring repayment of the bond at an earlier point of time.[2] The difference is simply the difference of the onus upon the investor. With the extendible bond, it will determine at the earlier point of time unless it is extended by notice, whereas with the retractable bond the investment gives notice. The difference may appear to be academic, but, in fact, investors very often do not give notice, and, therefore, retractable bonds tend to run for the full term, whereas extendible bonds tend not to be renewed for a period equivalent to the retractable.[3]

Mandatory redemption provisions Further specific terms with regard to the repayment of the security are mandatory and optional redemption provisions. The first of these provisions reflects the fact that where a large loan is obtained by an issuer, it may well be in the interests of both the issuer and investors that the loan represented by the securities be redeemed over a period of time. If the issuer has borrowed $100,000,000 onan issue of bonds with a ten-year life, the finding of such a vast sum on the last day of the tenth year may well cause the difficulties to the issuer. Where the results of the issue have invested in productive enterprise, whether by a company or a soveriegn borrower, it is likely that after two or three years the investment will be returning an income. Part, or all, of this income would, therefore, be available from then, not merely to service the interest represented by the coupons, but also to repay the principal. If, commencing at the end of year four, the bonds were redeemed by payment of $12,000,000 per annum, by the end of year ten there would only be a matter of $40,000,000 left for the issuer to find. The use of a provision which compels early repayment is often a useful discipline to an issuer, and an important way of boosting the confidence of investors and their advisers in an issue.

Mandatory redemption provisions come in two forms. The most common form is the provision of a straightforward sinking fund, by which the issuer contracts to repay a set number of bonds at specified periods (usually annual)

1 As it applies to shorter period borrowing the device is employed customarily on floating rate notes rather than bonds.

2 As the security is issued for a longer period although determinable earlier, it is a phenomenon of the international bond and not the floating rate note.

3 See Fisher *The Eurodollar Bond Market* Euromoney Publications plc (1979) p. 128.

before maturity. The company's obligation is to purchase the securities at par on the specified date. Clearly, the redemption of the investment at par may or may not be advantageous to an investor. If the secondary market price of the investment stands above par an investor would not willingly give up his investment for only its face value. Accordingly, it is important that the selection of the bonds to be redeemed is effected in a fair manner. It is usually provided that the securities to be redeemed within the sinking fund should be drawn by lot by the principal paying agent, and that a list of the bonds drawn, and the date on which they will be redeemed, will be notified to the bondholders not less than a specified period before such date.

Optional redemption provisions Issuers may also be unhappy at the prospect of being committed to purchase certain numbers of the bonds each year at par. If the bonds stand at less than par on the secondary market the issuer will be left in the uncomfortable position of purchasing back the securities, which represent the loan to it, at a price higher than it would need to pay on the secondary market itself. Accordingly, it is common for the issuer to be given the right to purchase bonds in the secondary market to enable them to buy bonds at a discount rather than at par. Sometimes the issuer is also given the right to purchase back the issue by private treaty, although usually a maximum price is imposed (eg 115 per cent of the principal amount exclusive of accrued interest and expenses). Any securities so purchased may be credited at their par value in satisfaction of all, or part, of any obligations of the issuer to redeem any part of the issue. Until they are so credited at the issuer's request they are deemed to be outstanding for the purpose of the drawing of securities for redemption under any such provisions. In the case of such voluntary redemption provisions certain specific provisions are usual. These are that any interest coupons not yet payable should be surrenderd in respect of all bonds to be redeemed, and all bonds so purchased should be cancelled for, if reissued or resold, they could give rise to potential problems or securities regulation in some of the jurisdictions in which they were sold. Further, the bonds will provide that the repurchase facility should be available to all bondholders alike to prevent discrimination. This latter is a London Stock Exchange requirement which also requires that the price for purchase to be not more than the average of the listed price for the previous ten days and, if purchase is made through the market, the price should not exceed the current market price which itself should not exceed 5 per cent more than the average of the previous ten days.[1]

The alternative manner of mandatory redemption is by means of a purchase fund. This has the benefit that the applicable price is the secondary market price of the securities, for they are simply purchased on the secondary

[1] The Stock Exchange *The Admission of Securities to Listing* Section 9, Chapter 2. On a domestic issue, these and the other required provisions with regard to redemption are to be included in the Trust Deed. In the case of Eurocurrency securities there is no requirement of a Trust Deed for the issue but the requirements must be complied with by the insertion of appropriate provisions in the terms and conditions of issue—Section 7, para 10.42

market. The working of the system if that the issuer is required to purchase on the secondary market a certain proportion of the issue if the secondary market price falls below a specified level (usually par). It therefore follows that should the price on the secondary market of the securities remain above par no obligation to purchase arises. The purchase fund is operated by the purchase agent, appointed by the issuer, which is simply a bank nominated for this purpose.

Where the obligation arises it may be that it is impossible for the agent to purchase the required number of bonds at a price below par, for the secondary market price, having dipped, may speedily rise again. In this situation if, at the end of the twelve months period the purchase agent has been unable to acquire the total number of bonds required, the obligation that has arisen in that year is continued for an additional period, (usually six months), during which the purchase agent remains responsible for purchasing in the secondary market, where the price falls below the specified level. Of course, in the subsequent year, the fact that it falls below the specified level may give rise to a further obligation to purchase a specified number under the issuer's obligations for the subsequent year. The purchase agent in these circumstances must remain purchasing in the secondary market so long as the price is under the specified figure. Acquisitions are initially credited against the outstanding obligation for the earlier year, and only subsequently against the obligation for the later year. Again, if the full obligation of the later year cannot be discharged within that year, it can be carried forward for six months of the subsequent year. The obligation lapses if, at the end of the specified extension period of six months, it has still not been possible to discharge the obligation because the price on the secondary market has fallen below the specified figure too infrequently.

As purchases take place under a purchase fund system on the secondary market, there is no need to have any provision within the terms and conditions dealing with the selection of the bonds required. As the obligation only arises where the price of the securities on the secondary market is below that specified, the effect of such a provision is to help support the price of bonds on the secondary market, and, therefore, is favourable to investors.

Clearly, the use of mandatory redemption provisions has the effect of reducing the average maturity of the bonds and, hence, the length of the loan. This is an important consideration for an issuer who needs to calculate carefully, prior to issue, the effect of the mandatory retirement provisions as to the average life of the loan to ensure that the financial effects are not too burdensome. It is also necessary for the issuer to look carefully as to when the compulsory redemption of the bond commences to ensure that, if he is depending upon the coming into production of an investment project for which the money has been borrowed, the project is, indeed, likely to be in full production by the first year of mandatory redemption to provide him with the means to pay.

Nevertheless, it must not be thought that provisions which have the effect of allowing early redemption of the bonds are necessarily against the issuer's interest. Where the bonds have been issued with a lengthy redemption at the time of high interest rates it may be very much in an issuer's interest to redeem those bonds, even, if necessary, financing the redemption by a new issue of bonds at a reduced interest rate on a subsequently kinder market. In such a situation a mandatory sinking fund is very much in the issuer's interest. It is otherwise where the issue was originally at a lower rate of interest and interest rates subsequently have risen.

A commonly used provision, which has the effect of giving an issuer the best of all worlds, is an optional redemption provision. Under this commonly used provision bonds may not be redeemed for a period of time after issue, but following a specified date (say at the end of three years from issue) the issuer may redeem some or all of the securities on giving a specified period of notice (usually thirty or sixty days). The price payable by the issuer on using this facility is usually fixed at a slight premium on the par value during the first twelve months that it is exercisable, declining by a fraction of a per cent on each subsequent anniversary, until par is reached for the last twelve months of the issue.

The option thus conferred upon the issuer is called a 'call'. Clearly, this right is of considerable importance to issuers and is now commonly inserted in bonds, particularly those issued at times of high interest rates.

ISSUES DENOMINATED IN COMPOSITE CURRENCY

We have already seen that a matter as significant to both issuer and investor as the rate of interest of an issue is the currency in which the issue is denominated, and the anticipation whether that currency will or will not decline relative to other currencies.[1] For obvious reasons issues denominated in currencies which are considered to be strong are more attractive to investors than those denominated in currencies considered to be weak. Equally, or even more, important are the future prospects of the economy of the country whose currency is denominated, for a strengthened economy will produce a stronger currency and a weaker economy a weaker currency. This is relevant both to the marketability of an issue, and to the rate of interest which will have to be paid by means of the coupons to support it.

Given the length of time during which an international bond may be outstanding there is an element of gamble for an investor, whatever the currency in which a bond is denominated. Over a ten- or fifteen-year span the most stable country, with a proud record of economic progress and currency stability, may run into difficulties, possibly consequent upon a change in economic policies following from the coming into power of a new government. It is no small wonder that investors have always shown some interest in having their investment denominated in some other way. A form of denomination, much used prior to the economic difficulties which manifested themselves in the years following the First World War, was by reference to the value of gold.[2] However, this approach now seems

[1] *ante* p. 22.

[2] See Mann *The Legal Aspect of Money* (1982) (4th Edn) Clarendon Press.

to have passed into the realms of history.[1] Modern attempts at giving monetary stability to investors have moved in the direction of tying the value of the bond applicable for redemption to the composite value of a number of currencies considered to be essentially stable.[2] A variety of possible permutations of this approach have been attempted in issues on the international bond market. The most usual choice for the basket of currencies underpinning the composite issue have been western European countries, because political and economic movements in this area have caused the currencies to be placed in relationship to one another.[3]

The oldest experiments with composite currency have been to denominate an issue in terms of the European Unit of Account (E.U.A). This had its origin as an artificial currency within a body known as The European Payment Union, comprising seventeen nations. The need for the artificial currency between the European countries, and the Payment Union was the means by which international obligations between the countries were cleared. In 1958, with the return of convertibility, the need for the European Payment Union came to an end and it was dissolved, but the European

1 In fact, a gold-backed Eurobond issue was made in January 1981 when Refinement International N.V. issued U.S. $1.9 million 3.25 gold-indexed bonds due 1996. Refinement is a U.S. recycler of precious and rare metals, holding substantial amounts of gold at any given time. The value of this was used as security for the borrowing by the appointment of a trustee for bondholders to hold delivery of certificates issued by the various holders of gold belonging to the issuer as it passed through their operations. The issue was always likely to be a problem to either borrower or lender. The price of gold has fallen since issue resulting in a loss of value and a failure to establish an effective secondary market, thus leaving the bonds virtually unsaleable—see Kerr *History of the Eurobond Market* p. 68

2 An early individual attempt arose in the agreement on German External Debts of 1953 when the terms of the original Young Loan bonds sold to finance German reparations for the First World War were renegotiated and the gold clause protection abrogated. In exchange the various currencies of denomination were placed in relationship to one another with a protecting clause by way of guarantee that on an alteration of the rate of exchange of any of the currencies payment should be calculated on the basis of the least depreciated. The terms of the agreement were not free from ambiguity and the circumstances of the surrounding negotiation confused. Inevitably there was much room for misunderstanding and disagreement as to what exactly had been agreed. When the issue eventually went to arbitration the parties seem to have been in disagreement on all points. *Case of Belgium (The Young Loan Arbitration)* (1980). 19 Int'l Legal Materials 1358 The case is analysed and the background explained in Bathurst 'Creditor Protection in a Changing World' (1980). 15 Texas Int Law J 519 The moral is clear. All such agreements should be precise, clear and free from ambiguity so that the events which trigger them are clearly specified and the arithmetical consequences beyond doubt.

3 Protection devices including multi-currency composites have attracted the attention of international organisations. See Report of the Secretary General, Clauses Protecting Parties Against the Effects of Currency Fluctuations 5, para.9; U.N. Doc. A/CN, 9/164 (1979); Report of the Working Group on International Negotiable Instruments 35-36, U.N. loc.A/CN/9/181 (1980); Report by the Committee on International Monetary Fund [1976] Report of the 57 Conf.—Madrid 165 (International Law Association).

Unit of Account, having been created, continued to exist as a concept to which reference could be made. The introduction of floating rates of exchange in the suceeding years, coupled with the increased volatility in the foreign exchange market, caused increasing problems for the member countries of the E.E.C. In an effort to deal with these problems in 1973, the nine member countries resuscitated the E.U.A. as a basis for dealing with transactions within the Community. Inevitably, the concept was redefined to link it to the currencies of the Community member countries themselves, and not the original seventeen members of the former payment union.[1] The value of the unit of account is fixed at a precise point representing the par value of the component currencies in relation to one another. A revaluation can only if all currencies within the unit change their par value and a majority of them move in the same direction, either upwards or downwards. If these conditions are satisfied, the unit of account is revalued.[2] As currency composite the European Unit of Account has been popular with both issuers and investors for the unit has proved to be remarkably stable point of reference at a time of great instability in currency markets. Over 90 public issues using the E.U.A. have been made. However, the coming into existence of the European Currency Unit caused the E.U.A. to fade away with the last issue being made in 1982.

The European Unit of Account has been replaced by the European Currency Unit (E.C.U.) as the composite currency formulation in active use by the international bond market for the making of new issues. The E.C.U. has been the unit of value for the European Economic Community since 1979 and is much used not merely by the various E.E.C. agencies but throughout the commercial activity of the Community. The E.C.U is used to manage the relative values of the various currencies of the Member States through the mechanism of the European Monetary System. Its value is derived from a basket of the currencies of the Member States (Spain and Portugal join the basket in 1989) but since it is now a convertible currency in its own right its value is actually determined by market forces.

There is, however, an important distinction between issues denominated in E.U.As. and those denominated in E.C.Us. The former is an entirely artificial unit of account suitable for achieving a valuation of the amount of the obligation to repay. Since the unit is merely artificial and not money, payment cannot be made in the unit. The unit must be translated into an equivalent value in a specified money for repayment to be effected. It would, of course, be possible to specify the currency in which payment is to be made at the time of the issue of the bonds. Thus, it could be specified that repayment would be an amount of dollars, equal to the value of the unit as at the date of repayment. The more usual provision, however, is to give the investor the choice of currency in which repayment is eventually to be made.

By contrast the E.C.U. is a convertible currency with individuals and

[1] In the past the value of the E.U.A. has also been linked to gold but this link was dropped in 1979. It is currently linked to the currencies in the European Monetary System.

[2] F G Fisher III *Eurobonds* Euromoney Publications (1988) p. 153.

companies being able to open an E.C.U. account with their banks and make and receive payments in E.C.U.s through a well established clearing system. Since 1984 there has been foreign exchange dealing in E.C.U.s and since the same year the Japanese have recognised the E.C.U. as a separate currency.

THE FLOATING RATE NOTE

If the problem of currency fluctuation gives rise to considerable difficulty for both investor and issuer, both also face difficulties in seeking to deal with the volatile interest rates on the world's capital markets, which have been a feature of recent years.[1] When international interest rates are low, it is likely that investors will be keen to take on a long term investment at a low rate of interest. If interest rates were to go up twelve months after the bonds had been purchased, an investor would be denied the opportunity of earning interest at the higher rates upon his capital unless he could capitalise his investment. Equally, a bond with a low rate of interest is likely to have a depressed value upon the secondary market, because prospective purchasers are conscious of the fact that they can get a better return upon their capital. Accordingly, an original investor in the bond will be confronted with the situation where he can only divest himself of his investment by taking a capital loss.

Equally bonds issued at times of high interest rates are potentially very expensive to an issuer. Were an issuer to issue a fifteen-year bond with a 15 per cent coupon at a time of high interest rates, his borrowing will look extremely expensive if, twelve months later, the same bonds could have been issued on the international market with the coupon at 10 per cent. In the most extreme manifestations of this phenomenon the issuer can protect himself by the inclusion of a call option, thereby enabling it to float a new issue of bonds at the lower interest rate to pay off the higher rate bonds pursuant to the use of the call option. This, however, is far from ideal. First, the usual form of call option involves the issuer in redeeming at a slight premium above par to make the inclusion of it palatable to investors. Secondly, the costs of a new issue at the lower interest rate are themselves not inconsiderable.

The answer which has evolved to these problems in an effort to satisfy both issuers and investors, is the floating rate note. This has been said to combine the 'characteristics of a long-term international bond with a medium-term syndicated bank loan'.[2]

Like the syndicated loan the interest payable on a floating rate note is set only a limited period of time. The most customary period chosen is six months. At the end of each period the rate of interest is recalculated by some bench mark of short-term interest rates as the variable base and adding a margin for profit. The amount of margin which is likely to be added depends upon the standing of the issuer, as this will determine the relative attractiveness of an issue to investors. Where the issue would be

1 The volatility of interest rates is aggravated by the volatility of exchange rates.
2 Fisher *Eurobonds* (1988) p. 171.

otherwise unattractive the margin would be increased. The amount of margin varies between one quarter of one per cent and one per cent. There is, however, usually a minimum interest rate underpinning the investment to protect the investor should minimum interest rates on the inter-bank market drop too severely. The minimum, however, is usually fixed at a low level.

The bench mark reference is fixed at the time of issue and specified in the note. There are various choices available related to short term borrowing costs on the inter-bank network. The choice is between the bid (LIBID) or the offered (LIBOR) rate, or the mean of the bid and offered rates (LIMEAN). LIBOR is most widely chosen. The note term will specify the length of time for which the bench mark rate will vary depending on which bench mark is chosen, currrent and prospective market conditions, and the attractiveness of the issuer.

The principal difference between floating rate notes and the straight international bond, lies in the length of term. The F.R.N. is typically issued for a shorter period (five to seven years). Mandatory redemption provisions are unusual, although typically a call option is included, exercisable after two or three years at par.

Floating rate notes have proved to be popular with industrial issuers as might be expected. It is noteworthy however, that they have also been especially popular with banks who use them to raise capital on a floating basis, which is then lent on at a higher, but still floating, margin to their customers.

To the usual documentation necessary for an international bond issue, an additional document is added for an issue of F.R.N.'s. This is the reference agency agreement which deals with the process of calculation of the interest payments. It appoints a bank to collect the bench mark quotes from banks specified by the agreement, who are the points of reference for the giving of the information. From the information supplied, the bench mark is ascertained and the appointed bank calculates the interest coupon for the current period. The first interest coupon is calculated two business days before the closing date.

It is necessary to include a clause to deal with the difficulty which might otherwise arise if it proved impossible to obtain the necessary quotes. A normal provision is that if an insufficient number of the prescribed London banks quote to satisfy the requirements of the interest fixing mechanism as specified in the notes then the rate should be (1) if ascertainable by the agent bank the margin above the lowest dollar lending rate which leading New York international banks selected by the agent bank are quoting to two reference banks or (2) if this is not ascertainable by the agent bank the rate which such leading New York banks are offered to leading European banks, or, if this cannot be ascertained, the interest rate previously chargeable.

It should be noted that as a result of the conceptual links between the F.R.N. and the syndicated eurocurrency loan is that in contrast to the interest on a fixed rate bond interest on a F.R.N. is calculated on the basis of the actual number of days in the particular interest period divided by the 360 days of the fictional year of the free currency markets.

A further sophstication can be introduced into a F.R.N. issue by providing that, while interest is payable every half year, the rates payable should be fixed at shorter periods, eg monthly. The result is called a 'mismatch F.R.N.'. They are used because short term interest rates (eg one month) are usually cheaper, and the result can be financially advantageous to both issuer and investor.

Because of the additional sophistication of the form of investment the costs of an F.R.N. issue are a little higher than those in respect of an international bond issue.

A variation of the floating rate note is a form of hybrid combining features of both the floating rate and the international bond. Under this, a floating rate note is issued for a typical period of seven years. The holder is given the right, under the terms of the note, to convert the medium-term note into a long term bond at a fixed rate of interest. The length of term of the bond is calculated from the date of the original issue, whatever the date of the subsequent conversion. If the investor does not exercise his conversion option, the floating rate note is redeemed by payment at the end of its term. If he does exercise his option, then thereafter, the security is converted into a long term bond.[1] An alternative is for the conversion of the note to depend not on the option of the investor, but on the happening of an extenal event, such as interest rates reaching a particular level. The danger of this latter possibility is, of course, that if the chosen rate of interest is too high or too low, the result is likely to be unsatisfactory to either the investor or the issuer.[2]

ZERO COUPON BONDS

As its name implies a zero coupon bond is a non-interest-bearing security. Its attraction to the investor arises from the fact that it is issued at a large discount, and thus has the possibility that it will give rise to considerable appreciation on redemption. From the issuer's point of view he is saved the necessity of having to find any money for the investor until redemption, since he does not have to pay interest. The potential drawback for an issuer arises if it is affected by any borrowing limits in making the issue. These may arise because of legal limits imposed by the terms of the articles of association of a corporation, or by central banks of countries in which the issue is to be marketed where their consent to make an issue is required, or, alternatively, the practical considerations of the size of issue which the creditworthiness of the issuer will support. In respect of legal limits the problem arises where the borrowing limit applies to the full principal amount as the issuer will receive only the discounted amount which may be inadequate for his needs; in the case of practical restrictions arising from the creditworthiness of the issue the problem is endemic to the actual situation.

The principal reason for a zero coupon issue, however, is the possibility of a tax advantage for the investor, which will depend on the revenue law of the jurisdiction of both issuer and investor. The intention is that the built-in discount should give rise to a capital gain thus avoiding income

1 In one case the length of term of the bond was 25 years.
2 These hybrids are discussed Fisher *Eurobonds* pp. 178-9.

tax, and the capital gain avoids capital gains tax either because the jurisdictions concerned do not tax capital, or because there are tax reliefs available which allow the appreciation to be written off over the lifetime of the security.

It would also, perhaps, be not over-cynical to point out the potential of the zero coupon as an instrument not merely of tax avoidance, but also of tax evasion. Since the instrument is in bearer form with no coupons the only transaction necessary after initial purchase is its sale. The smaller the number of transactions and the more anonymous their nature, the greater the likelihood that the tax evader will not be detected. The same considerations, however, make the zero coupon bond the more attractive to the forger. The only known example of an attempt to pass forged bonds concerned forged zero coupon bonds. The attempt was detected but the forger had chosen well. Without coupons the forged instruments might well have escaped examination until presentation for payment. In fact the forgers sought to evade even this by attempting to use the forged instruments as securities for a loan, where the bonds would probably only have been inspected on the grant of the loan prior to the forgers disappearing with the borrowed money.[1]

Because of the obvious difficulties involved in calculating the redemption price in the event of an issuer redeeming in the lifetime of the security, the issuer's powers to redeem are usually extremely restricted. Apart from the very necessary situation of early redemption on default it is normal that the issuer be only allowed to redeem voluntarily prior to the redemption date in the event of a change of applicable revenue law leading to the imposition of a withholding tax on the principal of the bonds. The bond terms contain careful provision for the calculation of the amount payable on early redemption in these restricted circumstances, so that an investor will receive a sum proportionally equal to the sum he would actually have received if the bonds had remained outstanding to redemption.

REFIXABLE BONDS

The refixable bond is a bond issued with a fixed rate of interest and is, therefore, not an F.R.N. However, the bond terms contain express machinery enabling the interest to be refixed intermittently (eg every two years) to reflect current interest rates. The new rate is published and bondholders are usually given the right to have their bonds redeemed if the new interest rate does not meet with their approval.

DROP LOCK BONDS

The drop lock bond is one which is issued as an F.R.N. but which contains in its terms a provision whereby the F.R.N. converts into a fixed rate bond if the interest rate falls below a stated minimum.

[1] Kerr *op. cit.* pp. 70 and 71.

CERTIFICATES OF DEPOSIT

The form of an issue of certificates of deposit has already been discussed. As has been seen, certificates of deposit may be issued on both a fixed interest and floating rate basis, thereby reflecting the essential characteristics of the international bond and the floating rate note. The form of the document is traditionally less complex than an international bond with a simpler range of terms endorsed upon it.[1] The terms include detailed provisions governing the obligation of the issuer to pay; the issuer's right to redeem the note compulsorily in the event that withholding taxes or duties are imposed which make the borrowing more expensive to the issuer; the obligation of the issuer to replace destroyed, lost or mutilated notes; details of the paying agent arrangement; a provision for notices to noteholders to be given by an authorized newspaper; a choice of law clause; a provision that the deposit note shall be valid only when countersigned by the manual signature of an authorized officer of the bank; and a provision commonly used to deal with unclaimed balances left in the hands of the paying agent is a term that if, at the end of three years from the date on which sums should have been claimed by the investor, they remain in the hands of the paying agent, the paying agent may return them to the bank, and thereafter the paying agent will have no responsibility to the investor, whose rights will exist solely against the bank. On the other hand the provision of fixed prescription periods are rare in certificates of deposit.

Certificates of deposit are thus much simpler documents, marketed much more informally, than are international bonds. This reflects both the comparative shortness of the term for which they are issued and the standing of the banking institutions which make use of them.

PARI PASSU CLAUSES

As previously indicated, because of the unsecured nature of a bond issue, the inclusion of a *pari passu* clause is standard form in an effort to ensure so far as possible that all the unsecured borrowing of an issuer ranks equally in the event of insolvency or default. A typical clause would be as follows:

> The bond and coupons are direct, general, unconditional and (subject to the provision of the negative pledge clause) unsecured obligations of the company and rank *pari passu* and rateably without any preference among themselves and (subject to the provisions of the negative pledge clause and with the exception of obligations in respect of national and local taxes and with certain other statutory exceptions) equally with all other unsecured obligations (other than subordinated obligations, if any) of the company from time to time outstanding.

While the basic form of a *pari passu* clause is standard its purpose varies depending on whether the issuer is a corporation or a sovereign borrower.[2] In the case of a corporate borrower the main consideration is the position

[1] *ante* p. 44
[2] See Wood *op. cit* p. 155 et seq.

of the bondholders in the event of a liquidation of the company on insolvency. In such a situation the bondholder is to be placed in an equal position with all other holders of unsecured debt issued by the corporate issuer. So far as such a clause is effective it ensures that on insolvency the assets of the corporation are distributed equally among all unsecured lenders. Unfortunately, however, such a clause is not totally effective. The reasons for this are that most jurisdictions have their own rules as to the priority of payments of debts on a corporate liquidation and those rules will take priority over the terms of the bond provision.[1] In particular in many jurisdictions outstanding taxes and wages due to employees of the company take priority over all other unsecured debt on the liquidation of a company.[2] Some jurisdictions give priority to depositors with banks or other financial institutions and to the holders of insurance policies in the event of the insolvency of an insurance company. Further, the rules of some jurisdictions may provide that unsecured debt ranks for payment in the event of corporate liquidation in the order of the date of creation—the earlier therefore having priority.

Nevertheless, the use of the clause does enable a bondholder at least to advance the argument that, subject to the laws of the jurisdiction involved, he is not to be discriminated against, and this argument might be of particular importance in negotiations with regard to the voluntary re-establishment and rescheduling of the totality of its unsecured debt by an issuer with financial difficulties.

If the primary purpose of the *pari passu* clause in the case of a corporate issuer is to put all unsecured creditors on the same basis in the event of insolvency, the same cannot be true of an international bond issue by a sovereign state. Since an insolvent state cannot be put into a formally structured bankruptcy and dissolved, the inclusion of such a clause can only be intended to have a different purpose. In such a case it would seem that the function of such a clause would be to prevent a government earmarking defined revenues or assets for the purposes of paying one set of creditors preferentially, thereby discriminating against the totality of its unsecured creditors. In such a situation there would seem to be little point in including the clause merely as a declaration of status as in the standard form applicable to a corporate issuer already given, rather it should be drafted as one of the responsibilities which the issuer undertakes, breach of which will constitute an act of default by the issuer.

To fall within the *pari passu* clause under its terms the obligations of the issuer must be direct, general and unconditional. The meaning of these terms is not entirely clear[3] but it has been suggested that 'direct' means non-contingent, and the use of the term 'unconditional' precludes an issuer from refusing payment unless the bondholder satisfies certain conditions such as qualifications as to residence and nationality, or performing a further obligation such as the making of a new compulsory loan. The word 'general'

1 Insolvency Act 1986, s 386(1); Sch 6.
2 ibid Sch 6, Category 5.
3 The meaning of these terms has been considered by Philip Wood *op. cit.* at p. 157 for which discussion the writer is indebted

probably connotes that the bonds are secured upon the general funds of the issuer, ie those funds generally available for meeting the issuer's obligations. In some instances an issuer may be required by the general law of the country in which it is incorporated or in which it carries on its business, to pay specific liabilities out of a specific earmarked and segregated fund. An obvious U.K. example lies in the field of life insurance where the claims attributable to an insurance company's life insurance business are payable out of a specially segregated life insurance fund. Equally, certain international organisations set aside specific designated funds for defined special purposes. It would follow from this that such funds would not be available for the purposes of the operation of the *pari passu* clause.

NEGATIVE PLEDGE CLAUSE

To understand the negative pledge and its limitations it is necessary to consider vital factors necessarily present in transnational borrowing as opposed to the traditional domestic model. Traditionally, the corporate trader was a company, often a family controlled corporation, manufacturing its product in a particular country and, if opportunities came its way, exporting its products overseas as well as selling them on its own domestic markets. If it needed to borrow various alternatives were, and are, open to it, all of the most used of which involved the giving of security to the lender. At its most basic it could borrow on the security of the factory building and surrounding land, which it would own. If it wished to borrow more than this would secure, it could borrow by making a domestic debenture issue containing a floating charge over all of its assets which would not, however, crystallise until the occurrence of events specified in the terms of the charge, eg the insolvency of the company. In the meantime the company would be free to use its assets in the course of its business including, where necessary, disposing of them.[1] Even where the modern domestic company raises finance by factoring its receivable accounts the creditor has the security of the outstanding accounts assigned to it.

Against this cosy picture the position of the multinational corporation raising much larger sums of capital on the markets of the world stands in marked contrast. The assets of the corporation will be scattered around the countries of the world and even on the high seas. Not all those countries will have highly developed systems of commercial law to be able to employ the full range of security devices developed in western legal systems. Even where the legal techniques are available in the system of law where a particular asset is placed, the local economy may not have the means to be able to finance the borrowing. Nor would the corporation wish to raise its finance in the piecemeal manner of negotiating individual loans in innumerable centres where particular parts of its assets were situate. Indeed, if the borrowings were to achieve the full credit potential of the corporation such a means of borrowing could not suffice even had it been possible, for the individual assets assumed their highest value in the hands of the

1 On the subject of the floating charge see R M Goode *Commercial Law* (1982) Penguin Books, Allen Lane Chapter 28.

multinational with its expertise to marshall the variety of the component parts of its wealth into a profitable whole of greater significance and potential than the sum total of the individual components.

If the multinational company sought to raise its finance internationally in one integrated borrowing therefore it could not offer security. Its main machinery to attempt this, derived from western legal devices, would have been the floating charge, but the use of this was impracticable because of the failure of the floating charge to win acceptance outside western common law systems, either because other legal systems have been too undeveloped for such a sophisticated concept, or, as in the civil law systems, antipathetic to it. To cover the gap left by the absence of security mechanisms the law of contract was pressed into service in the form of the negative pledge. However, as will be seen, the negative pledge for all the sophistication of its concept and the ingenuity of its possible drafting, shows all the drawbacks of its contractual origins and character.[1]

The negative pledge clause is an essential twin to support the policy underlying the *pari passu* clause, namely, that all lenders to the issuer should be kept, so far as possible, on an equal footing in the event of the insolvency of the issuer. Whilst the *pari passu* clause endeavours to put all unsecured creditors at equal rank, the negative pledge clause is included to try to prevent the borrower from issuing new secured debt once the unsecured issue has been completed. If such secured debt were allowed to be created it would have priority over the existing unsecured obligations to the detriment of the bondholders. Because of this the negative pledge clause is usually included. Indeed, IPMA regulations require that the absence of a negative pledge clause must be fully disclosed, as must also any significant variations from standard and accepted forms.

In the case of a corporate borrower, therefore, the functions of the negative pledge can be said to be essentially twofold. First, it seeks to prevent the charging of assets to a single secured creditor after the bond issue, leaving the bondholders and other unsecured creditors merely with rights against the balance of the issuer's assets (if any), and thereby establishing equality between the creditors. Secondly, the use of the negative pledge operates as a useful form of credit control preventing the issuer incurring excessive liabilities. Borrowers are anxious to give as little security as possible for their borrowings, as the greater the security the creditors have over the assets of the corporation the more limited the powers of management tend to be. It can be argued that in general with an efficient management the more power left in its hands to run the corporation's affairs the better for the success of the corporation's business. Further, given the bias of corporations to avoid the giving of security over assets if this is possible corporations are only likely to give security for loan where their credit worthiness is in decline and their bargaining position weak. The very fact that the issuer is prepared to countenance giving security is therefore one

[1] For these thoughts I am indebted to the seminal Seventh Crowther Memorial Lecture delivered by Professor D E Allan on 25 October 1982 at Queen Mary College London and printed subsequently as 'Credit and Security: Economic Orders and Legal Regimes' (1984) 33 ICLQ. 22.

of the earlier indications that it is developing financial difficulties, and it is precisely at this point of time that an unsecured borrower will be particularly anxious that assets should not be effectively withdrawn from the general fund available to unsecured creditors by being charged by way of security to finance new borrowing from a third party.

Similar considerations apply to the giving of security by sovereign borrowers. It is possible for a sovereign borrower to give as security for a loan charges over its assets such as gold bullion or foreign currency reserves held by a foreign bank on its behalf, or to charge future sources of income receivable by it. Clearly, the giving of such forms of security by a sovereign issuer takes the assets or income secured from the funds generally available for the payment of unsecured creditors.

A negative pledge clause can be drawn to cover the borrowing of both an issuer and also, where the issuer is a corporation, any subsidiary or associated companies. A common form is as follows:

> so long as any of the Bonds are outstanding the Borrower will not create or permit to subsist any mortgage, charge, pledge, lien or other encumbrance, on its assets or revenues.[1]

A more sophisticated form of covenant in an issue of covertible bonds, which controls the position of subsidiaries as well as the position of the issuer, has been as follows:

> So long as any of the Bonds remain outstanding (as defined in the Trust Deed), the Company will not and will procure that none of the Consolidated Subsidiaries shall:
>
> (a) create or permit to be outstanding any pledge, mortgage, charge or other security interest for the benefit of the holders of any international convertible bond issue upon the whole or any part of its property or assets, present or future, to secure (i) payment of any sum due in respect of such international convertible bond issue;
>
> or
>
> (b) permit to be outstanding any pledge, mortgage, charge or other security interest or any guarantee or indemnity given by a third party in respect of any international convertible bond issue of the Company or any of the Consolidated subsidiaries;
>
> without any such case at the same time according or procuring to be accorded to the Bonds, to the satisfaction of the Trustee, the same security, guarantee or indemnity (as the case may be) as is granted to or is outstanding in respect of such international convertible bond issue or such other security as the Trustee in its absolute discretion shall deem reasonably equivalent thereto or shall be approved by an Extraordinary Resolution (as defined in the Trust Deed) of the Bondholders.

The Trust Deed defines 'Consolidated Subsidiary' to mean:

> every Subsidiary the accounts of which were in the latest, or should, in the written opinion of the Auditors (as defined in the Trust Deed) given following

[1] Given by Wood *op. cit.* p. 147.

> a request from the Company or the Trustee, be in the next Consolidated Accounts (as defined in the Trust Deed) consolidated with those of the Company. A certificate by the Auditors that in their opinion a Subsidiary is or is not a Consolidated Subsidiary shall, in the absence of manifest error, be conclusive and binding on all parties.

The Trust Deed defines 'international convertible bond issue' as meaning:

> an issue of bonds, debentures, notes or other similar securities of the Company or any other person which (i) are convertible into or exchangeable for Shares or shares of capital stock of any of the Consolidated Subsidiaries or have attached thereto or are issued with rights or warranties to subscribe for or purchase Shares or shares of capital stock of any of the Consolidated Subsidiaries and (ii) either are by their terms payable, or confer a right to receive any payment, in any currency other than yen and more than 50% of the aggregate principal amount thereof is initially offered or distributed by or with the authorization of the Company or any of the Consolidated Subsidiaries outside Japan.

The form of the more sophisticated version is interesting because it shows something of the possibilities available to the draftsman within the basic concept. In the particular draft the negative pledge is limited to the giving of security to the holders of any international convertible bond issue. It does not prevent the issuer from giving security in respect of other forms of indebtedness, and consequently is limited with regard to the protection which it confers upon the bondholders of the issue having the benefit of the covenant whom it is supposed to protect. In short, the clause is drafted to put all holders of international *convertible* bond issues on the same footing, but has no wider impact than that. The second example also shows that the negative pledge can be extended to prohibit the granting of security by a corporate issuer's subsidiaries and prohibiting guarantees by the subsidiaries of the issuers indebtedness. Further, both the issuer and subsidiaries are prohibited from securing any payment under any guarantee or indemnity, or any other comparable obligation relating to an international bond issue. Thus, neither the issuer nor its subsidiaries can secure a subsequent convertible bond issue by the indirect method of obtaining a guarantee, possibly from the issuer's bankers in support of the issuer, giving security to the third party in return for its guarantee. Nor under the terms of the covenant can a subsequent convertible bond issue be guaranteed by a third party without security from the issuer, as the issuer and its subsidiaries are prohibited from permitting to be outstanding any guarantee or indemnity given by a third party in respect of any international convertible bond issue of the corporations or its subsidiaries.

In the case of an issue by a sovereign borrower the negative pledge may similarly be usefully extended to limit the actions of state agencies such as the central bank and political sub-divisions, treating them essentially on the same basis as subsidiaries of a corporate borrower. While it is clearly possible to draft a clause in such terms, persuading a sovereign issuer to accept such a clause is a different matter. Often the subordinate entities are constitutionally independent of the state which created them, and the state is reluctant to accept a clause which would detract from their autonomy, as well as placing yet further restrictions on the capacity of the government to act independently.

What, then, is the effect of the prohibition placed by a negative pledge clause? Subject to any relaxation such as that included in the more complex form already given, the clause is a general prohibition. The prohibition, however, is less simple than would appear at first sight. Not merely is the borrower prohibited from creating any security interest in the future, it is prohibited from permitting any security to exist. If, therefore, there is already in existence a security given by the borrower prior to the issue of the bonds, the borrower is prohibited from allowing the security to continue to exist. Further, if after the issue of the bond, but without any positive act by the issuer, a security interest comes into existence by operation of law (eg a repairer's lien over vehicles belonging to the borrower), the borrower is prohibited from permitting the security to continue to exist and must pay off the sum due to the secured creditor to bring the security interest to an end.

Second, it should be observed that the prohibition is against the creation or subsistence of security over the issuer's assets and revenues. In this connection it is irrelevant that the indebtedness secured is that of the borrower or any other person. The nub of the concern is the fact of security.

Finally, it should be noted that it is far from clear precisely what security interests are prohibited by the terms of the clause. The basis of the more widely drawn of the two example clauses quoted above is the prohibition of any outstanding pledge, mortgage, charge or other security interest. This is a list of specific forms of charge of assets together with a general phrase 'or other security interest'. What is far from clear is the nature of the different types of interest which may be swept within the general expression. The use of a list of specific forms of asset security, followed by words of more general application, would seem to demand an interpretation based upon *ejusdem generis*. Indeed, the general concept behind the giving of security itself is of a borrower having title to the asset charged and releasing this to a lender for the duration of the loan. In particular this is the specific form of the three actual types of security listed. On this basis, where the title never has been vested in the borrower, but is retained by him until such time as the loan is repaid, no security within the clause is given. Thus, such common commercial transactions as title retention, leasing, hire-purchase and conditional sale would not be prohibited by the clause for all that these common devices have the same financial and commercial effect as the giving of security; nor, *prima facie*, would transactions which affect the asset position of the issuer without any security being given. Thus, factoring by the corporation of its debts and receivables and the use of set off would not appear to fall within the terms of the standard clause, although, of course, any of these devices could be prohibited by specific provision.[1]

It may, however, be that a court will sometimes be prepared to look at the substance rather than the form of a transaction in deciding whether

1 Specific provision would be commercially inconvenient in all cases except probably factoring—See Wood *op. cit.* at p. 148.

or not a breach of a negative pledge clause has occurred. Thus, in one American case a company had entered into a negative pledge clause. Subsequently, it formed a subsidiary and proceeded to transfer to the subsidiary most of the parent company's assets. On receipt of the assets the subsidiary proceeded to issue debentures charged upon them. It was held that the parent had breached the terms of the negative pledge clause binding it because the effect of the various transactions was to charge what had been the parent's assets within the negative pledge for the benefit of the debenture holders of the subsidiary.[1]

If there are difficulties in the use of the negative pledge to prevent a corporation from using security type devices in breach of the terms of the negative pledge clause, there are even greater difficulties with regard to sovereign borrowers. Jealous of their constitutional power to make full use of the assets of the nation, governments are reluctant to enter into bond clauses which will seriously circumscribe their constitutional powers. A simple negative pledge clause in traditional form can be easily avoided by common commercial techniques available to a sovereign government. If sufficiently desperate a government can sell off receivables as sources of income for a limited period to service a borrowing rather than charging them. Foreign reserves can be left in overseas bank accounts thereby being available for set off. Assets can be 'sold' to a financial institution with the option for the state at a later point of time to buy back at a higher price, the difference being the interest on the loan.[2]

The basic structure of the negative pledge clause so far analysed consists purely of the negative prohibition, rather than an attempt to create any form of pledge of the assets of the issuer. Were the matter to rest there no security interest could be created, because the clause itself would not purport to confer upon the creditor any rights over the issuer's assets either present or future.

However, it is common for the basic prohibition to be modified to permit the charging of its assets by an issuer where the bondholders are protected. They may be protected by being secured in the same assets and by the same security as the new creditor, or alternatively by the existing bondholders being provided with a substantially equivalent security. The former is unlikely to be a satisfactory solution to the problem, for the new lender is not to accept the diminution of his security which its sharing with the existing bondholders would entail. Typically the international bond will provide both solutions as alternatives. In the example of the more sophisticated negative pledge clause already given, the issuer was prohibited from creating security interests in its assets 'without in any such case at the same time according or procuring to be accorded to the Bonds, to the satisfaction of the Trustee, the same security, guarantee or indemnity (as the case may be) as is granted to or is outstanding in respect of such international convertible bond issue or such other security as the Trustee in its absolute discretion shall deem reasonably equivalent thereto or as

1 *Re Associated Gas and Electric Co,* 61 F Supp (S.D.N.Y. 1944), aff'd 149 F 2d 996. (2nd Cir 1945) cert. denied 326 US 736 (1945).

2 All examples given by Wood *op. cit.* p. 148

shall be approved by an Extraordinary Resolution (as defined in the Trust Deed) of the Bondholders.'

Neither amendment to the underlying prohibition will create a security interest in favour of the bondholders in the assets of the issuer. With regard to the first alternative, where the bondholders are equally secured with the new lender by the same security and the same assets, the agreement is merely one to provide security on a contingency and does not purport to create a security interest itself. In short, it is merely an agreement to do a certain thing on a certain event and purports to be no more than that. With regard to the second alternative, namely the giving of an equivalent security, no security interest is created, not only because it similarly purports merely to be a contract and not a creation of a security interest, but also because the assets within the agreement, and on which any security would be imposed, are simply not identified.

However, to all this it may be objected that the nettle has not been grasped. The draftsman of the negative pledge clauses so far considered has failed to create a security interest because he has not seriously attempted to create a security interest. Could not the position be put right by the stroke of a draftman's pen in simply providing, after prohibiting the issuer's granting of security over its assets to a new lender, that, if it proceeds to grant such a security, a comparable security interest in favour of the bondholders should automatically attach to those assets securing the bond equally and rateably with the new lender. The twin arguments available against the two alternatives previously considered are overcome because the clause then purports to confer an automatic security interest and the assets concerned are identified.

It may in fact be that under U.S. law a security interest is created in such cases in the form of an equitable lien. Thus in *Connecticut Company v New York, N H and H R R Co*[1] a railroad company issued bonds containing a covenant whereby the bondholders would participate equally in the security of any mortgage created over its property at the date of the issue of the bonds. By a majority the court held that the covenant was effective in creating an equitable lien forthwith on the property owned by the issuer, which property was specific and identifiable, so that no valid mortgage could subsequently be created which would prevent the bondholders from participating in the security. Similarly, in *Kaplan v Chase National Bank*[2] the covenant prohibited the issuers creating any lien on, or pledge of, the stock of its subsidiaries without rateably securing the debentures. The bank made loans available to the issuer taking stock of the issuer's subsidiary as collateral security, and no steps were taken to secure the debenture holders. The court directed the bank to hold the stock which had been pledged as security for the loan as though provision had been made to similarly secure the debenture-holders.

In one U.S. case a court was prepared to infer security where the form of the negative pledge was merely a prohibition of the creation of security with no modification or expression of a conferral of an automatic security.

1 94 Conn, 23 107A 646 (1919).
2 156 Misc 471 281 N Y S. 825.

In *Coast Bank v. Minterhout*[1] the court held that the mere breaking of the prohibition on the granting of subsequent security created an equitable lien over the assets affected in favour of the bondholders enforceable against a purchaser of the security with notice of the prohibition. However, the pleadings in the case were decisive for the defendants had failed to answer the plaintiff's pleading that the prohibition was intended to create a security interest in the property. Thus, the issue for the court was 'not what meaning appears from the face of the instrument alone, but whether the pleaded meaning is one to which the instrument is reasonably susceptible. It is essentially the question that would be presented had the defendants denied that the parties intended to create a security interest and the plaintiff had offered extrinsic evidence to show that they did. Such evidence would be admissible to interpret the instrument, but not to give it a meaning to which it is not reasonably susceptible.'

Unfortunately for bondholders, however, the position in English law is that a provision for automatic attachment creates no more security interest than the situations already considered. It exists as a more contractual right in favour of the bondholders. At the time the issue is made no security interest can attach because no attachment is to take place until the occurence of the contingency (namely the attempt of the issuer to create a further security on its assets). Does attachment, however, take place subsequently when the contingency takes place? It would seem that it does not. Until the contingency occurs all that exists is an agreement to give security. While equity is prepared to treat that as done which ought to be done and to bring security into existence, it attaches conditions to its operations. The essential condition is that money should be advanced in consideration of the security. It is not sufficient that the creditor advanced the money against a mere contractual right. There must be an intention to confer a security interest upon him and the agreement must not be contingent on the occurrence of a future uncertain contingency.[2] At the time that the bondholders advance their money to the issuer there is no present intention that a security interest be created, but merely a contractual right which may subsequently, on the happening of a contingency, attach as a security interest. By the time the moment for attachment comes, the bondholder's money has been paid and the consideration is passed. There is therefore no consideration for attachment. In short, the agreement must be executed and the consideration given must be for the attachment and not the agreement itself.[3] The fact that the consideration requirements are those of equity, and not the simple common law concept, is emphasized by the fact that there is no executed consideration for the change, the lack of

1 61 Cal 2d 311, 392 P 2d 265, 38 Cal Rptr 505 (1964).

2 Goode *Legal Problems of Credit and Security* published jointly by Centre for Commercial Law Studies and Sweet & Maxwell (1988) 2nd edn p. 36. See, however, the contrary view of Peter Gabriel *Legal Aspects of Syndicated Loans*, Butterworths (1986) pp. 86-90.

3 *Re Jackson and Bassford Ltd* [1906] 2 Ch 467; *Re Gregory Love & Co* [1916] 1 Ch 203; *Williams v Burlington Investments Ltd* (1977) 121 Sol Jo 424.

consideration cannot be overcome by putting the agreement under seal.[1] It follows from this analysis that automatic attachment will not take place, and a creditor could obtain a security interest on the happening of the attachment only by advancing new funds by agreement with the issuer, and then only to the extent of the new advance. With regard to the money initially advanced by the bondholders, as there is no security interest a subsequent creditor will obtain priority even if he has advanced his funds with knowledge of the provisions of the original negative pledge clause.[2]

In short, it appears that under English law all forms of the negative pledge confer upon the bondholders merely contractual rights against the issuer and no form of security. It follows that the failure of the issuer to honour the terms of a negative pledge clause merely creates a right in contract under English law for the bondholders, and according to the terms of the issue a probable event of default in respect of the loan.[3] As it has been succinctly stated: 'the negative pledge reveals the limitations of contract; real securities in any system arise under the law and not under contract'.[4]

RELAXATIONS OF THE NEGATIVE PLEDGE

Tying as it does the issuer's capacity to deal with his own assets, the negative pledge clause has a great potential to prevent the proper commercial development of an issuing corporation or a sovereign issuer's capacity to exploit fully its potential to develop its resources. Not infrequently, therefore, efforts are made to effect modifications of the clause which will permit the issuer greater flexibility with regard to its own assets, while leaving the bondholders substantially protected. The equal and rateable security provisions already examined are examples of this. It enables a borrower to continue to raise unsecured credit so long as either the new creditor feels that the credit-worthiness of the issuer is such that its loan is sufficiently protected where security over the relevant assets of the issuer is shared

1 *Re Earl of Lucan* (1890) 45 Ch D 470.

2 *Palmer v Carey* [1926] AC 703; *Swiss Bank Corp Ltd, v Lloyds Bank Ltd* [1980] 2 All ER 419 affd [1981] 2 All ER 449.

3 It is conceivable that bondholders may be able to sue in tort for interference with the contract between the bondholders and issuer where they can show that the subsequent creditor took security with knowledge of the negative pledge clause but this is unlikely for the issuer's breach lies not in the giving of the security to the subsequent purchaser but in failing to give equal security to the bond holders. *Legal Problems of Credit and Security* p.51.
The bondholder might seek an injunction against the third party in reliance on the principle stated by Knight Bruce LJ in *De Mattos v Gibson* (1858) 45 ER 108 but it is unlikely that he will succeed for the third party when taking security is only doing what he is allowed to do by the express terms of a negative pledge clause requiring equal and rateable security—a point made by Professor R Cranston in 'Remedies in International Finance — why so few Formal Legal Proceedings', a paper given at University College, London, on 15 November 1988.

4 Allan *op. cit.*

with the existing bondholders, or alternatively where the existing bondholders are persuaded that the offer of some other security is adequate for their purposes.

Equally, however, both these methods of resolution of the problem are complex. Both methods involve the active co-operation of the bondholders and positive steps to effect the security. Where the same security is offered to the bondholders and the new creditor, the grant of the security will involve the appointment of a trustee to hold the security on behalf of all the creditors concerned. Where equivalent security is given the equivalent security must be approved on behalf of the bondholders and steps taken for the security to be given. All this involves considerable administration and some expense.

In the meantime the issuer will be anxious to go about its normal operations which, whether a corporation or a soveriegn issuer, will involve its normal commercial activities. Associated with these activities will inevitably be short-term routine commercial and financial borrowings and liens arising by operation of law. Thus, whenever an item of the issuer's property is repaired there will be a repairer's lien over the goods for the amount of the repairer's bill.[1] Similarly, bankers can exercise liens over the customer's securities deposited with them,[2] shipbuilders in respect of new ships until the price is paid,[3] and sellers of goods over the subject of sale until the sale price is paid.

The bondholders may well feel that it is unnecessary for the protection of their interests that such everyday commercial transactions giving rise to such short-term security should be a breach of the negative pledge clause and require in each case their approval. Indeed, in many cases it is doubtful whether the issuer could commercially carry on its day-to-day activities if constant approval for matters of this sort were required.

Equally, in respect of other matters such as guarantees, which are essentially of a long-term nature, the bondholders may feel that they do need protection for all that no security interest is given. After all, a guarantee will add nothing to the assets available in the event of insolvency of the issuer, but will simply add to its liabilities. Accordingly, there is almost endless potential to refine the drafting of a negative pledge clause to prohibit the issuer from entering into long-term transactions which weaken the position of the bondholders (for all that no security is given), while at the same time conferring upon the issuer wide power to enter into every day commercial transactions of a short-term nature without needing the bondholders' approval.[4] An example is the form of negative pledge clause used by the World Bank in its agreement with member countries.

> It is the mutual intention of the Borrower and the Bank that no other external debt shall enjoy any priority over the loan by way of a lien on governmental

[1] *Hatton v Car Maintenance Co Ltd* [1915] 1 Ch 621 at 624; *The Katingaki* [1976] 2 Lloyd's Rep 372.

[2] *Brandao v Barnett* (1846) 12 Cl Fin 787; *Re London & Globe Finance Corpn* [1902] 2 Ch 416.

[3] *Woods v Russell* (1822) 5 B and Ald 942.

[4] See the discussion and examples given by Philip Wood *op. cit.* pp. 151-155.

assets. To that end, the borrower undertakes that, except as the bank shall otherwise agree, if any lien shall be created on any assets of the Borrower as security for any external debt, such lien will *ipso facto* equally and rateably secure the payment of the principal of and interest and other charges on, the Loan and the Bonds and that in the creation of any such lien express provision will be made to that effect, provided, however, that the foregoing provisions of this Section shall not apply to: (i) any lien created on property, at the time of the purchase thereof, solely as security for the payment of the purchase price of such property; or (ii) any lien arising in the ordinary course of banking transactions and securing a debt maturing not more than one year after its date.

The term 'assets of the Borrower' as used in this Section include assets of the Borrower or of any its political sub-divisions or of any agency of the Borrower or of such political sub-division, including the Borrower's (named central bank) or any institution performing the functions of a central bank.[1]

[1] Quoted by Delaume *op. cit.* p. 254 n. 100.

7 Convertible bonds[1]

As it is possible to have a floating rate note convertible into a straight international bond, so it has proved possible to devise a form of bond, issued by a corporate issuer and convertible into equity shares within that corporation. The device appears to be American in origin, but has been cleverly adapted to make a significant impact upon international bond issues. The basis of a convertible issue is the issue of a bond which pays interest in the normal way. Within the rights conferred by the bond, and as part of its terms and conditions, the holder of the bond has the right, in certain circumstances, to convert the bond into shares of the issuing corporation or an associated corporation. The right may be conferred for a limited period or may apply for the whole life of the bond should it go to term. The terms on which the shares are to be acquired are laid out in the terms and conditions of the issue and this sets out the price which has to be paid for the shares. The price may remain constant or may be varied at specified intervals almost invariably in an upward direction. If the conversion is effected, then the bond is given up for a number of shares on the specified formula at the face value of the bond.

REASONS FOR THE ISSUE OF CONVERTIBLE BONDS[2]

The use of the convertible formula usually represents an attempt to meet the aspirations of both the issuer and the investor. From the investor's point of view the effect of conversion will be to convert an interest bearing investment, with a limited possibility of capital growth, into a participating investment within the corporation, likely to give less by way of income but a greater possibility of capital growth (dividends tend to be less than interest payments). The incentive for an investor to invest in a convertible is therefore the possibility of capital growth of the shares.[3] Consequently, the issuer must regard it as probable that the majority of investors will

[1] See generally Peregrine Aldred *Convertibles and Warrants*, Euromoney Publications (1987), and Roger McCormick and Harriet Creamer, *Hybrid Corporation Securities: International Legal Aspects,* Sweet and Maxwell (1987).

[2] See McCormick and Creamer *op. cit.* pp. 40–41.

[3] Nevertheless, there is truth in the following observation. 'The basic attraction of convertible securities to the investor is that they give him the best of two worlds. In the case of a debenture . . . convertible into common stock, the holder

convert and become shareholders in the issuing company.[1] Given that this is the common outcome one may wonder why issuers do not simply make a straight issue of equity without involving the intermediary of the bond. A common reason for the employment of the device is the view of the company that the current share price undervalues the shares and that an issue at that price would cause unnecessary dilution of the assets of the company.[2] In such a situation the interests of both investors and issuer can be accommodated by the usual formula of the convertible bond market, namely, by issuing the bond with the conversion price being fixed at a higher price per share than the market currently gives.[3] The investor thus will not convert unless the market price of the share goes up to that level and the effect, from the issuer's point of view, is that it will be getting on conversion a better price per share than the current market value.[4]

There is a further benefit from both the shareholders and the Company's point of view. It is probable that the company is raising capital to finance an expansion of its operations, which will be likely to lead to increased profits in years to come. By the time that the share price increases to the fixed exchange price it is likely that the investment in the company's operations will be actually yielding the increased profits. Thus, hopefully,

[1] has a reasonably certain source of income from a relatively secure investment which he can retain if the company shows no sign of economic expansion. On the other hand, if conditions improve, he can convert into a participating position in order to share in the equity growth': Loosemore 'Some Legal Problems Associated With the Use of Convertible Securities and Warrants as Corporate Financing Devices' (1975) 33 University of Toronto Faculty of Law Review p. 125 at p. 126. Another writer has referred to 'the convertible debenture's combination of advantages for it offers both the security characteristic of a straight bond and the growth opportunity associated with an equity investment'. Malstrom 'Stockholders Derivative Actions by Holders of Convertible Debentures,' (1973) 6 Univ. of Michigan Journal of Law Reform 760.

[1] It has in fact been demonstrated that many corporations issue convertible debentures to raise share capital rather than to make the debenture more marketable; Pelcher Raising Capital with Convertible Securities (1955) 12 Mich Bus Studies No 2 (1955).

[2] Klein 'The Convertible Bond: a peculiar package' (1975) 123 University of Pennsylvania Law Review at p. 539.

[3] In England and in many other jurisdictions the local company law demands that the company's capital be maintained by prohibiting the issue of shares at a discount. Thus the issue of debentures at a discount on terms that they can be immediately converted into shares of the same value is unlawful as an indirect means of issuing the shares at a discount *(Moseley v Koffyfontein Mines* [1904] 2 Ch 108). The doctrine would also be equally applicable where bonds issued by a subsidiary are convertible into equity of the parent. It is necessary to ensure that the parent receive full consideration for the shares issued.

[4] Other factors motivate an issuer's use of the convertible form. Stock markets are not immune from 'fashions' and an issuer's choice may be determined by the essentially irrational preference of investors at the time of issue. Further, the use of convertible bonds may be a necessary sweetener to promote the issue which would otherwise be unattractive to investors or enable an issuer to achieve a lower interest rate or fewer restrictive covenants. Loosemore *op.cit.* p.128.

three factors will be influencing the upward movement of the company's shares, namely, the adverse position of the stock market will have been overcome and the shares will have moved up in value merely in response to this. This rise will have proceeded further by reason of first the addition of further assets of the company, and secondly further injections of profits out of which dividends can be paid. Thus, the share price might well move above the exchange price, giving the investor the capital profit for which he was looking, while the increased assets and profits of the company diminish or avoid the dilution problem which was the issuer's concern. Further, the effect of conversion increases the shareholding and eradicates the company's debt enabling it to take up new borrowings, should it so desire, for the purpose of further capital investment.

If used when the market is favourable to a convertible issue, such a means of raising capital has the best of all bargains, namely an advantage for both issuer and investor.[1] Convertible bonds have proved to be attractive to investors and have often allowed issuers to obtain their finance at a rate of interest less than would have been possible had a straight debt issue been employed. A further advantage appears to be that some institutional investors may be prohibited from investing in shares in the issuer but may be allowed to invest in debentures with the conversion option.

CONVERTIBLE BONDS AND BONDS WITH WARRANTS – A COMPARISON

An alternative form of investment to the convertible bond, which has comparable features, is the issue of straight bond with a warrant giving the warrant–holder the option of purchasing shares in the issuer at a specified price. As with warrants annexed to domestic debentures the use of the warrant may take two forms. The warrant may be an integral part of the bond and not detachable from it, in which case the warrant–holder will always be the same person as the bondholder. Alternatively, the warrant may be detachable from the bond and independently negotiable and transferable. In these cases, the warrant may be detached and traded separately on the secondary market. The essential difference between the convertible bond and the issue of a bond with warrant is that the convertible bond involves only the provision of one set of capital funds to the company, being the amount raised by the company on issue which is subsequently converted from debt into share capital. By contrast the issue of the bond with a warrant enables the issuing corporation to raise two sets of capital as the bond is not converted into shares, for the warrant–holder has merely the right to purchase shares.[2] The first capital injection is thus loan capital

1 For a contrary view suggesting that the convertible bond typically creates a bad bargain for both user and investor seen Klein 'The Convertible Bond: a peculiar package' 123 (1975) University of Pennsylvania Law Review pp. 547–73

2 'The only essential difference is that a 'warrant is exercised by the payment of cash while a privilege of conversion is exercised by the surrender of a corporate obligation or a share of stock'. Hills 'Convertible Securities — Legal Aspects and Draftsmanship', (1930) 19 Calif L Rev 1 at p. 4.

on the issue of the bond, and the second, on the exercise of the warrant, is share capital.[1]

A further difference between the two forms of financing arises from the fact that the right to buy represented by the warrant will be for a specified period and exist independently of the bond. Thus if the bond is redeemed before maturity the option contained in the warrant will continue unlike a conversion right in a bond which will cease with the cessation of the existence of the bond.

In the case of both convertible bonds and bonds with warrants the equity linkage places great significance on the price of the shares which are to be obtained by conversion or purchase. This of necessity demands that the shares should be listed and in both cases the issuer will normally undertake at least to use its best endeavours to obtain or maintain a listing of the relevant shares on a designated stock exchange.

REVENUE ASPECTS

There are a number of special tax aspects relating to convertible bonds which must be taken into account by both the investor and the issuer.

(1) *Income taxes* In most jurisdictions the interest payable on bonds will be a deductible expense in calculating the taxable profits of the issuer which is a considerable tax advantage. By way of contrast the dividends paid on shares after conversion will not usually be deductible in the same manner.

From the point of view of bondholders the problem will usually arise because of withholding taxes. The issuer may be bound to withhold income tax at the standard rate on paying either interest or dividends, thus reducing the investors *prima facie* right to one of receiving net income only. The effect of the imposition of a withholding tax may be reduced by a double tax treaty between the issuer's jurisdiction and that of the investor. However, in the case of interest paid under the bond there is protection given to the investor in respect of the bond interest by reason of the grossing up provision. Such protection does not, however, extend to dividends payable net of tax. Normally, the prospectus will set out the position so that an investor can see the position as it will relate to him.

(2) *Capital taxes* Any gains realised on the disposal of shares or warrants may be subject to capital gains tax under the law of the jurisdiction of the investor. This in turn gives rise to the question of how the gain is calculated in the particular jurisdiction involved. Is conversion itself a disposal giving rise to a capital gains tax liability? Is roll over relief available which will delay the imposition of tax but will mean that in due course the shares will be taken as having been acquired not at their value at the time of conversion but at the original cost of the bond which will tend

[1] 'Thus, it is conceivable that when a company has issued bonds with warrants attached it may find itself with cash that it doesn't want. But this position is not really much different from what it would have been had it issued convertible bonds, because presumably funds generated by the exercise of warrants can be used to redeem, or purchase on the market, bonds from which warrants have been (or can be) detached.' Klein *op. cit.* p. 553.

to emphasise the size of the gain subject to tax? These are matters for the investor to consider carefully.

From the issuer's point of view the issue of shares on conversion (or on subscription under a warrant) may give rise to the payment of stamp duty or other issue taxes under the law of his own jurisdiction. Equally, such taxes may be imposed by the jurisdictions of some or all of the conversion agents, who are appointed to handle conversions in various financial centres through which the bonds are marketed, in respect of conversions actually effected through them. It is usual for an international convertible bond issue to specify clearly that such taxes are the responsibility of the issuer if imposed by the issuer's own jurisdiction, but otherwise that of the investor who has initiated the conversion through the particular conversion agent employed.

COVENANTS OF THE ISSUER ON A CONVERTIBLE BOND ISSUE[1]

Because of the necessity to protect the conversion element a number of covenants are entered into by the issuer in addition to those dealt with in greater detail in the pages which follow. These will usually include:

(1) *Sufficient shares* The issuer undertakes to maintain sufficient authorised capital unissued to cover the conversion rights granted.
(2) *Discount.* The issuer undertakes not to do anything which would have the effect of reducing the conversion price below par value thereby negating an issue at a discount, which may well be unlawful under the law of the issuer's jurisdiction.
(3) *Listing* The issuer undertakes to try to maintain the listing of the shares on the stock exchange on which they are currently quoted, and undertakes further that on conversion the shares will be listed on all stock exchanges on which are listed the classes of shares into which the bonds are to be converted.
(4) *Approvals* The issuer undertakes to try to obtain all necessary governmental approvals and consents for the share issue and, where registration of an issue is necessary, to try to have the share issue registered with the appropriate authority.
(5) *Share status* The issuer undertakes that the shares when issued will be valid securities of their type, fully paid and free of incumbrances.
(6) *Share ranking* The issuer undertakes that it will not modify the rights created by the shares or create other share capital on more favourable terms to the detriment of the conversion shares, eg as by issuing preference shares on a rights basis.

1 The London Stock Exchange has requirements for convertibles listed thereon see *Admission of Securities to Listing* Section 9 Chapter 2. In the case of domestic issues, the rights are to be covered in the terms of the trust deed. In the case of eurocurrency securities, there is no requirement to have a trust deed but in the absence of such a document the relevant requirements must be complied with by the inclusion of appropriate provisions in the terms and conditions of issue.

(7) *Evasion* The issuer undertakes not to grant conversion rights in shares of the issuer subsequent to the issue except on the same terms as the original issue, thereby preventing circumvention by this means of the anti-dilution provisions discussed later.

(8) *Notification of information* It is vital that if bondholders are to make sensible decisions as to whether or not to convert that they be kept fully informed of any changes of circumstances which might affect their decision. Accordingly, it is normal to provide that information be disseminated to bondholders, and some stock exchange regulations insist that this should be done. In particular, the issuer *will* undertake to publish changes in the conversion price and *may* also undertake to publish other events affecting the bondholder's rights eg dividends out of reserves, rights issues, mergers and liquidations.

FACTORS INFLUENCING THE TIMING OF CONVERSION

It is to be noted that, while the conversion option is exercisable by the investor, both the issuer and the investor will be interested in the timing of this. The investor will, of course, in any event not convert unless the market price of the shares goes beyond the agreed exchange price. However, where this occurs, he may well not convert at the earliest possible moment. If the return he is getting from the bonds is significantly in excess of the dividends being paid in respect of the appropriate number of shares the incentive for the investor is to continue his investment in the bond until the last possible moment for conversion. If a company accumulates its earnings, rather than reflecting increased earnings in increased dividends, it is not likely that the return on the appropriate number of shares will be anything like the return on the bond. In this situation the investor will be able to sit happily with his bond both collecting the income and watching the share price, which he will eventually be able to realise, increase as a result of the accumulations. There is unlikely to be an incentive for him to convert even to be able to take his capital appreciation early as the effect of this situation will be that the price of the bond may well increase at a faster rate than the increase of the stocks and shares, because the bond embraces, within the single instrument, both the healthy income and the increased capital value arising from the ever rising value of the shares.[1]

A further complicating matter affecting the investor's timing of his conversion decision arises where the bonds and the shares are denominated in different currencies. If this occurs the exchange rate between the two currencies may be fixed at the time of issue, and currency fluctuations, both existing and anticipated, will then have a significant bearing upon the choice of conversion timing.

The speculative element inherent in this situation is, if anything, emphasised by the normal provision in a convertible bond issue that the exchange rate prevailing at the time of issue of the bonds will continue to apply throughout the conversion period. This places the bondholder in the position that he will gain if the bond currency depreciates against

[1] Klein *op. cit.* p. 550.

the currency of the shares but lose if the currency movement is in the opposite direction. No such element exists in the case of a bond issue with warrants as the subscription price of the shares will be denominated in the currency of the shares.

AMORTISATION

Because of the conversion privilege contained within the bond mandatory amortisation is not usually considered a requirement on an issue, and is therefore, customarily, not included. It is anticipated that by the maturity date the bonds would have been converted into shares. Equally, the conversion right makes the inclusion of a call provision a sensitive matter between the issuer and the investor. For the investor the effective use of the call provision will bring to an end his conversion right.[1] Accordingly, call provisions are usually included in a form modified from the form incorporated in non-convertible bonds. A typical formula is that used in an issue of dollar denominated bonds made by a Japanese company in 1981, the terms of which were as follows:[2]

> *Redemption at the option of the Company* On or at any time after the 31 March 1987, and prior to maturity, the company may . . . having given not less than thirty nor more than sixty days notice to the bondholders (which notice shall be irrevocable) redeem all, or from time to time some only (being one million dollars in principal amount or any integral mutiple thereof) of the bonds at the following redemption prices (expressed as percentages of the principal amount of the bonds).

If redeemed during the twelve calendar months beginning 31 March, in any of the following years:

	Redemption Price
1987	103
1988	102½
1989	102
1990	101½
1991	101
1992	100½

1 It is, of course, vital to the bondholder that the notice requirements are sufficient to ensure that he receives the notice with adequate time to convert. If notice is to be given by advertisement in a particular newspaper it is vital that the bondholder peruse the relevant columns for if he does not he 'loses his right of conversion as well as the associated financial gain'. Malstrom 'Theories of liability under Convertible Debenture redemption notice requirements' (1976) 44 Fordham Law Review 817. However, as Mr. Malstrom points out in his article, it is possible that U.S. courts will intervene where a notice, although satisfying the bond requirements, is in fact insufficient to allow the bondholder to convert, see eg *Van Gemert v Boeing Co,* 520 F 2d 1373 (2d Cir), cert denied, 96 S Ct 364 (1975); *Kaplan v Vornado, Inc.* 341 F Supp 212 (N.D. I11. 1971).

2 Life Co, Ltd issue of U.S. $25,000,000 Convertible 6 per cent bonds redeemable 30 Sept 1996.

And thereafter at their principal amount, together in each case with interest accrued to the date of redemption.
Reference in these conditions to principal in respect of any bond shall, where the context so permits, be deemed to include a reference to any premium payable thereon.
Notwithstanding the foregoing, the Company may (on giving not less than forty-five days notice to the bondholders) redeem at any time on or after 31st March, 1985 all or any of the bonds at their principal amount, together with accrued interest to the date of redemption, provided that the closing price of the shares on the Osaka Securities Exchange (or the Tokyo Stock Exchange, if the shares are then listed on the Tokyo Stock Exchange) for each of twenty consecutive trading days, the last of which occurs not more than thirty days prior to the date upon which notice of such redemption is published, is at least one hundred and fifty per cent of the conversion price in effect on such day.

The company is also given the usual rights to redeem for taxation reasons and to purchase on the secondary market.

Under the terms of the bond the investors' right to convert continues, in the event of the bond being called for redemption, up to the close of business on the date on which redemption should take place.

The net effect of this is that *at any time* the issuer can call the bond where the share price is trading at one hundred and fifty per cent of the conversion price. Further, *during the specified years* the issuer can call the bond at a premium without regard to the trading position of the underlying shares. The effect of this is twofold. Since investors are not likely to lose money, the effect of the underlying shares going up in value to a level in excess of what the issuer would have to pay out if he redeemed the bond means that the issuer can effectively force the investors to convert by calling the bond. Thus, if the shares have increased in value to one hundred and fifty per cent, but the bond is trading only at a premium of five per cent, the natural response of an investor facing a call, is to convert to preserve in his hands the enhanced value of the shares. Indeed, the very point of the inclusion of the call provision is a reflection of the fact that most issuers have the clear intention of forcing the conversion once an appropriate price is reached. Equally, however, investors are aware of these intentions and it appears that the result of this is that, in advance of an expected call, convertibles trade only at a modest premium over their conversion value.[1]

EFFECT OF THE CONVERSION FACTOR IN BONDS

The conversion factor in the bonds has two effects. First, if the underlying value of the shares goes down, while the value of the bonds will be affected, the coupon interest will give some support so that the bonds are not likely to go down so far as the decline in value of the underlying shares because conversion does not have to take place. On the other hand, since the capital

[1] Fisher *op. cit.* p. 147.

appreciation of the bond is likely to be drawn from the rise in value of the shares, the inclusion of the call right in favour of the issuer has the effect that the bonds are not likely to trade at a price significantly in excess of the conversion value.

As a matter of practice, convertible bonds issued by U.S. companies or their subsidiaries are usually subordinated to the straight debt issues of the corporation. This is because financial analysts tend to regard convertible debt as equivalent to an issue of shares where it is issued in subordinated form, thereby increasing the ratio of the company's share–holding in relation to its debt.

Discretionary conversion by the trustee

Given the complex possibilites arising with regard to the timing of conversion and, in particular, the manner in which the issuer can often force a decision on the conversion issue, it has been traditionally felt that there may be a case for putting into a bond some machinery to protect the unsophisticated investor from the loss of the capital gain which he should make by affecting a conversion, but which his lack of sophistication and attention to his investment might cause him to overlook. This is by the inclusion of the so-called 'widows and orphans' clause which is, however, only possible if the issue is made with the support of a trust deed and trustee. The effect of the clause is that if redemption of the bonds is imminent but bondholders have neither exercised their conversion option nor presented their bonds for redemption, thus remaining totally passive, the trustee may subscribe for the shares into which their bonds would have been convertible if the trustee is of the opinion that the net proceeds of sale of the subscribed shares would exceed the amount payable on redemption of the bonds. If he elects to subscribe pursuant to this discretionary power the trustee must arrange the sale of the allotted shares, and ensure that the proceeds are sent to the principal paying agent for paying to the bondholders.

SECURITIES REGULATION CONSIDERATIONS

In general, there seems to be no greater securities regulation difficulty for the sale of convertible bonds or bonds with warrants than is the case of ordinary bond issues. Most countries, as has been seen, operate a private placement or professionals-only exemption to the regulation of issues of securities.

In many jurisdictions exchanging one security for another type issued by the same issuer does not consititute a public offer of the securities requiring registration and consequent control of the prospectus. It is assumed that holders of securities know about the issuer and that either disclosure requirements applied and were met at the time of the issue of the original securities, or an exemption applied and that there is no reason why the replacement security should be caught by the securities regulation provisions if the first was not.[1]

However, in respect of U.S. regulation, the position is more complex. The lock up procedure exists whereby issues of bonds are not sold in the U.S. and there is a complex mechanism to ensure that during a 90-day period from completion of the issue outside of the U.S., none of the bonds will be purchased by U.S. nationals, nor will they be sold within the U.S. In the case of the sale of convertible bonds or bonds with warrants, the instruments can be seen as necessitating two separate issues, the first, the initial issue of the bonds and the subsequent one, the issue of the corporation's shares when conversion takes place or the warrant exercised. With regard to issues of company shares rather than corporation debt, the S.E.C. has required not merely a 90-day lock up period, but also an effective mechanism which is designed to ensure that the securities will only be re-sold in the U.S. or to U.S. nationals, if either the corporation has registered the issue prior to the expiration of the 90-day period, or by that day there is an exemption available from registration in the U.S.[2] It would seem logical to suppose that the S.E.C. would take the view that, in the case of a convertible, either registration of the underlying shares of the corporation must be completed prior to their issue on conversion of the debenture or an applicable exemption therefrom must be demonstrated prior to that time.[3]

The question remains however, does this mean that convertibles can safely be allowed to be traded within the U.S. after the expiration of the 90-day lock up and before conversion takes place? The giving of the conversion right on a bond issue contemplates that in due course, the bond will be replaced by a share issue. In these circumstances, an issue of convertibles can be seen as being as much an issue of shares as of debt. On this analysis, registration of the underlying corporate shares should be effected, or an exemption should be available, before the expiration of the 90-day lock up period in respect of the original bonds since the bonds can be equated with the shares. This appears to be the analysis which appeals to the S.E.C., and would seem to reflect the commission's view that there is a greater

1 The London Stock Exchange requires that any convertible bond listed thereon should be exchangeable into securities which, at the time of exchange, are listed thereon or listed or traded on another regulated, regularly operating, recognised open market — see *Admission of Securities to Listing* Section 1, Chapter 2 para 17. Nevertheless, the Committee may admit such securities, options or warrants to listing in other circumstances if they are satisfied that holders have the necessary information available to form an opinion concerning the value of the underlying securities to which the convertible security option or warrants relates (ibid). Different stock exchange disclosure requirements relate to the different situations of a convertible issue by a listed company and a new applicant (Section 7 para. 6.4). However, apart from this, issue appears to be seen as a single issue of a debt instrument under English regulation.

2 Pan Amercian World Airways Inc, S.E.C. Action Letter (May 28, 1975) (Lexis Fedsec Library, No act file).

3 American Motors Corporation, S.E.C. No Action Letter (June 8th, 1982) (Lexis Fedsec Library, No act file).

risk of a flow back of bonds into the U.S. market when the issue is of a convertible nature, and particularly if the issue is by a U.S. issuer or overseas subsidiary.[1] Accordingly, if a convertible issue is to escape the attentions of the S.E.C., it seems that, not only should the bond issue be subject to the usual 90-day lock up period, but, so far as possible, all re-sales of the bonds to U.S. residents or within the U.S. should be prevented and the conversion or warrant rights should not apply to any U.S. national or resident.

Two further general considerations should also be borne in mind. First the law of some jurisdictions is quite nationalistic in its protection of its local companies and may prohibit foreigners from obtaining control of more than a relatively small proportion (eg 10 per cent) of the company's shares. This could affect a large institution which had acquired a lot of bonds and wished to convert them. Secondly, the company law of some jurisdictions demand that if a person acquires more than a specified percentage of the shares of a company he must make an offer for the remainder. In the U.K. the proportion under the Takeover Code is 30 per cent. Again this is of potential importance to the large institutional investor. Where the company law of the issuer contains any such prohibitions or requirements full disclosure should be made in the circulars and prospectus issued before sale to investors.

PRACTICAL CONSIDERATIONS OF CONVERSION

The terms of convertible bonds inevitably expend considerable space in defining the conversion period of the convertibles. Usually it commences about a month after the issue of the bonds and expires about a fortnight before maturity to enable a period of inactivity for the issuer to process redemption. It is usual for the bond terms to provide that, if the issuer fails to provide the paying agent with the funds to redeem, the conversion period continues until the funds are provided and the bondholder notified by the issuer. In general, the terms of the bond will also provide that the right of conversion terminates if the bonds are accelerated on default, or the issuer ceases to exist, or becomes insolvent. However, in such circumstances it is better for the bondholder that his claim be one for simple debt rather than a participant in the company, for a debt claim has greater priority on liquidation or dissolution.

The machinery of conversion is based upon the appointment of conversion agents in most of the jurisdictions in which the securities are marketed, and in the jurisdiction in which they are listed — in practice the same institutions as the paying agents. The issuer agrees to maintain a sufficient number of these throughout the life of the bonds in a sufficient number of centres. The agents are by the terms of their appointment the agent of the issuer and not that of the investor.

The procedure for conversion is that the bondholder serves notice of conversion at one of the conversion agents with whom he also deposits

1 K Mart (Australia) Properties Finance Limited, S.E.C. No Action Letter (March 31st, 1983) (Lexis, Fedsec, No act file).

his bond. The share certificate is sent by the conversion agent to the bondholder at the latter's risk within a specified period. Under the bond terms the shares on issue must rank *pari passu* with existing shares although ranking only for *future* dividends.

ANTI-DILUTION

For an investor the value of a convertible bond is the possibility that it represents acquiring at a lower price, fixed at the time of the issue of the bond, shares which have subsequently appreciated in value. To the extent that the issuer is free to take any steps which would depreciate the value of its shares, the investor is put at risk that his reasonable expectations will be thwarted. If left to its own devices, an issuer could bring about this very effect by sub-dividing its shares, by issuing bonus shares, or by making rights issues at a reduced price.[1] As an example, if the share capital of a company is \$1,000,000 comprising 100,000 shares with a face value of \$10 each all standing at par, a sub-division of the shares into 200,000 shares with a face value of \$5 is likely to halve the value of the shares on the secondary market as the assets and profits of the company will remain constant whilst the number of shares which those assets and profits have to service will have doubled.

To prevent this situation arising convertibles contain a number of provisions designed to protect the investor. Necessarily, when the investor is protected, the effect on an issuer may be to provide a practical limitation upon the exercise of its corporate powers.

CAPITAL DILUTION

The traditional manner in which the problem of sub-divisions of shares and bonus issues are dealt with, is by a provision that where these events take place, the price payable on conversion for the shares is reduced in the proportion which the sub-division or bonus issue had to the original share capital but the number of shares to which the bondholder is entitled is increased in the same ratio. A typical clause would provide as follows:

> 'If the Company shall (a) declare a dividend in, or authorize a free distribution of any Shares (b) sub-divide its outstanding Shares (c) consolidate its outstanding Shares into a smaller number of Shares or (d) reclassify any of its Shares into other securities of the Company, the conversion price shall be appropriately adjusted so that the holder of any bond, the conversion date in respect of which occurs after the coming into effect of the adjustment

[1] 'The interests of the holders of a convertible security will in many respects necessarily be in direct opposition to those of the holders of the underlying securities. Every advantage granted to the convertible security holders through the anti–dilution clause diminishes the interests of the holders of underlying securities; conversely any failure of the anti–dilution clause to protect against diminution in value of the conversion privilege will dilute the value of the senior securities.' Kaplan 'Piercing the Corporate Boilerplate: Anti-Dilution Clauses in Convertible Securities' (1965) 33 Univ of Chicago Law Revl at p. 3 footnote 7.

described in this subparagraph (i) shall be entitled to receive the number of Shares and/or other securities of the Company which he would have been entitled to receive after the happening of any event described above had such bond been converted immediately prior to the happening of such event (or, if the Company has fixed a prior record date for the determination of shareholders entitled to receive any such dividend or free distribution, immediately prior to such record date), but without prejudice to the effect of any adjustments to the Conversion Price made with effect from the date of the happening of such event (or such record date) or any time thereafter. An adjustment made pursuant to this subparagraph (i) shall become effective in the case of a sub-division, consolidation or reclassification, immediately on sub-division, consolidation or reclassification becoming effective, and shall become effective, in the case of a dividend in, or a free distribution of, any Shares, immediately after the record date for the determination of shareholders entitled to receive such dividend or free distribution. Provided, however, that in the case of a dividend in, or free distribution of Shares which must, under the issuer's applicable Corporation Law, be submitted for approval to A General Meeting of shareholders, or to a meeting of the Board of Directors of the Company ('the Board of Directors') before being legally paid or made, which is so approved after record date fixed for the determination of shareholders entitled to receive such dividend or distribution, such adjustments shall, immediately upon such approval being given by such meeting, become effectve retroactive to immediately after such record date'.

The vital effect of such a provision is to protect the investor, but it will be seen that there is also a protection to the issuer in that where shares are combined, thus reducing the total number of shares (which will have the opposite effect to dilution because the share price will go up proportionately to the combination) and where shares are converted into debt securities (which will also be likely to have a similar effect) the adjustment to the conversion price will work in the issuer's favour and not the investor's. In effect, whether shares are sub-divided or combined, exchanged for debt securities, or affected by a bonus issue, both issuer and investors will get that originally bargained for.

These provisions, of course, give no protection where a capital dilution takes place, not by way of sub-division or gift, but by issues of shares at below the price payable at conversion. With regard to this, basic philosophical problems are raised similar to the issue of categorisation involved in the securities regulation of convertible bonds. Is the bond to be viewed as a package of rights or is it merely a form of premature birth of shares in the issuing corporation? Either philosophy allows an adjustment of the conversion price to take place if there is a new issue of shares below the current market of the shares. However, the view that convertible bonds are merely prematurely born shares leads to the conclusion that, where the new issue of shares is at a price above the current market price but less than the conversion price, no adjustment should take place.[1] The bondholder is, in effect, a shareholder, and is therefore, not discriminated against if the company issues shares at the market price for this does not represent a dilution of the value of the shares with which the bonds are equated. For those who view the convertible bond as a package of rights, the issue of shares at less than the conversion price has the effect of diluting the conversion right within the package (for all that the new issue takes place at the current market price or above) and therefore the bondholder should be protected against this.

The two philosophies are patently mutually inconsistent and one or other of them must be adopted in the drafting of a clause to cover issues at below the appropriate price. Those adopted pursuant to the theory that the bond is a package of rights will seek to protect the bondholder from the effect of dilution arising from any issue below the conversion price. Accordingly, in these cases the trigger which gives rise to the operation of the clause will be the issue of shares at a price less than the conversion price. Beyond this, two formulae are available. Under the first, in any case there the trigger is operated, the conversion price is reduced proportionately to the effects of the new issue. Under the second, often referred to as the current quotient formula, the trigger is operated by an issue of shares either above or below the conversion price and the effect is that the conversion price is adjusted both upwards and downwards as appropriate, proportionally to the effect of the new issue. The logic behind this is that clearly, if bondholders are to benefit from reductions, they should also

1 Eg Loosemore, *op. cit.*, p. 130, 'It may be said that the purchaser of the convertible security is buying it because he thinks that management will be able to improve the profitability of the company and that its shares will rise in value. If further bonds are needed (for example to take advantage of a lucrative opportunity) and management chooses to raise these funds by means of a common share issue when the market price is still lower than the conversion price, the holder of the convertible will gain in the long run if the funds are used profitably. If they are not, management will be guilty of making a poor business decision, hardly a fundamental risk against which the purchaser of a convertible security can expect to be protected.

'The basic tenet of the market price clause is that the holder of the convertible security should be treated for purposes of protection against dilution, as if he were a common shareholder . . . The market price clause thus recognises the economic realities which require securities to be sold on the best term possible under the particular business conditions then applicable and does not deter a company from necessary financing by the sale of common stock when the market price is below the conversion price'. Kaplan *op. cit.* p. 21.

'The corporation may be ill-advised in selling stock at a time when the market is low, but it is not the function of anti-dilution provisions to protect convertible security holders against the possible bad judgment of the corporation's directors in timing its security issues, any more than to protect against bad judgment in production, or sales, or any other aspect of the management of the business.' Ratner 'Dilution and Anti-dilution: a Reply to Professor Kaplan' (1966) 33 Univ of Chicago Law Rev 494 at p. 496.

have the conversion price increased to take account of issues at above the conversion price which will have an anti-diluting effect.[1]

Where the bonds are viewed as a premature birth of shares, the market price formula is adopted. This is triggered only by an issue of shares at a price below the current market price and results in the conversion price being adjusted proportionately downwards.[2] The precise formulae adopted to effect these results are mathematical in nature and complex in form. They work with total mathematical precision.[3] On the modern international market it is the market price approach which is invariably used.

It should, however, be carefully noted that the analysis of convertible bonds and debentures as nascent shares is an economic one. Traditional legal analysis is in terms of a debt with a right attached and the holders are not members of the company with the consequent rights of shareholders.[4] If this were not the case interesting issues would arise with regard to directors conflicting obligations to the opposed interests of bondholders and shareholders in the dividend and call policies followed by the company.[5] It is precisely because of the traditional legal position of the bondholders as non-members of the company that protecting provisions are needed in the bond terms and trust deed.[6] This traditional approach indicates not only that if the bond terms contain no anti-dilution provisions it is unlikely that the courts will protect the bondholders, but that the courts will be unlikely to intervene if an anti-dilution provision, while included in the bond terms, is drawn insufficiently widely to protect the bondholders in the circumstances which have actually arisen.

1 The two formulae based upon sale under the conversion price are discussed with examples by Kaplan *op. cit.* pp. 7–10.

2 The conversion and market price based methods of anti-dilution are fully discussed and considered by Kaplan and Ratner in the works cited.

3 Bloomenthal Clark Boardman and Company, New York, (1985 rev.) Vol 3A 15.87.

4 *In re Sims Securities Trusts Ltd* [1971] 1 WLR 1455; *Gay v Burgess Mills,* 30 RI 231; 74A 714 (1909). However, a company may not use the convertible debenture formula to effect an issue of shares at a discount *Moseley v Koffeyfonte Mines Ltd* [1904] 2 Ch 108 (CA) discussed Macdonald 'The Evolution of the Debenture'(1907) 23 LQR.

5 The problems are discussed by Klein p. 566 *et seq.*

6 Indeed the rules of the English Stock Exchange covering listing require certain provisions in the trust deed before admission to listing will be allowed in the case of domestic issues. These *inter alia* limit the company's rights to reduce or increase its share capital and restrict its rights to capitalize profits or reserves by a share issue. The Stock Exchange *Memorandum on the Admission of Securities to Listing.* Appendix Sch VII. For U.S. authorities see, eg *Parkinson West End Street Railway* 173 Mass 446, 53 NE 891 (1899); *Broad* v. *Brackwell International Corpn,* 642F 2d 959 (5th Cir 1980) en bank), cert denied, 454 US 965 (1981).
It must not be thought that anti-dilution provisions on either the conversion or market price formulae however carefully drafted can resolve all difficulties or prevent a dilution if the issuer is determined to dilute and is sufficiently circumspect in the means adopted. Examples of how nearly every clause can be outflanked are given in the Kaplan and Ratner articles previously cited.

Mergers and share reclassifications

A further protection given to bond-holders, deals with the situation where the issuing corporation is taken over by another company or merged with it, or alternatively, there is a reclassification of its shares, or the distribution of substantially all of its assets to another company in such a way that the holders of the shares of the issuing company are entitled to receive shares in the company acquiring the issuer's assets. In these circumstances the bondholder is given the right, on subsequent conversion of his bond, to be treated in the same way as if he had been a shareholder in the original issuer at the relevant date (eg the date of the merger). A typical clause is as follows:

> 'In the case of any consolidation or amalgamation of the Company with, or merger of the Company into, any other corporation (other than a consolidation, amalgamation or merger in which the Company is the continuing corporation) or in the case of any sale or transfer of all or substantially all of the assets of the Company, the Company shall forthwith inform the Trustee of such event and if the Trustee deems it necessary, the Company shall cause the Corporation formed by such consolidation or amalgamation or the corporation which shall have acquired such assets, as the case may be, to execute a trust deed supplemental to the Trust Deed providing that the holder of each Bond then outstanding shall have the right (during the period such Bond shall be convertible) to convert such Bond into the class and amount of shares and other securities and property receivable upon such consolidation, amalgamation, merger, sale or transfer by a holder of the number of Shares into which such Bond might have been converted immediately prior to such consolidation, amalgamation, merger, sale or transfer. Such supplemental trust deed shall provide for adjustments which shall be as nearly equivalent as may be practicable to the adjustments provided for in the foregoing provisions of this Condition. The above provisions shall apply in the same way to any subsequent consolidations, amalgamations, mergers, sales or transfers'.

An alternative approach often adopted by the English draftsman to the takeover situation is the insertion of a provision that in the event of a takeover, the bondholder has the choice either of converting or calling for repayment at a price equal to the market price after the takeover bid.[1]

ILLEGALITY OF CONVERSION

It may be that after the issue of the convertible bond, the system of law under which the issuer is incorporated, and in the jurisdiction of which it carries on much of its business, will make it illegal for it to allow the debt represented by the bond to be converted into shares, usually through the introduction of exchange control regulations. This is commonly provided for in a convertible bond. Often the matter is dealt with by providing in the bond terms that the issue of shares is subject to all applicable laws and regulations so that the risk is assumed by the investor. Sometimes

1 Examples are given in Wood *Law and Practice of International Financial Law* pp. 189–190.

note is taken of the fact that the shares into which the bond might be converted will have a value, and that whilst conversion cannot be allowed, that value could be paid. A common clause taken from an issue by a Japanese corporation is as follows:

> 'If the company is prohibited under any applicable law of its place of incorporation for the time being in effect from delivering a certificate or certificates in respect of Shares issuable open conversion of bonds which certificate or certificates would have otherwise been deliverable in accordance with paragraph (B) of this Condition, then the Company shall pay or caused to be paid within fourteen calendar days of the relevant Conversion Date through the Custodian's Agent in the place of its incorporation to or to the order of the Bondholder converting such bonds cash in yen equal to the aggregate market value of the Shares for which the Company is prohibited from delivering such certificate or certificates and, upon receipt of such cash payment by the Custodian's Agent in the issuer's place of incorporation on behalf of such former Bondholder, the Company shall be discharged from its obligation to deliver such Shares or certificates thereof. The market value of each Share shall be (I) the last sale price (regular way) of a Share as reported by the stock exchange of the place of the issuer's incorporation if the shares are then listed thereon on the day which the relevant request for payment is made or, if no sale takes place on such Stock Exchange the price at which a Share is first traded (regular way) on such Stock Exchange subsequent to such day, less any applicable brokerage commission and tax payable by the converting Bondholder or (II) (if payment of a sum ascertained pursuant to item (I) above is not provided for under the applicable law of the issuer's place of incorporation, but such law provides an alternative method for determination of the price at which thereof an amount determined in accordance with the applicable provisions of the law of the issuers place of incorporation less any tax payable by the converting Bondholder'.

Since the issuer's capacity to allow the conversion of the bonds into shares will be governed by the place of its incorporation the failure to insert such a clause would mean that the conversion term would become impossible of performance in the event of that system of law- making conversion illegal.[1] The performance having become impossible the contractual obligation will have been frustrated and the issuer's liability thereunder brought to an end. The effect of the insertion of a clause in the terms set out above is to change the obligation to convert into an obligation to pay a sum of money in the event that conversion becomes impossible. In short, the effect of the clause is to alter the conversion obligation into a payment obligation.[2]

1 *First Russian Insurance Co v London and Lancashire Insurance Co* [1928] Ch 922 at 935; *Rae v Lazard Investment Co Ltd* [1963] 1 WLR 555 at p. 573.

2 Payment obligations are considered *post* Chapter 10. It should be noted that this obligation is an obligation to pay at one particular place, that of the issuer's place of incorporation.

8 Euronotes and eurocommercial paper

An international bond issue is a means of raising finance on a medium- to long-term basis by the issue of medium and long-term securities. However, other national markets, perhaps most particularly the U.S., had the means whereby similar issuers could raise finance by the issue of short-term notes and commercial paper. It was perhaps inevitable that sooner or later such a form of finance would be developed on the euro-markets. These developments, at least in a successful form, are comparatively recent, and give rise to the euronotes and eurocommercial paper issues which are now of great importance. Since euronote structures are most clearly related to those developed by the traditional bond and syndicated loan participants they will be examined first for all that eurocommercial paper issues are the simpler. This order of presentation also matches the order in which the two forms established themselves as market forces.

EURONOTES[1] R.U.F.S AND N.I.F.S

If convertible bonds are a means of linking an issue of corporate debt to ultimate equity participation R.U.F.s (Revolving Underwriting Facilities) and N.I.F.s (Note Issuance Facility) are hybrids showing features of both the international bond and the syndicated loan. The hybrids derive their names from the basic obligation undertaken under the facility by which a group of commercial banks agree for a fixed period of medium term to try to arrange sales of short-term notes issued by the borrower on a revolving tap basis.

It is of no little significance that the market fully developed these new techniques in the aftermath of the international debt crisis with the new hybrid procedures being fully used in 1984 and succeeding years. The development reflected the wish of banks to remove the loan risk inherent in the syndicated loan while remaining active in the euro-security market earning significant fees from their participation. The means of doing this was to step from straight lending to participating in the sale of short-term securities—in the language of this part of commerce, to securitise the market.

In evolving this development the market was noting two separate phenomena and bringing together the underlying ideas. First, by the early

1 See generally Lloyd Bankson and Michael Lee *Euronotes*, Euromoney Publications (1985); G Bullock *Euronotes and Eurocommercial Paper*, Butterworths (1987).

1980s there already existed an active short-term debt market in the short term C.D. market where short-term Certificates of Deposit of banks were commonly issued of only one, three or six months' maturity. It functioned because of the perception that the credit-worthiness of large banking institutions was of the highest. However, the debt-crisis itself called into question this generous traditional rating. The commercial paper of high quality governments, government agencies and market dominating corporations became equally or more attractive to investors. Secondly, from a bank's point of view if it was prepared to lend money for five or six years to a borrower there was no reason why it should not, if desired, enter into a five- or six-year underwriting commitment to its potential borrower for the issuance of short-term notes.

Since the euronote programme was premised on the fact that there was no eurocommercial paper market in existence and has proved to be the precursor of a fully developed market it is truer to say that both markets owe their inspiration and something of their form to the existence of the model represented by the U.S. commercial paper market and the institutions and their advisers which used it. This important development is therefore one further example of the influence of U.S. models and experience on the euromarkets.

NOTE ISSUANCE FACILITY

Under a N.I.F. the banks agree only to endeavour to sell the short-term notes under an issue by the issuer when called on to do so. There is thus no underwriting support falling on the group of managing banks and all risks that the securities do not sell fall on the issuer.[1] The banks offer only the facility of their endeavours. However, the means by which the notes are priced and placed will usually be as sophisticated as those used in a revolving underwriting facility.[2]

There is a slight variant on a N.I.F. which is called a S.N.I.F. S.N.I.F. stands for Stand-by Note Issuance Facility and the choice of title merely emphasises that the facility is not intended to be drawn on, but merely to operate as a stand-by facility in the event of other, more favoured, sources of finance failing.

REVOLVING UNDERWRITING FACILITIES[3]

A revolving underwriting facility contrasts directly with the N.I.F. of which it is a subsequent development. Under it the banks agree not merely to

1 However some N.I.F. arrangements come very close to imposing legal obligations akin to underwriting on the participant financial institutions—see R Beaumont 'The difference between N.I.F.s and R.U.F.s' IV IFLR June (1985) at p. 32. arrangements can also be made whereby N.I.F. and R.U.F. agreements are run in parallel on different financial terms with the more expensive R.U.F. representing the fall-back position.

2 See Bullock *op. cit.* p. 44.

3 For a description of the documentation and techniques used see S K Henderson 'Structuring and Documenting Euronotes' IV IFLR 18 (1985).

sell the notes issued by the issuer but also to underwrite the issue of the short-term notes by agreeing to buy any which are unsold at a fixed price or to make loans instead.[1] As a particular issue of short-term notes becomes repayable a new short term issue is made pursuant to the agreement until the agreement comes to an end thus constituting the revolving element in the name of the facility. The purpose of the arrangement is that the borrower is enabled to raise its requirement at low short-term market interest rates subject to the market finding its short-term notes acceptable on each issue. If the notes find market resistance the borrower is at least assured over the medium-term period of the facility that the banks will meet his needs at the higher fixed price.

The issuer pays for each constituent part of the services provided in a R.U.F. and will therefore pay a periodic underwriting fee, a margin for sales and a front-end management fee for the arranger and the underwriters. A R.U.F. can be arranged as a stand-by facility where the underwriting fees will be reduced but the structure will otherwise be weighted to deter the issuer from taking it up.

The banks have proved themselves enthusiastic in their wish to participate in the new free-currency market instruments perceiving a number of advantages to themselves. The sole obligation that a bank usually undertakes, in practice, in this form of financial accommodation is a contingent underwriting liability which makes little impact on the position shown on its balance sheet. Where exceptionally a bank has to purchase the securities its portfolio at least appears very liquid in view of the short-term nature of the instrument although factually its underwriting obligations in respect of securities which are not readily selling at a reasonable price makes its portfolio in reality not at all liquid. In addition on a healthy market with saleable instruments the banks will be making profits from both its underwriting fees and from on-sale of securities purchased by them at a discount. So long as the market remains active in taking up the securities the banks will feel that their profit margins benefit significantly from their activities in this field. Difficulties with the market could, however, change the position dramatically for, since the banks do not anticipate having to take up the notes, they seek a lower yield than they would do if giving a loan facility thus leaving them exposed if they did have to take up large quantities of low yielding securities. Further such difficulties with the market could well lead to the supervisory authorities reassessing the risks involved and making the contingent liability stand at more than the 0.5 per cent

1 The provision of support in the form of a commitment to make a loan is very important in the case of the participation of U.S. banks as managers for the Glass-Steagall Act prevents their undertaking to purchase securities—see S.K. Henderson 'The Impact of U.S. Law on Euronote Facilities' IV IFLR April p. 29 (1985).

of the capital value of the loan for calculating the adequacy of the capital base of a bank at present demanded by the Bank of England.[1]

The securities are not listed which has the consequence that institutions which are prevented from investing in unlisted securities either by reason of constitutional or internal prohibition or by reason of external regulatory controls cannot invest in them. However, the prestige credit assessment agencies such as Standard and Poors will rate a particular issue.

There is a variant on a R.U.F. known as a T.R.U.F. The structure is essentially the same but with the addition that the underwriting obligation of a participant bank can be transferred to another bank, hence the title behind the acronym—Transferable Revolving Underwriting Facility.

DRAMATIS PERSONAE

It follows from the description and analysis already given that a Revolving Underwriting Facility involves an issuer of short-term securities, a facility agent who will either offer the securities direct to the market or to a tender panel, a group of banks to act as managers to purchase any unsold notes or to make advances instead, and an issuing agent and a paying agent (who may in fact be the same) to perform the mechanical functions relating to the issue and payment of the securities.

(1) *Facility agent* The facility agent wears two hats. On the one hand he is the agent of the managers in administering the facility and on the other he is the agent of the issuer in offering the notes for purchase. His capacity is therefore dual. Occasionally, the structuring will avoid this by the documentation characterising the facility agent as offering the notes to the public as agent for the managers and not of the issuer but this is rare.

The actual marketing of the securities may be undertaken by the facility agent on one of two separate bases. The first of these is by a *sole placement facility* and the second is by means of a *tender panel*. The structuring of the latter will be examined in considering the tender panel. In a sole placement facility the facility agent will attempt to place the securities on the general market while also offering a portion to the managers. If placement is not wholly successful the back up obligation of the managers arises. The facility agreement will not allow removal of the agent by the manager/banks if his efforts are less than successful. The agreement will not place any positive obligation on the agent to effect any sales or even to use his best endeavours to that end although its role will often be advertised as being a 'best efforts' commitment. In practice, it is his reputation in the market which is being relied on.

(2) *The managers* The managers are the banks who undertake the residual underwriting obligation to purchase those securities at a predetermined

[1] Introduced April 1985. It contrasts with a weighting of 1 per cent for a straight loan by the bank. It applies only to U.K. incorporated banks because each central bank regulates only the national banks under its control. However other national regulatory bodies have introduced similar measures. The issue is discussed by Bullock *op. cit.* p. 77.

price which cannot be sold on the market at that price. Inevitably, the managers earn fees for the commitments which they undertake and typically the facility agreement makes the fee accrue regardless of whether the securities are issued and of whether or not the manager is called on to purchase any securities. The underlying basis of this is that the fee is payable for the legal commitment which is undertaken, not whether or not the commitment leads to repercussions. The question arises, however, as to whether a manager is entitled to his fee if the commitments themselves are terminated before the agreed date for cessation. One view is that the fees immediately stop accruing since the commitment which they purchased has ceased. A second view is that the managers' fee bought not only its commitment but also any subsequent obligation, as where outstanding securities were purchased by it or advances made in lieu and the securities or the advances remain outstanding. On this view as long as any of the securities held by or advances made by a manager remain outstanding the commitment fee should continue. A third possibility is that since the fee may accrue even if a particular manager has no outstanding securities or advances after termination of the commitment, because other managers do hold outstanding securities or advances all commitment fees should continue to accrue so long as any security or advance remains outstanding. In fact, it is the actual drafting of the facility agreement that is all important, with regard to the resolution of this particular matter in any particular case.

(3) *Issuing and payment agent* The formal parts of the transactions are undertaken by the issuing and paying agent or agents if, as is often the case, there is a separation of function. It is possible to have more than one paying agent acting on a joint basis and in any event sub-paying agents will be appointed in each of the major jurisdictions in which the securities are issued. The agents are, of course, the agents of the issuer. It is necessary that the paying agent, or one of them if several are used, should be appointed outside the U.K. for tax reasons. The appointment of a paying agent within the U.S. should be avoided for reasons of both tax liability and securities regulation avoidance.[1] The major concerns are therefore that the issuing agent should be assured that it will receive payment for all securities which it delivers, and that the paying agent should be assured that it will have adequate funds before repayment of the securities on maturity.

(4) *Investors* The investors are the holders of the notes purchased on the market. Their rights are the contractual rights conferred upon them by the terms of the notes held by them; they are not entitled to rely on the terms of the other documentation to which they are not parties. They are not represented by the issuing and paying agent or the facility agent who are not *their* agents. The terms of the documentation other than the securities themselves can thus be altered without the consent of the investors who will not be legally affected thereby.

[1] The implications of U.S. tax, banking and securities laws on Euronote distributions are considered in S.K. Henderson 'The Impact of U.S. Law on Euronote Facilities' IV IFLR April p. 29 (1985).

DOCUMENTATION

R.U.F.s are both too recent and too flexible in the use that is made of them for the documentation to have become at all standardised. Many different options are possible and any description of usual documentation must be read with this underlying reality in mind. Essentially, however, R.U.F.s are the adaptation to the needs and institutions of the international free-currency market of the techniques and short-term instrumentation characteristic of the U.S. commercial paper programme and yet one more example of U.S. know-how and experience applied to this esentially London-based market. Indeed, sometimes R.U.F. facilities are intended as cover for the replacement of maturing U.S. commercial paper. Where this is the position the facility agreement may contain either or both of two provisions not otherwise usual in a R.U.F. issue. First, the facility agreement in such circumstances may contain a provision that each bank will use its best endeavours to ensure that its particular commitment will be recognised by Standard and Poor's and Moody's Investor Service as constituting a back up facility for commercial paper issued or guaranteed by the borrower in the U.S. Secondly, the banks may well agree to make short-term advances on same day notice (often given by telephone) to redeem the maturing commercial paper in the U.S. through the banks U.S. offices at the bank's New York prime rate of interest. Given the very varied nature of the documentation employed by the market any account of the necessary documentation must of necessity be generalised but any issue would probably contain most or all of the following:

(1) *Facility Agreement* This is an agreement between the issuer, the banks who, of course, are also the underwriters and the facility agent which sets out the terms on which the bank will arrange the sale of the securities, and the terms on which, if necessary, the banks will purchase the securities themselves. The rights and the obligations of the managers are several, and in this they resemble the obligations undertaken in a syndicated loan agreement, on the documentation of which they are modelled rather than the underwriting obligation of an international bond issue. Unlike syndicated loan agreements it is unusual for the facility agreement to allow amendment with the consent of the majority of the managers thus leaving the general scheme of the obligations one that allows amendment only with the agreement of every manager, although the majority of the managers are usually empowered to initiate or waive action in respect of breach of conditions and events of default. By contrast the facility agent and, occasionally, even the issuer may be given discretion to make amendments to the tender panel and issuing and paying agent agreements, which may have an effect on the operation of the facility and thereby on the obligations of the managers.

Sometimes a Revolving Underwriting Facility will provide for a transfer of a manager's rights and legal obligations by novation to a new party. This is achieved by providing a form of a transfer certificate attached to the facility agreement thus obviating the necessity for each new party to the facility having to execute the agreement itself. Typically, where such a provision is included there is a requirement that the issue and sometimes also the facility agent should approve the incoming party.

It is usual for the facility agreement to contain conditions precedent to the right of the issuer to demand that the securities be issued. Failure of the conditions relieves the facility agent of its obligations to try to sell the securities, and the managers from their obligations to purchase the securities. Further, in a sale through a tender panel failure to satisfy a condition precedent releases the members of the tender panel and any members who have bid for the securities from their obligations in the event of acceptance of their bids. The conditions precedent usually required involve the delivery of the normal closing documentation usually required in international financial transactions such as copies of any necessary governmental consents, directors or corporate resolutions and legal opinions, together with other basic conditions of international financial transactions particularly the non-existence of defaults, that the issuer's warranties remain true, and that securities comply with the terms of the facility arrangement.

There are greater difficulties with regard to conditions precedent relating to adverse changes in circumstances inevitable to the type of borrowing facility represented by R.U.F.s.[1] Managers might well wish to include conditions that there should not have occurred a disruption in international conditions which materially adversely affect the marketability of the securities. Further, a condition precedent that there should not have occurred a material change adverse to the position of the issuer might be included. The full impact of these conditions will be appreciated when it is remembered that each condition would have to be satisfied each time a short-term issue is made within the period of the medium-term facility, and that often the terms permit the issue agent or a majority of the managers to determine conclusively whether the conditions are satisfied. While the managers would claim that such conditions are entirely reasonable, in that the sale of securities on a disrupted market or from an issuer in difficulties is not feasible, the issuer will point out that what it was paying its fee for was a facility extending over a period of time which, if taken up, should lead to what is effectively a medium term loan. This argument derives from the essentially split perception of this form of security issuance either as a medium-term banking transaction, or a participation in securities issue upon the world's capital markets. In any particular issue one or other approach will predominate and the detail of the specific structure should mirror the particular emphasis involved. This will usually be the banking transaction approach.

As has already been noted Standard and Poor will rate R.U.F. facilities at the request of an issuer to whom the quality of the rating will be a matter of considerable concern. The inclusion of a material adverse change clause increases the risk that additional funds will not be advanced on the maturity of a short-term issue thus effectively terminating the facility, and consequently Standard and Poor will rate such a facility on the basis of a short-term issue with an uncommitted back-up facility, which will

1 The importance of these in a R.U.F. where there is a continuing underwriting obligation is emphasised by R. Beaumont in 'The Difference between N.I.F.s and R.U.F.s' IV IFLR June p. 33 (1985).

adversely reflect upon the liquidity position of even a strong issuer and be devastating to the position of a weaker issuer.

In addition to the conditions precedent R.U.F.'s usually contain the standard protective terms usual in syndicated loan agreements, including cancellation of commitments in the event of illegality, and payment of additional costs resulting from a change in the law. Events of default also usually parallel those normal to syndicated loan agreements. One problem within this area is whether illegality or a default should result in acceleration of the securities and advances as well as terminating the facility commitments. If this form of finance is seen as a means of security issue then, while the commitment should be terminated, the securities should run to term. Alternatively, the facility can be structured so that all securities can be accelerated by the facility agent either unilaterally, or on the instructions of a majority of the managers. This is rare. More usually, if acceleration is to apply it is only the securities held by, or advances made by, the managers which the agreement provides should be subject to acceleration, thus distinguishing sharply the position of the managers from that of investors in general on the basis that the managers have undertaken a long-term obligation while the investors are only exposed for the short-term until the securities mature.

By the same rationale managers often receive rights of enforcement additional to those contained in the securities themselves. These will usually include a judgment currency clause, a contractual right to recover all costs of enforcement, and the issuer's submission to jurisdiction in desired locations although the latter is sometimes also included in the securities themselves. Further, a contractual right of set-off is also often excluded.

If a particular manager is relying on an associate company to finance the purchase of securities if this becomes necessary under the facility agreement, it will require that the protective terms of the agreement, including these particular ones, should also apply to the associate so that the associate is as fully protected as the manager itself.

(2) *Issue Agency Agreement* This appoints an agent of the issuer (in practice one of the banks) to issue the securities and deliver them to purchasers as payment is received. It will therefore contain detailed provisions for the authentication and insurance of the notes, their delivery to purchasers, and, most importantly, the receipt of the subscription price from the purchasers.

A particular problem arises in the case of securities denominated in U.S. dollars, for the issuing agent cannot deliver against immediate payment because of the time difference between Europe, where the notes must be delivered, and New York, where the dollars must ultimately be paid. The issue agency agreement usually provides quite expressly that the issuing agent should deliver notes only against payment so that if delivery takes place in advance of payment the risk is that of the issue agent vis à vis the issuer and the managers. Where delivery is to be effected by the issuing agent through one of the clearing centres the problem can be surmounted relatively easily by the agent placing the payment risk on the centre, which will usually have its own payment arrangements with its customer (although, of course, the issuing agent remains at risk of both the clearing centre and the purchaser proving insolvent). Greater problems arise where the sales are effected direct. Usually, the problem is overcome by the issuing agent requiring from the purchaser a bank undertaking. However, the issuing agent will wish to control the mode of payment in case it should be offered a mode or undertaking not acceptable to it. In strict law it does this in any event for, unless it has agreed to the contrary, it is entitled to payment in legal tender but it is usual to include an express provision to the effect that it retains absolute discretion to determine whether the mode of payment is acceptable to it for cosmetic reasons. By relying on a stated provision it is felt that it assists the issue agent in refusing a particular mode of payment or undertaking without impliedly impugning the bona fides or solvency of another institution.

(3) *Reference Agency Agreement* The securities can be sold on either an interest-bearing or a discount basis or, indeed, a combination of the two. The base rate of interest to be used to calculate either the discount or the interest actually payable must be defined, and this is accomplished by the terms of the Reference Agency Agreement, although this may not necessarily exist as a separate agreement but instead be incorporated as part of the facility agreement or the issue or paying agent agreement. The base rate used is usually one of the London based rates such as LIBOR (the London inter-bank offered rate) LIBID (the London inter-bank bid rate) or LIMEAN (the average of the other two rates) although inter-bank rates of other international financial centres may be used, e.g. NYBOR (New York inter-bank offered rate). The agreement will also set out the means of determining the appropriate rate and of the date on which it is to be ascertained. It usually provides that it should be determined on the basis of quotations obtained from specified reference banks.

(4) *Registration Agency Agreement* The introduction of TEFRA has had the effect that securities may be issued in both registered and bearer form. If a registered form is used or is an option the issuer appoints a registrar to register and transfer the securities. In practice, it is again usual to appoint one of the participating banks for this purpose.

(5) *Paying Agency Agreement* As with a bond issue a machinery for payment is necessary. The issuer appoints a bank paying agent. It is the paying agent's responsibility to pay the notes, cancelling and destroying the paid securities, and to issue replacement notes in the event of loss or destruction. Other banks will be appointed sub-paying agents in various financial centres through which the securities will be marketed. It is the function of the paying agent to make payment on the specified date. In the case of a dollar denominated security the paying agent will therefore have to make payment in Europe on the maturity date before New York's opening. If new securities are not to be issued to continue the borrowing under the underwriting commitment, the paying agent will need to receive sufficient funds from the issuer in New York on the business day before maturity. If other securities are being issued to fund the redemption of the matured security, the issuing agent will need to satisfy itself under its reserved discretion as to payment that the proceeds of the new issue will be forthcoming in time for redemption in New York.

Form of security

As there is no strict form of documentation evolved by the market for an issue so there is also no uniformity of security marketed in this way. Apart from forms of security already familiar the medium- or short-term certificate of deposit, the short-term FRN and the short-term fixed-rate note, a simple promissory note falling within the statutory definition of the Bills of Exchange Act 1882, s 83(1) or a special short-term euronote of one or several months may be used. While duration of the security is short the denominations are usually large. The securities may be either interest-bearing or discounted—in the latter situation it is the discount which provides the investor's return. Interest on a note of six months' duration or less, payable on maturity and not before, is treated as original issue discount for purposes of U.S. tax laws.

Apart from the inclusion of a choice of law clause the securities usually concentrate largely on the protection of the issuer's payment obligation by the inclusion of the promise to pay principal and interest, including on occasion default interest, prescribe the method of payment, and contain a grossing-up clause. The usual designated jurisdictions under the choice of law clause are unsurprisingly English law or the law of New York.

The tender panel

In a transaction in which a tender panel is used the facility agent will invite bids from the members of the tender panel and accept the highest priced which are offered until the necessary number of securities have been disposed of. There will be a minimum figure below which bids cannot be accepted agreed between the issuer, facility agent and manager which may or may not have been disclosed to the tender panel. In general, managers are likely to insist on the inclusion of themselves and their associate companies in the tender panel with the result that the managerial team and the tender panel may be identical.

The tender panel agreement

This is an agreement entered into by each tender panel member separately with the facility agent (and possibly the issuer) thus creating a separate contractual relationship with the facility agent and, where included, the issuer. As this is the sole contractual connection it is the sole source of the contractual rights and obligations of the member as a member of the tender panel although, where the member is also a manager, he may have separate rights and obligations as manager under the facility agreement. A copy of the tender panel agreement is annexed to the facility agreement as an exhibit.

The overall characteristic of the agreement is the amount of power concentrated in the hands of the facility agent. It will generally include a provision that the agent may drop any member from the panel and add additional ones at its discretion although the agreement may require that any additional or replacement member should be acceptable to the issuer. Sometimes protection from removal by the agent is conferred on managers who are also acting as tender panel members. However, mere inclusion within the panel does not really insulate from the power of the agent since the agreement will generally be quite express in specifying that the agent is not obliged to invite any particular panel member to bid in respect of any particular issue of securities. Further, the agreement customarily expressly preserves the agent's right not to accept any particular bid or bids (usually exercised, in practice, because the agent is doubtful that the member will be able to perform his obligation if the bid is accepted).

The documentation may or may not deal with the risk of an offeree, whose bid has been accepted, failing to perform its obligations. Often the risk is ignored. Where it is dealt with a number of solutions are possible. One possibility is that the managers be made to bear the risk. This does require specific provision within the documentation, for the managers' general underwriting obligations will usually require that they be notified of the lack of subscription by the facility agent several days before issue date, at which point of time it is probable that the failure of an offeree to perform its obligations will not have become apparent. A typical provision along these lines would be one requiring the facility agent to subscribe the relevant notes on the issue date, thus providing the funds due to the issuer, with the managers being obliged to purchase the notes from the facility agent the following day. Alternatively, the facility agent may bear the risk in which case the agreement will provide that the facility agent is obliged to purchase any notes not sold to defaulting offerees once it has accepted their bids, subject only to the satisfaction of the conditions precedent. The final alternative is for the issuer to bear the risk which can be simply accomplished by a provision in the facility agreement providing that the issuer only receives the proceeds to the extent that the successful offerees pay. Which solution is theoretically most appropriate will depend on who within the team represented by the issuer, his managers, and the agents has closest control over bids and the credit-worthiness of their makers.

There exists a potential conflict of interest inherent in the tender panel machinery whenever the issue agent is also a member of the tender panel. A similar problem arises in a sole placement transaction where the issue agent has an express right to make bids. Unless express provision is made there is nothing to prevent a manager from monitoring the bids of others as they come in and pricing its own bids on the basis of this information just immediately before the bid deadline. Apart from being arguably unfair to the other members of the tender panel who have no such advantage, it is also quite likely to result in the issuer getting a more adverse deal than would otherwise have been the result, for it is possible that if the issue agent had had to calculate its bid blind it would have done so more competitively to the advantage of the issuer.

Often this potential conflict of interest is ignored by the documentation but sometimes it is faced. There are three possible types of solution where the problem is expressly faced. Some agreements provide for bids by the facility agent as a member of the tender panel to be made previous to other bids being made. Others provide that a separate entity be the tender agent for the receipt of bids who may be either totally independent or, on some occasions, an associate company of the issue agent. An alternative solution is to permit the facility agent to acquire a portion of the securities (eg the last 10 or 20 per cent) at a price equal to the average of all bids by the tender panel which have been accepted or would have been accepted had the designated portion not been reserved.

The making of an issue involving a tender panel

The issue of securities under the underlying arrangements is initiated by the issuer giving notice of an issue to the facility agent five to ten days before issue. The facility agent requests bids specifying the amounts and denomination and the designated underwritten yield.

This permits the facility agent or the tender panel members to sound out their customers so as to presell the notes without contractual commitment from their customers subject to compliance with applicable tax and securities laws as in an ordinary bond issue. In a sole placement facility the selling restrictions will be contained in the main body of the facility agreement; in a tender panel transaction they will be contained in the tender panel agreement, although the managers will agree to them qua managers also in the facility agreement.

The tender panel members notify their bids to the tender agent in prescribed form which has, as its central factor, the bid yield. This must not, of course, exceed the underwritten yield. The tender agent on behalf of issuer accepts bids in ascending order of yields up to if necessary the underwritten yield. Equal bids are dealt with on a proportional basis. Successful bidders are notified of their success. Later on the same day the tender agent calculates the subscription price in accordance with a formula based on the accepted bids so that the securities all bear the same rate only the discounts varying in accordance with individual bids.

The tender panel members pay the subscription price to a specified bank account of the tender agent. The securities are delivered to a clearing agent or depository such as Euroclear or CEDEL.[1] A lock up or certificates of non-U.S. ownership may be required if the S.E.C. feel that there is otherwise any question of U.S. securities laws applying. The proceeds are paid to the issuer unless the issue is to replace a maturing issue when the proceeds will be transferred to the paying agent to use it for this purpose, he paying any balance to the issuer.

If insufficient bids are made the managers buy the unsold notes at the underwritten yield or make advances instead of similar yield (in the case of discount notes the discount is converted into a yield for this purpose).

It is to be noted that there is one unsatisfactory characteristic of this form of distribution in that neither the members of the tender panel nor ultimate investors know whether they respectively have bought, or will be able to buy, securities until the bids are in and accepted.

[1] In the field of Euronotes and Eurocommercial paper, apart from CEDEL and Euroclear there are two London depository and clearing systems, First Chicago Clearing Centre and Chase Manhattan Bank N.A. There are 'bridges' connecting the various systems.

EUROCOMMERCIAL PAPER[1]

The eurocommercial paper programme followed on from the success of the euronote programme. The parent programme had accustomed investors to making investments in the paper of good quality commercial issuers, but the marketing procedures were comparatively slow and complex. An earlier attempt to introduce a simple eurocommercial paper programme had failed to take hold. However, in the new environment a renewed programme became a clear success.

In form, eurocommercial paper represents a move to simplicity. The issuer appoints a dealer or dealers to an uncommitted programme of issue which is not underwritten. Usually, the issuer will have arranged back-up lines of credit. The securities in a particular tranche may not be issued forthwith but over a number of days, thereby spreading both the timing of the tapping of the market and the ultimate retirement of the paper. The dealer's responsibility is to place the paper and develop a stable background of investor demand to enable steady competetive marketing to take place. Both euronotes and eurocommercial paper are usually issued in large denominations and are aimed at institutional investors including banks.

Documentation

The basic documentation for a eurocommercial paper programme consists of four documents: (1) an information memorandum, (2) a dealer agreement, (3) the printed notes incorporating selling restrictions, and (4) an Issuing and Paying Agency Agreement.

(1) *The information memorandum* is equivalent to a prospectus on an international bond distribution. It will contain some account of the issuer's business and financial background, the terms and conditions on which the notes are issued, including a copy of a note, and any U.S. and other jurisdictional selling restrictions applicable to the issue.

(2) *The dealer agreement* is the underlying document establishing the programme and the legal relationship between the issuer and the dealers. If a parent company is guaranteeing the issue the guarantee will probably be found in this document. The document will also specify the terms on which the dealers have undertaken the issue (usually uncommitted and non-underwritten) and the conditions precedent to the purchase of notes by dealers which are broadly parallel to those applicable in a bond issue. The agreement will also contain representation and warranties similar to those undertaken by an issuer in a bond issue. There are also selling restrictions parallel to a bond issue. The issuer agrees to indemnify each dealer against misrepresentation in the information memorandum, and also to produce accounts and financial statements throughout the life of the programme and to notify any defaults which may occur or changes in its financial position. All representations and warranties are deemed to be repeated every time a note is delivered. The dealer agreement will provide that in

1 See generally Lucy Heller (ed) *Eurocommercial Paper* (1988) Euromoney Publications.

principle it cannot be amended, waived or supplemented except by the written agreement of all the parties. However, the issuer may usually terminate the agreement in respect of any dealer by 30 days' notice and any dealer can terminate his dealership on 30 days' notice.

The dealership agreement will also contain procedural provisions. In particular, there will be provisions concerning governing law and jurisdiction (usually English law, and the English courts non-exclusively). An agent in England will usually be appointed for the service of process. Usually, the agreement will allow for any legally significant communications to be made either in writing, or by telephone and then confirmed in writing.

(3) *The printed notes* undertake payment of principal and interest without deduction of taxes which are expressed to be fully negotiable. The note recites that it has now been registered under the Securities Act 1933 in the U.S. and details the selling restrictions applicable in both the U.S. and the U.K.

(4) *The issuing and paying agency agreement* establishes the procedure for the issue, delivery, payment, authentication and redemption of the notes.

LEGAL ISSUES

Many of the legal problems arising from eurocommercial paper and euronote issues are identical to the problems which arise from international bond and issues. However, in the area of securities regulation particular special issues arise and therefore attention will be given to this area both in the U.K. and the U.S.A. Further particular issues arise from U.K. federal income tax laws and these will also be considered. It should be noted that under a euronote programme of constant issues of securities the applicable securities and tax laws must be satisfied every time any particular security is issued or redeemed.

SECURITIES REGULATION

The U.K. position

(1) *Securities regulation* The short- and medium-term issue of securities under a eurocommercial paper or euronote programme almost certainly constitutes the carrying on of an investment business within the Financial Services Act 1986[1] and is therefore subject to the regime discussed in Chapter 4.

(2) *English banking laws* Under the Banking Act 1987 there is a wide regulatory framework for the control of banks and similar businesses in the U.K. under which the Bank of England and its independent advisory committee, the Board of Banking Supervision, have extensive supervisory powers.

The key regulatory provision is s 3 which makes it unlawful for a person in the U.K. to accept a deposit in the course of carrying on (whether in the U.K. or elsewhere) a deposit taking business, unless it is either an *authorised institution* under the Act or the acceptance of the deposit is covered

[1] Under the wide definition of debenture.

by one of the exemptions under the Act. Contravention gives rise to significant criminal penalties and civil liabilities including the responsibility to repay the unauthorised deposits. Since the taking of the money from the investor under a eurocommercial or euronote facility is short term, it can be seen as the taking of a deposit rather than the sale of a security. Consequently, it is important that the regulatory impact of the legislation be avoided.

The Act covers the acceptance of a deposit in the course of carrying on a business of deposit-taking whether in the U.K. or abroad. If therefore the issuer makes his arrangements so that the deposits are taken outside the U.K. the Act is avoided. Also, traditionally, the Bank of England have taken the view that euro-issues denominated in a currency other than sterling are not covered by the Act, because the deposits themselves are outside the U.K. However, it adds belt to braces in the case of an issue in a currency other than sterling to arrange for the proceeds to be first credited to an overseas bank account. This protection can be increased by express provision in the dealer agreement that the dealers are *not* the agent of the issuer, so that the initial deposits are taken when the dealers purchase the securities from the issuer, and not at the time of subsequent sale to purchasers from the dealer. If the dealers then credit a bank account of the issuer overseas the deposit has not been taken in the U.K.

The attitude taken by the Bank of England with regard to non-sterling deposits meant that in its view sterling deposits were clearly covered by the Act. However, even in respect of this it was prepared to grant exemption to issuers from the prohibition of deposit-taking in certain situations. This has now led to a system of legislation based exemptions currently by statutory instrument.[1] The requirements give rise to a number of conditions which must be met. These are as follows:

(i) *The issuer* The issuer, whether a U.K. or overseas company, must have net assets[2] of at least £25 million calculated on the basis of its latest audited accounts. A company which does not satisfy the requirement may issue if the programme is guaranteed by a parent company which satisfies the criteria or an authorised institution under the Banking Act. The minimum net asset restriction does not apply to overseas government, public authorities or international organisations.

The Bank of England has made it clear that it does not wish to see authorised deposit-taking institutions or their subsidiaries issuing commercial paper. The proper vehicle for such institutions is the C.D. market.

(ii) *The securities* These must be issued and transferable in minimum redemption amounts of £100,000. The maturities must exceed six days but may not exceed one year. It must carry on its face a statement that it is sterling commercial paper issued pursuant to the exemption and give details of the guarantor if it is guaranteed. If it is not guaranteed it should so declare.

1 SI 1988/646—Banking Act 1987 (Exempt Transactions) Regulations 1988 as amended by the Banking Act 1987 (Exempt Transactions) (Amendment) Regulations 1989 (SI 1979/465).

2 As defined under the Companies Act 1985, s 264(2).

(iii) *Supply of information to the Stock Exchange* There are different requirements with regard to the supply of information to the Stock Exchange depending on whether or not the issuer or its guarantor (where applicable) is quoted on the Stock Exchange or a recognised overseas exchange. If the issuer or guarantor is not so quoted the regulations set out detailed requirements of information which must be given to the Stock Exchange. If it is so quoted the issuer (or guarantor as appropriate) should declare that it is in compliance with the rules of the appropriate exchange and that; since the most recent information published under the rules, it is not aware, on the basis of reasonable enquiries, of any change of circumstances which could reasonably be regarded as significantly adverse to its obligations on its securities as they fall due.
(iv) *Notifications* Issuers must notify the Bank of England of the total amount of securities to be issued and, at periodic intervals, of the amount which has been issued.

In addition to the limitations on the taking of deposits under the 1987 Act, the Act also empowers the Treasury to make regulations about deposit advertisements, which could even extend to oral invitations.

The U.S. position: securities regulation

The Securities Act of 1933, requiring the registration of an issue and the filing of a prospectus in respect of any issue of securities, is so widely drawn as to have the potential to include notes and commercial paper. Since issuers will wish to avoid the cost, delay and regulation to which this gives rise, issues are structured to make use of an available exemption. However, in the case of short-term notes and paper, the exemptions applicable differ somewhat from those available for an issue of international bonds and certificates of deposits, and, where a common exemption is available, the requisite conditions to claim the exemption are not always identical. The available exemptions of potential interest are three in number.

1. *The commercial paper exemption* The 1933 Act includes an exemption specifically for commercial paper. To qualify four conditions must be satisfied:
   (i) the obligations must have a maturity that does not exceed nine months.
   (ii) the obligations must be of prime quality. Only highest standing issuers may rely on the exemption. Issuers have usually proved their quality to lay claim to the exemption by obtaining high ratings from recognised national U.S. rating agencies such as Moody's and Standard and Poor's.
   (iii) The obligation should be of a type not ordinarily purchased by the general public. This requirement is usually met by issuing the obligations in large denominations of at least $100,000, and placing them without advertising with institutions as a private placement.
   (iv) The obligations must be issued to facilitate 'current transactions' rather than as a 'general increase to the capital base'. The S.E.C. takes a restrictive view of what does and what does not constitute a current transaction, and this has rendered the use of the exemption in a euro-issue extremely unattractive.

2. *The implied foreign offering exemption* This is the standard means by which issues of international bonds avoid the registration requirements, and has already been discussed.[1] However, particular problems arise with regard to the 90-day lock up period. Euronote and eurocommercial paper issues are usually constructed on the basis that securities will be issued from time to time, so that the issuer is involved in a more or less continuous distribution of the securities. In such a situation the issue would never be completed and the 90-day period could never begin to run, prior to the securities coming to retirement. However, guidance has now been received from the S.E.C. as to how the exemption can safely be applied to issues of short-term obligations.[2] The requirements are:

(i) The maturities must be short-term (that is less than one year. In the case of U.S. issuers the limit is six months if U.S. withholding tax on any interest or discount is to be avoided).

(ii) The securities must be in minimum denominations of U.S. $500,000 (or its equivalent in another currency).

(iii) Each dealer agrees that it is not purchasing the securities for the account of any U.S. person, and that it has not offered, sold, or delivered the securities in the U.S. or to the account of a U.S. person, and will not do so.

(iv) Each dealer agrees that it will deliver to each purchaser to whom it sells paper, a notice whereby the purchaser acknowledges that no Securities Act registration has been obtained and warrants that it is not a U.S. person and is not purchasing from a U.S. person. It undertakes that it will obtain a similar acknowledgment and undertaking from any purchaser from it thereby creating 'cascading confirmations' down the sales chain.

(v) The restrictions on sale contained in (iii) and (iv) must appear in a prominent notice (legend) on the securities themselves.

(vi) No general solicitation or advertising of the issue may be made in the U.S. or to U.S. persons.

However, particular problems arise in the case of an underwritten euronote insurance facility, for whilst the securities themselves may have an appropriately limited maturity, the managing banks are extending a long-term credit facility to the purchaser, pursuant to which, arguably, any purchases made by them will be undertaken, *whether pursuant to their long-stop* underwriting obligations or otherwise.[3] Accordingly, in such cases the facility should be structured so as to ensure that any securities sold to the managers are exempt from U.S. withholding tax independently of the general short-term securities exemption. To achieve this two things must be done:

1. Given that the securities will be issued in bearer form the conditions necessary for the securities to qualify for the international bond

[1] *ante* ch 4.
[2] First Interstate Bancorp No Action Letter, 13 February 1985.
[3] A view taken by the S.E.C.

exemption to the anti-bearer bond rules enacted by TEFRA must be satisfied.[1]

2. Each manager must show that it qualified for an individual exemption from U.S. withholding tax on issue. This may be done by the manager showing either that he may rely on any exemption created by any tax treaty to which the U.S. is a party, or that interest received by it in respect of the securities will be connected with a U.S. trade or business carried on by it. In the latter case the interest will be exempt from the withholding tax but taxable as part of the income of the U.S. trade or business.

TEFRA REGISTRATION REQUIREMENTS

In general the Tefra requirements for registration of bearer securities have no direct significance for the short-term euro-security because registration is not required of securities having a maturity of one year or less. However, indirectly TEFRA requirements are significant because of their connection with the withholding tax exemption discussed above and the U.S. information reporting requirements discussed below.

U.S. INFORMATION REPORTING AND BACK UP WITHHOLDING TAX REQUIREMENTS

As part of its structures to try to collect tax from its citizens and in support of its general withholding tax provisions U.S. law required the payer of principal or interest on a debt obligation to report the payment to the Internal Revenue Service, and to withold a 20 per cent back up withholding tax from the payment if he is unable to give the payee taxpayer identification number. This applies not merely to the issuer but to others through whose hands the payment must pass before reaching the payee. While non-U.S. payees are exempt from these provisions it is necessary that the exemption be claimed by completing a form to show its entitlement which would give *inter alia* its name and address. Thus, for a payee to claim this exemption it must give up the very anonymity which has been one of the usual reasons for using the euro-securities markets for investment. Consequently, other exemptions have to be found. Two basic situations must be distinguished.

1. *Non-U.S. issuers without substantial U.S. connections* Obligations of a non-U.S. issuer with no substantial U.S. connection are exempt from the information reporting and back-up requirements provided that the payments on the obligation are not made within the U.S. Any paying or other agent of the issuer subject to the jurisdiction of the U.S. courts, with whom the issuer has a legal contractual relationship, must obtain a sworn statement from a duly authorised officer of the issuer stating that the corporation does not have a substantial U.S. connection to be able to rely on the exemption. Anyone else subject to the jurisdiction of the U.S. courts is entitled to assume that a corporate issuer is not a U.S. corporation, and has no substantial U.S. connection, unless its name

[1] Discussed in 3.

indicates the contrary, or the contrary was actually known by the person concerned.

A non-U.S. issuer has a substantial U.S. connection if the issuer derives (i) at least 50 per cent of its aggregate gross income from the conduct of a U.S. trade or business (ii) is a U.S. branch of a non-U.S. bank or (iii) is a controlled foreign corporation (ie more than 50 per cent of its voting shares are controlled by U.S. shareholders in certain circumstances).

2. *U.S. issuers and non-U.S. issuers with substantial U.S. connections* In order that these might not be frozen out of the euro-security markets, given the traditional requirements of anonymity by investors, the Internal Revenue Service have issued regulations containing exemptions which might be used. These are as follows:-

(a) *Short-term discount obligations of U.S. issuers and non-U.S. issuers and similar obligations of U.S. banks and U.S. branches of non-U.S. banks* This exemption includes (i) discount obligations of a U.S. issuer or of a non-U.S. issuer that derives at least 50 per cent of its aggregate gross income from the conduct of a U.S. trade or business, with a maturity of 183 days or less (ii) deposit obligations of a U.S. bank or of a U.S. branch of a non U.S. bank with a maturity of one year or less. To qualify for exemption such obligations must comply with the following conditions:

- (i) Interest and principal on the obligation must be both payable, and in fact paid, outside of the U.S.;
- (ii) The face amounts of the obligation must not be less than $500,000;
- (iii) The obligation must satisfy the TEFRA requirements for 'arrangements reasonably designed' to ensure that the security is sold or resold over the period of the issue only to non-U.S. persons;
- (iv) A prominent notice that the sale is made pursuant to the exemption appear on each security.

(b) *Short-term obligations of controlled foreign corporations with a maturity of one year or less provided that two conditions are satisfied.* First, principal and interest must be payable outside the U.S. Secondly, the obligation must satisfy the TEFRA requirements for 'arrangements reasonably designed' to ensure sales only to non-U.S. persons.

Securities issued subject to these exemptions escape the U.S. information and withholding tax arrangements.

3. *Private Placement* The existence of this has already been noted[1] and the requirements are considered elsewhere.[2] As with international bond issues, it is possible to avoid the registration requirements of the 1933 Act by combining the use of private placements exemption to place securities in the U.S. with the implied foreign offering exemption to distribute most of the issue.

U.S. TAX CONSIDERATIONS[3]

U.S. tax provisions, as they bear on the short-term euro-securities markets,

[1] *ante* Chapter 4.
[2] *post* Appendix 1.
[3] For a detailed account, see Bullock *op. cit.* pp. 116–124.

have become complex. A prospective issuer of eurocommercial paper or euronotes must now address three separate U.S. federal tax considerations. Firstly he must ensure that the issue is free of U.S. withholding tax.[1] Secondly if the securities, as is customary, are issued in bearer form, they must be exempt from the registration requirements imposed by TEFRA (Tax Equity and Fiscal Responsibility Act of 1982).[2] Thirdly the issue must be structured so that payments on them are exempt from U.S. information and reporting requirements.

U.S. withholding tax The tax falls on payments to non-U.S. persons of interest from sources within the U.S. Interest is treated as arising within the U.S. if it is paid in an obligation by a U.S. Corporation or, in certain circumstances, by a non-U.S. corporation. A non-U.S. corporation will be caught if (a) it derives at least 50% of its aggregate gross income from the conduct of a U.S. trade or business or (b) is a U.S. branch of a non-U.S. bank. If under the above rules there is a potential liability to the tax on exemption must be found.

Fortunately there is a general exemption to hand for the Internal Revenue Code provides an exemption for the interest (in the form of the discount at which the short-term obligations are issued), by exempting interest on notes having a maturity at issue of 183 days or less. Consequently it is usual for short-term euro-securities to be issued with a maturity limited to 183 days.

1 For the impact of U.S. withholding tax, currently at 30 per cent, on an international bond or certificate of deposit issue, see Chapter 3.

2 Also discussed in Chapter 3.

9 The secondary market and negotiability

For international bonds to function as a satisfactory means of raising investor money it is essential that the bonds, once issued, should be tradeable on a firmly established and reliable secondary market. To invest in bonds in the first place it is necessary for investors to be assured that the bonds which they purchase will be capable of resale before maturity, if the investor has need of the cash which the investment represents. Few institutions, let alone individuals, can afford to commit their money for a fixed ten- or fifteen-year term. Further, with increasing investor sophistication, investors who can commit large sums of money for a long period of time will require the possibility of switching investments in the light of changing economic developments and the performance of the economies of various countries, sectors of investment, and individual institutions. It is the secondary market in bonds which discharges this vital function, and enables an investor to realise his capital where the need arises and in the meantime to monitor the performance of his investment.

Ironically, when the international bond distribution system was developed and first used in the 1960s, little interest was shown in the establishment and development of a secondary market. The original distributions of bonds at this time were viewed largely as private placements, which would be kept to maturity. Stock Exchange listings were obtained but not for reasons of secondary dealing. When attention was turned to the desirability of establishing a secondary market, overtures were made to the London Stock Exchange but the participants there showed little interest. The secondary market had, therefore, to grow elsewhere. A secondary market for the sale and purchase of foreign bonds issued in New York already existed in Europe through the operations of a few specialist houses, and the secondary market for international bonds based itself on those houses. As the market became established, new houses showed interest and participated, but the market is still based upon a small core of closely-knit group of financial institutions who are prepared to make a market and deal even in difficult times.

While the market is based on a small core of institutions it does involve a much wider number of participants. It is necessary to distinguish between the market-makers, around whose operations the secondary market is based, and the much larger number of dealers who participate in that market. The second, larger group, contains an intermediate group, the brokers, who act as intermediaries between other market participants and do not purchase for their own account. The very nature of their operations necessitates their dissemination of information on issues and prices throughout the market. They are instrumental in bringing together willing dealers, who wish to sell, with willing dealers, who wish to purchase, thus assisting the market to operate. Finally, there is a vast number of dealers buying and selling on their own account, and for clients, to make the profits on which they are dependent. They may deal direct with each other, through a broker, or with a market-maker.

The market-makers are the core of the market, enabling it to exist as a market in varied circumstances. They are committed to trade in *both good and bad times* (although they may not be able to maintain this position in impossible times), and they do this by committing their own capital to hold securities under their own name and to their own account thereby carrying the risks of the market. Clearly, on a long-term basis such commitment must return good profits for it to be possible even through the trading position on any particular day may not be so rosy. To achieve this it is essential that a market-maker is sensitive to market conditions (market-makers cannot buck the market in the medium- or long-term although they can help it to achieve its longer-term movements more smoothly over the short term), and this is reflected in responsive attitudes to pricing and, where necessary, spreads.

As has been noted previously it is common practice for international bond issues to be listed on one or more stock exchanges. Exchanges chosen frequently are the Luxembourg Stock Exchange and the London Stock Exchange and, in the case of issues centred on the Far East, the Singapore Stock Exchange.[1] Apart from keeping the name of the issuer before the eyes of investors, listing has the very useful function of enabling investors to follow the performance of their investments, as prices of listed securities are regularly published in a variety of news publications. These show the price ranges at which the particular listed issues have been traded over the previous twenty-four hours or seven days depending on the frequency of publication. Further, some institutions will only invest in listed securities and by the laws of some countries, particularly their foreign exchange regulations, residents can only invest in foreign listed securities and are prohibited from investing in unlisted issues.

However, the secondary market in the bonds does not base itself upon the stock exchanges, where little trading in these international securities takes place. Because of the wide area of distribution of the securities the professionals interested in them are widely scattered geographically, and trade directly with one another using modern means of instantaneous communication such as the telephone, telex, and screen trading thereby by-passing the stock exchange. The true secondary market is therefore institutional, and based upon the professional firms that so deal.

It is the aim of the lead manager, by the steps that he takes in support of the issue, to ensure that a stable and realistic secondary market develops. The difficulties with regard to this have already been discussed.[2] However,

1 Of these, Luxembourg is the cheapest—Fisher *The Eurodollar Bond Market* Euromoney Publications (1979)p. 110.

2 *ante* p. 36

the lead manager is assisted to some extent in the initial pricing of the new offering by drawing comparisons from comparable seasoned bonds already being traded on the secondary market. In this way the security is related to its ultimate destination on the secondary market from its very inception.

MECHANICS OF TRADING

Given that the secondary market in international bonds is a world-wide market it makes much use of modern technology. It is typically, but not exclusively, based on the Reuter Monitor, a system of telecommunications network which allows market-makers to display the prices of the issues they follow on a screen. The many subscribers have their own screen on which they can read the prices displayed. If a dealer wishes to buy at the price he contacts the market-maker, usually by telephone, to make the deal. It should be emphasised that it is well understood by the market participants that the displayed prices are an indication only, and that the market-maker is not obliged to deal at that price. On receipt of a telephone call therefore the market-maker is free to quote a new price to the person who has responded to his displayed figure. In terms of legal concepts the displayed figure was an advertisement and offer to treat, and not a formal offer which was capable, by acceptance, of immediately becoming a contract.[1] However, a particular market-maker may feel, as a matter of professional reputation, that it is obliged to deal at the displayed price without being under any legal obligation to do so, for it may pride itself on its reputation for keeping its displays of prices constantly updated and dealing at those prices.

If as a result of a response to the price displays a deal is struck, the settlements offices both of buyer and seller record the transaction in a position book or ledger, and a sales and purchase confirmation is prepared with details of the transaction including the amount to be paid. When a deal is done it does not take effect immediately but at a future date, the value date, which is usually seven days after the date of the agreement. This allows for the settlement arrangements to be made. Thus, each party to a trade under the AIBD rules is required to dispatch a confirmation or contract note within one business day of agreement. The confirmation should include the name and address of the other party to the transaction, a proper description of the securities, the terms of the agreement (including the price), the trade (agreement) date and the value date, and detailed instructions as to the payment and delivery requirements. This enables arrangements to be made with the clearing systems of Euroclear and CEDEL. This is important because, as might be expected, payment is made against delivery of the bond, or looking at the settlement from the seller's point of view, delivery of the bond is made against payment. Further delivery is usually effected inside the clearing systems when settlement is effected, and therefore the making of arrangements with the clearing systems is important. Settlement inside the clearing systems is ultimately both simpler

1 *Fisher v Bell* [1961] 1 QB 394; *Grainger & Son v Gough* [1896] AC 325.

and more secure, typically involving the making of some book entries recording transfer of funds and transfer of securities within the system. By contrast settlement outside will usually involve a telegraphic transfer of funds, and a physical delivery of bonds in a particular financial centre.

In fact, securities can be delivered either in definitive form (the physical bonds themselves), or in global form where a temporary certificate represents the whole issue. Usually global bonds, as has been seen,[1] exist only for the first few months of a new issue where the lock-up procedure to avoid infringement of U.S. security regulation is employed. When the lock-up is finished they are replaced by an issue of physical bonds. Clearly, definitive bonds, having a physical existence can be removed from the clearing system and therefore traded, both within and outside the clearing systems. By contrast, a global bond must be retained within the system, and transfers can only be effected by book entries between accounts within the systems. If someone outside the clearing systems puchases bonds within a global bond a temporary account will be opened to allow the transaction to be carried through.

EUROBOND CLEARING SYSTEMS

The brief account of the mechanics of trading on the secondary market necessarily leads to a consideration of the two clearing systems, Euroclear and CEDEL, the importance of which has already been indicated. The first on the scene was Euroclear, founded in Brussels in late 1968 by Morgan Guaranty Trust. CEDEL was organized and established in Luxemburg within twelve months, commencing operations in 1971. Both systems are now owned and controlled by a number of shareholders.

The clearing systems were founded because they were necessary for the construction of the international bond market. Before the foundation of the automated systems both issue and trading depended on a system of physical delivery and transfer. The system could not keep up with the increasing number of trades and issues with the result that by 1967 the position was unsatisfactory and the system in difficulties. During the following year the problems approached crisis proportions. The very existence of the international bond market was at risk and without a solution its continued expansion would have been impossible. It was clear that what was needed was a system, which would resolve both the market's immediate delivery and settlement problems and have the capacity to support an expansion of the market. It was to meet this need that Euroclear was set up. CEDEL was set up subsequently, partly as a European reaction to an essentially U.S. initiative in Euroclear, and partly to prevent the existence of a monopoly in this sensitive area. However, while established as rivals it is obvious that two clearing systems in such an interlocking specialist area cannot work in total isolation from each other, and an electronic bridge exists between the two systems to allow securities to be moved from one to another to allow storage and dealings.[2]

1 See ch 4 *ante*.
2 Kerr *op. cit.* p. 98 *et seq.*

The underlying purposes of the two systems are ease of transfer of bonds and security. So long as most investors within the international bond market do not wish to have actual physical possession of their bonds, a physical delivery on initial issue or subsequent transfer would constitute a time-consuming, expensive, potentially insecure, and unnecessary function. Far better that the bonds should physically always remain in a safe and authorised depositary, and transfers merely be effected on the records of the two clearing systems. Risks are further reduced by the use of the systems because, when settlements are effected within them, they can be carried out by simultaneous transfers of cash and securities within the systems. Most investors on the international bond market being institutions, and the institutions being largely well satisfied with the depositary and bond clearing systems, most international bonds never leave the security of the systems from issue to maturity.

Behind the offices and electronic network of both systems is a network of depositary banks in major financial centres which provide custody services to the two systems in which the bonds are physically stored. It is usual, however, that all securities within a single issue should be placed in one particular depositary, which will usually be one of the paying agents for the particular issue. CEDEL keeps records of all certificate numbers held by it and can therefore offer both fungible and non-fungible accounts to its users.[1] The essence of the distinction is that in the case of non-fungible accounts the records of the clearing system identify precisely the bonds held by each individual account-holder.[2] In the case of a fungible account no records of the right to the individual bonds, and their physical situation is attempted. Instead, an account-holder is credited with the ownership of an appropriate number of bonds, which can be drawn to the appropriate quantity from the total pool of bonds held by the particular clearing system.

While CEDEL offers both fungible and non-fungible accounts to its users, in practice only 5 per cent of the securities deposited with it are held on non-fungible account.[3] This may explain why its rival Euroclear has never bothered with non-fungible accounts, and has only ever concerned itself with deposits held on a fungible basis.

Of course, in addition to their activities involving the secondary market, both systems are involved in new issue placements, and in particular the closing of a new issue. Since it is rare for the securities involved in a new issue to be removed from the depositary, closing is made easier than would otherwise be the case. At closing issues are generlaly delivered in global

1 This is of some significance to investor choice of system as some European investors are required by their national laws to maintain only non-fungible accounts.

2 The account holder may or may not be the ultimate investor. The account holders are institutions who will be making some investments on their own behalf and some on behalf of investors for whom they act. In the case of a non-fungible account it will be necessary to consult the records of both the clearing system holding the bonds and the account holder, to determine the ultimate ownership of the investment.

3 Fisher *Eurobonds'* Euromoney Publications (1988) p. 208.

form to one or other clearing system, and then credited to the accounts of participants within both systems, the last manager having notified the system in advance of the actual allocation. This can be arranged to be carried out against the credit of payment from accounts within the system as in the case of secondary market transactions, thereby making delivery and payment interdependent transactions.

POTENTIAL PROBLEMS ON INSOLVENCY[1]

This distinction may be of no small importance in the event of either of the systems becoming insolvent.[2] In the case of a non-fungible account where each investor's bonds are identified, under English law the bonds would be those of the individual investors, with the result that the securities would not be available to the creditors of the depositary. Such a straightforward analysis is not possible in the case of those accounts which are fungible. Here there are no specific bonds capable of being identified as being in the ownership of any particular investor.

In fact, under English law the difficulties in the way of the bondholder are insuperable. In the first place the ownership of the bonds cannot pass since the bonds are not identified, and therefore a transfer under the contract is impossible because of lack of certainty of subject matter. In the case of a sale of goods this principle is now embodied in the Sale of Goods Act 1979, s 16. Bonds and certificates of deposit are, of course, not goods within the Sale of Goods Act[3] and therefore s 16 is of no direct application, but s 16(b) is merely declaratory of the common law[4] and the reason is clear enough. How can the ownership in anything pass, whether goods or an investment, if the thing itself is not identified? The common law position is wider than the operation of s 16 and rests upon sturdy common-sense requirements.

If the ownership of the bonds or certificates cannot pass is there a solution to the problem through the operation of trust law? Can it be argued that the depositary is trustee of the bonds or certificates for the totality of the depositors as trustees in common in the proportion which the individual depositor's holding has to the whole? As a factual matter two situations are possible:

(1) that all the bonds or certificates of a particular issues are held in fungible account for the depositors;
(2) that some of the bonds of a particular issue are held in fungible account

1 See the discussion in R. M. Goode 'Ownership and Obligation in Commercial Transactions' (1987) 103 LQR 433.
2 Given the heavy institutional ownership of and commitment to both systems, insolvency is an unlikely outcome
3 'Choses in action' are excluded from the operation of the Act by s 61 (the interpretation section).
4 See the remarks of Byles J in *Heilbutt v Hickson* (1872) LR 7 CP 438 at p. 449.

for particular depositors whilst others are held for the issuer, the sales not yet having been arranged.[1]

With regard to the former the bonds in the fungible account will be a mass all of which are deposited for the depositors; in the latter only some will be held for this purpose. In the latter situation the claim of a trust for the depositors will fail for uncertainty of subject matter in the same way as a transfer under the contract fails. The position was well summed up by Oliver J. in *Re London Wine Company (Shippers) Ltd*[2]

> 'It seems . . . that any such trust must fail on the ground of uncertainty of subject matter . . . I appreciate the point taken that the subject matter is part of a homogeneous mass so that specific identity is of as little importance as it is . . . in the case of money . . . to create a trust it must be possible to ascertain with certainty not only what the interest of the beneficiary is to be but to what property it is to attach.'[3]

This problem does not exist in the former situation, but nevertheless an attempt to spell out a trust will be unsuccessful for what has been sold to the depositor are some bonds and not an interest in a trust. Any receipt given to him will reflect this underlying reality. As Oliver J went on to say in dealing with depositors' interests in wine held by an insolvent depositary in *Re London Wine Company (Shippers) Ltd.*

> 'I should find the very greatest difficulty in construing the assertion that "you are the sole and beneficial owner of" 10 cases of such and such a wine as meaning or intended to mean "you are the owner of such proportion of the total stock of such and such a wine now held by me as 10 bears to the total number of cases comprised in such stock.'

In short, there is nothing to prevent two or more persons from agreeing to buy a mass of bonds or certificates of deposit as trustees in agreed proportions and for these to be placed in a depositary under the agreed terms, but this must be the arrangement from its inception and the bonds must be purchased on those actual terms; purchases and deposits of bonds undertaken on a different basis cannot subsequently be artificially construed as transactions undertaken on a basis other than those actually undertaken.

Those arguments are relevant to the position of bonds held in fungible account in a depositary which have never been removed from the depositary, and therefore cannot be identified as ever having become owned by a particular depositor. Is the position any different where a depositor has removed a number of bonds thereby identifying them but has subsequently returned them to be held on a non-identified, fungible, basis? It is submitted

1 This is an unlikely situation since normally all the bonds will have been sold or held on behalf of the underwriters who had agreed to take them in the event of the issue being unsuccessful. The unlikely situation is, however, included for completeness of analysis.

2 Unreported, 7 November 1975. The full text of the judgment appears as an appendix to R M Goode *Proprietary Rights and Insolvency in Sales Transactions.* See also the opinion of Lord Hanworth, M R, in *Re Wait* [1927] 1 Ch 606.

3 At p. 19 of the transcript.

that the position is no different. It is true that it was held in the case of *Spence v Union Marine Insurance Co Ltd*[1] that, where goods are shipped on behalf of several separate owners and during the voyage lose the means of individual separate identification, the unidentified mass is held for each individual owner on trust as tenant in common in the proportion which the quantity shipped by him bore to the whole quantity shipped. However, even if all the bonds in an issue had left the depositary[2] and then been returned by the depositors to be held on a non-identified basis the depositors would still be unable to claim that the bonds are held on trust for them, at least in the absence of receipts declaring trusts in their favour, for their very act of returning the bonds on a non-identified basis is a clear indication of their intention that the bonds should lose their identity and the depositors' rights be purely contractual. The proposition actually decided by *Spence v Union Marine Insurance Co Ltd* was admirably summed up by Bovill CJ in that case as being that 'when goods of different owners become *by accident* so mixed together as to be indistinguishable, the owners of the goods so mixed become tenants in common of the whole in the proportions which they have severally contributed to it'.[3]

NEGOTIABILITY

International bonds and certificates of deposits are drawn in terms that they are negotiable, and the rights that they represent vest in the bearer, ie the person holding them for the time being. Plainly, it is necessary for the functioning of the secondary market that this should be so. However, the drawing of the securities in this form will help not one jot unless legal effect will be given to the form in which the securities are prepared.

The need for terminological clarity

What then is the effect of the preparation of the securities in this form? English law has two related concepts applicable to instruments intended to be capable of negotiation. These are negotiability and quasi-negotiability or transferability by delivery. The essential characteristics of a fully negotiable instrument are: (i) that the instrument and the rights which it embodies are capable of transfer by delivery; (2) that the person to whom the instrument is negotiated can sue on it in his own name; and (3) that the person to whom a current and apparently regular instrument has been negotiated who takes in good faith and for value obtains a good title to it even though his transferor had a defective title or no title at all.[4]

1 (1868) LR 3 CP 427 cited with approval *Smurthwaite v Hannay* [1894] AC 494 and *Sandeman & Sons v Tyzack Co* [1913] AC 680.

2 This is unlikely to occur in practice because in the case of any single issue of securities the majority of bonds held on a non-identified basis will never have left the depositary.

3 at p. 437, emphasis added

4 J Milnes Holden *The Law and Practice of Banking* 4th edn Pirman (1986) p. 121.

By contrast, quasi-negotiability or transferability by delivery recognises the first two characteristics only of the three attached to full negotiability. Thus, delivery of the document alone with any necessary endorsement thereon transfers the rights to the holder without the necessity for assignment or any notice to the person obliged thereunder. The consequences of this is that no new consideration needs to be given for the obligations to be enforceable, the original consideration being sufficient; that the contractual obligations represented by the documents lie between the person obligated thereunder and the holder so that the obligor can only discharge performance to the holder and not to the person to whom the document was originally given, or any person who held the document prior to the present holder; and consequent upon this the document may be safely treated as a chattel by being pledged, or, if possession is interfered with, used as the basis of an action in conversion or trespass to goods against the person interfering with the chattel.[1] However, the person to whom the instrument is negotiated cannot get a better title than that enjoyed by his transferor.

It is clearly advantageous to a holder of a document to know that it is in a category of documents treated by the law as fully negotiable in the narrow sense since a holder is thereby freed from the responsibility of enquiry into his transferor's title. This can be considered to be of the utmost importance in the case of negotiable securities available on a secondary market. A market in securities must function speedily with people being able to implement immediately their decisions to buy and sell. Further, if international bonds and certificates of deposit are not fully negotiable instruments, great difficulties would be caused to the working of the depositories and bond clearing systems. In particular, the consequences of international securities not being given full negotiable status would be most severe in the case of those held within one of the depositary systems in a pool covered by a multiplicity of fungible accounts. If it appeared that a transferor's title to some of them had been defective and an issuer took the point on whom should the loss fall? Should it fall on the particular investor who had withdrawn securities from the pool and whose allocation included the problem bonds? And what would be the position of those bonds left within the pool against which the issuer would take the same point? To which investor should they be notionally allocated? It is therefore essential that these international securities be recognised as being not merely transferable by delivery, but fully negotiable. The issue which then arises is whether the securities have, in fact, this characteristic.

Impact of the Bills of Exchange Act 1882

Are the instruments therefore negotiable instruments within the Bills of Exchange Act 1882? To be governed by that Act the securities would either have to constitute bills of exchange or promissory notes. They are clearly not bills of exchange because they do not contain any order to pay, but

1 Goode *Commercial Law* Penguin Books/Allen Lane (1982) pp.66, 67.

merely a promise that the issuer will in due course repay.[1] The greater difficulty is deciding whether the securities are or are not promissory notes. In the case of a certificate of deposit it would seem clear that the instrument is not a promissory note because it does not contain a promise of payment, but only evidences a prior agreement between a depositor and the depositee that the depositee will make repayment in due course in accordance with terms of the certificate.[2] With regard to the international bond in many cases the terms of the issue will contain uncertainties, eg as to the interest payable on a floating rate note which would take them outside the statutory definition.[3] Further, even where the instrument is a straight bond and not a floating rate note the fact that the bond terms make the sum owing repayable before the specified date for redemption if an act of default occurs will take the instrument outside the statutory definition of a promissory note, which requires a note to be payable 'on demand or at a fixed or determinable future time'. Nor is the instrument an 'unconditional promise' because of these very conditions as to time of repayment.[4] Further, the commercial community itself regards bearer securities as something apart from the forms of instruments dealt with by the Bills of Exchange Act.[5] This is hardly surprising. The Bills of Exchange Act codified the position with regard to negotiable instruments as known and identified in 1882. At that time the negotiable security had not evolved, and it is therefore hardly surprising if the Act does not apply to a form of instrument which was not in existence at the time that it was enacted. If it were to apply it would do so because of width of concept and not specific design. Further, traditionally the underlying purpose of the instruments dealt with in the Bills of Exchange Act is fundamentally different from the instruments at present under consideration which are true securities rather than convenient means by which everyday commerce may be undertaken. It is perhaps not without significance that the U.S. Uniform Commercial Code makes entirely separate provision for negotiable securities and negotiable paper.[6]

1 Within the Bills of Exchange Act 1882, s 3. Even where the Bills of Exchange Act does apply to the instrument not all matters arising from the instrument, its negotiation and acceptance will fail to be decided under English law — see s. 466 of the 1882 Act.

2 Within the Bills of Exchange Act 1882, s 83. Goode *Commercial Law* p. 524.

3 Goode *op. cit.* p. 524.

4 Bills of Exchange Act 1882, s 83(1). However, if the proposals of the Jack Committee are implemented a much wider statutory definition of negotiability will be introduced in a new Negotiable Instruments Act retaining much of the substance of the old 1882 Act. *Banking Services; Law and Practice Report* by the Review Committee, Chairman Professor R B Jack OBE Cm 622.

5 The attitude of the commercial financial community does seem to have an important bearing on categorisation, see *Bechuanaland Exploration Co v London Trading Bank* [1898] 2 QB 658 and *Edelstein v Schuler & Co.* [1902] 2 KB 144 discussed *post*.

6 Negotiable paper is dealt with in Article 3, negotiable securities in Article 8.

NEGOTIABILITY AND COMMERCIAL CUSTOM

That the commercial court will recognise the established custom of merchants in creating new categories of negotiable instrument cannot be seriously doubted. The case law is considerable and arises from the presentation to the courts of the bearer debentures issued to members of the public by limited companies where the obligations of the issuing company were expressed to be to the bearer on the instrument. The actual form of instrument went out of use because of the imposition of exchange control regulations[1] but given the close parallel between the international bond and the debenture[2] the attitude of the courts is most instructive. In *Crouch v Credit Foncier* while negotiability was recognised the decision was confined to an English instrument issued in England by an English company. The question therefore was whether the principle would be extended to foreign securities dealt with by English merchants as negotiable. The court showed a rugged common sense in dealing with the issue and proved themselves well able to give legal effect to the well established usages of commercial practice. The vitality of the courts is shown by Cockburn CJ, giving the judgment of the court in *Goodwin v Robarts:*[3]

> usage, adopted by the courts, having been thus the origin of the whole of the so-called law merchant as to negotiable securities, what is there to prevent our acting upon the principle acted upon by our predecessors, and followed in the precedent they have left to us? Why is it to be said that a new usage which has sprung up under altered circumstances, is to be less admissible that the usage of past times? Why is the door to be now shut to the admission and adoption of usage in a matter altogether of cognate character, as though the law had been finally stereotyped and settled by some positive and peremptory enactment[4]

The courts have been content to identify with the common-sense world of commercial men and have tried to avoid undermining the reasonable expectations of merchants and have striven to avoid the introduction of narrow distinctions. In *London Joint Stock Bank v Simmons*[5] Lord MacNaghten was clear and decisive:

> the Cedulas are foreign bonds with coupons attached payable to bearer. Admittedly they passed from hand to hand on the stock exchange and . . . are treated as negotiable instruments. I do not see on what grounds there are to be denied the quality of complete negotiability. In a matter of this sort, it is not . . . desirable to set up refined distinctions which are not understood or are uniformly and persistently ignored in the daily practice of the stock exchange.[6]

1 Exchange Control Act 1947, s 10.
2 Indeed the international bond when issued by a corporation will constitute a debenture under English Law.
3 (1876) LR 10 Exch 337.
4 At p. 352 ' . . . these words should be inscribed in letters of gold in every Court handling commercial litigation'. Lord Chorley in 48 LQR 51 at 55.
5 [1892] AC 201.
6 at p. 224.

The advantages of such a bluff commonsense approach are obvious. If the practices of merchants develop it is essential that the law develop to recognise their creations. If narrow distinctions were to be taken, so that only some of the securities expressed to be payable to bearer are recognised as negotiable, the only result could be general confusion and the failure of the market to develop.

The taking of a narrow distinction between English bonds and foreign bonds was rejected by Kennedy J in *Bechuanaland Exploration Co v London Trading Bank*[1] where he held that in deciding the issue of negotiability the important thing was the custom of English merchants. 'I think that both upon principle and upon authority, whether the instrument in question be an English instrument or a foreign instrument, the usage necessary to support a claim to rank as negotiable must be in either case a usage in England'.[2]

Thus, the sole matter to be determined is whether or not the necessary mercantile usage has been established, any distinction between English and foreign bonds being irrelevant. As, however, Kennedy J clearly indicated, the test of the usage is based upon the English market. Thus, the fact that an instrument is negotiable abroad in its country of issue will not make it negotiable here, unless it can be shown that the instrument was treated as negotiable by the usage of merchants in this country.[3]

In the subsequent case of *Edelstein v Schuler & Co*, [1902] 2 KB 144. Bingham J was prepared to recognise the negotiability of such bonds without further proof of usage in the light of judicial decisions previously made. Further, in a robust judgment the dynamic policy of the courts in recognising mercantile custom was stated at its bluntest in words, the application of which to both international bonds and certificates of deposit are clear and obvious.

> '. . . it is to be remembered that in these days usage is established much more quickly than it was in days gone by; more depends on the number of the transactions which helped to create it than the time over which the transactions are spread; that it is probably no exaggeration to say that nowadays there are more business transactions in a hour than there were in a week a century ago. Therefore the comparatively recent origin of this class of securities in my view creates no difficulty in the way of holding that they are negotiable by virtue of the law merchant; they are dealt in as negotiable instruments in every minute of a working day, and to the extent of many thousands of pounds . . . Our common law, of which the law merchant is but a branch, has in the hands of the judges the same facility for adopting itself to the changed needs of the general public; principles do not alter, but old rules of applying them change, and new rules spring into existence. Thus, it has been found convenient to treat securities like those in question in this action as negotiable, and the courts of law, recognising the wisdom of the usage, having incorporated it in what is called the law merchant, and

1 [1898] 2 QB 658.

2 at p. 676.

3 *Picker v London and County Banking Co.* (1887) 18 QBD 515 CA — Prussian bonds treated as negotiable in Prussia but not by English merchants held not negotiable under English law.

> have made it part of the common law of the country. In my opinion the time has passed when the negotiability of bearer bonds, whether government bonds or trading bonds, foreign or English, can be called in question in our courts. The existence of the usage has been so often proved and its convenience is so obvious that it must be taken that it should be part of the law; the very expression 'bearer bond' connotes the ideal of negotiability, so that the moment such bonds are issued to the public they rank themselves among the class of negotiable securities. It would also be a great misfortune if it were otherwise, for it is well known that such bonds are treated in all foreign markets as deliverable from hand to hand; the attribute not only enhances their value by making them easy of transfer, but it qualifies them to serve as a kind of international currency; and it would be very odd and a great injury to a trade if these advantages were not accorded to them in this country.'

Of course, for an instrument to be negotiable under the test of custom it must be expressed to be negotiable on its face; if it is not so expressed no amount of usage can confer a negotiability which the original obligor has declined to give.[1]

The necessity for positive assignment

The issues to which a consideration of this problem gives rise are compl and some further initial explanation is necessary. It will be remember that many bond issues are supported by, and subject to, the provisions of a trust deed, the terms of which are binding on bondholders.[2] Under the terms of the trust deed it is the trustee to whom the right to enforce the issuer's obligations is given, and a corresponding duty is imposed to act in certain circumstances.[3]

This raises the question of whether the interest of the bondholder has become an interest in a trust or a mere equitable interest, and that this is what is evidenced by the bond. In such a case a transfer of a bondholder's interest in the bond would need to be in writing under the Law of Property Act 1925, s 53 (1)(c), which provides that 'a disposition of an equitable interest or trust subsisting at the time of the disposition, must be in writing signed by the person disposing of the same or by his agent thereunto lawfully authorised in writing or by will'.

This must be seen in part against the overall background of the machinery created by the bond terms and trust deed. It will be recollected that an equal right to sue on the bonds is given to the bearer, and that it is only under the trust deed that the bondholder agrees that the trustee should have exclusive power of exercising the right. The purpose of the trust deed is not to confer benefits upon the issuer but upon the bondholders. It follows from this that the bonds are not mere evidence of an equitable

1 *London and County Banking Co v London and River Plate Bank Ltd* (1880) 20 QBD 232; *Jones & Co v Coventry* [1909] 2 KB 1029.
2 *ante* ch 2 p. 31.
3 *post* p. 242.

interest but direct obligations, the ownership of which entitles the bearer to benefit under the terms of the underlying arrangements.

Further, the nature of the trust of the second right to payment must be considered. The trust is a trust for the bondholders. Each bondholder is a participant as beneficiary of the right to payment conferred on the trustee. The significant consequence of this is that the equitable interest is always that of the bondholder, and not that of the individual to whom the bond was sold. Thus if A bought a bond on issue and sells it to B the equitable interest remains consistently that of the bondholder, the change of ownership of the bond merely changing the identity of the person entitled to demand performance of the trust as bondholder. This is entirely different to the situation where A personally has an equitable interest which he transfers to B where there is clearly a disposition by A to B. In the case of a bond issue there is never a disposition within s 53(1)(c), for the beneficial interest remains throughout exactly where it was conferred namely amongst the bondholders. Accordingly, a transfer of the bond in no way can represent an assignment of an equitable interest but merely extinguishes the previous owner's right to participate in the underlying arrangement whilst allowing the new bearer to participate as bondholders.[1]

Of course, no issue arising from the imposition of the trust can arise if, in fact, the trust is not imposed by the bond terms as was the case in *Venables v Baring Bros & Co.*[2] In that case the instruments under consideration were bonds issued by an American railroad company. Each bond contained an acknowledgment of indebtedness to bearer of the principal sum, promised that the principal would be paid to the holder of the bond on a specified date, and in the meantime interest would be payable to bear at half yearly intervals. The bonds were secured by a mortgage on the company's assets, and the mortgage contained various provisions relating to bondholders. However, the bond terms crucially omitted to subject the bonds to the terms of the trust deed.

Subsequently, some of the bonds were stolen and the plaintiff, a banker, advanced money against the deposit of the stolen bonds to a customer. The issuers subsequently refused to make payment of interest to the plaintiff and the plaintiff brought an action against the issuer to compel payment.

The defendant denied the negotiable nature of the bonds and on the basis of this assertion denied the title of the plaintiff to them. In rejecting the defendant's contention Kekewich J was able to base himself on the failure of the bond terms to subject the bonds to the terms of the trust deed.

> . . . it was said . . . the negotiable character of the bond depends on the bond itself, and that, unless you have on the face of the bond something

[1] It is a trust for beneficiaries identified by description. A parallel would be a trust for such of my nephews as qualify as solicitors for so long as they shall hold a practising certificate. Nephews could only participate in the trust by qualifying as solicitors (equivalent to buying the bond) but would be unable to participate if they ceased to hold a practising certificate (equivalent to selling the bond).

[2] [1892] 3 Ch 527.

> which shows that there is attached throughout a limitation essential to it which cannot pass, the negotiability, if otherwise established, stands unaffected, notwithstanding that the bondholder may not be able to enforce the provisions of the collateral instruments.[1]

By contrast there is clearly a simple trust situation if the bonds did not purport to confer upon the bearer the primary right to enforce them. If they contained only a covenant by the issuer with the trustee to make payment to the bearer the bearer's entitlement would not arise directly and it would seem the holder will be left with only an equitable interest under the trust. This was the position in the case of *Uruguay Central and Hygueritas Rly Co, of Monte Video.*[2]

It therefore follows that while the interest of the bondholder is an equitable interest in a trust of the second payment obligation, there is no disposition requiring a formal assignment complying with s 53(1)(c) of the Law of Property Act.[3] The negotiability, therefore, of international bonds and certificates of deposit falls to be determined solely according to the general principles applied by the commercial courts in determining whether or not legal effect should be given to mercantile usage. As has been seen by this test the bonds are indeed negotiable.

NEGOTIABILITY UNDER THE UNIFORM COMMERCIAL CODE

An examination of the U.S. law covering the recognition of negotiability reveals an equal capacity for adaptation to meet the changing customs of the market. However, under U.S. law this arises not because of the dynamism of the courts as in England, but from the uncompromising functionalism of the drafting of the Uniform Commercial Code.[4] That code defines a security as an instrument which (i) is issued in bearer or registered form; and (ii) is of a type commonly dealt in upon securities exchanges or markets or commonly recognised in any area in which it is issued or dealt in as a medium for investment; and (iii) is either one of a class or series or by its terms is divisible into a class or series of investments; and (iv) evidences a share, participation or other interest in property or in an enterprise or evidences an obligation of the issuer.[5] Where these conditions are satisfied a writing which is a security is governed by Article 8 and not by those provisions of the Uniform Commercial Code relating to commercial paper even though otherwise it meets the requirements of Article 3.[6]

1 at p. 537. However, in the particular case the bondholder had not surrendered his right of enforcement to the trustee.

2 (1879) 11 Ch D 372. Contrast the opposite result in *Re Olathe Silver Mining Co* (1884) 27 Ch D. 278 where there was a direct obligation to the bondholder.

3 It may well be that in any case the Law of Property Act 1925 has no application to situations which are primarily commercial and where application would lead to absurdity. *In Re AEG Unit Trust (Managers) Ltd's Deed* [1957] Ch 415.

4 For this we have to thank the principal draftsman of the original Article 8, Soia Mentshikoff, the wife of the UCC's main begetter Karl Llewellyn.

5 Article 8–102(1).

6 Article 8–102(2). Commercial paper is dealt with in Article 3.

The recognition of a transferable security therefore falls to be determined primarily from whether it is in fact dealt in upon securities exchanges or markets or recognised as a medium for investment.

The definition contains an express reference to bearer instruments as being issued in 'bearer form'. The code states that a security is in this form 'when it runs to bearer according to it terms and not by reason of any endorsement'.[1] It therefore follows that a security is in bearer form when its transfer does not require any endorsement. This is reinforced by Article 8–310 which provides that 'an endorsement of a security in bearer form may give notice of adverse claims but does not otherwise affect any right to registration the holder may possess'. As the official comment makes clear the concept of endorsement applies only to registered securities, and a purported endorsement of bearer paper is normally of no effect. The only effect to it is that it may by its terms give notice to the purchaser of any adverse claims in respect of any security.

However, the Uniform Commercial Code makes it far less important than under English law to determine whether or not a security is fully negotiable. Under its terms, any bona fide purchaser of an investment security, whether in bearer form and fully negotiable or depending upon a formal assignment, take free of any antecedent defect in his transferor's title. The functional drafting of Article 8–301 is worthy of quotation:

> (1) Upon delivery of a security the purchaser acquires the right in the security which his transferor had or had actual authority to convey except that a purchaser who has himself been a party to any fraud or illegality affecting the security or who, as a prior holder had notice of an adverse claim, cannot improve his position by taking from a later bona fide purchaser. 'Adverse claim' includes a claim that a transfer was or would be wrongful or that a particular adverse person is the owner of or has an interest in the security.
>
> (2) A bona fide purchaser in addition to acquiring the rights of purchaser also acquires the security free of any adverse claim.
>
> A 'bona fide purchaser' is a purchaser for value in good faith and without any notice of any adverse claim who takes delivery of a security in bearer form and of one in registered form issued to him or endorsed to him or in blank.[2]

As the official comment recognises, this defines bona fide purchaser in terms of three separate elements namely 'value', 'good faith', and lack of 'notice of any adverse claim'. What then constitutes notice of an adverse claim? It is expressly provided that a purchaser (including a broker for the seller or buyer but excluding an intermediary bank) of a security is charged with notice of an adverse claim in two specific situations. First, where the security whether in bearer or registered form has been endorsed 'for collection' or 'for surrender' or for some other purpose not involving transfer. Secondly, where the security is in bearer from and has on it an unambiguous statement that it is the property of a person other than the transferor. The mere writing of a name on a security is not such a statement.

1 Article 8–102(d).
2 Article 8–302.

The position with regard to fiduciaries is clarified by providing that the fact that the purchaser (including a broker for the seller or buyer) has notice that the security is held for a third person, or is registered in the name of or endorsed by a fiduciary, does not create a duty of enquiry into the rightfulness of the transfer or constitute notice of adverse claims.[1] If, however, the purchaser (excluding an intermediary bank) has knowledge that the proceeds are being used for, or the transaction is for the individual benefit of, the fiduciary or otherwise in breach of duty, the purchaser is charged with notice of adverse claims.[2]

It must not be thought that these provisions with regard to notice are exhaustive. It is still open to a court to decide a purchaser had notice in factual situations which do not fall within any of the express provisions which may be said to be included by way of common illustrative examples.

SECURITIES HELD BY A CENTRAL DEPOSITARY UNDER THE CODE

In stark contrast to the failure of English law to provide for modern developments in the transfer and holding of securities the U.S. Commercial Code makes express provision. This specifically provides for Central Depositary systems. Under the Code securities held by a depositary may be traded by book entries. The security must be in the custody of a clearing corporation or a custodian bank, or a nominee of either subject to the instruction of the clearing corporation. It must be in bearer form or indorsed in blank by an appropriate person, or registered in the name of the clearing corporation or custodian bank or a nominee of either. It must be further shown as held to the account of the person seeking to deal with it. When these conditions are satisfied then, in addition to other methods, a transfer or pledge may be effected by the making of appropriate entries on the books of the transferor or pledgor and increasing the account of the transferee or pledgee by the amount of the obligation or the number of shares or rights transferred or pledged.[3] In this connection it matters not that the securities dealt with are part of a fungible bulk for the entries may refer merely to the quantity of a particular security without reference to the name of the registered owner, certificate or bond number or the like and, in appropriate cases, may be on a net basis taking into account other transfers or pledges of the same security.[4]

A transfer or pledge carried out by these means has the effect of a delivery of a security in bearer form or duly authorised in blank representing the amount of the obligation or the number of shares or rights transferred or pledged. If a pledge or the creation of a security interest is intended, the making of entries has the effect of a taking of delivery by the pledgee or a secured party.[5] A transferee or pledgee is a holder. Once delivery

1 Article 8–304(1).
2 Article 8–304(2).
3 8–320(1).
4 8–320(2). This is in clear contrast to English law discussed *ante* p.235
5 8–320(3).

has been effected by the book entry the purchase of a security, which is part of a fungible bulk, is the owner of a proportionate property interest in the fungible bulk. Thus the insolvency of either his transferor or the depositary cannot affect him.[1] The very fact that ownership can pass in such circumstances enables the property held in common to be identified, a position impossible under English law.

NEGOTIATION AFTER MATURITY

It is a principle of English law that a holder of a negotiable instrument to whom it is negotiated after the maturity of the instrument takes subject to any defects in the title of his transferor. 'There is this distinction between bills endorsed before and after they become due. If a note endorsed be not due at the time it carries no suspicion whatever on the face of it, and the person receives it on his own intrinsic credit. But if it is overdue, though I do not say that by law it is not negotiable, yet certainly it is out of the common course of dealing, and gives rise to suspicion.'[2] By 1881 the rule was considered to be established beyond all doubt, and the reason for the rule stated as 'these instruments are usually current only during the period before they become payable, and their negotiation after that period is out of the usual and ordinary course of dealing, that circumstance is sufficient of itself to excite so much suspicion that, as a rule of law, the endorsee takes on the credit of and can stand in no better position than the endorser . . . '[3]

Under U.S. law the strict rule has been amended by the provisions of the Uniform Commercial Code, which recognises the reality that in fact securities are sometimes negotiated after maturity. The Code therefore provides that an act or event which creates a right to immediate performance of the principal obligation evidenced by the security or which sets a date on or after which the security is to be presented or surrendered for redemption or exchange, does not of itself constitute any notice of adverse claims except in two situations. First, a purchase made after one year from any date set for presentment or surrender for redemption or exchange, and, secondly, one made after six months for any date set for payment of money against presentation or surrender of the security if funds are available for payment on that day.[4] The latter limit is only applicable where it is shown that funds were available for redemption; the latter is the long-stop date applicable in any event. Consequently, under the terms of the Code it is

1 Article 8–313(2). In direct contrast to English law. There is similar protection given under the Code to the purchaser of an undivided share in an *identified* bulk of fungible goods which are treated as sufficiently identified to be sold and where such a sale takes place 'any agreed proportion of such a bulk or any quantity thereof agreed seller's interest in the bulk be sold to the buyer who then becomes an owner in common'. s 2–105(4).

2 *Brown v Davies* [1789] 3 TR 82 per Buller J at p. 82.

3 *London and County Banking Co, v Groome* [1881] 8 QBD 288 *per* Field J at p. 292. The principle is now incorporated in the Bills of Exchange Act 1882, ss 29 and 36.

4 Article 8–305.

now possible for there to be a bona fide purchase of a matured instrument provided that the negotiation of the security to the holder took place within the prescribed time limits. It is questionable whether this provision of the Code is beneficial, for when a security has matured the owner will normally surrender it to realise his investment in preference to negotiation, since negotiation is likely to be at a discount. It is this circumstance which under English law automatically puts the transferee upon enquiry. In the light of this it must be somewhat doubtful whether any alteration to the general principle of a transferee taking subject to any defects in the tranferor's title is beneficial for the sake of a minority of a non-representative transactions, even to the limited extent allowed under the Unform Commercial Code.

DEFINITION OF BONDHOLDERS

The examination of the issue of negotiability now enables us to proceed to define a term which has already been much used—that of the bondholder. It is usual for the term bondholders to be defined in the bond terms as 'the holders for the time being of the notes'. It will be remembered that the bonds are in bearer form, and the position of the bondholder is thus equated with that of a bare holder of a bearer instrument under the Bills of Exchange Act 1882, s 2 who is the person who is in possession of it. The important thing about a holder is not that he is entitled to receive payment from the issuer (he may be a thief in possession), but that if in good faith and without notice of any defect in the holder's title, the issuer pays to the holder the issuer will gain a good discharge. If the holder, however, had no title whilst the issuer is discharged the holder remains liable to an action from the true owner.[1]

1 Goode *Commercial Law* p. 442.

10 The obligation to pay[1]

INTRODUCTION

The fundamental obligation undertaken by the issuer of a bond or certificate of deposit is to pay the sums of money, the payment of which is promised by the terms of the security. Given the international distribution of the bonds extensive arrangements have to be made in respect of the actual mechanics. The provision of a single payment agent located in a single country would obviously be inappropriate, as investors will not find acceptable any system under which they have to travel across several countries, or, indeed, continents, to obtain payment of the sums due to them. Accordingly, an issuer will arrange a network of paying agents, with at least one in each of the main countries in which the bonds are to be marketed. From the network of paying agents one will be appointed the principal paying agent. Because of the need for a paying agent to dispense large sums of money in redeeming bonds paying agents are usually banks.

BOND TERMS

Plainly, an issuer will not be willing to pay twice against the same security, and accordingly the bond terms will specify that payment will only be made by a paying agent against surrender of the bond or interest coupon in respect of which payment is sought, thus preventing the same instrument being presented for payment twice at different paying agents. This provides a basic protection to the issuer in discharging his payment obligations, except in relation to forged instruments. The provisions with regard to payment are likely to be in a form similar to that which follows:

> 'Payments in respect of principal and interest will be made against surrender of Bonds or, as the case may be, Coupons at any specified office of any of the Paying Agents. The initial Principal Paying Agent and other Paying Agents and their specified offices are set out at the end of this Bond.
>
> The Issuer reserves the right, subject to the prior approval of the Trustee, at any time to vary or terminate the appointment of any Paying Agent and to appoint additional or other Paying Agents, provided that it will at all

[1] See generally Mann *The Legal Aspect of Money* 4th edn Clarendon Press (1982); Goode '*Payment Obligations in Commercial and Financial Transactions* Sweet and Maxwell (1983); The Law Commission (Law Com No 124) *Private International Law Foreign Money Liabilities*' (Cmnd 9064).

times maintain Paying Agents having specified offices in London, N. York City, and one other city in Europe, which so long as the Bonds are listed on the Luxembourg Stock Exchange will be in Luxembourg. Notice of any such termination of appointment and of any change in the specified offices of the Paying Agent will be given to the Bond holders.

Bonds should be presented for payment together with all Coupons appertaining thereto which, at the Relevant Date for the payment of Bonds remain unmatured, failing which the face value of any such missing Coupons (or, in the case of payment not being made in full, that proportion of the aggregate face value of such missing Coupons which the sum of principal so paidbears to the total principal amount due) will be deducted from the sum due for payment. Each amount of principal so deducted will be paid in the manner mentioned above against surrender of the relevant Coupon at any time within the period expiring five years after the Interest Payment Date specified on the face of such coupon.

If the due date for payment of any amount of principal or interest in respect of any Bond or Coupon is not on a business day, then the holder thereof shall not be entitled to payment of the amount due until the next following business day and shall not be entitled to any further interest or other payment in respect of such delay. In this paragraph 'business day' means any day on which banks are open for business in the place of the specified office of the Paying Agent at which the Bond or Coupon is presented for payment.'[1]

SOME REMAINING PROBLEMS

If the terms of the bonds themselves make clear provision as to the places at which payments can take place, and the times during which payment can be demanded, there remain a number of other issues of some complexity with which the terms of the bond do not deal, although on which they may have some effect. These issues can best be stated by giving an example to show the complexities of the situation.

A Japanese issuer has made a multimillion dollar issue of bonds denominated in U.S. dollars with paying agents in Singapore, the U.S., and the U.K. A German purchaser of bonds wishes to present his bond for payment in England. The terms of bonds specify that the trust deed, the bonds, and the coupons, are governed by, and are to be construed in accordance with, Japanese law.

As there is an English paying agent clearly the German bondholder can present his bonds and coupons for payment to the paying agent in England. However,

1. Is the German bondholder entitled to demand to be paid in dollars, or must payment be made in sterling, being the currency of the place of payment?
2. If payment is to be made in sterling how is the obligation to pay in sterling to be measured?

[1] Terms of issue by Life Co. Ltd. $25,000,000 6 per cent. Convertible Bonds 1996.

3. Is it possible for the payment obligation to be frustrated due to impossibility of performance, and if so by which set or sets of law is the issue of frustration to be considered?
4. If payment is not made on due demand and the English courts have jurisdiction in what currency is the German bondholder entitled to sue? Is he entitled to sue for dollars? Is he entitled in to sue in sterling as the currency of the place of payment where payment was demanded? Or, alternatively, is he entitled to sue in sterling as a currency of the court in which he is bringing his proceedings?
5. If he is entitled to bring his action as a claim for dollars is he entitled to a judgment in dollars, or must the judgment which is finally given on his action for dollars be converted into sterling?
6. If the German bondholder is entitled to a judgment in dollars can he insist that the judgment only be satisfied by payment in dollars, or can the issuer pay the English judgment in sterling?
7. Finally, if the German bondholder obtains a judgment in dollars which, because it remains unpaid, he then wishes to enforce against English assets of the issuer within the reach of the English courts, can he levy execution on those assets for a sum of dollars or, as he is using the process of the English courts, only a sum of sterling?

In considering these complex questions it is necessary to be aware of four legal systems each of which may have something to say with regard to the particular problem being considered. The first is the law of the obligation, that is the proper law or *lex causae* (in the example given Japanese law because the choice of law clause in the terms of the bonds); secondly the law of the country whose currency is stipulated to be payable, ie the *lex monetae* (in the example given the U.S. because of the denomination of the bonds in U.S. dollars); thirdly, the law of the due place of payment, i.e. the *lex loci solutionis* (in the example England because payment was to be made *inter alia* in that country); and, fourthly, the law of the state in which any proceedings are to be brought, i.e. the *lex fori* (in the example given England because it is in that country that the German bondholder is contemplating bringing his proceedings).[1]

THE ISSUER'S DISCHARGE OF HIS PAYMENT OBLIGATION

Money of account and the money of payment

To understand what the issuer must do to discharge his payment obligation it is necessary first to consider the nature of the distinction between the money of account and the money of payment. The nature of the distinction in English law has received its clearest judicial exposition from Lord Denning MR: '*The money of account* is the currency in which an obligation is measured. It tells the debtor *how much* he has to pay. The *money of payment* is the

1 See Mann *op. cit.* edn pp. 179–183; Goode '*Payment Obligations in Commercial and Financial Transactions*' (1983) p. 145.

currency in which the obligation is to be discharged. It tells the debtor *by which means* he has to pay.[1]

Determining the money of account

How then is the money of account to be determined? Essentially the starting place for the determination of the money of account is the proper law of the contract[2] and, in the example given, this would therefore fall to Japanese law. In this connection it has been well written:

> 'It cannot be gainsaid said the determination of the money of account is a matter of interpretation of the contract, and is so treated in all legal systems. As in connection with all other problems of construction so it is here necessary to have regard to all the circumstances of the case and so to deduce the true intention of the parties.'[3]

That intention may be perfectly clear from the contract itself as in the example given where U.S. dollars are specified. The real problems arise where there is ambiguity in the contract. This may be because an insufficiently precise description of the currency is used eg the case of the simple term dollar without specifying whether the dollar be a U.S., Australian, Canadian, or any other dollar. In cases of ambiguity attention may have to be paid to the detail of the transaction. Thus, in one Canadian case a transaction for '£3,500,000 = 88,060,000 francs' was held to constitute the franc as the currency of account to the exclusion of the £ because an examination of the text of the bonds and coupons actually issued revealed that they merely

1 *Woodhouse AC Israel Cocoa Ltd v Nigerian Produce Marketing Co Ltd* [1971] 2 QB 23 at 54. The distinction was subsequently recognised by the House of Lords on appeal [1972] AC 741 and further drawn by the Court of Appeal in *George Veflings Rederi AS v President of India* [1979] 1 WLR 59. The importance of the distinction in modern times of fluctuating exchange rates is emphasised by Lord Denning in a striking hypothetical example in the *Woodhouse* case at p. 54. The importance of currency fluctuation to the international bond market has already been stressed (*ante* ch 2 p. 22). As has been well-emphasised.
'The benefits of transnational financial transactions have always been closely intertwined with problems of valuation of the different national currencies of the parties involved. Every country has the ability to change the external value of its currency through revaluation or devaluation, within certain limits set by international law and the form of the international monetary system of the time. Additionally the value of a currency can be changed with respect to other currencies by market forces, through appreciation or depreciation.' Bathurst 'Creditor Protection in the Changing World'. 15 Texas Int LJ 519 [1980]

2 *Bonython v Commonwealth of Australia* [1951] AC 201; *Alan (WJ) & Co Ltd v EL Nasr Export and Import Co* [1972] 2 QB 189.

3 Mann *op.cit.* p. 224. See also Van Hecke *International Encyclopaedia of Comparative Law* vol. 3 Private International Law Chapter 36 'Currency' (1970) p. 3

provided for francs.[1] If the ambiguity or uncertainty cannot be solved by a close consideration of the available documentation then the 'nature of the transaction, the nationality, residence, and domicile of the parties, the valuation of the respective currencies at the time of the contract was made, the place where the contract was made and where it was to be performed, all these and similar facts will have to be looked at and weighed'.[2] There appears to be a general rule that where the debtor is a public authority there is a clear but rebuttable presumption that it intended to contract in its own currency.[3] If all else fails the foremost English writer on the subject has claimed that it is 'a rule of English (municipal) law, and, indeed, of most laws, that, in the absence of circumstances indicating a different intention of the parties, the money of the place of payment is the money of account meant by the parties'.[4]

The principle of nominalism

The principle that it is the money of account that fixes the amount of the financial obligation in an international monetary transaction connects with another important principle of monetary law, that of nominalism. This is that a payment of the nominal value of the designated currency discharges the obligation regardless of whether the purchasing power of the currency has declined since the obligation was incurred, either internally or externally in its relations with other currencies. The party to whom the money is due must be content with a payment of the nominal amount due, even though the real purchasing power of that nominal amount is less than it was when the obligation was created.[5] The principle of nominalism is generally accepted by states in relation to their currencies and is certainly a fundamental of English law.[6] The rule of English law is not confined to sterling. It will apply also where another currency is involved but the proper law of the obligation is English law. Nor is the principle of nominalism confined to English law. It is generally followed by developed legal systems.[7]

1 *Derwa v Rio de Janeiro Tramway Light and Power Co* [1928] 4 DLR 542.

2 Mann *op. cit.* pp. 224–5.

3 *Bonyton v Commonwealth of Australia; National Mutual Life Association of Australasia v A-G for New Zealand* [1956] AC 369.

4 Mann *op. cit.* p. 241

5 'Many do not realize that nominalism is a legal institution . . . [*had*] it been only a concept of political philosophy courts of law would not have been entitled to apply it. Nominalism is not self evident even if it is treated as such by many . . . It was adopted in the field of legal obligation as a corollary of the royal prerogative over coinage and to strengthen it.' Hirchberg 'Monetary Law in the Modern Era of Monetary Instability' 21 *Rev. de Derecho Puertorrigueno* 51 at p. 53.

6 *Treseder-Griffin v Co-operative Insurance Society Ltd.* [1956] 2 QB 127; Gilbert v Brett (*the Case de Mixt Moneys*) (1694) Davis, 18; *Bonyton v Commonwealth of Australia; Woodhouse AC Israel Cocoa Ltd v Nigerian Produce Marketing Co Ltd; Alan (W J) & Co Ltd v El Nasr Export and Import Co* [1972] 2 QB 189.

7 *Re Chesterman's Trust* [1923] 2 Ch 466; *Addison v Brown* [1954] 1 WLR 779; *Pyrmont Ltd. v Schott* [1939] AC 145; *Marrache v Ashton* [1943] AC 311.

For an issue of international bonds or certificates of deposit the major consequence of the choice of the money of account is that the obligation is linked to that unit for its measurement, and consequently is subject to change by the law of the *lex monetae*, with the result that where this occurs the debtor's obligation is similarly changed. Thus, on the conversion of all French francs into new French francs, and the conversion of the old German mark to the reichsmark and to the deutsche mark, debtors obligations denominated in those currencies became obligations to pay in the new currency created by the countries concerned at the conversion rate fixed by the law of those countries as the *lex monetae.*[1] A redefinition of the money of account is thus a matter for the *lex monetae.*[2]

Currency collapse and revalorisation.

Does this therefore mean that in no circumstances will a court ever revalorize or devalorise a monetary obligation to take account of a fall or increase of the money of account? Certainly in some countries where its currency has collapsed revalorisation of debts by the courts of that country has taken place. Probably the most dramatic example of currency collapse documented in modern times was the decline in value of the mark after the end of the First World War. So fast was the rate of decline that when the mark was transmuted into the reichsmark in 1924 it was at the rate of 1 billion old marks for one reichsmark. The effect of this was a massive distortion of the country's economy and people's perception of value.

When in Germany in 1924 the old mark was extingushed and the reichsmark introduced by legislation there was initially no formula within the legislation for revalorisation of debt.[3] Nevertheless, the German courts themselves intervened to revalorise debts when their intervention was sought, and did so in reliance on the general requirement of good faith imposed by s 242 of the German Civil Code to achieve justice between the parties.

There is no reported case of an English court being prepared to consider revalorisation of an obligation because of the decline in value of the *lex monetae.* On the other hand the case which is most likely to concentrate the minds of the courts of a jurisdiction with regard to revalorization, is where the currency which has collapsed is the currency of that jurisdiction. The pound has remained a relatively stable currency despite the ups and downs of inflation when compared with the drama of the German mark in the years immediately after 1918. A collapse of the pound could well lead to a radical rethinking by English courts. In such a situation it may well be that revalorisation would be permitted in the case of executed contracts. In the case of executory contracts the more likely route to be

1 See the comparative material included by Mann *op. cit.* ch 4.
2 Van Hecke *op. cit.* p.4.; Nussbaum *'Money in the Law, National and International'*, Brooklyn (1951).
3 Subsequently general rules were applied by statute for revalorisation.

employed by the English courts would be to view the obligations as frustrated.[1]

If, however, an English court will not in normal circumstances allow revalorisation of an obligation where the proper law of the obligation is English law, will they allow revalorisation where the proper law of the obligation is a foreign system of law which does allow revalorisation? The answer appears to be that in these circumstances the English court will indeed allow revalorisation to bring about the same result that would have arisen had the matter been litigated in the courts of the legal system whose law applied to the obligation. Both authorities arose from ligitation in England of obligations affected by the collapse of the German mark in the years after 1918, and in both cases the English court having ascertained that German law was the law governing the *obligation* revalorised the debt as a German court would have done.[2]

The classification of the issues of revalorisation and devalorisation of the debtor's obligation as a matter for the proper law of the obligation is logical and consistent. It is followed not merely by English private international law, but also by the courts of Germany, Austria and Switzerland, and appears generally accepted by writers on the subject.[3]

Multiple currency and gold clauses

It is, of course, to protect investors against the possible effects of the principle of nominalism that use has been made of denomination of issues in composite

[1] Goode *op. cit.* p. 129.; Mann *op. cit* p. 111. In support of the underlying pragmatism of the English courts with regard to payment obligations one can point to the *Miliangos Case*, an obvious reaction to ever-increasing exchange rate fluctuations. It is in this sense and with these probable effects that there is truth in Hirschberg's assertion that 'monetary law must develop its own attitude to hyperinflations and very severe inflations the practical result' [of which] 'would be that all savings and liquid private rights would become practically valueless and whole sectors and classes of the population would be ruined'. Hirschberg *op. cit.* p. 52. For a comparative survey of English, French, and U.S. judicial attitudes to the problem of inflation and responses thereto, see Downs 'Nomination, Indexation, Excuse and Revalorisation: A Comparative Survey' (1985) 101 LQR 98.

[2] *Franklin v Westminster Bank Ltd* (1931) reproduced in Mann *op. cit.* Appendix 11 at p. 562. *Re Chesterman's Trusts* [1923] 2 Ch 466; a complex problem is that where a currency disappears on the dismemberment of an independent state, eg Austria/Hungary in 1918 and Germany in 1948. The most logical and generally accepted solution would appear to be to translate the debt into the new currency of the state with which the debt is most closely connected in the intentions of the parties. See Mann *op. cit.* Chapter 9. The solution employed must, of course, be that of the proper law of the obligation which necessarily governs the transaction. It seems that most legal systems will determine the effect of revalorisation by application of the law of the obligation. There are some conflicting German decisions but the weight of authority even in Germany is in favour of this solution. There is a similar general support from the writers. Van Hecke *op. cit.* p. 7.

[3] Mann *op. cit.* pp. 276 and 277 and authorities cited therein.

currency units. In previous years the use of gold clauses were intended to produce the same effect. The effectiveness of such clauses and their interpretation are governed by the law of the obligation.[1] Similarly, clauses have sometimes been incorporated in the past into international debt obligations, giving the creditor the option of demanding payment in one of several currencies, and often with a correlative right to demand payment in one of several places. Again the effect of such a clause is decided according to the proper law of the obligation. Depending on the wording and the circumstances, clauses may be construed as true alternative currency clauses, or merely a denomination in a single currency with an option conferred upon the investor to obtain repayment at one of various alternative centres[2] The latter is the usual form of the modern international bond.

The inclusion of a gold clause or multiple currency clauses in a monetary obligation may cause considerable problems for a debtor, where the value of gold or the selected currencies appreciate at a much faster rate than the debtor's domestic currency or the currency of the country where the funds are utilised. In addition, countries may feel that the widespread use of such devices places an unacceptable burden upon the value of their domestic currency. Faced with these problems in the 1930s many countries passed legislation invalidating gold clauses, the then source of the problem. It may therefore be not unreasonable to suppose that were similar problems to arise in modern circumstances from the use of multiple currency clauses a similar reaction might be provoked.

Among the statutory attempts to invalidate gold clauses a considerable variety of aim and effect can be discerned. Some legislation has invalidated gold clauses permanently.[3] In others gold clauses effected before a specified date have been invalidated without affecting the validity of subsequent clauses.[4] Usually, the legislative essay has been limited to those obligations expressed in the domestic currency;[5] in others any gold clause has been invalidated whatever the currency of account.[6] Neither the U.K. nor Switzerland have felt the need to make use of any legislation at all.[7]

1 *R v International Trustee* [1937] AC 500; *New Brunswick Rly v British and French Trust Corpn Ltd* [1939] AC 1; *Kricorian v Ottoman Bank* (1932) 48 TLR 247; *Feist v Societe Intercommunale* [1934] AC 161; *Multiservice Bookbinding v Marden* [1979] Ch 84. See on the whole subject Mann *op. cit.* p. 290 et seq.

2 Contrast *R v International Trustee; Rhokana Corpn Ltd v IRCrs* [1938] AC 380; and *Montreal Trust Co v Stanrock Uranium Mines Ltd* (1965) 53 DLR (2d) 594 with *New Brunswick Rly v British and French Trust Corpn Ltd* [1939] AC1; *Auckland City Corpn v Alliance Assurance* [1937] AC 587 and see generally Mann *op. cit.* p. 207 et seq.

3 U.S. Joint Resolution 5 June 1933 (48 Stat L.112).

4 Belgium Royal Decree 11 April 1935; Netherlands Act of 24 May 1937.

5 U.S. Joint Resolution; Belgian Decree; Dutch Act.

6 Canadian Act of 10 April 1937 (Geo. 6, c 33).

7 With regard to English law see *Multiservice Bookbinding v Marden* [1979] Ch 84.

Where legislation invalidating gold clauses has been enacted it will be applied by the courts of the country concerned. However, the scope of the application will depend on the interpretation of those courts based upon its language and legislative history. The U.S. legislation has been held to apply to all dollar debts regardless of the place of payment; but it appears that the Belgian Decree does not apply to obligations governed by foreign law. Neither the Dutch nor Austrian[1] legislation appears to apply to obligations where the place of payment is outside the enacting country. In France the restriction on gold clauses has been evolved by the courts, who have not applied the doctrine to contracts involving an international payment.[2]

While the courts of the enacting state will give effect to an invalidating statute by interpreting and applying the products of its own legislature, it is less likely that the courts of other jurisdictions will give effect to the legislative policy of what to them is a foreign legislature. In general, such legislation will be applied by a foreign court only in those circumstances where effect would be given to the legislation by the proper law of the obligation.[3] Where it would not be so recognised a foreign court will not usually apply it, apparently for public policy reasons, except where their own legislature had enacted similarly draconian legislation. The French courts have applied their distinction between domestic obligations and obligations involving an international payment to a gold clause subject to foreign law.[4]

Two things which are implicit in these comments with regard to the money of account and the principle of nominalism should perhaps be made clear with regard to English law. While the English courts will intervene to allow revalorisation of the debt where revalorisation is allowed by the law of the obligation, they will not intervene merely because the debt would be revalorised under the money of account. The relevant law with regard to this is the law of the obligation itself.[5]

The only relevance which an allowance of revalorisation by the money of account could have would be where the proper law of the obligation was prepared to give effect to the revaluation of the *lex monetae,* which English law alone was not. The only relevance of the *lex monetae* is to fix the unit of account and to identify it if change takes place.[6] Equally, English law will only apply a foreign invalidating statute to a gold clause where the proper law of the obligation would apply it.[7] Secondly, the

1 Goldklauselverordreung of 23 March 1933.
2 Van Hecke *op. cit.* p. 9. Mann *op. cit.* pp. 163–172.
3 Van Hecke *op. cit.* p. 9.
4 Van Hecke *op. cit.* p. 10.
5 *Anderson v Equitable Assurance Society* (1926) 134 LT 557.
6 *Pyrmont Ltd v Schott* [1939] AC 145; *Marrache v Ashton* [1943] AC 311; *Anderson v Equitable Assurance Society* (1926) 134 LT 557; *British Bank for Foreign Trade Ltd v Russian Commercial and Industrial Bank* (1921) 38 TLR 65.
7 Dicey and Morris '*The Conflict of Laws*' 11th edn Stevens (1987) Rule 208. p. 1431; *R v International Trustee* [1937] AC 500.

principles discussed are merely relevant to identify the payment obligation of the issuer at the due date of payment which is, of course, when the bond or coupon is presented for payment at a paying agent at a date after the maturity of the bond or coupon. The principles are not applicable to resolve the question of the investor's rights in the event of the issuer failing to pay on presentation. The obligations discussed are implied into the bargain between the issuer and investors; they do not extend to a breach of those obligations by the issuer and any entitlement to damages which may arise.

The money of payment

From this we can now see the significance and workings of the money of account as quantifying the obligation owed. Reverting to our initial questions, when the investor presents his bond for payment in London is he entitled to insist on payment in dollars, sterling, or some other currency? In general, it is open to the parties to a transaction to agree that payment might be made in some currency other than that identified as the money of account, thus designating a money of payment, but the practice in issues of international bonds and certificates of deposit is for no separate designation to be made for a currency of payment, the intention of the parties being that repayment of the bonds will be in the currency of account. Further, where the money of account, and therefore of payment, is a foreign currency there is a second rule of English law to consider, for under English law in such circumstances *prima facie* the debtor has the option of tendering either the foreign currency itself or its sterling equivalent. In this English law merely accords with other systems of law, which generally confer a faculty of conversion for payment in their own currency unless the parties have expressly or impliedly agreed to the contrary. The existence of the faculty of conversion, and the possibility of the parties providing for its exclusion, are matters for the law of the place of payment as these matters relate to performance. It would seem clear, however, that in the case of an issue of international bonds or certificates of deposit, it is the intention of the parties that the *prima facie* rule should be superseded and that repayment should be in the money of payment. The very international nature of the issue is a clear indication that the payment obligation can be discharged in the currency of the denomination of the issue and that currency alone. Only in this way can uniformity across the varying jurisdictions be obtained. To take a contrary view would make the bondholders' rights depend on the situation of the particular paying agent at which the bond was presented for repayment—a matter which cannot be predicted at the time of issue when the parties' intention must be identifiable. Further, as a matter of commercial reality, the sale and purchase of bonds being in the currency of denomination it is likely that both parties have in mind redemption in that currency and that currency alone.

In fact, issues of international bonds often make very precise provision for payment. Payment of large sums of money in cash is inconvenient in modern commercial transactions and increasingly the payment terms contained in bonds modify dramatically the payment obligation. An example is as follows:

> 'payments in respect of principal and interest will be made against surrender of Bonds or, as the case may be Coupons at any specified office of any of the Paying Agents. Such payment will be made at any specified office of any Paying Agent in New York City in dollars or, at the option of the holder, at any specified office of any Paying Agent by a dollar cheque drawn on, or by transfer to a dollar account maintained by the payee with, a bank in New York City, subject in all cases to any fiscal or other laws and regulations applicable thereto'.

The other terms of the payment clause previously given are set out but there is modification of the clause specifing due date of payment as follows:

> 'If the due date for payment of any amount of principal or interest in respect of any Bond or Coupon is not a business day, then the holder thereof shall not be entitled to payment of the amount due until the next following business day and shall not be entitled to any further interest or other payment in respect of such delay. In this paragraph 'business day' means any day which banks are open for business in the place of the specified office of the Paying Agent at which the Bond or Coupon is presented for payment and (in the case of payment by transfer to a dollar account as referred to above) on which dealing in foreign currencies may be carried on in both New York City and such place'.[1]

Both the identification of the money of payment and the construction of such a clause as above would fall to the proper law of the obligation.[2]

The procedural rules in an action to enforce payment

The above rules set out the basis on which the issuer's responsibility with regard to payment is determined. Where, however, an issuer does not pay voluntarily an investor will be faced with having to sue to recover the investment that he has made. It is the procedural rules of the jurisdiction in which he seeks to bring his action which will determine whether he can sue in a foreign currency or only the currency of the jurisdiction in which proceedings are being commenced.

Under English law it is now the rule that where proceedings are commenced in respect of a foreign money obligation proceedings can be brought in

1 The above modification will also have an interesting effect on the possibility of frustration of the payment obligation discussed *post* p. 273.

2 Van Hecke *op. cit.* p. 13.

the foreign currency concerned, and a judgment obtained in that currency.[1] The English rule is a recent innovation and brings English law into line with civil law countries, where the courts traditionally have been able to give judgments in a foreign currency or for the equivalent of local currency. By way of contrast in the U.S. the Supreme Court insists on conversion into dollars at the date of giving judgment, and the courts of New York traditionally accept the breach date rule.[2]

The English rule applies whether the proper law of the contract is a foreign law[3] or English law.[4] The rule is not confined to liquidated claims but extends to claims for unliquidated damages in either contract[5] or tort,[6]

1 *Miliangos v George Frank (Textiles) Ltd,* [1976] AC 443 affirming the approach adopted by the Court of Appeal in *Schorsch Meier GmbH v Hennin* [1975] QB 416; *Jugoslavenska Oceanska Plovidba v Castle Investment Co Inc* [1974] QB 292. This approach was entirely revolutionary reversing the previous principle of English law that proceedings could only be brought in sterling—a principle centuries old in origin and reaffirmed by the House of Lords as recently as 1960 in *Re United Railways of the Havanas* and *Regla Warehouses Ltd* [1961] AC 1007. The old approach was based on the simple concept that the obligation to deliver foreign money was an obligation to deliver a commodity (the foreign currency), breach of which was a simple breach of contract to deliver the commodity for which damages might be claimed, assessed by reference to the market price of the foreign money at the date of breach. The approach worked well while sterling was a relatively stable currency but came under increasing criticism as currencies including sterling became much more unsettled in their relationships with one another. Lord Denning was typically graphic in his declaration of the need for review. While noting that from 1605 it had always been accepted that a court could give judgment only in sterling, he went on: 'This is because of our faith in sterling. It has always been a stable currency which had no equal. Things are different now. Sterling floats in the wind, it changes like a weathercock with every gust that blows. The change compels the court to think again about our rules. The reasons for the rule have now ceased to exist.' *Schorsch Meier GmbH v Hennin* at pp. 424 and 5.

2 There are, in fact, a few cases in whch the New York courts have converted at judgment date on the ground that in the particular case this would produce a more equitable result. *John S Metcalf Co v Mayer,* 213 App Div 607, 211 N.Y. s 53 (1925); *Sirie v Godfrey,* 196 App Div 529, 18 8 NYS 52 (1921). See also *Librairie Hatchette v Paris Book Center Inc* 62 Misc 2d 873, 309 NYS 2d 701 (1970). Two more recent decisions where the breach date rule was not applied are *Sodivin v Peartree Imports,* 83 Civ 6478 and *Vishipco Line, et al v Chase Manhattan Bank,* 660 F 2d 854 (2d Cir 1981) cert. denied, 456 US 924 (1982). For a spectacular illustration of the potential injustice of the breach date rule, see *Competex SA v Labow,* 81 Civ 2550 (SDNY Oct 17 1983) discussed by Freedman 'Judgments in foreign currency—when to convert?' IFLR (1984) Part 9 p. 22.

3 *Miliangos v George Frank Textiles* [1975] QB 487.

4 *BP Exportation Co (Libya) Ltd v Hunt (No 2)* [1979] 1 WLR 783; [1981] 1 WLR 232 CA; [1982] 2 WLR 253 (HL).

5 *The Folias* [1979] AC 685; *Jean Kraut A.G. v Albany Fabrics Ltd* [1977] QB 182; *Services Europe Atlantique Sud v Stockholm Rederiaktiebolag Svea* [1979] AC 685.

6 *The Despina R* [1979] AC 685; *Hoffman v Sofaer* [1982] WLR 1350.

and to a claim for a restitutionary award under the Law Reform (Frustrated Contracts) Act 1943.[1] The new rule does not give the creditor an alternative choice of currency in which to proceed (either sterling or the foreign currency) for he must use the currency which most accurately expresses his loss.[2] If further compensation is needed for a failure to pay on time, either because of a decline in value of the appropriate currency on the foreign exchanges or of a decline of internal purchasing power, the loss will be recoverable, if, and only if, it should have been within the contemplation of the defendant under the rule in *Hadley v Baxendale.*[3]

While a judgment can now be obtained in a foreign currency it remains necessary to convert the English judgment into sterling at current rates if the judgment is to be enforced.

Under English law there is one important restriction upon the application of the principles adopted in *Miliangos* in the case of a corporate debtor. Where insolvency proceedings are started in the case of a corporate debtor the *Miliangos* rule ceases to be applicable as from the commencement of

1 *Barclays Bank International Ltd v Levin Bros (Bradford) Ltd* [1977] QB 270; *Federal Commerce and Navigation Co Ltd v Tradax Export SA* [1977] 2 QB 324; *The Folias* [1979] AC 685; *Services Europe Atlantique Sud v Stockholm Rederiaktiebolag SVEA.*

2 *Ozalid Group (Export) Ltd v African Continental Bank Ltd* [1979] 2 Lloyd's Rep 231 as explained by Goode.
See the comments of the Law Commission *op. sit.* at pp. 29 and 30. It was for this reason that the Law Commission recommended that the United Kingdom should not become a party to the European Convention on Foreign Money Liabilities (1967) which would impose on a debtor an *automatic* obligation to compensate for an exchange loss arising from late payment. Law Com No 109; Scot Law Com No 66. The Law Commission's recommendation has been accepted by the Government.
The Miliangos principle is really an extension of nominalism. As Lord Wilberforce pointed out in that decision: 'The creditor has no concern with pounds sterling—for him what matters is that a Swiss Franc for good or ill should remain a Swiss Franc.' (at p. 466).
Creditor option of currency in which to sue would be particularly anomalous in the case of international bonds in view of the lack of debtor choice of the currency in which to make payment.

3 With regard to losses arising from currency fluctuations see *Isaac Naylor and Sons Ltd. v New Zealand Co-operative Wool Marketing Association ltd.* [1981] 1 NZLR 361, discussed Rickett 'Contract damages for exchange losses—a New Zealand development' [1982]LMCLQ 566. See also *Aruna Mills Ltd v Dhanrajmal Gobindram* [1968] 1 QB 655 approved by the House of Lords in *President of India v Lips Maritime Corporation* [1988] AC 395. However, it will not apply to losses arising from failure to pay liquidated damages within a reasonable time unless the contract required payment in such a time scale (which will not be lightly implied) and the decline in value of the currency on the foreign exchanges should have been within the contemplation of the defendant when the contract was made—see the *President of India Case.* With regard to losses arising from a decline in purchasing power of the currency see—*Ozalid Group (Export) v African Continental Bank ante; Wadsworth v Lydell* [1981] 1 WLR 598, CA; *Compania Financiera Soleada, SA v Hamoor Tanker Corpn Inc* [1981] WLR 274.

the winding up. To hold otherwise would be arguably to give an unfair preference to the creditor entitled to a debt expressed in foreign currency, and cause unacceptable difficulties for those involved in the administration of the assets of the insolvent company. Accordingly, in this situation despite the *Miliangos* revolution foreign currency claims must be converted into sterling at the date of the winding up order where the company is being wound up compulsorily,[1] or, in the case of the creditor's voluntary winding up, at the date of the resolution to that effect.[2] This exception has the support of the Insolvency Law Review Committee and is, therefore, unlikely to be reversed.[3] This modification, of course, has the potential to effect only those issues made by corporate borrowers, the winding up of which is undertaken by the English courts; sovereign borrowers which either cannot or will not pay their obligations cannot face comparable proceedings.

INTEREST

Interest on the granting of an English judgment

Where payment is delayed the plaintiff has lost the use of his money for the period of time from which payment should have been made to the date when it is in fact tendered. The purpose of an award of interest by the court is to compensate him for being kept out of the use of his money for this period. It must be distinguished from compensation for a recoverable loss sustained as a direct consequence of late payment.[4]

The period in respect of which interest in designed to compensate may well fall into two distinct parts, the first arising before a judgment being given and the second thereafter. The issues raised are separate and distinct. The initial period raises the question of how far the court when giving judgment can include in its award an amount of interest to cover the loss down to the date of judgment. The second issue falls to be determined by the question whether or not the judgment itself carried interest.[5] It is the first situation with which we are here concerned. The right to interest until the date of judgment on an award itself raises two separate issues. First, the entitlement to interest, and secondly, the rate at which interest is to be paid. The right to recover on a contractual debt is a matter governed by the proper law of the contract whether the right to interest does or

1 *Re British American Continental Bank Ltd, Goldzieher and Penso's Claim* [1922] 2 Ch. 575; *Re Dynamics Corpn of America* [1976] 1 WLR 757.

2 *Re Lines Bros Ltd* [1982] 2 All ER 187.

3 *Insolvency Law and Practice* Cmnd 8558 (1982) paras 1306–1309.

4 The distinction is, however, artificial; see Mann 'On Interest, Compound Interest and Damages' (1985) 101 LQR 30. Should not it be foreseeable in these days that a failure to pay an obligation promptly or to pay compensation promptly will occasion interest charges to the payee in the normal course of events, and should not interest be automatically recoverable under the first rule in *Hadley v Baxendale?*

5 As to which see *post* p. 266.

does not depend on an express or implied term of the contract.[1] Where the proper law of the contract is foreign the court will have to determine whether or not under the applicable foreign law the plaintiff is entitled to interest.[2] Where the proper law of the contract is English law, the plaintiff is entitled to interest as of right if there is a term in the contract to that effect.[3] Where there is no such term the court has a general discretion to award interest on any sum for which judgment is given, or of which payment is made after the commencement of proceedings but before judgment.[4]

The position with regard to the right to interest in tort cases is less clear. It may be that the right is to be determined by the *lex fori* but by analogy with the position in contractual matters it would seem more logical for the matter to be determined by the law or laws governing tortious liability. In fact, in the English conflict of laws there is some support for this proposition.[5] However, even this approach is somewhat circuitous under English law for, under the English conflict of law principles, the defendant's conduct must be actionable both in the law of the country where the tort was committed and under English law as the *lex fori*.[6] Thus, in the English courts a plaintiff will have no entitlement to interest unless he can establish such entitlement both by the law of the place where the tort was committed and under English law as the *lex fori*. Under the latter there is no right to interest but merely a discretion conferred upon the court[7] which renders the plaintiff's position doubly insecure.

The position thus achieved by English law in contractual matters has a twofold potential relevance to non-payment of an international security. Where ligation occurs for compensation for breach of some agreement under which the obligation breached was not interest bearing, the right to interest is essentially discretionary. Where, however, the obligation is specified as interest bearing, as the payment obligation itself is, the right to interest is non-discretionary and exists as part of the general law of damages, the *interest bearing nature of the obligation itself* bringing the situation within the first rule of *Hadley v Baxendale*. The situation was well summed up by Lord Cairns LC in the leading case:

> 'any claim in the nature of a claim for interest after the date up to which interest was stipulated for, would be a claim really, not for a stipulated sum and interest, but for damages, and then it would be for the tribunal before

1 *Mount Albert Borough Council v Australasian Temperance and General Mutual Life Assurance Society Ltd* [1938] AC 224; *Miliangos v George Frank (Textiles) Ltd (No 2)* [1977] QB 489 at 496–497; *Societe des Hotels du Touquet-Paris-Plage v Cumming* [1922] 1 KB 451.

2 *Societe des Hotels du Touquet-Paris-Plage v Cumming.*

3 *London Chatham and Dover Rly Co v South Eastern Rly Co* [1893] AC 429; *Cook v Fowler* (1874) LR 7 HL 27.

4 Supreme Court Act 1983, s 35A.

5 *Ekins v East-India Co* (1717) 1 P Wms 395; Morse *Torts in Private International Law* North Holland Publishing Company, Amsterdam, (1978), p. 204.

6 See *post* Chapter 13 p. 336.

7 Supreme Court Act 1981, s 35A.

> which that claim was asserted to consider the position of the claimant and the sum which properly and under all the circumstances should be awarded for damages. No doubt, *prima facie,* the rate of interest stipulated up to the time certain might be taken and generally would be taken as the measure of interest, but that would not be conclusive'[1]

The position with regard to the rate of interest is also less than totally certain. Where the claim for interest arises by virtue of a contractual term giving the right, there can be little doubt that it is the proper law of the contract which determines the rate at which the interest be paid, and also whether it be simple or compound.[2] However, the position is less clear where that is not the case. There is a total absence of authority with regard to tort cases, and a conflict of authority with regard to contractual claims for interest on damages. Here it may be that the matter is to be determined by English law as the *lex fori* where litigation is brought in the English courts,[3] or it may be that the matter should be determined by the proper law of the contract.[4] The latter seems to be the preferable solution.

Where English law is applicable either as the *les fori* or the proper law of the contract, the court has a general discretion to award simple interest.[5] It is now quite clear that where a judgment is given in a foreign currency, *prima facie* the interest should be at the rate applicable to that currency rather than to the rate generally given by the courts on internal sterling judgments.[6] The reason for this is that rates of interest applicable to a particular currency will depend on whether it is strong or weak, with stronger currencies generally securing a lesser rate of interest. For an award of interest to be made in a currency other than that in which the judgment was expressed will generally tend either to over or under compensate the plaintiff.

These principles of English law govern the right to interest on compensation for breach of an obligation not specified as interest bearing. Where the obligation breached is specified as interest bearing then, under English law, the issue is categorised as a damaged issue, and the proper law of the contract would *prima facie* be applicable. Where that law is English law the usual rules with regard to contractual damages will apply,

1 *Cook v Fowler* (1874) LR 7 HL 27 at p. 32.

2 *Mount Albert Borough Council v Australasian Temperence and General Mutual Life Assurance Society Ltd* [1938] AC 224; *Fergusson v Fyffe* (1841) 8 Cl & Fin 121.

3 Cheshire and North *'Private International Law,* (1980) (10th Edn) Butterworths pp. 712–3; *Miliangos v George Frank Textiles Ltd (No. 2)* [1977] QB 489 at p. 497; *The Funabashi* [1972] 1 W.L.R. 666 at p. 671; *Van Der Zijden Wildhandel NV v Tucker and Cross Ltd* [1976] 1 Lloyd's Rep 341 at p. 342.

4 Dicey and Morris *'The Conflict of Laws' Rule* (1987) (11th Edn) Stevens 199(2) p. 1332 *et seq.; Helmsing Schiffahrts GmbH Co K.G. v Malta Drydocks Corpn* [1977] 2 Lloyd's Rep, 444.

5 Supreme Court Act 1981, s 35A.

6 *Shell Tankers (UK) Ltd v Astro Comino Armadora SA The Pacific Colocotronis)* [1981] 2 Lloyd's Rep 40, 45, 47.

subject to the general principle that interest at the same rate as that specified by the instrument should, *prima facie,* compensate.[1]

Enforcement of foreign judgments

Apart from having international financial transactions litigated before them the English courts may be called on to enforce a judgment given by a foreign court.

Foreign judgments may be enforced in England either at common law or pursuant to some statute.[2] The statutory material concerned is the Administration of Justice Act 1920, the Foreign Judgments (Reciprocal Enforcement) Act 1933, the Civil Jurisdiction and Judgments Act 1982 and a statutory instrument the European Communities (Enforcement of Community Judgments) Order 1972.[3]

Traditionally, enforcement of foreign judgments by action at common law by the English courts has proceeded upon the same basis, and in accordance with the same principles, as those courts adopt in giving judgment on a foreign currency claim litigated before them. Accordingly, before *Miliangos* English courts converted a foreign judgment into a sum of sterling at rates of exchange applicable when the prior foreign judgment was given, and gave judgment for that sum.[4] This approach, however, has been exploded by the decision in *Miliangos* itself. Since the purpose of obtaining the English judgment by action at common law is to enforce the foreign judgment, it would seem probable that conversion will now be effected at the date of the later English judgment.[5]

With regard to the applicable statutes the Administration of Justice Act 1920 is silent on the date on which conversion should be effected. In contrast, the Foreign Judgments (Reciprocal Enforcement) Act 1933 originally provided for conversion into sterling of a sum payable on a foreign judgment in accordance with the breach date rule then in force.[6] Following the decision in *Miliangos* the statutory provision was repealed by the Administration of Justice Act 1977.[7] The effect of the repeal under the 1933 Act is that the foreign judgment expressed in foreign currency will now be registered in its original form, and thereafter will be subject to the English rules applicable to judgments in foreign currency.[8] The 1920 Act while silent on the point has always been operated on the same basis as the 1933 Act

1 See Lord Cairns in *Cook v Fowler* quoted *ante* p. 264.
2 See *post* Chapter. 346.
3 This latter covers judgments not given by foreign national courts but by specified European Community bodies particularly the European Court of Justice. Accordingly, it is not likely to effect the purely private law matters now under consideration and need not concern us further.
4 *Scott v Bevan* [1831] 2 B & Ad 78; *East India Trading Co Inc v Carmel Exporters and Importers Ltd* [1952] 2 KB 439.
5 See the Canadian case of *Batavia Times Publishing Co v Davis* (1978) 88 DLR (3d) 144 at 153; Law Com No 124 p. 19.
6 S. 2(3)
7 Section 4(2)(b)(i) and Sch 5 Part 1
8 Law Com No 124 at p. 20.

and will, therefore, adopt the amendment to the later Act in respect of its future operation.[1]

The Civil Jurisdiction and Judgments Act 1982 implements the E.E.C. Convention of Jurisdiction and the Enforcement of Judgments in Civil and Commercial Matters 1968. It makes no express provision for the conversion into sterling of a foreign currency judgment falling within its provisions leaving the courts to implement the *Miliangos* rule. This, no doubt, will be the principle adopted.

The procedural rules applied by the English courts in dealing with foreign money liabilities have recently been extensively considered by the Law Commission in their report 'Private International Law— Foreign Money Liabilities'.[2] Apart from forming an erudite summary of the applicable rules the report is of particular interest for, while noting the present evolution of their rules and making recommendations for their future development, it has, with one exception, been content to leave the future development with the judges and the courts. Since the Commission have expressly taken this attitude it may well be that their report and its comment is given considerable weight, whether overt or unexplained, by the English courts in their dealings with these issues.

Interest on judgment debts

Under English law there is statutory provision under the Judgments Act 1838 whereby every judgment debt carries interest from the time of the entering up of the judgment until the judgment is satisfied, and express provision is made that 'such interest may be levied under a writ of execution on such judgment'.[3] The applicable rate of interest is fixed by Statutory Order from time to time.[4]

It therefore follows that English High Court judgments carry interest at the applicable statutory rate. The Law Commission have taken the view that this is anomalous. The statutory rate will usually be fixed at a level reflecting the scale of interest rates currently prevailing in the U.K. which may well fail to reflect the rates currently earned on the foreign currency

1 Law Com No 124 at p. 20.

2 Law Com No 124 (Cmnd 9064).

3 S 17. Somewhat anomalously the Judgments Act 1838 was held not to apply to the county court *R v County Court Judge of Essex* (1887) 18 QBD 704 although this was doubted by Lord Denning MR in *K v K* [1977] Fam 39 at 49. In 1981 the County Courts Act 1959 was amended to empower the Lord Chancellor to provide by order for county court judgments to carry interest. See now County Courts Act 1984, s 74. No order has been made.

4 The statutory orders are made pursuant to the Administration of Justice Act 1970, s 44. A judgment creditor cannot recover more than the statutory rate unless there is an express statutory term entitling him to a different rate of interest which is specifically expressed to apply after judgment and to be a part of that judgment: *Halsbury's Laws* (4th edn) para 110.

in which judgment is given. The result is twofold. First, the creditor may be either under or over compensated because of the difference in the rates. Secondly, the rate of interest, given to him under the discretionary power in respect of late payment before judgment, will be different from that obtained by him pursuant to the statute on the judgment itself. As the Law Commission pointed out the result is that 'the judicial development of the rules concerning interest on foreign currency claims to the date of judgment has not been matched by legislative change relating to the rate of interest that automatically runs on foreign currency judgment debts'.[1] As a consequence the Law Commission has recommended legislation to empower the High Court to direct that a sum awarded by a judgment in a foreign currency should carry interest at such fixed or variable rate as the court should think fit rather than the prescribed statutory rate. If implemented apart from empowering the court to chose a rate of interest related to the particular currency in which the judgment is expressed, further flexibility can be incorporated by the power to award a variable rate such as a fixed percentage above a particular bank's base rate or above.

The proposed power would be qualified in one important respect so as to obviate unnecessary difficulties for sheriff's officers on whom the duty of levying execution falls. The Law Commission felt that it would cause unnecessary difficulties for sheriff's officers if execution itself were to proceed subject to a variable rate imposed by the court. Accordingly, the Commission has proposed that when enforcement procedure is initiated the rate of interest applicable at the date of the commencement of execution should continue thereafter.[2] Given that it is the creditor's responsibility to calculate the debt and recoverable interest to the date of commencement of execution, the freezing of the rate of interest thereafter should keep the responsibilities of the sheriff's officer to manageable proportions.

Indeed, it may be that the assistance given to sheriff's officers by English law in the primary principle established by the *Miliangos* decision that conversion should take place into sterling on the commencement of enforcement proceedings is itself unnecessary. Ontario, which has now adopted a comprehensive currency conversion code effective from 1 January 1985, has felt no such inhibitions. Pursuant to the Code the conversion date for a foreign currency obligation is fixed in relation to the receipt of the payment by the creditor, or the sheriff's officer on his behalf, being the dollar rate for the particular currency quoted by a chartered bank in Ontario on the first date that it quotes such a rate before receipt by the creditor.[3] It appears that any Canadian chartered bank will do for the

1 Law Com No 124 at p. 47.
2 Law Com No 124 at p. 49.
3 Courts of Justice Act s 131. This now brings to an end the previous divergence of approach whereby foreign money judgments would be converted in general at the date of the Canadian judgment thereon whereas original claims would be converted on the breach date pursuant to the Supreme Court decision in *Gatineau Power Co v Crown Life Insurance Co* [1945] SCR 655. On the whole subject of Canadian developments see J Michael Robinson QC 'Canada adopts a currency of conversion code' 3 IFLR. (1984) No 11 p. 27.

purpose of ascertaining the rate and the purpose of the provision is that the defendant or the sheriff can simply obtain a quote from a Canadian chartered bank of the rate of conversion for the particular foreign currency on the day immediately preceding payment. Such a quote could be obtained from a bank direct or from the financial press. Further, the Courts of Justice Act has been amended[1] to confer discretion upon the Ontario court to allow interest at a rate higher or lower than the statutory rates similar to the English Law Commission's recommendations for this country. The Ontarian government has indicated that it intends to clothe this general provision with a practice direction under which the court's discretion will be exercised in foreign currency claims by permitting interest to run at the equivalent to the 'bank rate' applicable to the particular foreign currency until conversion is made in Canadian dollars on receipt of payments by the creditor. This would seem to envisage interest running after judgment at a fluctuating rate, with the consequent responsibilities of calculation upon the creditor and, on enforcement, on the sheriff's officer. Thus, the Canadian reforms accept the full and pure logic of the policy behind the *Miliangos* decision, and rely on the creditor and the sheriff's officer to overcome any particular practical difficulties which arise. The practical impact of these changes in Canada will merit detailed examination by those interested in the development of English law in future years.

THE FRUSTRATION OF PAYMENT OBLIGATIONS

Can the issuer's obligation to repay the loan be frustrated? This is a complex and difficult issue with a number of subtleties involved, which are not immediately apparent. Under English law frustration of a contractual obligation can arise either because of physical impossibility of performance, or because performance has become illegal. The potential of physical impossibility with regard to payment would appear to be non-existent. The creditor's monetary obligation to pay is an abstract obligation not limited to any particular notes or coins. The reference to money is merely to use money as a unit of account, by which his obligation might be quantified. Accordingly, the destruction to specific notes and coins, out of which the issuer had envisaged making payment through the paying agents, is irrelevant as it was no part of the contract that the coins or notes would come from any specific source.[2]

The possibilities arising for frustration of the obligation by reason of supervening illegality are much more considerable. In general terms, it would appear that problems of illegality can arise where an obligation to pay is to pay at a particular and identified place. If subsequently the law of the place of performance changes so that payment at that place does become unlawful, or alternatively executive action taken within the existing law of that place makes payment unlawful, the debtor may, indeed, find himself legally unable to make the payment in accordance with his contractual obligation. The effect of such illegality must, however, be determined not

[1] S 134.
[2] The issue is more fully considered by Goode *op.cit.* p. 131.

by the law of the place of performance, but by the proper law of the obligation.[1] Therefore, if an Israeli company supplies goods to a Syrian purchaser under a contract governed by English law and payment is to be made in Syria, should the making of such payment subsequently become illegal under Syrian law it is a matter for English law as the proper law of the contract to determine the effect of the supervening illegality upon the obligations of the parties.

Under English law the effect of supervening illegality in such a situation is not necessarily to frustrate the contract. While performance of the contract can no longer be compelled damages for breach can still be given. Damages will be granted if the impossibility was self-induced by the party seeking to rely upon it,[2] or where the party seeking to rely upon the impossibility has contracted that he will perform in spite of any subsequent developments making performance illegal, thereby assuming the risk thereof.[3]

Where the frustrating event is not self-induced and the debtor has not specifically contracted to bear the risk, it does appear that under English law supervening illegality will have the effect of frustrating the obligation.[4] This has been criticised by Dr Mann, relying on the abstract nature of the payment obligation, and pointing out that the place of payment is usually of little importance to the creditor but the fact of payment is all important.[5] It follows therefore, he argues, that the parties' true intent would be, were they asked at the time of contracting, that if payment at the place of payment became impossible payment would simply be made elsewhere. It would follow from this that a payment obligation could only be frustrated if it was impossible to pay anywhere in the world. While Dr Mann's approach is attractive it is ultimately untenable for there is nothing to identify the place where payment is to be made in the alternative. Who is to choose? What if the choice is commercially disastrous to the other party? Unless the alternative place of payment is identified in the payment obligation, which will rarely be the case, it must be correct to claim that 'the supposed right to make an alternative tender fails for uncertainty'.[6]

What, however, does all this have to do with the position with regard to payment on international bonds? As has been seen, these are payable not merely in one place, but a number of different places, all of which

1 *Toprak Mahsulleri Ofisi v Finagrain Compagnie Commerciale Agricole et Financière SA* [1979] 2 Lloyd's Rep 98; *Power Curber International v National Bank of Kuwait SA* [1981] 1 WLR 1233.

2 *Agroexport State Enterprise for Foreign Trade v Compagnie Européene de Cereales* [1974] 1 Lloyd's Rep 499.

3 *Toprak Mahsulleri Ofisi v Finagrain Compagnie Commerciale Agricole et Financière SA; Peter Cassidy Seed Co Ltd v Osuustukkukauppa* [1957] 1 Lloyd's Rep 25.

4 *Ralli Bros v Compania Naviera Sota y Aznar* [1920] 2 KB 287; *A V Pound & Co Ltd v M W Hardy & Co Inc* [1956] AC 588; *Toprak Mahsulleri Ofisi v Finagrain Compagnie Commerciale Agricole et Financière SA.* The authority of the Ralli Bros case is, in fact, a matter of doubt: see Mann *op. cit.* p. 421 n. 91.

5 Mann *op. cit.* p. 421.

6 Goode *op. cit.* p. 134

are carefully chosen to mirror the wide geographical area over which the bonds are distributed. In such a case frustration could not occur because payment became illegal in one place because the parties had themselves agreed that various alternative places of payment are available. In such circumstances the obligation could only be frustrated if payment at all places of payment became illegal by their respective laws. Such would be an event unlikely in the extreme.

It is at this point that it becomes necessary to consider complexities of the international finance market affecting primarily the international dollar market. To explain these complexities it is worth first looking at their application to the eurocurrency Market rather that to the international bond market. It will be recollected that the eurocurrency market is a system of bank deposits connected ultimately to a deposit in the currency of denomination.[1] Thus a eurodollar is a deposit of dollars outside the U.S. through a system of bank transfers and connected ultimately to an actual deposit of dollars within the U.S. What then if the country of the currency of the denomination of the deposits, which holds the underlying deposits to which the euro-currency deposits outside that country are connected, takes steps to block payment of that underlying deposit?

This issue was raised but not decided as a result of the dispute between the U.S. and Iran. During the course of that dispute the President of the U.S., by executive order made on 14 September 1979, blocked all property of the government of Iran and the central bank of Iran which either were, or in the future would become, subject to the jurisdiction of the U.S. or would come or had come within the possession or control of persons subject to that jurisdiction.[2] This, of course, raised the issue of the legal effect of such an order on the substantial dollar deposits held by the government of Iran at banks in financial centres around the world including London. If such a bank refused to make payment, and certainly the London branches af American banks would wish to do this, would the English courts order payment to be made?

Clearly, it is not likely that an English court would be willing to give extra-territorial effect to actions of the U.S. government. The argument, however, was more subtle. It was claimed that on the eurocurrency market, where extremely large sums of money are transferred, it is the well understood commercial custom that sums due to a depositor cannot be collected in cash, but only through the interconnecting system of deposits which depend on the payment of the ultimate deposit and often ultimately involve the

1 See *ante* Chapter 1 p. 4.

2 Executive Order No 12170, 44 Fed Reg 65729 (1979). The events are outlined in J Gold *'The Fund agreement in the Courts'* Vol 2 p. 363. International Monetary Fund, Washington D.C. (1982).

clearing system and the central bank of the currency concerned.[1] In the case of eurodollar deposit use of the clearing system would involve the use of Chips in New York, and entries by Federal Reserve Board as the central bank of the United States.[2] Accordingly, payment abroad could not be legally effected, not because of any extra-territorial effect to the executive order, but simply because the system of payment depended upon operations within the U.S. which were lawfully prevented as a purely internal operation. In short, by coming to the particular market the Iranians had by implication accepted the customs as to payment of that market as implied terms of their contract with the bank obliged to them, and were therefore subject to the risk that payment may became impossible because of legal moves in the country whose currency denominated the deposit.[3]

The issue was never litigated to a conclusion as the immediate problems between the U.S. and Iran were resolved by negotiated agreement between those countries which led to the release of the frozen deposits. Nevertheless, the issues did not terminate with the agreement. Instead, they were raised again by President Reagan in relation to Libyan funds.[4] The matter came to be litigated in London in the case of *Libyan Arab Foreign Bank v Bankers Trust Company.*[5] Here the Libyan bank had over $ 130 million deposited with the London branch of Banker's Trust, a New York corporation, when all Libyan funds were frozen by Presidential decree. Under the law of New York the London deposits were included within the Presidential ban. English law did not take the same view. The Libyan bank sued Bankers Trust in London for, *inter alia,* recovery of its deposit. Bankers Trust defended on the basis that New York law applied as the governing law of the contract, and further that law made unlawful the making of a transfer from the U.S. to allow payment in London to be made. In 1980 it had become a term of the banking arrangement that all transactions should pass through a New York demand account.

1 'Should the parties fail to make express provisions on the mode of performance, it is most probable that the courts would accept as a fact that it is a custom of the trade that foreign funds be placed by a bank at the disposal of another bank at a bank in the country of the currency involved.' Dach 'Legal Nature of the Euro-Dollar' 1964 13 AJCL 38. In fact, express provision to this effect may be made. Dach *op. cit.* pp. 39 and 42.

2 See *ante* ch 1 p. 5.

3 The arguments deployed can be seen from the unresolved litigation to which they gave rise. ie *Central Bank of the Iranian State, Bank Markezi Iran v Citibank Paris* Revue critique de droit international privé, Vol. 69 (1980) pp. 382–84 (France) and the proceedings in England detailed in Iranian Assets Litigation Reporter 2 May 1980 pp. 639–50; 16 May 1980 pp. 790–802; 20 June pp. 1028–65; 3 July 1980 pp. 1098–*1104 summarised in* J Gold *'The Fund Agreement in the Courts Vol. II. p. 372 et seq.* The Iranian counter-argument was that while the procedure for London inter-bank dealings in Eurodollars was admitted as being the norm it was not the only procedure which could be, or indeed had been, followed. The procedure for clearing in the U.S. was carried out for convenience only and was not an implied term of the contract.

4 U.S. Executive Order 12544 of 8 January 1986 appears 25 ILM 181 (1986).

5 26 ILM 1600 (1987).

Staughton J held that the proper law of the contract was, in accordance with general principles, English law as the law of the place where the account was kept. Consequently, the fact that the deposits were included within the Presidential prohibition was not decisive of the case. However, the U.S. bank put forward the argument that the contract was unlawful by English law since it was a contract to perform an act which had become illegal at the place of performance, because the payment could only be made by the use of transfers via the U.S. In fact, this last involves two separate principles, one of public policy that illegal contracts prejudicial to friendly states should not be enforced, and the other of practicality that it is usually impossible to perform contracts which are illegal at the place of performance and they must be viewed as frustrated, a distinction emphasised by Robert Goff J in *Toprak Mahsulleri Ofisi v Finigrain Compagnie Commerciale Agricole et Financière SA*[1] and accepted by Staughton J.[2] The first such principle was not involved because that principle only applies where *both* parties intend to do the illegal act, whereas in the particular case the Libyan had no real object and intention that any illegal act should be undertaken in New York. They simply wanted to be paid in London. Further, the principal authority relied on by Bankers Trust in support of the principle was *Regazzoni v KC Sethia (1944) Ltd*[3] which was a case where the parties intended to perform the common illegal act at the time of contracting whereas the present case was one of supervening illegality.[4]

For the second aspect of the illegality argument to succeed (the frustration argument) it was necessary that there should be an express or implied term of the contract to the effect that payments should pass through New York, where such payments would certainly be unlawful. Bankers Trust relied on the express term of the contract, but Staughton J construed this narrowly. It was, in his view, intended to regulate the contractual relations of the parties only as long as the particular banking relation continued, but that the arrangement would be terminated by reasonable notice from the Libyan bank which had been given in April 1986. Therefore, the deposit was still held by Bankers Trust as an interest bearing account for the Libyan bank, under which Bankers Trust were obliged to make transfers of funds on the instructions of the Libyan Bank provided that no infringement of U.S. law in the U.S. was involved.

If the express term fell could the implied term approach arising from the very nature of wholesale eurodollar transactions be called in aid? Bankers Trust alleged that there was an implied term that transfer of funds from the London account, whether or not effected through New York 'would be effected by instructing a transfer to be made by the defendants' New York Head Office through a U.S. clearing system to the credit of an account with a bank or branch of a bank in the U.S. nominated or procured to be nominated by or on behalf of the Libyan Bank for that purpose'. In

1 [1979] Lloyd's Rep 98.
2 At 1613.
3 [1958] AC 301.
4 At p. 1614.

short, the contention was that all transactions would ultimately depend on Chips or Fedwire. The term would be implied (i) from the usage of the international market in eurodollars, and (ii) from the course of dealing between the parties. Staughton J. rejected the contention, because the evidence before him revealed that at least some of the transactions undertaken between the parties had not conformed to the term to be implied, consequently no uniform usage was demonstrated.[1]

As there was no express or implied term demanding that payment be made through New York, the final vital question to be determined was whether payment would be made in any way which did not involve the use of facilities in New York, in particular transactions leading ultimately to Chips. Staughton J. considered in depth the various means of payment which could be used namely (i) in-house transfer at Bankers Trust London; (ii) correspondent bank transfer; (iii) Chips or Fedwire; (iv) banker's draft on London account; (v) banker's payment; (vi) London dollar clearing (vii) other clearing systems outside the U.S.; and (viii) certificates of deposit. These were all rejected mostly because the use of New York facilities would be involved. However, payment would always be made in cash in London, in either U.S. dollars or sterling, and consequently a mode of legal payment remained available and the contract was not frustrated. The court would have required very strong evidence before being satisfied that such a term should be implied, that it was understood to apply throughout the market, and no such evidence had been produced.

The Libyan litigation gives a ruling on the position with regard to eurodollars. The application to the position of international bonds must now be considered. Clearly, where there is no special term requiring payment through New York, no issue of frustration can seriously be raised as payment can clearly be made in England. However, where there is such a special term the implication of the decision is that, if it is still subsisting, payment would be affected. In the Libyan litigation the express term had ceased to be relevant for the terms under which the account had been held were brought to an end in April 1986, and with that termination of terms went the express requirement of payment via New York. However, in the case of an international bond the right to repayment will always arise from the bond itself and depend on the bond terms. Consequently, it is submitted that litigation of a special bond term such as that cited would give rise to a different result to that achieved in the *Libyan Arab Foreign Bank* case. The effect of frustration is considered later.[2]

1 Staughton J expressly left open the issue as to whether some such implied usage might not apply in the case of time deposits traded between banks but found that the Libyan deposit was not of this class of business.

2 The effect of frustration is considered ch 11 *post*.

11 Modifications to the payment obligation

The world-wide distribution of international bonds and other securities creates considerable potential for difficulties to arise due to legal developments in the issuer's jurisdiction or elsewhere, which can result in modifications to the payment obligation. The most threatening areas for such legal development lie in the fields of exchange control and taxation. The potential effect may be a partial modification, or a total extinction of the principal underlying obligation of the securities.

EXCHANGE CONTROL REGULATIONS[1]

Introduction

Individual countries have shown a considerable interest in capital flows into and out of their individual jurisdictions. This is hardly surprising. The capital flows can have considerable impact upon the international value of their currency, can reduce or expand investment in their own native industries, can affect their own money supply and inflation, and can generally impair an individual country's capacity to carry out the independent economic policies which it wishes to implement. For all these reasons the movement of capital has proved to be a major political interest for the governments of individual countries.

The consequence has been that individual countries have sought to control capital flows out of their jurisdictions, and the means employed to do this have been given the general title of exchange controls. The controls used may be of a general regulatory nature, such as restrictions on borrowing in foreign currency by resident enterprises without central bank consent, and, where such borrowings are made, requiring a percentage of the funds to be deposited with the central bank thereby reducing the effectiveness of the borrowing to the borrower or issuer. Further, access to the domestic capital market may be prohibited to foreign borrowers. At their most draconian exchange control measures may prohibit the payment of existing foreign currency liabilities, whether arising from external trade or financial operations without central bank consent, thereby reducing, or even terminating, the capacity of the borrower or issuer to pay interest or capital on its existing liabilities.

[1] See generally Dicey and Morris *The Conflict of Laws* (1987) 11 edn Stevens p. 1466 et seq.

The effect of exchange control needs to be considered in two stages for, while there is a general body of law which has evolved, specific provision has been made to impose a new international legal structure on members of the International Monetary Fund under the 1944 agreement entered into at Bretton Woods, which is generally referred to as 'the Fund Agreement'.

It should be noted that exchange control regulations could have an impact on an international bond issue in two separate and distinguishable situations. First, the issue may be in breach of the exchange control regulation of the issuer's country at the time that the issue is made. Where this occurs pre-issue investigation will discover it, and, if the problem cannot be overcome, the issue will be aborted. Secondly, an issue which has been made perfectly lawfully and with no exchange control problem, can subsequently find itself in difficulty due to new exchange control regulations introduced by the issuer's country after the issue has been made.

THE GENERAL POSITION

English conflicts of laws have developed specific rules for dealing with the problems raised by exchange control. First, irrespective of the proper law of the contract and of the place of performance, English courts will refuse to enforce a contract, including its payment obligation, the performance of which is prohibited by duly enacted English exchange control regulations.[1] Given the high element of public policy underpinning such regulations this is hardly surprising, and in fact the courts of most jurisdictions will similarly enforce their own exchange control regulations.[2] Secondly, under English conflict of laws, where exchange controls are part of the law of the jurisdiction whose law governs the obligation (the proper law of the obligation), the English courts will give effect to them.[3] A similar position applies in the U.S.[4]

Thirdly, under the English conflict of laws where exchange control regulations would render performance of the contract illegal at its place of performance, if the proper law of the contract is English law the parties are discharged from their contractual obligations on the basis that those obligations have become impossible of performance.[5] Where the proper law of the contract is not English law, the effect of illegality at the place of performance arising from exchange control regulations would fall to be considered by the proper law of the contract unless principle of comity

1 *Boissevain v Weil* [1950] AC 327.

2 G Van Hecke *Currency* The International Encyclopedia of Comparative Law, Private International Law, Tubingen: JCB Mohr (Paul Siebeck) (1971) Vol 8 Ch 36.

3 *Re Helbert Wagge and Co Ltd* [1956] Ch 323.

4 *French v Banco Nacional de Cuba* 23 NY 2d 4b 242 NE 2d 704, 295 NYS 2s 433 (1968).

5 *Ralli Bros v Compania Naviera Sota y Aznar* [1920] 2 KB 287. A contrary situation seems to apply in the U.S. where the courts may order the payment to be made at a new venue where payment is lawful if this produces a just result: *Pan American Life Insurance Co v Blanco*, 362 F 2d 167 (5th Cir 1966).

between friendly nations were in issue.[1] Where the proper law would give no effect to the exchange control regulations English and United States courts dealing with the matter will ignore them,[2] even though the issue is left with an obligation to make a payment illegal by the law of its own jurisdiction.

A complicating issue in some jurisdictions may be the unwillingness of the courts to give effect to exchange control regulations, even when introduced by the legal system of the proper law of the contract, on the grounds that the enforcement of exchange control regulations would be to enforce a foreign country's revenue laws or laws of a public nature, or that enforcement would otherwise be against the public policy of the particular jurisdiction. In general, English law does not appear to take the view that it is against public policy to enforce a foreign country's exchange control regulations,[3] nor does it classify such regulations as a foreign country's revenue or public law falling outside the scope of private international law.[4] It would be otherwise if the regulations were oppressive and discriminatory, for here their enforcement would offend public policy.[5] However, this permissive approach adopted by the English courts has not been uniformly adopted by other jurisdictions, some of which have held much stronger views of public policy limiting their recognition of foreign exchange regulations.[6]

At this level the potential legal problem therefore arising from the impact of exchange control regulation on an international bond issue can be circumvented without too great a difficulty, bearing in mind that capital and interest on the bonds are repayable in several jurisdictions. Provided that the governing law of the payment obligation is sensibly selected, and, in particular, is not made the law of the issuer's jurisdiction, and provided that jurisdiction is conferred on courts other than the courts of the issuer's jurisdiction, potential legal problems should be avoided. That does not mean that practical problems are avoided. If the issuer is faced with the unenviable choice of defaulting on its payment obligation or breaching the exchange control regulations of its own jurisdiction, it may decide that its interests are best served by taking the former rather than the latter action. This then would leave bondholders able to enforce the payment obligation by bringing action, but the ultimate success of such a move is dependent upon the presence of assets of the issuer outside its home

1 Mann (1937) 18 BYIL 107–113; Cheshire and North *Private International Law* (1987) 11th edn, Butterworths pp. 485–9; Dicey and Morris *op. cit.* p. 1220 *dubitante*.
2 *Kleinwort and Sons & Co v Ungarische Baumwolle Industrie AKT* [1939] 2 KB 678; *Lann v United Steelworks Corp* 1 NYS 2d 951 (1938).
3 *Kahler v Midland Bank* [1950] AC 24; *Zivnostenska Banka v Frankman* [1950] AC 57.
4 *Frankman v Prague Credit Bank* [1948] 1KB. 730, 746; *Kahler v Midland Bank* [1950] AC 24, at 46, 47.
5 *Re Helbert Wagg & Co Ltd's Claim* [1956] Ch. 323, at 352.
6 The comparative position of various jurisdictions is discussed by Mann *The Legal Aspect of Money* (1982) 4th edn Clarendon pp. 401–406.

jurisdiction against which enforcement of any judgment obtained could take place. Greater complications arise, however, in situations to which the Fund Agreement applies.

THE FUND AGREEMENT

Its purpose

The general principles already considered are substantially modified in important respects by the Fund Agreement. Unfortunately the precise impact of the Fund Agreement at an international level is impossible to define with precision, as there are many difficulties arising from its apparently simple basic provisions. The constitution of the IMF, through its governing Fund Agreement in 1944, was intended to prevent a recurrence of the nationalistic and protectionist policies of the 1930s which, it was considered, instead of ameliorating the consequences of the world recession had made them worse and, indeed, institutionalized a downward spiral of economic activity on a worldscale.[1] The Fund Agreement seeks to achieve its ends by recognising that the protection of a country's capital is a matter of importance, not merely to the individual country concerned, but to the international economic community as a whole.[2] The major provision of

[1] Article 1.

[2] Article 1(11). The full objectives disclosed by Article 1 are as follows:

(i) To promote international monetary co-operation through a permanent institution which provides the machinery for consultation and collaboration on international monetary problems.

(ii) To facilitate the expansion and balanced growth of international trade and to contribute thereby to the promotion and maintenance of high levels of employment and real income and to the development of the productive resources of all members as primary objectives of economic policy.

(iii) To promote exchange stability, to maintain orderly exchange arrangements among members, and to avoid competitive exchange depreciation.

(iv) To assist in the establishment of a multilateral system of payments in respect of current transactions between members and in the elimination of foreign exchange restrictions which hamper the growth of world trade.

(v) To give confidence to members by making the general resources of the Fund temporarily available to them under adequate safeguards, thus providing them with opportunity to correct maladjustments in their balance of payments without resorting to measures destructive of national or international prosperity.

(vi) In accordance with the above, to shorten the duration and lessen the degree of disequilibrium in the international balances of payments of members.

A failure to consider *all* the objectives in relation to each other is likely to lead to a court misunderstanding the effect of the Agreement's provisions—see the telling criticism by Joseph Gold of the English cases of *Wilson Smithett and Cope Ltd v Terruzzi* [1976] QB 683 (Kerr J), 709 CA and *United City Merchants (Investments) Ltd v Royal Bank of Canada* [1982] 2 WLR 1039 in 'Exchange Contracts, Exchange Control and the IMF Articles of Agreement' (1984) 33 ICLQ 777. Over 140 countries are members of the IMF.

the Agreement is deceptively simple. The agreement provides simply and starkly in Article VIII, s 2(b):

> Exchange contracts which involve the currency of any member and which are contrary to the exchange control regulations of that member maintained or imposed consistently with this Agreement shall be unenforceable in the territories of any member.

The Fund Agreement further goes on to provide that 'any question of interpretation of the provisions of this Agreement arising between any member and the Fund or between any members of the Fund shall be submitted to the Executive Board for its decision.[1] Given the politically sensitive matters with which the Agreement deals the Fund has shown itself to be reluctant to lay down detailed rulings on the meaning of the terms of the Agreement, preferring to leave the detail to be supplied by the rulings of the individual courts of the member countries, even though this leads to an inevitable diversity of approach.[2] However, where the Fund does give an interpretation through its Executive Board such an interpretation is binding on the member countries.[3]

This divergence is clear in the approach of the court of individual member countries to a number of the terms employed within the Fund Agreement, but nowhere more starkly than in their approach to the fundamental term 'exchange contract'. While all jurisdictions and scholars appear to agree that for there to be an exchange contract the claim must involve a consensual transaction[4] (and the concept would not cover, for instance, an action in tort), some jurisdictions (principally the common law jurisdictions) and writers have confined the concept to a contract[5] involving the exchange of the currency of one country into that of another[6] while others (principally the civil law countries) have been prepared to apply the concept to any

1 Article VIII 2(b).

2 The differences of approach are discussed by the General Counsel to the fund, Joseph Gold, in *The Fund Agreement in the Courts* International Monetary Fund, Washington D.C., Vol. 1. 1982.

3 Article XXIXa.

4 See Mann *op. cit.* at p. 384.

5 Dicey and Morris at p. 1029; Nussbaum 'Exchange Control and the International Monetary Fund' (1950) 59 Yale Law J pp. 421–430; Nussbaum *Money in the Law, National and International* (1950) pp. 539–45.

6 Nussbaum 'Exchange control' etc. *op. cit.* at p. 426, *Money in the Law* etc *op. cit.* at pp. 542–3; *Wilson Smithett and Cope Ltd v Terruzzi* [1976] 1 All ER 817 (England); *Banco do Brasil SA v AC Israel Commodity Co,* 12 NY 2d 371, 190 NE 2d 2352, 239 NYS 2d 872 (1963) cert. denied 376 U.S. 906 (1964) (U.S.A.); *Emek v Bossers and Mouthaan* I.R.L. (1955) 722 (Belgium); *United City Merchants (Investments) Ltd v Royal Bank of Canada* [1983] 1 AC 168 H.L.

transaction which affects a country's foreign exchange resources.[1]

Under the narrow definition adopted by the common law jurisdictions a certificate of deposit or international bond would not constitute an exchange contract unless its payment provision specifically required repayment in a currency other than that in which it had been issued. On the other hand in respect of the wider definition adopted by the civil law jurisdictions, since repayment can clearly affect a country's exchange and capital resources, an international bond or certificate of deposit is capable of being an exchange contract.

Further, the Fund Agreement itself does not seek to regulate all exchange contracts. For the member states to be bound to enforce a particular set of exchange control regulations, they must be consistent with the terms of the Fund Agreement. This provides quite specifically that no member faced with the scarcity of its currency shall impose restrictions on the making of payments and transfers for current international transactions without the approval of the Fund itself.[2] Thus, an individual member is left free to impose restrictions on capital transactions. Current transactions are defined to include interest on loans and a 'moderate amount' by way of repayment of capital.[3]

The consequences of an exchange contract falling within the Fund Agreement are specified by the Agreement as being that it should be unenforceable in the territories of any member. To a common lawyer the choice of the word unenforceable suggests that the bar is procedural, and merely prevents the exchange contract being enforced, so long as the bar represented by the terms of the Fund Agreement remains.[4] This coincides with the Fund interpretation of the consequences of the IMF Agreement. On the other hand it is more natural for civil law jurisdictions more used

1 *Lessigner v Miray* IRL (1955) 725 (West German); *Société Filature et Tissage X Jourdain v Epoux, Heynen Bintner* (ILR (1955) 727 (Luxembourg); *de Boer, Widow Moojen v von Reichert* 89 J Droit Int'L 718 (1962) (France). See also J Gold *The Fund Agreement in the Courts*; and the many instances of the concept of 'Exchange Contracts' being given a wide meaning. Gold Exchange Control and the IMF Articles of Agreement' *ante* pp. 796–798 Mann *op. cit.* at pp. 385–389, which discusses the comparative material. In one important respect, however, it is submitted that Dr Mann is wrong for he considers that a transaction can only be characterised as an exchange contract if it offended exchange control regulations at the time the contract was made and that it will not be an exchange contract if it is in breach of exchange control regulations *subsequently* introduced (ibid at p. 389). This is clearly wrong on both a textual construction and an economic analysis: see Gold *The Fund Agreement in the Courts* (1962) at p. 65.

2 Article VIII 2a.

3 Article 30(d).

4 However, a court must take the point that the contract is unenforceable regardless of the attitude of the parties. See *Gold The Fund Agreements in the Courts (1962) at p. 61.*

to treating such obstacles as substantive rather than procedural and, from this approach, to conclude that exchange contracts are a complete nullity.[1]

Against this background it is now possible to examine the impact of exchange control regulations on an international bond issue where the Fund Agreement is potentially applicable.

Let us suppose that there is an issue by a Swedish issuer denominated in U.S. dollars with six countries nominated as places for payment including Sweden. After the issue has been made, but before repayment becomes due, Sweden introduces stringent exchange control regulations.

First, it will be necessary to determine, in relation to each jurisdiction in which enforcement proceedings are contemplated, whether or not that particular jurisdiction is a member of the IMF In the case of any jurisdiction not a member of the IMF the Fund Agreement can be ignored, and attention devoted to the general considerations previously discussed. Where a particular jurisdiction is a member of the IMF it will be necessary to consider whether that particular jurisdiction takes a wide or narrow view of the meaning of exchange contract. It is only if it takes a wide view that it is likely to characterise the contract represented by the bond as an exchange contract, and similar considerations will apply to whether or not it is prepared to view the contract as one involving the currency of the issuer's country, namely Sweden. In the case of any jurisdiction which does not recognise the bonds as exchange contracts there will be no *procedural* obstacle to enforcement.

There may, however, be a substantive effect upon the rights represented by the bonds arising from these procedural considerations. Six places of payment were postulated. If three of the places of payment recognise the bond as an exchange contract and three do not, there is no substantive effect upon the payment obligation, because total repayment can be effected in the three jurisdictions which do not recognise the bond as an exchange contract and therefore are not bound by the fund agreement. In the unlikely event that all six recognise the bond as an exchange contract falling within the Fund Agreement, payment is prohibited at all six places of payment, and the effect of this must be considered according to the proper law of the payment obligation.

The effect of impossiblity of performance under English law in such a situation was considered by Staughton J in the *Libyan Arab Foreign Bank* case[2] The Libyan Bank had pleaded, as an alternative to its main contention that, if the Presidential decree had frustrated the contractual obligation to repay, they were entitled to rely on the Law Reform (Frustrated Contracts) Act 1943 to reclaim their deposits as 'sums paid or payable to any party in pursuance of the contract before the time the parties were discharged' from further performance by the frustration of the contract. Staughton J. held that had he had to consider dealing with the argument (which was

1 See Mann *op. cit.* as p. 396 et seq. Gold's argument is in fact, the more convincing. The exchange contract is unenforceable for the very good reason that, under the Articles of the Fund Agreement, exchange control regulations are seen as an essentially temporary phenomenon.

2 26 ILM 1600 (1987).

unnecessary as he had decided the case on other grounds), he would have concluded that the obligations of Bankers Trust were suspended, and not discharged by reason of frustration. On the other hand, if the effect of the Presidential decree had been permanently to avoid the payment obligation the result would have been otherwise.

Similarly, in the hypothetical case of the Swedish exchange control regulations if the proper law of the payment obligation were English law legal impossiblity of performance at the places of performance would frustrate the contract. This must necessarily be the result if the payment obligation is avoided in each of the six places of payment. Where, however, it is merely unenforceable in each of the six places of payment the overall effect upon the payment obligation in each place is merely a temporary interruption which may be brought to an end. The lack of enforceablility in each jurisdiction could be brought to an end by either that jurisdiction, or the country of the issuer (Sweden) which had enacted the exchange control regulations, ceasing to be a member of the IMF. Alternatively, the abrogation of the particular set of exchange control regulations would have a similar result. In such a situation payment could then be demanded in each of the jurisdictions where payment has become legal, provided that applicable periods of prescription and limitation had not expired.[1] However, where English law is the proper law of the obligation temporary impossibility of performance in all places of payment will have the effect of frustrating the payment obligation where the effect of impossibility 'would render it a thing radically different from that which was undertaken by the contract'.[2]

Where frustration has taken place would it be possible to reclaim the amount due under the Law Reform (Frustrated Contracts) Act 1943 as contended by the Libyan bank in the recent case? Staughton J was of the opinion, *obiter*, that it would not since the deposits made by the Libyan bank with Bankers Trust were not paid 'in pursuance of the contract' since there was no obligation on the Libyan bank to deposit any sums with Bankers Trust. Such an argument is not so strong with regard to the money paid to purchase the bond from the issuer. While it is true that there was no obligation to purchase any bonds upon the investor, the payment of the purchase price is in fact the payment of a sum to enter into a transferable contractual relation with the issuer, and the price can therefore be said to be paid pursuant to the contract.

TAXATION AFTER ISSUE

The problems of tax laws in existence at the time of issue can usually be overcome by appropriate planning.[3] The alternative, should the problems

1 For prescription and limitation see *ante* 6 p. 165.

2 *Davis Contractors Ltd v Fareham UDC* [1956] AC 696 *per* Lord Radcliffe at p. 729. To hold a party to a contract in such circumstances would be 'not to maintain the original contract, but to substitute a different contract for it'. *per* Viscount Finlay LC in *Metropolitan Water Board v Dick Kerr & Co* [1918] AC 119 at 127 quoting Rowlatt J in *Distington Hematite Iron Co v Possehl & Co* [1916] 1 KB 811 at 814.

3 *ante* ch 2 p. 45.

prove to be insuperable, is that the issue should not proceed. Neither of these alternatives is however available in circumstances where, after the issue has been made, new taxes are introduced.

An example of the express terms with regard to taxation which are inserted in the bond terms reads as follows.

> All payments of principal and interest by the Company in respect of the Bonds will be made without withholding and deduction for, or an account of, any present or future taxes, duties, assessments or governmental charges of whatever nature, imposed or levied by or on behalf of Japan (the country of the issuer) or any authority therein or thereof having power to tax, unless the withholding or deduction of such taxes, duties assessments or governmental charges is required by law. In that event, the Company will pay such additional amounts as may be necessary in order that the net amounts received by the holders of the Bonds and Coupons after such withholding or deductions shall equal the respective amounts of principal and interest which would have been receivable in respect of the Bonds or as the case may be Coupons in the absence of such withholding or deduction, except that no such additional amounts shall be payable with respect to any Bond or Coupon presented for payment—(1) by or on behalf of a holder (a) who is for Japanese tax purposes treated as a resident of Japan or a Japanese corporation (b) who is for Japanese tax purposes treated as a non-resident of Japan or a non-Japanese corporation having a permanent establishment in Japan in cases where (x) the payment of principal or interest is attributable to the business of such non-resident or non-Japanese corporation carried on in Japan through such permanent establishment or (y) such permanent establishment consists of or includes a branch office, factory, mine or other similar fixed place of business and there is no applicable tax treaty, convention or agreement or the applicable tax treaty convention or agreement does not distinguish between income which is and income which is not attributable to a permanent establishment in Japan, or (c) who is otherwise subject to such taxes, duties assessments or governmental charges by reason of his being connected with Japan otherwise than by reason only of the holding of any Bonds or Coupons or the receipt of principal or interest in respect of any Bonds, or (2) more than 30 days after the Relevant Date except to the extent that the holder thereof would have been entitled to such additional amounts on presenting the same for payment at the expiry of such 30–period.
>
> The 'Relevant Date' in respect of any payment means the date on which such payment first becomes due, except that if the full amount of moneys payable has not been duly received by the Principal Paying Agent or the Trustee on or prior to such date it means the date on which, the full amount of such moneys having been so received, notice to that effect shall have been duly published in accordance [with the requirements to notice of the bond terms].
>
> Any reference in [the bond terms] to principal or interest in respect of the Bonds shall be deemed also to refer to any additional amounts which may be payable under this condition or any undertakings or covenants given in addition thereto or in substitution therefore pursuant to the Trust Deed.[1]

The effect of this is that:

1 Issue of $25,000,000 9 per cent Convertible Bonds by Life Co Ltd redeemable 30 September 1996.

(1) The principal and interest is to be made free of all taxes or duties of whatever nature so that the bondholder receives the agreed net sum. The protection extends not merely to withholding taxes but also to capital and inheritance taxation.

(2) However, the protection is drawn so as to extend only to taxation levied by the issuer's jurisdiction; if therefore the bondholder's own jurisdiction were to enact legislation imposing unexpected taxation upon a bondholder, the bondholder is, understandably, left to face this alone.

A further thing to be noted is that there are two separate provisions which are effectively in the alternative. The first provision is that payments are to be free of taxes. The clause also provides that if taxes are obliged to be deducted the issuer is to pay additional amounts so that the lender receives the full amount of the interest. The reason for the alternatives is that it is most unlikely that the withholding tax imposed will be other than mandatory, and therefore the issuer will be compelled to deduct tax whether it wishes or not, and will have to account to the tax authorities of its own jurisdiction for the amount so deducted. On this basis, the first provision, namely that payment should be free of taxes, is broken by events. However, the bondholder then has the protection of the grossing-up provision, which compels the issuer to pay additional sums so that the loss of the tax falls on the issuer's shoulders and not upon those of the bondholder.

Clearly, no issuer will accept the responsibility of prejudicial changes in the tax burden where these occur because of the failure of the bondholder promptly to present the bond or coupon for payment. It will be observed that the bond term is drawn to exclude this risk falling on the issuer to the extent that the additional tax liability arises due to the failure of the bondholder to present the bond or coupon within 30 days of the relevant date, which is precisely defined.

A further aspect of the bond term to assist the issuer arises from the imposition of the grossed up liability on the issuer. This inevitably increases dramatically the cost of the borrowing represented by the issue. Because of this it is normal market practice that where a tax is imposed on an issuer, with the result that the issue has to pay grossed-up amounts, it is given a right to prepay the loan. Often, however, a small penalty is imposed upon an issuer who exercises this right to compensate the bondholders for early repayment of their investment.

A typical clause is:

> Should the Company at any time satisfy the Trustee that on the occasion of the next payment in respect of the bonds it will be obliged to pay any such additional amounts as are referred to in [the bond term dealing with taxation] the Company may on giving not less than thirty days but not more than sixty days notice to the bondholders, redeem all (but not some only) of the bonds then outstanding at par plus accrued interest in each case[1]

Variations can be incorporated in such a clause by requiring the issuer, at least for the first few years of an issue, to redeem at a little above

1 Issue of $50,000,000 9 per cent bonds by A/S Eksportfinans due 1986.

par, the percentage reducing each year, until par is reached for the later years of the issue. This percentage is unlikely to be sufficient to induce an issuer to decide not to redeem, but it will at least confer a small 'sweetener' on the bondholder.

The importance of securities within euro-issues being structured to be free of taxation and so that investors are able to collect principal and interest without being required to sign certificates or otherwise identify themselves is emphasised by IPMA regulations. These note the importance of the issue and specify that it is presumed that the initial payments are free of income tax and the withholding tax regime. Any deviation should be disclosed in the screen or telephone invitation issued by the syndicate and in the invitation telex. Standard form clauses for a typical issue are suggested for inclusion in the invitation telex to confirm that the issue is free of such taxes. Further, the rules specify that it should be disclosed whether there is a gross up provision and a tax call possibility, in the latter case with a redemption price. If the tax call can be triggered by events other than the imposition of a withholding tax, they should be specified. In all cases it should be stated whether the redemption date must be an interest payment date. In the case of U.S. issuers it should be stated whether there is protection against the imposition of certification or identification requirements. If such protections differ materially from the suggested IPMA clauses the differences should be spelled out. The recommended IPMA clause relating to bonds and floating rate notes for inclusion in the invitation telex is as follows:

> *U.S. Information Reporting and Back-up Witholding Taxes (Fixed & Floating Rate Notes):*
>
> Under temporary regulations, payments of principal and interest on the notes to a holder made by the issuer or its payment agents outside the U.S. will generally not be subject to information reporting or back-up withholding unless the issuer or its paying agent has actual knowledge that the holder is a U.S. person. With certain exceptions the issuer will be required to redeem the notes at par without additional amounts plus any accrued interest within one year in the event that payments thereon outside the U.S. should become subject to certain U.S. certification, information or other reporting requirements, the effect of which is the disclosure to the issuer, a paying agent or a governmental authority of the nationality, identity or residence of a beneficial owner who is a U.S. alien. If such requirements can be satisfied by the payment of a back-up withholding tax or similar charge, the issuer will have the option to pay additional amounts in respect of such charges rather than redeem.

Under IPMA rules optional tax redemption provisions in circumstances where withholding tax has been or will be imposed should comply with the following principles:

1. The right to call only should arise when a change in law or in the application or official interpretation thereof has occurred and, as a result, the issuer has or will become obligated to gross up.
2. Notice of redemption should not be given earlier than the date 90

days before the earliest date on which grossing up would be required were a payment in respect of the relevant securities then due.

3. An issuer should be required to take reasonable measures available to it to avoid the incidence of withholding tax and the obligation to gross up.
4. An issuer should satisfy the trustee of its securities (if any) and/or provide certification that the necessary conditions precedent to the right to redeem have been met.
5. In the case of floating rate securities, redemption should be made only on an interest payment date.

IPMA gives both a model English law tax redemption clause and a model U.S. tax redemption clause.

Model English law tax redemption clause

The Notes may [also] be redeemed at the option of the Company in whole, but not in part, at any time, on giving not less than 30 nor more than 60 days' notice in accordance with Condition [Notices] (which notice shall be irrevocable), at the principal amount thereof, together with interest accrued to the date fixed for redemption, if (1) the Company [satisfies the Trustee immediately prior to the giving of such notice that it]* has or will become obliged to pay additional amounts as provided or referred to in Condition [Taxation] as a result of any change in, or amendment to, the laws or regulations or any political subdivision or any authority thereof or therein having power to tax, or any change in the application or official interpretation of such laws or regulations, which change or amendment becomes effective on or after [date of Subscription Agreement], and (2) such obligation cannot be avoided by the Company taking reasonable measures available to it, provided that no such notice of redemption shall be given earlier than 90 days prior to the earliest date on which the Company would be obliged to pay such additional amounts were a payment in respect of the Notes then due. Prior to the publication of any notice of redemption pursuant to this paragraph, the Company shall deliver to the [Trustee]* [Fiscal Agent]** a certificate signed by two [Directors] of the Company stating that [the obligation referred to in (2) above cannot be avoided by the Company taking reasonable measures available to it and the Trustee shall be entitled to accept such certificate as sufficient evidence of the satisfaction of the condition precedent set out in (2) above in which event it shall be conclusive and binding on the Noteholders and the Couponholders]* [the Company is entitled to effect such redemption and setting forth a statement of facts showing that the conditions precedent to the right of the Company so to redeem have occurred, and an opinion of independent legal advisers of recognised standing to the effect that the Company has or will become obliged to pay such additional amounts as a result of such change or amendment].**

* Applies to issues constituted by a Trust Deed
** Applies to issues under a Fiscal Agency Agreement

Model U.S. tax redemption clause

The Notes may [also] be redeemed at the option of this Company in whole but not in part, at any time, on giving not less than 30 nor more than 60 days' notice in accordance with 'Notices' below (which notice shall be irrevocable), at the principal amount thereof, together with accrued interest to the date fixed for redemption, if the Company has or will become obligated to pay additional interest on the Notes as described under 'Payment of Additional Interest' as a result of any change in, or amendment to, the laws (or any regulations or rulings promulgated thereunder) of the U.S. or any political subdivision or taxing authority thereof or therein, or any change in the application or official interpretation of such laws, regulations or rulings, which change or amendment becomes effective on or after [date of Underwriting/ Subscription Agreement], and such obligation cannot be avoided by the Company taking reasonable measures available to it, provided that no such notice of redemption shall be given earlier than 90 days prior to the earliest date on which the Company would be obliged to pay such additional interest were a payment in respect of the Notes then due. Prior to the publication of any notice of redemption pursuant to this paragraph, the Company shall deliver to the Fiscal Agent a certificate stating that the Company is entitled to effect such and setting forth a statement of facts showing that the conditions precedent to the right of the Company so to redeem have occurred, and an opinion of independent counsel of recognized standing to the effect that the Company has or will become obligated to pay such additional interest as a result of such change or amendment.

12 Default and bondholder representation and meetings

DEFAULT

When the bond issue has been completed, it is plainly the hope of all of the parties that the issue will run smoothly to term, while in the interim being traded on the secondary market, and, at maturity, that it will be redeemed by the issuer in accordance with its contractual obligations. The vast majority of bond issues behave in this predictable and exemplary manner. However, there are always bound to be exceptions, and occasionally an issue will run into difficulties with an issuer breaching its obligations, and, even in extreme circumstances, failing to redeem the issue on maturity at all. In such circumstances, it becomes a matter of great importance to investors to have clear and enforceable legal rights, by the use of which their position may be protected. The bond terms include provisions to cover the position of investors in this situation. As the most important matter for investors is that the issuer's payment obligation should be met, the most significant of the provisions are directed to securing the investor's position where payment does not occur in accordance with the issuer's obligation, or circumstances arise which make it probable that the repayment obligation will not be performed when it becomes due. The means employed are by the inclusion within the terms of the bond of a clause defining events on the occurrence of which the issuer may be taken to be in default of his obligations (events of default), and setting out clear consequences where one of the events occurs.

EVENTS OF DEFAULT

The actual events of defaults specified in any particular set or terms vary with the particular draftsman and his perception of the requirements of the particular issue. The following events are usually dealt with.

(1) *Non-payment* The most obviously vital events for the investor to try to secure is that the bonds should be redeemed and interest paid promptly. For this reason the first and most important provision is that the failure in this respect constitutes an event of default. A typical provision would be that default should arise where:

> there is failure for more than 7 days to make payment of any amount of

principal of, or premium, if any, on any bond or failure for more than 15 days to make payment of any amount of interest on the bond.[1]

(2) *Failure to comply with the terms of the trust deed or bond* An investor will also be concerned to ensure that an issuer complies with his other obligations under the terms of the bond and, where the issue is supported by a trust for the bondholders, the trust deed. Failure to comply is invariably constituted an event of default in terms such as:

> the issuer shall fail duly to perform or observe any other term of, or undertaking or agreement in, the Trust Deed or Bonds required to be performed or observed by the issuer and any such default shall continue for a period of 30 days after written notice is received by the issuer from the Trustee specifying such a default and requiring the issuer to remedy the same.[2]

(3) *Cross-default* The concept of cross default is that the investor is empowered to call a default with regard to the bond issue where the issuer defaults on any other borrowing it may have from third parties, or fails to perform any other analogous financial obligations, eg a guarantee of a third party's borrowing. The rationale is twofold. First, failure to perform financial obligations may well be a general prelude to financial disintegration and default with regard to the bonds themselves. Secondly, the provision reinforces the *paripassu* and negative pledge clauses by conferring equal rights on all lenders with the benefits of a cross default clause on the event of default on one source or credit. Such a creditor may secure preferential terms from the issuer as part of an agreement not to take immediate enforcement action where there is no cross default provision in other loans, or alternatively be able to enforce and recover money due to it thereby reducing the credit-worthiness of the issuer before the bondholders could take action (no event of default having occurred on the bonds in the absence of a cross default clause). Cross default clauses seek 'to bar these preferential attempts by giving all the lenders the same sanction'.[3]

A typical provision would be in terms constituting as events of default:

(a) the security for any mortgage or charge created by the issuer becomes enforceable and steps are taken to enforce the same or any indebtedness for or in the nature of borrowed moneys created or owing by the issuer becomes repayable prior to its date of maturity by reason of default or is not paid when due (or on the expiry of any applicable grace period); or

(b) the issuer refuses or fails to discharge any guarantee or obligations contracted by it of any indebtedness for or in the nature of borrowed

1 Terms of issue U.S. $50,000,000 9 per cent notes of $1,000 each due 1986 issued by A/S Eksportfinans of Norway.

2 ibid.

3 Wood *Law and Practice of International Finance* Sweet and Maxwell, London (1980) p. 166.

moneys when due to be discharged (or on the expiry of any applicable grace period).[1]

(4) *Creditor's enforcement* Not all of an issuer's credit will be in a form analogous to borrowing. Credit may have arisen due to the supply of goods, services or materials on one or two month account. Nevertheless, failure to pay for any protracted period may be as significant with regard to the issuer's credit-worthiness as failure to repay its borrowings. The clearest indication that failure to pay such credit is assuming serious proportions arises when a creditor is so frustrated that he takes action against the issuer's assets by way of enforcement, thereby clearly signalling the seriousness of the issuer's failure to pay while at the same time diminishing the issuer's credit-worthiness. Consequently, a provision is usually included in the bond terms constituting as events of default:

> an encumbrancer takes possession of the whole, or any substantial part of the assets of the issuer or a distress or execution or other process is levied or enforced upon or sued out against any substantial part of the assets of the issuer and is not in any such case discharged within 14 days or a receiver, administrator or other official is appointed of the issuer or of any substantial part of its assets.[2]

(5) *Insolvency* Clearly, if an issuer is insolvent there is a substantial likelihood that it will be unable to pay both the bonds and any other borrowing which it has undertaken. In such circumstances, it is clearly desirable for the bondholders to be able to put the bonds into default. If the bondholder were unable to do this he would be left with merely contingent rights in the resultant insolvency as his debt is payable only in the future. Consequently, clauses have been devised which list as well as the general ground of insolvency certain objective and easily proved facts indicative of insolvency as events of default, eg:

> the issuer shall stop payment of its debt generally or shall be unable to pay its debts as they fall due or shall become bankrupt or insolvent or shall institute (by petition, application, answer, consent or otherwise) any bankruptcy, insolvency, dissolution, liquidation or similar proceeding, or any such proceeding shall be instituted by petition, application or otherwise against the issuer and shall remain undismissed for a period of 30 days.[3]

(6) *Liquidation and dissolution* Clearly, in the case of an issuer which is a corporation the liquidation of the company and the subsequent dissolution of its legal personality removes its capacity to continue as issuer and to make payment. Equally, a corporation's cessation of its business operations is likely to remove from it the ability to generate income from which the bonds can be repaid. Such events are constituted events of default although inevitably there is considerable overlap with the previous clause.

1 Terms of issue U.S. $50,000,000 9% notes of $1,000 each due 1986 issued by A/S Eksportfinans of Norway.
2 ibid.
3 ibid.

A typical clause would be:

> an order of a competent court is made or an effective resolution is passed for the winding up or dissolution of the issuer or any analogous proccedings are taken in respect of the issuer or the issuer shall cease or threaten to cease to carry on the whole or substantially the whole of its business (other than in each case for the purposes of and followed by amalgamation or reconstruction previously approved in writing by the Trustee) or the issuer convenes a meeting for the purposes of making or proposes or enter into, any arrangement or composition for the benefit of its creditors.[1]

Consideration of these various events of default indicates that they fall into two categories. Events (1) and (2) above are for direct breaches of the obligations that the issuer has undertaken in the terms and trust deed. Events (3) and (6), however, constitute as events of default matters which themselves would not constitute any breach by the issuer of any of the obligations, which it has undertaken, were it not for their specification as events of default. The reason for this is simply that the occurrence of these events of default render it highly likely that it will only be a matter of time before the issuer is in breach of its obligations to the investors. When such probabilities arise, it is clearly both right and inevitable that investors should not have to wait until the probable consequences of the events of default produce the actual result of breach by the issuer of its obligations to investors.

Subsidiaries

Where an issue is made by a corporation the issuing corporation may not be a single isolated company but part of a group of companies, the other being subsidiaries of the parent issuer. In such circumstances, despite the individual legal personality conferred upon each member of the group, the reality is that the total group is one economic unit, of which the loss of any individual constituent member is bound substantially to weaken the remaining parts of the enterprise. Further, in reality, a parent is not likely to allow a subsidiary to go into liquidation unless the parent is itself in such financial difficulties that it cannot carry the burden of preserving its offspring.

Where a group of companies constitutes one economic enterprise, bonds issued by one constituent member are not likely to be viewed favourably by the market on issue unless the terms of the events of default apply equally to the subsidiaries as well as to the parent issuer. In such situations the terms of the events of default will be amended accordingly, as in the following example relating to execution upon the assets of the enterprise:

> (5) if any distress, execution or seizure before judgment is levied or enforced upon or sued out against a part of the property of the issuer or any Consolidated Subsidiary which is (in the opinion of the Trustee) material in its effect upon the operations of the issuer or the relevant Consolidated Subsidiary (as the case may be and is not discharged within 30 days thereof (or such longer

[1] ibid.

period as the Trustee may consider appropriate in relation to the jurisdiction concerned)).[1]

A consolidated subsidiary will be defined in such terms as 'every subsidiary the accounts of which were in the latest or should, in the written opinion of the Auditors given following a request from the Company or the Trustee, be in the next, Accounts consolidated with the Company'.[2] A certificate by the auditors that in their opinion a subsidiary is or is not a consolidated subsidiary would, in the absence of manifest error, be conclusive and binding on all parties. This is of some importance as the auditors are given the sole effective right of determination of a wide and important issue.

Guarantor

Sometimes a bond issue will be guaranteed by another legal personality. Where this occurs the usual explanation is that the credit-worthiness of the guarantor is greater than that of the issuer (it makes little sense for a less creditworthy legal person to guarantee the debt of one more creditworthy)! Effectively therefore, the credit-worthiness of the guarantor is substituted on the marketing of the issue for the credit-worthiness of the issuer itself.[3] Consequently, investors are concerned that the events of default applicable to the issuer should also be applicable in respect of the guarantor, with whose capacity to discharge (if necessary) the obligations of the issuer investors may have more concern than that of the issuer itself. Consequently, once again the draftsman will ensure that the events of default relate to both guarantor and issuer. The use of guarantees is, in many ways, the reverse situation to an issue of the parent where the position of the subsidiary is involved by the draftsman as an event of default. Often the subsidiary will issue and the parent company will guarantee the issue of its subsidiary. In practice, it is far more usual for bond issues to be made by subsidiaries than parent companies for reasons of taxation and securities regulation.

EFFECT OF AN EVENT OF DEFAULT

The effect of the occurrence of an event of default depends in part upon the consequences attached to it in the drafting of the terms, and in part

1 Terms of issue U.S. $25,000,000 6 per cent Convertible Bonds redeemable 1996 by Life Co Ltd of Japan.

2 This contrasts with the requirements for the drawing of group accounts under English law where the Companies Act 1985 requires accounts to be prepared for the holding company and the subsidiaries except where the *directors* are of the opinion that certain circumstances have arisen. Companies Act 1985, s 229 'Holding company' and 'subsidiary' under the 1985 Act are defined in s 736.

3 The giving of a guarantee may constitute a transfer at an undervalue within the Insolvency Act 1986, s. 423, and therefore be at risk that the court will set it aside in the event that the guarantor becomes insolvent, but only if given to prejudice the guarantor's other creditors.

upon general provisions of law. It is possible for a clause to be drafted under which the occurrence of any event of default automatically accelerates the loan so that it forthwith becomes repayable. While this might sound an excellent solution for the draftsman to achieve, the resultant inflexibility is far from desirable.[1] In particular, as has been seen, one of the events of default is a cross default clause under which default by the issuer on any of its other borrowing automatically constitutes an event of default under the terms of the bond. Since cross default clauses are usual in all forms of international lending, the result of the issuer's bonds going into automatic default on the occurrence of an event of default is that all its other international borrowing will go into default under the various cross default clauses. The whole would constitute a complex domino effect right across the issuer's main international borrowing. When it is recollected that for an issuer inadvertently to incur a lien in respect of some of its property will constitute a breach of its obligations under the terms of issue and hence a potential event of default under (2), the desirability of flexibility can be seen to be of compelling dimensions.

Thus, has been seen, if an issuer inadvertently allows a repairer's lien to arise in respect of its equipment or by oversight fails to pay interest on the loan on the stipulated date of payment, an event of default may arise with the whole of the principal of many millions of pounds becoming payable forthwith under the issue. Further, the effect of cross default clauses in its other borrowing may have the effect of accelerating its obligations several times over and taking the total well beyond its capacity to pay immediately. If such consequences to an issuer may be said to be catastrophic, the potential to an investor of a non-performing investment, which may prove to be irrecoverable *in toto*, are equally serious. It is therefore of importance to both issuer and investor for the decisive step of default to arise only as a last resort. Like the nuclear deterrent default is a weapon

1 See the comments of Professor RM Goode on the parallel problem of automatic crystallisation clauses in Goode *Legal Problems of Credit and Security* (1988) 2nd edn Sweet and Maxwell for the centre for Commercial Law Studies London (1980) p. 74 *et seq*. The issuer cannot rely on equity to give relief even if the relevant default is technical or due to clerical error — *TC Trustees Ltd v JS Darwen (Successors) Ltd* [1969] 2 QB 295 at 301-2. See also *Scandinavian Trading Tanker v Flot Petroleum Ecuatoriana* [1983] 2 AC 694; *Sport International Bussum BV v Inter-Footwear Ltd* [1984] 1 WLR 776; *BICC plc v Burndy Corp* [1985] 2 WLR 132 — discussed by Professor R Cranston in 'Remedies in International Finance: Why so Few Formal Legal Proceedings?' A paper given at University College London on 15 November, 1988.

where the threat of use is likely to be more effective than actual employment.[1]

The possible solutions to the problem depend on whether or not the issue is underpinned by the appointment of a representative for the bondholders (in common law jurisdictions a trustee is appointed for the purpose), or merely a fiscal agent appointed on behalf of the issuer.[2] If the bondholder representative is used an exclusive discretion to call default can be vested in him;[3] if not flexibility can be built into the terms of the events of default themselves.[4] Indeed, even where a bondholder's representative is appointed flexible default terms may be employed as well. One of the most obvious and frequently used methods is the allowance of grace periods in respect of events of default. In the examples quoted the amount of grace was seven days in respect of payment of principal, 15 days in respect of interest, and 30 days in respect of breach of any other of the issuer's obligations to the investors under the terms of the bond and the trust deed. Again, given the widespread use of grace periods in international loans, cross default and other clauses referring to additional borrowing of the issuer will only become effective at the expiration of any grace period under that additional borrowing.[5]

As an alternative or addition to the use of grace periods to bring flexibility with regard to default, the draftsman may use a test of materiality of the breach. The object of this is that an event of default should only lead to default if it is of such a nature as to be material to the risk of the committed investors on the bond issue. The problem here is for the draftsman to achieve a workable test of materiality. The means employed must depend upon the particular event of default, the modification of which is being considered. Thus, in the case of cross default the clause may be modified so that only default on one of the larger loans of the issuer would give

1 One thinks of a default occurring on the part of a financially troubled company. 'Often, however, the content of the default will have been fashioned at a time when the borrowing company was not financially troubled. Thus, the elements constituting the default may have been drafted in form and substance for a company which was healthy and was expected to remain healthy. Both lender and borrower, then, will have conceived of the default as a rather routine provision in their agreement, but when the default materializes, they may have to cope with it in an entirely different context — in a harsh world for which they and their earlier notions about default may be ill-adapted.
Further '[d]efault' connotes wrong doing and questionable motive. The borrower's motive, however, is to make money, not to lose it . . .'. Cone 'The Treatment of Default' in *Default and Rescheduling Corporate and Sovereign Borrowers* ed Suratgar, Euromoney Publications (1984) p. 25. See also the comments of professor R. Cranston in 'Remedies in International Finance: Why so Few Formal Legal Proceedings', *op.cit.*

2 *post* p. 296.

3 *post* p. 300.

4 Flexibility is important in both issuer and bondholder. See the excellent analysis of Cone *op. cit.* p. 16. See, as examples, events of default nos. 3 and 4 *above.*

5 See, as examples, events of default nos. 3 and 4 *above.*

rise to the operation of the cross default clause in the bond issue. A typical modification would be as follows:

> If any indebtedness for money borrowed (hereinafter called 'indebtedness') of the issuer and/or of any of the Consolidated Subsidiaries having an aggregate principal amount of $1,000,000 (or its equivalent in any other currency or currencies) or more shall become prematurely repayable following a default or steps taken to enforce any security therefore or the issuer and/or any of the Consolidated Subsidiaries defaults in the repayment of any such indebtedness at the maturity thereof (or, in the case of Indebtedness due on demand, upon demand therefore) or at the expiration of any applicable grace period therefore or any guarantee or indemnity in respect of any Indebtedness of others having on aggregate principal amount of $1,000,000 (or its equivalent in any other currency or currencies) or more given by the issuer and/or any of the Consolidated Subsidiaries shall not be honoured when due and called upon.[1]

This, of course, is quite specific and definite. The alternative is to be general by simply requiring the breach to be material, but this leaves difficulty for either issuer or investor to know whether a particular breach is material with the adjudication of a court. One possible way out of the difficulty where the bond issue is supported by a trustee is to leave the decision with regard to materiality of any particular breach to the certification of the trustee which shall be conclusive for all purposes.[2]

IPMA recognises the existence of a variety of types of cross default clause. It identifies the strongest type as one which allows the acceleration of a eurobond (both capital and interest).

> if any indebtedness of the issuer, the guarantor, a significant subsidiary or agency [in the case of sovereign issues] (i) shall become or be capable of becoming repayable prior to the due date by reason of default by the issuer, guarantor, significant subsidiary or agency or (ii) shall not be repaid at maturity, or (b) if any guarantee given by the issuer, guarantor, significant subsidiary or agency shall not be honoured when due and called upon, or (c) if a security for any such indebtedness or guarantee is enforced in favour of the creditors of such indebtedness

Further IPMA recognises that such an absolute provision can be limited in any of the following six ways:

(a) limitation of the level of indebtedness covered: only external indebtedness, indebtedness for borrowed money, publicly issued debt or funded debt.
(b) limitation of whose debt is included: only issuer's and not guarantor's significant subsidiaries' or agency's.
(c) elimination of immaterial defaults: only defaults in respect of an indebtedness or guarantee which exceeds a threshold which may range from $1,000,000 to as high as $50,000,000. The threshold may also be expressed in terms of a percentage of the issuer's net

1 Terms of issue of Life Co. Ltd. of Japan, footnote p. 291 *ante*.
2 As in event of default nos. 5, p. 290, *ante*.

worth or may be on an aggregate basis to cover a succession of small defaults.

(d) limitation of the triggering events only actual acceleration as opposed to capability of being accelerated.

(e) inclusion of a grace period: they often range from 5 to 60 days. Many clauses also provide that they are not triggered if and so long as the issuer is contesting the acceleration in good faith. It is sometimes provided that the grace period starts running only after the holders of a specified percentage (10 per cent to 25 per cent) have given notice to the issuer.

(f) inclusion of a materiality test: some cross-default clauses provide that they are not triggered unless the trustee certifies in writing that the default is, in his opinion, material.

The existence of a cross default clause should be disclosed, as should the manner in which it differs from the absolute form above where such difference exists. Where there is a guarantee any applicability of the cross default to the guarantor's own debt should be disclosed.

BONDHOLDER REPRESENTATION

When it is necessary to enforce their rights under the terms of a bond issue, investors start from a basic disadvantage arising from the necessarily fragmented nature and inherent secrecy of bondholding in an international issue. Consequently, it is probable that bondholders will be scattered through a wide range of jurisdictions which, in itself, would make communication between them difficult. Their difficulties are likely to be compounded, as it is most unlikely that they know the identity of each other, and, especially in the case of an issue of bearer bonds, have no reasonable opportunity of identifying each other. This is compounded by the deliberate anonymity and secrecy demanded by investors in international bonds. Consequently, in the event of default on the bonds either looming or occurring the holders are not likely to be able to organise themselves as a group, and would be reduced to taking individual action. This has two consequences. First, in some situations default may occur which could be avoided if adjustments to the performance of the obligations of the bond could be achieved, which may be in the interests of the bondholders as a group, for payment delayed is preferable to no payment at all. Secondly, if steps on default are necessary, a greater weight and effectiveness can be achieved if the bondholders move as a corporate entity and speak with one voice than if there is merely the fragmented activity of a group of individuals.

For such unity of direction and action to be achieved machinery is necessary whereby action can be taken on behalf on bondholders rather than by them, and where there is disagreement as to the action to be taken, a decision of the majority of the bondholders ascertained. The machinery developed for these purposes, although not invariably used, is, first, the use of a representative for the bondholders to act on their behalf, and, secondly, the bondholders' meeting.

The central figure in this arrangement is the bondholders' representative, who has delegated to him certain powers by the terms of the issue including, usually, the power to call default. Where the representation is by a trustee, the representative derives his powers from the trust deed. He is the common point of reference through whom the bondholders organise themselves. In addition to the powers devolved to him, further powers can be voted to him by the bondholders in meeting pursuant to the terms of the trust deed. If the trust deed does not enable the conferral of additional powers by majority, unanimity amongst bondholders would be necessary which is probably impossible to achieve in practice. The representative calls and organises such meetings where necessary, either on his own intiative or at the request of a percentage of the bondholders themselves. Out of this comes unity of action undertaken by the representative on behalf of the bondholders and binding on them all, and the means by which a majority view can be ascertained. The bondholders' position can be further improved by the selection of a representative who has expertise and resources far beyond those possessed by non-institutional bondholders.

Nor are the advantages arising from the use of a representative exclusively those of the bondholder, for the representative machinery enables greater flexibility to be used in the drafting of the events of default and in the operation of the bonds after issue. Where default is to arise on the occurrence of an event materially adverse to the interests of the bondholders, the decision with regard to the materiality of the event can be left to the discretion of the representative. Further, if during the period that the bonds are outstanding some adjustment is necessary of no significance to the bondholders (eg the issuance of security in technical breach of a negative pledge cause which does not in fact affect the security of the bondholders), power can be conferred on the representative to waive the bondholders' right of action in respect thereof, or the representative may call a bondholder's meeting for this purpose. If an issuer runs into liquidity difficulties before redemption, which are plainly surmountable given a little time, and it wishes to put before the bondholders proposals renegotiating the bond terms, the bondholders' representative and meeting give a machinery through which this can be accomplished.

TRUST DEED OR FISCAL AGENCY AGREEMENT

As has been seen a bond issue undertaken in an issue based on a common law jurisdiction may be supported by using either a trust deed or a fiscal agency agreement.[1]

In making the issue, the issuer will have evaluated the advantages and disadvantages of the alternative possibilities before deciding on which basis the issue was to proceed. An important consideration to the issuer, which is sometimes decisive with regard to the choice which is made, is the question of cost. It is undoubtedly cheaper in most cases to use a fiscal agent rather than a full trustee in making the issue. The legal consequences are fundamentally different, however, and in many cases it will be these consequences rather than the saving of money which is the decisive

[1] *ante* p. 31

consideration, for it is only the use of the trustee which will create a true bondholders' representative.

As the name implies, a fiscal agent is simply an agent and is, in fact, the agent of the issuer. On the other hand a trustee is the representative of the bondholders, and, as might be expected, is subject to fiduciary responsibilities to them.

Since the fiscal agent is simply the issuer's agent, the responsibilities given to him are limited to the various administrative tasks, which will necessarily arise from time to time during the term of the issue. The primary responsibility placed upon the fiscal agent is the supervision of the payment of the bonds and coupons on presentation; the initial delivery of the bonds at the closing date and subsequent release of the definitive bonds on exchange of the global bond; drawing of bonds on partial redemption; replacement of bonds which are lost or destroyed; and holding financial information including annual accounts of the issuer for inspection by the bondholders, if they are sufficiently inquisitive to wish to peruse them. On some issues the fiscal agent can call default of an issue but only on the specific request of a bondholder, there being no power for the agent to take the intitiative and consequently no responsibility upon the agent.

The position of a trustee is markedly different. The underlying concept of trusteeship is that one person (the trustee) should hold property on behalf of another (the beneficiary), and this, indeed, was the original function of the ancestor of the trustee for the bondholders. Unsurprisingly, this ancestor was the trustee for debenture holders — a vital part of the machinery of the secured debenture from the last century. The very fact that the first issues of debentures were secured necessitated a mechanism for the security to be held. Clearly, the documents of title of the various assets used as security needed to be held in one place and by one person for the debentures themselves would be held by a wide ranging group of debenture holders. The obvious solution was the use of a trustee, responsible to the debenture holders as his beneficiaries, and this indeed was the device employed. The advantages were obvious. The trustee as holder of the legal title could deal with the charged assets in the interests of the beneficiaries without having to obtain the consents of all members of a widely scattered and numerous group. If he acted in breach of the terms of the trust the debenture holders could trace the assets into the hands of third parties, with the exception of the protected bona fide purchaser for value in good faith; equally in these circumstances they could bring action against the trustee for breach of trust. Finally, for all that the assets were held by the trustee with full legal title, the mere fact that the beneficial interest lay with the debenture holders meant that, in the event of the insolvency of either the issuer or the trustee, the assets would not be available to the creditors.

While the development can be seen as perfectly logical and consistent in relation to secured debentures, the same consistency is not immediately apparent in relation to unsecured issues of debentures or bonds; here there is no property for the trustee to hold by way of security and therefore no such clear function for him to discharge. However, experience of issues of secured debentures indicated that the machinery had considerable potential for development. The trustee proved an excellent medium in the common law jurisdictions as the bondholders' representative taking action on their behalf in accordance with the powers conferred as necessary, and organising debenture holders' meetings when circumstances required.

The underlying effectiveness of this commonsense approach was reinforced by the fact that the trustee owed a fiduciary responsibility to the debenture holders for the manner in which his powers were exercised, which gave some legal control over the behaviour of the trustee.

It is for these reasons that the use of the trust has continued in unsecured issues. In fact, even in such issues the potential of the trustee to hold property can be useful. Thus, if after a bond issue has been made, the issuer desires to raise further monies giving security, but is constrained by the terms of the negative pledge clause requiring him to make comparable security for his existing bondholders, it would be the trustee who would hold this security on their behalf. Further, even in the case of a fiscal agency agreement it is common form to stipulate that funds paid by the issuer for use on redeeming either bonds or coupons should be held as trustee for the bondholders, thereby protecting the investors against the risk of the insolvency of either the issuer or the trustee fiscal agent after the latter has received the monies on behalf of the bondholders.[1]

In fact, the trustee has proved to be of such great use in protecting debenture and bondholders that in some jurisdictions the use of a trustee is a precondition of an issue falling within the scheme of protection of a jurisdiction's securities regulation. The precondition may arise either by reason of statute as in the U.S. under the Trust Indenture Act 1939 or as a requirement of a stock exchange for listing to take place as in the case of Singapore, Amsterdam, and the U.K. However, such requirements do not usually apply to international issues where the issuer is left with a choice as to whether he proceeds by way of using a trustee or a fiscal agent. Where it is decided to proceed by appointment of a trustee the normal practice would be the appointment of a professional trust corporation.

Powers to monitor performance

The issuing of bonds without security sounds inherently risky, but it is doubtful whether the risks are so substantially greater than most issues of debentures with the mechanism of a floating charge. The following perceptive comparison between the position under a mortgage and debenture issue contains much truth:

> with a mortgage the mortgagee can within reason dictate the terms of the loan. With a debenture issued to the public the lender has only the choice to invest or not invest. With a mortgage the lender is more concerned with the security of his loan than the success or failure of the borrower's business.

1 In terms of debt issue within the U.S by corporations, the U.S. Trust Indenture Act 1939 requires that money held by fiscal agents should be held as trustee for the security holders, s 317 (b). The 1939 Act does not, however, apply to international bond issues, which escape the control of U.S. securities regulations; *ante* Chapter 4.

> If he is prudent he will have sufficient security even if the borrower fails. With a debenture the lender's own funds provide, in many cases, the major part of the assets backing a loan. The security for the loan is the assets of the company and the value of these assets is dependant on the success of the company. This makes the debenture holder dependant on the profitability of the borrowing company. If the company fails, heavy losses are likely to result on the forced sale of assets.[1]

As has been seen, some fiscal agency agreements show a modest recognition of this underlying fact by requiring the issuer to file with the fiscal agent copies of its most recent accounts as they become available so that bondholders may inspect them if they wish. However, if this is to be more than a matter of form the bondholder must himself exercise the opportunity of inspection, given the legal nature of the relationship between the agent and the issuer, which determines that the fiscal agency should merely be the alter ego of the issuer.

Greater possibilities arise where a trustee is used for effective demands of the issuer to run its business profitably thereby ensuring its financial viability. The trustee is a representative of the bondholders and not an agent of the issuer, and is therefore in a legal relationship from which independent action on behalf of the bondholders would be possible. This is reflected by the terms of most trust deeds which impose considerable responsibility upon the issuer with regard to its financial and business affairs by means of extensive covenants with the trustee. In particular, covenants are likely to be included whereby the issuer undertakes at all times to carry on and conduct its affairs in a proper and efficient manner, and to keep properly such books of account as it is obliged to keep under the law and accountancy practice applicable to it under the jurisdiction in which it carries on business. The trustee is given a right of access to the books of account either personally or by appointee. Where the issuer is part of a group with subsidiaries, similar obligations are undertaken by the issuer on behalf of the subsidiaries.

Further, covenants traditionally include one requiring the issuer to give the trustee such information as the trustee may reasonably require for the purpose of discharging the trustee's duties, powers, trusts, authorities and discretions, arising both by operation of law and under the terms of the trust deed itself, and to send the trustee copies of every balance sheet, profit and loss account and annual report, and of any circulars issued by the issuer, to its shareholders or creditors as soon as reasonably practicable after the time of issue. In addition, the issuer will covenant to send such periodical auditors' or directors' reports as the trustee may reasonably require.

The information provided to the trustee, or available to the trustee on demand, is such that an active and diligent professional trustee is well placed to monitor and comprehend the financial situation of the issuer's business, and thereby the risks of potential default upon the bonds. Further, where an issuer runs into financial difficulties with the consequent risk

1 IRM 'Trustees for Debenture Holders' (1968) 5 Victoria University of Wellington Law Review p. 40.

of default, and such financial difficulties are a consequence of the issuer's failure to carry on and conduct its affairs in a proper and efficient manner, the trustee is enabled to take positive action on the covenant on behalf of the bondholders to protect their position. Failure to correct this position would constitute an act of default.

Enforcement on default

When an event of default occurs the consequences vary, depending upon whether the issue is supported by a fiscal agency agreement or trust deed. In the case of the former each bondholder is left to fend for himself and must make his own arrangements with the issuer for repayment or, alternatively, must make his own legal action to enforce payment. Where there is a trust deed the position is more complex. Where an act of default takes place the responsibilities to deal with the situation are heaped upon the trustee. Typically, the trust deed will provide that in such situations the trustee *may* at its discretion and, if so requested in writing by the holders of a proportion, often not less than one fifth of, in principal amount of the securities then outstanding, or if so directed by an extraordinary resolution of the bond holders *shall*, call the securities due and repayable for the total amount outstanding. The consequences of the occurrence of an event of default therefore in this situation do not apply automatically, and depend instead upon the trustee calling the default, although he can be forced to take this action by holders of the specified proportion in value of the securities or by an extraordinary resolution. The element of discretion which is therefore given to the trustee is considerable and potentially of vital importance. Given the fragmentation of the bondholders it is often unlikely that holders of one fifth in value will be able to identify each other to make a positive requisition upon the trustee until the lapse of considerable time. Similarly, an extraordinary resolution of bondholders arising from a bondholders' meeting will also take considerable time to arrange. When default looms urgent action is usually essential, and failure to take prompt action can be prejudicial to the bondholders. The element of discretion conferred upon the trustee is usually emphasised by a provision that any event of default, other than that of nonpayment, should in any event only be the cause of acceleration where the trustee has certified to the issuer that the occurrence of the event is, in the opinion of the trustee, materially prejudicial to the interests of the security holders. Consequently, by failing to give such a certificate the trustee can prevent itself being forced to take any action whatsoever, even if enjoined to do so by the written demand of all bondholders.

Nor where there is a trust deed can the trustee be outflanked by the bondholders acting independently, for the deed customarily includes a provision that only the trustee may enforce the rights and remedies of the bondholders and the coupon holders against the issuer, and that no bondholder or coupon holder shall be entitled to proceed directly against the company unless the trustee, having become bound to take action under the terms of the trust deed, fails to do so continues in such failure.

This typical structuring of the powers in the event of default of an issue based upon a trust deed can also be seen as having sinister aspects from the point of view of the bondholders, whose individual rights of action have been taken away. It is easy to take an individualistic and censorious stance with regard to the resultant structuring. However, the placing of the rights and responsibilities upon the shoulders of the trustees is, in intention at least, entirely defensible. The structuring is intended to produce the best overall result. First, it is intended to prevent a free-for-all in which the most diligent, best informed, and wealthier are likely to be able to preserve their own personal positions at the expense of those bondholders who do not have these characteristics. As these characteristics are most likely to be found in institutional bondholders rather than individual investors, the overall effect is intended to strengthen the position of the individual bondholders at the expense of the institution. Secondly, it is intended that the structure will prevent multiplicity of actions by each individual bondholder, which could only squander investors' resources in fragmented litigation, and possibly result in an indefensible diversity of result. Finally, the intended result recognises that not all bondholders' interests are necessarily the same, enables a single evaluation to be made of the best interests of the bondholder as a group, and prevents an individual, and possibly perverse, bondholder taking isolated action to the detriment of the majority interest. Given the powerful arguments in support of the structure it is submitted that English courts, if called upon so to do, will support the discretion conferred upon the trustee in accordance with the terms of the trust deed, and restrain action by individual bondholders in breach of its terms.[1]

The existence of a trust

If the trustee has these powers on behalf of the bondholders what are his potential liabilities to them? In order to consider this matter it is necessary to consider a central issue arising from bond structures and that is the

[1] This approach has also been followed in France see *Kerr v Société Pyrenées Minerals* Cass 19 February, 1908, Clunet 1912, 243 affirming Court of Appeals of Toulouse 18 July 1905, Clunet 1906, 451. In general, however, common law jurisdictions have been unsympathetic to the machinery and have attacked the structuring. Ambiguous terms have been construed *contra proferentem* as in *Perry v Darlington Fireproofing Co*, 76 Ohio App 101 63 NE 2d 222 (1945); *Hirschfield v Astoria Associates, Inc* 139, NYS 2d 519 (Sup Ct 1955) ; or by testing the reality of the bondholder's consent to the terms as in *Oswianza v Wengler and Mandell Inc*, 358 ILL 302, 193 NE 123 (1934); *Roittenhouse v Lukens Steel Co,* 116 Pa Super 303, 176 Atl 543 (1935); and *Cunningham v Pressed Steel Car Co*, 238 App Div 624, 265, NY Supp 256 (1933). In respect of issues to which it applies, the Trust Indenture Act of 1939 now contains in s 316 a total prohibition on restrictions of an individual bondholder's power of enforcement for non-payment without the consent of the particular bondholder. In Canada there has been a straight-forward assertion of the individual bondholder's right to enforce at least where the machinery seems incapable of effective operation *Re Imperial Steel Corpn Ltd* (1925) 28 OWN 242; *Shaughnessy v Imperial Trusts Co* (1904) 3 NB Eq Rep 5

position of the trustee. The relevant provisions of the actual documentation produces the following.

(1) Each bond contains a promise by the issuer to pay to the bondholder on maturity and in the meantime to pay interest on the interest days.
(2) As has been seen the bond is bought subject to the terms of the trust deed. The trust deed contains a covenant by the issuer to pay the trustee the principal sum and interest. However, every payment made to the Principal Paying Agent to enable payments to be made to the bondholders, which is, in fact, paid to the bondholders, is to be taken in satisfaction of the issuer's obligation to the trustee, and is to be deemed to have been made to the trustee.
(3) If an act of default occurs the trustee is empowered, and in some circumstances obliged, to take action on behalf of the bondholders to recover the money payable in such an event.
(4) In situation 3 the bondholders are, in general terms, prohibited from taking independent action.[1]

The central issue, which arises from the above, is the identification of the subject matter of the trust, for the English concept of trust revolves around property being held by one person for the benefit of another. As recently as 1945, Cohen J was prepared to accept the definition of *Underhill on Trusts* (8th edn) p. 3:

> A trust is an equitable obligation, binding a person (who is called a trustee) to deal with property over which he has control (which is called the trust property) for the benefit of persons (who are called the beneficiaries or *cestui que trust*) of whom he may himself be one and anyone of whom may enforce the obligation.[2]

The idea that a trust presupposes a trust property lies deep in the thinking of the common law jurisdictions. Thus, Mayo J. in an Australian case[3] has said: 'Strictly it refers . . . to the duty or the aggregate accumulation of obligations that rest upon a person described as trustee. The responsibilities are in relation to property held by him, or under his control'.

A secondary difficulty in seeing the situation as a real trust situation is the lack of real duties imposed on the trustee before default occurs.[4] In considering the position of the secured debenture trustee the New York Supreme Court has denied the existence of a true trusteeship at all in the following words:

> In such indentures the use of the word 'trustee' is clearly a misnomer. The corporate trustee has very little in common with the ordinary trustee, as we generally understand the fiduciary relationship. The ordinary trustee is

1 A typical clause would be as follows. 'Only the trustee may enforce the rights and remedies of the Bondholders and the Coupon holders against the Company and no Bondholders or Coupon holders shall be entitled to proceed directly against the Company unless the Trustee, having become bound to do so in accordance with the terms of these presents, fails to do so and such failure is continuing.'

2 *Re Marshall's Will Trusts* [1945] Ch 217 at 219.

3 *Re Scott (decd)* (1948) SASR 193 at 196

4 The trustee's position on default is considered *post* p. 317

> supposed to represent the interests of the beneficiary alone. The courts impose upon him an undivided loyalty to the *cestui que trust*. So strict is the rule of undivided loyalty to the beneficiary that the mere fact that a trustee has an interest inconsistent with the interest of his *cestui*, casts upon him the burdens of explanation and justification . . . The trustee under a corporate indenture, on the other hand, has his rights and duties defined, not by the fiduciary relationship, but exclusively by the terms of the agreement. His status is more that of a stakeholder than one of a trustee. Indeed, in the earlier indentures the documents were rather in the form of escrow agreements and no duties were assigned to the trustee.[1]

These comments and their own extensive deliberations led the distinguished authors of the classic U.S. treatise on the subject to conclude 'that the anomalous position, the confusion of thought referred to above, result in part, at least, from failure to recall that synonymity of title will not inevitably engender synonymity of function or duty'.[2]

The parallel of a stakeholder for the model of the trustee of a secured corporate debenture issue is attractive but is hardly a viable model in the case of an unsecured issue, where the 'stakeholder' holds nothing. Here a better parallel is that of agent. Thus, the undertaking by the bondholder with the trustee would not destroy the bondholder's right to sue, but merely bars his own individual remedy. It would thus confer an irrevocable authority on the trustee to be able to take action on behalf of the bondholder, who would become thereby not a trustee of the debt but representative of the right to bring the action. In this respect it would be not a trustee but the representative of the bondholders as a class and, as such representative, agent of each bondholder with all the fiduciary responsibilities which arise from the agency relationship.[3]

Superficially attractive though this approach is, it is confronted by the undoubted fact that the English courts in dealing with the trust for debenture holders have consistently used the usual terminology and concepts of trust law. Perhaps the most striking case is that of In *Re Magadi Soda Co Ltd*[4] where the court treated purchases of secured debentures by the trustees from the debenture holders at an undervalue as a purchase by a trustee of a *cestui que trust*. Eve J stated explicitly:

> Trustees for debenture holders are in no different position from other trustees,

1 *Hazzard v Chase National Bank*, 159 Misc 57, 83, 287 NY Supp 541, 570 (Sup Ct 1936).

2 Ralph A McClelland and Frederick S Fisher Jr *The Law of Corporate Mortgage Bond Issues* Chicago, Callaghan and Company (1937) reprinted by William S Hein and Co, Buffalo (1983) in their Historical Reprint in Jurisprudence and Classical Legal Literature series.

3 For a discussion of the fiduciary duties, see *Bowstead on Agency* (1985) 11th Edn Sweet and Maxwell, London bt FMB Reynolds p. 156-204. There is a close parallel from the law of agency, where the relationship is fiduciary, but without there being a trust relationship. However, on occasion the agent may hold property for his principal as trustee with all the incidents of a trustee — Bowstead at p. 162.

4 (1925) 41 TLR 297

> except that, unlike many other trustees, they are remunerated for their services and whether the mortgagor company is a going concern or whether the security is being realized for the benefit of the debenture holders, the conduct of the trustees is controlled by the same rules, subjected to the same restrictions, and will be measured by the same standards as are applied to other fiduciary agents. The receiver not only fills a fiduciary position towards all the debenture holders, but his appointment to an office of such responsibility presupposes that he will discharge his duties with punctilious rectitude.[1]

Since English law apparently sees no difficulty in treating the trustee as a full trustee in the case of a secured debenture is the position different in the case of an unsecured bond on the argument that the absence of security results in a lack of subject matter around which a trust can be constructed? There is no doubt that there can be a trust of a right to be paid[2] including a chose in action.[3] Logically, therefore, the trustee is trustee of the right to payment given to him by the trust deed. However, this right itself is worthy of fuller consideration.

The trustee's right to payment will in general be satisfied by payment to the bondholders via the paying agent, and it is only if this does not take place or some other act of default occurs, that it is envisaged that payment will be made to the trustee or that he will take steps to enforce payment. To a property lawyer this looks very much as though there is a primary right to payment given to the bondholder and a secondary, contingent, right given to the trustee. It is questionable whether a mere contingent right to payment could give rise to an immediate trust with the contingent right being its subject matter, but that problem could be overcome by concluding that the trust was only intended to commence when the contingency occurs and the trustee becomes obliged to take positive steps under the trust deed.[4]

However, it is submitted that such arguments are based on a misconception. In fact, there is neither a primary and secondary payment right nor a contingency. There are, in fact, two separate payment rights of equal importance conferred respectively on the bondholder (first payment right) and the trustee (second payment right) under which payments made under the first are by definition payments under the second. The terms of the trust deed are quite precise and mean neither more nor less than they say: the trustee is the trustee under a trust of the second non-contingent payment right which he holds for the beneficiary. This accords well with the expectation of those who draft trust instruments who clearly envisage that the terms of the Trustee Act 1925 will apply even though no effort to incorporate that statute is made.

[1] at p. 298.
[2] *Trendex Trading Corpn v Credit Suisse* [1980] 3 All ER 721.
[3] *Fletcher v Fletcher* (1844) 4 Hare 67.
[4] Such a trust is valid if it does not offend the rule against perpetuities. See *Re Lord Stratheden and Campbell* [1894] 3 Ch 265.

LIABILITY OF THE TRUSTEE

Exculpation clauses

The English form of trust deed is construed traditionally in such a way as to modify the trustee's potential liability to the bondholders. The overall position has been well summed up as follows:

> The trustee is permitted to rely on advice of professional advisers, upon compliance certificates given by responsible officers of the issuer and on minutes of bondholders' meetings, is not concerned to enquire as to whether an event of default has occurred and is not responsible for the application of the proceeds of the issue. He is indemnified by the issuer for liabilities incurred in the execution of the trust (a claim which expressly ranks prior to the claims of the bondholders) and he can delegate his powers and appoint agents without being responsible for their actions.[1]

In addition a provision is usually inserted in an international bond trust modifying the trustee's active duty to be a watchdog.[2] While the potential responsibilities of the trustee are thus considerably modified, the overall effect is not to attempt a total release of all potential obligations. However, the modification of the trustee's obligations is sufficiently wide to be viewed as as exculpation attempt. The courts in the U.S., following their general approach to the trust deed as being a contract of adhesion, have traditionally viewed exculpatory clauses as provisions to be construed *contra proferentem*, and have been ingenious in finding good reasons for holding that they did not cover the particular breach complained of.

In an English law based issue, the trust deed usually expressed states that nothing within it shall, in any case in which the trustee has failed to show the degree of care and diligence required of it as trustee (having regard to the powers, authorities and discretions conferred by the trust deed), indemnify it against any liability for breach of trust, or any liability which by virtue of any rule of law would otherwise attach to it, in respect of any negligence, default, breach of duty or breach of trust of which it may be guilty in relation to its duties thereunder.[3] This, of course, closely parallels the main provision of the Companies Act 1985, s 192, which is applicable to a domestic issue but not an international corporate issue, since the issuer will not generally be incorporated under the 1985 Act which is a requirement of applicability.[4]

At common law the provision in a debenture trust deed indemnifying

1 Wood *op. cit.* p. 226.

2 Discussed *post* p. 321. See, eg *Starr v Chase National Bank* NYLG 21, Sept. 1936 (Sup. Cr.) 771; *Hazzard v Chase International Bank*, 159 Misc 57, 287 N.Y. Supp 541. (Sup Ct 1936)

3 Typical wording generally employed in a trust deed.

4 See the definition section 735(1) discussed *ante* p. 85.

the trustee for debenture holders from liability for breach of duty is enforceable for the beneficiaries' rights are determined by the terms of trust instrument and bind him.[1] The purpose of s. 192 is to prohibit blanket indemnities for breach *conferred in advance*. The power for indemnity to be conferred by bondholders as beneficiaries existent at common law *after the breach* has occurred remains. However, even in its implication with regard to future breaches the clause, like s. 192, is probably of limited effect, for it would seem to allow the trust deed to define narrowly the trustees' obligations in the first place, so that a breach needing indemnity is unlikely to occur. This is of considerable potential future effect as will be seen later.[2] However, while, in principle, the courts will give effect to the limitation on liability, it has been well observed that in the present judicial climate clauses relieving trustees from liability should be viewed with reserve.[3] Certainly, the court in the recent case of *Bartlett v Barclays Trust Co*[4] was not prepared to construe the clauses within the trust deed proferred as exculpatory clauses by the bank as having that effect, ascribing their insertion and effect to other purposes.

Trustee Act 1925 s 61

If the courts may well prove to be reluctant to give anything but limited effect to clauses limiting a trustee's liability, to what extent can a trust corporation seek protection in the powers conferred on a court under the Trustee Act 1925, s. 61 to excuse a trustee from liability for breach of trust where the trustee 'acted honestly and reasonably and ought fairly to be excused'. In considering the failure of the trustee in *Bartlett* the court took the view that clearly the trustee had acted honestly. However, in failing to take the positive action required by the serious professional responsibilities it had undertaken, it had not acted reasonably nor could the court take the view that it would be fair to excuse the bank at the expense of the beneficiaries.[5] It seems therefore that the court's discretion is likely to be favourably exercised only where the breach of trust is technical and not a substantive failure to fulfil the principal purposes for which trust corporations are appointed.

Unfair Contract Terms Act 1977

Since the relationship between trustee and bondholder is that of trustee and beneficiary there is no contractual relationship and the Unfair Contract Terms Act 1977 has no application to the trustee exemption clauses. This

1 *Wilkins & Hogg* (1861) 3 Giff 116 affd. (1862) 8 Jnr (NS) 25; *Pass & Dundas* (1880) 43 LT 665. A similar situation applies with regard to personal representatives *Re Tankard* (1942) Ch 69.
2 *post* p. 323.
3 Wood *op. cit.* p. 226.
4 [1980] 1 Ch 515 at p. 536.
5 at pp. 537–8.

is because the exemption does not arise by reference to any contract term or notice within s 2(1) of the Act.[1]

BONDHOLDERS' MEETINGS

If the machinery of bondholder's representation gives some measure of protection to bondholders and flexibility to an issuer, further protection and assistance is customarily conferred in an issue of international bonds by means of provisions for meetings of bondholders, where their views can be democratically ascertained. Further, provision is usually made whereby a majority decision, democratically achieved at a properly convened meeting, will bind all bondholders, so that an arrangement beneficial to the bondholders as a whole, and acceptable to the majority, cannot be blocked by a minority.

The potential usefulness of such an arrangement is obvious, and it is not surprising that some national systems of bondholder protection should make their use compulsory in some form or another. In the case of the U.K., rules of the Stock Exchange require that provision for meetings should be included in the trust deed of any issue of debentures quoted on the Stock Exchange.[2] The range of matters which may arise for discussion and resolution at a bondholders' meeting are many and varied. They range from concerns of relatively minor importance to the individual bondholder (e.g. a relaxation of the technical requirements of a negative pledge clause to allow the issuer to raise further funds where the original was drawn over-restrictively and there is no significant adverse affect upon the bondholders), to such vital matters as a postponement of payment of interest, or reduction in the amount of principal of the bonds when the issuer cannot meet its liabilities. It follows that as a practical matter the degree of protection needed by an individual bondholder varies with the degree of importance of the actual issue raised.

Accordingly, the general provision inserted in an English law trust deed permits the trustee (and possibly also the issuer) to convene a meeting of bondholders upon receipt of a request in writing of the holders of at

1 For a contrary view, see William Goodhart QC 'Trustee Exemption Clauses and the Unfair Contract Terms Act 1977' [1980] *Conv* 333. By contrast the restriction on the bondholder's right to sue is contractual in nature but is not an exclusion of liability for negligence or liability within the Act.

2 In contrast North America has a more laissez faire attitude to issues to which their domestic requirements apply. There the trustee and the issuer are obliged to provide lists of known bondholders to any bondholder requesting one, so that the bondholders can organize themselves. The effect of the provision is therefore to encourage bondholders to leave their names and addresses with the issuer so that contact can be made — Trust Indenture Act 1939, s 312 (U.S.); Canada Business Corporations Act 1974-5-6, s 58. In civil law jurisdictions in contrast the statutory scheme for bondholder representation often contains provision enabling bondholders representing a proportion of the total of the banks outstanding to call meetings to discuss and vote on matters arising from the issue. The proportions vary from 5 per cent in Brazil, France and Germany to 20 per cent in Belgium.

least 20 per cent of the principal amount of the securities. The notice given must be at least 21 days, the quorum is a simple majority of the holders of the principal amount of the bonds, and any vote is carried on a simple majority of these attending. If insufficient bondholders attend, the meeting is adjourned, but at the adjourned meeting two bondholders are constituted a quorum, empowered to pass any resolution, and make decisions for the purpose of which the meeting was called.

Plainly, with such modest requirements for a quorum it would be possible for the machinery to be manipulated by a small but more organised group to oppress a substantial number of bondholders. This possibility is traditionally approached by entrenching the more fundamental bondholder rights so that they can only be modified by extraordinary resolution involving a larger quorum and majority. A typical clause is as follows:

> A meeting of the bondholders shall in addition to all other powers have the following powers exercisable by Extraordinary resolution, namely:
>
> (A) to sanction any proposal by the Issuer for any modification, abrogation, variation or compromise of or arrangement in respect of, the rights of the bondholders and/or the Coupon-holders against the Issuer, whether such rights shall arise under these presents or otherwise;
>
> (B) to sanction any proposal by the Issuer for the exchange or substitution for the Bonds of, or the conversion of the Bonds into, shares, stocks, debenture stock or other obligations or securities of the Issuer or any other body corporate now formed or hereafter to be formed;
>
> (C) to assent to any modification of the provisions contained in these presents, the Bonds or the Coupons which shall be proposed by the Issuer or the Trustee;
>
> (D) to approve a person proposed to be appointed a new trustee under these presents and to remove any trustee for the time being hereof;
>
> (E) to authorize the Trustee to concur in and execute and do all such documents, acts and things as may be necessary to carry out and give effect to any Extraordinary Resolution;
>
> (F) to discharge or exonerate the Trustee from any liability in respect of any act or omission for which the Trustee may have become responsible under the presents or under the Bonds;
>
> (G) to appoint any persons (whether Bondholders or not) as a committee or committees to represent the interest of the Bondholders and to confer upon such committees any powers or discretions which the Bondholders could themselves exercise by Extraordinary Resolution[1]

Matters required to be resolved by extraordinary resolution require, traditionally, a quorum of three-quarters of the holders of the principal value of the outstanding bonds and a majority of three-quarters of those

[1] Provisions for meetings of bondholders in Trust Deed constituting U.S. $50,000,000 9 per cent notes due 1986 between A/S Exportfinans and the Law Debenture Corporation Ltd.

present, which is, as has been pointed out by one experienced writer 'an almost impossible quorum in the case of bearer bonds'.[1]

While the usual provisions of the trust deed contain provisions which are of protection to the individual bondholders, there can be no protection from the terms of the provisions themselves against a majority of bondholders, who can achieve the specified quorum and majority, from oppressing a small minority by passing discriminatory resolutions to the minority's detriment. However, in many jurisdictions the courts will intervene, either pursuant to statutory power[2] or by means of general equitable supervision. It is clear in England the courts will intervene where the majority power is abused. The principles applicable were stated by Parker J in *Goodfellow v Nelson Line*[3] in the following terms:

> The powers conferred by the trust deed on a majority of the debenture holders must, of course, be exercised bona fide, and the Court can no doubt interfere to prevent unfairness or oppression, but subject to this, each debenture holder may vote with regard to his individual interests, though these interests may be peculiar to himself and not shared by other debenture holders . . . Where . . . there is, as between different holders, a diversity of interest, it may be necessary or advisable as a matter of business fairness, to make special provision for special interests and I do not think there is any equity preventing a debenture holder voting for or against a scheme containing such a special provision merely because he is interested thereunder . . . However . . . where there are diverse interests . . . where those diverse interests are specially provided, the Court ought to consider carefully the fairness of any scheme whereby a majority of debenture holders seek to bind a minority.

In the actual case before him there was a diverse interest of a minority, who had special protection under guarantees attached to the debentures in the particular circumstances which had arisen. However, the minority had voted in favour of the scheme, which involved their giving up their protection, and which had the support of a clear overall of the bondholders. The dissentient was not in fact entitled to the protection, and the court therefore refused to intervene. If those holding the protected interest were prepared to give it up it was not for the court to prevent them.

In another case a scheme of reconstruction of a company, under which secured bonds were to be exchanged for income unsecured bonds subordinated to a first issue of income bonds, and where a committee, one only of whom was to be appointed by the secured bondholders, was to have power to modify the scheme without the approval of the bondholders, was sanctioned by the majority of the bondholders requisite under the trust deed. In fact, the required majority would not have been obtained without the vote of the holder of a large number of bonds, whose support was

1 Wood *op. cit.* at p. 230. The legislation of individual countries will often specify the powers of the bondholders' meeting and contain any limitations on the powers of a simple majority of any meeting convened. Examples are considered by Wood *op. cit.* at the same page.

2 As in Japan where Article 326 of the Commercial Code subjects the resolution to the approval of the court. (Quoted by Wood *op. cit.* p. 231.)

3 [1912] 2 Ch 324 at 332.

obtained by the promise of a large block of ordinary stock. This reconstruction was invalid. Effectively, the power of the single but crucial bondholder has been used to further his own interests pursuant to a secret bribe.[1] Equally, an attempt to pass a majority resolution under the terms of the trust deed, which would have the effect of ending the treatment of debenture holders *pari passu* and selecting by tender some only of the debenture holders to have their debentures redeemed, has since been held invalid.[2]

If an issuer comes forward with a set of proposals with regard to the reconstruction of a bond issue which is placed before a meeting of bondholders and a particular bondholder wishes to oppose its implementation, it cannot under English law prevent information as to the way it has cast its vote being given to the issuer. This is a matter of some real concern to dissentient bondholders, for they may well feel that an issuer, which is secure within its own jurisdiction may discriminate against them, either with regard to the particular bond issue, or more likely with regard to other financial and commercial transactions, in which it is interested. The matter came before Hirst J for decision in *Haarhaus & Co GmbH v Law Debenture Trust Corporation p.l.c.* (Financial Times LR 9 February 1988) in proceedings arising from a meeting of holders of U.S. holder promissory notes held at the Wembley conference centre on 14 January 1988. The notes themselves had been issued for approximately $3.2 million to uninsured trade creditors of Nigerian importers under a scheme constituted by a trust deed between the Central Bank of Nigeria as issuer, the Federal Republic of Nigeria as guarantor, and the Law Debenture Trust Corporation as trustee. The notes provided for payment of principal and interest by instalments with final redemption in 1990. During 1987 Central Bank had defaulted on its obligations under the trust deed and the purpose of the meeting was to put before the noteholders proposals extending the completion date to 2010.

The meeting was, in fact, convened by the Central Bank; the chairman was nominated by the trustee. The extraordinary resolution, which was before the meeting to allow the reconstruction, required a two-thirds majority and this was secured on a show of hands, However, the chairman then demanded a poll.

The voting slips bore the noteholders' polling numbers which would allow them to be identified. The boxes were opened by the issuer's agent, for the purpose of counting the votes, Chase Manhattan Bank. The vote numbers were entered into a computer and removed to Chase Manhattan's premises. The resolution was passed with the requisite majority.

One of the bondholders who had voted against the resolution issued writs, claiming that the voting was confidential, and seeking injunction to prevent disclosure as to the way in which votes had been cast to the Nigerian Central Bank. It did so in a representative capacity on behalf of all noteholders, claiming that there was a risk of damage to them if

1 *British America Nickel Corpn v O'Brien Ltd* [1927] AC 369. See also the remarks of Parker J in *Goodfellow v Nelson Line (Liverpool) Ltd* [1912] 2 Ch 324 at 333.

2 *Re New York Taxicab Co Ltd* [1913] 1 Ch 1.

the information was disclosed. However, since the majority, who had voted for the resolution had reason to fear discrimination or reprisals, the proceedings could not be continued on a representative basis, and the case had to be viewed as the action of the individual bondholder alone.

The bondholder based his claim on two grounds. First, he alleged that it was an express or implied term of the trust deed that information as to how individuals voted was confidential. However the court had no difficulty in rejecting the submission that at common law there was any special requirement of confidentiality for polls. Nor was there anything in the provisions of the trust deed to support the notion that the poll was to be confidential vis-à-vis the Central Bank.

Secondly, the bondholder contended that the information was subject to a duty of confidentiality in equity in view of the risk of damage to the dissentient bondholder. However, the court also dismissed this contention. The same considerations, which had precluded the success of the contention that there was a term in the contract that the information was confidential, indicated that it had never been impressed with confidentiality in the first place, and, indeed, since Chase Manhattan was the issuer's agent it was difficult to see how its own principle was not entitled to the information which it held. Further, the bondholder could not reasonably have understood that Chase Manhattan was receiving the information in confidence, and nor could Chase Manhattan itself. Finally, the bondholder had failed to establish that there was any reason for its fear of discrimination and reprisals. Its evidence in this regard was woefully inadequate and the court strongly deprecated the making of serious allegations of the kind without any proper evidential support.

It thus appears that under English law there is no protection to a bondholder, who votes against a proposed reconstruction of a bond issue, unless it is agreed from the beginning that the manner of voting should be confidential and should not be disclosed to anyone other than the institution which takes the votes or, alternatively, unless the dissentient bondholder is able to establish by evidence that there is a real possibility of discrimination or reprisals. This is a heavy burden for dissentients to bear, and it might well have been better to have treated voting records as confidential, given that there seems little public interest to be served by allowing them to be disclosed and considerable public interest to be served in forbidding disclosure.

THE MACHINERY IN PRACTICE

The problems which can arise with this machinery where a bond issue does not have a trustee, or, alternatively, the precise nature of the machinery is misunderstood by those seeking to operate it, can be seen from the attempts by Costa Rica to renegotiate its international loans in 1981 and 1982.[1] Costa Rica had been caught in the perennial trap awaiting a poor undeveloped country struggling to keep its democratic traditions and

[1] For a full account see 'Costa Rica: A Case History' in *Default and Rescheduling: Corporate and Sovereign Borrowers* ed. Suratgar, *op. cit.*

institutions viable. 1976 and 1977 were boom years on the world coffee market with prices reaching high levels. As an exporter of coffee Costa Rica did well out of this situation and its government, conscious of elections pending for 1978, proceeded to borrow to finance large-scale developments on the strength of this substantial income. When the bottom feel out of the coffee market, Costa Rica was left with massive debt obligations, which it could not service. It sought to renegotiate the whole of its international borrowing.

Confronted with this the creditors split into two separate groups for the purpose of negotiation.[1] One group consisted of holders of notes and bonds represented by prominent lead managers of the various issues, Banque Nationale de Paris, D.G. Bank and European Banking Company. The second group consisted in banks participating in syndicated loans to Costa Rica, who were organised into a ten-bank committee led by the Bank of America. The twin grouping represented a difference of interests which quickly moved towards conflict.

The syndicated loan group took the view that the syndicated loans and the bonds and notes should all be treated equally, so that if payment was delayed in respect of one form of borrowing, it should be delayed in respect of all. It pointed out that the vast majority of the securities issued by Costa Rica had been purchased by institutions, and therefore that there was no good reason why any distinction should be drawn between the two forms of finance. This group became increasingly incensed, as interest and capital was repaid on the bonds in accordance with their terms, while payments on the syndicated loans were withheld.

For the bondholders the absence of a machinery for renegotiation was put forward as being fatal to the argument of the syndicate lenders. A renegotiation with the lead managers of the issue could only be abortive, because they had no authority or power to agree anything on behalf of any individual bondholder. They were not trustees. The Costa Rican government agreed with the bondholders but came close to buckling under pressure from the syndicated lenders. This prompted a telex from the European Banking Company in 1982, exposing the fallacy of the argument of the syndicated lenders in the following terms:

> 'You refer to the meeting which took place in London between your government's representatives and the lead managers of Costa Rican issues. Whilst this meeting was of course useful, it should have been explained to you by your advisers that the lead manager of Eurobond issues do not represent the noteholders and have no right to commit noteholders either, since they are not in a position to ensure that all bearer noteholders are in receipt of any form of communication. In this respect the lead managers of your bond issues are not the same as the committee of creditor banks who have the right to represent all the commercial banks. This is only the beginning of a basic misunderstanding which persists about the nature of the contract your government entered into when it issued its bonds'.

1 There was a third group of creditors being those whose lending had been part of a short-term credit lead managed by Libra Bank International. This group simply commenced proceedings.

There is a traditional argument that, in fact, bondholders should have priority with regard to repayment over syndicated loans on the basis that bonds might be held by unsophisticated investors little able to face the loss — the so-called widows and orphans argument. To meet this it had been suggested, and under pressure the Costa Rican had been disposed to agree, that the bonds in institutional hands should be included in the renegotiation, while those in private hands should be repaid in accordance with their terms. The effect of this would have been to create two classes of bonds. The telex from the European Banking Company went on to demolish this approach.

> 'You refer to the requirement of your commercial bank creditors that all bonds and FRNs held by non-natural persons be included in any rescheduling. The commercial banks have no right to make such a requirement since you are not in a position to meet it. This request by the commercial banks is an entirely unreasonable one and is clearly made in ignorance of the legal and technical characteristics of your contractual obligations under the terms of the bond issues.
>
> No distinction exists between so-called natural and non-natural persons since, as any legal adviser will explain to you, the rights of bondholders are uniform, regardless of their nature. It is most unfortunate that this misunderstanding should have arisen because it has placed your government in an invidious position. While you are correctly pursuing negotiations with your commercial bank creditors, utilising the legal process called for in the documentation relating to your commercial bank loans, you appear to be neglecting another important group of creditors, namely your bondholders and, what is far worse, you would appear to have been willing to entertain a repudiation of your obligations with respect to some of these bondholders without any attempt to seek their consent.'

Faced with the clear correctness of these arguments, and the threat that all assistance from multilateral institutions necessary to make any renegotiations and financing practicable would be withdrawn, the attempt to renegotiate the bond financing was abandoned, it being left to individual bondholders to make their arrangements with the Costa Rican government with regard to the repayment of their bonds or their exchange into some other security. The renegotiation of the syndicated loans proceeded independently.

CIVILIAN JURISDICTIONS

While trusteeship is a concept well established in common law jurisdictions, it is little known in civil law systems. These have great difficulty in comprehending a concept which separates the legal and beneficial interests in the same items of property. Nevertheless, so effective has the use of the trustee been as a piece of commercial machinery that some countries with a basically civil law system have been moved to produce a statutory basis for bondholders' representation into the body of their commercial law, often by use of an approximation to trusteeship. Legislatures which have been active in this field include those of Panama, Argentina, Chile and Mexico in Central and South America, and Switzerland, the Netherlands, Luxembourg and Liechtenstein in Europe.[1]

Further, legislation in civil law countries has commonly created a mechanism for bondholders' meetings, at which resolutions can be proposed and if adopted, will bind all bondholders. Such a provision is widespread in jurisdictions in South America, and almost invariable in Europe. In short, the same needs, which demanded the evolution of trust law by essentially individual utilisation in common law countries, have dictated public law interference in those jurisdictions which lacked the private law concepts and machinery capable of evolution to meet them.

PROBLEMS OF DEFAULT AND BONDHOLDERS' REPRESENTATION—CONFLICT OF LAW CONSIDERATIONS[2]

Where an issue is based on a common law jurisdiction and used a trustee, it is usual for the trust deed to contain a clause expressly selecting a proper law for the trust. Where this is employed it is clear that in an English court the clause will be given effect, and the trust operated according to the chosen law.

An attempt, however, to create a trust in reliance on a selected civil law system which does not recognise the trust concept will usually fail, because that system does not have, and therefore cannot recognise, the relationship attempted. However, where a trust is created in reliance on a selected common law system, it appears that in the absence of any avoiding public policy considerations to the contrary, the courts of a civil law system will recognise the creation and give it effect.[3] To this fundamental situation the recent Hague Convention on the law applicable to Trusts and their Recognition,[4] to which effect has now been given in the U.K. by the Recognition of Trusts Act 1987, has now brought some relief. Article 6 provides that a trust shall be governed by the law chosen by the settlor whether such choice be express or implied. If, however, such chosen law 'does not provide for trusts or the category of trust involved' the choice shall not be effective and the trust shall be governed by the law with which

1 Wood *op. cit.* pp. 217–218.

2 On this subject generally see Delaume *'Transnational Contracts'* Oceana Pubs, Dobbs Ferry. New York (1983 rev) Chapter 5 and 'Choice of Law and Forum Clauses on Eurobonds' 11 Colum J. Transnational Law 240; Rich *'International Debt Obligations of Enterprises in Civil Law Countries; The Problem of Bondholder Representation'* (1981) 21 Virg J of Int Law.

3 *Kerr v Société Pyrenées Minerals* Cass 19 February 1908, Clunet 1912, 243 Affirming Court of Appeals of Toulouse 18 July 1905, Clunet 1906, 451. *Sohege v John Palmer, The Singen Manufacturing Co* Rev Dr Int Pr 1908, 239, Clunet 1910, 1229; *Courtois v De Gamay, Rev* Crit, Dr Int Pr 1971, 518; Clunet 1973, 207. There may be a problem of understanding in applying the trust concept as civil lawyers find it difficult to understand a divided concept of ownership between legal and beneficial interests. Frequently the trust is applied but as an agency arrangement!

4 See generally Hayton (1987) 36 ICLQ 260; Gaillard and Trautman (1987) 35 Am J Comp L 307.

it is most closely connected under Article 7. Thus, where the Convention is applicable the trust will only fail if it is not a form recognised by both the chosen law and the law with which it is most closely connected if these differ. However, it is by no means certain that the Convention is applicable to a trust for bondholders on an issue of international bonds for it applies only where a legal relationship has been created whereby *assets* have been placed under the control of a trustee by virtue of Article 2. The use of the word assets does seem to suggest that some tangible assets or fund should be held by the trustee and not merely the right to enforce the issuer's payment obligation which is given to him on an international bond issue. At the very least, there is a substantial risk that the Convention will be read in this light in civil law jurisdictions as they wrestle to come to grips with a concept new to their jurisprudence.

A problem, however, remains in that a trust deed with a designated proper law, the validity and effect of which falls to be resolved in another jurisdiction, may not comply with the internal requirements for bondholder representation of that jurisdiction. Clearly, if under the terms of the statute of the adjudicating jurisdiction the internal system is applicable to the issue, its requirements will be paramount and the provisions of the trust deed, at least so far as they conflict, invalid.[1]

Whether or not a jurisdiction's bondholder representation statutes apply to an issue is a matter to be determined from the terms of the statute itself. Usually statutes apply to issues made within the jurisdiction which passed the statute. However, in every case the statute of the particular jurisdiction must be considered for its specific effect.

Nevertheless, while the terms of an applicable bondholder statute will take precedence over the trust deed, the requirements of the international bond market have on occasion had the ultimate triumph by causing the bondholder legislation to be amended. This is well illustrated by the history of the French legislation. Under French law since 1935 bondholders in an issue made in France by foreign issuers were grouped by law into an association called a *masse des obligatiores.* In 1966 a new French company law was enacted, which extended the applicability of the statutory *masse* to bonds issued outside France by French corporations, thereby giving the French bondholders' representation statute effective extra-territorial effect.[2] Inevitably, the practical effect of this was to cause great difficulties for French companies attempting to raise international finance on the international bond market. Accordingly, the following year the law was amended[3] to exempt from its operations the raising of capital by French

1 Even if the recent Hague Convention does cover the trust for bondholders, this problem is not overcome because recognition of a trust created under a designated system of law is subject to the mandatory rules of the forum under Article 15.

2 Article 339, Company Law of 24 July 1966.

3 Article 25 Law of 12 July 1967.

companies on foreign markets, thus enabling French companies to participate freely in the international financial market.[1]

Public policy considerations outside private international law

It must not be thought that public policy considerations are limited to conflicts within the sphere of private international law. A further problem can arise on an international bond issue where the trust deed purports to confer wider powers on the trustee than those contained within the bondholder representation statute of the system of law law governing the trust. Here there is no problem of recognition, for the trust is created by the system of law whose bondholder statute gives rise to the difficulty. Further, it is probable that the conflict will be litigated before the courts of the jurisdiction whose law governs. The essential question which is raised is whether or not the terms of the bondholder representation statute are mandatory in fixing a maximum power which may be conferred on the trustee. This very issue was raised by an interesting case arising from Luxembourg which caused great concern in financial circles when it was first decided. To understand the case some knowledge of Luxembourg law and the workings of the Luxembourg market are necessary. The importance of that market, and the frequent use of quotation on the Luxembourg Stock Market, have already been stressed. Where an issue is made subject to Luxembourg law, it is usual to appoint as trustee a Luxembourg bank or financial institution to represent the bondholders. The terms of the trusteeship, as in an English based issue, are invariably fully contained in a lengthy trust indenture subject to the terms of which all purchases are made.

The relevant statutory scheme for bondholder representation in Luxembourg is contained in the Luxembourg Law on Commercial Companies. That statute confers considerable powers on the bondholders' meeting, including *inter alia,* the power to make conservatory measures *(actes conservertoires)* in the general interest of the bondholders, and the power to appoint agents to carry out the decisions of the meeting.[2] However, under the statute the overall grouping of the bondholders ceases on the insolvency of the issuer and/or the issuer making any composition with its creditors.[3]

It may, of course, be argued with some justification that it is precisely in the situation of insolvency that the bondholder representation provisions and the restriction on individual action can be most important, and this is the view commonly taken on the international financial markets. Consequently, trust deed drafting for international issues organised under Luxembourg law has customarily conferred on the trustees wider powers than those given by the Luxembourg bondholder statute, and provided further that these powers continue after insolvency or the issuer making

[1] French legal developments are discussed by both Delaume *op. cit.* and Rich *op. cit.*

[2] Article 88.

[3] Article 92.

a composition with its creditors. The restrictions of the statute and the width of the trust deed provisions customarily employed cannot be reconciled, and the stage was set for conflict. The inevitable collision occurred spectacularly in 1971 with the decision of the Tribunal Civil of Luxembourg in 1971 in *Faillite Four Seasons Overseas NW v SA Finitrust.*[1]

The case arose from the liquidation and insolvency of a Luxembourg company Four Seasons, NV. On the date of the insolvency SA Finitrust filed two claims. The first corresponded to the total amount of bonds issued by the insolvent corporation together with interest. The second was for the same amount, subject to reduction in the future proportionate to the amount of claims filed by individual bondholders. Subsequently, the bondholders ratified the trustee's action, and authorised the trustee to proceed to represent the bondholder and their claims 'without prejudice to the rights of the bondholders to proceed individually'. The trustee in bankruptcy contested the claims. On his behalf it was argued that the claim was invalid because of the uncertain amount of the claim, and because both the filing of the claim and the subsequent ratification were invalid in the light of the provisions of the bondholder statute.

The court accepted these arguments. The provisions of the Luxembourg Law on Commercial Companies were mandatory. It followed that the powers of the trustee contained in Article 88 were exhaustive and they did not cover the actions of the trustee (who was referred to in the judgment as an agent). As such it could not be ratified by the bondholders' resolution. In addition, the powers of the bondholders' organisation had been abrogated on the insolvency of the corporation under Article 92.

The potential of this decision to damage Luxembourg's standing as an international financial centre was clear. The court had rightly applied the mandatory provisions of Luxembourg domestic law, but the effect of the decision was to deny the bondholders the protection that they believed they had, and had shown the inability of Luxembourg law to allow the effective machinery essential to the protection of bondholders on the insolvency of an international issuer, where speed of organisation and action is all important. Inevitably, commercial necessity triumphed and the law was amended the following year.[2] Under the amendment a bondholder representative *(representant fiduciaire)* can be appointed with the wide powers commonly conferred on the trustee of common law jurisdictions.

THE POSITION OF THE TRUSTEE[3]

[1] Trib. d'Arrondissement Luxembourg, 21 Jan 1971; Rev Crit Dr Int, Fr 1973, 51. This decision is discussed by Delaume *op. cit* and Rich *op. cit.*

[2] Arrête Grand Ducal of 22 December 1972 Concernant la Representation Fiduciare, Memorial (Off Gaz), 29 December, p. 2113.

[3] The position and responsibilities of the trustee both under the Trust Indenture Act 1939, and at common law, has been the subject of greater litigation and academic interest in the United States than in this country. A classic exposition is that of Louis S. Posner 'The Trustee and the Trust Indenture; a Further Study' 46 YLJ 737. See also W.A. Johnson 'Default Administration of the Corporate Trust Indenture' (1971) 15 St LULJ at pp. 203, 374, 509.

Where the machinery of an issue uses a trust deed placing the rights and responsibilities of enforcement firmly on the shoulders of the trustee it is important that within that machinery the trustee should be, and be seen to be, an effective representative of the bondholders. At a practical level there are two major areas in which the trustee may not be perceived to be the effective bondholders' representative which their interests demand. The first is where the trustee is faced with a conflict of interests, being either a conflict between the bondholders' interests and his own individual interests, or, alternatively, a conflict between his duties to two independent interests, one being that of the bondholders, both of which he is supposed to represent. The second area arises if the trustee is merely required to be passive reacting only to situations notified to him rather than an active watch-dog monitoring the situation of the issuer on behalf of the bondholders. Finally, a third area of difficulty arises from the performance of trust duties in the light of knowledge obtained in a fiduciary capacity. The first area of difficulty, that of conflict on interests, will be considered first.

(i) *Conflicts of interest*[1] Conflicts of interests for trustees for bondholders usually arise because in many countries trusteeship is customarily undertaken by financial institutions and in particular banks. Traditionally, the remuneration to which trusteeship gives rise has been significantly less than the profits which can be earned from banking and financial services. In such circumstances, the institutions which have gained the experience of trusteeship, have been reluctant to give up their more remunerative work to be able to concentrate on the less remunerative duties of trusteeship.

Sometimes an issuer's own bank will be chosen to be trustee of an issue, and in such circumstances, when default looms, the trustee bank may find itself with its obligation as trustee to look after the bondholders, but with a conflicting temptation to secure the issuer's overdraft with it by the taking of security or the exercise of set-offs. Further, the bank may be tempted not to notify bondholders of events of default, thereby giving itself time to secure the issuer's indebtedness to it, or to delay accelerating the payment of the bonds for the same purpose. A second potential area of conflict for a bank acting as trustee arises where it has a trustee investment department, responsible for the investment of many securities on behalf of trustee and investment accounts which it holds. In such circumstances difficulties may arise for it with regard to its investment decisions on behalf of the discretionary accounts that it handles when the issuer, of whose bonds it is trustee, faces increasing financial difficulties. In particular, should it sell bonds held by the investment accounts before informing the other bondholders of the difficulties arising, thereby enabling those investors to clear their investment with minimum loss, or should it delay its sale decision on behalf of those investors until all bondholders have been notified, but when the market price of the bonds on the secondary market is likely

1 This subject is more fully discussed by T Prime in 'Conflicts of Interest, Legal Rules and Equitable Principles' in '*Conflicts of Interest in the Changing Financial World*' ed Prof RM Goode The Institute of Bankers, London (1986) and BAK Ryder 'The Fiduciary and the Frying Pan' (1978) 42 Conv. NS 114.

to be significantly lower? Finally, the bank trustee may also run a corporate finance department which advises the issuer, and which is given access to confidential information by the issuer. Where the bank trustee is informed of impending default by the issuer in confidence as the issuers' adviser, difficulties may arise for the trustee in deciding whether or not that information should be made available to the bondholders via the trustee department.

Of course, potential conflicts of interest are not limited to situations where trusteeship is undertaken by a bank offering a full range of commercial and financial services. It can also arise if there is a community of ownership or personnel between two independent companies as where there are cross-sharings between issuer and trustee or cross-directorships. In particular, is an individual who is a director of both the issuer and the trustee responsible for making available to the trustee corporation information given to him in confidence as trustee of the issuer? Finally, a conflict of interest can arise where the trustee is a trustee of two issues by the same issuer, where the bond or debenture holders of each issue will be in pursuit of the same assets if financial difficulties arise for the issuer.

In England many of the potential conflict of interest problems are avoided on an institutional basis. In *Re Dorman, Long and Co Ltd*[1] a trenchant criticism of institutions courting conflicting roles was voiced and as a result banks have not undertaken trusteeship work in this country.

As a consequence in England trusteeship has been undertaken by specialist corporations, in particular the Law Debenture Corporation Ltd.

Nevertheless the principles of equity have been utilised by the courts to set out general guide lines of the standard to be expected of all trustees. In particular, a trustee is expected to discharge his obligations with the standards of honesty and care that an ordinary prudent and conscientious man brings to the discharge of his own affairs. The trustees must therefore avoid misleading the debenture holders, make full disclosure of all information within their possession which may assist the debenture holders in appreciating the position of their investment, and in particular must not purchase debentures at an undervalue on their own account, withholding information from the bondholders in the trustee's possession which would affect the value of the bonds.[2] If investors seek the advice of the trustees disinterested advice, ignoring any conflicting interest of the trustee, must be given.[3]Indeed, the courts are so anxious to preserve the highest standards of conduct from those in a fiduciary situation that there are judicial pronouncements to the effect that all potential conflicts of interest should be avoided. In *Aberdeen Rly Co v Blaikie Bros* [4] Lord Cranworth LJ was firm that equity will not allow a fiduciary 'to enter into engagements in which he has, or can have, a personal interest conflicting, or which possibly may conflict, with the interest of those whom he is bound to protect'.

1 [1934] Ch 635 at p. 671.
2 *Re Magadi Soda Co Ltd* (1925) 94 LJ Ch 217.
3 *Re Dorman Long and Co* [1934] Ch 635
4 [1854] 1 Macq 461 at 471.

Perhaps the most extensive judicial statement is that of Lord Herschell in *Bray v Ford*:[1]

> 'It is an inflexible rule of a Court of Equity that a person in a fiduciary position, such as the respondents, is not, unless otherwise expressly provided, entitled to make a profit; he is not allowed to put himself in a position where his interest and duty conflict. It does not appear to me that this rule is, as has been said, founded upon principles of morality, I regard it rather as based on the consideration that human nature being what it is, there is danger in such circumstances, of the person holding a fiduciary position being swayed by interest rather than by duty, and thus prejudicing those whom he was bound to protect. It has, therefore, been deemed expedient to lay down this positive rule. But I am satisfied that it might be departed from in many cases, without any breach of morality, without any wrong being inflicted, and without any consciousness of wrong-doing.

If the institutional protection general in English appointments is ignored, and a bank appointed under a trust deed which English law is to govern, difficult issues may arise. [2] While under an English trust deed it is customary for the appointed trustee to be institutionally independent, a provision is usually included within the trust deed sanctioning actual and potential conflicts of interest. A typical example would be as follows:

> 'A trustee hereof or any subsidiary or holding company of any trustee hereof or director or other officer of any such company shall not be precluded from underwriting, guaranteeing the subscription of or subscribing for some or all of the securities with or without commission or other remuneration or from purchasing or otherwise acquiring, holding, dealing in or disposing of the securities, the coupons or any of them or any notes, bonds, debentures, debenture stock, shares or securities whatsoever of, or from acting as banker or paying agent for, the Company, or any of its subsidiaries or from otherwise at any time contracting or entering into any financial or other transactions, including contracts of insurance, with the Company or any of its subsidiaries or from being interested in any contract or transaction or from accepting and holding the office of trusteeship for the holders of any securities of the Company or any of its subsidiaries and shall not be liable to account to the Company or any of its subsidiaries or to the bondholders or coupon-holders for any profit made by it or him thereby or in connection therewith.'

It will be seen that the effect of this is to allow a wide power to the trustee, its directors and officers, to enter into financial transactions with the issuer, to deal in securities including bonds of the issuer, and to deal as trustee

1 [1896] AC 44 at 51, 52.

2 In the U.S., where the use of banks for debenture trust work is commonplace, statutory provision has been made in the Trustee Indenture Act of 1939 to regulate and avoid the problems which arise either actually or potentially with regard to a trustee's conflict of interest. However the application of the Act does not mean that the general equitable responsibilities of a trustee are not also applicable; indeed, it is quite clear that they remain. It therefore follows that these general equitable responsibilities similar to those imposed by the English courts would apply to a trust governed by the law of one of the states of the U.S. which, as in an international bond issue, falls outside the application of the 1939 Act. *Morris v Cantor* 390 FF Supp 817 (S.D.N.Y 1975).

for another issue by the same issuer. In addition, cross-directorships are also often sanctioned. While such a clause obviously effectively permits the trustee to undertake transactions for profit and to keep any profits arising therefrom, which it would not otherwise be able to do, such clauses do not themselves constitute an exculpation clause relieving the trustee from liability, which would otherwise arise for failing effectively to look after the bondholders' interests. In short, while the trustee is empowered to undertake activities which would not otherwise be available to it, the activities must not be performed in such as way as to prejudice the position of the bondholders, and if prejudice occurs the trustee will remain fully liable for its general equitable responsibility to the beneficiary. The problem can be controlled by making a full disclosure to bondholders where a conflict of interest arises, for transactions undertaken by the fiduciary with the knowledge and approval of the beneficiary will be effective and bind the beneficiary.[1] Further, it is essential that the disclosure of the conflict must be full disclosure so that the beneficiary fully understands the nature of the conflict, the potential effect upon him, his legal rights and the extent to which he is giving up those rights.[2]

(ii) *Responsibility to monitor performance and default* If an issuer runs into financial difficulties making default on the bonds likely, it is plainly in the interests of the bondholders that these difficulties should be identified at the earliest possible time, so that effective action can be taken before the disaster overtakes the issue. If an issue is not properly monitored it is all too likely that bondholders will only become aware of the issuer's financial problems when the issuer fails to meet its payment obligations, whether with regard to the bonds or with regard to other debts and borrowings owed by it. As has been seen, the terms of the trust deed oblige the issuer to make available to the bondholder considerable amounts of financial information as a matter of course, and the trustee is empowered to demand further information if it wishes to call for this. Since the issue is so constructed that the power of action is vested in the trustee, both with regard to collecting the information and being able to take enforcement action on behalf of the bondholders, it might be thought that there were strict requirements upon the trustee requiring full and prompt action to be taken by it. For all that the trust deed requires the issuer to notify the trustee of any act of default which occurs known to it, effective monitoring by the trustee is essential if the bondholders are to be protected. An issuer, facing financial difficulties and knowing that an act of default has occurred, is not necessarily going to meet its contractual obligations under the trust deed and inform the trustee.

The general requirement at equity is for a trustee 'to bring to the management of trust affairs the same skill and diligence which a man of ordinary prudence may be expected to use in his own concerns'.[3] However, it may well be that an even higher duty is required of a trust corporation

1 *Boardman v Phipps* [1967] 2 AC 46.

2 *Boulting v Association of Cinematograph Television and Allied Technicians* [1963] 2 QB 606 at 636; *Phipps v Boardman.*

3 *Knox v McKinnon* (1888) 13 App Cas 753.

offering a specialist service. In *Bartlett v Barclays Trust Co Ltd* [1] Brightman J. considered the position of a trust corporation carrying on the specialist business of trust management and his judgment brought little joy for these institutions. He said:

> 'A trust corporation holds itself out in its advertising literature as being above ordinary mortals. With a specialist staff of trained trust officers and managers, with ready access to financial information and specialist advice, dealing with and solving trust problems day after day, the trust corporation holds itself out, and rightly, as capable of providing an expertise which it would be unrealistic to expect and unjust to demand from the ordinary prudent man or woman who accepts, probably unpaid and sometimes reluctantly, from a sense of family duty, the burdens of trusteeship. Just as, under the law of contract, a professional person possessed of a particular skill is liable for breach of contract if he neglects to use the skill and experience which he professes so . . . a professional corporate trustee is liable for breach of trust if loss is caused to the trust fund becaue it neglects to exercise the special care and skill which it professes to have.'[2]

In that case the trustee had held nearly all the shares in a property company on behalf of the beneficiaries. The objects of the property company had been altered so that it could undertake development of an inherently speculative nature. The bank trustee had operated on the basis that the change of objects and the resulting ventures were primarily a matter for the board of the company. Their view of the trustee's function therefore had been largely passive. In the view of Brightman J they had a legal duty to be more active:

> 'It was not proper for the bank to confine itself to the receipt of the annual balance sheet and profit and loss account, detailed annual financial statements and the chairman's report and statement, and to attendance at the annual general meetings and the luncheons that followed, which were the limits of the bank's regular sources of information. Had the bank been in receipt of more regular information it would have been able to step in and stop, and ought to have stopped . . . the board embarking on the projects . . . Even without the regular flow of information which the bank ought to have had, it knew enough to put it on enquiry.[3]

In the circumstances the learned judge found that the trustee had failed

1 [1980] Ch 515.

2 at 534. In *In Re Magadi Soda Co Ltd* (1925) 41 TLR 297. Eve J held that the trustees for debenture holders are in no different position to other trustees except that, unlike many other trustees, they are remunerated. This is significant for it is the remuneration which gives rise to the higher standard of care. Such a higher standard on the part of a professional trustee has been denied in Canada—see *Fales v Canada Permanent Trust Co* [1977] 2 SCR 302 at 318, 70 DLR (3d) 257 cited by DWM Waters *Law of Trusts in Canada* (2nd edn 1984) at p. 753. In the U.S. the Uniform Probate Code (1974 ed.) S.7–302 adopts the higher duty. The decision in the *Bartlett Case* had been foreshadowed years before by the obiter remarks of Harman J in *Re Waterman's Will Trusts* [1952] 2 All ER 1054 at 1055.

3 at pp. 534 and 5.

to discharge its duty, whether judged from the standpoint of the prudent man of business, or the higher requirements attributable to a trust corporation. This general requirement would seem to contemplate an active trustee taking full steps to monitor the performance of the bonds, including collecting in and considering all financial and other information with regard to the issuer available to the trustee. This is clearly what the judge required of a trust corporation as its general duty, and would appear also correct for a prudent man of business when put on enquiry, at least where he had the skills whereby the detailed financial information available conveyed meaning to him. However, under English law the general strict equitable requirement is not supplemented by any precise statutory provisions, and the duties of the trustee in equity can be modified by the provisions of the trust. In reliance thereon it is customary for the trust deed on a bond or debenture issue to be modified, so as to remove from the trustee the positive obligation to be an active watch-dog on behalf of the 'bondholders and instead constitutes him a much more passive recipient of information. A typical modification would be as follows;

> 'The Trustee shall not be bound to give notice to any person of the execution hereof or to take any steps to ascertain whether any event has happened which causes, or which with the lapse of time and/or upon the giving of a certificate, would cause the principal amount of the securities to become repayable and, until it shall have actual knowledge or shall have express notice to the contrary, the Trustee shall be entitled to assume that no such event has happened and that the Issuer is performing all the obligations on its part contained in the Trust Deed and under the Securities'.

The effect of this is that the trustee is entitled to assume that the issuer is performing all of its obligations in the absence of knowledge or notice to the contrary. It is only when it has such knowledge or notice that a duty to investigate, and if necessary to enforce the issuer's obligations, can arise.

The problem which arises here is what is knowledge in the context of an institution. Is knowledge of each and every member of the institution to be imputed to it even though the individual with particular knowledge is only in a comparatively minor position? Equally, even with senior officials, are they to be expected to carry in their minds all the wealth of detail of the documents within the institution's care? As an example of the second issue let us suppose that the manager of a trustee bank knows that it is trustee of a bond issue, and, further, that the issuer is granting security over some of its assets to a third party. He takes no action. The bondholders allege negligence. In fact, but unbeknown to the official, the granting of the security will constitute a breach of a negative pledge clause under the terms of issue of the bonds thereby constituting an act of default. While the particular official did not know of the precise terms of the bond issue, a copy of the relevant terms was filed in the bank as part of its store of documentation. Clearly, if the official had known of the precise terms of the negative pledge clause he would have had personal knowledge of the default, and therefore all the ingredients would have come together in his own mind and negligence would be clear. Would it make any difference if the official concerned knew that the bond terms contained a negative pledge cause, did not know its precise terms, but could have ascertained the details from the bank's records? Would the bank escape liability if its official was aware of the prior issue, but not specifically aware that it contained a negative pledge clause, although the use of such a clause is usual? However, would the bank further remain liable if the particular issuer did not usually include a negative pledge clause on an issue of bonds but had done so on its most recent issue? Could the particular official rely on his knowledge of the normal practice of the issuer even though, from the bank's own records, he could ascertain that they had not been followed in the one particular issue, with the result that a breach of covenant could be effected by the issuer's action?

Of English law's answers to problems thus revealed, a general picture has been well sketched by Professor Atiyah:

> 'The principles upon which the knowledge of a servant will be imputed to his master has rarely received much discussion in cases of tort, although analogous questions arise in the law of agency, and receive more discussion there. In that branch of the law it is well settled that the knowledge of an agent will generally be imputed to his principal if the agent receives the information in connection with a transaction in which he is acting for his principal, and it is his duty to communicate that information to his principal. Although this principle has been treated as applicable to the law of tort in at least one case; it is questionable whether the second of these requirements is necessary in many tort situations'.[1]

It may well be that the law implies a general responsibility on the employee to communicate information obtained during his employment to his employer whether he sees fit in any particular case to do so or not.

The position is well illustrated by the facts of *Lloyds Bank Ltd v EB Savory & Co.*[2] In the case the respondents were a firm of London stockbrokers who had employed two dishonest clerks. Over a period of time the clerks had misappropriated a number of crossed cheques made payable to bearer drawn on the branch with which the respondents dealt. These were paid into various London branches for the credit of two other country branches, one being the account of one clerk, the second that of the wife of the other. The cheques were cleared. The bank had a rule that no cheque made payable to a firm, company or anyone in the capacity of a principal, should be accepted for the credit of the private account *inter alia* of a partner, agent, or clerk. There was a further unwritten rule that banks do not take, in payment without enquiry, cheques drawn by a firm in favour of a third party and paid in by a person other than the payee, who is known or ought to be known to be an employee of the drawing firm.

On receipt of the cheques by the various London branches into which they were paid, they were cleared through the Clearing House, and the paying in slips were sent to the country branches but with no mention

1 Atiyah *'Vicarious Liability in the Law of Torts'*, Butterworths (1967)p. 188.
2 [1832] AC 201.

of the names of the drawers. Thus while the country branches knew, or should have known, of the fact that their customer or her husband was in the employment of the respondent, they were not informed of the fact that the respondent was the drawer of the cheque. On the other hand, in the branches where the cheques were accepted, and in the clearing system, it was known that the respondent was the drawer, but not that the accounts to be credited were those of employees of the respondents.

The bank sought to avoid liability, pleading that they had acted in good faith and without negligence, and were entitled to rely on s 82 of the Bills of Exchange Act. While protection was refused by a majority of the House of Lords[1] on the ground that the bank had failed to obtain adequate references in opening the accounts in the first place, two of their lordships[2] were quite clear that the bank could not be allowed to escape liability in reliance on the fragmentation of their knowledge and a third seemed disposed to concur.[3] No less a commercial lawyer than Lord Wright said that 'the Bank cannot in virtue of the system which it voluntarily adopts, no doubt for general convenience and in the general interest of its customers, put itself in a better position than if the cheques had been paid into one branch: the Bank cannot in that way claim to have split up its knowledge'.[4] In short, the knowledge of an employee obtained in the course of his employment, will be imputed to the employer under the general principles of agency for determining liability under ordinary principles of civil law.[5]

In the U.S. there seems to be a similar willingness to impute all knowledge within the institution to the institution. Thus, in the important case of *Browning v Fidelity Trust Co*[6] trust property was released by the trustee under a power allowing such release, where there was no default on the loan. In fact, a teller in the trustee's banking department was aware of two defaults on the payment of interest. This was not known to the trustee

1 Lords Buckmaster, Warrington and Wright. Lord Blanesborough and Lord Russell dissenting would have allowed the Bank the protection of the section.
2 Lord Buckmaster and Lord Wright.
3 Lord Warrington.
4 at p. 235.
5 No precise equitable authority has been discovered. Plainly the underlying policy of the approach of English law is commercial but so is the policy behind the increased demands on the corporate trustee shown in *Bartlett v Barclays Bank.* In that case, the court treated the knowledge of two bank employees as knowledge of the bank but both were in senior positions as were the employees in *Quistclose Investments Ltd v Rolls Razors Ltd* [1970] AC 507 and *Warren Metals Ltd v Colonial Catering Co Ltd* [1975] 1 NZLR 273, two cases of constructive trusts where knowledge was important. Increasing demands on the situation of the trustee can be seen elsewhere in trust law, for no longer is it sufficient for a trustee properly to appoint an agent for issues of supervision now also arise—see *Re Lucking's Will Trusts* [1968] 1 WLR 866 and the discussion in Hanbury and Maudsley *'Modern Equity'*, 12th edn Stevens and Sons (1985) ed. Jill E. Martin, p. 549 et seq. Passive trustees have always been at risk that they will be held liable in consequence of a co-trustee's breach of trust for failing to supervise and correct the others breach.
6 250 Fed 331 (CCA 3d 1918).

department. The court held the trustee negligent, and refused to consider their departments as separate entities.

However, it may be that under U.S. law not all the knowledge of the servants of the company can be imputed to the company. The fullest discussion of the problem occurred in *Hazzard v Chase National City Bank of New York,*[1] which analyses the situation by drawing a distinction between senior and junior personnel, between knowledge obtained privately and that obtained through the work of the trustee, and between that on the files of the bank and that not so recorded. The judgment is explicit.

> 'Therefore, in the conclusions here reached, I have taken as the knowledge of the defendant . . . the sum total of all the knowledge and information which its various officers themselves had, as officers, and also the material which was contained in the various credit and investment files of the bank on the date. Whatever knowledge might have been in the possession of officers of the bank, in their individual capacities rather than as officers, should of course not be considered. Nor should every paper or letter which came to the attention of subordinate clerks. However, the bank is made up of all its officers, its board and its files. When the bank was retained and paid as a corporate trustee, when it gave its name to the trust indenture itself, all of these things were included. It was the bank, and not Mr . . . who was trustee, and for that reason, all of the component parts of the bank must be taken together . . . [2]

However, this may avail the trustee little, for it is clear that it includes the officers of the company within the English concept and extends to any official of the company exercising discretionary powers in carrying out the trustee's work, including in the *Browning* case, a teller. Further, the distinction between senior and junior employees may well not be recognised by English law.

If that is the general position is there any alteration arising from the fact that the modification of responsibility contained in the average trust deed uses the term *actual* knowledge and not merely knowledge. There seems to be no English case in point, but the actual result of the U.S. case of *Browning v Fidelity Trust Co* is instructive for in fact the trustees escaped liability because the court held that the imputed knowledge of the cashier was not the actual knowledge of the trustee department, and that therefore the trustee could rely on an exemption clause in the trust deed relieving it of liability for all but gross negligence. It follows from this that the court did not regard the matter as one of actual knowledge.

It would seem therefore that English courts may well take the view that the use of the term actual knowledge evades responsibility for knowledge imputed generally from the trustee's various employees under the principle of *Lloyds Bank v EB Savory and Co.*, and in the case of a corporation requires the actual knowledge of the directing minds of the company, or of its alter ego where appropriate, to whom the particular powers of decision have been delegated. Within the concepts used by English law it would

1 159 Misc 57, 287, NYS 541 (Sup Ct 1936).
2 287 NYS 561.

seem that only in this way could effect be given to the requirement of actuality of knowledge.

(iii) *Knowledge obtained in a fiduciary capacity* The final area of difficulty with regard to the meaning of actual knowledge arises where the trustee acquires the knowledge in a different and conflicting capacity giving rise to a problem of conflict of interest as previously discussed. The issue here is whether the trustee is bound to act on the basis of the information that it has received, or whether action only becomes necessary when knowledge comes to it in its capacity as trustee in relation to the particular trust in question. Thus, if a particular trustee is trustee of two bond issues by the same issuer, and knowledge comes into its possession in relation to trust 'A' suggesting that it should take action on behalf of the bondholders, does it have knowledge in relation to trust 'B'? Plainly, to take action on behalf of the first set of bondholders without taking parallel action on behalf of the second will be prejudicial to the holders of the second issue. On the other hand efforts taken to protect the holders of the second issue may be prejudicial to the interests of the holders of the first issue, who may find their interests better protected if they have a clear run before the other creditors of the issuer are alerted to the difficulties arising.

The problem thus identified has been but little considered in England.[1] In England the issue has been discussed in the House of Lords in passing in *Boardman v Phipps,*[2] but otherwise seems not to have disturbed judicial equanimity. Fortunately, small though the discussion in England has been it is at least instructive. First, it seems clear that information obtained in one fiduciary capacity is not, *per se,* prohibited from use in another. In *Boardman v Phipps* Lord Hodson pointed out 'that in these times corporate trustees, eg the Public Trustee and others, necessarily acquire a mass of information in their capacity of trustees for a particular client and cannot be held liable to account if knowledge so acquired enables them to operate to . . . (the) . . . advantage of trusts. Each case must depend on its own facts . . .'.[3]

Lord Upjohn gave greater thought and guidance in the matter:

> 'There is no general rule that information learnt by a trustee during the course of his duties is property of the trust and cannot be used by him. If that were to be the rule it would put the Public Trustee and other corporate trustees out of business and make it difficult for private trustees to be trustees of more than one trust. This would be the greatest possible pity for corporate trustees and others may have much information which they may initially acquire in connection with some particular trust put without prejudice to that trust can make it readily available to other trusts to the great advantage of those other trusts.
>
> The real rule is . . . that knowledge learnt by a trustee in the course of his duties as such is not in the least property of the trust and in general may be used by him for his own benefit of other trusts unless it is confidential information which is given to him (1) in circumstances which, regardless of

1 But see Rider *op. cit.:* Prime *op. cit.*
2 [1967] AC 46.
3 at p. 107.

> his position as a trustee, would make it a breach of confidence for him to communicate to anyone for it has been given to him expressly or impliedly as confidential, or (2) in a fiduciary capacity, and its use would place him in a position where his duty and his interest might possibly conflict. Let me give one or two simple examples. A, as a trustee of two settlements X and Y holding shares in the same company, learns facts as trustee of X about the company which are encouraging. In the absence of special circumstances (such, for example, that X wants to buy more shares) I can see nothing whatever which would make it improper for him to tell his co-trustees of Y who feel inclined to sell that he has information that this would be a bad thing to do. Another example: A as trustee of X learns facts that make him and his co-trustees want to sell. Clearly, he could not communicate this knowledge to his co-trustees of Y until at all events the holdings of X have been sold for there would be a plain conflict in the prices that might or might possibly be obtained.'[1]

Lord Upjohn's guidance would seem to combine principle with practical pragmatism in a very English manner. The essence of the matter would appear to be that where information is received in confidence the trustee *must* not communicate the knowledge to the second trust so long as the exclusive possession of the information is necessary for the proper protection of the interests of the first trust. Implicit in Lord Upjohn's statement are two separate ideas. First, that were a trustee to use the information for the purposes of the second trust in breach of his fiduciary duty to the first trust that action would constitute a breach of his responsibility to the beneficiaries of the first trust and be actionable by them. Second, so long as the fiduciary duty to the first trust continues the failure of a trustee subject to the duty to communicate the information to the second trust does not constitute a breach of duty to that trust, and is not actionable by the beneficiaries thereof.[2]

1 at p. 128–129.

2 Pragmatic though this approach may be, it cannot be pretended that all practical problems are avoided. The preservation of the knowledge within the first trust so long as it is needed for the proper administration of that, trust 'could well place a professional fiduciary or trustee . . . in a very difficult position with regard to the expectancies of . . . other beneficiaries. Problems of definition might also arise as to when and where the information was acquired first and in what context. This also assumes that information is unitary, complete and specific, whereas so much investment information is piecemeal, suggestive and to some extent uncertain.' Ryder *op. cit.*, p. 125. Nevertheless this approach is very necessary in modern conditions. 'Of course as in most instances where such problems are likely to arise the fiduciary is a professional person who has intentionally entered conflicting relationships for the purpose of monetary gain, one might argue that this is the concern of those who choose to court such fate. The argument ignores the facts of present day life, which increasingly requires professional expertise to administer often vast sums of capital for the benefit of large sections of the public.' Ryder *op. cit.*, p. 127.

13 Private international law considerations

INTRODUCTION

Because of their wide geographical distribution, international bonds and certificates of deposit from a single issue may give rise to an attempt to litigate them in any one of a number of jurisdictions in which they have been distributed. The same is potentially equally true of the documentation which formed the framework for the making of the issue and the trust deed or fiscal agency agreement which supports it. In order that a particular bond issue may be litigated, and the result of that litigation predicted with any degree of certainty, it will be necessary to decide three questions. First, in the courts of which jurisdictions may the individual bond issue be litigated? Secondly, in dealing with a particular bond issue the law of which legal system will the court entertaining the claim apply as governing the particular dispute? Thirdly, if a judgment is granted in the courts of a specific jurisdiction, will the courts of other jurisdictions allow enforcement of that judgment against assets within their jurisdiction? These are all matters traditionally answered by the body of substantive law of a legal system known alternatively as the conflict of laws or private international law. It should be emphasised that the questions are separate and distinct. The mere fact that the courts of a particular legal system will entertain jurisdiction in a particular action does not necessarily mean that they will apply the substantive rules of their own system of law in resolving the dispute. Nor does it mean that a judgment of a particular jurisdiction will be enforceable in a second jurisdiction even if made on the basis of the law of the second jurisdiction. However, all questions fall to be determined by a legal system applying its particular conflict of laws rules.

It should be clearly understood from the outset that the term legal system is carefully chosen in preference to the laws of a country. Countries do not necessarily have a unified legal system, either because they were planned on a federal basis from their inception, as in the case of the U.S. where there is a system of federal law, but where each constituent state also has its own individual body of law representing a separate legal system, or because of the historical evolution of the nation as in the case of the U.K. where, while England and Wales share a common legal system, Scotland and Northern Ireland each have separate and distinct systems. Whenever there is an issue as to which legal system is the appropriate one to determine a particular dispute there is a conflict of laws issue to be determined, and it matters not that the competing legal systems are in separate nations or within one particular nation.

It might have been thought that the system of conflicts of law would have been developed on a truly international basis so that all legal systems applied the same body of law in determining these issues, with the result that wherever issues of jurisdiction enforcement and applicable law are raised the result would be uniformly the same, the courts of only one legal jurisdiction would be entitled to hear the dispute, and only one predictable body of law applied to it. Unfortunately, such a tidy result does not obtain in practice, and each legal system has its own individual body of private international law which it applies, and which may radically differ from others. Further, there is a difficulty of categorisation. The body of rules applicable will fall to be determined within any system of private international law on differing bases, depending upon whether the particular dispute is categorised for instance as contract, tort, or a matter of procedure. Since legal systems have developed differently and based their development upon differing concepts, categorisation within systems varies from one to another. The result is an untidy tangle, on which simplification and unification can necessarily only be imposed slowly, because of the depth of the underlying obstacles and the sheet complexity of the overall mass.

Nor would a unified body of law resolve all the difficulties for the lawyer in ascertaining the law governing a particular transaction or dispute. Clearly, identifying a specific system of law as the one governing the dispute is but a beginning where that body of law is different to that in which the lawyer has been trained. The second necessary process then to be undertaken is the ascertainment of the content of the appropriate law. A third stage in the process is to prove the content of that law where it is not the same law as the law of the courts having jurisdiction; all this constitutes considerable difficulty in an internationally complex transaction, where the judge hearing the matter might well be felt to have enough difficulties without having to come to terms with unknown concepts and rules from a legal system with which he is not familiar.

GOVERNING LAW — CHOICE OF LAW CLAUSES

As has been seen widespread use is made in international bond transactions of clauses specifying a particular system of law as governing contractual disputes between the parties. These are commonly inserted not only in the bond terms themselves, but also in the syndicate documentation and the trust deed or fiscal agency agreement. Clearly, it is desirable that a system of law should be chosen which has a developed body of commercial law, so that the legal results of commercial disputes are predictable. Further, it is desirable that the system selected and the courts which will administer it should be felt to be neutral so that the parties to any contract, including in the case of bonds the investors, can have confidence in it. Practice on the international bond market indicates a clear preference in choosing the system of law of the place where the issue is centred — on the London market, English law. This is perhaps inevitable in a system of distribution which is so institution biased. Inevitably, institutions feel most confident with systems of law with which they are familiar, and which have been habitually applied to financial transactions around which their experience has been built. Further, the expense of a large scale investigation of the provisions of a foreign legal system with which the institutions are not familiar is thereby avoided.

Under English law the parties to a contract are entitled to specify the proper law of the contract and where this is done the English courts will give effect to the parties' choice.[1] Nor is it fatal that the system of law chosen has no obvious contact with the transaction to which it is applied.[2] Strong commercial reasons can be advanced in support of this.

> In international transactions, particularly on commodity markets where the same shipment of goods may be bought and sold many times before delivery of the actual goods to the last buyer, it is of great commercial convenience that all contracts relating to such sales should be subject to the same proper law irrespective of the place of shipment or discharge, the residence or nationality of the parties, or the place where the contract was made.[3]

Nor are the legitimate interests of the parties necessarily limited to obtaining conformity in interconnecting transactions. It is a perfectly reasonable aspiration of the parties to wish to subject their transaction to a neutral and well known legal system which has their confidence. Indeed, it must be borne in mind that not all legal systems have a developed and sophisticated

1 *Miller and Partners Ltd v Whitworth Street Estate Ltd* 1970] AC 583.

2 *Vita Food Products Inc v Unus Shipping Co Ltd* [1939] AC 277 *per* Lord Wright at p. 291. In *Tzorztis v Monark Line A/B* [1968] 1 WLR 406 Lord Denning MR stated that an express clause should be 'conclusive in the absence of some public policy to the contrary' (at p. 411).

3 *Compagnie d'Armement Maritime SA v Cie Tunisienne de Navigation SA* [1971] AC 572 *per* Lord Diplock at p. 609. It is hardly surprising that deliberate choice of law should be of particular benefit to international transactions since it arises directly from the proper law of the contract concept developed by the English courts on abandoning the old rule that a contract was governed by the law of the place where it was made in the middle of the last century.
Abandonment was in fact a reaction to changing patterns of international trade in the nineteenth century. 'Until the beginning of that century merchants had owned the ships carrying their goods and they themselves or their agents had bought and sold their cargoes in the ports. When at about 1840 international trade increased rapidly, shipping had already become a separate trade; the merchants and their agents accompanied the ships less often and contracts of sale were not concluded so frequently as before at the place where the goods were loaded and unloaded. From 1850 onwards postal and telegraphic services were developed for the convenience of international trade, and the activities of banks also increased through the use of a new form of credit. All this broke up the unity of place and time in the making and performance of contracts . . . The intention of the parties took over the role which the place of contracting had occupied.' Lando, *Contracts*, The International Encyclopedia of Comparative Law,
Private International Law Tubingen: JCB Mohr (Paul Siebeck) 1971 – Vol 8 Chapter 24, p. 7. Because of this a great English jurist has been able truthfully to write:-
'The English doctrine of the proper law is one of the outstanding contributions made by English lawyers to the general science of the conflict of laws' — Morris *The Conflict of Laws* (1980) 2nd edn Sweet and Maxwell p. 225.

body of commercial law of their own. However, a more complex issue is whether a choice of English law will be recognised in other jurisdictions if litigation arises there.

Fortunately, English law is not alone in recognising party autonomy in selecting a proper law to govern their contractual obligations, at least where those obligations are truly international in character. Where the parties have made an express choice of a system of law the courts of most jurisdictions will give effect to it. Thus France, Belgium, Holland, West Germany, Switzerland, Scandinavia, the Socialist countries of eastern Europe, Italy, Grece, India, Israel, Japan, Thailand and Taiwan, and the countries of the Spanish and Portuguese speaking world all recognise party autonomy in such circumstances.[1] It has thus been submitted that the phenomenon is 'a general principle of law recognised by civilized nations' within article 38 of the Statute of the International Court of Justice.[2] Certainly, the principle was honoured by the International Court of Justice in the Serbian and Brazilian loans cases.[3]

GOVERNING LAW IN THE ABSENCE OF A CHOICE OF LAW CLAUSE

While the inclusion of a choice of law clause in a bond issue and the pertinent documents is the norm, it is by no means a universal practice. In the case of international bond issues the problem is occasionally posed of sovereign borrowers who, possibly because of a constitutional prohibition but more frequently because of considerations of national prestige, are unwilling to submit to the issuer's own system of law because of the possible detriment to investors if subsequently the issuer was to use its power to amend its own laws, as by introducing a lawful abrogation of, or moratorium upon, its obligations. The result is an impasse which is compromised by the choice of law issue being ignored and no provision being inserted in the documentation. In such a situation the next step applied by the English courts is to try to see whether they can infer any common intention of the parties on the point. The intention is to be inferred from the terms and nature of the contract, and from the general circumstances of the case . . .[4] It has been stated judicially that the only certain guide is to be found in applying sound ideas of business convenience and sense to the language of the contract itself, with a view to discovering from it the true intention of the parties.[5]

Finally, if the intention of the parties cannot be deduced the contract will be held to be governed 'by the system of law with which the transaction

1 See Lando *op cit.* pp. 14–33
2 Lando *op. cit.* p. 33
3 ICJ 12 July 1929, Clunet 1929 977. See also the international arbitration decision *Saudi Arabia v Arabia Oil Co (Aramco)* (1963) 27 ILR 117, 165 ss.
4 Dicey and Morris *The Conflict of Laws* (1987) 11th edn at p. 1182 rule 45. Sub-Rule 2.
5 *Jacobs v Credit Lyonnais* (1884) 12 QBD 589 at p. 601.

has its closest and most real connection'.[1] Given that the intention of the parties when not expressly stated is to be found primarily by objective assessment, it may be thought that the addition of a third rule for objective decision is unnecessary. The implied intention approach may be said to ask what a reasonable person would take the parties to have intended to have chosen in fact; the closest and most real connection places the responsibility on the court (the omnipresent reasonable person) to impute an intention or to determine for the parties what is the proper law which, as just and reasonable persons, they ought to or would have intended if they had thought about the question when they made the contract.'[2] Seen in this light the concepts are very close, the significant difference being that the second frankly recognises that often the parties will have had no real ascertainable intention because they never gave thought to the issue when contracting. The degree of overlap is potentially enormous. For instance, the courts have shown a strong tendency to view as a weighty, and often decisive, factor in their determination provisions giving an exclusive jurisdiction to the English courts or to English arbitrators in deciding that English law should be applied.[3] This approach has an undoubted convenience in that it leaves the tribunal with jurisdiction applying its own system of law with which it is familiar. It can, however, be rationalised either as showing by implication the intention of the parties that the law of the system to which jurisdiction was granted was to apply, or alternatively as saying that the conferral of jurisdiction gave the transaction its closest and most real connection with the law of the country on which jurisdiction was conferred. The principal effect of the division into two rules does, however, have some practical importance, because the search for the implied intention of the parties enables the terminology of the contract to be considered, which may indicate that the parties had in mind a particular legal system.[4] Further, it has been authoritatively laid down that it is only where the court is unable to ascertain an implied choice by the parties under the first branch of the rule that enquiry as to the system of law with which the contract is most closely connected should be commenced.[5] As an objective connecting factor the place of

1 Dicey and Morris *op. cit.* at p. 769 rule 3; *The Assunzione* [1954] 150; *Whitworth Street Estates Ltd v James Miller and Partners Ltd* [1970] AC 583; *Coast Lines Ltd v Hudig and Veder Chartering NV* [1972] 2 QB 34.

2 *Mount Albert Borough Council v Australasian etc. Assurance Society Ltd* [1938] AC 224, 240 PC. See also *The Assunzione* [1954] 150; *NV Handel Maatschappij J. Smits v English Exporters Ltd* [1955] 2 Lloyd's Rep 317.

3 *Re United Railways of the Havana and Regla Warehouses Ltd* [1960]Ch 52; *Hamlyn v Talisker Distillery* [1894] AC 202; *Spurrier v la Cloche* [1902] AC 446; *NV Kwik Hoo Tong Handel Maatschappij v James Finlay & Co* [1927] AC 604. Jurisdiction is, however, only a strong indication of the proper law and is not necessarily decisive: *Compagnie Tunisienne de Navigation SA v Compagnie d'Armement Maritime SA* [1971] AC 572,

4 *The Industrie* [1894] P. 58; *Rossano v Manufacturers Life Insurance Co* [1963] 2 QB 332; *Re International Trustee for the Protection of Bondholders A/G v R.* [1937] AC 500.

5 *Amin Rasheed Corpn v Kuwait Insurance* [1984] AC 50 at p. 61.

performance is given considerable weight, but this is of little help in an international bond issue, where the performance of the contract (namely the payment of the bonds) is to take place in a wide range of jurisdictions.

Like English law most other developed systems will give effect to the tacit choice of the parties where the parties have failed to state this expressly, but it can be clearly inferred from the surrounding circumstances and the contractual document itself. Thus, the use of drafting techniques or legal terms characteristic of a particular system of law may lead to the courts inferring the choice of that system. A similar inference may often be drawn from a clause submitting the contract to the jurisdiction of the courts of a particular jurisdiction or providing for arbitration at a place within a particular state or country.[1]

In the absence of an effective choice of law by the parties the legal systems of the world display a bewildering variety of approaches in fixing the system of law which shall govern the contract.[2] Some (eg Belgium) will select the system which they feel that the parties would have selected had they given thought to the matter. Others will select the system with which the court feels that the contract is most closely connected (eg France, the Netherlands, England, Scandinavia, Switzerland, Czechoslovakia, and, largely, the U.S. and Greece.) Yet others will impose a rigid rule usually applying the law of the place of contracting (eg Austria, Italy, Portugal, Societ Union, Taiwan, Iran, Japan, Zaire, Brazil, Costa Rica, Peru) sometimes immediately, or alternatively as a last resort, where presumptions arising from case law or statute do not apply to the particular conflicts issue (eg Poland, East Germany, Spain). Many of those jurisdictions with a flexible system may be influenced by the justice of the particular case in their ultimate decision, although this tends to occur infrequently in a truly transnational situation such as an international bond issue. Flexible systems also show a definite tendency to link the transaction to the *lex fori* but again this phenomenon appears to be rare in truly transnational contracts.[3]

1 Lando *op. cit.* p. 46–51.

2 If the EEC Convention on the Law Applicable to Contractual Obligations is implemented a widespread revision of the laws applicable to the ascertainment of the proper law of the contract throughout the EEC will be occasioned. In the absence of the choice of the parties either specifically expressed or *demonstrated with reasonable certainty* by the terms of the contract or the circumstances of the case the proper law will fall in general to be determined by ascertaining which party is to effect the contractual performance most characteristic of the contract (eg, in a contract for the sale of goods, the seller) and applying the law of his jurisdiction. This Convention has, however, been subject to massive criticism by English commentators, see eg Collins (1976) 25 ICLQ 35; Diamond (1979) 32 CLR 155; Mann (1983) 32 ICLQ 265; also both Collins and North in *Contract Conflicts*, (ed. North), North Holland Pub. Co. (1982) p. 371. However, see the spirited and thought-provoking defence of Jaffey (1984) 33 ICLQ 531.

3 The approaches of the various legal systems of the world to this issue are carefully considered by Lando *op. cit.* pp. 51–93, a study notable as much for the distinguished evaluation of the material used (comparative law is made to fulfil its function of comparing) as for the width of the scholarship displayed.

THE CURRENCY OF CONTRACTUAL DAMAGES IN THE ENGLISH CONFLICT OF LAWS

The various contracts and documents underlying an issue may impose obligations on the parties which are breached and which, therefore, give rise to an award of damages. Given the wide distribution of the bonds, issues may arise as to the currency in which the damages are to be awarded. In some cases the parties may have expressly or by implication fixed the money of account by which the obligation is to be measured. In bond issues this principle covers the payment obligation of the issuer which is discussed in Chapter 10. However, where breach occurs of some other contractual obligation, the currency in which the obligation is to be measured will not have been contemplated by parties at all.

Damages for breach of contract fall to be determined under the proper law of the contract. Where the proper law is English law the principles applicable were laid down by Lord Wilberforce in *The Folias*.[1] First, *prima facie*, a judgment should be given in the currency designated in the contract either expressly or implied to be the money of account,[2] for in such a case the contract itself indicated the intention of the parties as to the currency in which damages for its breach should be payable. However, where the parties' intention as to the currency in which damages for breach should be expressed cannot be deduced from the contract, damages should be given in the currency in which the loss 'was felt by the plaintiff' as this most truly expresses his loss. This will usually be the plaintiff's own currency rather than the currency in which the loss first arose. In *The Folias* the French charterers of a ship sued the shipowner for damages. In circumstances for which the shipowners were liable the cargo had arrived at its destination damaged and the French charterers had had to pay a sum of money in Brazilian cruzeiros which of necessity they had purchased with French francs. Their real loss had, therefore, been in French francs expended to discharge their own contractual commitment and not the Brazilian cruzeiros which had been used to make payment. Accordingly, judgment was given in French francs.

NEGOTIATION IN THE ENGLISH CONFLICT OF LAWS

While the proper law of the obligation will determine most issues arising from the contract represented by the bonds, questions of negotiation fall within a separate and distinct branch of the law. If A negotiates his bond to B questions may arise as to whether the negotiation is effective to transfer the rights represented by the obligation to B so that B can give a good discharge to the issuer.

1 [1979] A.C. 685. See also *Food Corpn of India v Carras (Helles) Ltd* (*The Dione*) [1980] 2 Lloyd's Rep 577; *Jean Kraut AG v Albany Fabrics* [1979] QB 182.

2 For identification of the money of account and discussion of the payment obligation itself — an obligation to pay a *liquidated* amount, see ch 10 *ante*.

From the point of view of people handling negotiable instruments the claims and rights represented by the instrument are fully represented by the tangible document which they actually handle, and which must ultimately be produced for payment to be made. The instrument is seen essentially as a chattel and is so dealt with by passing from hand to hand. In English conflict of laws this practical commonsense approach is applied, and issues of negotiation are decided according to the law of the place where negotiation took place, which is necessarily where the instrument was at the time of delivery.[1] A similar result appears to apply in the U.S.A.[2]

Applying these principles to concrete situations capable of arising, one may take the following situation. Alan holds an international bond, which is obtained from him by fraud in England by Brian after its maturity date for redemption has passed. Brian flies to Ireland and transfers it to Colin who acts in good faith and gives valuable consideration. Colin travels to Vienna and transfers the bond to Dieter who acts in good faith and for valuable consideration. The bond is governed by Luxembourg law. Alan sues Dieter for the bond in the English courts.

The first issue for the English courts to consider is whether Brian obtained a good title in England when Alan was induced by fraud to transfer the bond to him. In deciding this the English courts will apply English law not as the *lex fori* or the law of the obligation of the bond, but as the law of the place where the bond was transferred. If Brian obtained a good title under English law the sole remaining questions are whether the transfer to Colin and Dieter were valid under Irish and Austrian law respectively. If so Alan's action will fail.

If, however, under English law Brian did not obtain a good title the English courts will have to consider not merely whether the transfers to Colin and Dieter were *in themselves valid* between the parties under the appropriate systems of law but what the effect of the transfers was since *ex hypothesi* neither Brian nor consequently Colin would have a title to transfer in respect of the Bond, and the *nemo dat* rule would apply. Thus, on the basis that Brian did not obtain a good title under English law, the question would be what effect does Irish law give to the transfer of a matured bond to which the transferor has no title? The defect would only be overcome if under Irish law Colin became a holder in due course capable of taking free from defects of title. If a transfer of a matured bond is incapable of conferring this status Colin would obtain no title. In that situation the effect of the transfer to Dieter under Austrian law would have to be considered. If under Austrian law Dieter became a holder in due course the defect would be cured and Alan would fail in his action.

TORT ISSUES IN THE CONFLICT OF LAWS

Inevitably tort issues with regard to international bond sales are capable of being extremely complex. The relevant torts likely to be committed are

1 *Alcock v Smith* [1892] 1 Ch 238; *Embericos v Anglo-Austrian Bank* [1904] 2 KB 870; affd [1905] 1 KB 677.

2 Second Restatement *Conflict of Laws* para. 216.

deceit and negligent misrepresentation. If bonds are sold in twenty-five different jurisdictions as a result of a prospectus printed in a twenty-sixth jurisdiction, it is difficult to see how one single system of law can be selected in priority to all others to determine the various tortious claims which are likely to result. Whereas contracts are carefully pre-planned operations and, as such, capable of judicious conflict avoidance by use of a choice of law and jurisdiction clauses, tort claims all too frequently occupy the traditional position of the illegitimate child being not merely little loved but unplanned and unforeseen.

The position is further complicated by the fact that there is little uniformity of approach of the courts of different jurisdictions in deciding what law should be applied to any particular contractual situation. Whereas in the field of conflict of laws pertaining to contracts English law has given to international jurisprudence the widely accepted and versatile concept of the proper law of the contract, no such simple base can be found in the field of tort.

Further, most jurisdictions demonstrate a remarkable lack of authority as to the principles involved. The reasons and effects have been clearly identified:

There are essentially two different approaches to the problem.

1. Law of the place of the commission of the tort (lex loci delicti)

Under this approach, which historically has been a much favoured one, the governing law is that of the place where the event occurred which is alleged to be a tortious interference with the plaintiff's rights. The arguments in favour of this approach are strong. First, it fixes a particular system of law and eliminates thereby any opportunity to the plaintiff to obtain a remedy not otherwise available by forum shopping. Secondly, in general, it is clearly reasonable that the liabilities to be attached to conduct should be judged by the standards of the place where it is committed. Against this it has been pointed out that in modern circumstances the place where a tort occurs is simply fortuitous, and, further, in particular circumstances, there may be no real and substantial connection between the tort and the place where it occurs. This has proved to be particularly true of the potential liability of a driver to his passenger when the journey has started in one jurisdiction, of which both parties are nationals, and the accident has occurred in another jurisdiction, with which they have no connection, but through which they were travelling at the time. Similarly, with international securities a sale of securities between two Englishmen in Switzerland, while making a connection at Basle airport to return to London, would have only the most artificial connection with Switzerland if the vendor was guilty of a misrepresentation to the purchaser.[1]

Whatever the limitations of the *lex loci delicti* as the means of resolving the conflicts issue it is nevertheless the basis of most civil law systems. Thus it is the solution adopted in Austria and Switzerland, France, Belgium,

1 Adaptation of a hypothetical example given by Wood *Law and Practice of International Finance* Sweet and Maxwell p. 213.

Holland, Spain and through South America, as well as the Scandinavian countries although the proper law of the tort approach does show some support in Norway.[1]

2. The proper law of the tort

The final possibility is the creation of an artificial concept parallel to the proper law of the contract namely the proper law of the tort. This has been seized on in the U.S., where the previously applicable solution of the application of the *lex loci delicti*[2] has been replaced by this new concept. The American Law Institute's Restatements (2nd) of the Conflict of Laws, s 145[3] embodies the central expression of this by providing that 'the rights and liabilities of the parties with respect to an issue in tort are determined by the local law of the state which, as to that issue, has the most significant relationship to the occurrence and the parties'. Certain factors are listed to be taken into account in determining the significance of the relationships of the applicable systems of law namely (1) the place where the injury occurred; (2) the place where the conduct causing the injury occurred; (3) the domicile, nationality, place of incorporation and place of business of the parties; (4) and the place where the relationship, if any, between the parties is centred.

Inevitably, the inclusion of this test in the prestigious Restatement has led to its widespread adoption by American courts, particularly with regard to motor accidents where one at least of the vehicles involved has been a stranger to the state in which the accident actually occurred. The underlying concept is sophisticated and flexible to enable just decisions to be arrived at, and is closely analagous to the concept of the proper law of the contract to which it is clearly related. It has, however, been criticised, with some justification, on the ground that it is unpredictable, and the unpredictability of its effect cannot be avoided by the participants as the parties to a contract can bring certainty to their relations by the inclusion of a choice of law clause.[4]

Influence of the lex fori

Even where the law applied by a legal system is that of the proper law of the tort or the *lex loci delicti*, the *lex fori* often retains a considerable influence upon the resolution of a conflicts problem in tort matters. First,

1 Stromholm *Intentional Torts* The International Encyclopedia of Comparative Law, Private International Law, JCB Mohr (Paul Siebeck), Tubingen (1980) Vol. 8, Chapter 33, pp. 6–8.

2 See American Law Institute *First Restatement of the Conflict of Laws* (1934).

3 This approach rejects the approach of the First Restatement of the Conflict of Laws (1934) which by s 378 provided that 'the law of the place of the wrong determines whether a person has sustained a legal injury'. In general the tortious nature of the alleged tortfeasor's acts was to be decided by reference to the law of the state where the last event had occurred necessary to complete the alleged tort.

4 *Boys v Chaplin* [1971] AC 356. *per* Lord Hodson at p. 377–8 *per* Lord Wilberforce at p. 391.

the initial categorisation of the problem as one of tort is usually undertaken by the *lex fori* applying its own law.[1] Thus, in civil law countries fraudulent misrepresentation inducing a contract are taken to be subject to the law governing the essential validity of that contract.[2] Secondly, where the *lex fori* under its own conflict rules applies the *lex loci delecti*, the location of the tort is usually regarded as a matter for the *lex fori*.[3] This is a matter of some significance in transnational securities issues. If a prospectus containing a misrepresentation is issued in country A, and in reliance thereon investors in countries B and C purchase securities and bring actions in countries D and E respectively, the courts of D and E will determine whether the action is properly tortious or contractual according to their own rules as *lex fori*. Further, those courts if applying the *lex loci delicti* will apply their own laws in deciding where the tort is located. Thus, if the courts of D take the view that the tort is located where the prospectus was issued, the liability of the issuer will be decided by the application of the tort laws of country A. On the other hand, if the courts of E take the view that the tort is located in C, where the misrepresentation was acted upon, the courts of E will apply the tort of law C in deciding liability. Therefore the commission of the same act by an issuer can lead to the application of different laws in jurisdictions applying the *lex loci delicti*, depending on the different countries in which the act has an effect, and whether the *lex fori* regard the act as completed by the commission of the act or only by the act causing an effect (the purchase of the securities).

English law

If U.S. law has embarked upon an innovative attempt to evolve practical solutions from a potentially fruitful new concept, the English conflict of law rules with regard to tortious liability probably embody all three of the principles already discussed. Propositions must be modified with the deliberate use of ambivalent terms such as probable because the present state of the law is an undoubted blot upon our jurisprudence, not merely because of the conservatism of the content but also because of its uncertainty and obscurity of the rules. The uncertainty is a direct consequence of the content, because so restrictive is the approach of the English judges in dealing with tortious situations with a foreign element that foreign law is only likely to be pleaded by a defendant to reduce or eliminate a liability, rather than by a plaintiff in establishing one. The consequence has been to worsen the factor already noted, tending to an inevitable dearth of authority. Unfortunately, when the issue finally reached the House of Lords so that an authoritative declaration of English principles could be made in *Boys v Chaplin*,[4] while their Lordships could unite in a fundamentally

1 Stromholm *op. cit* p. 4.
2 Stromholm *op. cit.* p. 19 citing Batiffol and Lagarde *Droit international* 11 (ed 5 Paris) (1971) no. 596; Raape *Internationales Privatrecht* (ed 5 Berlin and Frankfurt) (1961)
3 ibid, p. 492.
4 [1971] AC 356.

restrictive approach, they could not agree sufficiently in their various speeches to enable clear and undoubted principles to be enunciated.[1] It would appear probable that to be actionable in English courts the wrong complained of must be actionable under English law (the *lex fori*) *and* under the law of the place where it was committed (the *lex loci delicti*).[2]

The English approach has been widely adopted in those parts of the Commonwealth with a common law system and even, somewhat surprisingly, in Quebec.[3]

THE CURRENCY OF DAMAGES IN TORT UNDER ENGLISH LAW

As with contractual liabilities arising from international transactions so tortious liabilities give rise to issues as to which currency a court dealing with the issue should select for its award. This should be determined under the system of law properly applicable to the tort. Originally, under English law, damages arising from tort should be determined in the currency of the place where the loss was suffered.[4] A similar rule obtains in Germany.[5] More recently, in England, a similar approach to that used with regard to unliquidated damages for breach of contract was applied to damages in relation to tort by Lord Wilberforce in *The Despina R.*[6] The principle applicable is that damages should be given in the currency in which the loss was effectively felt or borne by the plaintiff, rather than the currency or currencies in which it was immediately sustained. In that case the costs of repair had been initially incurred in various currencies. However, the principal place of business of the managing agents of the plaintiff was New York, and the payments had been made by drawing on their U.S. dollar account in that jurisdiction. Judgment was accordingly given in U.S.

1 It might even be doubted whether the case does have a *ratio decidendi*2. See the discussions by North and Webb (1970) 19 ICLQ 24 and Karsten (1970) 19 ICLQ 35.

2 This seems the most likely *ratio* and is the one generally accepted.

3 Stromholm *op. cit.* pp. 5 and 6. In Civil Law jurisdictions an interesting parallel with English law can be found in German law where the basic principle is the continental one of the *lex loci delicti*. However, this is modified by a requirement that where a claim exists against a German national the alleged tort must be actionable under both German law and the *lex loci delicti*. Further actions in tort between German nationals will be decided according to German law wherever committed.
The identification of the place of the wrong has been put on a broad footing to include every place where the tort has an impact, thus leaving the injured party to select which system of law he wishes to choose from those available. In the case of publication of a misleading prospectus in a wide range of jurisdictions, the range would thus be wide indeed in the event of the issuer's *act being categorised as tortious in nature.*

4 *The Canadian Transport* (1932) 43 Ll L Rep 409.

5 B G H 6 Nov 1951 B G HZ 3, 321 cited Van Hecke *Currency* The International Encyclopedia of Comparative Law, Private International Law, Tubingen: JCB Mohr (Paul Siebeck) (1971) — Vol 8, Chap 36.

6 [1979] AC 685; *Hoffmann v Sofaer* [1982] 1 WLR 1350.

dollars. However, it should be emphasised that the principle is flexible, and Lord Wilberforce contemplated that circumstances could arise in which the plaintiff would be unable to show that in the normal course of events it would be contemplated that he would use the currency in which he normally conducted his business operations, and, in such a case, his loss would be felt in the currency in which it immediately arose, and consequently in those circumstances judgment would be given in that currency. The position in tort thus now closely parallels the principles applicable to the granting of damages in contractual matters.[1]

JURISDICTION

Merely because the parties to a transaction have selected a particular system of law as governing that transaction does not mean that the courts of the chosen system shall have, or shall have exclusively, jurisdiction to hear any dispute arising between the parties. The applicable law and the jurisdiction for trial are two entirely separate matters in the conflict of laws, and are uniformly treated as such. Whether or not the courts of a particular legal system have jurisdiction is a matter for the *lex fori* to decide for itself in accordance with its own substantive rules of private international law.

It may be that an investigation of those substantive rules will indicate that the courts of more than one jurisdiction will entertain the proceedings thereby giving the potential plaintiff a choice of venue for his action. In such circumstances a plaintiff will be likely to give serious consideration to practical financial considerations. In particular, he will be concerned that any judgment eventually obtained should be effective. To this end he will be particularly interested in whether the defendant has assets in any of the available jurisdictions against which, if necessary, execution can be levied. Further, he will tend to favour any jurisdiction in which assets of the defendant are situate, and where the courts of that jurisdiction have a summary procedure available to him whereby the defendant's assets can be secured against removal to another jurisdiction, if removal appears at all likely, pending the outcome of the proceedings. Also the plaintiff will be anxious that the courts of the jurisdiction eventually chosen will give him a fair hearing and that its machinery of justice should be sophisticated, prompt and effective. In addition, he will be interested in choosing a jurisdiction which is geographically convenient to himself and his witnesses, in which his evidence can be fully deployed without unnecessary expense, and in which the resultant expense is minimised so far as this is consistent with total development of his case. Finally, if no forum is available in which the defendant has assets, the plaintiff will be concerned at least to use a forum, a judgment of which will be recognised and enforced in a jurisdiction where the defendant's assets lie.

1 *ante* p. 259.

SUBMISSION TO JURISDICTION CLAUSE

It is usual for the issuer and its advisers to give active consideration to these issues before marketing the issue as the marketability of the securities will often be linked to the perception of the investors and their advisers of the effectiveness of the enforcement procedures in the event that the bond terms are breached. It is therefore usual that the bond terms should include a clause conferring jurisdiction on the courts of some specified legal system or legal systems within whose territorial ambit the bonds will be sold.[1] Similar care is usually taken to include a similar choice of jurisdiction clause in the five syndicate agreements. In both cases the clauses are usually specified as being non-exclusive, so that a litigant is free to bring his action either in the courts of the specified jurisdiction or in the courts of any other legal system which will accept jurisdiction under its own individual rules of private international law. In such a situation there can be little doubt that the courts of most developed legal systems will accept jurisdiction on the basis of a non-exclusive choice of jurisdiction clause if so nominated.[2] Such a clause will also be given effect under European Community law with regard to truly international transactions such as international bond distributions.[3]

As most jurisdictions will therefore endeavour to give effect to a choice of forum clause on what basis can such a clause be successfully attacked? In general terms one of the most promising avenues of attack in many jurisdictions would be that the clause was never really agreed by both parties,

1 It is not usual that all jurisdictions within which the bonds are to be sold will be covered.

2 See Delaume *Transnational Contracts* Oceana Pubs Inc, Dobbs Ferry New York (1983) Chapter 6. The theoretical basis of the approach of the developed legal systems of the world is that by their contractual choice the parties have submitted to the jurisdiction of the designated forum. A similar result is obtained if a defendant participates in litigation within a non-designated jurisdiction after a dispute has arisen other than to deny the jurisdiction of the courts.

3 Article 17. However, under Community law the express conferral of jurisdiction is stated to be exclusive and will be so treated by the courts of the Community members.

Under U.S. law, restrictions have customarily been imposed on granting effect to an express choice of law clause. Traditionally the courts insist that the transaction giving rise to the cause of action and the parties should have sufficient connection (minimum contacts) with the jurisdiction to warrant the U.S. court accepting jurisdiction even if a purely technical case has been made out. *Companie de Astral SA v Boston Metals Co* 205 Md 237, 107 A 2d 357 (1954) cert denied 348 US 943, 75 SG 365, 99 L Ed 738 (1955); *Longines Wittnaver Co v Barnes Reinecke* 15 NY 2d 443, 261 NYS 2d 8 (1965), cert denied 382 US 905, 86 S Ct 241, 15 L Ed 2d 158 (1965); *Standard Fitting Co v Sapag SA* 448 F Supp 426 (WDLa 1977). However, it must be admitted that in many instances the

as so often the clause is included in a standard form contract bearing all the hallmarks of a contract of adhesion. In this connection, a choice of forum clause in a bond issue would appear to be a typical example for the inclusion of such clauses is negotiated by the issuer and the promoting syndicate, with the bondholders being presented with a take it or leave it situation. Nevertheless, as has been noted by one eminent writer 'cases

1 minimum contacts required have been few and with some courts within the wide U.S. jurisdiction a defendant seeking to avoid jurisdiction would rely on the due process requirements only as a last resort born of utter desperation. *McGee v International Life Assurance Co*, 355 US 220, 78 St Ct 199, 2 L Ed 2d 223 (1957); *Scovill Manufacturing Co v Dateline Electric Co* 461 F 2d 897 (7th Cir 1972); *Microelectronic Systems Corpn v Bambergers* 434 F Supp 168 (E.D. Mich. S.D. 1977); *Transatlantic Cement Inc v Lambert Frères et Cie* 448 F Supp 816; *Tamori v Bache and Co Lebanon SAL* 431 F Supp 1226 (N.D.Ill. 1977) aff'd 565 F2d. 1194 (7th Cir 1977) cert. denied 98 S. Ct 1450 discussed Delaume *op. cit.* chapter 7. pp. 37–43. Thus where there has been an express submission to jurisdiction there will always be a residual doubt as to the effectiveness of the submission, for a court may refuse jurisdiction on the ground of either *forum non conceniens* or by finding that the minimum contacts are not available.

It was felt that the resultant unpredictability was adverse to the development of New York as an international financial centre where progress could best be maintained as in England by dealing with clauses which had not greater connection with New York than the choice of its laws as governing a contract and the submission to its courts. Consequently the law of New York was reformed in 1984 with regard to choice of forum as well as choice of law. As a consequence of this reform contained in s 5–1402 of the New York General Obligations Law any person may maintain an action or proceeding against a foreign corpoiration, non-resident or foreign state where the action or proceeding arises out of or relates to any contract, agreement or undertaking for which a choice of New York law has been made in whole or in part provided that two conditions are fulfilled. Firstly the contract agreement or undertaking (which may be contingent) must be made in consideration of, or relate to an obligation arising out of, a transaction covering in the aggregate not less than one million dollars. Secondly it must contain a provision or provisions whereby the proposed defendant agrees to submit to the jurisdiction of the courts of New York.

Where the conditions of applicability are satisfied the action can be maintained notwithstanding any provision in any Act purporting to limit or affect the right of any person to maintain an action or proceeding, eg Business Corporation Law 314; Banking Law s 200(b).

The result of the amendments of New York law is that the parties of an International financial transaction including a bond issue or issue of certificates of deposit now have substantial autonomy in selecting the law and courts of New York to govern their transaction without their efforts being frustrated by lack of distribution in the U.S. See G Penn and T Cashel 'Choice of Law Clauses under English and New York Law' [1986] JBL Part I p. 333 part II p. 497; part III [1987] JBL p. 238.

are few in which a bondholder has challenged, usually without success, the binding character of such a clause'.[1] The reason for his is probably a combination of the wide publicity given to choice of forum clauses in the documentation before issue,[2] coupled with the perceived practical advantages to both issuers and bondholder of the arrangement. Both sides benefit from the certainty that proceedings can be brought within the permitted fora. Issues of interpretation of choice of jurisdiction clauses do arise but in general can be disposed of easily. Often a forum or fora are specified as being available to both parties with one party (often the bondholders) being given the option to sue in alternative fora if they so elect. Provided that the drafting is clear both parties may proceed with the specified fora but only the party to whom the option is given may utilise the alternative fora. A greater difficulty of construction can arise where an election of domicile clause is included which is a common device in civil law countries to confer jurisdiction.[3] Here the problem that emerges is that such a clause has two possible functions. It may operate as a submission to the courts of the chosen domicile, or it may merely designate the place to which all notices or legal communications must be made. However, the draftsmen clauses in international bond issues are well aware of the trap and draft carefully to avoid ambiguity. The election of domicile is thus clearly reduced to the provision of a place for service of notices and legal communications, a clear choice of forum being expressly made.

JURISDICTION WITHOUT A SUBMISSION CLAUSE

The private international law rules of jurisdiction apart from the recognition of an effective choice of jurisdiction clause vary widely from legal system to legal system. At common law the rules are esentially procedural in nature and depend upon the service of the writ on the defendant either within the jurisdiction or outside it pursuant to leave granted under Order 11 of the Rules of the Supreme Court. Under Civil Law jurisdictions jurisdiction tends to depend on more substantive principles, the domicile of the defendant being particularly important. A discussion of them would take a great amount of space and has been excellently dealt with elsewhere[4] and the matter will not be further pursued here. However, brief mention should be made of the European Convention on Jurisdiction and the Enforcement of Judgments to which effect is given in the U.K. by the Civil Jurisdiction and Judgments Act 1982.

Under the Convention, which is binding within the E.E.C., the available bases of jurisdiction depend on whether or not the defendant is domiciled

[1] Delaume *Transnational Contracts* Chapter 8, p. 34. The position contrasts with the more successful challenge mounted under U.S. law to a clause restricting the individual's right of action to enforce the bond to promote the position of the trustee — see *ante* p. 301.

[2] Customarily the matter is mentioned in the prospectus, *ante* Chapter 3.

[3] The domicile of the defendant is a common test of civil law jurisdiction now adopted by the EEC Convention on Jurisdiction and the Enforcement of Judgments.

[4] See Dealume *Transnational Contracts* part II.

within the Community. If he is so domiciled common bases of jurisdiction applicable to all community states are prescribed which are used to determine whether a state has jurisdiction, including the domicile of the defendant and, where the action is in contract, where performance of the contract is due. In the case of a company domicile is determined by ascertaining where the company has its seat.[1] Once jurisdiction is undertaken by the courts of a particular legal system other courts will not involve themselves in the matter.[2] Bases of jurisdiction traditionally utilised by individual Member States which are viewed as excessive, such as nationality used by French law and mere temporary presence used by common law jurisdictions, may not be used under the Convention against a defendant domiciled within the Community but may still be used against a defendant domiciled outside the Community.[3]

As has been seen under the Convention a possible basis of jurisdiction under contract arises from where performance of the contract was due. In construing whether or not there has been a failure to perform within a particular jurisdiction, and hence a breach arising from non-performance, it is necessary that the non-performed term of the contract should have been one under which the promisor was obliged to perform in that particular jurisdiction.[4] If, therefore, under the terms of the contract the promisor could perform his obligation either in the specified jurisdiction or elsewhere and failst to perform in that particular jurisdiction there is no failure to perform within the jurisdiction.[5] It will be recollected that under the terms of payment of an international bond various paying agents will be appointed in various parts of the world. It does not, however, follow that if a bondholder presents a bond for payment in a particular jurisdiction at a payment agent and is refused payment, that an issuer can argue that the courts of that jurisdiction have no jurisdiction because he could perform the contract through any of the paying agents. What has been offered to bondholders by the contractual terms is that payment will take place at any of the paying agents selected by the bondholder. A presentation of the bond at a specific paying agent crystallises the payment obligation to an obligation to pay through that particular paying agent; failure to do so is therefore a breach of a contractual term to perform within the jurisdiction.

1 Article 53(1).
2 ibid.
3 Those grounds of jurisdiction characterised by the Convention as excessive are those based upon nationality found in France, Luxembour, Belgium, Holland and Italy, those based upon the domicile of the plaintiff found in Belgium and Holland, those based on the presence within the jurisdiction of property belonging to the defendant found in Denmark, Germany and the U.K. (this has particular relevance to Scotland within the U.K.) and those based on the service of the document instituting the proceedings on the defendant during a temporary presence within the particular jurisdiction found in the Republic of Ireland and the U.K. (within the U.K. this has particular relevance to England and Wales, and Northern Ireland).
4 This at least is the position under English law *Rein v Stein* [1892] 1 QB 753.
5 Again under English law *Bell and Co v Antwerp London and Brazil Line* [1891] 1 QB 103; *Comber v Leyland* [1898] AC 524.

ENFORCEMENT OF FOREIGN JUDGMENTS

Clearly, it is of little practical advantage for a plaintiff to obtain a judgement for a sum of money which remains ultimately unsatisfied. In international litigation it can easily transpire that a judgment is obtained in the courts of one jurisdiction which cannot be satisfied within that jurisdiction as the defendant has no assets there. On the other hand, there may be an abundance of the defendant's assets within a different jurisdiction. The question will then arise as to whether the courts of the second jurisdiction will recognise and, if necessary, enforce the judgment that has been obtained elsewhere. For instance, where a plaintiff litigating a matter arising from a bond issue obtains a judgment in Luxembourg only to find that there are no assets of the defendant in Luxembourg, as they are all situated in England, he will necessarily be limited to seeking a practical remedy from the English courts. Must he bring a fresh action involving re-litigation of the merits or may he seek to enforce the judgment of the foreign court? In fact, there is under English law a complex web of procedures both by statute and common law whereby the original judgment may be recognised and enforced by the English courts.

The important thing to note about this, however, is that the rules applicable to the enforcement of a judgment in a foreign court are the private international law rules of the courts of the jurisdiction which are asked to enforce the judgment not those of the jurisdiction which granted the judgment. The details of these rules vary considerably from jurisdiction to jurisdiction and there is little point in examining the individual rules in great detai.[1] Within the E.E.C. the European Convention on Jursidiction and the Enforcement of Judgments creates a regime under which the judgment of a court of any jurisdiction within the community is automatically enforceable through the courts of other Community jurisdictions, whether granted under one of the permitted heads of jurisdiction against someone domiciled within the Community, or even under one of the 'excessive' heads of jurisdiction if the defendant is domiciled outside the Community.[2]

1 For the English rules see Dicey and Morris*The Conflict of Laws* Chapter 33 and for a comparative description and analysis of common and civil law systems Delaume *Transnational Contracts* Part II.

2 Article 26.

14 Sovereign immunity

While the rules applicable to jurisdiction and the enforcement of judgments will often give all the information necessary for a bondholder or other person entitled to enforce a contract to assert their rights, further complications can arise. Where the issuer or proposed defendant is a sovereign state, constituent territory within a sovereign state, or state agency, difficulties may arise because different systems of law have conferred upon such bodies immunity from both action and execution. The degree and confines of the immunity unfortunately vary from jurisdiction to jurisdiction.

The subject of sovereign immunity is a fast developing and expanding one. Traditionally, most civil law jurisdictions have adopted a qualified concept of immunity, whereby the sovereign body is open to action in respect of its commercial activities, but could otherwise claim immunity. In contrast to this, the common law jurisdictions conferred an absolute immunity upon the sovereign defendant. However, increasingly the absolute immunity concept has been regarded as outmoded as states and their agencies have become ever more involved in commercial activities for a variety of social, economic, and political reasons during the twentieth century. As a result the basic common law doctrine has been limited by statute in many jurisdiction; in England by the State Immunity Act, brought about by a combination of judicial development of the common law[1] and the influence of the European Convention of State Immunity, which has been ratified by the U.K.[2]

Before proceeding further it is desirable to underline the fact that as the concepts of jurisdiction and recognition of judgments are separate and, in most jurisdictions, depend upon different bodies of law, so with sovereign immunity the issues of immunity from suit and immunity from execution are separate and, in some legal systems where immunity from suit in respect of commercial transactions is denied, immunity from execution of the sovereign's assets may be conferred. The adviser of a proposed defendant seeking to bring action against a sovereign body must therefore consider separately the two issues of whether he can bring the action against the

1 *Trendrex Trading Corpn Ltd v Central Bank of Nigeria* [1977] 2 WLR 356; 16 ILM 471 (1977) CA.

2 Ratified by U.K. on 3 July 1979. The Convention is also ratified by Austria, Belgium and Cyprus and signed by Germany, Luxembourg, Portugal, Switzerland and the Netherlands.

sovereign and, if judgment is obtained, proceed to execute against the assets of the sovereign body in the event that the judgment is not met.

In addition, the twin concepts of commercial and sovereign acts, while useful, inevitably leave unresolved many other issues of immunity from suit which have to be faced by all legal systems. One such issue is whether the immunity extends only to the central government of a federal state or to its constituent political sub-divisions. Further, does the immunity of the central government extend to its instrumentalities or agencies including nationalised industries?

With regard to the first of these questions it appears that in France and other common market countries in general the immunity extends only to the central government of a federal state, and not to its constituent parts on the grounds that only the central government enjoys external sovereign prerogatives in relations with foreign states.

The European Convention largely draws its concepts and policies from continental civil law systems, as is clear from its provisions as to the entities which are entitled to claim immunity. Its starting point is to deprive any entity other than a foreign state of the right to immunity, and it clarifies this by defining the expression 'contracting state' as not including 'any legal entity of a contracting state which is distinct therefrom and is capable of suing or being sued, even if that entity has been entrusted with public functions'.[1] Thus, an entity is not part of the state and therefore not entitled to immunity where both of two conditions are satisfied, namely that the entity is legally distinct from the contracting state and, secondly, is capable of suing or being sued. However, in respect of the separate entities the courts of any contracting state are forbidden to 'entertain proceedings in respect of acts performed by the entity in the exercise of sovereign authority (*acta jure imperii*)'.[2]

As might be expected in many of its policies and concepts the State Immunity Act 1978[3] fits into the pattern established by the European Convention. Not least is this true of the way in which the Act deals with establishing which bodies are entitled to rely upon the defence of sovereign immunity. In this respect the Act provides that only the central government of a foreign state can claim immunity together with its agencies which, although capable of suing or being sued in their own name, are not regarded as distinct from the government involved.[4] Their immunity does not, however, extend to commercial transactions and contractual obligations performed in the U.K.[5] Any other entity is, under the Act, a separate entity with more restricted immunity. The Act follows the European Convention in allowing the constituent states of a federal structure to be accorded

1 Article 27(1).
2 Article 27(2).
3 See generally White 'The State Immunity Act 1978' [1979] JBL 105; Laws 'The State Immunity Act' [1980] LMCLQ1 (Feb.) and the splendid discussion by Mann 'The State Immunity Act 1978' (1979) 50 BY 42.
4 S 14(1).
5 S 3.

an equal immunity to the federal body by means of Orders in Council dealing with individual cases.[1]

With regard to separate entities the structure of the European Convention is again followed for such entities are entitled to claim immunity only in respect of acts undertaken in a sovereign capacity in circumstances such that a state itself would have been immune.[2]

The U.S. Foreign Sovereign Immunities Act, while passed to undertake a parallel reform to that undertaken by the English State Immunity Act, had no reason to model itself upon the concepts of the European Convention, and, indeed, its starting points are in contrast with the Convention and the English Act. The applicable immunity rules apply to central governments and also to the political sub-divisions of a foreign state,[3] to all its agencies and instrumentalities,[4] and to all the agencies and instrumentalities of any one of its political sub-divisions.

By way of contrast to both the English and U.S. Acts, the Canadian State Immunity Act combines something of both the U.S. and English approach. The Canadian Act includes within the definition of foreign state the foreign sovereign, its agencies and its political sub-divisions and their agencies. However, the meaning of political sub-division under the Canadian Act is limited to provinces or states of a federal state. Further in dealing with agencies the Canadian Act defines agency as 'any legal entity that is an organ of the foreign state but that is separate from the foreign state'.[5]

WAIVER OF IMMUNITY

As the parties to a dispute can confer jurisdiction on a forum not otherwise possessing it by express contractual choice, so a sovereign body can confer jurisdiction by similar means. Express waiver of immunity from jurisdiction and execution are commonly included in international bond terms. Such terms are generally recognised by most systems of law and are acknowledged by recent legislative and treaty developments.

Such waivers of immunity from jurisdiction will be given effect by most

1 Made pursuant to s 14(5).

2 S 14(2).

3 Political subdivisions include 'all governmental units beneath the central government, including local governments—Section by Section Analysis.

4 Agencies and instrumentalities are defined by a cumulative test as any entity
'(1) which is a separate legal person, corporate or otherwise, and
(2) which is an organ of a foreign state or political sub-division thereof, or a majority of whose shares or other ownership interest is owned by a foreign state or political sub-division thereof, and
(3) which is neither a citizen of a State of the United States . . . nor created under the laws of any third country.' s 1603(b).

5 S 2.

Continental systems of law,[1] the U.S., [2] and under[3] the European Convention.[4]

> 'A State may submit after the dispute giving rise to the proceedings has arisen on or by a prior written agreement; but a provision in any agreement that it is to be governed by the law of the U.K. is not to be regarded as a submission.'

While this does not specify that such waiver is irrevocable it would seem that this is the effect, for the consequences should be the same as those arising from other forms of submission under s 2(1).[5]

However, a question nevertheless arises with regard to all systems of law. Does the fact that a particular individual has authority to enter into a contract on behalf of a sovereign body mean that he has also necessarily authority to waive immunity? The U.K. legislation makes specific provision in s 2(7). First, the head of a state's diplomatic mission in the U.K. (or the person performing those functions) is deemed to have authority to submit to jurisdiction on behalf of the state. Secondly, 'any person who has entered into a contract on behalf and with the authority of the state shall be deemed to have authority on its behalf in respect of proceedings arising out of the contract'.

Other systems of law seem to proceed on the basis that authority to waive is to be assumed from authority to contract on the simple principle that waiver is contractual in origin. In any event, a party wishing to rely on an express waiver, whether under the U.K. or any other legal system, must satisfy itself that the agent of the state has authority to enter into the contract itself for, at the very least, the waiver must stand or fall with the effectiveness of the contract of which it is part.

Waiver of sovereign immunity and submission to jurisdiction in the case of a party appearing to proceedings can be implied from his conduct.[6] The issue therefore arises as to whether waiver will be inferred from some provision of the contract or bond terms short of an express submission to jurisdiction. In the U.S. jurisdiction has been asserted over a state entity which issued bonds on the New York market, on the ground (among others) that the bond terms conferred a right on the bondholders in the event of default to give notice accelerating payment to American banks acting as agents for the issuer. In the view of the court this indicated that the issue envisaged that proceedings might be brought in the U.S. courts.[7] On

1 Delaume *Transnational contracts* Oceana Pubs, Dobbs Ferry, New York (1982 rev.) Chapter 11, p. 43.

2 Foreign Sovereign Immunities Act, s 1605(a)(1).

3 Canadian State Immunities Act, s 1605(a)(1).

4 Article 2.

5 The provisions of the U.K. Act are not retrospective and do not apply to waivers of immunity entered into before the coming into force of its provisions (s 23(3)). Earlier waivers are governed by the law in force prior to the Act.

6 Dicey and Morris *The Conflict of Laws* 11th edn, Rule 20 exception 1 and the authorities therein cited.

7 *Hannes v Kingdom of Rumania Monopolies Institute* 20 NYS 2d 825, 260, App Div (1st Dept, 1940), rearg denied 24 NYS 2d 994, 260 App Div, resettled 26 NYS 866, 260 App Div 1058.

the other hand the mere choice of the law of a particular system as governing an issue will not *per se* constitute a submission by the sovereign to the courts of that jurisdiction in either U.S.[1] or English law.[2]

Given that most developed systems of law no longer confer immunity upon states and sovereign bodies in respect of commercial transactions, the question necessarily arises as to whether the inclusion of an express waiver of immunity clause in a contract or the terms of a bond remains necessary to accomplish that end. It can certainly be argued strongly that the mere fact of coming to the international capital markets of the world with a bond issue is itself the undertaking of an act of a commercial nature. In the case of the U.K. argument is strengthened by the detailed categorisation of acts of a commercial nature contained within the State Immunity Act.[3] However, the use of express terms continues and considerable practical advantages ensure. Often the submission to jurisdiction is linked to choice of fora in the same clause, and certainly fora selection remains a necessary part of contractual planning not least in the careful selection of fora with a restricted view of sovereign immunity. Further, within the waiver clause express categorisation of the contract or bond issue as an act of a commercial nature makes it much more difficult subsequently for the sovereign to be heard to argue the contrary. This is a matter of particular importance outside the U.K. where the categorisation of acts is left to the courts even under such recent legislation as the Canadian and U.S. A matter of great importance is service of process to ensure that the proceedings can be commenced, and the sovereign brought within the jurisdiction of the forum. The provisions with regard to these matters under many systems of law are cumbersome, and such that a determined sovereign defendant may well be able to avoid or delay.[4] Express provision may considerably enhance the position of a prospective plaintiff in this respect.

The importance of express waiver, however, is at its greatest when issue of execution rather than submission to jurisdiction are concerned. Some systems of law do not automatically allow a sovereign's assets to be the subject of execution in all situations where immunity from jurisdiction is denied. Thus, under the European Convention it is expressly provided that no measure of execution, whether to enforce a judgment or to preserve property for a plaintiff in the event of success in the litigation, shall take place against the property of a contracting state unless that state has expressly consented thereto in writing in any particular case.[5] Further, while in general civil law systems and common law systems with statutory modification allow execution where there is no immunity from suit, so that sovereign

1 *Frazier v Hanover Bank* 119 NYS 2d 319 (1953), aff'd 119 NYS 2d 918, 281, App Div 861 (1953), reargument and appeal denied 127 NYS 2d 815, App Div 655.

2 State Immunity Act, s 2(2).

3 S 3(3).

4 Delaume *Transnational Contracts* Chapter 11.

5 Article 22. The restriction relates to the State's property alone and does not protect the property of other public entities where these lack immunity from suit under the Convention.

assets can be executed against when used for purely commercial purposes, the burden of proving that the assets are used for commercial purposes lies on the creditor, a burden which he will often find it impossible to discharge.[1] From this point of view an express waiver clause in the widest possible terms, is of great importance. Such a clause may waive immunity, not merely with regard to the assets of the sovereign within the jurisdiction, but its assets wherever located. While such clauses call for complex advice and planning by the legal adviser depending, as they do for their ultimate efficacy, upon the rules of each jurisdiction in which immunity is sought pertaining to both sovereign immunity[2] and recognition and enforcement of foreign judgments, properly drafted examples undoubtedly keep open avenues of redress which would otherwise be closed to plaintiffs.[3] Ideally, such waivers should also be clear that immunity from execution is waived with regard to both pre-judgment attachment and post-judgment enforcement so that all doubt is removed.[4]

The power of an express waiver of immunity from execution to open up remedies for a plaintiff otherwise closed to him is particularly important with regard to the property of central banks. A central bank's immunity from suit rests upon general principles and therefore allows some prospects of success to a prospective plaintiff, but the immunity of the bank's assets to execution is much more widely based, putting a litigant in a much more hopeless situation. Central banks in the modern world have very definite functions, in part carrying out the functions of government, in part carrying out financial and commercial activities utilizing funds held to their own account. On the other hand the position of a state's central bank and the immunity of its assets from seisure is often a matter of the greatest concern to that state seeing, as it usually will, its very prestige and ability to carry out its own governmental policies sacrificed if its central bank's assets are attached or garnished as a consequence of litigation. Recognising this delicate reality among the sovereign bodies of the international community many systems of law confer wide immunity from execution on the assets of foreign central banks in their jurisdiction.

The increasing trend in Continental countries is to deny immunity to central banks unless the bank concerned satisfies the court that the act giving rise to the liability arose from the fulfilment of a governmental function, and the property against which execution is sought was used for that purpose.[5] The burden of proof is therefore on the central bank concerned and the forum will not necessarily accept its assertion[6] although, in practice, the claims of the central bank will usually be decisive.

1 Article 26.
2 See the examples quoted and discussed by Delaume *Transnational Contracts* Chapter 12 pp. 24–33.
3 The issues of sovereign immunity alone are relatively straightforward since most developed systems of law will give full effect to the waiver if it is properly drawn.
4 Thereby avoiding the arguments presented by the sovereign defendant in *Libra Bank Ltd v Banco Nacional de Costa Rica* 676 F2d47 (2d Cir 1982).
5 Delaume *Transnational Contracts* Chapter 12 p. 22.
6 Ibid.

In the common law jurisdictions both the Foreign Sovereign Immunities Act and State Immunity Act have special rules protecting central banks. With regard to immunity from suit the State Immunity Act makes a distinction between central banks trading as separate entities and those which operate as a branch of the government of the state concerned, the former, pursuant to the basic philosophy of the Act, enjoying no immunity from suit.[1] However, by way of contrast, when it comes to immunity from execution the English Act provides that the assets of a state's central bank (or other monetary authority) should not be regarded 'as used or intended for use for commercial purposes' thereby removing all such assets from the reach of execution.[2]

Under the U.S. Foreign Sovereign Immunities Act the property of a central bank or monetary authority held 'for its own account' is immune from attachment.[3] Given that such funds can be held both for governmental and commercial purposes it appears that the immunity conferred is a blanket immunity given to central banks for the protection of all of their assets making the position of a prospective plaintiff extremely difficult.

The position of a prospective plaintiff in all such jurisdictions can be improved by properly drafted waiver provisions. Continental countries will give effect to clauses giving general waiver of immunity and there is no reason to suppose that the general principle will not be applied in the case of the property of central banks; equally, the problem in these jurisdictions could be addressed by characterising the assets of the bank as held for commercial purposes. In the U.K. and the U.S. the relevant statutes contain provisions allowing immunity from execution to be waived[4] in the case of assets otherwise immune, and again there is no reason to suppose that this does not extend to the property of central banks.

ABSENCE OF WAIVER

Sovereign borrowers are, however, often unwilling to waive their immunity. From their point of view, waiver may be seen as a denial of both their dignity and ultimate sovereignty for the preservation of which their governments may feel ultimately accountable to their people. Usually such reluctance is overcome by the harsh attitudes of the market place which may well adopt an attitude of no waiver, no issue. Nevertheless, from time to time sovereign issues have been made with no waiver of immunity. The effect of this must be considered.

In general civil law systems have drawn a distinction between acts of sovereigns which they consider to be of a commercial nature and those of a non-commercial nature, with immunity being recognised in respect of the latter but not in respect of the former. This distinction has been

1 S 14(4).

2 Thereby reversing the effect of *Trendrex Trading Corpn v Central Bank of Nigeria* [1977] QB 529. See the cutting criticism by Mann (1979) 50 BYBIL p. 62.

3 S 1611(b)(1). It may not be that this is the intention of the legislature; see the Section by Section Analysis 15 ILM 101 (1976), 116.

4 In the U.K. State Immunity Act, s 13(3).

adopted as the basis of the amending legislation in the common law jurisdictions.

Given the broad consensus which is reached among so many systems of developed law that sovereign immunity should not attach to commercial acts, the question then arises whether the issue of securities by foreign states, their political sub-divisions and public agencies constitute commercial acts. On the one hand the very use of the normal international market place for the raising of money by the issue of securities strongly suggests that the issuer is engaged upon a normal commercial activity. On the other hand, the capital sums thus realised will often be designated for essentially public purposes which may be declared in the prospectus. In any event, the different concepts of sovereign immunity applicable to different jurisdictions may give rise to complication. However, under the important European Convention a contracting state does not have immunity where the proceedings arise from a contract falling to be discharged in the territory of the forum. An issuing sovereign borrower and the supporting syndicate of financial institutions effecting the issue are clearly all bound together by contract and consequently under the European Convention proceedings can be taken against one another in the jurisdictions in which the contracts are to be performed. Similarly, each security issued constitutes a package of contractual rights between the issuer and the security holder for the time being, which can, under the Convention, be enforced in the jurisdictions in which the contracts are to be performed, which are in the case of a securities issue where payments of interest on the coupons and repayments of the principal of the securities are to take place.

In the case of the U.S. Foreign Sovereign Immunities Act and the Canadian legislation, immunity does not exist in respect of acts of a commercial nature. Here the creation of the contractual relationships between the issuer and the supporting syndicate for the issue is essentially commercial in character, as is the issue of securities upon the market, and logically should be so categorised by the courts. However, it must be borne in mind that for proceedings to lie under the Foreign Sovereign Immunities Act there are jurisdictional requirements which must be satisfied.

In the U.K. much more specific provision is made for international security transactions than under the U.S. legislation. Clearly, similar arguments as to the commercial characterisation of the contractual connections between the issuer and the syndicated institutions apply as under the U.S. and Canadian legislation. With regard to the obligations arising from the issue of the securities themselves it should be noted that the Act includes within the definition of commercial transactions 'any loan or other transaction for the provision of finance and any guarantee or indemnity in respect of such transaction or *any other financial obligation*'.[1] As the U.K. legislation, unlike the U.S., does not require any connection between the transaction in question and the U.K., it would appear that it is in the U.K. that the greatest opportunity for litigation of issues arising from the sale of international securities free of the restrictions of sovereign immunity arises.

On occasion, sovereign issuers have been unwilling to accept full waiver

[1] S 3(3).

clauses but have been prepared to include provisions in the securities themselves characterising the security issue as a private and commercial act. While such a categorisation by the parties may not be treated as final by the courts of any particular jurisdiction it clearly makes it more difficult for a court to categorise as a public act that which the parties have categorized as a commercial one and, indeed, makes it far more difficult for a sovereign issuer to raise the argument of public act in the first instance.

Nevertheless, none of this removes the underlying difficulty of enforcement. Immunity from suit in a number of jurisdictions does not make any easier a creditor's situation in seeking to enforce without an express waiver clause if a jugment is not met once granted.

The problem of comity

It might be thought that armed with recent legislation admitting the principle of the restrictive doctrine of sovereign immunity the U.S. and English courts would adopt a vigorous approach in their dealings with sovereign defendants. This has, however, proved to be far from the situation which has arisen. There is a residual problem which the termination of the blanket concept of sovereign immunity has thrown into sharp relief—that of comity. The problem is the greater because it seems probable that it is not avoided by the inclusion of a waiver clause as it rests ultimately on public policy and the national interest. In its English and civil law manifestations it can at least be avoided by the normal practice of bond issues of choosing as the governing law a system other than that of the issuer.

Problems can arise where the system of law applicable to the contractual relations between the parties is that the sovereign whose trading entity or private issuer is one of the parties involved, for here the sovereign can by legislative act alter or abrogate those very relations. The other party will thus lose the benefit of their contract without having any remedy against the sovereign, unless the English courts refuse to recognise the change to the proper law on the grounds of public policy as they will where the alteration is shown to be penal and discriminatory. It is at this stage that the problem of comity can arise. In *Settebello Ltd v Banco Totta and Acores (a body corporate)*[1] the English courts allowed the actions of the state to remove the liability of its state trading organisation. The case concerned a contract between a Portuguese state shipyard and a western company for the construction of an oil tanker. Under the terms of the contract Settebello Ltd were entitled to cancel the contract and claim compensation if the ship was not ready for delivery by 30 April 1982. The shipyard's performance was guaranteed by the defendant bank. Shortly before the delivery date the Portuguese government made a decree enabling Portuguese companies, declared to be in a critical economic condition, unilaterally to suspend their customers' rights of cancellation of a contract where substantial financial penalities would ensue. The declaration was made. The bank refused to pay under the guarantee relying on the new law.

The contract was governed by Portuguese law and therefore the shipyard

[1] (1984) Times, 4 August—A full transcript is available on Lexis.

could *prima facie* rely on the governmental decree in proceedings before the English courts. The plaintiff's case was that the action was discriminatory being designed purely to remove the liability of the individual shipyard, and the English courts should therefore decline to give effect to it on grounds of public policy. It sought letters of request to obtain evidence in Portugal that the decree had in fact been made only on the initiative of the shipyard and drafted by the shipyard's lawyers. The application was refused on the ground that to grant it would be to allow an inquiry into the motives of foreign legislation which should be refused 'as a matter of principle on grounds of comity'.[1] The decision and its reasoning has now been upheld on appeal.[2]

The significance of the decision lies not in the English courts' general willingness to give effect to changes in the law governing the contract, but in their unwillingness to enquire into the motives of the foreign legislation and the true purpose of the legislation in its exaggerated respect for apparently sovereign acts under the principle of comity. If no real regard is to be given to the true purpose of a foreign legislative act, then under English law no substantial protection is given to those who trade with or finance state trading entities, however discriminatory the actions of the sovereign government may be.

The principle that an English court will not examine the legislative,[3] or executive,[4] actions of a foreign state in exercising its jurisdiction to give its effect to its public interests is long established in English law. The underlying concept is that the English courts will not examine the validity of a sovereign act of a foreign state. As such the concept would appear to be the same as that now applied in the realm of sovereign immunity of *acta jure imperii.* The significant difference is in the operation of the principle of comity and that of sovereign immunity. For sovereign immunity to be applicable it is the state itself which must be party to the proceedings; for the principle of comity to come into play the proceedings need not involve the sovereign at all as a party but merely call into question the sovereign acts that it has undertaken. While the two doctrines are capable thus of operating in two separate situations, it appears that the concept of sovereign act which has already underpinned the principle of comity is the residual principle of immunity under the restrictive doctrine of sovereign immunity now adopted by the English courts.[5]

1 Hirst J was expressly applying judicial restraint in accepting the justiciability before the English court on the basis of the House of Lords decision of *Buttes Gas and Oil Co v Hammer (No 3)* [1982] AC 888. See IAE Insley and Frank Wooldridge 'The Buttes Case: The Final Chapter in the Litigation' (1983) 32 ICLQ 62. The Buttes case was, however, somewhat remarkable. It involved private rights ultimately dependent on no less than three sovereign states.

2 [1985] 1 WLR, [1985] 2 All ER 1025.

3 *Blad v Blamfield* (1674) 3 Swan 604.

4 *AM Luther v James Sagor & Co* [1921] 1 KB 718.

5 For a discussion and criticism of the basis of this distinction see Crawford 'International Law and Foreign Sovereigns: Distinguishing Immune Transactions' (1983) 54 BYBIL 75.

It may, indeed, be desirable that the principle of comity be given increased weight to solve the complex political problems which the restriction of sovereign immunity may give rise to for sovereign immunity itself had real political arguments to support it. However, that is not to say that it should be given unrestricted operation. Even states are subject to the operation of international law under which the discriminatory use of national law is controlled.

The objectionable feature of English law in this respect is its failure to inquire into the actions of foreign states, at least to ascertain whether or not international law has been adhered to.[1] However, it may be that the decision in the particular case rested upon the fact that in the particular circumstances of the *Settebello* case the inquiry could only be pursued with the co-operation of the Portuguese courts and legal procedures which would be clearly unlikely to be forthcoming.[2]

The concept that certain sovereign actions by the state will not be examined by the courts of another country is widely utilised in civil law systems. Thus, the basic concept has been accepted in Austria,[3] Belgium,[4] France,[5] Italy,[6] Germany[7] and Holland.[8] It appears from this therefore that this concept, which is also recognised by the U.S. in its Act of State doctrine is of a general application in most legal systems. The issue therefore arises as to whether it is a rule of international law, which must be applied by national courts unless its application would lead to breach of an alternative rule of international law (such as nationalisation without compensation), or whether it is a rule of private international law, which has gained acceptance within the international rules of most legal systems and which, as a mere rule of private international law, may give way to national concepts of public policy adopted by any particular jurisdiction. In the latter situation, of course, one of the matters which national law can take into account

1 *Settebello case ante;* see, however, *Anglo Iranian Oil Co v Jaffrate* [1953] 1 WLR 246; *Frankfurther v WL Exner Ltd* [1947] 1 Ch 629.

2 ibid.

3 *Hungarian Soviet Government Case,* Austrian Supreme Court in Civil Matters 31 Oct 1922 (Ob 1055/22 [1922] 4 EOGZ 274 (No 110).

4 *Propetrol, Petroservice, et Petrolest, v Companio Mexicano de Petroleo,* Civil Tribunal of Antwerp, 21 Feb 1939, [1939] Belgique Judiciaire 11, 12

5 See, eg *Société Hardmuth* Court of Appeal of Paris, 2 Dec 1950, 44 Rev Cr Dr Int'l Priv 501 (1955); *De Keller v Maison de la Pensée Francaise,* Tribunal de la Seine, 12 July 1943, 44 Rec Cr Dr Int'd Prive 503 (1955), [1954] Int'l Rep 21.

6 *Campione v Peti Nitrogenmurek and Popular Government of Hungary,* Riv DI (1974) 101.

7 *Prince Dabisita–Kotromaniez v Societe Lepke,* Tribunal of Berlin, 1 Nov. 1928 56 Clunet 184 (1929), *NV Verenigde and Deli-Maatschapijen v Deutsch-Indonesische Tabak-Handelsgessellschaft* ILR 28 (1929).

8 See, eg *United States of Mexico v NV De Bataafsche Petroleium Maatschappij,* District Court of Middleburg 2 Aug. 1938, [1938] Ned jur No 790, *Petroservice SA and Credit Minier Franco-Roumain SA v Compania Mexicana de Petroleo 'El Aguila',* Court of Appeal of the Hague, 4 Dec 1939 [1940] Ned Jur No 27, aff'd on other grounds, 7 Feb 1941 Ned Jur No 923.

within the concept of public policy is the state's obligations under international law. The latter appears to be the view of civil law system and has been expressly adopted in the jurisprudence of France,[1] and Germany,[2] and Holland where the courts have decided that a breach of international law is a matter falling within their public policy concept which could lead them to refuse to apply the Act of State to any particular set of circumstances.[3] This approach is cleary potentially more secure for bondholders unwise enough to find themselves in *Settebello* situation.

The English principle of comity is recognised in the U.S. under its Act of State doctrine. The classic statement of the principle in U.S. law was made by Chief Justice Fuller in *Underhill v Hernandez:*

> 'Every Sovereign State is bound to respect the independence of every other Sovereign State, and the courts of one country will not sit in judgment of the acts of the government of another within its own territory. Redress of grievances by reason of such acts must be obtained through the means open to be availed of by sovereign powers as between themselves.[4]

The modern exposition of the rule can be found in the Restatement. This provides that:

> Except as otherwise provided . . . a court in the United States having jurisdiction to determine a claim asserted against a person in the United States or with respect to a thing located there, or other interest localised there, will refrain from examining the validity of an act of a foreign state by which that state has exercised its jurisdiction to give effect to its public interest.[5]

The effect of this is clearly potentially disastrous in the case of an issue where the issuer's own law is made the law governing the issue, and its government subsequently changes the law to avoid or delay payment even though the change of law is effect on an entirely discriminatory purpose.

The purpose of the Act of State doctrine is unashamedly to prevent the actions of the U.S. courts becoming an embarrassment to the executive in its conduct of foreign relations.

This being the purpose of the doctrine the U.S. courts have not traditionally been prepared to question the validity of the Act of State of a foreign government, even where the act has violated international law.

1 See, eg *Martin v Banque D'Espagne,* Cour de Cassation, 3 Nov 1952, Rev Cr Dr Int'; Priv 425 (1953) [1952] Int'l L: Rep 202 (No 42); *Société Potasas Ibericas v Bloch,* Cour de Cassation 145 March 1939 [1939] Dalloz Rec Heb Jur 257.

2 *NV Verenigde Deli–Maaschappijen and NV Senembah–Maatschappij v Deitsche–Indonesiche Tabak Handelssgesellschhaft mbH,* Court of Appeal of Bremen, 21 Aug, 1959, 9 Archive de Volkerrechts 318 (1961).

3 *Senembah Maatschappij NV v Republiek Indonesie Bank Indonesia and De Twentsdche Bank NV,* 4 June 1959, Archive der Volkerrechts 318 (1961).

4 168 250 (1897) at 252; approved in *inter alia Oetjen v Central Leather Co,* 246 US 303 (1918); *United States ex rel Von Heymann v Watkins* F2d 650, 652 (2nd Cir 1947).

5 Restatement of the Foreign Relations Law of the U.S. (2nd) at p. 125.

Thus, in the leading case of *Banco Nacional de Cuba v Sabbatino*[1] the Supreme Court refused to make an inquiry on the express grounds that, if the result of the enquiry would be that they adjudicated that the act of the foreign government was indeed in breach of international law, this would make even more difficult the executive's position in the sensitive matter of handling the foreign relations of the U.S.

On the other hand, since the Act of State doctrine of the U.S. expresses a clear policy the courts have held that it does not apply where the executive branch has clearly indicated that it has no objection to the validity of the act of a foreign state being examined—The Bernstein Exception.[2] The *Sabbatino* case itself led to legislative intervention in 1965 when Congress enacted and exception to the general Act of State doctrine ('the Hickenlooper Amendment'), which amended the Foreign Assistance Act of 1965 to require U.S. courts to adjudicate all cases where a breach of international law is in issue notwithstanding the Act of State doctrine. The only general exception to this is that the court is forbidden to proceed to adjudicate even though a breach of international law is alleged 'in any case with respect to which the President determines that application of the Act of State doctrine is required in that particular case by the foreign policy interests of the U.S. and a suggestion to this effect is filed on his behalf in that case with the court'.[3]

It is quite clear that the combined effects of the Bernstein exception and the Hickenlooper Amendment is to put the attitude of the executive to the forefront in determining these delicate matters, as well as making available the machinery whereby the executive's attitude can be made manifest to the court. Such power in political hands will inevitably be utilised with a view to the political advantage of the state rather than the demands of justice of the individual case. The placing of the doctrine on substantially political lines has led to the U.S. courts being prepared to give effect to foreign decrees expropriating property within the U.S. where the executive has indicated to the courts that recognition should be given as a matter of comity.[4]

The willingness of U.S. courts to be guided by the executive with regard to the needs of foreign relations have recently given rise to important and controversial litigation in New York, which has general implications for the payment of international financial transactions, the litigation of which is centred for U.S. purposes on that state. It further indicates that U.S. courts retain a residual jurisdiction to give effect to sovereign acts on the basis of comity where that Act of State doctrine itself cannot apply. The litigation in *Allied Bank International v Banco Credito Agricola de*

1 376 US 398 (1964).

2 *Bernstein v Van Heyghen Freres SA,* 163 F 2d 246 (2nd Cir), cert denied 332 US 772 (1947); *Bernstein v NV Nederlandsche-Amerikaansche, Stoomvoart-Maatschappij* 210 Fed 375 (2nd Cir 1954).

3 Foreign Assistance Act 1965 Pub L No 88–663, 78 Stat 1009.

4 *U.S. v Pink* 325 US 203 (1942); *State of the Netherlands v Federal Reserve Bank of New York,* 201 Fed 455 (1953).

Cartago[1] involved a number of promissory notes payable in New York issued by a Costa Rican government bank. The promissory notes themselves had been issued as a result of the restructuring of the obligations of a failed Costa Rican bank in 1976. In the renegotiation Allied Bank International had acted as the agent for 39 banks which had accepted the promissory notes in the restructuring of the failed bank's debts. The notes themselves were to be repaid by three Costa Rican banks. No governing law was specified but the agreement provided concurrent jurisdiction in respect of disputes in both New York and Costa Rica. The obligations undertaken by the three banks were registered with the central bank of Costa Rica, which was to supply the necessary U.S. dollars as the notes became payable. Payment proceeded on a regular basis until 1981 when, with approximately half of the principal of the notes still outstanding, the Costa Rican government imposed severe exchange control regulations under which insufficient U.S. dollars were available to allow the Costa Rican banks to continue making payment on the notes. The notes were payable in New York. Under the exchange control regulations the three Costa Rican banks were specifically prohibited from making payment of their foreign debts.

The immediate result of the Costa Rican governmental action was that further talks were put under way in an attempt to restructure the Costa Rican public sector debt including the outstanding notes. However, before these could be brought to fruition one of the syndicate of 39 banks, Fidelity Union of New Jersey, brought proceedings against the Costa Rican banks which were heard initially before the New York district court for the Southern District, which dismissed the case on the ground that the Act of the Costa Rican government was an Act of State into which it would not enquire and which conferred upon the Costa Rican banks a defence.

Allied Bank International, as agent of the New Jersey bank, appealed to the U.S. Court of Appeals for the second circuit. The Appeal Court ruled in favour of the defendants. However, in doing so it did not rely on the Act of State doctrine which was, indeed, weak ground as the performance of the obligation to pay was to be effected in New York and not Costa Rica.[2] Instead, it based itself purely on grounds of comity, on the basis that the Costa Rican Presidential decree and the resultant central bank action were consistent with the policy of the U.S. and had the support of the U.S. executive and legislation.

In the view of the Court of Appeals the Costa Rican action was analagous to a declaration of the bankruptcy by a U.S. corporation under Chapter 11, under which a corporation's debts are not repudiated but deferred whilst the corporation is put in a viable form to make payment. As such it constituted a mode of operation consistent with U.S. legal institutions.

More importantly the Court of Appeals inferred U.S. executive approval of the Costa Rican attempts to restructure its debts from the fact that the President of the U.S. had approved the continuation of the foreign

[1] 23 ILM 742 discussed by Brown 'Enforcing Sovereign Lending' 3 IFLR No 7 (July 1984) at p. 5.

[2] *Garcia v Chase Manhattan Bank* 735 F2d 645 (2nd Cir 1984).

aid programme to that country despite its default and, indeed, Secretary of State George Schultz had written approving the reorganisation efforts undertaken by the Costa Ricans. Further evidence of executive approval was inferred from the participation of the U.S. government in the signing of 'a Paris Club Agreement' approving the restructuring of Costa Rica's inter-governmental debt.

This led to application being made to the U.S. Court of Appeals to rehear the case en banc. The position of the appellants was considerably strengthened by the fact that the U.S. government joined the dispute on the side of the appellants and filed its own brief in the court. The government brief pointed out that, in holding that Costa Rican law was consistent with the policy of the U.S. the court did not have before it the views of the U.S. government, and the court's decision was based on an inaccurate understanding of the policy of the U.S. In the brief the U.S. government made it perfectly clear that its policy was *not* that Costa Rican debt to private lenders should be rendered unenforceable by the actions of the Costa Rican government to which creditors did not agree. Indeed, as the brief stressed, in its view the result of the Court of Appeals' decision would be to make restructuring and renegotiation of private debt more difficult, which will be adverse to debtor governments and their governmental and private institutions, and adverse to U.S. policy which is to promote harmonious renegotiation agreements in all circumstances where this is possible.

Significantly, the appeal was also supported by the powerful New York Clearing House Association which also filed a brief. One point emphasised by the Association is that the effect of the decision might well be that financial institutions would find that participation in international financial arrangements payable in New York State becomes less attractive than on those payable in other jurisdictions, and hence the markets in London and Europe would be promoted to the detriment of those of New York, the major U.S. centre.

The case proceeded to a rehearing where the Court of Appeals reversed its previous decisions.[1] It rejected the defence of Act of State on the grounds that the operation of that doctrine was restricted to the territorial jurisdiction of the actor state which would, in any event, be unlikely to give effect to the decisions of U.S. courts operating against its own executive's acts. The principle of comity was likewise rejected, great reliance being placed upon the declared U.S. governmental position which was decisive to its reasoning. It appears therefore if the U.S. governmental position had been otherwise, and it had given a declaration that the Costa Rican acts were consistent with U.S. policy, the defendants' arguments would have been upheld. In the particular circumstances declared by the U.S. government the defence was rejected. Clearly, the court took the view that it would only be in the most exceptional circumstances that the government would declare acts taken by a foreign government to abrogate payment obligations performable within the U.S. to be consistent with U.S. policy for it expressly declared:

1 757 F2d 516 (2d Cir) cert dismissed 106 SC 30 (1985); [1985] ILM 762.

> 'The United States has an interest in ensuring that creditors entitled to payment in the United States in dollars under contracts subject to the jurisdiction of United States courts may assume that, except under the most exceptional circumstances their rights will be determined under recognised principles of contract law.'[1]

INTERNATIONAL ORGANISATIONS

The importance of international organisations as issuers in the international bond market is considerable. Two main varieties of such borrowers have used the market. The first is the development banks including the International Bank for Reconstruction and Development (World Bank),[2] the Asian Bank, the Inter-American Development Bank and the Nordic Investment Bank.[3] The second is institutions connected with the E.E.C. including the Community itself, the Council of Ministers, the European Coal and Steel Community, the European Investment Bank, Eurofina and Euratom.[4]

1. *The position by charter and constitution*

The immunities from suit attaching to international organisations in the contractual field is determined from their charters and other supporting instruments. Generalisations are difficult to make as to the content of these, and therefore the question must be considered in the light of each specific contractual situation. Clearly, however, regard must be had to the organisation's charter and treaty documentation dealing with the subject, as well as the terms of the issue or contract itself.

In general, international organisations enjoy immunity from suit except in so far as this is waived. However, in practice, the charters or other treaty documentation of such organisations commonly limit the immunity to acts *jure imperii* by making provision for the settlement of private disputes (*jure gestionis*), including some machinery to allow a hearing of the dispute to take place.[5]

In the case of international organisations involved in lending money, and with a consequent need to raise capital on the markets of the world, the requirements of the market place have caused this distinction to be deeply embedded in their constitutional organisation. Such organisations customarily are protected from facing general litigation brought by member states in the courts of the world for, where the organisation is in conflict with its member states, its charter or treaty documentation usually provides

1 This resolved the immediate problem but has left many difficulties—see the criticism by M Erin Kelly 'The Act of State Doctrine and Allied Bank' (31 Villanova LR 291 (1986)).

2 Peter Gallant *'The Eurobond Market'* Woodhead-Faulkner Group (1988) p. 110.

3 FG Fisher III *'Eurobonds'* (1988) p. 57.

4 ibid.

5 For example, any disputes involving the organs of the European Community are allocated to the European court. ECSC Treaty of 18 April 1951 (261 UNTS 140, Article 42); EEC Treaty of 25 March 1957 (298 UNTS 169), Articles 153, 155 and 185.

that the matters are to be resolved by determination of the organs of the organisation itself or by international arbitration.[1]

By way of contrast, such international financial organisations do not usually have an equivalent immunity in respect of contractual claims brought by non-member states. In drafting their charters regard has been paid to their need to raise money on the capital markets of the world, and it has been realised that a general immunity from suit would be detrimental to their efforts to raise capital, and would have made any bonds issued by them less attractive to investors. The charters consequently uniformly allow action to be brought against them.

However, even though international organisations are uniform in this respect differences of detail remain. Some organisations allow suit to be brought in any court having jurisdiction,[2] but more usually there is some restriction often limiting the available fora to the courts of competent jurisdiction in the territory of member countries where the organisation maintains an office or has appointed an agent to accept service or notice of process or has issued or guaranteed securities.[3] Further, some organisations by their charter allow any person to bring his claim whatever its nature, whereas others, following a more recent pattern, limit the actions which may be brought to those arising from their financial transactions such as the sale or guaranteeing of securities.[4]

As the laws of individual legal systems draw a distinction between immunity from jurisdiction and immunity from execution so a similar distinction is drawn in the law and practice of international organisations. As has been seen those international organisations not involved in the provision of finance are usually immune from suit in the absence of waiver and are similarly immune with regard to execution. Since in practice they do not waive their immunity from execution, and a waiver of immunity from suit does not, *per se,* amount to a waiver of immunity from execution, the immunity is retained intact to prevent their assets falling to the disposal of creditors.[5]

International lending organisations, however, are forced to operate here, as with immunity from suit, with an eye to the demands of the world capital markets where investors would be disturbed if they did not have the power ultimately to seek a remedy against the property of the international organisations who raise capital on those markets. In general,

1 Eg IRBD, Articles of Agreement (2 UNTS 134), Article IX.

2 E1B Statute (298 UNTS 120) Article 29 paras. 1 and 2; ECSC Treaty *ante* Article 40 para. 3; EEC Treaty *ante* Articles 183 and 21.

3 Eg IBRD Articles of Agreement *ante* Article VII Section 3; IADB Articles of Agreement (389 UNTS 69), Article XI, Section 3

4 Asian Development Bank Agreement (57 UNTS 123), Article 50; African Development Bank Agreement (510 UNTS 3, 46) Article 52.

5 In fact, no significant difficulties have emerged. Practice of the United Nations, the Specialised Agencies and the International Atomic Energy Agency concerning their Status Privileges and Immunities A/CN 4/L 118 (8 March 1967), A/CN 4L 118/Add 1 (5 May 1967) and A/CN 4/L 118 dd2 (23 May 1967).

in the case of such organisations, post-judgment execution is possible against the assets of the organisation but pre-judgment attachment is not.

2. *The position under English law*
The mere fact that the charters and constitutions of international organisations contain provisions defining and limiting their liability as though they were sovereign does not lead necessarily to the conclusion that the domestic law of even the member countries will recognise the privilege claimed. In *Standard Chartered Bank v International Tin Council*[1] the English courts refused to recognise such an international body as inherently sovereign. Bingham J explained, 'first the absolute doctrine of sovereign immunity grew up in reliance on a theory that sovereign states were characterized by what Marshall CJ in *Exchange Schooner v M'Fadden* (1812) 7 Cranch 116 described as "perfect equality and absolute independence". It followed from this that one sovereign would not insult the dignity or undermine the independence of another by seeking to assert jurisdiciton over him. Whatever the merits of this doctrine as between personal sovereigns or sovereign states, it is not obviously apt to be applied to a body such as the International Tin Council of which sovereign states are no more than members and whose own sovereign status is said to have a Cheshire cat quality. The ITC could scarcely be seen as enjoying perfect equality with the U.K. or the same absolute independence . . . Second, . . . international organisations such as I.T.C. have never been recognised at common law as entitled to sovereign status. They are accordingly entitled to no sovereign or diplomatic immunity in this country save where such immunity is granted by legislative instrument, and then only to the extent of such grant.'[2]

The privileges reserved by the charters and constitutions of international organisations will only be effective under English law to the extent that English legislation gives effect to them. The position is otherwise under the Second Restatement of the Foreign Relations Law of the United States for Rule 83(1) provides that 'an international organisation has such immunity from the jurisdiction of a member state to prescribe or enforce rules of law as is necessary for the fulfilment of its purposes as they are stated in its constitution'. Consequently, the privileges reserved in the constitution of the body will be recognised to the extent that they are necessary for the fulfilment of its purposes. Perhaps if no privileges are reserved by the constitution it is to be assumed that none are necessary to achieve its purposes!

In fact, the position in England is less antagonistic to the status of international organisations than the bare common law exposition would lead one to suppose. By virtue of the International Organisations Act 1968 privileges and immunities can be conferred on designated international organisations by Order in Council and this is customarily done. Indeed, privilege was conferred on the International Tin Council. The extent of the privilege will be defined by the precise terms of the particular Order

1 [1987] 1 WLR 641.
2 At p. 648.

in Council and the empowering Act but can, for instance, free from the threat of discovery all of its documents.[1]

3. *The European Community*

In the case of the European Community specific provision is found in Article 1 of the Protocols on the Privileges and Immunities of the various communities;

> 'The property and assets of the Community may not be subject to any administrative or legal measure of constraint without the authorisation of the Court of Justice'.

This, of course, binds the courts of the member countries of the community.[2] Outside the Community its effectiveness would depend on the willingness of the courts of other jurisdictions to give effect to it and that in turn would depend a great deal on the respect of the forum for the integrity of the Community itself.[3]

1 *Shearson Lehman Bros v Maclaine Watson & Co Ltd International Tin Council Intervener (No 2)* [1987] WLR 16.

2 Court of Justice 13 March 1962, Demande d'autorisation de pratiques saisie -arrêt entre les mains de la Haute Autorité de la CECA, Case 4/62, Recevil de la Jurisprudence de a Court, Vol VIII 83; and 11 May 1971, Demande en autorisation de pratiques saisie - arrêt entre les mains de la Commission des Communautés Européenes, Case 171 Recevil etc Vol XVII, 363.

3 In case of a bond issue it is customary of the bond terms themselves to recite the restriction on enforcement except through the European Court — see the example given by Delaume *Transnational Contracts* Chapter 12 p. 38 n18.

Appendix 1

The U.S. Congress enacted the Securities Act 1933 and the Securities Exchange Act 1934 to dictate disclosure of detailed financial and other information relating to the issuer, underwriters and the security which is being offered by means of a registration statement. However, even in enacting the two pieces of legislation Congress recognised that registration would not always be appropriate and included exemptions within the legislation. In particular, the 1933 Act exempts from the registration requirement 'transactions by an issuer not involving any public offering'[1] and also empowers the Securities and Exchange Commission (the S.E.C.) to enact rules and regulations exempting issuers from registration requirements 'if it finds that . . . registration is not necessary in the public interest and for the protection of investors by reason of the small amount involved or the limited character of the public offering . . .'[2]

SECURITIES ACT 1933 s 4(2)

'Transaction by an issuer not involving any public offering' is an obvious general private placement exemption and is contained in s 4(2) of the Act. It has always been the principal exemption relied upon in connection with the distribution of securities not registered under the 1933 Act. At first sight it would appear to denote an offering made to a restricted group of persons and not available to the public as a whole, and seems to have been so understood in the U.S. for a period of some 20 years. While factors other than the pure restriction on numbers were to be considered in deciding whether an issue was public or private it was generally felt, at least outside the S.E.C. responsible for enforcing the legislation, that an offer restricted to no more than 25 persons would not be considered public.

In 1953 this simple approach was shattered in the decisive case of *S.E.C. v Ralston Purina Co*[3] when the Supreme Court rejected the numerical basis of the concept. The purpose of the statute was to protect the public and therefore the exemption was limited to offers to those who were not in need of protection. The issue turned upon 'whether the particular class

1 S 4(2).
2 S 3(b).
3 346 US 119 (1953).

of persons affected needed the protection of the Act'.[1] This, in turn, would depend first upon the sophistication of the offerees and whether they would be able to look after themselves by making an intelligent investment decision if presented with sufficient information on which to make that decision. Secondly, the offerees would have to have access to 'the kind of information which registration would disclose'.[2]

The *Ralston Purina* case has undoubtedly been a landmark decision. The implications were clearly that the numerical criterion had been extinguished. Thus, an offer to only three sophisticated investors has since been held to be a public offering where they did not have access to the kind of information which would be included in a registration statement.[3] The principles of the *Ralston Purina* case have been applied since to a range of cases.[4] It does appear, however, that there is a relationship between the amount of information which needs to be available and the sophistication of the investor. If the investor is sophisticated and experienced in business and has substantially all the information before him that would have been contained in a registration document, the offering will not cease to be a private offering simply because a registration document would have contained more information. An experienced businessman with substantially all the information needed for an intelligent appraisal of the investment is able to look after himself, if necessary by demanding any additional information.[5] Further, the degree of sophistication is to be measured by the investor's capacity to understand the particular transaction rather than by general investment experience.[6] As has been judicially observed:

> If sophistication or lack thereof is relevant, the focus must be not so much upon prior experience with the purchase and sale of securities, but rather upon whether the offerees knew what to look for in, and how to interpret, the available information concerning the issuer's business and profit potential.[7]

Unfortunately, these developments devolved considerable responsibilities upon the issuer, who battled with the uncertainty arising from the generality of the tests. If the exemption was available where the offeree had access to the same kind of information which would have been made available under the Act in the form of a registration statement, how could an issuer be sure in advance that a court would hold that a particular offeree had

1 At p. 125.
2 At p. 127.
3 *Gilligan Will & Co v SEC* 267 F 2d 461 (2nd Cir 1959).
4 *SEC v Continental Tobacco Co* 463 F 2d 137 (2nd Cir 1972); *Lively v Hirschfield* 440 F 2d 631 (10th Cir 1970); *Bowers v Columbia General Corpn* 336 F Supp 609 (D Del 1971). The cases, however, while seeking to apply the Ralston tests do not always seem to do so accurately, see Harold S. Bloomenthal *Securities and Federal Corporate Law* at p. 4–42.2 et seq.
5 *Bowers v Colombia General Corpn* 336 F Supp 609 (1971). However, it is to be noted that in the particular case the plaintiffs were found to have access to the additional information if they wished to call for it and were advised by experienced lawyers and accountants.
6 Ibid.
7 Ibid.

available to him such information? Further, how could an issuer be sure that a court would hold a particular offeree to be sophisticated?

With regard to the first part of the test the obvious means of ensuring that the offeree had access to information of the correct quality was to furnish to each offeree a disclosure statement which supplied the same information as would have been available in a registration statement. The effect has been well put: 'The literary style of the offering circular came more and more to resemble the prospectus, both to protect the exemption and to meet the test for full and fair disclosure'.[1] The effect of discharging such a high disclosure obligation was that an issuer achieved certainty.

However, from the point of view of many would-be issuers the cost was too high. The whole purpose of seeking an exception was often to avoid the cost of putting together all the information required to be filed in a registration statement. However, it was precisely the provision of identical information in a non-registration statement which the *Ralston Purina* test seemed to require. The only exception of any degree of certainty was the case of a private offering to managerial executives of the issuer, who could normally be expected to know as much about the issuer's business as anyone, and who would normally be responsible for the making of the issuer's offer themselves.

With regard to the sophistication of the offerees, there could not even be certainty secured at a high price. It was the responsibility of the issuer to ensure that the issue was made to investors capable of fending for themselves and up to the issuer to estimate the offeree's sophistication accurately. To try to secure themselves, issuers commonly obtained the signature of investors to purchase agreements which acknowledged their financial sophistication and acumen. Such moves could only be a marginal protection. There could be no doubt that a court would make an independent assessment of an offeree's sophistication and would substitute its own findings for the purchaser's self-evaluation.[2] The best that could be said for the purchaser's declaration was that if he endeavoured to sue for breach of the regulatory provisions it would make his position more difficult when being cross-examined.

A final factor in deciding whether the offering is truly private is whether the purchaser had bought the securities with the intention of retaining them. The issuer must show that the initial group of purchasers of the private placement did not purchase the securities with a view to resale.[3] If the purchaser from the issuer resold the securities the issuer was considered to have distributed the securities in two steps, the initial purchaser acting as underwriter. The position of all the initial purchasers is therefore relevant, and if any subsequent disposition by them of securities is of a public nature

1 Parnall, Kohl and Huff 'Private and Limited Offerings after a Decade of Experimentation: the Evolution of Regulation D' (1982) 12 NMLR 633 at p. 642. The mere fact that an issue is exempted from registration does not absolve the issuer from the obligation to make full and fair disclosure.

2 *SEC v International Scanning Devices Inc* [1977–1978] Transfer Binders Fed Sec L Rep (CCH) 96 147.

3 In *Re Ambrosia Minerals Inc* 39 SEC 734.

the issuer will lose his exemption.[1] A prudent issuer would seek to cover this loophole by four steps: first, by taking from an investor a written undertaking that he would not distribute; secondly, by instructing its agent not to register any subsequent transfers by one of the initial purchasers; thirdly, by limiting the number of certificates issued to an initial purchaser to make fragmented dispositions more difficult; and fourthly, by stamping the security on issue with a legend making clear the non-public nature of the initial offering under which they were issued.[2]

The disadvantages of their system have been seen by the Americans themselves[3] and this has resulted in a good deal of experimentation over the last fifteen years.

RULE 146

Because of the increasing confusion as to the effect of s 4(2) the S.E.C. adopted Rule 146 in 1974 as a general private placement exemption pursuant to s 4(2) of the 1933 Act. Without removing an issuer's right to rely on the wording of s 4(2), and the judicial interpretation which had arisen, it provided a safe harbour by providing that if the conditions which it required were met by an offering it was considered exempt from the registration requirements. The conditions demanded were, however, extensive and the safe harbour went substantially unused. It has been characterised as 'an ill-conceived exemption, and its flaws were apparent from the beginning'.[4]

RULE 506

By the early 1980s it had become clear that S.E.C. intervention to clarify exemptions under the 1933 Act including Rule 146 had failed totally. In August 1981 the S.E.C. proposed Regulation D and after allowing half a year for public comment the S.E.C. adopted Regulation D on 8 March 1982. The regulation is concerned to provide safe harbour provisions for both large private placements within the concepts of s 4(2) and also limited offerings by small companies within s 3(b). Its declared purpose is:

1 Ibid In *re Unity Gold Corpn* 3 SEC 618 (1938) *In re Gilligan Will and Co* 38 SEC 387. 'Disclosure to investors: a Reappraisal of Federal Administrative Policies under the '33 and '34 Acts' (The Wheat Report) at 160–177.

2 It was the subjective element involved which caused the SEC to evolve a set of 'safe harbor' formulations now embodied in Regulation D. (Sec Act Rel No 6389 (8 March 1982) [1981–82] Transfer Binders Fed Sec L Rep (CCH 83, 106)). They are objective in form and threefold in number, *vis* rule 504, 505, 506. An issuer is, of course, entitled to ignore the safe harbor formulations and rely on the criteria established by the courts.

3 See McDermott, 'The Private Offering Exemption', 59 Iowa L Rev 23 (1974); Meer, 'The Private Offering Exemption under the Federal Securities Act — A Study in Administrative and Judicial Contraction', 20 Sw L J 503 (1966); Victor and Bedrick, 'Private Offering: Hazards for the Unwary', 45 Va L Rev 869 (1959)

4 R B Campbell Jr. 'The Plight of Small Issuers (And Others) Under Regulation D; Those Nagging Problems That Need Attention', 74 Kentucky LJ 127 (1985–86).

> to simplify existing rules and regulations, to eliminate any unnecessary restrictions that those rules and regulations place on issuers, particularly small businesses, and to achieve uniformity between state and federal exemptions in order to facilitate capital formation consistent with the protection of investors.[1]

The crucial provisions within Regulation D relevant to general private placement are contained in Rule 506 and central to the workings of Rule 506 is the concept of the 'accredited investor'.

The accredited investor

The purpose of establishing the concept of the accredited investor was to move away from subjective tests of sophistication. Instead, objective tests enable the investor to be 'accredited' as not in need of the protection of the legislation quickly and without difficulty. Ironically, the term arises out of the statutory definition in s 2(15) of the Securities Act which incorporated a generalised standard which includes reference to financial sophistication, net worth, knowledge and experience in financial and investment matters. However, the S.E.C. has carried out its own redefinitions of the concept in Rule 501 for the purpose of, *inter alia*, Rule 506.

There are two basic categories of accredited investor, institutional and individual. Institutional investors include banks, insurance companies, investment companies, business development companies, employee benefit plans having total assets in excess of $5 million and tax exempt organisations having assets in excess of $5 million.

The approach to individuals is focused principally on objective wealth tests in the interests of predictability and certainty rather than subjective sophistication standards under s 4(2) itself. However, there is an exception to the wealth-based test which makes directors, executive officers, or general partners of the issuer 'accredited' on the basis of their status. The policy this represents is that they are business insiders who have the knowledge and business experience to be able to evaluate the risk of investment in their own securities.

With this exception the individual investor must meet one of three tests to be accredited, namely, (1) the net worth test (2) the income test or (3) the big hitter test. The net worth test requires that the investor *either singly or together with* his or her spouse should have assets that exceed liabilities by $1,000,000 at the time of purchase. The income test requires that the investor, without his or her spouse, has had annual income of at least $200,000 for each of the two preceding tax years, and, further, that the investor reasonably expects that level of income to continue during the year of the purchase of the investment. The big hitter test is more complex. It requires that the investor *either singly or together with* his or her own spouse should purchase an interest of at least $150,000 in the security. Further, the purchase must exceed 20 per cent of the issuer's net worth at the time of purchase thus requiring him to hold net assets of at least $750,000 at the time of the purchase of the securities.

1 S.E.C. Securities Act Release No 6389.

The three tests to determine individual qualification are inflexible rules and must be precisely met if accreditation is to exist.

RULE 506

The private offering exemption under Rule 506 has been described as 'the heir to the former Rule 146 exemption'. However, while continuing the policies of the Rule 146 exemption changes have been made with a view to standardization and ease of application. At the core of Rule 506 is the 'accredited investor' exemption defined in Rule 501. It will be appreciated that the effect of the accredited categorisation is that investors so labelled are deemed to be able to look after themselves, and it is because of this that the protection of registration of the issue is removed from them. Thus, substantial investment institutions are deemed to be able to look after themselves as are wealthy individuals.

The rule allows exemption from registration of the issue of securities sold exclusively to accredited investors and to no more than thirty-five non-accredited investors. Thus, provided the offer is limited to accredited investors it can be made to any number that the issuer cares to approach. If, however, the issuer wishes to sell to someone who does not meet the strict accreditation tests of Rule 501 he may sell to no more than thirty-five non-accredited purchasers. Each of the non-accredited purchasers must meet a sophistication requirement based not on an economic test but on business acumen and experience. In this the test is similar to that required under the replaced Rule 146 for it is the *purchasers* who must meet the sophistication test whereas under Rule 146 all *offerees* were required to meet the test. However, if a non-accredited investor does not possess enough business knowledge and financial acumen to evaluate the investment for himself he is permitted to rely on a suitably knowledgable and experienced financial adviser (the 'purchaser representative'). It is nevertheless the issuer's responsibility to make reasonable steps to ensure the suitability of the non-accredited investor for the particular investment and to this end the issuer usually asks for a detailed description of the investor's educational and business background and his or her financial position from the investor often through a questionnaire as part of the private placement memorandum.

Rule 506 has no condition attached to it limiting the size of offering and therefore constitutes an unlimited exemption with regard to the amount of capital which may be raised provided that the securities are limited in distribution to accredited investors and the permitted number of qualified but non-accredited investors. However, it appears that a large offering may be carefully scrutinised by the S.E.C. for violation of the conditions attached to distribution under Rule 156. Apart from the limitation with regard to type of investor Rule 156 has a further restriction against general advertisement or solicitation reflecting the fact that it is indeed a private placement exemption, and is therefore only appropriate if the general public is unlikely to be tempted to invest in it. Obviously, solicitations can take place in very varied factual backgrounds with varying degrees of privateness. It is a question of fact whether they are sufficiently private to fall within the exemption and the S.E.C. decides this issue on a case-by-case basis.

It appears that advertisements in trade journals or at events aimed at an audience which is likely to be wealthy and sophisticated are not acceptable because the method of solicitation is essentially public.[1] Presumably, solicitation by brokers to the general public would not be acceptable for the same reason. However, general solicitations by brokers seeking qualified offerees for *subsequent* issues are permitted[2] for the broker-dealer is able to screen the investors before the future offering and the sale is therefore selective and not the result of indiscriminate solicitation.

THE RESALE PROBLEM

An investor who purchases a security in a private placement under Rule 506 takes a restricted security within Rule 144(a)(3). To resell the security to the public the purchaser must either seek to register the security or sell himself pursuant to an exemption or otherwise avoid classification as an underwriter under s 4(1) and 5 of the Securities Act 1933. While there is a 'safe harbour' resale exemption contained in Rule 144 this has proved to be very restrictive and this had had a detrimental effect on the liquidity of investors. If no lawful buyer is available the investor must usually hold the securities for an extended period of time (as long as two or three years) so that any connection between initial issue and resale is clearly broken. In practice, resales to institutions have been tolderated by the S.E.C. in order that there might be some secondary market and liquidity in these investments. It has now proposed a new regulation, Rule 144A, to legitimise this practice, reflecting its belief that institutional investors are able to protect themselves, routinely deal in non-registered securities, understand traditional restrictions on resale, and can be relied on to observe traditional restrictions when imposed.[3]

The consequence of failure to avoid ss 4(1) and 5 of the 1933 Act, is that the purchaser will be classified as an underwriter and the issue classified as a two-stage distribution. It may well be that to protect itself against such complications an issuer must make enquiries as to whether the purchaser is purchasing for his own account, inform the purchaser that the sale is under the exemption and with restrictions on resale and put an appropriate endorsement on the securities.[4]

THE RELATIONSHIP OF RULE 506 AND S 4(2)

Rule 506 does not replace s 4(2). It merely offers a safe harbour into which issuers can steer. If they prefer they can rely on s 4(2) of the 1933 Act with its general wording and judicial interpretation. Inevitably, however, since a safe harbour has been provided issuers generally make use of it.

1 E.g. Aspen Grove, No Action letter from S.E.C. (8 Nov 1982). See the discussion in Campbell *op. cit.* p. 112.
2 E.g. Arthur M. Borden, No Action letter from S.E.C. (6 Oct 1978).
3 The proposals are discussed by Glenn M Reitner and Stephen B Grant in 'Resales of US Privately Placed Securities' 8 IFLR 20 (1989).
4 Rule 502(d) Securities Act Release No 6389 (8 March 1982) 1 Fed Sec L Rep (CCH) 11 para. 2374.

Index